MANAGEMENT

Challenges in the 21st Century

MANAGEMENT

Challenges in the 21st Century

Second Edition

Pamela S. Lewis
Drexel University

Stephen H. Goodman
University of Central Florida

Patricia M. Fandt
University of Washington, Tacoma

SOUTH-WESTERN College Publishing

An International Thomson Publishing Company

Publishing Team Director: John Szilagyi
Development Editor: Katherine Pruitt-Schenck
Marketing Manager: Steve Scoble
Production Editor: Sandra Gangelhoff
Production House: WordCrafters Editorial Services, Inc.
Composition: GGS Information Services
Cover Designer: Tin Box Studio, Cincinnati, Ohio
Cover Photograph: © Les Jorgensen/Photonica
Team Assistant: Linda Chaffee

Photo Credits

Pages 2, 40, 496 © Steven Peters/Tony Stone Images; p. 76 © Alan Oddie/PhotoEdit; p. 118 © Ken Fisher/Tony Stone Images; pp. 152, 568 © Bruce Ayres/Tony Stone Images; p. 188 © Jon Riley/Tony Stone Images; pp. 220, 532 © Dan Bosler/Tony Stone Images; pp. 260, 330 © Michael Newman/PhotoEdit; p. 296 © Comstock; p. 368 © 1996, PhotoDisc, Inc; pp. 400, 432, 462 © Walter Hodges/Tony Stone Images; p. 606 © David Ash/Tony Stone Images

Copyright © 1995
by West Publishing Company
St. Paul, Minnesota

Copyright © 1998
by South-Western College Publishing
Cincinnati, Ohio

Library of Congress Cataloging-in-Publication Data
Lewis, Pamela S.
    Management : challenges in the 21st century / Pamela Lewis,
Stephen H. Goodman, Patricia M. Fandt. — 2nd ed.
        p.   cm.
    Includes bibliographical references and index.
    ISBN 0-538-87899-1
    1. Management. I. Goodman, Stephen H.   II. Fandt, Patricia M.
III. Title.
HD31.L388   1998
658—dc21   97-20809
                                                                          CIP

        3 4 5 6 7 8 9 WST 5 4 3 2 1 0 9 8

Printed in the United States of America

I(T)P® International Thomson Publishing
South-Western College Publishing is an ITP Company.
The ITP trademark is used under license.

To my family—for your unwavering support of my efforts.
PSL

To Cynthia and Whitney—for the joy you continue to bring into my life each day.
SHG

To Jim—for your love and confidence in me; to my students, who challenge me to be an effective educator.
PMF

ABOUT THE AUTHORS

PAMELA S. LEWIS

Pamela S. Lewis is a Professor of Management and Dean of the College of Business Administration at Drexel University in Philadelphia, Pennsylvania. She completed her Ph.D. at the University of Tennessee in the area of strategic management and international business. Throughout her career, Dr. Lewis has distinguished herself for her commitment to providing innovative and high-quality business education. She has been invited to make numerous presentations to academic groups regarding the need for change in business curricula and the importance of industry/academic partnerships in business education today. Dr. Lewis is also active in research and has published numerous journal articles in the areas of strategic planning, international strategy, and entrepreneurship. She is active in executive education as well, and her seminars in strategic planning, entrepreneurship, and international management have been well received by both domestic and international audiences.

STEPHEN H. GOODMAN

Stephen H. Goodman is an Associate Professor of Management at the University of Central Florida. He received his Ph.D in Business Administration from Pennsylvania State University, where he specialized in operations management and operations research. Prior to his doctoral study he received a B.S. in Aeronautical Engineering and an M.B.A., also from Penn State. During his 25 years in academia, he has taught, researched, and published primarily in production planning and control. He has also served as a coauthor of a textbook in the field of production/operations management. Currently he has a major teaching and research focus in quality management. He is an active member of the Decision Sciences Institute (DSI) and the American Production and Inventory Control Society (APICS), having held offices in each, has engaged in journal review activities, and has conducted professional training classes. He has achieved the distinction of Certified Fellow in Production and Inventory Management (CFPIM) from APICS.

PATRICIA M. FANDT

Patricia M. Fandt is an Associate Professor and Director of the Business Administration Program at the University of Washington Tacoma. She acquired more than 12 years of professional experience in sales and management prior to being awarded her Ph.D in Organizational Behavior from Texas A&M University. During her academic career, she has taught, researched, and published primarily in the areas of team development, management skill assessment, decision making, impression management, and classroom/training techniques for enhancing learning and student performance. Her current focus involves the integration of technological and multidisciplinary concepts to create curriculum that better prepares students facing the dynamic and challenging new century. She is the author of *Management Skills: Practice and Experience*. She is an active member of the Academy of Management, Southern Management Association, and the Organizational Behavior Teaching Society. She has held officer positions in the Southern Management Association and the Management Education and Development (MED) Division of the Academy of Management.

BRIEF CONTENTS

CONTENTS

PART 2   PLANNING CHALLENGES IN THE 21ST CENTURY   117

---

10 Managing Human Resources   331

11 Organizational Culture, Change, and Development   369

PART 4   LEADERSHIP CHALLENGES IN THE 21ST CENTURY   399

12 Communicating Effectively within Diverse Organizations   401

13 Understanding Leadership in a Dynamic Environment   433

---

17 Productivity and Quality in Operations   569

18 Information Technology and Control   607

PREFACE

Approaching the 21st Century

As we move closer to the 21st century, you are about to begin studying one of the most important and interesting disciplines of business: the field of management. This continues to be an exciting time to be a student of management! Times are continuing to change and so are the functions and roles of the manager. It is still imperative that tomorrow's managers be prepared to meet the challenges of a highly dynamic and rapidly changing business environment. Our overriding objective in developing this book was to capture the excitement and challenge of management in the business environment of the 21st century.

Change is coming from all directions: quality management has radically changed the way many organizations do business; the global marketplace has redefined the competitive structure of many industries; and the increasing predominance of entrepreneurial and service-based organizations has altered the structure of our economy. Diversity in the workforce has become the rule rather than the exception; organizations are being restructured and redesigned to be lean, flexible, and adaptable to change; and managers in all areas and at all levels of the organization are expected to be proactive, team-oriented, and focused on results. Succeeding as a manager in the organization of today and tomorrow requires a special set of management skills and competencies.

One of the first things you were told in the preface to the first edition of this book was that this was an exciting time to be a student of management, for tomorrow's managers will need to be prepared to meet the challenges of a highly dynamic and rapidly changing business environment. In the few short years since that first edition was prepared, much has happened in the business environment that needed to be captured in this new edition. As authors, we also have had to adapt to change. While the theoretical content of the chapters remains true to the first edition, significant changes have been made in each chapter.

New to this Edition

- The well-received *Managerial Incident* that opens each chapter and its corresponding closing *Managerial Incident Resolution* have been changed to provide fresh illustrations of situations or problems, and how they were dealt with within the realm of the content and theory of the chapter.

- The boxed material (highlighted examples) in each chapter has been replaced with updated or new illustrations and applications of contemporary management practice. These highlighted examples fall into the categories of *Managing for Excellence, Global Perspective, Entrepreneurial Approach, Meeting the Challenge, Managerial Incident, Information Technology: Insights and Solutions, Video Case,* and *Case.*

- Every chapter has been updated to reflect the numerous changes that have occurred in the business world during the past few years. Along with the major new features noted above, many new illustrative examples have been woven into the fabric of each of the chapters.

- A timely and exciting new feature at the end of each chapters is called *Information Technology: Insights and Solutions.* This feature consists of a set of information technology exercises. These exercises give students the opportunity to use the Internet to search for information in some area related to the materials in the chapter, and to use the latest technology in spreadsheet, word processing, and presentation software to present the information to the class.

In all, over 70 new company situations and scenarios have been developed to accompany the theoretical content of the chapters, as well as numerous additional company examples interspersed through the text.

TEXT HIGHLIGHTS

This book includes a number of features designed to prepare students to be managers in the year 2000. These features focus on: (1) meeting the challenges inherent in a dynamic, rapidly changing business environment, (2) developing the competencies and skills that managers will need in the future, and (3) responding to the contemporary management trends that will affect both organizations and managers in the 21st century.

- *Meeting the Challenge.* The underlying, integrating theme that forms the foundation of this book is meeting the challenge on the eve of the new century. Contemporary managers will be challenged continually to respond to opportunities and threats that arise in the dynamic, global environment of business. As competitive pressures continue to escalate and consumers around the globe demand increasing levels of quality, managers must strive for excellence in all facets of their organizations. Our focus in this book is on meeting these challenges as they affect the functions of management and the roles and activities of the manager.

- *Competencies and Skills.* Beyond our theme of meeting the challenge, we have developed this book with an emphasis on the competencies and skills needed by contemporary managers. Students of management must be prepared to translate theory into practice as they move into the workplace. To do so, they will need to develop fully their skills in such important areas as teamwork, critical thinking, problem solving, communication, and adapting to change.

- *Theory and Practice.* This text bridges the gap between management theory and practice by using an interdisciplinary, applied approach to the material in the text. Because managers come from all areas of an organization (e.g., production departments, finance and accounting departments, sales and marketing departments), it is important to understand how the concepts of management are applied in the various functional areas of organizations of all sizes. Further, an interdisciplinary approach to the study of management is essential given the blurring of the lines separating the traditional functions of business (e.g., management, marketing, finance, etc.) and the increasing predominance of interfunctional work teams within contemporary organizations.

- *Contemporary Management Trends.* Finally, we have identified and highlighted several contemporary management trends that present challenges for organizations and managers today. They include global management, entrepreneurship, service management, quality, team-based management, ethics, and cultural diversity. Rather than adding a separate chapter on each of these trends, we introduce them very early in the text and then integrate the topics into each and every chapter of the book.

Organization

Part 1 of the text addresses the basic concepts of management, the roles of the manager, and the changing nature of both the contemporary organization and the contemporary manager. The contemporary management trends discussed above are introduced, and a foundation is laid for examining how these trends affect management theory and practice. In addition, the history of management thought is reviewed, and the topics of social responsibility and ethics are addressed in light of their increasing importance in modern organizations.

Part 2 explores the managerial function of planning. This section examines the basic principles of the planning process, as well as planning from a strategic perspective. Strategy is examined as a tool for responding to challenges in today's highly competitive, global business environment and for achieving quality in every aspect of an organization's operations. Further, decision making is addressed as a key managerial responsibility, and a number of tools and techniques for decision making are presented.

Part 3 of the text focuses on the organizing function of management. More specifically, this section addresses the fundamental principles of organizing, as well as the models of organizational design that are appropriate for contemporary, team-oriented organizations. Issues of organizational culture, change, and human resource management are also addressed in this section. Particular emphasis is placed upon organizing to improve flexibility, facilitate change, utilize team management, and respond to the challenges of a diverse and heterogeneous work environment.

Part 4 explores the managerial function of leadership. This section focuses on factors that influence the behavior of people. Separate chapters examine individual and group behavior, what motivates members of the workforce, the nature of leadership, and communicating with others. Special attention is given to developing a leadership style that empowers the members of diverse organizations to excel in everything they do and to work as a team to achieve the goals and objectives of the organization.

Part 5 examines the management function of control. The foundational principles of control are addressed, and specific attention is given to productivity, quality control, and information systems control. Control is presented as a principal tool for achieving quality in the products, services, and processes of the organization, as well as a tool for developing a competitive advantage based on enhanced productivity, increased efficiency, and superior quality.

Applications-Oriented Approach

Consistent with our application-oriented approach to the presentation of contemporary management trends, we have included the following elements, which are designed to help you become a more effective manager:

- *Chapter Overview.* Every chapter opens with a summary that describes the general content of the chapter. This opening summary highlights the primary topics and concepts to be covered in the chapter and explains why the information is important to the manager of the future.
- *Learning Objectives.* Each chapter contains a well-defined set of learning objectives. These objectives focus on the specific topics covered in the chapter and provide a checklist of important points discussed in the chapter.
- *Managerial Incident/Resolution.* There is a Managerial Incident in each chapter that details a real-life organizational problem or situation that is re-

lated to the content of the chapter. This incident is referred to often as the chapter unfolds. At the close of the chapter, a Management Resolution describes how the problem was solved or the situation was addressed using the management concepts discussed in the chapter. This allows the student to see how the concepts and theories presented in each chapter are applied to business situations in actual companies.

- *Information Technology: Insights and Solutions.* A set of information technology exercises is presented at the end of each chapter. These exercises give students the opportunity to use technology to search for information in an area related to the materials in the chapter. Much of the information can be gathered via the Internet, or by phone or fax from the appropriate company sources. Each of these exercises typically has some classroom presentation aspect associated with it, requiring the use of spreadsheet, word processing, and presentation software to arrange and present the information.

- *Ethics: Take a Stand.* An ethical dilemma related to the material presented in the chapter appears at the end of each chapter. Students evaluate various alternative courses of action in terms of their ethical implications and select one that is both ethical and meets the objectives of the organization. The *Ethics: Take a Stand* feature highlights the increasing importance of making managerial decisions founded on strong individual and organizational ethics.

- *Thinking Critically: Debate the Issue.* Each chapter contains a debate topic related to the content of the chapter. Students are asked to work in teams to develop arguments to support a particular position. The instructor selects two teams to present their findings to the class in a debate format. This exercise helps students to develop critical thinking skills, teamwork skills, and oral communication skills.

- *Chapter Video Cases.* At the end of every chapter there is a video case that presents a real organization that uses contemporary management practices. Many of these video cases were produced specifically for use in this book. Cases include an ethics case involving the Bank of Alma and small business cases featuring Rheaco, Inc. and A. C. Petersen Farms, Inc.

- *End-of-Chapter Cases.* In addition to the video case at the close of each chapter, a second case outlines a fictitious situation that provides an opportunity for students to apply the concepts and tools presented in the chapter. These cases are designed to help students develop their analytical thinking skills and to apply the knowledge they gained from the chapter to resolve problems or address situations that often occur in contemporary organizations.

- *Chapter Summary.* Each chapter closes with a summary of the major points presented in the chapter. This overview of the chapter contents provides students with an overall perspective of the topics covered.

- *Review/Discussion Questions.* A set of review and discussion questions is provided at the end of each chapter. The review questions relate directly to the content of the chapter. The discussion questions are application-oriented in that they require students to respond to real-world situations or issues using the knowledge gained from the chapter.

- *Experiential Exercises.* Structured experiential exercises are provided at the close of each chapter. These exercises can be used in either large or small class environments and are designed get students directly involved in the learning process by requiring them to apply management theory to real-world situations. Many of these exercises involve "self-assessment" and will help students gain a greater understanding of their own management competencies and skills.

- *Highlighted Examples.* Throughout the book, organizations that provide examples of contemporary management practices are highlighted. These examples are designed to profile real companies that are confronting management challenges and responding in proactive and innovative ways. Some of these examples are supplemented by video segments. The highlighted examples include:

  Managing for Excellence. Companies that have achieved excellence through their management practices are featured in Managing for Excellence. Of particular interest are those organizations that have adopted a quality orientation in everything they do.

  Global Perspective. Organizations that have pursued international business strategies and compete effectively in the global marketplace are profiled in Global Perspective. The focus in these examples is on how management practices must be adapted to cope with the complexities of the international business area.

  Entrepreneurial Approach. Businesses both large and small that have succeeded as a function of their entrepreneurial approach to management are profiled in Entrepreneurial Approach. These examples highlight the importance of innovative and creative management in today's rapidly changing business environment.

  Meeting the Challenge. Meeting the Challenge provides an opportunity for students to practice the management principles they have studied. For example, students are given the opportunity to use self-assessment instruments to describe their own personal management styles and organizational assessment skills to evaluate organizations.

- *Integrative Case—IBAX.* Each of the five parts of the book concludes with a comprehensive and integrated case that is supplemented by a 7- to 12-minute video that shows IBAX's real-life executives, managers, and team members employing the contemporary management concepts, tools, and techniques described in that section to facilitate the IBAX turnaround.

Supplement Package

A professor's job is demanding. Because of this, we expect professors to demand a lot in return from the publisher and the authors of *Management.* Both the textbook and the accompanying ancillary materials have been developed to help instructors excel when performing their vital teaching function. For the first edition of *Management,* a variety of supplemental materials was tested and provided. In this edition, we include those supplements instructors found most helpful.

Instructor's Manual with Complete Video Guide and Transparency Masters (ISBN 0-538-87900-9)

The instructor's manual for *Management* was prepared by Bruce R. Barringer of the University of Central Florida and provides important information for each chapter. Each chapter of the manual includes the following information:

- Learning Objectives for each chapter.
- A detailed outline of the chapter material, including appropriate points at which to use the transparency support material.
- An Extended Outline with narratives under each major point to flesh out the discussion and show alternative examples and issues to bring forward.
- Detailed responses to the review questions, discussion questions, Ethics: Take a Stand exercises, cases, video, and experiential exercises.
- Additional Cases with suggested answers are also included in the manual for those instructors who wish to supplement the case material included in the text.

- A Multimedia Guide describing the video cases that accompany each chapter, including questions for discussion and detailed responses.
- A full set of transparency masters.

Test Bank (ISBN 0-538-87901-7)
Special attention was given to the preparation of the test bank because it is one of the most important ancillary materials. Bruce R. Barringer of the University of Central Florida has expanded significantly the original test bank that was prepared by Ned D. Young of Sinclair Community College. The test bank contains over 3,500 multiple choice, true/false, matching, case, and essay questions.

Westest (ISBN 0-538-88042-2)
Westest is the computerized version of the test bank, provides instructors with a convenient means of generating tests. The menu-driven testing package has many user-oriented features, including the ability to edit and add exam questions, scramble questions within sections of the exam, and merge questions. Westest is available for DOS, Windows, and the Macintosh. Call-in testing is also available.

PowerPoint Presentation Slides (ISBN 0-538-88037-6)
Almost 600 electronic slides to be used with PowerPoint, a state-of-the-art presentation graphics program for Microsoft Windows, are provided on 3.5" disks. These slides provide a comprehensive review of each chapter in the book. Using PowerPoint software, instructors can:

- Present the slides electronically in the classroom.
- Edit and change any of the slides, or add new material as needed.
- Animate and present a slide show with transition effects.

All-New Video Program (ISBN 0-538-Assorted)
In this edition we have incorporated 27 new video segments that highlight all aspects of today's management. One video segment ranging from 5 to 30 minutes accompanies each of the 18 chapters and helps to explain the concepts of that chapter. In addition, nine supplemental videos are offered separately to highlight various management practices in modern small and corporate businesses. The videos were selected from Learnet, CNBC, and Blue Chip (Small Business Management).

Management On-Line
Professors will never be out of touch with the changing environment of management with free access to South-Western Publishing and the Internet. You'll receive monthly updates to information in the text, additional annotations for use in lectures, suggested readings, and more through South-Western's electronic bulletin board. More specifically, updates will be provided to cases, the chapter highlighted examples, the ethics feature, and the critical thinking feature. In addition, a Thought Question of the Month will be provided along with two clue based identification challenges: CEO of the Month and Company of the Month.

Transparency Acetates (ISBN 0-538-88041-4)
One-hundred full-color transparency acetates are provided with *Management*. The transparencies were selected from the book and also from materials that do not appear in the book.

INSIGHTS: Inc. Readings in Small Business Management (ISBN 0-538-88036-8)
A readings book prepared by Lynn Bowes-Sperry of James Madison University is available for those faculty who wish to supplement text assignments with articles from the current business press. This soft-cover book contains multi-

ple selections from the popular *Inc. Magazine* that discuss contemporary issues and challenges in small business management.

Student Study Guide (ISBN 0-538-88034-1)

The extended study guide for *Management* was written by George Carnahan of Northern Michigan University. For each chapter, this comprehensive guide includes learning objectives with detailed descriptions; a chapter outline; multiple choice and agree or disagree questions with answers; exercises; and a chapter summary.

Student Notetaking Guide (ISBN 0-538-88035-X)

This unique bound supplement includes selected copies of the transparency masters for students to use while taking notes during lectures. Detailed outlines are also provided for each chapter of the book.

ACKNOWLEDGMENTS

A book such as this does not come to fruition solely by the hands of the authors. Many individuals have had significant involvement with this project, and their contributions must not go unrecognized. Many reviewers made insightful comments and valuable suggestions on the preliminary drafts of this book. Although criticism is sometimes a bitter pill to swallow, we can now look back and agree that the reviewer comments led to modifications that greatly strengthened the final product. We would like to express our gratitude to each of the following reviewers:

Second Edition Reviewers:
Royce L. Abrahamson, Southwest Texas State University
Lynn Bowes-Sperry, James Madison University
Janice M. Feldbauer, Austin Community College
Robert A. Figler, University of Akron
Edwin L. Hoying, Jr., University of Phoenix
Natalie J. Hunter, Portland State University
Gerald H. Kramer, Northwestern Missouri State University
Thomas R. Mahaffey, Siena College
Sandra M. Martinez, New Mexico State University
Daniel W. McAllister, University of Nevada—Las Vegas
Joseph F. Michlitsch, Southern Illinois University
James D. Oldson, The George Washington University
Robert J. Paul, Kansas State University
Khush K. Pittenger, Ashland University
John Wallace, Marshall University
John Washburn, University of Wisconsin—Whitewater
Terrence E. Williamson, South Dakota School of Mines and Technology

First Edition Reviewers:
Royce Abrahamson, Southwest Texas State University
Jeffrey Bailey, University of Idaho
Edward Bewayo, Montclair State University
Allen Bluedorn, University of Missouri
Peggy Brewer, Eastern Kentucky University
Deborah Brown, Santa Fe Community College
George Carnahan, Northern Michigan University
James F. Cashman, University of Alabama
Daniel S. Cochran, Mississippi State University
Roy Cook, Fort Lewis College

John Cotton, Marquette University
Marian Crawford, University of Arkansas, Little Rock
Carol Danehower, Memphis State University
Arthur Darrow, Bowling Green State University
Richard V. Dick, Missouri Western State University
Kenneth K. Eastman, Oklahoma State University
Stanley W. Elsea, Kansas State University
Roy Farris, Southeast Missouri State University
Jan Feldbauer, Austin Community College
Diane Ferry, University of Delaware
Robert A. Figler, University of Akron
George Foegen, Metro State College
Sonia Goltz, University of Notre Dame
Richard Grover, University of Southern Maine
Ted Halatin, Southwest Texas State University
John Hall, University of Florida
Dorothy Heide, California State University, Fullerton
Marvin Hill, Northern Illinois University
Phyllis Holland, Valdosta State College
John Jackson, University of Wyoming
Dewey Johnson, California State University, Fresno
Forest Jourden, University of Illinois, Champaign
Marvin Karlins, University of South Florida
Robert E. Kemper, Northern Arizona University
Russell Kent, Georgia Southern University
David G. Kuhn, Florida State University
James M. Lahiff, University of Georgia
Lars Erik Larson, University of Wisconsin, Whitewater
Esther Long, University of West Florida
Barbara Marting, University of Southern Indiana
Dan McAllister, University of Nevada, Las Vegas
James McElroy, Iowa State University
Joseph Michlitsch, Southern Illinois University
Edward J. Morrison, University of Colorado, Boulder
Diana Page, University of West Florida
Robert J. Paul, Kansas State University
Allayne Pizzolatto, Nicholls State University
Paul Preston, University of Texas, San Antonio
Richard Randall, Nassau Community College
Bill Ryan, Florida Atlantic University
Jerry D. Scott, Southeastern Oklahoma State University
Dawn Sheffler, Central Michigan University
Jane Siebler, Oregon State University
Mary Thibodeaux, University of North Texas
Ronald Vickroy, University of Pittsburgh at Johnstown
John Villareal, California State University
John Wallace, Marshall University
Deborah Wells, Creighton University
Carolyn Wiley, University of Tennessee, Chattanooga
Mimi Will, Foothill College
Jack Wimer, Baylor University
Lou J. Workman, Utah State University

In addition to these manuscript reviewers, other colleagues have contributed greatly by developing several of the high-quality, comprehensive sup-

plements that support this book. These individuals, and their contributions for which we are so grateful, include:

Instructor's Manual	Bruce R. Barringer, University of Central Florida
Study Guide	George Carnahan, Northern Michigan University
Test Bank and Computerized Testing	Bruce R. Barringer, University of Central Florida and Ned D. Young, Sinclair Community College
Videos	Bruce R. Barringer, University of Central Florida
INSIGHTS	Lynn Bowes-Sperry, James Madison University
PowerPoint Slides	Bruce R. Barringer, University of Central Florida
Web Site Updates	Bruce R. Barringer, University of Central Florida

A project of this magnitude is never undertaken without a great deal of commitment on the part of the author team. However, it is important to acknowledge someone who was equally committed to the project—our original executive editor, Rick Leyh. It is doubtful that we would have undertaken such an immense project with another editor. Rick's commitment to quality, attention to detail, never-ending enthusiasm for the project, and encouragement to continue throughout the long process of writing this book were strong motivators. The torch was passed to John Szilagyi for this second edition, and John continued the tradition of pushing and prodding to make each draft a significant improvement over the prior one. The end result has been a product in which we take great pride.

In addition to John, other individuals at South-Western made valuable contributions to this project. They include Katherine-Pruitt Schenck, our developmental editor, who played a critical role in linking the huge network of contributors to this project. We also acknowledge the stamina of Sandy Gangelhoff, our production editor, who not only tolerated our continual changes to the manuscript as it moved through production, but actually encouraged us to change whatever was necessary to make this product the very best possible. Our thanks also go to Steve Scoble, Marketing Manager, for coordinating the outstanding sales and marketing efforts awarded this text.

It is our belief that the IBAX cohesion case adds an important dimension to the book. IBAX provided us with an opportunity to follow and detail the turnaround of a company and to tie that turnaround to contemporary management practices. The cooperation and candor of IBAX's managers in the video interviews were greatly appreciated. In particular, we'd like to thank Jeff Goodman for giving rise to the story and taking the time to share it with us, as well as with many students of management.

Finally, we'd like to thank our families for their support throughout this project. Their tolerance of our absence from many family activities, their understanding of the time commitment a project like this requires, and their continual encouragement to push on enabled us to endure the long nights and lost weekends that made it possible for us to complete this book. For that support and commitment, we will always be grateful.

1

MEETING THE CHALLENGES OF THE 21ST CENTURY

Management and Managers: Yesterday, Today, and Tomorrow

CHAPTER 1

■ CHAPTER OVERVIEW

The world of business has undergone radical and dramatic changes in the last decade—changes that present extraordinary challenges for the contemporary manager. These challenges include escalating global competition, an unprecedented demand for quality and value on the part of consumers, and an ever-pressing need to capitalize on the technological advances that are reshaping the operations of most organizations. More important, tomorrow's managers will face an even more demanding business environment. To meet the challenges of the business environment of today and tomorrow, managers must be flexible, proactive, and focused on quality in everything they do.

In this chapter, we examine the manager of yesterday, today, and tomorrow. Our primary focus is on the manager's job and how it will change as a result of changes in the business environment. We explore the competencies that tomorrow's managers must possess if they are to achieve success.

■ LEARNING OBJECTIVES

When you have finished studying this chapter, you should be able to:

- Define the concept of management within an organizational context and as a process.
- Identify the roles played by managers.
- Describe how managers spend their time.
- Discuss the responsibilities of functional and general managers.
- Describe the three levels of managers in terms of the skills they need and the activities in which they are involved.
- Describe the environmental trends that are affecting the way organizations operate and the way managers do their jobs.
- Identify and discuss the organizational changes that are affecting managers' jobs.
- Describe the manager of tomorrow in terms of both managerial style and the competencies that will be necessary for success.

Managerial
Incident

IBAX: A COMPANY IN NEED OF LEADERSHIP

IBAX, a provider of information services software to the health care industry, was created in 1989, as a partnership between IBM and Baxter. For IBM, the venture provided entry into the software side of the computer business. For Baxter, the partnership with IBM provided much-needed credibility in a computer-related business.

IBAX got off to a very rocky start and posted a loss of millions of dollars in its first two years of existence. The market for health care information systems was extremely competitive, and gaining market share proved more difficult than was originally thought. In addition, the health care industry was experiencing significant change due to a continuing stream of technological improvements and an uncertain regulatory environment. The company seemed to lack an identity of its own, and the absence of a strong organizational culture made it difficult to build a team of people who were committed to achieving the organization's goals. Quality was not the first priority, and customer orientation was lacking throughout the organization. Finally, and perhaps most important, IBAX lacked strong leadership and, as a result, couldn't seem to correct its problems.

That was the situation when Jeff Goodman assumed the role of chief executive officer of IBAX. Goodman knew that he faced many challenges in turning IBAX around, but he was committed to doing whatever was necessary to make this venture a success.[1]

INTRODUCTION

The situation Jeff Goodman faced was not an enviable one. How could he take a company that was struggling to survive to a position of leadership? Improving technology, escalating demands for quality and value, and growing pressures from government regulation had created a business environment characterized by rapid and dramatic change. IBAX's ability to survive and prosper would depend upon the abilities of Jeff Goodman and his management team to adapt to this environment.

Unfortunately, IBAX's predicament is not uncommon. Today, organizations of all sizes and types are operating in a business environment that is more competitive and changing more rapidly than ever before. As a result, contemporary managers are facing extraordinary challenges and are being forced to rethink the way they manage their operations. Yesterday's management styles, practices, and processes may simply be ineffective given the very different challenges that the manager of today faces and the manager of tomorrow will confront.

The purpose of this book is to introduce students to the field of management. Management, as a discipline, has been greatly affected by the significant environmental and organizational changes that have occurred in recent years. We will explore the effect of these changes on the contemporary manager and learn how managers can achieve success in the highly dynamic business environment of the 21st century.

In this chapter we define and discuss the concept of management. Next, we examine the research that describes the roles managers play, the way they spend their time, and the skills they need to be successful. Finally, we examine how environmental and organizational change is affecting the manager's job, in terms of the competencies that will be necessary to be a successful manager in the 21st century.

MANAGEMENT AND WHY WE STUDY IT

Everything that we will address in the subsequent chapters of this book relates to managing the organization and the job of the manager. Consequently, it is important to develop a clear understanding of the concept of management at the outset. Let's look at a definition of management, the organizational context in which management occurs, and the process of management from a functional perspective.

MANAGEMENT DEFINED

Management has been defined in many ways. Mary Parker Follett, an early management scholar, offered what has come to be known as the classic definition when she described management as "the art of getting things done through people."[2] Although this definition captures the human dimension of management, a more comprehensive definition is needed.

For the purposes of this book, **management** is defined as the process of administering and coordinating resources effectively, efficiently, and in an effort to achieve the goals of the organization. **Effectiveness** is achieved when the organization pursues appropriate goals. **Efficiency** is achieved by using the fewest inputs (such as people and money) to generate a given output. In other words, effectiveness means "doing the right things" and efficiency means "doing things right."[3]

Managing for success requires a focus on achieving superior performance in every aspect of an organization's activities by all the individuals and groups within the organization. Achieving excellence has become a priority for many organizations as they face the challenges of a more competitive business environment. Thomas Peters and Robert Waterman originally drew attention to the concept of excellence in their classic book *In Search of Excellence,* in which they profiled some of America's best-run companies.[4] Based on their study of these organizations, Peters and Waterman identified eight characteristics of

Management
The process of administering and coordinating resources effectively and efficiently and in an effort to achieve the goals of the organization.

Effectiveness
Pursuing the appropriate goals—doing the right things.

Efficiency
Using the fewest inputs to generate a given output—doing things right.

TABLE 1.1   Characteristics of excellent organizations

- A bias for action, favoring "doing" over "planning."
- Simple form and lean staff, that is, a small number of staff relative to production or line employees, few levels in the hierarchy, and a relatively simple structure.
- Close to the customers, with customer needs, goals, and satisfaction considered as important as any other factor (including profit).
- Productivity through people, for all employees, and a focus on improving productivity by increasing people's desire and authority to make such improvements and then recognizing their contributions.
- Encouragement of entrepreneurship, by expecting managers to act as innovators and giving them the authority to do so.
- Focus on key business values, to provide clear and focused organizational goals and a strong and shared culture.
- Emphasis on what the organization does best, and on building on strengths, rather than on branching out into new areas that the organization has few resources for dealing with.
- Controls that are both "tight" and "loose," that is, very clearly defined limits but with great freedom and autonomy within those limits.

SOURCE: Selected excerpt from *In Search of Excellence: Lessons from America's Best-Run Companies,* by Thomas J. Peters and Robert H. Waterman, Jr. Copyright © 1982 by Thomas J. Peters and Robert H. Waterman, Jr. Reprinted by permission of HarperCollins Publishers, Inc.

well-managed organizations (see Table 1.1). Many of today's managers regard these attributes as indicators of organizational excellence and success.

THE ORGANIZATIONAL CONTEXT OF MANAGEMENT

Management, as we have defined it, occurs within an organizational context. The management processes, tools, and techniques that we will examine and discuss in this book are those appropriate for managers who work in organizations. But what is an organization?

Organization
A group of individuals who work together toward common goals.

An **organization** is a group of individuals who work together toward common goals. Organizations can be for profit, such as the business organizations with which we are all familiar (for example, Microsoft, Pizza Hut, J. C. Penney), or not for profit, such as churches, fraternities, and public universities. Whether they are for profit or not for profit, organizations have one characteristic in common: they are made up of people. The efforts of these people must be coordinated if the organization is to accomplish its goals.

The Process of Management

Four major functions are associated with the process of management: (1) planning, (2) organizing, (3) leading, and (4) controlling. Figure 1.1 illustrates these functions and shows how they relate to the goals of the organization. These four functions form the foundation of this book. Although each is examined in detail in a separate part of the book (planning in Part II, organizing in Part III, leading in Part IV, and controlling in Part V), a brief introduction of these functions is appropriate here.

Planning

Planning
Setting goals and defining the actions necessary to achieve those goals.

Managers at all levels of the organizational hierarchy must engage in **planning.** Planning involves setting goals and defining the actions necessary to achieve those goals. While top management establishes overall goals and strategy, managers throughout the hierarchy must develop operational plans for their work groups that contribute to the efforts of the organization as a whole. All managers must develop goals that are in alignment with and supportive of the overall strategy of the organization. In addition, they must develop a plan for administering and coordinating the resources for which they are responsible so that the goals of their work group can be achieved.

FIGURE 1.1
The functions of management

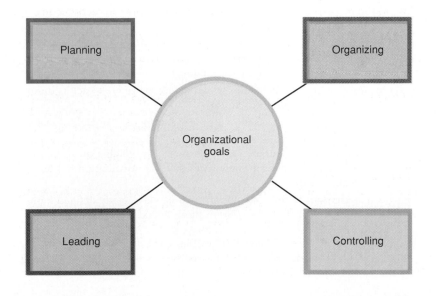

Organizing

The managerial function of **organizing** involves determining the tasks to be done, who will do them, and how those tasks will be managed and coordinated. Managers must organize the members of their work group and organization so that information, resources, and tasks flow logically and efficiently through the organization. Issues of organizational culture and human resource management are also key to this function. Most important, the organization must be structured in light of its strategic and operational goals and so that it can be responsive to changes in the business environment.

Leading

Managers must also be capable of **leading** the members of their work group toward the accomplishment of the organization's goals. To be effective leaders, managers must understand the dynamics of individual and group behavior, be able to motivate their employees, and be effective communicators. In today's business environment, effective leaders must also be visionary—capable of envisioning the future, sharing that vision, and empowering their employees to make the vision a reality. Only through effective leadership can the goals of the organization be achieved.

Controlling

Managers must monitor the performance of their organizations, as well as their progress in implementing strategic and operational plans. **Controlling** requires identifying deviations between planned and actual results. When an organization is not performing as planned, managers must take corrective action. Such actions may involve pursuing the original plan more aggressively or adjusting the plan to the existing situation. Control is an important function in the managerial process because it provides a method for ensuring that the organization is moving toward the achievement of its goals.

With the four functions of management in mind, let's move on to examine the manager. **Managers** are the people who plan, organize, lead, and control the activities of the organization so that its goals can be achieved. Over the years researchers have examined managers in detail to find out who they are and what they do. These studies can help us develop a general understanding of managers.

WHAT WE KNOW ABOUT MANAGERS

Regardless of your particular career interest, you may someday become a manager. Accountants become managers, salespeople become managers, and so do computer scientists and engineers. Some musicians are managers, as are some actors. In fact, even professors become managers. If you are successful in your chosen career and have administrative and leadership skills, you may be called upon to manage others.

Much of the research of the 1970s and 1980s focused on who managers are and what they do.[5] More specifically, many studies examined the roles managers play, the skills they need, and how they spend their time.[6] Others examined how roles, skills, and time allocation vary according to managerial level and scope of responsibility.[7] The next paragraphs examine some of the more enlightening research on the subject of managers.

In addition to fulfilling the functions of planning, organizing, and controlling, managers must be capable of leading the members of their work-group toward the accomplishment of the organization's goals. They must be effective communicators, they must understand the dynamics of individual and group behavior, and they must be able to motivate their employees.
© Walter Hodges/Tony Stone Images

Organizing
The process of determining the tasks to be done, who will do them, and how those tasks will be managed and coordinated.

Leading
Motivating and directing the members of the organization so that they contribute to the achievement of the goals of the organization.

Controlling
Monitoring the performance of the organization, identifying deviations between planned and actual results, and taking corrective action when necessary.

Managers
Organizational members who are responsible for planning, organizing, leading, and controlling the activities of the organization so that its goals can be achieved.

MANAGERIAL ROLES

According to a widely referenced study by Henry Mintzberg, managers serve three primary roles: interpersonal, informational, and decision making.[8] Figure 1.2 illustrates Mintzberg's theory of managerial roles, and the following discussion describes each role in greater detail.[9]

Interpersonal Roles

Interpersonal roles
The manager's responsibility for managing relationships with organizational members and other constituents.

The first set of roles identified by Mintzberg are **interpersonal roles.** These roles, which arise directly from the manager's formal authority base, involve relationships with organizational members and other constituents. The three interpersonal roles played by the manager are those of figurehead, leader, and liaison.

As the heads of organizational units, managers must perform certain duties that are primarily ceremonial in nature. For example, managers may have to appear at community functions, attend social events, or host luncheons for important customers. In doing so, managers fulfill their role as figureheads.

Because managers are largely responsible for the success or failure of their organizational units, they must also play the role of leaders within their work groups. In this capacity, managers work with and through their employees to ensure that the organization's goals are met.

Finally, managers must also serve as organizational liaisons. They act as liaisons both in working with individuals and work groups within the organization and in developing favorable relationships with outside constituents. Managers must be politically sensitive to important organizational issues so that they can develop relationships and networks both within and beyond their organizations.

Informational Roles

Informational roles
The manager's responsibility for gathering and disseminating information to the stakeholders of the organization.

The second set of managerial roles identified by Mintzberg are informational roles. In their **informational roles,** managers are responsible for ensuring that the people with whom they work have sufficient information to do their jobs effectively. By the very nature of managerial responsibilities, managers become the communication centers of their units and are a communication source for other work groups within the organization. People throughout the organization depend upon the management structure and the managers themselves to disseminate or provide access to the information they need to do their job.

One of the informational roles that a manager must assume is that of monitor. As monitors, managers continually scan the internal and external environments of their organizations for useful information. Managers seek out information from their subordinates and liaison contacts and may receive

FIGURE 1.2

The roles of the manager

SOURCE: Henry Mintzberg, "The Manager's Job: Folklore and Fact," *Harvard Business Review,* March-April 1990, 49–61.

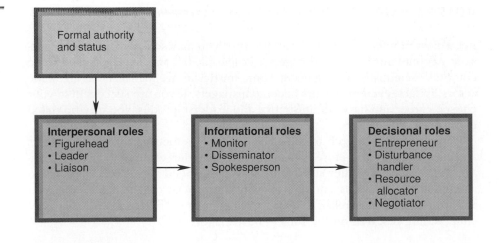

unsolicited information from their networks of personal contacts. From this information, managers identify potential opportunities and threats for their work groups and organizations.

In their role as disseminators, managers share and distribute much of the information that they receive as information monitors. As disseminators, managers pass on important information to the members of their work group. Depending on the nature of the information, managers may also withhold information from work group members. Most important, managers must ensure that their employees have the information necessary to perform their duties efficiently and effectively.

The final informational role played by managers is that of spokesperson. Managers must often communicate information to individuals outside their units and their organizations. For example, directors and shareholders must be advised about the financial performance and strategic direction of the organization; consumer groups must be assured that the organization is fulfilling its social obligations; and government officials must be satisfied that the organization is abiding by the law.[10] Lawrence Rawls, the former chief executive officer of Exxon, was acting in a spokesperson role when he personally delivered a message to the American public about the Exxon Valdez oil spill in Alaska.

Decisional Roles

Finally, managers also play the role of decision maker. In their **decisional roles,** managers process information and reach conclusions. Information in and of itself is nearly meaningless if it is not used to make organizational decisions. Managers make those decisions. They commit their work groups to courses of action and allocate resources so that the group's plans can be implemented.

Decisional roles
The manager's responsibility for processing information and reaching conclusions.

One of the decisional roles played by managers is that of entrepreneur. Recall that in the monitor role, managers scan the internal and external environments of the organization for changes that may present opportunities. As an entrepreneur, the manager initiates projects that capitalize on opportunities that have been identified. This may involve developing new products, services, or processes.

A second decisional role that managers play is that of a disturbance handler. Regardless of how well an organization is managed, things do not always run smoothly. Managers must cope with conflict and resolve problems as they arise. This may involve dealing with an irate customer, negotiating with an uncooperative supplier, or intervening in a dispute between employees.

As a resource allocator, the manager determines which projects will receive organizational resources. Although we tend to think primarily in terms of financial or equipment resources, other types of important resources are allocated to projects as well. Consider, for example, the manager's time. When managers choose to spend their time on a particular project, they are allocating a resource. Information is also an important resource. By providing access to certain information, managers can influence the success of a project.

The final decisional role played by the manager is that of negotiator. Studies of managerial work at all levels have found that managers spend a good portion of their time negotiating. Managers may negotiate with employees, suppliers, customers, or other work groups. Regardless of the work group, the manager is responsible for all negotiations necessary to ensure that the group is making progress toward achieving the goals of the organization.

SCOPE AND LEVELS OF MANAGERS

We have looked at the various roles that managers play within the organization. To this point, however, we have not distinguished among types of managers. Is it true that all managers are alike? No, it is not. Managers often differ with regard to both the scope of their responsibilities and their level within the vertical structure of the organization.

Scope of Responsibility

The nature of the manager's job will depend on the scope of his or her responsibilities. Some managers have functional responsibilities, whereas others have general management responsibilities.

Functional managers

Managers who are responsible for managing a work unit that is grouped based on the function served.

Functional managers are responsible for a work group that is segmented according to function. For example, a manager of an accounting department is a functional manager. So are the managers of a production department, a research and development department, and a marketing department. Work groups segmented by function tend to be relatively homogeneous. Members of the group often have similar backgrounds and training and perform similar tasks. Functional managers often have backgrounds similar to those of the people they manage. Their technical skills are usually quite strong, as they are typically promoted from within the ranks of the work group. The greatest challenge for these managers lies in developing an understanding of the relationship between their work groups and the other work units within the organization. Equally important, functional managers must convey information back to their work groups and ensure that the members of their unit understand the group's role within the organization as a whole.

General managers

Managers who are responsible for managing several different departments that are responsible for different tasks.

In contrast to functional managers, **general managers** manage several different departments that are responsible for different tasks. For example, the manager of a supermarket is responsible for managing all the departments within the store. The produce manager, grocery manager, bakery manager, and floral manager all report to the general manager. Because general managers manage diverse departments, their technical skills may not be as strong as the skills of the people they manage. The manager of the supermarket, for example, may not know the difference between a chrysanthemum and a violet or have the faintest idea how croissants are made. Whatever general managers lack in technical skills, however, they make up for in communication skills. General managers must coordinate and integrate the work of diverse groups of people. They are responsible for ensuring that all the discrete parts of their organizations function together effectively so that the overall goals of the organization can be achieved.

Levels of Management

Managers exist at various levels in the organizational hierarchy. A small organization may have only one layer of management, whereas a large organization may have several. Consider, for example, the number of levels of management in a single-unit family restaurant versus a large restaurant chain such as Chili's. While the small family restaurant may have only one level of management (the owner), Chili's has several layers, such as general store managers, area directors, and regional directors.

In general, relatively large organizations have three levels of managers: first-line managers, middle managers, and top managers. Figure 1.3 illustrates these managerial levels, as well as the "operatives," or the individuals who are not in the managerial ranks, but who actually deliver the product or service of the organization. The pyramid shape of the figure reflects the number of managers at each level. Most organizations have more first-line managers than middle managers, and more middle managers than top managers. As we will see later in this chapter, however, the trend of the 1990s has been to reduce the number of employees in organizations in an effort to improve efficiency. The net effect of such downsizing has been a significant reduction in the number of middle managers within many corporate structures.

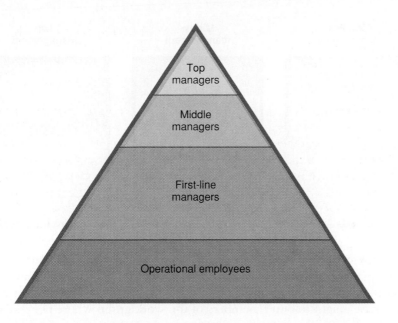

FIGURE 1.3
Levels of management

The skills required of managers at different levels of the organizational hierarchy vary just as their job responsibilities vary. In other words, managers at different levels have different job responsibilities and therefore require different skills. The skills necessary for first-line managers to be effective are not the same as the skills needed by middle or top-level managers, just as the skills needed by middle managers differ from those needed by top-level managers.

While managers at each level must generally possess planning, organizing, leading, and controlling skills, certain job-specific skills are more important at one level than at another. Figure 1.4 illustrates three broad types of managerial skills that vary in importance according to the level of management. As we will discuss, technical skills are likely to be most important for first-line managers, human skills for middle managers, and conceptual skills for top-level managers. Nevertheless, it is important to note that managers at all levels use these skills to some degree, and human skills, in particular, are very important at all three levels of the management hierarchy.[11]

Just as skills vary across levels of management, so do the activities in which managers are involved. A recent study of over 1,000 managers examined the extent to which managers at each level engaged in certain basic activities such as managing individual performance, instructing subordinates, planning and allocating resources, coordinating interdependent groups, managing group performance, monitoring the business environment, and representing one's staff. The results of the study suggest that managers at different levels of the organizational hierarchy are involved in these activities to varying degrees.

As we examine the levels of management in more detail, we will look at the skills that are required of managers at each level, as well as the activities in which they are involved. By doing so, we can gain a better understanding of how managers' jobs vary according to their positions within the organization.

First-Line Managers: One-to-One with Subordinates   First-line managers supervise the individuals who are directly responsible for producing the organization's product or delivering its service. They carry titles such as production supervisor, line manager, section chief, or account manager. First-line managers are often promoted from the ranks based on their ability to deliver the product or service of the organization, as well as their ability to manage others who do the same. The primary objective of first-line managers is to ensure that the products or services of their organization are delivered to the customer on a day-to-day basis.

FIGURE 1.4

Skills needed at different levels of management

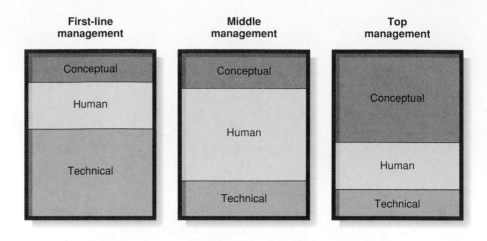

Technical skills

The ability to utilize tools, techniques, and procedures that are specific to a particular field.

Human skills

The ability to work effectively with others.

Technical skills are most important for first-line managers. **Technical skills** enable managers to use their knowledge of the tools, techniques, and procedures that are specific to their particular field. These skills are usually trainable and can be taught to other members of the work group where necessary. Surgeons, secretaries, computer programmers, and auto workers use technical skills every day.

First-line managers are most involved in two of the basic activities listed earlier—managing individual performance and instructing subordinates. Managing individual performance involves motivating and disciplining subordinates, monitoring performance, providing feedback, and improving communications. Instructing subordinates includes training, coaching, and instructing employees on how to do their jobs. Both of these activities become less important as managers rise in the managerial ranks.

Middle Managers: Linking Groups   Middle managers supervise first-line managers or staff departments. They carry titles such as department head, product manager, or marketing manager. Middle managers may come from the ranks of first-line managers in a particular department or from other areas of the organization. These managers are typically selected because they have a strong understanding of the overall strategy of the organization and a commitment to ensuring that it is implemented well. The primary objective of most middle managers is to allocate resources effectively and manage the work group so that the overall goals of the organization can be achieved.

Middle managers must possess strong human skills, commonly known as interpersonal or people skills. **Human skills** involve the ability to work effectively with members of one's work group, as well as with other work groups within the organization. Within the work group, middle managers must manage group dynamics, encourage cooperation, and resolve conflicts. They must listen to the opinions of others and be tolerant of differing beliefs and viewpoints. Further, they should create a work environment where members of the work group can express themselves freely, offer ideas, and participate in the planning activities of the unit. When interacting with outside work groups, middle managers serve as liaisons, communicating the needs and issues of their work group to other members of the organization and conveying information from other work groups back to their units. Fulfilling these responsibilities requires the constant use of human skills.[12] Managers who do not possess these skills are unlikely to be effective middle managers.

Consistent with their linking function, middle managers are most involved in three basic activities—planning and allocating resources, coordinating interdependent groups, and managing group performance. The importance of these three activities rises sharply as one moves from first-line to middle management, but interestingly, it declines slightly for the top management group.

Planning and allocating resources involves setting target dates for project completion, estimating resource requirements, determining where resources should be spent, interpreting the implications of overall organizational strategy for the activities of the work group, and developing evaluation criteria to measure the group's performance. Coordinating interdependent work groups includes reviewing the work and plans of the manager's unit, as well as those of other work groups, and setting priorities for activities. This may also require persuading others to provide the information or resources needed by the manager's group. Finally, in managing group performance, managers must define areas of responsibility for managerial personnel, monitor the performance of group members, and provide feedback on their performance.

Top Managers: An Eye on the Outside   Top managers provide the strategic direction for the organization. They carry titles such as chief executive officer (CEO), president, chief operations officer, chief financial officer, and executive vice-president.

Occasionally, top-level managers work their way up the organizational hierarchy from the first-line management level. More often, however, CEOs of large organizations come with management experience gained from many other organizations. For example, when Lou Gerstner was hired as CEO of IBM, he came with many years of experience with several organizations, including American Express and RJR Nabisco.

Regardless of their background, top-level managers should be selected because they have a vision for the organization and the leadership skills necessary to guide the organization toward reaching that vision. Top managers must set the strategic direction of the organization in light of organizational resources, assets, and skills and the opportunities and threats that exist in the external environment. This was the primary challenge that Jeff Goodman faced when he took the helm of IBAX. A strategic vision was essential if this firm was to survive and prosper.

Top-level managers need to have strong conceptual skills if they are to be effective. **Conceptual skills** enable managers to process a tremendous amount of information about both the internal and the external environment of the organization and to determine the implications of that information. Conceptual skills also enable top-level managers to look at their organization as a whole and understand how separate work groups and departments relate to and affect each other. Finally, strong conceptual skills enable top managers to develop a distinctive personality or culture for the organization.

Conceptual skills
The ability to analyze complex situations and respond effectively to the challenges faced by the organization.

Research indicates that top managers are much more heavily involved in one particular management activity than are their first-line and middle manager counterparts—monitoring the business environment. Though this activity ranks lowest in importance for both first-line and middle managers, it is extremely important at the executive level. Monitoring the business environment involves scanning the external environment for sales, business, economic, and social trends that might affect the organization. In addition, it involves developing and maintaining relationships with outside constituents of the organization. It is important to note that while historical research has suggested that this activity is important only at the top level of the organization, that may change in the future. Later in the chapter, we will examine some changes in the business arena that suggest that monitoring the environment will become an important activity at all levels of the organization.

It is interesting to note that one managerial activity was considered equally important by all three levels of managers—representing staff. From the lower to the upper ranks of management, managers felt that this was an important responsibility. Representing staff is consistent with the spokesperson role outlined by Mintzberg, for it involves communicating on behalf of one's work

TABLE 1.2   Levels of management and associated skills and activities

First-line	Technical	Managing individual performance
		Instructing subordinates
		Representing staff
Middle	Human	Planning and allocating resources
		Coordinating interdependent groups
		Managing group performance
		Representing staff
Top/executive	Conceptual	Monitoring the business environment
		Representing staff

group with other work groups and helping subordinates to interact with other groups. In essence, this activity requires managers to be ambassadors for their units.

All managers must have technical, human, and conceptual skills if they are to be successful. Further, most managers are responsible, to some degree, for all of the managerial activities discussed here. As we have seen, and as is illustrated in Table 1.2, each level of management requires a slightly different mix of skills and involves a somewhat different set of activities. Further, since managers will be involved in different activities at various levels of the organization, they need to develop new skills as they move up the corporate ladder.

We have examined a number of research studies that have focused on managers—who they are, what they do, and how they spend their time. At this point, it is important to examine some environmental and organizational trends that are influencing the job of the manager. Contemporary management theory has begun to recognize the accelerating rate of change in today's business environment and the significant impact of such change on the manager's job. Accordingly, we turn our attention to a review of the changes that are occurring and their effect on the job of the manager of tomorrow.

MANAGING IN THE 21ST CENTURY

Hyperchange
A condition of rapid, dramatic, complex, and unpredictable change that has a significant effect on the ways in which organizations are managed.

Virtually everyone would agree that we live in a dynamic and rapidly changing world. While some might argue that change is nothing new, others would suggest that we are now experiencing hyperchange. **Hyperchange** involves changes that come more quickly; are more dramatic, complex, and unpredictable; and have a more significant impact on the way organizations are managed than did the changes of the past.[13] Further, and most important, the success both of an organization and of individual managers is often dependent upon their ability to respond to hyperchange.

Recognizing change is insufficient— responding proactively is essential. For example, as early as the 1970s, top management at McDonald's recognized the trend away from eating red meat and high-fat foods. Nevertheless, they continued to focus almost exclusively on hamburgers and to fry their french fries in animal fat. Similarly, the three major U.S. car manufacturers knew that the American public wanted smaller, more fuel- efficient automobiles, yet they continued to turn out large, gas-guzzling cars. And although Xerox recognized that demand for the low-end copiers produced by its Japanese competitors was rising, it continued to market only high-end products.

In each of these cases, managers realized that changes were occurring, but failed to react proactively. And in all of these cases, they responded only when the competition forced them to do so. Increasing competition from Wendy's and other restaurants that offered healthy food alternatives finally drove Mc-

Donald's to respond to consumers' growing health consciousness (although the company still struggles to attract the adult consumer).[14] Foreign competition forced U.S. automobile manufacturers to respond to the needs of the consumer. And competition from both domestic and Japanese organizations caused Xerox to open its eyes to the changing marketplace.

Though all of these companies were slow to respond to change, there are also numerous examples of organizations that have capitalized on economic, social, political, and technological changes. Consider Starbucks as a coffee peddler,[15] Sony as the world's largest provider of electronic products,[16] and Gateway Computer as a provider of high-quality, low-cost computer equipment—each of these companies has achieved success by proactively addressing changing market conditions. Managing for Excellence illustrates how Jack Shea, CEO of Spiegel, Inc., has built his business by being a "trend-spotter." Over the last 20 years, Spiegel has achieved success by focusing on changes that occur in the marketplace. From catalogs to specialty retail to Internet shopping, Spiegel has always focused on finding the best distribution channels to reach its time-conscious customers.

The success of both organizations and individual managers depends on their ability to respond to hyperchange. Managers and organizations that succeed realize what changes are occurring and react proactively.
© Michael Newman/PhotoEdit

Change will continue at a relatively rapid rate.[17] Though the 1980s were called the "White Knuckle Decade" and the 1990s have been characterized by dramatic changes, most believe that the changes experienced in those periods will pale in comparison to what will be seen in the future. Competition is brutal and is coming from sources unimaginable 20 years ago. Advances in transportation, communication, and information technology have made it possible to do business across the globe with a level of efficiency that has redefined the competitive structure of many industries. Further, companies can't win with just the lowest price or the highest quality anymore—they have to have both. We are living in a radically different world, and it calls for different methods of management. Achieving organizational success will be extremely challenging in the business environment of the future.

Tomorrow's managers must be prepared to cope with change if they are to be effective. Let's take a look at some of the changes, both environmental and organizational, that will influence the job of the manager and how organizations will function in the future.

ENVIRONMENTAL TRENDS

Many changes have affected and will continue to affect the modern business environment.[18] The next paragraphs describe five of the most significant developments. These five deserve special emphasis because of the far-reaching and profound effect they will have on managers and organizations. Because each of these trends will be addressed in greater detail throughout the book, here we will only briefly consider how they will affect the ways in which organizations are managed.

Globalization of the Marketplace

One need only glance at the recent trends in international trade and foreign direct investment to recognize that the global marketplace is growing in size and economic importance. Most organizations today are involved, in some way,

SPIEGEL: STAYING AHEAD OF THE CROWD

Jack Shea, CEO of Spiegel, Inc. is a trend-spotter—and that's how he stays one step ahead of the crowd. As early as the 1980s, Shea was looking at social, demographic, and technological trends and adjusting Spiegel's strategy accordingly. While the company had traditionally targeted sleepy, rural communities, Shea realized that there were several trends that suggested new target markets. The combination of women entering the work force in substantial numbers, the introduction of the 1-800 number, and the increasing use of credit cards made upscale customers in urban areas more attractive. As a result, he changed the merchandise mix to include upscale brand merchandise, adopted the slogan "a fine department store in print," and set out to reach the urban consumer. The strategy was a huge success.

In 1985, Shea led the charge to expand Spiegel in niche markets through the use of specialty catalogs. He realized that the trends were away from buying merchandise in broad-based department stores and toward shopping in specialty stores. He designed a strategy to capitalize on those trends as well and led Spiegel into the specialty shopping market.

The identity of Spiegel really changed in 1988 when the company purchased Eddie Bauer and its 400 retail outlets. According to Shea, "Eddie Bauer came on the market when the catalog industry was peaking. We looked at it twofold. We didn't have a big men's business by design. Our market was working women. Of Eddie Bauer's $250 million in sales, the majority of it was in men's, which didn't overlap with us. Of that $250 million, $150 million was in retail. Retail gave us another outlet of distribution."

Today, Shea is developing strategies for distributing products through electronic media. In 1994, Spiegel formed a partnership with Time Warner and launched Catalog 1, the first catalog-based cable television shopping channel. That same year, the company began experimenting with catalogs on CD-ROM. In 1995, Spiegel discontinued Catalog 1 and began marketing its products on the Internet through an interactive shopping mall called Dreamshop. While sales have not been as strong as expected, Shea is still hot on the new medium. "We are using it as a marketing tool, to get people to visit us. We get about 100,000 hits a day. Over 53 percent of them are international, and that tells us a lot about potential expansion."

Jack Shea is a leader who knows the importance of meeting customers' needs and responding to changes in the business environment. In his words, "If all of a sudden the American public wanted to buy all their merchandise from a pushcart we would have the biggest and best pushcarts." Now that is an attitude that will win every time![19]

in the international business environment. The level of involvement varies dramatically from company to company, however. Some organizations maintain relatively simple import or export relationships with foreign suppliers or customers. A more significant commitment may involve a contractual, franchising, or licensing agreement with a foreign company. A strategic alliance with an organization from another nation may involve an equity investment in foreign assets. At the far end of the continuum of international business involvement would be the organization that owns and operates foreign subsidiaries.

Organizations that are involved in the international business arena often face unique managerial challenges.[20] The global business environment is more complex than the domestic environment, and organizations operating in the international marketplace face a much broader set of environmental forces.

Capitalizing on today's global opportunities demands managerial skills that were not required of yesterday's manager.[21] For example, decisions about where to locate a plant to minimize labor and transportation costs, how to coordinate production schedules across national borders, and how to disseminate new technology on a global basis are far more common today than in the past. Further, many organizations are finding that they must enter partnerships with other firms to maintain their competitiveness worldwide. The recognition of the need to "cooperate to compete" has led to many global partnerships that require very special international management skills.[22]

Not only has the evolution of the world marketplace forced many organizations to radically change the way they operate, but it will continue to influence the way industries will be structured and the way companies will function for many years to come. Consequently, we have focused on issues of global management throughout this book.

Advances in Information Technology

One of the most significant trends affecting organizations today is the increasing availability of sophisticated information technology.[23] In the 1960s, big, cumbersome mainframe computers existed within individual organizations to support a specific business function. In the 1980s, the development of the personal computer (PC) brought the power of information technology to the individual user. Today, the Information Highway provides access to a worldwide network of information that goes far beyond the individual organization or individual user. Rather it provides a link between users and organizations across the globe and, in doing so, has transformed the ways in which firms are organized and operated.[24]

Information technology has become an integral part of both our personal and professional lives. As Joel Birnbaum, the senior vice-president of research and development at Hewlett-Packard, stated:

> Information technology is becoming pervasive in our society, and that means it will be more noticeable by its absence than its presence. Electricity is an example of a pervasive technology. One assumes its availability (in the developed world), and only its absence is notable. Although information technology is commonplace today, it is not yet integrated into our environment the way telephones, televisions, and automobiles are. Alan Kay, the great visionary who dreamed of a portable, hand-held computer 20 years ago while he was at Xerox, once said that technology is only technology for people who are born after it was invented. From that viewpoint, it's too late for us to become the great application pioneers of the information highway.
> However, just as our children don't think of TVs as technology, children born today are not going to think of computers as technology.[25]

Today, three central themes of change in the area of information technology are affecting business:

1. *The Internet and other forms of globally connected networks.* This infrastructure provides the ability to share information on a worldwide basis. It creates the need to think beyond our individual jobs or organizations and toward the capabilities of operating on a global basis.

2. *Electronic commerce.* Increasingly, the complete operating process, from manufacturing to distribution to human resource

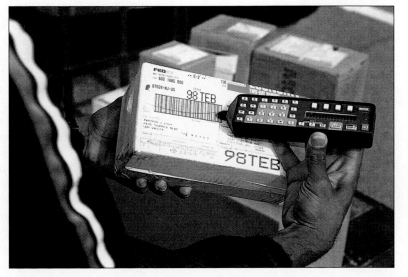

Organizations today are being affected by changes in information technology through the Internet, electronics, and mobile computing. The entire operating process is becoming automated using EDI systems, which allow managers to improve their response time and efficiency and to reduce costs.

© Jeff Greenberg/Unicorn Stock Photos

management, will be automated using electronic data interchange (EDI) systems. This technology will enable managers to reshape their business processes to improve response time and efficiency and reduce costs.

3. *Mobile computing.* Increasingly, individuals will have access to information technology irrespective of their physical location. The increasing availability of portable computing devices will enable individuals to access information and communicate with others from remote sites across the globe.[26]

Federal Express provides an excellent example of an organization that is capitalizing on all three of these trends. Information systems internal to the organization ensure the efficiency of the company's operations. Employees who travel beyond the physical location of the organization are provided with portable computing devices that allow them to communicate directly with the central system. Additionally, the Internet provides customers with the ability to track the location of their package in just seconds by simply entering the

N-E-S-T-L-E-S . . . Nᴇꜱᴛʟᴇ́ Mᴀᴋᴇꜱ ᴛʜᴇ Vᴇʀʏ Bᴇꜱᴛ . . . Iɴғᴏʀᴍᴀᴛɪᴏɴ Sʏꜱᴛᴇᴍꜱ?

Nestlé S.A., known for such products as Perrier water, Nescafé coffee, and Stouffer's frozen foods, is the epitome of a global organization. Headquartered in Vevey, Switzerland, Nestlé generates 98 percent of its business from sales made outside its home country. The organization is comprised of close to 400 operating companies that employ 220,000 employees across 100 countries. Clearly, the complexity of managing such broad-based operations presents significant operational challenges.

To complicate things further, Nestlé is committed to being both decentralized and centralized—simultaneously. Decentralization has been one of the keys to the company's product success. The operating companies are given significant latitude in developing and distributing products that are well suited for their local clientele. Yet Nestlé still wants to achieve the economies of scale that come from centralizing operations on a worldwide scale. These dual goals, products that are local and systems that are global, are a tall order by anyone's measure.

Key to achieving these goals is a sophisticated information system (IS). This system is developed and coordinated at the central level, but is adapted as necessary to meet the specific needs of the operating companies. Once the core global information system has been developed at corporate headquarters and the functionality of the applications has been established, it is transferred to a field IS organization for further adaptation to the local conditions. Once modified to meet local requirements, the applications are deployed internationally. This system provides corporate headquarters and the operating companies at Nestlé with the information necessary to function efficiently and effectively.

The ability to develop IS solutions that are adaptable to multiple markets has been one of the keys to achieving economies of scale across markets, while still maintaining a product focus at the local market level. Nestlé provides an excellent example of how information technology can be used to support highly complex and far-reaching global operations.[27]

ID number of their shipment. Federal Express is capturing the power that is possible through the use of a worldwide information technology infrastructure and sophisticated information systems. Global Perspective provides an example of another company, Nestlé, that uses information technology to manage its highly complex international operations.

According to *Technology Forecast: 1996,* an understanding of emerging trends in today's technological environment is critical to making informed business decisions. In fact, as Paul Turner, executive director of the Price Waterhouse World Technology Centre, observed, "For anyone intending to stay on the leading edge there are two important questions: What are the new key technologies? What are the current trends that should direct my planning for the future of my business?"[28] Today's business leaders must be prepared to address these questions if they intend to remain competitive within their industries.

Increasing Predominance of Entrepreneurial Firms

Large organizations have long been considered the cornerstone of the U.S. economy. While few would argue against the economic benefits of these organizations, there are many economic benefits that come from entrepreneurial firms as well. Although estimates vary widely, entrepreneurship is believed to be responsible for the creation of 40 to 80 percent of all new jobs in the United States. In fact, millions of new jobs are created annually from business start-ups alone.[29] The role of the entrepreneurial company in fostering the vitality of the domestic and world economy is indisputable.

The spirit of the entrepreneur has entered the mainstream of American management philosophy, and entrepreneurial companies are influencing the business environment in many ways. Consider the following:

- Entrepreneurial firms are responsible for a disproportionate number of new products, services, and processes. And those new products, services, and processes are coming faster than ever before. Consider, for example, that gunpowder took 200 years to move from the laboratory to artillery. Today, the equivalent innovation would travel the same path in only a few months.

- Entrepreneurial activities place pressure on large, bureaucratic firms to be more innovative and proactive. In fact, some would suggest that entrepreneurship represents a key solution to problems in product and service quality, poor productivity, and the declining competitiveness of American industry.

- Entrepreneurship provides opportunities for minorities and others who may face barriers in traditional corporate environments.[30] Both immigrants and women have benefited greatly from entrepreneurial activities. Additionally, entrepreneurship may be appropriate for individuals who prefer greater independence than is possible in traditional corporate environments. Entrepreneurial Approach describes how one large company, Wal-Mart, is helping such individuals "get their start."

While the benefits of entrepreneurship are widely recognized, a number of criticisms have been leveled at entrepreneurship in general. Some argue that continuous innovation can cause the premature obsolescence of many products and processes. This forces many organizations to invest heavily in research and development in order to imitate others' innovations. In addition, some critics argue that an economic system that facilitates small entrepreneurial companies at the expense of large established firms weakens the global competitiveness of the nation. This problem is particularly acute in industries where success is dependent upon size and economies of scale.

Despite these arguments, entrepreneurs and entrepreneurially spirited companies will continue to create pressures for change in organizations of all

Entrepreneurial Approach

WAL-MART GIVES A LEG UP TO ENTREPRENEURS

Despite the fact that Wal-Mart is one of the largest companies in the United States, this organization is doing its part to help much smaller businesses. Wal-Mart maintains two programs designed to help entrepreneurs get their start through the company's extensive distribution system. These programs, known as Wal-Mart Innovation Network (WIN) and Support American Made, have already assisted more than 3,000 inventors and entrepreneurs by evaluating their products and prototypes for possible distribution by the chain.

For a small fee, entrepreneurs submit the products and detailed company information to a team of analysts. Those analysts evaluate the entries for product quality, packaging, service capacity, and capitalization levels. A report is provided to the entrepreneurs with either a stamp of approval or suggestions on what must be corrected in order to receive a more favorable report.

While winning a stamp of approval from the program does not guarantee that Wal-Mart will purchase the product for distribution in its stores, it does get vendors special notice by Wal-Mart buyers. Additionally, the entrepreneurs are also provided with information on where to find other support resources and, in some cases, even references to other retail outlets to test-market their products.

"Talk about location, location, location," says one entrepreneur who received a favorable evaluation from the WIN program and now distributes his product in Wal-Mart stores. "It's the kind of foot traffic you dream about."[31]

sizes and types.[32] In fact, innovation, proactiveness, and flexibility will become a prerequisite for success in most industries. Managers must be prepared to respond quickly to changing customer demands and to be proactive with regard to product, service, or process innovation. For that reason, we have highlighted entrepreneurial management practices throughout this book.

Growth in Service-Based Organizations

Though the U.S. manufacturing sector will never be insignificant, the fastest-growing segment of our economy is the service sector.[33] Nearly 80 percent of U.S. jobs and 60 percent of gross domestic product come from the performance of services rather than the production of goods.[34] Further, *Fortune*'s 1996 list of the 100 largest U.S. service corporations includes some of the world's most respected companies, including American Express, Disney, and Wal-Mart.

The shift to a service-based economy has created challenges for many managers. The manufacturing environment requires certain tools, techniques, and managerial practices that may be inappropriate for service organizations.[35] Employees, customers, and managers play dramatically different roles in service firms than in manufacturing firms. As a result, many managers have had to change their approach and redefine relevant performance measures.

If service organizations are going to prosper in the long term, they must develop and maintain management systems that are suited to their unique and special needs.[36] An effective model for service management would:

- Value investments in people as much as investments in machines.
- Use technology to support the efforts of workers on the front line, not just to monitor or replace them.
- Make recruitment and training as crucial for salesclerks and housekeepers as for managers and senior executives.
- Link compensation to performance for employees at every level, not just for those at the top.[37]

The message is clear—frontline workers are the key to success in service organizations. Whereas the old model fails to adequately recognize the importance of recruiting, selecting, and supporting the people who deliver the service to the customer, the new model puts the service delivery employee at the forefront of the management system. The potential benefits of such a system are profound, and senior managers at firms that have adopted such an approach to service management (such as retail company Dayton Hudson and hotel chain Fairfield Inn) have found that service delivery can be the cornerstone of a competitive strategy. As we study the fundamental principles of management, we will apply those principles to service organizations throughout the text.

Focus on Quality

The decade of the 1990s has been the decade of quality management. In fact, quality has been touted as one of the principal solutions to the decline in competitiveness experienced by many U.S. firms throughout the 1980s. But what exactly is quality?

Quality is a term that is used to describe a product or service. A quality product or service is one that meets the customers' needs and provides the value that they want and expect. **Quality management** is a formal approach to management in which the overriding priority of the organization is to deliver a quality product or service and to work toward excellence and continuous improvement in everything it does.

Quality management
A formal approach to management where the overriding priority of the organization is to deliver a quality product or service and to work toward excellence and continuous improvement in all areas of the organization.

Many organizations today face increased competitive pressures from both domestic and foreign sources. As these organizations strive to develop or maintain a competitive advantage within their industries, quality management becomes essential.[38] By improving quality, an organization may achieve benefits such as reduced costs, increased sales, and better customer satisfaction.[39] The promise of such benefits has encouraged many organizations to invest millions of dollars in training and development and new equipment and facilities in an effort to improve their competitiveness.

Quality has become, and will continue to be, a key competitive determinant for most companies. As Robert Stempel said during his tenure as chair of General Motors, "The worldwide quality revolution has permanently changed the way we all do business. Where once quality was limited to technical issues, it is now a dynamic, perpetual improvement process involving people in all aspects of the business."[40] Quality is a fundamental business strategy for many organizations, and few businesses, if any, will survive without a quality orientation. Jeff Goodman certainly found this to be true in the health care information systems industry. In fact, as we will see in the Managerial Incident Resolution at the close of this chapter, Goodman credits the turnaround at IBAX largely to its new quality orientation.

Not only is improving quality vital to increasing the profitability of corporations around the world, but it is also vital to improving the competitiveness of nations. A quality orientation enables organizations to compete in global markets and to capture a share of the worldwide demand for their products. U.S. corporations originally looked to the principles of quality management as a means of combating the increasingly competitive and quality-oriented organizations from Japan. Today, firms from around the globe are looking to quality management as a means of improving overall competitiveness. Providing the highest-quality product or service has been the managerial challenge of the 1990s and will continue to be a key competitive challenge long into the future.[41] As you study management and work your way through this book, you will find that we have focused on quality management all along the way.

The five environmental trends outlined here have had a significant impact on the business environment of today and will continue to influence the business environment of the future. Related to these environmental changes are a number of fundamental changes that are occurring within organizations. The nature of the workplace is changing dramatically, and these changes will also have significant implications for the manager of the future.

ORGANIZATIONAL CHANGES

Contemporary organizations are experiencing a number of important changes that revolve around achieving excellence.[42] The inflexible, authoritarian rulers of the past are being replaced by charismatic, visionary leaders. Similarly, you'll find far fewer middle managers who provide little added value to their companies. In their place are self-managed work teams with a focus on quality and bottom-line results. The relative homogeneity that once characterized the management teams of most U.S. organizations has vanished as the U.S. work force has become more heterogeneous and culturally diverse. Finally, the rigid, vertically integrated corporate structures that were predominant in American corporations over the last several decades are increasingly being abandoned for streamlined, flexible structures that permit greater adaptability to change. While these topics will be discussed in detail elsewhere in the book, let's examine each briefly here.

The Changing Chief Executive Officer
Over the last several decades, most public organizations have grown significantly. With that growth came a larger and more fragmented shareholder base. As the relative power of individual shareholders began to decline, the model for chief executive officers became that of "professional managers"—in theory, accountable to everyone, but in actuality, accountable to no one. Such managers built self-sufficient hierarchies with explicit chains of command. The command-control military model of management was often characteristic of these World War II–generation managers.[43] But today things have changed—dramatically.

The decade of the 1990s was characterized by resignations of once-prominent CEOs[44]—James Robinson from American Express,[45] John Akers from IBM,[46] and Paul Lego from Westinghouse Electric, to name just a few. A fundamental reason for the fall of these mighty CEOs had to do with the inappropriateness of their leadership styles for the rapidly changing and highly dynamic business environment of the 1990s. And if predictions hold true, the 21st century will be even more rapidly changing and highly dynamic than the past decade. These conditions call for a special kind of leader and leadership style.[47]

Today's CEOs can't be afraid of change—they have to love it and be eager to influence its course. They have to be willing to shake things up and make what some might see as radical decisions to ensure the competitive strength of their organizations. They must be willing to abandon the tall hierarchy in favor of flatter, more flexible, participatory designs, encourage dialogue and tolerate dissenting opinions and views, and instill a team-oriented culture that makes quality the first priority.[48] CEOs who embrace this new form of leadership will be those who prosper in the highly volatile business environment of the future, and therefore, we will focus on this style of management throughout the book.

From Middle Managers to Self-Managed Teams
One of the most pervasive trends in American corporations in the last decade has been to "right-size" corporate structures. What does that mean? It means

that companies of all sizes and types have reduced their employee base in an effort to streamline their operations and achieve greater productivity.[49]

The hardest-hit segment of the organization has been the middle manager. Although middle managers make up only about 5 percent of the total work force, they accounted for a disproportionately larger percent of the total layoffs in the last decade.[50] Why have middle managers become so dispensable?

Employees at all levels of the organization are being held accountable for their value-added contribution to the firm. And given the changing times, many middle managers simply cannot be justified based on that criterion. Computers are swiftly altering the way we communicate. With the increasing power of information technology, the informational role of the manager is less critical today. Employees throughout the organization have ready access to the information necessary to do their jobs effectively.

But how are organizations coping with fewer middle managers? Many companies are replacing their traditional hierarchies with self-managed teams (SMTs). **Self-managed teams** are groups of employees who work together toward the development of strategy for their work unit and the achievement of established goals and objectives.[51] Many companies today use SMTs to reduce middle-management costs and foster teamwork throughout the organization. In most cases, the team-oriented culture that results leads to better organizational performance.[52]

In the future, the middle-management function will be performed by managers who are prepared to be team leaders for SMTs. Their primary responsibility will be to empower others to do whatever is needed to achieve the goals of the team. This new breed of middle manager may carry the title of coach, facilitator, sponsor, or team leader rather than manager.

There are numerous examples of organizations that have moved toward a team-oriented work environment. Nabisco, Citicorp, Chrysler, General Foods, General Electric, and Honeywell are just a few of the organizations that have made the shift.

Although the implementation of an SMT work environment has not been problem-free for all organizations, today's competitive business arena will encourage many organizations to consider its use.[53] In fact, SMTs may dominate the organizational design of companies in the future. Consequently, we will focus on this team-oriented approach to management as we work our way through this book.

Increasing Diversity in the Workplace

Closely connected to the globalization of business has been the globalization of the labor market. Just as goods and services flow relatively freely across national boundaries, so do human resources. The result is increased diversity of the population base in this country (and in others as well) and increased diversity in the workplace.[54] **Diversity** refers to the heterogeneity of the work force. No longer does the workplace include only individuals who are very similar to one another (that is, white men); now it includes individuals of both sexes,[55] as well as people of various races, nationalities, and ethnic backgrounds.

Diversity presents new challenges for businesses and managers. As we will see in subsequent chapters, organizational success often requires strong organizational culture and group cohesiveness. Achieving this may be more difficult when the workplace includes people with different backgrounds, from different nations, or with different cultural frames of reference. Men, women, Caucasians, Hispanics, African Americans, and others with diverse racial, national, and ethnic backgrounds often have very different perceptions about the same

Self-managed teams
Groups of employees who design their jobs and work responsibilities to achieve the self-determined goals and objectives of the team.

Diversity
The heterogeneity of the work force in terms of gender, race, nationality, and ethnicity.

situations. As a consequence, it may be more difficult for diverse groups to reach a consensus on common goals and on the methods for achieving those goals.

Many organizations today have established training programs to help employees develop an appreciation for diversity and to foster cooperation among culturally diverse groups. These programs focus on valuing, perhaps even celebrating, diversity and the breadth of thought and experience that results from diverse work groups. Issues of diversity will continue to influence the activities of organizations and the behavior of managers long into the future. Consequently, this topic is discussed in much greater detail throughout the book.

A New Organizational Model

For decades organizations have aspired to be large. Growth was considered to be synonymous with success, and the "bigger is better" syndrome governed the strategic decision making of most firms. Some of the largest and most successful companies of the past (for example, IBM and General Motors) used this model very successfully for decades. Today, however, the model presents problems for many companies. Maintaining flexibility and responding quickly to change are often impossible in large, complex organizations.[56] Being lean and flexible has now become preferable to being big for many organizations.[57] This is particularly true for organizations that operate within rapidly changing industries.

Further, while an organization may be able to develop superior skills in certain core areas of its business, maximizing effectiveness over a broad range of business activities is becoming increasingly difficult. As a result, a number of successful organizations today have adopted an alternative organizational model that offers advantages over the traditional model.[58] While this new model goes by a number of names—the modular corporation, the virtual corporation, and the network corporation, to name a few—the concept is similar.[59] The strategy is to focus on core business activities and outsource other business functions to organizations that can perform those functions more effectively and efficiently. For example, an organization may outsource the production function, the marketing function, the distribution function, or all three. The central organization simply coordinates the activities of others so that the product reaches the ultimate consumer in the most efficient manner possible.

Success with this model requires an ability to develop a set of relationships with organizations that can fulfill business functions that are best outsourced. Consider, for example, the strategies of Dell Computer and Chrysler as compared to IBM and General Motors. Dell and Chrysler have been gaining market share from their more established and heavily integrated counterparts.[60] Why? Because they have a competitive advantage—flexibility and efficiency. This competitive advantage is made possible by a set of relationships with other organizations that perform many business functions for the core organization.

The modular corporation is not a fad, but rather a streamlined organizational model that fits the rapidly changing environment of today and tomorrow. It provides maximum flexibility and efficiency because partnerships and relationships with other firms can be created and disbanded as needed. In addition, this model allows companies to direct their capital and other critical resources toward developing a core competency that provides a competitive advantage. As Donald Beall, CEO of Rockwell International, recently commented, "Without a doubt, focusing on a core competency—and outsourcing the rest— is a major trend of the 1990s."

The environmental and organizational changes we have just described will undoubtedly have a far-reaching impact on tomorrow's business leaders and managers. Table 1.3 provides a list of urgent questions that arise given the rapidly changing business conditions we can expect in the 21st century. These questions are difficult to answer, but doing so is critical to the success of all organizations.[61]

TABLE 1.3   Coping with the challenges of the 21st century

The unprecedented complexity and uncertainty that characterize today's business environment, coupled with the rapid-fire developments in information technology and organizational dynamics, pose a host of urgent questions for today's business leaders.

- *Learning to Adapt.* How can an organization effectively deal with constant and multidimensional change? How can it boost its capacity for learning and adaptability?
- *Structure.* How should a company be organized for maximum responsiveness to continuous and often unpredictable changes in the marketplace? How should it relate to its network of customers and suppliers?
- *Skills.* What leadership qualities are needed to guide tomorrow's organizations? What skills will be crucial to success at all levels of an organization operating in such a dynamic environment?
- *Management Styles.* What happens when command-and-control styles of management collide with ongoing efforts to empower workers? When more workers have greater access to more information, how should business decisions be made?
- *Impact of Information Technology.* What will happen to industry structures when electronic markets and information highways make it possible for buyers and sellers of any size to find each other easily anywhere in the world without human intermediaries?
- *New Ways of Working.* With greatly increased capabilities for communication and coordination, how will individuals work together? How will their work be evaluated? Will there be less need for large offices and factories? Will more people become telecommuters?
- *Innovation.* In such a competitive world where the winners are likely to be companies that are the first to recognize new ideas and implement them, how can an organization create the environment needed to spur continuous innovation?
- *Measures of Success.* As intellectual capital and other intangibles play a larger role in a firm's success, can we adapt traditional accounting measures to more accurately portray the true assets, liabilities, and long-term prospects of a company?

THE CONTEMPORARY MANAGER

What effect will these changes have on the managers of tomorrow? Will they depend on the same set of skills and competencies as managers of the past or will there be new requirements for managerial success? As we begin our study of management, it is helpful to identify the characteristics of managers who will be successful in the future.[62]

THE NEW MANAGER PROFILE

Successful managers will have a different managerial style in the future.[63] Managers will no longer think of themselves as "the boss," but will view themselves as sponsors, team leaders, or internal consultants. The chain of command will be less relevant as managers seek out whomever they need to get the job done. They will work within a fluid organizational structure, involve others in decision making, and share information freely. They will develop their cross-functional skills so they can be more flexible. And, perhaps most important, these new managers will demand results, not just long hours, from

TABLE 1.4   Old versus new manager profile

WHICH KIND ARE YOU?	
OLD MANAGER	**NEW MANAGER**
• Thinks of self as a manager or boss • Follows the chain of command • Works within a set organizational structure • Makes most decisions alone • Hoards information • Tries to master one major discipline, such as marketing or finance • Demands long hours	• Thinks of self as a sponsor, team leader, or internal consultant • Deals with anyone necessary to get the job done • Changes organizational structures in response to market changes • Invites others to join in decision making • Shares information • Tries to master a broad array of managerial disciplines • Demands results
SOURCE: Brian Dumaine, "The New Non-Manager Managers," *Fortune*, February 22, 1993, 80–84. © 1993 Time Inc. All rights reserved.	

their work teams. Table 1.4 lists the key characteristics of the old and new managers.[64]

COMPETENCIES OF TOMORROW'S MANAGERS

This profile implies that the new managers will require certain competencies to be successful.[65] As you study about management and business, you must try to develop these competencies.[66] In effect, the manager of tomorrow must be all of the following:

- *The great communicator.* Communication skills can make or break a career as well as an organization. A good leader spends more time speaking—informing, persuading, and inspiring—than doing anything else. Though speaking is essential, listening may be the key managerial talent of the 1990s. Your ability to understand and apply the techniques of business does not occur in a vacuum. Solutions are hardly ever simple. It is imperative that you learn to read with comprehension, listen intently, question effectively, and write persuasively.

- *The team player.* Managers of the future must be capable of functioning effectively both as team members and as team leaders. Whether these are work teams within the organization or partnerships and team efforts between organizations (for example, the modular corporation), managers will require strong team management skills. Productivity and effectiveness can be greatly enhanced when people work together toward common goals. Team leaders are responsible for ensuring that individual team members are selected appropriately, trained well, encouraged to contribute in meaningful ways to the group effort, and rewarded equitably for their contributions.

- *The technology master.* The information age is now! As Tom Peters notes in his book *Thriving on Chaos,* "Technology is . . . a wild card affecting every aspect of doing business."[67] Almost every business, large and small, has come to view the new technologies of the 1990s as key technologies for the next century. Certainly, managers of the future must be proficient in information technology. Business has transformed from manufacturing

In order to be successful, today's managers must be competent in a wide variety of areas, one of the most important of which is technology. In the past, businesses manufactured products, but today they manage information, and organizations have high expectations of their computers and of those who use them.

© /PhotoEdit

products to managing information, and managers must be capable of making this transition as well. Organizations have exceptionally high expectations of their desktop computers—and the people who use them.

- *The problem solver.* The ability to solve problems is essential for the contemporary manager. The problem solver does not confuse opinions with arguments or association with causality. He or she can both evaluate arguments and construct them. The ability to think incisively, evaluate evidence judiciously, recognize hidden assumptions, and follow lines of reasoning to the sometimes tortuous end is an essential competency for the successful manager.

- *The foreign ambassador.* As was suggested earlier, the global marketplace has become an economic reality. Though the United States continues to be a dominant player, its relative position in the world economy has declined in comparison to Germany and Japan. Maintaining a strong international position will require managers who are prepared to function effectively in a global environment. These managers must appreciate cultural diversity, understand the complexities of the global environment, and be willing to adapt their skills and strategies to cope with international business challenges.

- *The change maker.* Managers of the future must be capable of adapting to change when appropriate and creating change when necessary. Effective managers cannot be threatened by change, but rather must embrace change and desire to influence its course.[68] In fact, tomorrow's managers will be the architects of change to the extent that they respond proactively to environmental trends, look for new ways to meet the needs of their customers, and explore methods of increasing the efficiency and effectiveness of their organization.

- *The 21st-century leader.* In the highly competitive business environment of today and tomorrow, managers can't wield total control from the top of a pyramid; nor can they control the action from the sidelines. Rather, they must empower the individual employees of the organization to do whatever is necessary to achieve its goals and work with them to ensure that they have the resources to get the job done.

Meeting the Challenge

ARE YOU READY TO MANAGE IN THE YEAR 2000?

Use the following scale to rate the frequency with which you perform the behaviors described below. Place the number (1–7) in the blank preceding the statement.

Rarely	Irregularly	Occasionally	Usually	Frequently	Almost Always	Consistently
1	2	3	4	5	6	7

____ 1. In dealing with others, my major concern is getting what I want; what happens to others is not very important to me.

____ 2. If I had to choose between working hard on some task and working very little but still doing more than other persons, I would prefer the latter.

____ 3. I am not satisfied with a relationship or business arrangement unless the other people in it are satisfied too.

____ 4. I like it best if my peers and I are about equally successful.

____ 5. In doing my work, I tend to set my own standards; I'm not very concerned with how others do their work.

____ 6. It is exciting to pit my abilities, skills, and intelligence against those of others.

____ 7. If I were to receive a larger reward than another person, even though we both did the same work, I would be quite unhappy.

____ 8. If I were to receive a bigger raise than my coworkers, I would feel uncomfortable.

Transfer your answers to the scoring form below and total the four columns. Circle your highest score.

Column A	Column B	Column C	Column D
Question 1 ____	Question 2 ____	Question 3 ____	Question 4 ____
Question 5 ____	Question 6 ____	Question 7 ____	Question 8 ____
Total ____	Total ____	Total ____	Total ____

If your highest score was for column A, you are considered an *individualist*. Your are mainly concerned with your own outcomes and have little interest in those of others. If your highest score was for column B, you are probably a *competitor*. Your main concern is being better than others, overcoming them in competitive situations. If your highest score was for column C, you are a *cooperator*. You prefer to maximize the other person's outcomes as well as your own. If your highest score was for column D, you are an *equalizer*. You prefer to minimize differences between yourself and others. Of course, you may well show a mixed pattern. In any case, examine your answers to these questions carefully—they may reveal much about your management orientation. Managers in the future need to be oriented toward working with, not against, others.

SOURCE: Robert A. Varon and Paul B. Paulus, *Understanding Human Relations: A Practical Guide to People at Work*, 312–13. Copyright © 1991 by Allyn and Bacon. Adapted by permission.

Meeting the Challenge provides a questionnaire that will help assess your readiness to be a manager in the year 2000. It evaluates your management orientation with regard to being a team player. If you find that your orientation is to work independently or to be highly competitive with others in your work group, you may want to focus on building your teamwork skills as you continue your education.

Students of management who have already begun their careers may want to look at Experiential Exercise 1.2. This "Test for Success" will give you a sense of whether a promotion is likely or you need to be looking for a new organization to join.

MANAGERIAL IMPLICATIONS

The managers of the future must be better and brighter and have more energy, enthusiasm, and insight than the managers of the past. The flatter, leaner structures that characterize today's organizations leave fewer avenues for promotion.[69] As a result, only the very best will make their way up the corporate ladder. The jobs of tomorrow's managers will be increasingly demanding and challenging, but will be rewarding for those who perform well. To be an effective manager in tomorrow's business environment, you must:

- Keep abreast of changing conditions that affect the organization.
- Develop an understanding of the major environmental trends that are affecting organizations across the globe.
- Be flexible and adaptable to organizational changes, as well as proactive in initiating change when appropriate.
- Understand the changing role of the manager within the corporate structure.
- Make the most of your education and develop the skills and competencies necessary for managerial success.
- Focus on excellence and quality in everything you do.

As you read this book and study the field of management, you must focus on learning how to be an effective manager. Only through a conscious effort to develop your managerial talent can you hope to prosper as a leader in the business environment of tomorrow.

IBAX: A COMPANY IN NEED OF LEADERSHIP

When Jeff Goodman joined IBAX in 1990, the company was millions of dollars in the red. By the close of 1993, the company had posted a profit of $2.1 million. What happened to cause such a turnaround? Many say it was strong leadership and a focus on doing things differently.

In three years, Goodman reduced the company's staff from 750 to 580—which included slashing management ranks from 100 to 60. By cutting these salaries and eliminating unnecessary travel and consultants' fees, Goodman cut $20 million from IBAX's operating expenses.

Then Goodman really went to work. He decided that IBAX could grow best if it was freed from its monolithic structure. Instead, Goodman created six self-running companies within the corporation. Each has its own leaders, who have formed employee teams to handle operations. A look at IBAX's hiring process shows just how deep-rooted the teamwork concept is. Goodman and other top executives don't hire people for openings. That's left up to the rank and file—the other team members. Goodman thinks they're best suited to determine whether a position needs to be filled, create job descriptions, interview candidates, and hire them if they fit in.

Goodman also focused the company's attention on quality. Continuous improvements in product and service quality became the driving force behind decision making at IBAX. In fact, Goodman's relentless pursuit of quality earned him comparisons to a pit bull. But such dogged traits produced results—both customer satisfaction and sales began to grow.

Managerial
Incident
Resolution

IBAX responded to its changing environment by implementing modern management practices such as team building and a quality orientation.[70] The Integrative Case that appears at the close of each part of this book provides a more detailed description of how IBAX's performance was improved dramatically through effective planning, organizing, leading, and controlling. You can follow the IBAX story as you move through the book and learn more about effective management practices.

SUMMARY

- Management is defined as the process of administering and coordinating resources effectively, efficiently, and in an effort to achieve the goals of the organization. Management typically occurs in an organizational setting. Organizations comprise a group of individuals who work together toward common goals. The process of management involves four primary functions: planning, organizing, leading, and controlling.

- Henry Mintzberg identified three primary roles played by managers—interpersonal roles, informational roles, and decisional roles. In their interpersonal roles, managers act as figureheads, leaders, and liaisons. In their informational roles, managers serve as monitors, disseminators, and spokespeople. Finally, managers in their decisional roles function as entrepreneurs, disturbance handlers, resource allocators, and negotiators.

- Managers' scope of responsibility varies depending on whether they are functional or general managers. Functional managers are responsible for a work group that is segmented according to function. General managers oversee several different departments that are responsible for different tasks. Functional managers typically have strong technical skills, whereas general managers require strong human skills.

- Most large organizations have three levels of managers: first-line, middle, and top managers. These managers differ both in terms of the skills they require and the way they spend their time.

- Five environmental trends will continue to have a significant effect on the way organizations operate and the way managers do their jobs. These trends are (1) the globalization of business, (2) advances in technology, (3) the increasing predominance of entrepreneurial firms, (4) the growth of service-based organizations, and (5) the focus on quality management.

- A number of important organizational changes are occurring today. The autocratic and inflexible CEOs of the past are being replaced by charismatic, visionary leaders. Team leaders of self-managed teams are replacing traditional middle managers in many corporate structures. Further, culturally diverse work groups have become the norm rather than the exception. Finally, the large, complex corporate structures of the past are being replaced by streamlined, flexible structures that depend on outsourcing to achieve efficiency.

- The managers of tomorrow will be quite different from the managers of yesterday. They will be more team-oriented, participatory, flexible, and focused on results. Further, they must be strong communicators, team players, masters of technology, problem solvers, foreign ambassadors, change makers, and leaders.

KEY TERMS

Management	Controlling	Technical skills
Efficiency	Managers	Human skills
Effectiveness	Interpersonal roles	Conceptual skills
Organization	Informational roles	Hyperchange
Planning	Decisional roles	Quality management
Organizing	Functional managers	Self-managed teams
Leading	General managers	Diversity

REVIEW QUESTIONS

1. Define the concept of management within an organizational context. What are the functions of management and why are they important?
2. Describe the roles of the manager as outlined by Mintzberg.
3. Describe the responsibilities of the functional manager. Describe the responsibilities of the general manager. How do the skills needed by each type of manager differ?
4. Distinguish among the three levels of managers in terms of the skills they need and the activities in which they are involved.

5. What are the five environmental trends that are affecting organizations today? Explain how each of these trends may affect the job of the contemporary manager.
6. Identify and discuss the organizational changes that are occurring today. What is the anticipated impact of these changes on the job of the contemporary manager?
7. Describe the manager of tomorrow in terms of both managerial style and the competencies that will be necessary for success.

DISCUSSION QUESTIONS

Improving Critical Thinking

1. How is the increasing diversity of this nation influencing the student body at your university? Is the university administration taking proactive steps to ensure diversity on your campus? Do they maintain programs to ensure that diversity is celebrated rather than simply tolerated? Brainstorm on additional ways in which your university could encourage and support diversity on your campus.
2. Review the business curriculum at your university. In what ways is it designed to support the development of the managerial style that will be needed by the manager of the future? What could you do outside the classroom to further develop this profile?

Enhancing Communication Skills

3. What can you do to ensure that you develop the competencies you need to succeed as a manager? Write a one-page plan to develop these competencies.

4. Identify a company that you feel has a quality orientation and one that you feel does not. Compare and contrast these organizations. Present your assessment to the class orally.

Building Teamwork

5. We have concluded that the contemporary manager is somewhat different than the manager of the past. If Mintzberg were to conduct his research on managerial roles today, how would you expect his results to differ? With a small group of your fellow students, formulate a response that can be presented to the class.
6. As organizations continue to downsize and the ranks of middle managers are reduced, how might the responsibilities of both top-level managers and first-line managers change? How might technology be used to facilitate these changes? Form a student team to respond to these questions.

1. Identify a medium- to large-sized company in your community. Contact a member of upper-level management at this company and request an interview. During the interview, ask the manager the questions listed in Table 1.3. Focus on learning more about how information technology is affecting the ways in which the company operates. Share what you learn with the rest of the class.

2. Select one of the five environmental trends identified in the chapter. Using the Internet, research what is currently happening with respect to that trend. In particular, look for statistics that show the strength of the trend and how it is affecting the business environment.

3. Identify a lower-, middle-, and upper-level manager in a specific organization. Using e-mail, contact these managers and share with them what you know about the three primary roles of managers according to Mintzberg—interpersonal, informational, and decision-making. Ask them to give examples of how they serve in each of these roles within their organization. Also ask them to estimate the percentage of their time spent in each role. Compare and contrast the three managers' responses.

INFORMATION TECHNOLOGY: Insights and Solutions

ETHICS: Take a Stand

Bob Wise is the vice-president of operations for Work Station, a national distributor of office supplies. Bob has just come from a meeting with store managers where he listened to the ideas and philosophies of the company's management team. One manager, Sally Mims, made a particularly good impression on Bob. Sally, a recent MBA graduate from the local university, was the most creative and proactive of the managers on Bob's team. Her employee group is the most cohesive and has won virtually all of the sales and promotion contests held by the company for the last year. Further, and not surprisingly, Sally's store has consistently outperformed stores in similar market areas.

As Bob walked back to his office, he thought about the other managers on his team. Most of the store managers were older men, over the age of 50. All of them had been with the company for over ten years, many had a complacent attitude about their work, and most of the managers seemed to be very resistant to change. Although the company had held numerous management development workshops over the last several years, the managers resisted attending. Even when they did attend, they seemed to gain very little from the experience. They almost ridiculed the team approach to management, preferring to rely on authoritarian relationships with their subordinates to get the performance they desired—even though that approach did not seem to be working.

As Bob contemplated the situation, two alternative courses of action came to mind. Perhaps what his managers needed was more extensive training. Maybe he should find a two- or three-week management development program that would help the older managers see the light. Though such a program would be expensive, it might be the only way to instill some creativity into the company's current management team. Bob was doubtful that the training would help many of the managers, however.

As Bob looked for another alternative, he could not help thinking about how impressive Sally Mims had been in the store managers' meeting. Her MBA training and her youthful enthusiasm were definite advantages in this business. "If only we had a management team composed of managers like Sally," Bob thought. As this image formed in his mind, Bob began to think of ways to build such a team. It would require terminating many of the current managers, but to the extent that they could be replaced by younger, more effective managers, the company could reap great benefits. From a cost perspective, this alternative was quite attractive, as the younger employees would come in at lower salaries and could be given less expensive benefit packages.

Though the second alternative seemed to have much greater long-range potential for the company, Bob was concerned about the impact of terminating his present management team. Where would they go? Could they get other jobs? Would it be fair to treat people who had given ten years of their lives to the company in such a way?

For Discussion
1. Do you think it is ethical to replace managers with ten years' seniority with younger, less expensive managers? Why or why not?
2. What are the advantages and disadvantages of each of the alternatives that Bob identified?
3. Which alternative would you choose if you were Bob? Why?

THINKING CRITICALLY: Debate the Issue

PROTECTIONISM VERSUS FREE MARKETS

As this chapter explained, the world is fast becoming a global marketplace. As this transpires, many continue to argue the benefits of free-market economies versus independent-market economies that do not encourage free trade and follow protectionism policies.

Form teams with four to five students on each team. Half of the teams should prepare to argue the benefits of free markets, while the other teams should prepare to argue the benefits of protectionist policies. This will require significant research into the topic of world trade. Your instructor will select two teams to present their findings to the class in a debate format.

UPS: THE COMPLETE PACKAGE

Home Page: {http://www.ups.com/}

The UPS Story: {http://www.ups.com/about/about.html}

Video Case

From its humble beginnings in 1907, United Parcel Service has grown to be the largest package delivery provider in the world. In 1996, the company had sales of $22.5 billion, based on an average daily delivery volume of 12 million parcels and documents. Today, UPS has the capacity to deliver to every address in North America. Worldwide, the company has more than 4 billion people within its reach. This total exceeds that of any other package delivery firm and is twice as much as any phone company.

What makes UPS successful is an uncompromising commitment to customer service. For instance, through a program called UPS Worldwide Logistics, the company can tailor its operations to facilitate the needs of almost any business, which might include rate negotiation, customs clearance, warehousing, electronic data exchange, and inventory control. Another program, called Inventory Express, is a logistic management service in which UPS stores the customer's merchandise, then ships it as needed— "just in time." In addition, the company provides its customers with many information services, such as TotalTrack and MaxiShip. TotalTrack, which is available on the Internet as {http://www.ups.com/tracking/tracking.html}, can instantly provide customers with tracking information for all bar-coded air and ground packages. MaxiShip is a system that lets customers manage the entire distribution process, from the rating and zoning of packages to preparation of user-defined management reports.

To achieve a high degree of customer service, UPS relies on a highly dedicated work force and state-of-the-art technology. The dedication of the company's employees is achieved through three long-standing company policies: employee ownership, training, and promotion from within. UPS stock is owned by its employees. This makes each employee a part owner of the firm, which encourages a high level of customer service. Technology at UPS spans an incredible range, from aircraft specially designed to accommodate packages to global computer and communication systems. One computer system, referred to as UPSnet, links more than 1,300 UPS distribution sites in 46 countries.

UPS considers itself to be not just in the delivery business but in the customer satisfaction business. The highest priorities for the company over the next five years will be to continue to introduce new services, provide customers with comprehensive information about their shipments, and provide updated training to the company's 339,000 employees. As when the company began in 1907, the future success of UPS depends upon its ability to continue to meet the evolving needs of its customers.

For Discussion

1. Provide examples of both efficiency and effectiveness in UPS's current operations. What steps will the managers of UPS need to take to ensure that the company remains both efficient and effective in the future?

2. Four environmental trends that will influence the manner in which firms compete in the future include the globalization of the marketplace, the increasing predominance of entrepreneurial firms, the growth in service-based organizations, and the increased focus on quality. Is UPS well positioned to take advantage of these trends? Why or why not?

3. Have you had personal experience dealing with UPS? Was your experience consistent with the way UPS is portrayed in the video?

CASE

A DAY IN THE LIFE OF BECKY JOHNSON

Becky Johnson is the operations manager for ABE Manufacturing Company. She arrives at work every day at 7:30 A.M. Today, she must prepare for a meeting that is scheduled for 8:30 A.M. The meeting lasts one hour, and the managers attending it discuss budget problems that have resulted from an increase in a supplier's prices. The group decides that Becky will call the supplier to negotiate a better price. If a lower price cannot be negotiated, ABE will drop this supplier and seek out another.

At 9:30 A.M. Becky goes back to her office where four phone messages (one personal, three business) are waiting for her. She has time only to return two business calls. She makes an appointment for next week with one of the callers. At 10:10 A.M. she writes a letter to another important supplier and takes a phone call from the marketing department about a current product's safety record. At 10:40 A.M. she holds a meeting with office personnel to talk about new office procedures that will speed up the process of ordering raw materials. She stresses how important it is to keep improving inventory management. She mentions some minor problems that, if corrected, could improve productivity, but also commends everyone on what a great job they are doing otherwise. At 11:30 A.M. she goes to the production floor to meet with floor supervisors and workers.

At 12:10 P.M. Becky goes to a well-deserved lunch and bumps into fellow managers from several other departments. During lunch the manager from the marketing department discusses several potential product ideas for ABE. Several of the managers, including Becky, set up a time when they can meet formally to discuss these ideas.

At 1:00 P.M. Becky returns from lunch to discover three new messages. She has time only to return two phone calls, including one from earlier in the morning. Afterward, she prepares for a meeting with her boss that is scheduled for 2:00 P.M. During this meeting, the boss talks to Becky and other managers about ways to reduce inventory levels. The meeting lasts until 3:30 P.M.

Since Becky likes to make sure all of her employees understand company policies and procedures, she goes back to her office and writes a brief report about the inventory improvement meeting for their review. Later, on the way down the hall to get a drink, Becky sees the marketing manager and they continue their conversation about the new product ideas. She then proceeds to the production floor to talk to the production employees and supervisors. She asks specifically if they've had any problems with components or raw materials.

Finally, at 4:45 P.M. Becky returns to her office to make a couple of final phone calls. One call is an inquiry to a manager in another division. Becky asks if he has experienced any difficulty with a certain piece of equipment that has been a real problem spot for one of Becky's production lines. At 5:30 P.M. Becky Johnson goes home.

For Discussion

1. At what points in the day was Becky acting in (1) interpersonal roles, (2) informational roles, and (3) decisional roles?

2. In what activities (as outlined in the chapter) did Becky engage throughout the day?

3. Did Becky spend her time appropriately? How might she have adjusted her management style to be more effective?

EXPERIENTIAL EXERCISE 1.1

What Is Excellence?

Purpose: To identify the characteristics of excellent organizations and to see if the class can come up with a common set of characteristics that people agree are associated with sustained high performance in organizations.

Step 1 For ten minutes, have each class member make a list of characteristics of "excellence."

Step 2 Form groups of four or five people. Each group will review the individual lists of each of its members. After discussion a group list should be developed. If most of the members disagree with a particular characteristic, it should be deleted from the list. Display the final group list on the chalkboard or flip chart.

Step 3 Reassemble the class to discuss the group lists. Make a new combined list of those characteristics identified by several groups.

Step 4 Discuss how the combined class list compares to the set of eight factors identified by Peters and Waterman in Table 1.1.

For Discussion

1. Were the original individual lists very different or fairly similar? Why?

2. How easy or difficult was it for groups to agree on a list? Why?

3. Did the class list resemble the Peters and Waterman list? Why?

EXPERIENTIAL EXERCISE 1.2

Test for Success[71]

To stay or not to stay—that is the question. Use the first part of this quiz to figure out whether you're in line for a promotion. If not, the second part will help you determine when's the right time to make a move.

Will I be promoted soon?

If your answer is YES, add:

1. *Is your company doing well?* Is it posting good financial results, drumming up new business, hiring and promoting others? . . . .   10 points _____

2. *Do you get choice assignments?* Are you put on projects that showcase your talents? Are you pushed to learn new things and increase your skills? . . . . .   10 points _____

3. *Are you popular?* Does your boss like you? Do you like your boss? Are you getting along well with your peers? . . . .   10 points _____

4. *Is your input solicited?* Are you included in key meetings? Do people come to you with questions about matters outside your usual domain? . . . .   5 points _____

5. *Do you have the skills?* Can you take the next logical step in your company right now without further training or experience? . . . .   5 points _____

6. *Are you golden with the grapevine?* Do others drop hints that you're in good standing? Hear any rumors that your boss likes your work? . . . .   5 points _____

7. *Have you groomed a successor?* Were you to be promoted, is there someone who could step into your job right away? .   5 points _____

If you scored higher than 40, start thinking about how to decorate that corner office. You're primed for a promotion.

Total points: _____

If you scored 25 to 40, stay tuned.

If you scored less than 25, move to the second part of this quiz.

Is it time to move on?

1. *Have you stopped learning?* Are you getting stale? Do you no longer get the chance to increase your skills and broaden your experience? . . . .   10 points _____

2. *Has your status slipped?* Are exchanges with your boss becoming increasingly one-sided? Do you feel as if you have less freedom to act than in the past? . . . .   10 points _____

3. *Is your company faltering?* Has it lost market share, taken a major hit on its stock price? Has it been sharply criticized by Wall Street, the press, or its own employees? . . . .   10 points _____

4. *Are big changes on the horizon?* Has your company merged with another recently? Any kind of major organizational restructuring under way? Have new high-level executives come in from the outside? . . .   5 points _____

5. *Are you out of the loop?* Have you stopped hearing gossip? Do you feel you're the last to know about key decisions? . . . .   5 points _____

6. *Do you dread going to work?* Are you anxious on Sunday nights? Have your eating and sleeping habits changed? Do friends and family comment that you look tired or seem unhappy? . . . .   5 points _____

7. *Is your salary stagnating?* Are your raises on a downward trend percentagewise? . . . . . .   5 points _____

If you scored higher than 40, close this book, take a deep breath, then start your search immediately!

Total points: _____

If you scored 25 to 40, put out feelers.

If you scored less than 25, your situation may improve, but remain open to outside opportunities.

ENDNOTES

1. Based on an interview with Jeff Goodman, CEO of IBAX; G. Yasuda, "IBAX's Goodman Gets to the Heart of Problems," *Orlando Sentinel,* January 17, 1994.

2. M. P. Follett, "Dynamic Administration," in *Dynamic Administration: The Collected Papers of Mary Parker Follett,* ed. H. Metcalf and L. F. Urwick (New York: Harper & Row, 1942).

3. P. F. Drucker, *The Effective Executive* (New York: Harper & Row, 1967).

4. T. J. Peters and R. H. Waterman Jr., *In Search of Excellence: Lessons from America's Best-Run Companies* (New York: Harper & Row, 1982).

5. See, for example, C. P. Hales, "What Do Managers Do? A Critical Review of the Evidence," *Journal of Management Studies,* 23, 1986, 88-113; C. M. Pavett and A. W. Lau, "Managerial Work: The Influence of Hierarchical Level and Functional Specialty," *Academy of Management Journal,* 26, 1983, 170-77; H. Willmott, "Images and Ideals of Managerial Work: A Critical Examination of Conceptual and Empirical Accounts," *Journal of Management Studies,* 21, 1984, 349-68; H. Willmott, "Studying Managerial Work: A Critique and a Proposal," *Journal of Management Studies,* 24, 1987, 249-70.

6. A. I. Kraut, P. R. Pedigo, D. D. McKenna, and M. D. Dunnette, "The Role of the Manager: What's Really Important in Different Management Jobs," *Academy of Management Executive,* 3, 1989, 286-93.

7. C. M. Pavett and A. W. Lau, "Managerial Work."

8. H. Mintzberg, "The Manager's Job: Folklore and Fact," *Harvard Business Review,* September-October 1974, 91.

9. H. Mintzberg, "The Manager's Job: Folklore and Fact," *Harvard Business Review,* July-August 1974, 49-61.

10. Ibid.

11. R. L. Katz, "Skills of an Effective Administrator," *Harvard Business Review,* September-October 1974, 91.

12. R. L. Katz, "Skills of an Effective Administrator," 92.

13. G. Land, *Grow or Die: The Unifying Principle of Transformation* (New York: Random House, 1973).

14. S. Branch, "McDonald's Strikes Out with Grownups," *Fortune,* November 11, 1996, 157-62.

15. See, for example, J. Reese, "Starbucks: Inside the Coffee Cult," *Fortune,* December 9, 1996, 190-98.

16. K. Harris, "Mr. Sony Confronts Hollywood," *Fortune,* December 23, 1996, 36.

17. W. Kiechel III, "How We Will Work in the Year 2000," *Fortune,* May 17, 1993, 38-52.

18. J. Huey, "IS Impossible," *Fortune,* September 23, 1991, 135-40.

19. L. Strohl, "Ahead of the Crowd," *Managing,* Fall 1996, 12-14.

20. P. F. Drucker, "Behind Japan's Success," *Harvard Business Review,* January-February 1981, 83-90; E. Thornton "50 Fateful Years: From Enemy to Friend to ?" *Fortune,* December 16, 1991, 126-34.

21. E. Thornton, "Japan's Struggle to Be Creative," *Fortune,* April 19, 1993, 129-34.

22. J. W. Slocum Jr. and D. Lei, "Global Strategic Alliances: Payoffs and Pitfalls," *Organizational Dynamics,* 19, 3, 1991, 44-61.

23. I. T. Siegel "Catching the Ninth Wave: Information, Technology and Strategic Change," *Planning Review,* 23, September/October, 1995, 21-23; *Globalization, Technology, and Competition,* eds. S. P. Bradley, J. A. Hausman, and R. L. Nolan (Boston, Mass.: Harvard Business School Press, 1993).

24. See, for example, A. B. Shani and J. A. Sena, "Information Technology and the Integration of Change: Sociotechnical System Approach," *Journal of Applied Behavior Science,* 30, 2, June 1994, 227-47; P. W. Yetton, K. D. Johnston, and J. F. Craig, "Computer-Aided Architects: A Case Study of IT and Strategic Change," *Sloan Management Review,* Summer 1994, 57-67; E. K. Clemons, "Information Technology and the Boundary of the Firm: Who Wins, Who Loses, Who Has to Change," in *Globalization, Technology, and Competition,* eds. S. P. Bradley, J. A. Hausman, and R. L. Nolan, (Boston, Mass.: Harvard Business School Press, 1993), 219-42.

25. Price Waterhouse World Technology Centre, *Technology Forecast: 1996* (Menlo Park, Calif.: 1996), 645.

26. Ibid.

27. J. Greenbaum, "Nestlé Makes the Very Best . . . Standard?" *Information Week,* August 23, 1993, 22-26; J. Greenbaum, "Nestlé's Global Mix," *Information Week,* April 25, 1994, 44-46; F. Hect, "Nestlé Takes On the World," *Eurobusiness,* February 15, 1996, 18-23.

28. Ibid, vii.

29. Ibid.

30. For examples of six successful entrepreneurs, see M. Barrier, "Entrepreneurs Who Excel," *Nation's Business,* August 1996, 18-28.

31. H. Plotkin, "Wal-Mart Throws the Book at Small-Biz Vendors," *Inc.,* January 1997, 24.

32. For readings in the area of entrepreneurship, see K. J. Marshack, "Copreneurs and Dual-Career Couples: Are They Different?" *Entrepreneurship Theory & Practice,* Fall 1994, 49-69; E. L. Hansen, "Entrepreneurial Networks and New Organization Growth," *Entrepreneurship Theory & Practice,* Summer 1995, 7-19; K. Stephenson, "The Formation and Incorporation of Virtual Entrepreneurial Groups," *Entrepreneurship Theory & Practice,* Spring 1995, 35-52.

33. M. Magnet, "Good News for the Service Economy," *Fortune,* May 3, 1993, 46-52.

34. R. Zemke, "The Emerging Art of Service Management," *Training,* January 1992, 37-42.

35. M. E. Mangelsdorf, "Making It: Service Firms Have a Lot to Learn from U.S. Manufacturing Companies These Days," *Inc.,* October 1991, 20-24.

36. K. Bertrand, "In Service, Perception Counts," *Business Marketing,* April 1989, 44-51; R. Zemke, "The Emerging

Art of Service Management"; G. Foster, "What Service Firms Can Learn from Manufacturing," *Across the Board,* March 1992, 55.

37. Ibid.

38. P. F. Drucker, "The New Productivity Challenge," *Harvard Business Review,* November-December 1991, 69-79.

39. B. M. Cook, "Quality: The Pioneers Survey the Landscape," *Industry Week,* October 21, 1993, 240, 20, 68-73; P. B. Crosby, "The Next Effort," *Management Review,* 81, 2, 1992, 64.

40. "International Quality Study: The Definitive Study of the Best International Quality Management Practices" (joint project of Ernst & Young and American Quality Foundation: 1996), 1.

41. R. Jacob, "TQM: More Than a Dying Fad?" *Fortune,* October 18, 1993, 66-72.

42. T. A. Stewart, "The Search for the Organization of Tomorrow," *Fortune,* May 18, 1992, 92-98.

43. J. A. Byrne, "Requiem for Yesterday's CEO: Old-Style Execs Who Can't Adapt Are Losing Their Hold," *Business Week,* February 15, 1993, 32-33.

44. T. A. Stewart, "The King Is Dead," *Fortune,* January 11, 1993, 34-41.

45. B. Saporito, "The Toppling of King James III," *Fortune,* January 11, 1993, 42-43.

46. C. Loomis, "King John Wears an Uneasy Crown," *Fortune,* January 11, 1993, 44-45.

47. Ibid.

48. R. Jacob, "Thriving in a Lame Economy," *Fortune,* October 5, 1992, 44-54.

49. L. S. Richman, "When Will the Layoffs End?" *Fortune,* September 20, 1993, 54-56; J. Fierman, "When Will You Get a Raise?" *Fortune,* July 12, 1993, 34-36.

50. S. Sherman, "A Brave New Darwinian Workplace," *Fortune,* January 25, 1993, 50-56.

51. See, for example, S. J. Wall and S. R. Wall, "The Evolution (Not the Death) of Strategy," *Organizational Dynamics,* 24, 2, Autumn 1995, 6-19.

52. D. Barry, "Managing the Bossless Team: Lessons in Distributed Leadership," *Organizational Dynamics,* Winter 1992, 31-47.

53. D. Barry, "Managing the Bossless Team."

54. W. B. Johnstone, "Global Work Force 2000: The New World Labor Market," *Harvard Business Review,* March-April 1991, 115-29.

55. N. J. Perry, "More Women Are Executive VPs," *Fortune,* July 12, 1993, 16.

56. R. Miles, H. Coleman Jr., and W. E. D. Creed, "Keys to Success in Corporate Redesign," *California Management Review,* 37, 3, Spring 1995, 128-45.

57. N. Nohria and J. D. Berkley, "An Action Perspective: The Crux of the New Management," *California Management Review,* Summer 1994, 70-92.

58. R. E. Miles and C. C. Snow, "Organizations: New Concepts for New Forms," *California Management Review,* 28, 1986, 62-73.

59. H. H. Hinterhuber and B. M. Levin, "Strategic Networks—The Organization of the Future, *Long Range Planning,* 27, 3, 1994, 43-53; S. Tully, "The Modular Corporation," *Fortune,* (February 8, 1993)A, 106-14; John Byrne, "The Virtual Corporation," *Business Week,* February 8, 1993, 98-103; R. E. Miles and C. C. Snow, "Organizations: New Concepts for New Forms," 62-71.

60. See, for example, A. Taylor III, "Chrysler's Great Expectations," *Fortune,* December 9, 1996, 101-104.

61. T. W. Malone, M. S. S. Morton, and R. R. Halperin, "Organizing for the 21st Century," *Strategy & Leadership,* July/August 1996, 7-10.

62. E. Thornton, "Japan's Struggle to Be Creative."

63. B. Keys and T. Case, "How to Become an Influential Manager," *Academy of Management Executive,* 4, 1990, 38-49.

64. B. Dumaine, "The New Non-Manager Managers," *Fortune,* February 22, 1993, 80-84.

65. See, for example, K. C. Green and D. T. Seymour, *Who's Going to Run General Motors* (Princeton, N.J.: Peterson's Guides, 1991).

66. L. R. Dorsky, "Producing Managers Right the First Time," *Quality Progress,* February 1992, 37-41.

67. T. Peters, *Thriving on Chaos: Handbook for a Management Revolution* (New York: Random House, 1988).

68. W. Kiechel III, "Facing Up to Denial," *Fortune,* October 18, 1993, 163-66.

69. J. Fierman, "Beating the Midlife Career Crisis," *Fortune,* September 6, 1993, 52-62.

70. G. Yasuda, "IBAX's Goodman Gets to the Heart of Problems."

71. *Fortune,* January 13, 1997, 52.

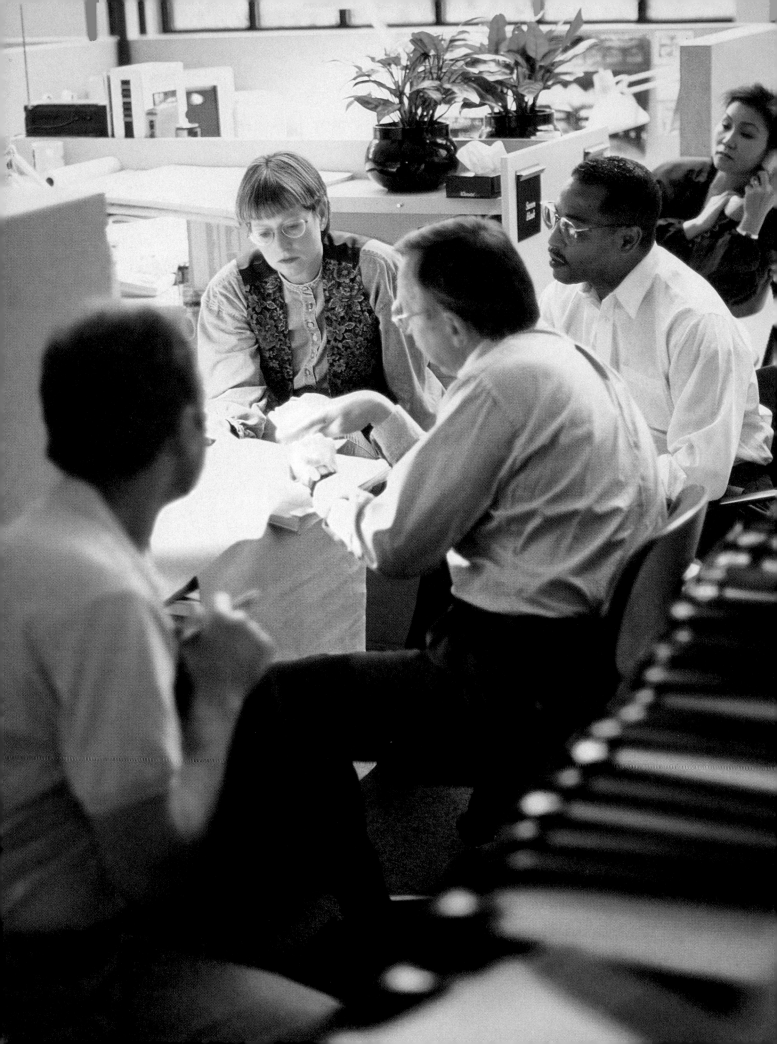

Evolution of Management Thought

■ ## CHAPTER OVERVIEW

The concept of management and the basic management functions are not new phenomena. Throughout recorded history, activities have been conducted that most certainly would have required careful attention to the management functions. Without management it is doubtful that the massive stone fortifications stretching across northern England and northern China would ever have been erected. The Great Pyramids of Egypt and other wonders of the ancient world would not have advanced beyond a vision in a dreamer's mind without management. Endeavors such as these require planning, organizing, leading, and controlling. Not only was management important in the past, but it continues to be important in the present, both in the erection of modern-day edifices and monuments and in the conduct of business and industry around the globe. Management will continue to be important as long as humans survive on earth.

Despite management's lengthy tenure, formal theories on management began to emerge only during the past one hundred years or so. In this chapter we will examine the historical evolution of management theories and philosophies and the factors that helped influence their development. This historical tour will explore the five major schools of management thought that have emerged over the years. Our trip through time will reveal that the degree of support for and use of these different perspectives have shifted, as times, conditions, and situations have changed. Components of each of these schools of thought still exist in current management thinking, however. Furthermore, they are likely to continue, perhaps in different degrees, to influence management thought in the future. If we understand the managerial philosophies of the past and present, we will be better equipped to be successful managers in the future.

■ ## LEARNING OBJECTIVES

When you have finished studying this chapter, you should be able to:

- Describe the major influences on the development of management thought.
- Identify the five major perspectives of management thought that have evolved over the years.
- Describe the different subfields that exist in the classical perspective of management and discuss the central focus of each.
- Describe the theories of the major contributors to the behavioral perspective of management.

- Identify the major events that gave rise to the emergence of the quantitative perspective of management.
- Describe the structure of the building blocks of systems analysis.
- Discuss the nature of the contingency perspective of management.
- Discuss the future issues that will affect the further development of management thought.

Managerial Incident

UNITED PARCEL SERVICE: THE OLD MANAGEMENT PRACTICES MEET WITH RESISTANCE

United Parcel Service (UPS) is the largest transportation company in the United States, controlling more than 75 percent of the market for domestic ground delivery of parcels and about 25 percent of the air-express delivery market. UPS maintains a fleet of more than 120,000 trucks and 450 airplanes to provide these services. The company has long been renowned for its ability to provide dependable, low-cost delivery of small parcels, competing with the United States Postal Service for most of its life. Over the years UPS has built a reputation for efficient and reliable deliveries. To a large extent these successes are attributable to a managerial philosophy that embraces structure and rigidity within the organization. Rules, regulations, policies, and procedures at UPS maintain a well-defined hierarchy of workers and a well-defined division of labor. Explicit policies exist for performance of each job, hiring, and promotion. Engineers have determined the number of workers needed to deliver a given daily volume of packages, and have prescribed the best way for each worker to perform each task down to the most minute detail. Until recently, UPS workers seemed to accept this highly regimented system.

UPS has always been a fierce competitor, responding decisively to any threat from its competitors. In fact, it was the success of Federal Express that prompted UPS to introduce air-express delivery in addition to the services it already offered. Shortly after Federal Express acquired Emery Air Freight, UPS increased its parcel weight and size limits in order to compete for the delivery of larger parcels. The company also expanded its guarantee of 10:30 A.M. delivery of overnight letters to most of the country. Recently UPS workers have begun to feel stress brought on by competition-induced changes. UPS drivers have had to learn how to deliver new services, some of which require speedier deliveries, more lifting, and heavier loads. In addition, drivers have had to learn how to use UPS's sophisticated and technical package-tracing systems. In the early- to mid-1990s, worker complaints were on the rise, and UPS's productivity actually suffered a slight decline. A Teamsters Union local produced a study claiming that "UPS employees scored in the 91st percentile of U.S. workers for job stress, while many suffered from anxiety, phobias, or back strain."[1]

INTRODUCTION

United Parcel Service was beginning to realize that the management style and practices that had worked well in the past were beginning to cause discontent within the work force, which quite possibly might lead to major problems within the organization. Although it was the contention of UPS management that the Teamster local study was biased and unscientific, and that much of the labor unrest resulted from "muscle flexing by an embattled Teamsters Union leadership," it was clear that the traditional management practices would need some refinement to appease a rather vocal contingent of UPS employees. Despite the company's tradition of well-paid employees with meaningful opportunities for advancement and job security, the ripple of discontent would have to be dealt with before it became a disruptive wave. The dilemma UPS management faced was whether they should deal with this situation by continuing the practices that had proven so successful in the past, or should they consider making some changes?

As we saw in Chapter 1, changes are occurring that are causing managers to revise their managerial styles and become more creative in their thinking. But change is nothing new—all that is new are the types of change. Management thinking has evolved throughout the centuries to deal with the ever-changing environment. In this chapter we examine the evolution in management thought by describing several management theories and philosophies that have emerged over the years. The majority of the evolutionary changes and new perspectives of management have occurred since the nineteenth century, when the pace of change quickened as the Industrial Revolution transformed agricultural societies into industrial societies. Today, management thinking continues to evolve to meet the challenges raised by rapid and dramatic societal changes, and these factors will undoubtedly continue to influence future management developments. Before examining the historical developments in management thinking, let's first identify those factors that have influenced the evolution of modern management thought.

ENVIRONMENTAL FACTORS INFLUENCING MANAGEMENT THOUGHT

Through the years many environmental factors have caused management theorists and management practitioners to alter their views on what constitutes a good approach to management. These environmental factors can be conveniently categorized as economic, social, political, technological, and global influences. We will examine each of these influences in turn and the effects they have had on the evolution of management thought.

ECONOMIC INFLUENCES

Economic influences relate to the availability, production, and distribution of resources within a society. With the advent of industrialization, the goal of most manufacturing organizations was to find the most profitable way to provide products for newly emerging markets. They needed a variety of resources to achieve this objective. Some resources were material and some were human, but in each case, they tended to become scarcer over time.

When there was a seemingly endless expanse of virgin forests, loggers didn't think twice about clear-cutting a mountainside. Coal reserves were once stripped away with no thought of depletion. Flaring off (burning in the atmosphere) surplus natural gas was once a common practice. But as resources became scarce, it became increasingly important that they be managed effectively. Time and circumstances dictate that supplies will not always be unlimited: through gradual depletion over time, resources can run out, and disruptions of supplies can occur due to temporary but immediate circumstances. Witness the OPEC oil embargo of the 1970s and the ripple effect it had on the oil industry, the petrochemical industry, and countless related industries. Or consider the sudden and dramatic impact of Hurricane Bertha as she skirted the southeast coast of the United States before moving inland through the mid-

Business must be ready to respond immediately to changing conditions. Following Hurricane Bertha in 1996 and Hurricane Andrew earlier, manufacturers and distributors of construction materials had to rethink their strategies so they could act in a socially responsible manner. And retailers monitored the storm carefully in order to be able to keep emergency items in stock.

© Bill Bachman/PhotoEdit

Atlantic and northeast states in July 1996. Manufacturers and distributors of construction materials had to quickly rethink their manufacturing and distribution strategies so they could act in a socially responsible manner. Businesses that engaged in the retail sale of these commodities also found it necessary to manage their resources differently. For example, Home Depot closely monitored the track of the storm so it would be able to move such items as emergency generators and building materials into affected areas. In short, scarcity makes it necessary for resources to be allocated among competing users.

SOCIAL INFLUENCES

Social influences relate to the aspects of a culture that influence interpersonal relationships. The needs, values, and standards of behavior among people help to form the social contract of the culture. The social contract embodies unwritten rules and perceptions that govern interpersonal relationships, as well as the relationships between people and organizations. Management needs to be familiar with these perceptions if it is to act effectively. The ethnic, racial, and gender composition of today's work force is becoming increasingly diverse. Recognizing and satisfying the varying needs and values of this diverse work force present a challenge to management.

Throughout modern business history, management thinking and practice have been shaped, in part, by work stoppages, labor insurrections, and strikes by mine workers, auto workers, teamsters, and many others. Most of these incidents were precipitated not just by demands for more pay, but by safety concerns, welfare issues, and other social considerations.

Although these examples of social influence have a negative flavor, this need not always be the case. In recent years the social contract of our culture has been changing. Workers have become more vocal in their desire to be treated as more than just muscle to do the job. They are insisting on using their mental abilities as well as their physical skills. As we will see throughout this book, these changes have led to some of the contemporary approaches that empower workers, giving them decision-making authority and responsibility for their activities. This approach has had a positive impact on organizations that have tried it.[2] Empowered workers often exhibit pride of ownership for their work and a dedication to quality and excellence in all that they do. Later in this chapter, we will see in Managing for Excellence that changing its view of the work force was one of the factors that contributed to the dramatic resurgence of the Harley-Davidson Motorcycle Company.

POLITICAL INFLUENCES

Political influences relate to the impact of political institutions on individuals and organizations. At a basic level are the various civil and criminal laws that influence individual and organizational behavior. In addition, the political system has bestowed various rights upon individuals and organizations, including the right to life and liberty, contract rights, and property rights, among others, and these also have an impact. Finally, government regulations are yet another source of political influence. The laws, rules, and regulations that form the political influences on management in many instances have been the outgrowth of economic and social influences. Environmental regulations have often been precipitated by reckless disregard for the preservation of our natural resources. Child labor laws and OSHA (Occupational Safety and Health Administration) regulations trace their origin to social outcries over exploitative and dangerous working conditions.

Political forces have influenced management thinking in a variety of ways. For example, over the years increasing concern for individual rights has forced management to adapt to a shorter work week for employees, provide a safe work environment, and make increasing contributions to employees' welfare. Regulations against monopolies have caused some businesses to restructure and some industries to reorganize. Increased environmental regulation has caused many changes in many organizations. Deregulation of banking and trucking has had a dramatic influence on organizations in these industries. In short, evolving laws, rules, and regulations have tended to transform the way many organizations conduct business, necessitating changes in their management philosophies and styles over the years.

TECHNOLOGICAL INFLUENCES

Technological influences relate to the advances and refinements in any of the devices that are used in conjunction with conducting business. As was noted in Chapter 1, advances in transportation, communication, and information technology have made it possible to conduct business on a global basis. Managers in the global economy must be alert to all opportunities for improvement. They must stay abreast of the new technology so they can make intelligent, informed decisions. The stakes are high because these decisions affect both the human and the technical aspects of operations. Whether an organization adopts the new technology may determine whether it retains its competitive edge.[3] This is evident in the UPS situation described in the opening Managerial Incident. UPS spent more than $2 billion to update its technology by developing its own computer-based parcel tracking system to match the feature introduced by Federal Express.

Managers are seeing constant innovations in communications and information exchange capabilities, including voice mail, electronic mail, fax machines, and electronic data interchange. Cellular telephones and portable computers provide two familiar examples of dramatic technological advances that have occurred in the past few years. Early cellular telephones were not very portable and required separate battery packs carried over the shoulder in briefcase-sized satchels. Motorola, one of the premier innovators in this technology, now has battery-powered units that can fit into a shirt pocket. These will no

Communications and information exchange capabilities are changing constantly. Cellular telephones are much more convenient than their early counterparts, and notebook-style computers may now contain modem, speakerphone, answering machine, and fax machine. Such innovations are changing workers' job responsibilities—and the way in which they should be managed.

© Amy C Etra/PhotoEdit

doubt shrink even more as technological innovations continue. Notebook-style computers that weigh a few pounds now allow managers to exchange information with their company computers while flying virtually anywhere in the world. For example, in mid-1996 Compaq unveiled a notebook-style computer that contains a modem, speakerphone (cellular or regular), answering machine, and fax machine.[4] Similarly, advances in transportation are rapidly "shrinking" the globe. Factories of the future will incorporate such technologies as computer-aided design (CAD), computer-aided manufacturing (CAM), computer-integrated manufacturing (CIM), computerized numerically controlled machines (CNCM), automated storage and retrieval systems (AS/RS), and flexible manufacturing systems (FMS). Innovations such as these are transforming workers' job responsibilities and, consequently, the way in which they should be managed.[5]

GLOBAL INFLUENCES

Global influences relate to the pressures to improve quality, productivity, and costs as organizations attempt to compete in the worldwide marketplace. The international, or global, dimension of an organization's environment has had the most profound impact on management thinking in recent years. In the world of business, national boundaries are quickly disappearing. Global competition has begun to affect all businesses. For example, U.S. automakers can no longer claim this country as their exclusive domain. Foreign competitors continually penetrate the U.S. market with high-quality, low-priced cars. To survive, U.S. automakers have found it necessary to compete on the same quality and price dimensions as their foreign competitors and to seek foreign markets of their own.[6]

As time progresses, even the lines between domestic and foreign automobiles continue to become more blurred. "U.S. automobiles" continue to incorporate more and more imported components, while "foreign automobiles" are increasingly being manufactured in the United States with U.S.-made parts and U.S. labor. For example, Marysville, Ohio, boasts a Honda manufacturing plant and Georgetown, Kentucky, can claim a Toyota manufacturing plant.

Similar situations in electronics and other industries could be cited. In all cases, increasing global competition has caused organizations to focus on using all the skills and capabilities of their workers in an effort to improve quality, productivity, and costs. Contemporary and future perspectives on management have been and will continue to be influenced most heavily by the global dimension of the environment.[7]

SCHOOLS OF MANAGEMENT THOUGHT

Beginning in the late 19th century, and continuing through the 20th century, managers and scholars have developed theoretical frameworks to describe what they believed to be good management practice. Their efforts have led to five different perspectives on management: the classical perspective, the behavioral perspective, the quantitative perspective, the systems perspective, and the contingency perspective. Each perspective is based on different assumptions about organizational objectives and human behavior. To help place these perspectives in their proper chronological sequence, Figure 2.1 displays them along a historical time line.

You might wonder why it is important to study the historical development of management thought. In general, studying history allows us to learn about mistakes made in the past so that they can be avoided in the future. Further-

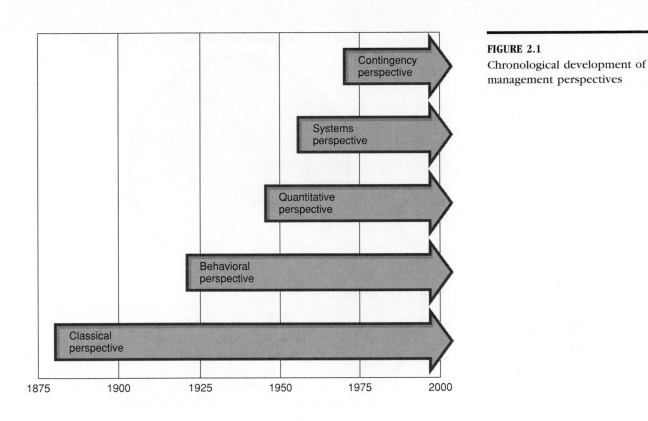

FIGURE 2.1
Chronological development of
management perspectives

more, it allows us to learn of past successes so that they can be repeated in the appropriate future situation. This certainly applies to the study of management history.

In addition, as Figure 2.1 shows, all these perspectives continue to influence managers' thinking, although opinions differ as to how influential each is. Consequently, it is important that future managers become familiar with the basic concepts of each school of thought. The following sections examine these major perspectives on management thought in more detail.

CLASSICAL PERSPECTIVE

The oldest of the "formal" viewpoints of management emerged during the late nineteenth and early twentieth centuries and has come to be known as the **classical perspective.** The classical perspective had its roots in the management experiences that were occurring in the rapidly expanding manufacturing organizations that typified U.S. and European industrialization. Early contributions were made by management practitioners and theorists from several corners of the world.

The classical perspective consists of three main subfields: (1) scientific management, (2) administrative management, and (3) bureaucratic management.[8] As we will see, scientific management focuses on the productivity of the individual worker, administrative management focuses on the functions of management, and bureaucratic management focuses on the overall organizational system. Nevertheless, as Figure 2.2 illustrates, these three subfields also contain some overlapping elements and components.

Scientific Management
Scientific management focuses on the productivity of the individual worker. As nineteenth-century society became more industrialized, businesses had difficulty improving productivity. Frederick Winslow Taylor (1856–1915), an American mechanical engineer, suggested that the primary problem lay in poor management practices. While employed at the Midvale Steel Company in

Classical perspective
Comprising the oldest formal viewpoints of management, it includes the scientific management approach, the administrative management approach, and the bureaucratic management approach.

Scientific management
Focuses on the productivity of the individual worker.

FIGURE 2.2

Subfields of the classical perspective on management

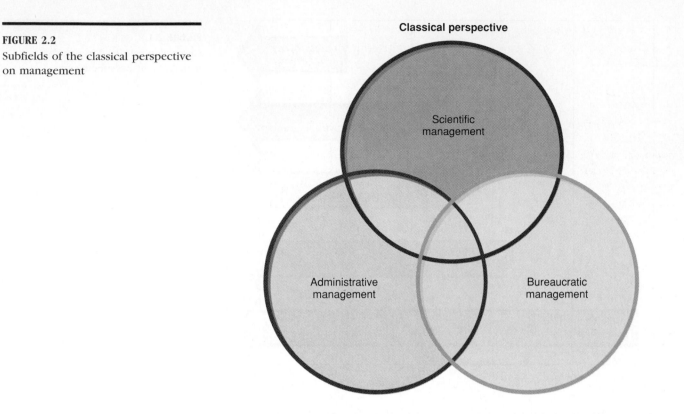

Philadelphia, Pennsylvania, Taylor began experimenting with management procedures, practices, and methods that focused on worker/machine relationships in manufacturing plants. He contended that management would have to change, and that the manner of change should be determined by scientific study. Taylor's observations led him to formulate opinions in the areas of task performance, supervision, and motivation.[9]

Task Performance   Taylor was convinced that there was an ideal way to perform each separate work task, and he attempted to define those optimal procedures through systematic study. His celebrated "science of shoveling" refers to his observations and experiments on the best way for workers to perform this manual task during the manufacture of pig iron. Taylor experimented with different shovel sizes and designs to find the one that was most comfortable. He varied the size of the load scooped up onto the shovel to find the least fatiguing amount. He experimented with different combinations of work time and rest intervals in an attempt to improve the worker recovery rate. Ranges of physical motion on the part of the workers were also examined. Based upon Taylor's suggestions, Midvale was able to reduce the number of shovelers needed from 600 to 140, while at the same time more than tripling the average daily worker output.[10]

These types of observations and measurements are examples of time and motion studies. Time and motion studies identify and measure a worker's physical movements while the worker performs a task, and then analyze the results to determine the best way of performing that task. In the attempt to find the best way of performing each task, scientific management incorporates several basic expectations of management, which include the following:

- *Development of work standards.* Standard methods should be developed for performing each job within the organization.
- *Selection of workers.* Workers with the appropriate abilities should be selected for each job.

- *Training of workers.* Workers should be trained in the standard methods.
- *Support of workers.* Workers should be supported by having their work planned for them.

Taylor's scientific management contributions went well beyond determining the one best way of performing a task. He also maintained rather strong convictions about supervision and motivation.[11]

Supervision   In the area of supervision, Taylor felt that a single supervisor could not be an expert at all tasks. This was because most supervisors were promoted to their positions after demonstrating high levels of skill in performing a particular function within the organization. Consequently, each first-level supervisor should be responsible only for workers who perform a common function familiar to the supervisor, such as machine operator, material handler, or inspector. Each supervisor's area of expertise would become an area of authority. Since in Taylor's era these supervisors were referred to as *foremen,* Taylor called this concept *functional foremanship.* Several foremen would be assigned to each work area, with each having a separate responsibility for such duties as planning, production scheduling, time and motion studies, material handling, and so forth.

Motivation   In the area of motivation, Taylor felt that money was the way to motivate workers to their fullest capabilities. He advocated a piecework system, in which workers' pay was tied to their output. Workers who met a standard level of production were paid at a standard wage rate. Workers whose production exceeded the standard were paid at a higher rate for all of their production output. Taylor felt that such financial incentives would induce workers to produce more so that they might earn more money. He also felt that management should use financial incentives judiciously. If the increased employee earnings were not accompanied by higher profits generated by the productivity increases, then the incentives should not be used.

While Frederick Taylor is generally acknowledged to be the father of scientific management, the husband-and-wife team of Frank and Lillian Gilbreth also made some pioneering contributions to the field.[12] Frank Gilbreth specialized in time and motion studies to determine the most efficient way to perform tasks.[13] He identified seventeen work elements (such as lifting, grasping, positioning, etc.) and called them *therbligs* (a loose reverse spelling of his last name).[14] In one of his more notable studies, Gilbreth used the new medium of motion pictures to examine the work of bricklayers. He was able to change that task's structure in a way that reduced the number of motions from eighteen to five, resulting in a productivity increase of more than 200 percent. Contemporary industrial engineers still use Frank Gilbreth's methods to design jobs for the greatest efficiency.

Lillian Gilbreth concentrated her efforts on the human aspects of industrial engineering. She was a strong proponent of better working conditions as a means of improving efficiency and productivity. She favored standard days with scheduled lunch breaks and rest periods for workers. She also worked for the removal of unsafe working conditions and the abolition of child labor. The Gilbreths' time and motion experiments attracted quite a bit of notoriety. In fact, their application of time and motion studies and efficiency practices to their twelve children was eventually chronicled in the long-running Broadway play and subsequent motion picture *Cheaper by the Dozen.*

While Taylor and the Gilbreths with their focus on the productivity of the individual worker dominated the scientific management subfield of the classical perspective, their views were not embraced by all classical thinkers. Others focused on the functions of management or the overall organizational structure, as will be seen in the next two sections.

Administrative management
Focuses on the managers and the functions they perform.

Administrative Management

Administrative management focuses on the managers and the functions they perform. This approach to management is most closely identified with Henri Fayol (1841–1925), a French mining engineer, whose major views emerged in the early twentieth century.[15] Fayol made his mark when he revitalized a floundering mining company and turned it into a financial success. He later attributed his success as a manager to the methods he employed rather than to his personal attributes. Fayol was the first to recognize that successful managers had to understand the basic managerial functions. He identified these functions as planning, organizing, commanding (leading), coordinating, and controlling. He also contended that successful managers needed to apply certain principles of management to these functions. Fayol developed a set of fourteen general principles of management, which are listed in Table 2.1.[16]

Many of Fayol's principles are quite compatible with the views of scientific management. For example, the object of Fayol's principle on the division of work is to produce more and better work with the same amount of effort. Taylor was attempting the same thing with his shoveling experiments. Fayol's

TABLE 2.1   Fayol's general principles of management

1. *Division of work.* By dividing the work into smaller elements and assigning specific elements to specific workers, the work can be performed more efficiently and more productively.
2. *Authority and responsibility.* Authority is necessary to carry out managerial responsibilities. Managers have the authority to give orders so that work will be accomplished.
3. *Discipline.* To ensure the smooth operation of the business, it is essential that members of the organization respect the rules that govern it.
4. *Unity of command.* To avoid conflicting instructions and confusion, each employee should receive orders from only one superior.
5. *Unity of direction.* Similar activities within an organization should be coordinated under and directed by only one manager.
6. *Subordination of individual interest to the common good.* The goals of the overall organization should take precedence over the interests of individual employees.
7. *Remuneration of personnel.* Financial compensation for work done should be fair both to the employees and to the organization.
8. *Centralization.* Power and authority should be concentrated at upper levels of the organization with managers maintaining final responsibility. However, managers should give their subordinates enough authority to perform their jobs properly.
9. *Scalar chain.* A single, uninterrupted chain of authority should extend from the top level to the lowest position in the organization.
10. *Order.* Materials should be in the right place at the right time, and workers should be assigned to the jobs best suited to them.
11. *Equity.* Managers should display friendliness and fairness toward their subordinates.
12. *Stability of personnel tenure.* High rates of employee turnover are inefficient and should be avoided.
13. *Initiative.* Subordinates should be given the freedom to take initiative in carrying out their work.
14. *Esprit de corps.* Team spirit and harmony should be promoted among workers to create a sense of organizational unity.

SOURCE: Based on Henri Fayol, *General and Industrial Management*, trans. by Constana Storrs. (London: Pittman & Sons, 1949).

order principle stating that everything and everyone should be in their proper place is consistent with the orderly objective of time and motion studies.

Some of Fayol's classical theories and principles may not seem compatible with contemporary management as described in Chapter 1. For example, his principle of centralization of power and authority at upper levels of the organization is contrary to the contemporary management view of allowing front-line workers more autonomy and authority for making and carrying out decisions. Furthermore, contemporary managers rarely demand that the goals of the overall organization take precedence over the interests of individual employees. Contemporary management thinking views employees as a valuable resource whose interests must be considered. Therefore, considerable importance is placed on satisfying the wants, needs, and desires of individual workers.

Despite the apparent incompatibility between some of Fayol's principles and the philosophies of contemporary management, several of his principles continue to be embraced by today's managers. His managerial functions of planning, organizing, leading, and controlling are routinely used in modern organizations. In fact, these functions form the framework for the organization of the material in this textbook. In addition, Fayol's principles on subordinate initiative, harmony, and team spirit are particularly applicable to the modern trend toward encouraging creativity and teamwork in the workplace.

Whereas scientific management focuses on the productivity of the individual worker and administrative management focuses on the functions of the manager, bureaucratic management, the final subfield of classical management, shifts its focus to the overall organizational system.[17]

Bureaucratic management
Focuses on the overall organizational system.

Bureaucratic Management

Bureaucratic management focuses on the overall organizational system and is based upon firm rules, policies, and procedures; a fixed hierarchy; and a clear division of labor. Max Weber (1864–1920), a German sociologist and historian, is most closely associated with bureaucratic management.[18] Weber had observed that many nineteenth-century European organizations were managed on a very personal basis. Employees often displayed more loyalty to individuals than to the mission of the organization. As a consequence, resources were often used to satisfy individual desires rather than the organization's goals.

To counter this dysfunctional consequence, Weber envisioned a system of management that would be based upon impersonal and rational behavior.[19] Management of this sort is called a *bureaucracy,* and it has the following characteristics:

- *Division of labor.* All duties are divided into simpler, more specialized tasks so that the organization can use personnel and resources more efficiently.

- *Hierarchy of authority.* The organization has a pyramid-shaped hierarchical structure that ranks job positions according to the amount of power and authority each possesses. Power and authority increase at each higher level, and each lower-level position is under the direct control of one higher-level position, as in Figure 2.3.

- *Rules and procedures.* A comprehensive set of rules and procedures that provides the guidelines for performing all organizational duties is clearly stated. Employees must strictly adhere to these formal rules.

- *Impersonality.* Personal favoritism is avoided in the operation of the organization. The specified duties of an employee dictate behavior. The rules and procedures are impersonally and uniformly applied to all employees.

- *Employee selection and promotion.* All employees are selected on the basis of technical competence, and are promoted based upon their job-related performance.[20]

Max Weber sought to counter the loyalty of employees to individuals rather than to the organization—which had resulted in the use of resources to satisfy individual desires rather than the organization's goals—by implementing *bureaucracy,* a system based on impersonal and rational behavior.

©/Archive Photos

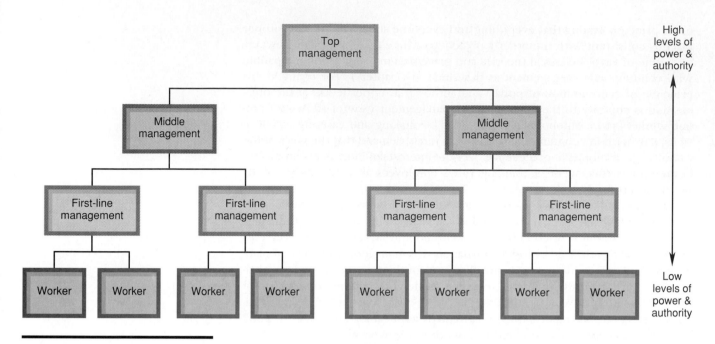

FIGURE 2.3
Bureaucratic hierarchical power
structure

Traditional authority
Subordinates comply with a leader because of custom or tradition.

Charismatic authority
Subordinates voluntarily comply with
a leader because of her special personal qualities or abilities.

Rational-legal authority
Subordinates comply with a leader because of a set of impersonal rules and
regulations that apply to all employees.

Weber believed that an organization exhibiting these characteristics would
be more efficient and adaptable to change, for such a system would be able to
maintain continuity. Regardless of the individual personalities who might enter or leave the system over the years, the formal rules, structure, and written
records would allow the organization to continue to operate as it had in the
past.

Weber believed there were three different types of authority: (1) traditional, (2) charismatic, and (3) rational-legal.[21] **Traditional authority** is based
upon custom or tradition. **Charismatic authority** occurs when subordinates
voluntarily comply with a leader because of her special personal qualities or
abilities. **Rational-legal authority** is based upon a set of impersonal rules and
regulations that apply to all employees. Superiors are obeyed because of the
positions they hold within the organization. Table 2.2 briefly describes these
three types of authority and provides examples of each.

TABLE 2.2   Weber's three authority types

AUTHORITY TYPE	DESCRIPTION	EXAMPLES
Traditional	Subordinate obedience based upon custom or tradition.	Indian tribal chiefs, royalty (kings, queens, etc.)
Charismatic	Subordinate obedience based upon special personal qualities associated with certain social reformers, political leaders, religious leaders, or organizational leaders.	Martin Luther King, Jr., Cesar Chavez, Mahatma Gandhi, Billy Graham, Bill Gates (Microsoft), Mary Kay Ash (Mary Kay Cosmetics)
Rational-legal	Subordinate obedience based upon the position held by superiors within the organization.	Police officers, organizational executives, managers, and supervisors

The term *bureaucracy* has taken on a negative connotation today. In many cases negative opinions about a bureaucracy are fully justified, especially when its rules and regulations are imposed in an inflexible and unyielding manner. Who among us has not been frustrated by an encounter with the "bureaucratic red tape" of some government agency or university office? An inflexible and unyielding imposition of the rules and regulations is in direct conflict with the changing face of contemporary organizations as described in Chapter 1. There we noted that future managers will typically display a greater reliance on work teams that are empowered to use their creativity, self-motivation, and initiative to make decisions and solve problems as they work toward achieving the organization's goals.

Even though the trend is toward less bureaucracy, we should not be too quick to bury its basic tenets. Despite its associated rules and "red tape," it can still provide some effective control devices in organizations where many routine tasks must be performed. Low-level employees should be able to accomplish such work by simply following the rules. Consider for the moment the situation described for United Parcel Service in the opening Managerial Incident. UPS has become quite successful and efficient in its package delivery service. In fact, UPS can deliver packages more efficiently and cheaply than the U.S. Postal Service. Despite its recent problems, the early success of UPS was due in part to its bureaucratic structure. Rules, regulations, policies, and procedures at UPS maintained a well-defined hierarchy of workers and a well-defined division of labor.

Not all bureaucratic organizations can claim the success and efficiency of UPS, however. Sometimes the rules and red tape can be carried to an unhealthy extreme. When General Motors wanted to construct a truck assembly plant in Egypt, the proposal had to pass through many ministries and required a multitude of signatures to gain approval. As a result of this sea of red tape, more than three years elapsed before final approval was granted.[22]

The classical thinkers of the late nineteenth and early twentieth centuries made many valuable contributions to the theory and practice of management. However, their theories did not always achieve desirable results in the situations that were developing in the early twentieth century. Changes were occurring in the workplace that gave rise to new perspectives on management. As a result, the behavioral perspective of management, which represents a significant departure from classical thinking, emerged.

BEHAVIORAL PERSPECTIVE

During the first few decades of the twentieth century, the industrialized nations of the world were experiencing many social and cultural changes. Standards of living were rising, working conditions were improving, and the length of the average work week was declining. Although these improvements temporarily stopped during the Great Depression and World War II, they have continued during the rest of this century. One of the most profound changes was the newfound ability of workers to influence managerial decisions through the formation of powerful labor unions. Amid these changes, managers were increasingly finding that workers did not always exhibit behaviors that were consistent with what classical theorists had called rational behavior. Furthermore, effective managers were not always being true to the principles laid down by these traditionalists. Managers were being presented with more and more evidence that human behavior has a significant impact upon the actions of workers. Observations and evidence such as this gave rise to the behavioral perspective of management, which recognizes the importance of human behavior patterns in shaping managerial style. The next sections describe the observations and research findings of several of the major contributors to this behavioral perspective.

Mary Parker Follett

In the first decades of the twentieth century, Mary Parker Follett, an early management scholar, made several significant contributions to the behavioral perspective of management. Follett's contributions were based upon her observations of managers as they performed their jobs. She concluded that a key to effective management was coordination. It was Follett's contention that managers needed to coordinate and harmonize group efforts rather than force and coerce people. She developed the following four principles of coordination to promote effective work groups:[23]

1. Coordination requires that people be in direct contact with one another.
2. Coordination is essential during the initial stages of any endeavor.
3. Coordination must address all factors in and phases of any endeavor.
4. Coordination is a continuous, ongoing process.

Follett believed that management is a continuous, dynamic process in which new situations and problems are likely to arise as the process is applied to solve a problem. She felt that the best decisions would be made by those people who were closest to the decision situation. Consequently, she thought that it was inappropriate for managers to insist that workers perform a task only in a specifically prescribed way. She argued that subordinates should be involved in the decision-making process whenever they are likely to be affected by the decision. Follett's beliefs that workers must be involved in solving problems and that management is a dynamic process rather than a static principle are certainly in contrast to the earlier views of Taylor, Fayol, and Weber, but are more consistent with contemporary management philosophy. Her views on coordination, teamwork, and employee decision making were put to good use by Growing Green, Inc., a family-owned business specializing in plantscaping and plant care, described in Entrepreneurial Approach.[24] In this illustration we see how the creation of work teams possessing decision-making authority helped to overcome a crisis situation in the company.

Follett also made early contributions in the area of conflict management. She felt that managers could help to resolve interdepartmental conflict by communicating with one another and with the affected workers. She recognized that conflict could actually be a positive force in an organization, for, if managed properly, it could serve as an integrating factor that stimulates production efforts.[25]

Elton Mayo

Beginning in 1924, studies of several situational factors were being performed at the Western Electric Company's plant in Hawthorne, Illinois. One of these experiments was designed to demonstrate that increased levels of lighting could improve productivity.[26] Test groups and control groups were formed. The test group was subjected to a variety of lighting conditions while the control group operated under constant lighting conditions. The results demonstrated that when illumination levels were increased, the productivity of the test group improved, as was expected. The experimenters were surprised, however, to find a similar increase in productivity when the test group's level of illumination was dramatically decreased. Equally puzzling was the fact that the control group's productivity also increased, even though its lighting conditions remained constant.

Elton Mayo, a Harvard professor and management consultant, was brought in to investigate these puzzling results. After reviewing the results of these and other newly designed experiments, Mayo and his colleagues explained the results by what has come to be known as the **Hawthorne effect.** Productivity

Hawthorne effect
Phenomenon where individual or group performance is influenced by human behavior factors.

GROWING GREEN, INC.: WORK TEAMS OVERCOME CRISIS SITUATION

Growing Green, Inc. of St. Louis, founded in 1973 by entrepreneur Teri Pesapane and her husband, Joel, was formed to operate as a plantscaping and plant care business and small gift shop. Their venture was capitalized with $3,200 from their savings. In the early years of operation Teri and Joel were able to handle all aspects of the business. Generally, Teri negotiated the deals, and Joel handled the deliveries. By 1988 the Pesapanes had seen their business grow to the point where their revenues were $700,000, and their staff consisted of sixteen employees. It seemed that this two-person operation had come a long way. Unfortunately, all was not as rosy as this picture might seem. The Pesapanes had a real crisis on their hands. Employee morale was low, turnover was high, and employees either couldn't or wouldn't make decisions. They felt compelled to check with Joel on everything, even for such routine decisions as what sprays or fertilizers needed to be applied to certain plants and when they should be applied. Teri and Joel felt that they were prisoners of the business; they couldn't even go away for a weekend without fear that their business might fall apart.

Realizing that they had to relinquish some control, the Pesapanes attended a seminar on work team management. Armed with the insights gained from the seminar, they divided the staff of Growing Green into small action teams, each with decision-making authority. A sales team was formed to bring in new business, an operations team was designated to handle plant installations, a service team was assigned the responsibility of maintaining plants at customer sites, and an administrative team took care of billing and other financial matters. The senior-level employees from each of these teams compose a management team. Teri and Joel no longer get involved in the daily decision making; this responsibility has been taken over by the various work teams. In fact, the two have been able to be away from the business for extended periods of time without the previously feared catastrophic results. With this new structure, Growing Green has seen its client base more than double to approximately 250 and its revenues grow to approximately $1 million.

---

increases were not being caused by a physical event but by a human behavior phenomenon. Workers in both groups perceived that special attention was being paid to them, causing them to develop a group pride, which in turn motivated them to improve their performance. The Hawthorne studies revealed that factors not specified by management may directly influence productivity and worker satisfaction. It was found, for example, that an informal group leader in a task group may have more power among group members than the formal supervisor. Although the Hawthorne studies were conducted between 1924 and 1933, they did not have much impact until the 1950s because of world events (the Great Depression and World War II).[27]

It has been said that the Hawthorne studies "represent the transition from scientific management to the early human relations movement" and that they "brought to the forefront the concept of the organization as a social system, encompassing individuals, informal groups, and intergroup relationships, as well as formal structure."[28] In short, the Hawthorne studies added the human element to management thinking, an element that had been missing in the classical approaches to managerial thought.

Douglas McGregor

Douglas McGregor, whose background and training were in psychology, had a variety of experiences as a manager, consultant, and college president. McGregor was not totally satisfied with the assumptions about human behavior that were to be found in the classical perspective and the early contributions to the behavioral perspective. His experiences and background helped McGregor formulate his Theory X and Theory Y, which pose two contrasting sets of assumptions with which managers might view their subordinates. Table 2.3 provides a summary list of the assumptions inherent in these contrasting views.[29]

McGregor proposed that **Theory X** managers perceive that their subordinates have an inherent dislike of work and that they will avoid it if at all possible. This theory further suggests that subordinates will need to be coerced, directed, or threatened in order to get them to work toward the achievement of organizational goals. Finally, Theory X assumes that subordinates have little ambition, wish to avoid responsibility, and prefer to be directed. Managers who subscribe to this theory are likely to exercise an authoritarian style, telling people what to do and how to do it.

In contrast, **Theory Y** managers perceive that their subordinates enjoy work and that they will gain satisfaction from performing their jobs. Furthermore, this theory assumes that subordinates are self-motivated and self-directed toward achieving the organization's goals. Commitment to the organization's goals is a direct result of the personal satisfaction that they feel from a job well done. Finally, Theory Y assumes that subordinates will seek responsibility, display ambition, and use their imagination, creativity, and ingenuity when working toward the fulfillment of organizational goals. Managers who subscribe to Theory Y are likely to exercise a participatory style, consulting with subordinates, soliciting their opinions, and encouraging them to take part in decision making.[30] In Chapter 1 we looked at the ways management and managers are changing. The greater reliance on employees as decision makers, problem solvers, and team players is a strong endorsement for McGregor's Theory Y assumptions. Meeting the Challenge provides a self-assessment exercise that allows you to assess your own tendency toward Theory X or Theory Y assumptions. This exercise can be used to apply the theory to yourself and others with whom you work to assess your management styles.[31]

Chester Barnard

Chester Barnard studied economics at Harvard, and although he never completed the requirements for his degree, he had a very successful management career. He started in the statistical department of AT&T, and by 1927 he had become the president of New Jersey Bell. Barnard made two major contributions to management thought: one dealt with the functions of executives, and the other was his theory of authority. He felt that executives serve two primary functions. First, executives must establish and maintain a communica-

Theory X
Managers perceive that subordinates have an inherent dislike of work, and will avoid it if possible.

Theory Y
Managers perceive that subordinates enjoy work, and will gain satisfaction from their jobs.

TABLE 2.3   Comparison of Theory X and Theory Y assumptions

FACTOR	THEORY X ASSUMPTIONS	THEORY Y ASSUMPTIONS
Employee attitude toward work	Employees dislike work and will avoid it if at all possible.	Employees enjoy work and will actively seek it.
Management view of direction	Employees must be directed, coerced, controlled, or threatened to get them to put forth adequate effort.	Employees are self-motivated and self-directed toward achieving organizational goals.
Employee view of direction	Employees wish to avoid responsibility; they prefer to be directed and told what to do and how to do it.	Employees seek responsibility; they wish to use their creativity, imagination, and ingenuity in performing their jobs.
Management style	Authoritarian style of management.	Participatory style of management.

THEORY X AND THEORY Y

Complete the following questionnaire. Indicate your agreement or disagreement with each of the statements by placing the correct number next to the statement. This is not a test, and there are no right or wrong answers. Use the following scale: Strongly Agree—5; Agree—4; Undecided—3; Disagree—2; Strongly Disagree—1.

_____ 1. Most people prefer to be directed and want to avoid responsibility.

_____ 2. Most people can learn leadership skills regardless of their particular inborn traits and abilities.

_____ 3. The best way to encourage high performance is by using rewards and punishment.

_____ 4. A leader will lose influence over subordinates if he/she allows them to make decisions without direction and strict rules.

_____ 5. A good leader gives detailed and complete instructions to subordinates, rather than depending on their initiative to work out the details.

_____ 6. Because groups do not set high goals, individual goal setting offers advantages over group goal setting.

_____ 7. A leader should give subordinates only the information necessary for them to do their immediate tasks.

_____ 8. People are bright, but under most organizational conditions their potentials are underutilized.

_____ 9. Most people dislike work and, when possible, avoid it.

_____10. Leaders have to control, direct, and threaten employees to get them to work toward organizational goals.

_____11. Most people will exercise self-direction and self-control if they are committed to the objectives.

_____12. People do not naturally dislike work; it is a natural part of their lives.

_____13. Most people are internally motivated to reach objectives to which they are committed.

_____14. People are capable of innovation in solving organizational problems.

_____15. Most people place security above all other work factors, and will display little ambition.

Scoring Key: Reverse score items 2, 11, 12, 13 (1 = 5, 2 = 4, 3 = 3, 4 = 2, 5 = 1). Sum all 15 items. Score of more than 55 indicates a tendency to manage others according to the principles in Theory X. Score of less than 35 indicates a tendency to manage others according to the principles in Theory Y. Score between 35 and 55 indicates flexibility in the management of others.

tions system among employees. Barnard regarded organizations as social systems that require employee cooperation and continuous communication to remain effective. Second, executives are responsible for clearly formulating the purposes and objectives of the organization and for motivating employees to direct all their efforts toward attaining these objectives.

Barnard's other major contribution was his theory on authority. According to Barnard, authority flows from the ability of subordinates to accept or reject an order. His acceptance theory of authority suggests that employees will accept a superior's orders if they comprehend what is required, feel that the orders are consistent with organizational goals, and perceive a positive, personal benefit.[32] Many management scholars consider Barnard the father of the behavioral approach to management. In fact, many believe that his work laid the foundation for several contemporary approaches to management.

As we approach the mid-twentieth century on the timeline of Figure 2.1, we begin to encounter new problem-solving and decision-making tools that gave rise to a quantitative perspective on management. As you will see, the quantitative school provided managers with sophisticated new analytical tools and problem-solving techniques.

QUANTITATIVE PERSPECTIVE

The quantitative perspective had its roots in the scientific management approaches and is characterized by its use of mathematics, statistics, and other quantitative techniques for management decision making and problem solving. The most significant developments in this school of thought came during World War II, when military strategists had to contend with many monumentally complex problems, such as determining convoy routes, predicting enemy locations, planning invasion strategies, and providing troop logistical support.[33] Such massive and complicated problems required more sophisticated decision-making tools than were then available. To remedy this situation, the British and the Americans assembled groups of mathematicians, physicists, and other scientists to develop techniques to solve these military problems. Because the problems often involved the movement of large amounts of materials and the efficient use of large numbers of people, the techniques they devised could be readily transferred from the military arena to the business arena.

The use of mathematical models and quantitative techniques to solve managerial problems is often referred to as *operations research*. This term comes from the names applied to the groups of scientists during World War II (*operational research teams* in Great Britain and *operations research teams* in the United States).[34] This approach is also referred to as *management science* in some circles. Regardless of the name, the quantitative perspective has four basic characteristics:

1. *Decision-making focus.* The primary focus of the quantitative approach is on problems or situations that require some direct action, or decision, on the part of management.
2. *Measurable criteria.* The decision-making process requires that the decision maker select some alternative course of action. To make a rational selection, the alternatives must be compared on the basis of some measurable criterion, or objective, such as profit, cost, return on investment, output rate, or reject level.
3. *Quantitative model.* To assess the likely impact of each alternative on the stated criteria, a quantitative model of the decision situation must be formulated. Quantitative models make use of mathematical symbols, equations, and formulas to represent properties and relationships of the decision situation.
4. *Computers.* Although many quantitative models can be solved manually, such a process is often time-consuming and costly. Consequently, computers are quite useful in the problem-solving process (and often necessary for extremely complex quantitative formulations).[35]

In the past few decades, giant strides in microchip capability have enabled computer sophistication to advance tremendously. Computer hardware that fits in the palm of one's hand can outperform hardware that filled rooms a few decades ago. It has been said that today's average consumers wear more computing power on their wrists than existed in the entire world before 1961. Similarly, a host of quantitative decision-making tools evolved in this century, including such tools as linear programming, network models, queuing (waiting line) models, game theory, inventory models, and statistical decision theory. Several of these are described in more detail in Chapter 7.

SYSTEMS PERSPECTIVE

Systems analysis
An approach to problem solving that is closely aligned with the quantitative perspective on management.

An approach to problem solving that is closely aligned with the quantitative perspective is **systems analysis.** Because many of the wartime problems re-

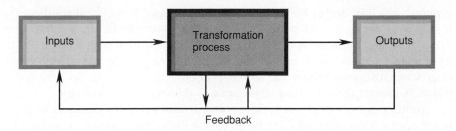

FIGURE 2.4
Basic structure of systems

flected exceedingly complex systems, the operations research teams often found it necessary to analyze them by breaking them into their constituent elements. Since any system is merely a collection of interrelated parts, identifying each of these parts and the nature of their interrelationships should simplify the model-building process. Systems can be viewed as a combination of three building blocks: inputs, outputs, and transformation processes. These blocks are connected by material and information flows.[36] Figure 2.4 illustrates the interaction of these blocks and flows.

Although a more thorough discussion of inputs, outputs, and transformation processes can be found in Chapter 17, the basic components of the systems model can be briefly introduced here. **Inputs** can vary greatly depending upon the nature of the system. Such diverse items as materials, workers, capital, land, equipment, customers, and information are potential inputs. **Outputs** typically consist of some physical commodity or some intangible service or information that is desired by the customers or users of the system. The **transformation process** is the mechanism by which inputs are converted to outputs. We usually think in terms of a physical transformation process, in which material inputs are reconfigured into some desired output. This scenario would be typical of a manufacturing system. Several other types of transformation processes are found in nonmanufacturing types of systems, however.[37] For example, in a transportation or distribution system such as Delta Airlines or United Parcel Service, the transformation process merely alters the location of the inputs, not their form. In storage systems such as a U-Haul Storage Facility or a Bank of America Safety Deposit Box Division, the inputs change in the time dimension, but not in form or location. **Feedback** represents information about the status and performance of the system.

Systems are often further distinguished by whether or not they interact with the external environment. **Open systems** must interact with the external environment to survive. The interactions can be reflected in the exchange of material, energy, information, and so forth. **Closed systems** do not interact with the environment. In both the classical and early behavioral perspectives, systems were often thought of as closed. In fact, the quantitative perspective often uses a closed-system assumption to simplify problem structures. Nevertheless, the difficulty of totally eliminating environmental interactions makes it hard to defend the concepts of open and closed systems in the absolute. Perhaps more appropriately, we might view systems as relatively open or relatively closed.[38] Thus, we might think of the production department of an organization as a relatively closed system. It can manufacture products in a continuous fashion while maintaining little interaction with the external environment. Meanwhile, the marketing department would be more appropriately viewed as an open system, for it must constantly interact with external customers to assess their wishes and desires. Long-run organizational survival requires that all organizations have some interaction with the external environment; therefore it is appropriate to think of contemporary business organizations as open systems.

Most complex systems are often viewed as a collection of interrelated subsystems. Because changes in any subsystem can affect other parts of the orga-

Inputs
Such diverse items as materials, workers, capital, land, equipment, customers, and information used in creating products and services.

Outputs
The physical commodity, or intangible service or information, that is desired by the customers or users of the system.

Transformation process
The mechanism by which inputs are converted to outputs.

Feedback
Information about the status and performance of a given effort or system.

Open systems
Systems that must interact with the external environment to survive.

Closed systems
Systems that do not interact with the environment.

Synergy
A phenomenon where an organization can accomplish more when its subsystems work together than it can accomplish when they work independently.

Entropy
The tendency for systems to decay over time.

Contingency perspective
A view that proposes that there is no one best approach to management for all situations.

nization, it is crucial that the organization be managed as a coordinated entity. If decisions are made independently at the subsystem level, the organization as a whole will often achieve less-than-optimal performance. But when all organizational subsystems work together, the organization can accomplish more than when the subsystems are working alone. This property, in which the whole is greater than the sum of its parts, is referred to as **synergy.**

Another important property of systems is **entropy,** which refers to their tendency to decay over time. As is the case with living systems, organizations must continuously monitor their environments and adjust to economic, social, political, technological, and global changes. Survival and prosperity often require that new inputs be sought. A system that does not continually receive inputs from its environment will eventually die.

CONTINGENCY PERSPECTIVE

In the 1960s managers were becoming increasingly aware that the effectiveness of different management styles varied according to the situation. With this awareness came the emergence of the **contingency perspective,** which proposes that there is no one best approach to management. This perspective recognizes that any of the four previously discussed management perspectives might be used alone or in combination for different situations.[39] In the contingency perspective, managers are faced with the task of determining which managerial approach is likely to be most effective in a given situation. This requires managers to first identify the key contingencies, or variables, in the given organizational situation. For example, the approach used to manage a group of teenagers working in a fast-food restaurant would be quite different from the approach used to manage a medical research team trying to discover a cure for AIDS.

The young fast-food workers might best be managed in a classical, authoritative style. Bureaucratic rules and regulations might be put in place to guide all worker actions and behaviors. Scientific management principles would probably be used to define the best way to perform each work task. Variation from the prescribed method would not and probably should not be tolerated in this situation. This is not the time or place to experiment with different ways to fry the burgers or mix the shakes!

It is doubtful that the medical research team would succeed under this approach to management. The team is faced with a very complex, unstructured endeavor that will require the team members to bring together all of their unique problem-solving skills. Such a situation requires that the team be given the autonomy to try out different solutions, pursue different avenues, and take risks that would simply be out of the question for the teenaged burger flippers.

Because the contingency perspective proposes that managerial style is situation-specific, it has not yet developed to the point where it can dictate the preferred way to manage in all situations. A particularly important factor to consider in the contingency approach is the type of technology being used by the organization. In pioneering contingency studies conducted in the 1960s, Joan Woodward discovered that a particular managerial style was affected by the organization's technology. Woodward identified and described three different types of technology:

1. *Small-batch technology.* Organizations of this type exhibit job-shop characteristics in which workers produce custom-made products in relatively small quantities.
2. *Mass-production technology.* Organizations of this type exhibit assembly-line characteristics in which standardized parts and components are used to produce large volumes of standardized products.

TABLE 2.4 Production technology examples

PRODUCTION TECHNOLOGY	EXAMPLES
Small-batch technology	Custom fabrication machine shop, manufacturer of neon advertising signs, print shop specializing in personal business cards, trophy engraving shop
Mass-production technology	Manufacturer of automobiles, manufacturer of refrigerators, manufacturer of hair dryers, manufacturer of pencils
Continuous-process technology	Oil refinery, flour mill, soft drink bottler, chemical processor

3. *Continuous-process technology.* Organizations of this type have a process in which the product flows continuously through the various stages of conversion.

The level of human interaction varies with each of these technology types. Small-batch technology tends to have the most human involvement (is the most labor-intensive) due to the customized outputs. Mass-production technology tends to have less human involvement due to the automated and robotic equipment that typifies assembly-line operations. Continuous-process technology has the lowest level of human involvement as the product flows through the stages of conversion. Consider, for example, how little "hands-on" human involvement is needed in an Exxon oil refinery as crude oil flows through the various processing stages on its way to becoming gasoline. Examples of each of these production technologies appear in Table 2.4, and all three are discussed more thoroughly in Chapter 17.[40]

Some of Woodward's findings showed that bureaucratic management methods were most effective in organizations using mass-production technology. Conversely, organizations using small-batch and continuous-process technologies had little need for the formalized rules and communication systems of the bureaucratic style.[41] Continued studies of this type will fill in all the gaps and eventually provide more definitive guidelines as to which managerial style is desirable for a particular situation.

Other important factors to consider in defining the contingencies for each situation include environment, organizational size, and organizational culture.[42] For example, large organizations may find it necessary to use more structured and rigid rules, regulations, and policies to control organizational activities. On the other hand, smaller organizations may find that they can rely less on the formal structure and allow workers the autonomy to make decisions for the situations and problems that they encounter. In this example, the larger organization would undoubtedly tend toward a more bureaucratic management style, while the smaller organization would display a more behavioral orientation. As Figure 2.5 shows, parts of all of the management perspectives we have examined might be combined to form a contingency approach.

INFORMATION TECHNOLOGY AND MANAGEMENT STYLE

In recent years we have all been witness to the tremendous advances that have occurred in the systems and devices that can process, disseminate, and transfer information. Most of our lives have already been touched by cellular tele-

FIGURE 2.5

Blending components into a
contingency perspective

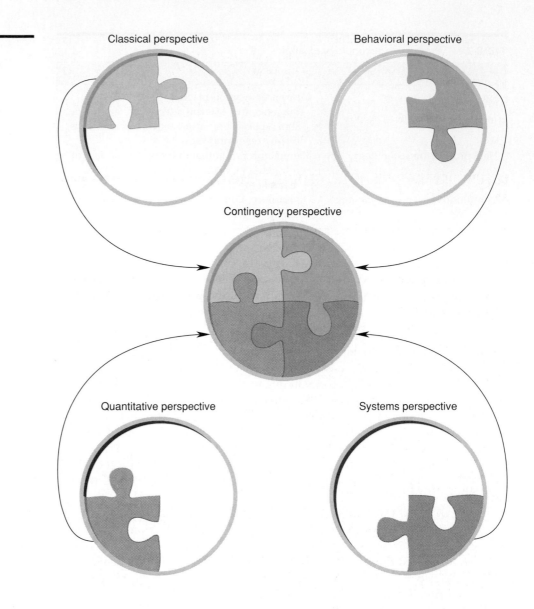

phones, microcomputers, fax machines, and specialty software packages. These
same devices and systems can have a profound effect on the choice of a management style. In many instances they can facilitate the adoption of a particular style.

The most obvious areas in which technological advances in information
processing facilitate the use of a particular style are the quantitative and systems perspectives. The geometric increase in microchip processing capability
makes it easier to develop ultrasophisticated quantitative models of complex
management systems. Rapid processing and feedback of information in these
system models allow the organization to be managed as a coordinated entity.
Perhaps less obvious is the impact that information processing technology has
on the subfields of the classical perspective on management. For example, classical theories might suggest how many workers should report to a single superior (span of control), and how many hierarchical levels of authority are
needed in a particular organization. But these can be altered when each employee has at her disposal devices that relay critical decision-making information. In addition, the centralization principle of Fayol may not be desirable in
these new situations. When low-level workers are empowered to make decisions and have the needed information readily available, it is not necessary for
all decisions to be made at upper levels of management.

But technological advances can be a two-edged sword. In addition to facilitating the adoption of a particular management style, they may at times force a change. This is evident for UPS as described in the opening Managerial Incident. The additional workload and stress to drivers brought on by the new, computerized package-tracing system has forced UPS to ease up on its traditional bureaucratic management style.

FUTURE ISSUES: DIVERSITY, GLOBALIZATION, AND QUALITY

As you might expect, the theories and ideas that have emerged thus far do not represent the end of the road in the evolution of management thought. Economic, social, political, technological, and global forces that influence management thinking continue to change. A major trend in recent years has been heightened concern for diversity within the workplace. The work force has become increasingly more varied, as has the number of minority-owned businesses. Census Bureau data indicate that the recent growth rate of Hispanic-owned businesses in the United States is triple that of general business growth. In the words of one Commerce Department official, "entrepreneurship is the flame that heats the American melting pot; it is the vehicle through which racial and ethnic minorities can enter the American mainstream, and it is visibly their most productive method for doing so."[43] The ranks of management need to exhibit a level of diversity that is similar to these levels of work force and entrepreneurial diversity. Diversity within an organization can have an added side benefit. When government contracts stipulate that minority suppliers must be used, businesses displaying cultural, ethnic, and gender diversity stand a better chance of winning government business.

In recent years, Japanese management styles have received considerable scrutiny due to the tremendous successes achieved by Japanese industries. Most readers are surely aware of the degree to which the Japanese have taken control of the global automobile and electronics markets. There are technical reasons for much of this success, for it has been achieved in part because of a managerial philosophy that is committed to quality and a just-in-time operating philosophy (a concept that is treated in more detail in Chapter 17).[44] The Harley-Davidson Motorcycle Company, described in Managing for Excellence, illustrates the dramatic impact this philosophy can have on a company's operations. Harley-Davidson, which was nearly bankrupt, emerged as a giant in the global motorcycle market. It is ironic that Harley-Davidson's re-emergence as a very desirable motorcycle has also resulted in it being the number one target for motorcycle theft.[45]

The successes of the Japanese management style are not due entirely to the technical operating system, however. Many aspects of the Japanese management style follow the prescriptions for successful management in the 21st century that were discussed in Chapter 1. A focus on quality is certainly central to the Japanese style. It is somewhat ironic that the Japanese emphasis on quality was a result of the teachings of the noted American quality philosophers W. Edwards Deming and Joseph Juran. Another noted American, Armand Feigenbaum, originated the

Recent growth of Hispanic-owned businesses in the United States is triple that of general business growth, providing minorities a means of entering the American mainstream. Such a level of diversity is desirable in the ranks of management as well.

© Jeff Greenberg/Unicorn Stock Photos

Managing for Excellence

HARLEY-DAVIDSON: A DRAMATIC RE-EMERGENCE IN THE WORLD MARKET

Harley-Davidson, an 80-year-old U.S. motorcycle manufacturer, experienced a rather dismal reversal of its fortunes during the late 1970s and early 1980s. Although Harley once held a dominant position in the U.S. motorcycle market, its market share slipped to less than 4 percent in the late 1970s. Honda, Kawasaki, and Yamaha motorcycles had come roaring in from Japan, offering not only lower prices but also higher-quality, state-of-the-art machines. Unable to compete with the Japanese imports on quality and price, Harley tried to prove in court that the Japanese were dumping their cycles in the United States at prices below cost to gain market share. However, it was revealed in court that the Japanese manufacturers' operating costs were 30 percent lower than Harley's. Harley's problems were many and varied. It had been laboring under an outmoded production technology and a rather tall, cumbersome hierarchy in its organizational structure. Performance was suboptimal due to lack of coordination between subsystems. Opinions of employees were seldom solicited—instead, employees were simply viewed as the muscle to carry out their prescribed job duties. The outmoded technology, organizational structure, and use of personnel all contributed to production inefficiencies and problems that resulted in motorcycles that were inferior in quality and price.

It was after these revelations that company president Vaughn Beals realized that he would have to turn his attention inward to reverse Harley's downslide. Many significant changes and improvements were made, and continue to be made, at Harley-Davidson. Its tall vertical hierarchy was replaced with a flatter structure. Management revised its view of the work force; it stopped assigning workers to narrowly defined jobs and no longer disregarded their opinions and expertise. This Theory X–like practice was replaced with a Theory Y–type attitude in which job descriptions were enlarged and workers were cross-trained to provide them with more flexibility, variety, and job security. Perhaps even more important, workers were brought into the decision-making and problem-solving processes. The result has been a complete reversal of fortunes. Both employee productivity and product quality have increased. At the same time, significant reductions in material costs, production costs, and inventory levels have been achieved. Productivity increased by 30 percent, inventory has been reduced by 40 percent, the costs of scrap and rework have dropped by 60 percent, and machine setup time has gone down by 75 percent. Perhaps most important, the company has been continuously profitable since beginning to implement these changes. All of these improvements helped to ensure that Harley-Davidson would continue to be a key player in the global motorcycle market.

concept of total quality control, which was quickly adapted by the Japanese. Many American firms have now embraced the concept of quality and have been successful enough to win the coveted Malcolm Baldrige National Quality Award. Some of the more recognizable recent winners of this award include AT&T, Cadillac, Eastman Kodak, Federal Express, GTE, IBM, Motorola, Ritz-Carlton Hotels, Texas Instruments, Westinghouse, and Xerox.[46]

It would be difficult to dispute that the Japanese maintain a global focus. Although not as apparent to observers from abroad, their management style also incorporates the concept of workers as decision makers, problem solvers, and team players. These were all identified in Chapter 1 as keys to operating successfully in the 21st century. Consider for the moment Global Perspective and note how these concepts were central to the success enjoyed by Toyota as they expanded their worldwide manufacturing operations into the United

TOYOTA MOTOR MANUFACTURING U.S.A., INC.

Toyota Motor Manufacturing U.S.A., Inc. (TMM), located in Georgetown, Kentucky, represents Toyota's first venture into the manufacture of Toyota automobiles on American soil. TMM manufactures the Toyota Camry sedan and station wagon at this plant. When plans for this facility were first announced, many were skeptical as to the likelihood that the company would be able to adapt its production system to the American work force, or that American workers would adapt to Japanese manufacturing philosophies. Doubters were quickly quieted, for the venture has been an enormous success, with 6,000 employees fully committed to teamwork and continuous improvement philosophies.

Before arriving on U.S. soil, CEO Fujio Cho was worried about the successful operation of the plant, in his words, "I didn't know of the American ways." Cho approached the challenge by approaching the situation as a cultural learning experience. He quickly formed an effective work force that assimilated the Japanese work methods. TMM workers have adapted readily to the Japanese practices that stress teamwork and continuous improvement. Cho has noted that "our team members come up with numerous bright ideas on their own. The employees are independent minded, but they are also professional in their thinking." The opinions and ideas of TMM employees are solicited, and quite often put into practice. Some 38,000 of the nearly 40,000 productivity-enhancing and cost-cutting suggestions made in 1993 have been implemented. Cho's lofty goals include having TMM become the number one auto plant in the United States in terms of quality, productivity, safety, and team members' morale.

Global Perspective

States. Employees working in teams developed thousands of cost-cutting and productivity-enhancing ideas that were implemented by management.[47] It should also be noted that the Japanese management style embraces aspects from several of the historically evolving management perspectives discussed in this chapter. There is a hint of bureaucratic management in the Japanese philosophy of lifelong career commitment to employees. At the same time, the Japanese philosophy includes a strong behavioral component, for it recognizes the importance of workers as decision makers and problem solvers.

The Japanese management style spawned the development of Theory Z by William Ouchi, a contemporary management scholar.[48] **Theory Z** is a management approach that advocates trusting employees and making them feel like an intimate part of the organization. According to the theory, once a trusting relationship is established with workers, production will increase.

Many question whether the Japanese management style has developed and evolved to the point where it can be considered a major school of management thought. Perhaps the bigger question is whether we should be calling this style "Japanese management" or something else. Much of what we call the Japanese management philosophy originated in the Japanese automobile industry. However, these manufacturers readily admit that most of their technical innovations and ideas were borrowed from the methods used by U.S. automobile manufacturers in the heyday of Henry Ford. The Japanese simply refined these technical practices and principles, as they did the behavioral and classical components that form the total package. With this awareness, perhaps a name other than "Japanese management" would be more appropriate. Whatever the name, we must still ask whether this management style has

Theory Z
Advocates that managers place trust in the employees and make them feel like an intimate part of the organization.

evolved to the point where it can be considered a major school of management thought. Probably not yet, for it still must stand the test of time. Nevertheless, in time this philosophy or another might be more thoroughly developed and added to the list of major management schools of thought. Any new philosophy that emerges will undoubtedly contain bits and pieces from prior theories, but these will most assuredly be combined with new elements that have evolved in response to political, economic, social, technological, and global influences. New eras present new problems and challenges, and new management styles arise to deal with them.

MANAGERIAL IMPLICATIONS

Over the years, management theorists have developed several views on the best way to manage an organization. Each of these views is based on differing assumptions about organizational objectives and human behavior. To demonstrate quality in the management of an organization, it is important that managers use the appropriate management approach. Therefore, it is critical that tomorrow's manager be:

- Thoroughly schooled in the different management perspectives that have evolved over the years.
- Able to understand the various economic, political, social, technological, and global influences that have affected management thinking over the years, and will continue to shape future evolutionary changes in management thought.
- Capable of identifying and understanding such key variables as environment, production technology, organization culture, organization size, and international culture as they relate to his organization.
- Prepared to select elements from the various management perspectives that are appropriate for her situation.
- Adaptable to change, because future conditions and developments can quickly render his chosen approaches obsolete.

In this chapter we toured the major historical developments in the evolution of management thought. We saw the emergence of five major perspectives on management, and many subfields within those major classifications. This march through time has revealed that certain aspects of every one of these evolutionary views are still appropriate for use in both today's and tomorrow's organizations. The successful managers of tomorrow will be the ones who can blend together the appropriate components from the wide body of management theory.

Managerial Incident Resolution

UNITED PARCEL SERVICE: THE OLD MANAGEMENT PRACTICES MEET WITH RESISTANCE

In the mid-1990s, UPS management began reacting positively to the employee discontent issues. Changes are occurring that reflect less regimentation and greater attention to behavioral issues. Management has acknowledged that the degree of difficulty has increased for many jobs. The UPS guarantee of 10:30 A.M. delivery for overnight letters often requires drivers to make duplicate runs during the day. A morning run is made to deliver the overnight letters, while a later run is made to deliver the remaining parcels. Heavier parcels add a level of difficulty, as does the requirement to log in information for the parcel-tracing system. Historically, UPS hires have been predominantly high school graduates. However, UPS has begun to hire more skilled and college-educated workers to deal with these new job demands. As the diversity of UPS's work force has increased, management is encountering an increasing number of workers who are less tolerant of rigid work rules. UPS has included language in its new contract with employees stating that management will not coerce, harass, intimidate, or overly supervise any employee. These measures have helped placate matters for now, but as change continues to be a part of this work environment, UPS management must continue to be receptive to further modifications to its management policies.[49]

SUMMARY

- As agricultural societies were transformed into industrial societies as a result of the Industrial Revolution, managerial thinking was shaped by a variety of economic, political, social, technological, and global influences. Such influences continue to affect the way in which managers function.

- In the past century, five major perspectives of management thought have evolved: the classical, behavioral, quantitative, systems, and contingency perspectives. The classical perspective developed in the later part of the nineteenth century and the first part of the twentieth century. The behavioral perspective began to evolve in the early third of the twentieth century. Development of the quantitative perspective began in earnest during World War II. The systems perspective began to evolve in the 1950s, while the contingency perspective is the most recent, having begun in the 1960s.

- The classical perspective includes scientific management, administrative management, and bureaucratic management subfields, each of which has a different focus. Scientific management focuses on the improvement of individual worker productivity. Time and motion studies observe and measure a worker's physical movements in order to determine the best way of performing a task. The expectation in scientific management is that managers will develop standard methods for performing each job, select workers with the appropriate abilities for each job, train workers in standard methods, and support workers by planning their work. Scientific management proponents believe that financial incentives are the major motivating factor that will induce workers to produce more. Administrative management focuses on the managerial process and the functions of the manager. Fayol identified planning, organizing, leading, coordinating, and controlling as the basic managerial functions. Bureaucratic management has as its primary focus the overall structure of the organization. This subfield emphasizes the division of labor into specialized tasks, a hierarchy of authority in

which power and authority increase at higher levels of the organization, a comprehensive set of rules and procedures for performing all organizational duties, a climate of impersonality in which personal favoritism is to be avoided, and an employee selection and promotion process that is based on technical competence and performance.

- The behavioral perspective of management had several major contributors. Mary Parker Follett emphasized the importance of coordination and harmony in group efforts. Elton Mayo recognized that the human element could play a significant role in determining worker behavior and output. Douglas McGregor proposed Theory X and Theory Y to explain employee attitudes and behavior. Chester Barnard examined the functions of executives. He contended that executives are responsible both for establishing and maintaining a communications system among employees and for clearly formulating the purposes and objectives of the organization and motivating employees toward attaining those objectives. Barnard also contributed an acceptance theory on authority, which was a new way of describing how subordinates accept or reject orders from their superiors.

- The major impetus for the emergence of the quantitative perspective of management was World War II and the many monumentally complex problems associated with the war effort. The quantitative perspective has a decision-making focus in which an alternative course of action must be selected as a solution to some problem. It requires the establishment of some measurable criteria so that alternatives can be compared prior to selection. Quantitative models are used to assess the impact of each alternative on the stated criteria, and computers are often quite helpful in the problem-solving process.

- The systems perspective takes a set of inputs and subjects them to some transformation process, thereby generating some type of output. Inputs, transformation processes, and outputs can be quite varied, but the basic structure remains the same. Throughout this process, feedback loops constantly filter information about the status and performance of the system.

- The contingency perspective of management suggests that there is no one best approach to management. It is a situational approach, for the proper managerial style is dependent upon the key variables, or contingencies, within the given situation.

- In the future, cultural, racial, and gender diversity will have a huge influence on management thinking. In addition, quality and globalization will have enormous impacts upon how businesses and industries are managed.

KEY TERMS

Classical perspective
Scientific management
Administrative management
Bureaucratic management
Traditional authority
Charismatic authority
Rational-legal authority

Hawthorne effect
Theory X
Theory Y
Systems analysis
Inputs
Outputs
Transformation process

Feedback
Open systems
Closed systems
Synergy
Entropy
Contingency perspective
Theory Z

REVIEW QUESTIONS

1. List and briefly describe the major factors that have influenced the evolution of management thought.

2. Identify the five major perspectives of management thought.

3. Briefly describe the main focus of scientific management and its basic expectations.

4. Briefly describe the purpose of time and motion studies.

5. What does the scientific management approach view as the major motivator for workers?

6. Briefly describe the main focus of administrative management.

7. Identify and briefly describe the basic managerial functions identified by Fayol.

8. Describe the Hawthorne effect and how it changed managerial thinking.

9. Discuss Follett's four principles of coordination.

10. Briefly describe the two functions of executives attributed to Barnard.

11. What is the acceptance theory of authority?

12. What event had the greatest impact on the evolution of the quantitative perspective of management?

13. Discuss the four basic characteristics of the quantitative perspective of management.

14. Discuss the systems concepts of synergy and entropy.

15. What is the main contention of the contingency perspective of management?

DISCUSSION QUESTIONS

Improving Critical Thinking

1. Reexamine Fayol's fourteen general principles of management, identify which seem most appropriate for contemporary management situations, and discuss why you feel that way.

2. Some suggest that Japanese management is just the same old stuff in a new package, while others suggest that this style is a new and different departure. Provide arguments in support of both of these views.

3. Suppose you overheard one of your peers comment that "The contingency approach to management is a cop-out. They're just making it up as they go along!" What would you say to try to convince this student

that this approach is a valid way of dealing with unique and different situations?

4. Japanese management—wave of the future or passing fancy? What do you think, and why?

Enhancing Communication Skills

5. In your own life experiences, you probably have had some occasion to use aspects of the scientific management approach. Try to recall some physical task that you analyzed to determine the best or most efficient way to perform it. To enhance your oral communication skills, prepare a short (10–15 minute) presentation for the class in which you describe that task and the results of your analysis.

6. Based upon your observations of businesses with which you have interacted, try to identify one where employees seemed to fall into McGregor's Theory X category and one where they seemed to fit Theory Y. To enhance your written communication skills, write a short (1–2 page) essay describing these businesses and explaining why you classified them as falling into the Theory X or Theory Y category.

Building Teamwork

7. Have you ever been influenced by the Hawthorne effect? Try to recall some incident in which your performance was affected because you knew you were being watched. To refine your teamwork skills, meet with a small group of students who have been given this same assignment. Compare and discuss your experiences and then reach a consensus on the group's two most interesting experiences with the Hawthorne effect. The group members whose experiences were judged the most interesting will act as spokespersons to describe these experiences to the rest of the class.

8. Try to recall from your own experiences an encounter that you had with a bureaucratic organization. Think about both the positive and negative aspects of that encounter. To refine your teamwork skills, meet with a small group of students who have been given this same assignment. Compare and discuss your experiences, and then reach a consensus on which two experiences represented the most rigid and unwavering bureaucratic response from the organizations. The group members whose experiences were judged to have the most rigid bureaucratic response will act as the spokespersons to describe these experiences to the rest of the class.

INFORMATION TECHNOLOGY: Insights and Solutions

1. Use the Internet to search for the names of all Malcolm Baldrige National Quality Award winners since its inception. Then arrange this information into an electronic spreadsheet that will allow you to provide three lists. The first list will use the year of the award as the primary sort and category of award as the secondary sort. The second list will use category as the primary sort and year as the secondary sort. The third list will use company name as the primary sort.

2. Using whatever search vehicle you prefer (Internet, fax, telephone, etc.), develop a list of services provided and fees charged by Federal Express and United Parcel Service. Then, using any presentation software package, prepare a slide show presentation for your classmates that compares the services of these two companies.

3. Use the Internet to search for information on foreign automobile companies that have manufacturing plants in the United States. Then put this information into an electronic spreadsheet that can be sorted by manufacturer, state, or model name of automobile. Compare your lists with the lists of classmates to discover who performed the most thorough search.

ETHICS: Take a Stand

In the continuing evolution of management thinking, much attention is currently being paid to what is called the "Japanese style of management," which is often associated with a just-in-time (JIT) operating philosophy. In a manufacturing environment, JIT proposes many departures from the traditional Western way of operating. In a high-volume, repetitive manufacturing environment, one of the traditional Western ways of thinking advocates a division of labor coupled with a highly specialized work force. Worker responsibilities are often very narrowly defined, and each worker's skill expectations are quite specific. In fact, over the years union contracts have often evolved that specify precisely what a worker can and cannot be expected to do.

The emerging JIT philosophy holds that there is no room in such an environment for highly specialized workers. Instead, multiskilled, cross-trained workers are essential to make the system operate effectively. Often longtime, specialized workers find that they are out of their element in such situations and are in danger of being phased out.

For Discussion

1. Discuss the ethical issues and dilemmas when workers no longer fit the mold.

2. Discuss potential remedies for this problem.

THINKING CRITICALLY: Debate the Issue

BUREAUCRATIC MANAGEMENT—GOOD OR BAD?

Form teams of four or five students as directed by your instructor. Research the topic of bureaucratic management, identifying both its positive and its negative aspects. Look for situations where it works effectively and others where it seems to be ineffective. Prepare to debate either the pros or cons of this approach. When it is time to debate this issue in front of the class, your instructor will tell you which position you will take.

Video Case

VALASSIS COMMUNICATIONS

Related Web Site: {http://www.marketingjobs.com/cpwp/valasswp.html}

Valassis Communications, headquartered in Livonia, Michigan, is one of the nation's largest publishers of printed sales promotion materials. The company is best known for its freestanding promotional inserts, which are distributed across the country in Sunday newspapers. The inserts contain coupons, refund offers, sweepstakes information, and advertising for the firm's many clients. By building a solid reputation of quality, service, and reliability, in its short 20-year history Valassis has captured over 45 percent of the market for freestanding inserts and serves 3,000 customers through 340 different newspapers. The company's clients include some of the best-known corporate names in America, including Kellogg, Procter & Gamble, Nabisco Brands, and General Mills. Along with its commercial success, in 1993 Valassis was named one of the "100 Best Companies to Work for in America" by an independent rating agency.

Valassis believes that employee teamwork has been an important part of its success. Rather than ask employees to meet tough deadlines by working separately or to solve problems alone, the company has created an environment in which employees work together in teams. The premise of teamwork is that to be highly effective, employees require the knowledge, skill, and creativity of each other. At Valassis, this concept has produced remarkable results. In one instance, a team worked together to meet a 72-hour deadline to produce a promotional video for Disney. On a more routine basis, teams work together to complete projects, generate ideas, cut costs, reduce waste, and solve problems. These initiatives have resulted in both increased performance and improved employee morale.

Through its experiences, Valassis has learned that teamwork requires a highly supportive environment. As a result, the company keeps teamwork skills in mind when making hiring decisions, provides employee cross-training, and arranges its office suites in a manner that facilitates employee communication and feedback. On a more personal basis, the employees of Valassis have learned that teamwork works best when team members are open minded, are willing to cooperate, and have mutual respect for one another.

By embracing teamwork, Valassis Communications believes that it is getting the most out of its employees, which is important in the company's highly competitive environment. It is clear that teamwork will remain an important management technique for Valassis Communications as it prepares for the future.

For Discussion

1. Is the concept of teamwork more consistent with the classical perspective or the behavioral perspective of management? Explain your answer.

2. Several environmental factors, including economic influences, political influences, social influences, technological influences, and global influences, have shaped the evolution of management thought. Which of these factors have had an influence on the increasing importance of teamwork at Valassis Communications and similar organizations?

3. Do you believe that teamwork is an effective management technique or a management fad that will eventually disappear? Explain your answer.

DESIGNTECH PRODUCTS: LET'S FIND THE BEST WAY

CASE

DesignTech Products is a small, privately owned manufacturer of specialty computer circuit boards. These boards are used in conjunction with computer-aided design software primarily for architectural and construction applications. DesignTech was founded by Rodman W. Spilling, a licensed architect by vocation and a computer tinkerer by avocation. Spilling was able to combine his knowledge of computer circuitry with his expertise in architecture to fabricate a "better mousetrap" in his home workshop. Realizing the vast potential of his improved circuit board, Spilling mortgaged his home, borrowed from his life insurance and his in-laws, and secured some bank loans in order to start DesignTech.

Since DesignTech's circuit boards had unique features for different customers, they could not be manufactured in a high-volume, assembly-line fashion. Instead, Spilling designed small work pods, where individual workers were required to perform a variety of tasks to produce a board. For example, a single worker might select and install components and chips, wire circuits, and solder connections, among other tasks. Spilling gave the workers complete autonomy to decide how they would perform these tasks.

Early operations of DesignTech did not go quite as Spilling had planned. He noticed that workers seemed to vary considerably in the way they per-

formed these routine tasks; consequently, there was no way to predict the amount of time it would take to manufacture a specific circuit board. Many times Spilling would observe his workers and say to himself, "I wonder what would possess someone to do it that way." When he asked one of his workers why a particular procedure was used, the worker responded, "Well, R.W. (as Spilling was referred to throughout the company), nobody ever sat us down and told us there was a perfect way."

For Discussion

1. Do you think that Spilling provided his workers with too much autonomy in selecting work procedures?

2. Review the principles of scientific management, and discuss how they might be used to improve the task performance of DesignTech's workers.

EXPERIENTIAL EXERCISE 2.1

To Which School Do You Subscribe?

Purpose: To give class members an opportunity to observe how each of the various schools of management thought affects individual and group behaviors.

Procedure: Prior to the experiential exercise that follows, conduct a class in which the theories and ideas associated with each of the various schools of management thought are presented and discussed. Before dismissing the class, perform Steps 1, 2, and 3 of the following procedure. Then, in a subsequent class meeting, perform Steps 4 and 5.

Step 1 Divide the class into small groups of approximately three to five students per group. Be sure that at least five groups are formed. Depending upon the class size, it may be necessary to vary from this guideline.

Step 2 Randomly assign each of the groups to a particular school of management thought. If more than five groups were formed, more than one group will be assigned to a particular school of thought. This is perfectly acceptable. The assignments of groups to schools of thought are to be secret. Groups must not divulge to other groups which school of management thought they were assigned.

Step 3 Instruct each group to design a brief skit that shows a manager in a work situation engaging in the type of behavior that their school of management thought would predict or advocate. Inform the groups that these skits are to be presented before the entire class in the next class session.

Step 4 In the following class meeting, the skits will be presented before the entire class. Class members are to guess which school of management thought was represented in each skit.

Step 5 After the skits have been presented and student guesses made, the class will conclude with a discussion that might include the following issues:

- What are the similarities and differences among the schools of management thought?

- Does any one school of management thought seem more appropriate for use by contemporary managers in today's business organizations?

- Would certain types of organizations be more likely to subscribe to a particular school of management thought?

- Are any of the schools completely out of date and no longer appropriate for use by contemporary managers?

EXPERIENTIAL EXERCISE 2.2

Fayol's Principles versus Woodward's Technology Types: How Do They Fit?

Purpose: To assess how well each of Fayol's fourteen principles fits with Woodward's three technology types.

Procedure: Follow these steps:

Step 1 Construct a matrix containing fourteen rows and three columns. Label each of the rows with one of Fayol's principles and each of the columns with one of Woodward's technology types.

Step 2 Place a rating between 1 and 10 in each of the cells of the matrix. The rating in a cell is to be your subjective assessment of how well the principle identified by the row fits or applies to the technology type identified by the column. A rating of 1 indicates the least applicable (or worst fit), and a rating of 10 indicates the most applicable (or best fit). Since your ratings for a principle might vary for different companies in the same technology type, try to make each rating an average of your observations, experiences, or knowledge of different companies in each technology type.

Step 3 With the aid of your instructor, assemble the ratings from your classmates who have had this same assignment. Compute a class mean rating for each cell of the matrix.

ENDNOTES

1. F. Robert, "As UPS Tries to Deliver More to Its Customers, Labor Problem Grows," *The Wall Street Journal,* May 23, 1994.

2. J. A. Conger, "Leadership: The Art of Empowering Others," *Academy of Management Executive,* 3, 1989, 17–24.

3. L. J. Krajewski and L. P. Ritzman, *Operations Management: Strategy and Analysis,* 4th ed. (Reading, Mass.: Addison-Wesley, 1996).

4. "Virtual Office," *USA Today,* June 27, 1996, B11.

5. J. R. Evans, D. R. Anderson, D. J. Sweeney, and T. A. Williams, *Applied Production and Operations Management,* 3d ed. (St. Paul, Minn.: West Publishing, 1990), 423–28.

6. J. Evans and W. Lindsay, *Production/Operations Management: A Focus on Quality* (St. Paul, Minn.: West Publishing, 1993).

7. B. Brocka and M. S. Brocka, *Quality Management* (Homewood, Ill.: Business One Irwin, 1992), 18.

8. D. Wren, *Evolution of Management Thought,* 2d ed. (New York: Wiley, 1979).

9. F. W. Taylor, *Scientific Management* (New York: Harper & Row, 1911).

10. C. Wrege and A. G. Peroni, "Taylor's Pig-Tale: A Historical Analysis of Frederick W. Taylor's Pig-Iron Experiments," *Academy of Management Journal,* 17, March 1974, 6–27.

11. C. Wrege and A. M. Stotka, "Cooke Creates a Classic: The Story behind F. W. Taylor's Principles of Scientific Management," *Academy of Management Review,* 3, October 1978, 736–49.

12. D. Wren, *Evolution of Management Thought.*

13. F. B. Gilbreth, *Principles of Scientific Management* (New York: Van Nostrand, 1911).

14. M. K. Starr, *Operations Management: A Systems Approach* (Danvers, Mass.: Boyd & Fraser, 1996), 375.

15. H. Fayol, *Industrial and General Administration* (New York: Sir Isaac Pitman and Sons, 1930).

16. C. George Jr., *The History of Management Thought* (Englewood Cliffs, N.J.: Prentice-Hall, 1968).

17. J. F. Mee, "Pioneers of Management," *Advanced Management—Office Executive,* October 1962, 26–29.

18. M. Weber, *General Economic History,* trans. F. H. Knight (London: Allen & Unwin, 1927).

19. D. Wren, *Evolution of Management Thought.*

20. M. Weber, *The Theory of Social and Economic Organizations,* ed. and trans. A. M. Henderson and T. Parsons (New York: Free Press, 1947).

21. Ibid.

22. D. Ignatius, "The Egyptian Bureaucracy Galls Both the Public and Foreign Investors," *The Wall Street Journal,* March 24, 1983.

23. M. P. Follett, *Creative Experience* (London: Longmans, Green, 1934).

24. B. Buchholz and M. Crane, "Nurturing the Team Spirit at Growing Green," *Your Company,* Spring 1995, 11.

25. M. P. Follett, "Dynamic Administration," in *Dynamic Administration: The Collected Papers of Mary Parker Follett,* ed. H. Metcalf and L. F. Urwick (New York: Harper & Row, 1942).

26. H. M. Parson, "What Happened at Hawthorne?" *Science,* 183, 1974, 922–32.

27. J. A. Sonnenfeld, "Shedding Light on the Hawthorne Studies," *Journal of Occupational Behavior,* 6, 1985, 111–30.

28. F. Kast and J. Rosenzweig, *Organization and Management: A Systems and Contingency Approach* (New York: McGraw-Hill, 1979).

29. D. McGregor, *The Human Side of Enterprise* (New York: McGraw-Hill, 1960), 33-58.

30. Ibid.

31. R. A. Baron and P. B. Paulus, *Understanding Human Relations: A Practical Guide to People at Work* (Needham Heights, Mass.: Allyn & Bacon, 1991), 312-13.

32. C. Barnard, *The Functions of the Executive* (Cambridge, Mass.: Harvard University Press, 1938).

33. B. Render and R. M. Stair Jr., *Introduction to Quantitative Models for Management* (Englewood Cliffs, N.J.: Prentice-Hall, 1996).

34. L. Austin and J. Burns, *Management Science* (New York: Macmillan, 1985).

35. T. Cook and R. Russell, *Introduction to Management Science* (Englewood Cliffs, N.J.: Prentice-Hall, 1985), 6-20.

36. K. Boulding, "General Systems Theory—The Skeleton of Science," *Management Science,* 2, April 1956, 197-208.

37. L. J. Krajewski and L. P. Ritzman, *Operations Management,* 3-4.

38. Kast and Rosenzweig, Organization and Management, 102.

39. F. Luthans, "The Contingency Theory of Management: A Path out of the Jungle," *Business Horizons,* 16, June 1973, 62-72.

40. J. Woodward, *Industrial Organizations: Theory and Practice,* 2d ed. (London: Oxford University Press, 1980).

41. Ibid.

42. F. Kast and J. Rosenzweig, *Contingency Views of Organizations and Management* (Chicago: Science Research Associates, 1973).

43. "More Businesses Hispanic-Owned, Government Says," *The Orlando Sentinel,* July 12, 1996, B1.

44. M. A. Vonderembse and G. P. White, *Operations Management: Concepts, Methods and Strategies,* 3d ed. (Minneapolis: West Publishing Company, 1996), 638-651.

45. Based on E. Eldridge, "Thieves Hog Wild over Motorcycles," *USA Today,* July 19, 1996, B1; R. Willis, "Harley-Davidson Comes Roaring Back," *Management Review,* March 1986, 20-27; J. Van, "Message to American Companies: Rebuild from Scratch," *The Orlando Sentinel,* December 8, 1991, F1; D. Hutchins, "Having a Hard Time with Just-in-Time," *Fortune,* June 9, 1986, 64-66; J. A. Conway, "Harley Back in Gear," *Forbes,* April 20, 1987, 8.

46. M. K. Starr, *Operations Management,* 144.

47. C. P. Prather, "Company of the Year: Remaining Positive and Leading Kentucky into the Future," *The Lane Report* (Lexington, Ky.), January 1, 1994.

48. W. Ouchi, *Theory Z: How American Business Can Meet the Japanese Challenge* (Reading, Mass.: Addison-Wesley, 1981), 60.

49. F. Robert, "As UPS Tries to Deliver More to Its Customers, Labor Problem Grows," *The Wall Street Journal,* May 23, 1994.

Social Responsibility and Ethics

■ CHAPTER OVERVIEW

Corporate social responsibility and business ethics have been the focus of a great deal of attention in recent years. Organizations are increasingly being held accountable for the contributions they make to society, as well as for the degree to which their individual members adhere to an appropriate code of ethical conduct. Further, managers of the future will be expected to address important social issues proactively and to maintain a high standard of ethical behavior if they are to succeed within the corporate environment.

This chapter begins with a discussion of the stakeholder view of the firm. With that view in mind, we will explore the concept of social responsibility, examine three perspectives of social responsibility, and consider four strategies for approaching social issues. In addition, recommendations for developing a socially responsive position are offered. The topic of business ethics can be approached in several ways. Here we will consider values and the role they play in shaping one's ethical behavior. Approaches for addressing ethical dilemmas are discussed as well. Our examination of ethics concludes with a discussion of ways to encourage and support ethical behavior in a corporate environment. Implications for tomorrow's managers are also discussed.

■ LEARNING OBJECTIVES

When you have finished studying this chapter, you should be able to:

- Discuss the stakeholder view of the firm.
- Describe the concept of corporate social responsibility and the primary premises upon which it is based.
- Distinguish among the three perspectives of corporate social responsibility.
- Identify and evaluate different strategies for responding to social issues.
- Discuss the ten commandments of social responsibility.
- Explain what values are and how they form the basis of an individual's ethical behavior.
- Distinguish between terminal and instrumental values.
- Identify and discuss the differences in the utility, human rights, and justice approaches to ethical dilemmas.
- Explain the methods used by an organization to encourage ethical business behavior.
- Describe the different approaches used in ethics training programs.
- Discuss what is meant by whistleblowing in monitoring ethical behavior.

C H A P T E R

3

Managerial Incident

Astra: Power and Sexual Harassment

It's a familiar routine. A scandal erupts in a large corporation. Bowing to public pressure, the Board vows to get to the bottom of the mess, hiring a retired government big shot or blue-chip law firm to conduct an "independent" investigation. Name a major company that has been in trouble in recent years and it has probably gone through the drill.

No company knows that better than the Swedish pharmaceutical company, Astra AB. It was in June 1995—the final night of the national sales meeting for its U.S. subsidiary, Astra USA, Inc. Pairs of employees were dancing in the ballroom of a suburban Boston hotel. Astra USA's president and chief executive officer, Lars Bildman, had his arms wrapped around a 25-year-old sales representative, Pamela L. Zortman. Onlookers saw that Bildman, extremely drunk, was running his hands along her back and nibbling at her neck.

Suddenly, Zortman rushed into a nearby restroom. There a distraught Zortman told other women that Bildman had tried to kiss her. She didn't get much sympathy from the two longtime female managers present. "That's the way it is at Astra and you'd better get used to it."

In May 1996, *Business Week* was about to publish the results of a six-month investigation into allegations of rampant sexual harassment at Astra USA. Given the impending *Business Week* report, top executives at the parent company had to decide how to handle this very difficult situation.[1]

INTRODUCTION

Management at Astra was facing a very difficult situation. The negative publicity surrounding the investigation of sexual harassment at their U.S. subsidiary would undoubtedly damage the image of the company. Additionally, if the allegations were in fact true, the company could be vulnerable to legal action on the part of the complainants. The management team of the parent company needed to act quickly and appropriately to head off further damage to the organization.

Unfortunately, such situations are far too common in today's business environment. Many respectable organizations have faced allegations of socially irresponsible or illegal behavior. Such accusations can have serious consequences for an organization's image in its local community, the financial community, and society overall. Consequently, managers must take care to act responsibly and ethically with regard to issues that affect the general welfare of society.

As we examine corporate social responsibility and ethics, you will see examples that illustrate the benefits of responsible and ethical behavior, as well as others that illustrate the negative consequences of irresponsible or unethical behavior. First, however, we must answer a very important question. To whom is business responsible? Is it the stockholders of the company? The customers? The employees? Answering such questions requires an understanding of the stakeholder view of the firm.

ORGANIZATIONAL STAKEHOLDERS IN A GLOBAL ENVIRONMENT

Stakeholders
People who are affected by or can affect the activities of the firm.

Central to the issues of corporate social responsibility and ethics is the concept of stakeholders. **Stakeholders** are all those who are affected by or can affect the activities of the firm.[2] While it has long been accepted that a corporation must be responsible to its stockholders, contemporary social responsibility theory maintains that a corporation has obligations to all of its stakeholders. This perspective broadens the scope of the business's obligations beyond a relatively narrow group of shareholders to a much broader set of constituents that includes such groups as government, consumers, owners, employees, and communities throughout the globe.[3]

Figure 3.1 illustrates the many and varied constituent groups that can be stakeholders in a given organization. The primary stakeholders of a firm are those who have a formal, official, or contractual relationship with the organization. They include owners (stockholders), employees, customers, and suppliers. Peripheral to this group are the secondary stakeholders, who include other societal groups that are affected by the activities of the firm. Consider, for example, who might represent primary and secondary stakeholders for your college or university. As a student, are you a primary or secondary stakeholder? What about the employers in your community? Are they primary or secondary stakeholders? Consider what happened at Malden Mills Industries, profiled in Entrepreneurial Approach. Who were primary and secondary stakeholders for this firm and how were they affected by the decisions of the owner?

As organizations become involved in the international business arena, they often find that their stakeholder base becomes wider and more diverse. Organizations that must cope with stakeholders from across the globe face special challenges that require a heightened sensitivity to and awareness of economic, political, and social differences among groups. For example, international firms must be responsive to customers with very different needs, owners with varied expectations, and employees with distinct, and perhaps dissimilar, motivations.[4] Dealing effectively with such groups requires a focus on understanding the global nature of stakeholders and developing strategies that recognize and respond to such differences.

Consider, for example, the experiences of socially conscious ice-cream giant Ben & Jerry's. While being socially proactive has worked well in the

FIGURE 3.1

The stakeholder view of the firm

SOURCE: A. Carroll, *Business & Society: Ethics and Stakeholder Management* 3e. Copyright ©1996. By permission of South-Western College Publishing, a division of International Thomson Publishing Inc., Cincinnati; Ohio 45227.

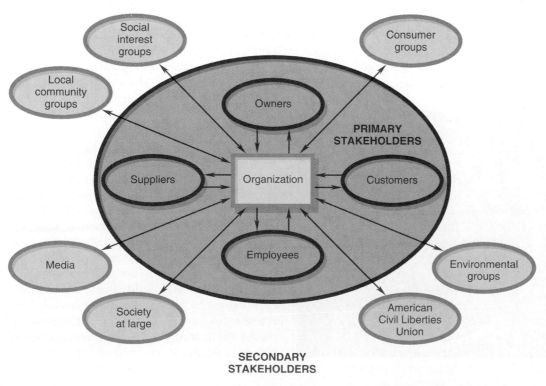

Entrepreneurial Approach

MALDEN MILLS: COMPASSION COMES FIRST

It was just two weeks before Christmas when a fire broke out at Malden Mills Industries in Lawrence, Massachusetts. Four of the five buildings that composed the plant were destroyed in the fire. It was clear that operations would cease at Malden Mills for at least several months—and perhaps for good.

With sales over $400 million annually, Malden Mills was the largest employer in Lawrence, Massachusetts. The company's work force consisted of approximately 2,400 employees, many of whom were immigrant workers. As the company's employees watched the fire destroy their plant, many thought of the difficult times that lay ahead. The possibility of long-term unemployment was weighing heavy on everyone's mind.

But Aaron Feuerstein, the owner of the fire-damaged Malden Mills, had a different message to send his work force. In addressing approximately 1,000 of his employees on the morning after the fire, Feuerstein announced that he would continue to pay their salaries for at least 30 days despite the mill being closed. In addition, the 70-year-old owner made a commitment to rebuild the mill as quickly as possible, right where it once stood.

Why were some surprised at that decision? Because many had doubted that Feuerstein would rebuild at all. According to Feuerstein, "most people would have been happy at their 70th birthday to take the insurance money and go to Florida. I just don't want to do that." Feuerstein's decision was based on his commitment to his work force and his community. His concern and compassion was greatly appreciated not only by the employees at Malden Mills, but by the citizens of Lawrence as well.

The Christmas spirit was alive and well in Lawrence after all.

Firms in the international arena face special challenges that require them to be sensitive to and aware of economic, political, and social differences among groups. While their social proactivism has worked well for Ben & Jerry's in the U.S. market, their strategy has not transferred without effort to the international market.

© Jean Higgins/Unicorn Stock Photos

U.S. market, transferring their "caring capitalism" strategy to new international markets has proven difficult. For example, when President Robert Holland wanted to start shipping products to France in December of 1995, Ben Cohen (one of the original founders) insisted that their advertisements take a stand against the French government's nuclear testing policy in the South Pacific. Holland resisted, saying, "If the decision is to punish French consumers because of their government's foreign policy, that didn't make sense."

In the end Holland prevailed. But the incident has caused onlookers to wonder if Ben & Jerry's will have to modify its social agenda in order to grow in the international marketplace.[5]

With the stakeholder view of the organization in mind, we will move on to examine the concepts of social responsibility and ethics. Although these two topics are integrally related, they can and should be addressed independently. Corporate social responsibility is an organizational issue that relates to the obligation of business to society. In contrast, ethical issues are most relevant at an individual level, for ethics is maintained by people, not organizations. Nevertheless, both are important topics that have significant implications for the long-term success of any organization.

SOCIAL RESPONSIBILITY

Few issues have been the subject of more heated debate than corporate social responsibility. For decades, practitioners and academics have argued over the nature and extent of the obligations business has to society. Perspectives on the issue of corporate social responsibility have varied dramatically over the years, and even today achieving a consensus on the subject is difficult.[6]

What is corporate social responsibility? It is a complex concept that resists precise definition. In a very general sense, **corporate social responsibility** can be thought of as the interaction between business and the social environment in which it exists. Most would agree that being socially responsible means acting in a way that is acceptable to society and that all organizations should act in a socially responsible manner.

Corporate social responsibility
The interaction between business and the social environment in which it exists.

The debate over corporate social responsibility focuses on the nature of socially responsible behavior. Does being socially responsible mean that the corporation's actions must not harm society, or does it mean that the corporation's actions should benefit society? How does one determine harm and benefit? These issues are at the heart of the controversy over corporate social responsibility.

To gain a better understanding of corporate social responsibility, we will first examine the two basic premises of the concept. Then, with these premises in mind, we will explore three perspectives of corporate social responsibility that exist today, as well as a model for evaluating corporate social behavior.

THE PREMISES OF THE SOCIAL RESPONSIBILITY DEBATE

Many would argue that the controversy over the responsibility of business was inevitable, given the moral and ethical challenges that corporate America has faced over the last several decades. You don't need to look far to find examples of organizations that have acted "irresponsibly" in the eyes of some segment of society. Whether it involved a violation of worker safety regulations, insufficient attention to product safety for consumers, or the relocation of a plant (and numerous jobs) to a foreign country with lower labor costs, corporate America has been besieged with accusations of social irresponsibility in recent years.[7]

The discussion of social responsibility began over 35 years ago when H. R. Bowen proposed that businesses and managers have an obligation to "pursue those policies, to make those decisions, or to follow those lines of action that are desirable in terms of the objectives and values of our society."[8] This simple proposition inspired the modern debate about social responsibility.

Bowen's assertions rest on two fundamental premises, **social contract** and **moral agent,** which can be summarized as follows:

Social contract
An implied set of rights and obligations that are inherent in social policy and assumed by business.

Moral agent
A business's obligation to act honorably and to reflect and enforce values that are consistent with those of society.

- *Social contract.* Business exists at the pleasure of society, and as a result, it must comply with the guidelines established by society. An implied set of rights and obligations is inherent in social policy and assumed by business. This set of rights and obligations can be thought of as a social contract between business and society.
- *Moral agent.* Business must act in a way that is perceived as moral. In other words, business has an obligation to act honorably and to reflect and enforce values that are consistent with those of society. Further, business can be held accountable as a moral agency.

These two premises have provided the foundation for the concept of social responsibility, but they have also served as targets for critics of the concept. In fact, there are several perspectives on social responsibility, which differ mainly in their view of these two premises. Let's examine these perspectives in greater detail.

THE THREE PERSPECTIVES OF SOCIAL RESPONSIBILITY

Three primary perspectives of corporate social responsibility have emerged over the years: (1) economic responsibility, (2) public responsibility, and (3) social responsiveness.[9] Table 3.1 outlines the primary tenets of these perspectives. Each perspective views Bowen's two premises somewhat differently and, consequently, offers a different view of the concept of corporate social responsibility.[10]

Economic Responsibility

Although many hold the economic responsibility perspective, one of its most outspoken proponents is Milton Friedman. Friedman maintains that the only social responsibility of business is to maximize profits within the "rules of the game." In his opinion, the only constituents to which business is responsible are the stockholders, and it is the firm's responsibility to maximize the wealth of this constituent group. This is the only social contract to which business should be committed. If socially responsible behavior on the part of the corporation serves to reduce the financial return to the stockholders, the managers of the business have undermined the market mechanism for allocating resources and have violated the social contract of business as it should be in a free market society.

Proponents of the economic responsibility perspective also argue that corporations cannot be moral agents. Only individuals can serve as moral agents. When individuals choose to direct their own assets or resources toward the public good, that behavior is appropriate and to the benefit of society. However, when they begin to direct corporate resources toward that end, they have violated their commitment to the owners (that is, the stockholders) of those assets or resources.

Critics of the economic responsibility perspective argue that many of today's business organizations are not merely economic institutions and to view them as such is both unrealistic and naïve. Many large corporations wield sig-

TABLE 3.1   Three perspectives of social responsibility

PERSPECTIVE	BASIC TENETS
Economic responsibility	• The responsibility of business is to make a profit within the "rules of the game." • Organizations cannot be moral agents. Only individuals can serve as moral agents.
Public responsibility	• Business should act in a way that is consistent with society's view of responsible behavior, as well as with established laws and policy.
Social responsiveness	• Business should proactively seek to contribute to society in a positive way. • Organizations should develop an internal environment that encourages and supports ethical behavior at an individual level.

SOURCE: S. L. Wartick and P. L. Cochran, "The Evolution of the Corporate Social Performance Model," *Academy of Management Review,* 10, 1985, 764.

nificant political power and have tremendous influence on a wide variety of public policies and regulations across the globe. Further, the activities of many corporations are essential to realizing important social goals such as equal opportunity, environmental protection, and increased global competitiveness in critical industries. Viewing the modern corporation as simply an economic institution is myopic and ignores the reality of the worldwide evolution of business.[11] Figure 3.2 illustrates, in a somewhat humorous way, how decisions that are economically desirable can be very negative from a social welfare perspective, reinforcing the view that business has a significant impact on society.[12]

Public Responsibility

The public responsibility perspective represents an alternative view of social responsibility. Focusing almost exclusively on the social contract premise, proponents of public responsibility argue that business should act in ways that are consistent with public policy. Rather than viewing public policy as simply the laws and regulations with which business must comply, supporters of this philosophy define public policy as "the broad pattern of social direction reflected in public opinion, emerging issues, formal legal requirements, and enforcement or implementation practices."[13] In other words, public policy refers to the overall perceptions and expectations of the public with regard to the interaction between business and society.

Critics of the public responsibility position argue that it lacks clarity. If public responsibility means adhering to existing public policy, which is traditionally considered to be the laws and regulations of the legal system, then this perspective differs little from the economic perspective. Like the economic perspective, this view would imply only that business should comply with the "rules of the game." If, however, a broader view of public policy is assumed, the public responsibility perspective differs little from the traditional view of social responsibility and Bowen's concept of social contract. Consequently, critics of the public responsibility position argue that it does not reflect a unique philosophy and that, unless it is defined more clearly, it is redundant to other perspectives.

Social Responsiveness

The third perspective of social responsibility is that of social responsiveness. Proponents of this perspective argue that corporate social responsibility should

FIGURE 3.2

Economic consequences versus social consequences

SOURCE: "A CEO Forum: What Corporate Social Responsibility Means to Me," *Business and Society Review*, 81, pp. 87–89, ©1989 by Sage Publications, Inc. Reprinted by Permission of Sage Publications, Inc.

The negative consequences of irresponsible social behavior can have long-term and far-reaching effects on society. As an example, consider the impact of the Valdez oil spill on the surrounding environment.

© Ken Graham/Tony Stone Images

not be simply an obligation on the part of business to meet the minimum expectations of society. Viewing social responsibility in this way suggests that it is a burden. Rather, modern corporations should proactively seek to act in ways that improve the welfare of society. Social responsiveness implies a proactive and tangible effort to contribute to the well-being of society.

The social responsiveness perspective also recognizes the moral agency aspect of corporate social responsibility. While proponents of this perspective agree with the economic responsibility proponents that morality is an individual rather than an organizational obligation, they maintain that the organization is responsible for creating and maintaining an environment where moral behavior on the part of individual organizational members is encouraged and supported.

Although many have endorsed the social responsiveness perspective, it has also sparked some legitimate questions. Most pervasive, perhaps, has been the

TABLE 3.2   Socially irresponsible behaviors

Unfortunately, you need not look far to find examples of socially irresponsible corporate behaviors. Consider the following "classic" incidents:

- Swiss conglomerate Nestlé marketed infant formula in developing countries by encouraging new mothers to give up breast-feeding and switch to formula. The company used so-called "milk nurses" to promote their products in maternity wards. These women, who were actually sales representatives for the company, dressed as nurses, increasing their credibility with new mothers. As a result, many new mothers made the switch. But there were problems: (1) the formula had to be mixed with water, which was contaminated in many countries, causing health problems for many infants; (2) the mothers could not easily afford the product so they would overdilute it, causing malnutrition problems for their babies; and (3) once these mothers had given up breast-feeding, they were completely dependent on this product to feed their babies. Eventually bowing to organized protests and boycotts from numerous activist groups, the company finally agreed to alter its marketing practices. Did Nestlé have an obligation to fully educate mothers in these Third World countries about product usage and safety issues?

- A chemical leak at a Union Carbide plant in Bhopal, India, killed 2,500 people and injured 200,000 more. Investigations revealed that appropriate safety precautions had not been taken and that the deficiencies were made possible because of lax regulation and enforcement practices in India. (For example, while the Environmental Protection Agency in the United States has a staff of over 4,000, the counterpart organization in India has a staff of about 150.) Did Union Carbide have an obligation to pursue the same safety measures in India as it did in the United States, irrespective of the government's ability to monitor and enforce such standards?

- When the dangers of silicone breast implants became apparent in the United States, the Food and Drug Administration asked all domestic manufacturers to adopt a voluntary moratorium on exports. Dow Corning ceased all sales in the international marketplace, citing the need to apply the same standards internationally as it follows domestically. Three other manufacturers continued to export their silicone breast implants. Should multinational companies apply the same product standards internationally as they do domestically?

question of how much social responsiveness is enough. The perspective fails to define the extent to which an organization should proactively attempt to benefit society. At what point do the efforts of the organization come at the expense of profitability?

Critics of this perspective also argue that it ignores issues of social irresponsibility. Acting irresponsibly is often of greater consequence than failing to act responsively. Consider, for example, how Exxon's irresponsible behavior during the Valdez oil spill affected the environment. Table 3.2 provides some examples of socially irresponsible behavior that have occurred in the last two decades. As is clear from these incidents, irresponsible behavior by organizations can have far-reaching and long-term effects.

Evaluating the social behavior of organizations can be quite difficult given the diversity of perspectives regarding social responsibility. The following section describes one framework for evaluating the extent to which organizations demonstrate socially responsible behavior.

THE FOUR FACES OF SOCIAL RESPONSIBILITY

In a very general sense, an organization's social behavior can be categorized according to two dimensions—legality and responsibility. As illustrated in Figure 3.3, four combinations of legal and responsible behaviors are possible: (1) legal/responsible, (2) legal/irresponsible, (3) illegal/responsible, and (4) illegal/irresponsible.[14]

Although one would hope that all organizations would operate in a legal and responsible manner, the evidence suggests otherwise. In fact, there are far too many examples of firms that have behaved in an illegal or irresponsible way. Why would a company choose to behave illegally or irresponsibly? Let's consider a situation where that might happen.

Suppose a manufacturing company has been notified of a new pollution regulation that will affect one of its plants. The cost of complying with the regulation is $1.2 million, while the fine for failing to comply is $25,000. The likelihood of being caught in noncompliance is 10 percent, and even if the organization is caught, there will be little publicity. Although noncompliance would be both illegal and irresponsible, a cost-benefit analysis might suggest that the organization not comply with the regulation. Is this an appropriate decision? Absolutely not. Yet some companies facing such a situation might make that choice. When the penalty associated with breaking the law is less costly than complying with the law, an organization may make an inappropriate decision.

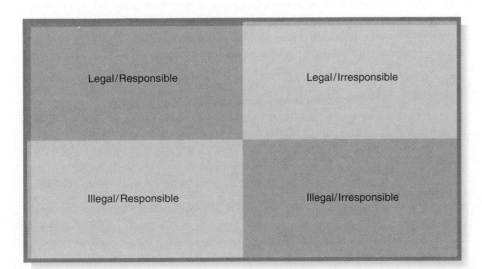

FIGURE 3.3

The four faces of social responsibility

SOURCE: D. R. Dalton and R. A. Cosier, "The Four Faces of Social Responsibility," *Business Horizons,* May/June 1982, 19–27.

Consider the other two quadrants in the model. Can you think of examples of organizations that have acted legally, but irresponsibly? Illegally, but responsibly? Under what conditions might an organization choose to act in such ways? Consider the incidents profiled in Table 3.2. In which quadrant would each of these incidents fall?

Organizations will typically behave in ways that are consistent with their overall strategy for responding to social issues. Social responsibility strategies may range from doing nothing to making an attempt to benefit society in very tangible ways. The following section identifies four different strategies for social responsibility and examines reasons why an organization might choose a particular strategy.

SOCIAL RESPONSIBILITY STRATEGIES

As we know, organizations take widely different approaches to corporate social responsibility. Some organizations do little more than operate to ensure profitability for their stockholders while others maintain very aggressive and proactive social responsiveness agendas.

Figure 3.4 illustrates a continuum of social responsibility strategies that range from "do nothing" to "do much." Four distinct strategies can be identified along this continuum: reaction, defense, accommodation, and proaction. They vary according to the organization's tendency to be socially responsible or responsive.[15]

Reaction

An organization that assumes a reaction stance simply fails to act in a socially responsible manner. Consider, for example, the classic case of Manville Corporation.[16] Over 40 years ago, the medical department of Manville Corporation (then known as Johns Manville) discovered evidence to suggest that asbestos inhalation causes a debilitating and often fatal lung disease. Rather than looking for ways to provide safer work conditions for company employees, the firm chose to conceal the evidence.

Why? That's hard to say. But there is evidence to suggest that the company was more concerned about profitability than about the health and safety of its employees. Presumably, top executives at Manville thought it would be less costly to pay workers' compensation claims than to develop safer working conditions.

Manville's irresponsibility did not go without notice, however. Eventually, as a result of litigation, the company was forced to pay a $2.6 billion settlement, which forced a reorganization that left the company on very shaky ground. Was shareholder wealth maximized by the irresponsibility of Manville's leaders? Obviously not. The stockholders of the firm lost a substantial amount of money as a result of the company's reactive social responsibility strategy.

Defense

Organizations that pursue a defense strategy respond to social challenges only when it is necessary to defend their current position. Consider, for example, the three major automobile manufacturers in this country. How did they react to the social issues of air pollution, vehicle safety, and gas shortages in the 1970s?

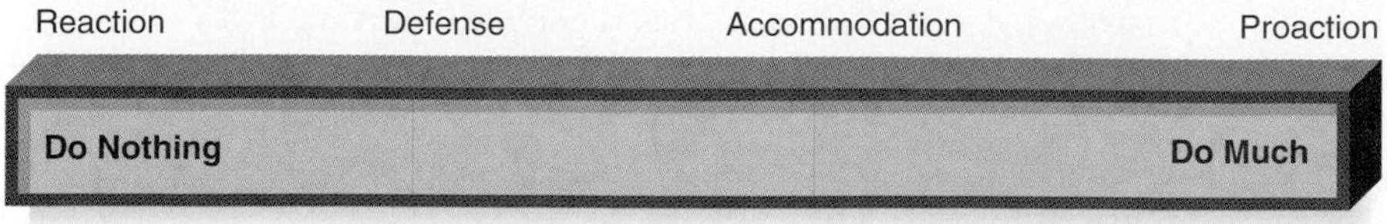

FIGURE 3.4

Social responsibility strategies

SOURCE: A. Carroll, "A Three-Dimensional Conceptual Model of Corporate Performance," *Academy of Management Review*, 4, 1979, 497–505.

Reaction	Defense	Accommodation	Proaction

Do Nothing   **Do Much**

When Dr. Haagan-Smit, the prophet of smog, proclaimed that automobiles were the major contributor to U.S. smog, domestic car manufacturers argued that the problem was really a function of poorly maintained vehicles. When Ralph Nader brought the issue of vehicle safety to the foreground of social consciousness, the automakers argued that bad drivers were the problem, not unsafe cars. And when the oil crisis struck and consumers demanded more fuel-efficient automobiles, car manufacturers continued to give them new models of the same gas hogs of the past.[17]

Can we call this social responsiveness? Hardly. The U.S. car manufacturers' strategy was one of defense. Not until the Japanese automakers stepped up with solutions to these social issues, and the U.S. automakers begin to see the effect of their complacency on the bottom line, did they begin to act in a socially responsible manner. They were forced to respond to the needs of society (and their customers) as a result of pressures from foreign competitors.

Accommodation

Corporations with an accommodation strategy of corporate social responsibility readily adapt their behaviors to comply with public policy and regulation where necessary and, more importantly, attempt to be responsive to public expectations.[18]

Bank of America, for example, has always readily disclosed information required by law. This policy has not differentiated the company from its competitors, however, because virtually every financial services company meets the minimum requirements of disclosure regulation. But in contrast to many of its competitors, Bank of America has pioneered a code for voluntary disclosure of bank information requested by its customers or by any other member of the public. This policy of "ask and you shall receive" is an example of an accommodation strategy of social responsibility.[19]

Proaction

Organizations that assume a proaction strategy with regard to corporate social responsibility subscribe to the notion of social responsiveness. They do not operate solely in terms of profit; nor do they consider compliance with public policy, regardless of how it is defined, to be sufficient. These organizations proactively seek to improve the welfare of society.

Many organizations have gone above and beyond the call of duty to address important social issues (see Table 3.3 for some examples). General Electric stands out as one organization that has aggressively worked to contribute to society in the area of education. General Electric's CEO, Jack Welch, considers it the responsibility of business to "teach and lead" students who represent the future of this country. Several GE plants have developed volunteer programs that support mentoring relationships between GE employees and local high school students. As a result of these programs, several high schools have dramatically increased the number of their students who go on to college.[20]

Another example of a proactive organization is Starbucks Coffee Company. Starbucks has been long recognized for its proactive programs to support and develop its employees. But more recently, the company is making an effort to export its employee-oriented philosophy to its Third World suppliers. Global Perspective describes how Starbucks is making a difference in the lives of people in other parts of the world, as well as those at home.

Which strategy is the best? Should all organizations assume a proaction strategy with respect to corporate social responsibility? Not necessarily. There are, however, some basic social responsibility principles to which all organizations should subscribe.

TABLE 3.3   Examples of proactive social responsiveness

- *Honda.* Voted #1 by *Consumer Reports* for its safety-oriented self-propelled lawn mowers. It beat its competitors to the market with the mower even before safety legislation was passed.
- *Pennsylvania Power & Light Company.* Set up a citizen advisory board to discuss company issues that affect the general public.
- *Xerox Corporation.* Allows employees with at least three years of company service to take a one-year leave of absence to participate in a community service project. Employees receive normal pay and raises from Xerox and are promised a comparable job when they return.
- *3M Company.* Initiated an environmental protection program called "Pollution Prevention Pays." As part of the program, 3M set a goal of reducing its air, land, and water releases 90 percent by the year 2000. So far it has been successful in cutting pollutants by more than 500,000 tons since 1975. The National Wildlife Federation's Corporate Conservation Council gave 3M an Environmental Achievement Award in recognition of its progress to date.
- *Kaiser Aluminum.* Agreed to an affirmative-action plan that would place more racial minorities in craftwork positions.
- *GE Plastics.* At GE company conferences, employees teamed up to discuss ways of renovating old community buildings in San Diego.
- *Merck & Company.* Spent millions of dollars to develop Mectizan, a drug that prevents river blindness, a disease found mostly in West Africa. The company also distributed the drug free of charge in all countries where river blindness is found.
- *Gulf Power Company.* Pensacola, Florida–based Gulf Power Company helped find and fund a new home for wildlife when the original site of a wildlife sanctuary was sold. The company helped recruit its employees to volunteer and also donated money to the effort.
- *Kraft General Foods.* Now uses recycled plastic for its salad dressing bottles, making it the first company to use recycled plastics in food containers other than soft-drink bottles.
- *Rubbermaid.* Came out with a litterless lunch box called the "Sidekick." It features plastic sandwich, drink, and snack containers and means that plastic wrap, cans, and milk cartons will no longer be necessary to pack a lunch. The box has developed a strong market share and become the rage among grade-schoolers.
- *Monsanto.* Chairman and CEO Richard J. Mahoney pledged that the company would be environmentally responsible by reducing emissions, eliminating waste, working for sustainable agriculture, and managing corporate land to benefit nature.
- *Eastman Kodak.* Encourages its 100,000 employees to volunteer in local community programs by allowing them to take time off from work with pay (up to 40 hours a year) to volunteer for public service. The time does not offset vacation or sick leave and is typically used for volunteering at churches, schools, shelters, and environmental organizations.

SOURCES: "Corporations Going Green," *Business Ethics,* March/April 1992, 10; D. Bihler, "The Final Frontier," *Business Ethics,* March/April 1992, 31; and "On Company Time: The New Volunteerism," *Business Ethics,* March/April 1992, 33. Reprinted with permission from Business Ethics Magazine, 612/962-4701, 52 South 10th St., Ste. 110, Minneapolis, MN 55403.

SOCIAL RESPONSIBILITY PRINCIPLES FOR THE YEAR 2000

All evidence points to a growing emphasis on social responsibility in the future.[22] This may be, in part, a result of the increasing concern for quality in many organizations. While achieving quality clearly requires a focus on meeting the needs of customers, it may also require increased concern for meeting

STARBUCKS: MAKING A DIFFERENCE IN THE THIRD WORLD

Starbucks Coffee Company, the Seattle-based organization that is fueling the coffee-bar craze in the United States, is well recognized for its proactive employee-oriented programs. With over 500 company-owned stores throughout the country, Starbucks projects itself as a progressive business, touting its "Bean Stock" employee ownership plan, its full medical and dental benefits available even to part-time workers, and its annual six-figure donations to nonprofit organizations. In fact, Michael Moe, a growth stock analyst at Lehman Brothers securities brokerage firm, says, "They're a bunch of idealistic people who believe Starbucks is their vehicle to contribute to society and accomplish a broader mission." And management realizes that the only way to get anywhere is by treating employees well. At a time when 'the customer comes first' is the adage of the day in most organizations, Starbucks' philosophy is "the employee comes first."

Transferring this mentality to its Third World suppliers has been the company's most recent challenge. According to the U.S./Guatemala Labor Education project, workers in Guatemala toil in inhumane conditions in Guatemala to earn two cents a pound picking beans, while Starbucks sells the same beans for up to $8 a pound. While the majority of specialty coffee firms had not considered working conditions in coffee-producing countries a top ethical priority, Starbucks was committed to taking the lead in addressing this difficult social issue.

Starbucks' recently released a "code of conduct" that encourages Third World suppliers to ban child labor and to provide workers with increased wages, improved working conditions, and at least minimal health care. According to Eric Hahn, the Starbucks Campaign Coordinator for the U.S./Guatemala Labor Education Project, "Starbucks has gone a long way to deal with a very new situation. There is nothing else like this code of conduct in the coffee or agricultural industries."

Starbucks has made a commitment to carrying its social mission beyond the boundaries of the United States. What will be the effect the company's efforts? Only time will tell.[21]

Global Perspective

the needs of all stakeholders of the organization. In fact, organizations that strive to respond effectively to the expectations and needs of all of their stakeholders may have a competitive edge over others in their industry.

As corporations and managers look for ways to fulfill their obligations to society, they should keep the following ten commandments in mind:[23]

- *Commandment I: Thou Shall Take Corrective Action before It Is Required.* Compliance with self-imposed standards is almost always preferable to compliance with standards that are imposed by outside constituencies. Organizations should continually look for ways to improve product safety and reliability before they are forced to do so by lawsuits, regulatory bodies, or competition. (See Table 3.3 for an example of how Honda demonstrated this commandment.)

- *Commandment II: Thou Shall Work with Affected Constituents to Resolve Mutual Problems.* Organizations should not make decisions that have significant social implications in isolation. Instead, they should work with those involved to try to find mutually acceptable solutions. For example, many organizations that have considered closing plants have found that discussing the issues with plant employees has led to alternative solutions (cost-cutting measures, employee stock-option plans, and the like) that have been preferable for all parties involved.

- *Commandment III: Thou Shall Work to Establish Industrywide Standards and Self-Regulation.* Companies and industries can preserve their freedom to conduct business as they see fit by behaving responsibly before a regulatory body forces them to do so. Although developing industrywide standards requires cooperation and coordination among the players in the industry, the effort is well worth the price if it can avert ill-conceived regulations.[24] Always remember that regulations developed by those who know less about the industry than the major players are likely to be less effective than self-developed policy.

- *Commandment IV: Thou Shall Publicly Admit Your Mistakes.* Few things are worse for a company's image than being caught trying to cover up socially irresponsible behavior. It is far better to admit mistakes as soon as they are discovered, make restitution as expediently as possible, and establish control systems to ensure that such mistakes never happen again. If, for example, it turned out that there was widespread sexual harassment at Astra AB, top executives at the parent company would be well advised to confront the issue head-on by openly acknowledging the problem and implementing systems to avoid such problems in the future.

- *Commandment V: Thou Shall Get Involved in Appropriate Social Programs.* Most organizations that are truly concerned about their responsibility to society become involved in one or more social programs. Where possible, organizations should look for programs that have a need for some special talent or skill that they possess, so that the benefits of their contribution are magnified.

- *Commandment VI: Thou Shall Help Correct Environmental Problems.* Regardless of the industry in which a firm operates, there are always opportunities to address environmental issues in a proactive manner. At a minimum, doing so can help a company build a favorable image in its community, and in many cases, it can even lead to significant cost savings. Managing for Excellence describes how social crusader Gunter Pauli is helping organizations across the globe build what he calls the "zero-emissions" manufacturing plant of the future—at a net cost benefit to those who do so.

- *Commandment VII: Thou Shall Monitor the Changing Social Environment.* Like other components of the external environment, the social environment is ever changing. Socially responsible organizations should monitor these changes and act proactively to address social trends as they occur. For example, the increasing diversity of the work force requires organizations to make an aggressive effort to ensure that people of different racial, ethnic, and cultural backgrounds are given equal opportunities for advancement. Being on the "cutting edge" of social responsiveness will enhance the image of the organization and provide greater benefits for those affected by such trends.

- *Commandment VIII: Thou Shall Establish and Enforce a Corporate Code of Conduct.* Every business organization should establish a code of conduct that governs the actions of the organization as well as the behavior of its individual members. This code of conduct should be distributed throughout the organization and should be used as a guide for decision making and action by all individuals and groups in the organization.

- *Commandment IX: Thou Shall Take Needed Public Stands on Social Issues.* Organizations should never ignore social issues or refrain from tak-

GREEN MACHINE

Social crusader Gunter Pauli has a mission in life—to challenge the logic of how conventional factories work. Pauli wants to help organizations build manufacturing plants that function as closed-loop systems, or in other words, factories that completely eliminate waste by reusing or recycling all the raw material they take in. He calls it "zero-emissions" manufacturing and it's Pauli's answer to the environmental problems that result from traditional manufacturing.

One of Pauli's zero-emissions plants, a brewery, is located in southern Africa. Water flows from the brewery into ponds designed for fish farming. Mushrooms grow on piles of spent grain from the fermentation process. Chickens feed on earthworms set loose in the grain. It seems part science experiment, part environmental theme park. But according to Pauli, it is serious business: "It's a small plant, but it will generate more sales than a traditional brewery of the same size," he declares. "And it will create more jobs. That's what 21st-century entrepreneurship is about. Companies have to be financially sustainable. They also have to be socially sustainable." And Gunter Pauli is determined to do his part to help organizations do just that.[25]

ing a position. Clearly, many organizations would prefer to avoid controversial issues, but it is important that they stand up for what is right, whether the issue is discrimination, unsafe products, or disregard for the environment. It is important to take a stand.

- *Commandment X: Thou Shall Strive to Make Profits on an Ongoing Basis.* Ignoring the need to make profits is one of the most severe acts of irresponsibility. An organization cannot provide jobs and employ workers if it is not in a position to make consistent profits. To fail to recognize the importance of profitability is to threaten the livelihood of the employees of the organization.

Managers today must act in a socially responsible fashion. Their actions will be in vain, however, if the individual members of the organization do not have strong ethical values. In the next section of the chapter, we will examine more closely how ethics influences the behavior of individuals in the organization.

ETHICS

Ethics is everyone's business, from top management to employees at all levels of the organization. One of management's most important challenges is to conduct business ethically while achieving high levels of economic performance. Why ethical problems arise in business and what can be done about them are some of the issues that will be addressed in this section.

UNDERSTANDING BUSINESS ETHICS

Should you pay a bribe to obtain a business contract in a foreign country? Is it acceptable to allow your company to dispose of hazardous waste in an unsafe fashion? Can you withhold information that might discourage a job candidate from joining your organization? Is it appropriate to conduct personal business on company time? These are just a few examples of ethical and moral dilemmas you may face as a manager.

In recent years, increasing attention has been focused on ethics in business, due in large part to media coverage of a number of unethical actions.[26] Embezzlement, Defense Department favoritism to suppliers, fraudulent billing practices—these are just a few of the issues recently raised by the news media and stockholders. Consider, for example, how insider trading and other improprieties on Wall Street captured the attention of many people. Books such as *Liar's Poker* and *Nightmare on Wall Street* provide an all-too-vivid depiction of the corruption and unethical behavior that characterized the "jungle" of trading stocks and bonds.[27] In fact, as described in one book, the hapless trainee who was new to the jungle "didn't worry much about ethics—he was just trying to stay alive."

But the investments business was not the only industry to attract attention for ethical violations. Consider, for example, the scandals profiled in Table 3.4—all of which involved charitable institutions.[28]

Ethics reflects established customs and morals and fundamental human relationships that may vary throughout the world. Often ethical issues are controversial because they raise emotional questions of right and wrong behaviors. For our purposes, we will define **ethical behavior** as behavior that is morally accepted as "good" and "right" as opposed to "bad" or "wrong" in a particular setting. Right behavior is considered ethical behavior, while wrong behavior is considered unethical. In the business world, however, the difference between right and wrong behavior is not always clear.[29] Although many unethical behaviors are illegal, some may be within the limits of the law.

Corporate executives are concerned with business ethics because they want to be perceived as "good" by resolving conflicts in values and analyzing the impact of decisions on organizational members. In many cases, the goal is to avoid illegal or unethical corporate behavior leading to adverse governmental or societal reactions, such as warnings, recalls, injunctions, monetary or criminal penalties, adverse public opinion, or loss of contracts.[30]

Foundations of Ethics

Although ethical behavior in business does reflect social and cultural factors, it is also highly personal and is shaped by an individual's own values and experiences. In your daily life, you face situations where you can make ethical or unethical decisions. You make your choices based on what you have learned from parents, family, teachers, peers, friends, and so forth. In addition, your ethics are also determined by your values.

Ethics
The established customs, morals, and fundamental human relationships that exist throughout the world.

Ethical behavior
Behavior that is morally accepted as good or right as opposed to bad or wrong.

TABLE 3.4   Examples of ethical problems in charitable organizations

- *UNICEF.* Staff personnel in Kenya were charged with fraud when they stole $10 million by mismanaging funds, padding expense accounts, double-billing for services, and channeling money to phony organizations.
- *United Way.* President William Aramony and two associates defrauded the national charity of $1 million, partly to fund Aramony's high living.
- *American Parkinson Disease Association.* Executive director Frank Williams embezzled about $80,000 a year for ten years, in part because he felt undercompensated by the association.
- *Foundation for New Era Philanthropy.* Founder John G. Bennett, Jr. was charged with fraud when he bilked $100 million from other charities by way of a pyramid scheme.

SOURCE: D. Stipp, "I Stole to Get Even: Yet Another Charity Scam," *Fortune,* October 30, 1995, 24. ©1995 Time Inc. All rights reserved.

Values are the relatively permanent and deeply held preferences of individuals or groups; they are the basis upon which attitudes and personal choices are formed. Values are among the most stable and enduring characteristics of individuals. Much of what we are is a product of the basic values we have developed throughout our lives. An organization, too, has a value system, usually referred to as its organizational culture. We will discuss organizational culture in more detail in Chapter 11.

To better understand the role of values as the foundation for ethical behavior, let's look at a basic values framework. Rokeach developed a values framework and identified two general types of values: instrumental values and terminal values.[31] **Instrumental values,** also called *means-oriented values,* prescribe desirable standards of conduct or methods for attaining an end. Examples of instrumental values include ambition, courage, honesty, and imagination. **Terminal values,** also called *ends-oriented values,* prescribe desirable ends or goals for the individual and reflect what a person is ultimately striving to achieve. Terminal values are either personal (peace of mind) or social (world peace). Examples of terminal values are a comfortable life, family security, self-respect, and a sense of accomplishment.

Different groups of people tend to hold different values. For example, business school students and professors tend to rate ambition, capability, responsibility, and freedom higher than people in general do. They tend to place less importance than the general public on concern for others, helpfulness, aesthetics, cultural values, and overcoming social injustice.[32]

In most cases, the ethical standards and social responsibility of an organization or business reflect the personal values and ideals of the organization's founders or dominant managers. Over the years, those values and ideals become institutionalized and become integral to the organization's culture. For example, Thomas Watson's personal values and ethics formed the basis of IBM's culture. At Johnson & Johnson, the culture is based on the ideals of General Robert Wood Johnson. At Hewlett-Packard, the values reflect the personality and beliefs of Bill Hewlett and David Packard. At General Motors, Alfred Sloan was credited with being the moral voice of the culture. In each case, these individuals were the source of their organizations' experiences, values, and principles. They were the behavioral role models for the organizations' ethical behavior and commitment to social responsibility.

An organization's culture and the practices of its senior managers can influence the ethical behavior, not only of its employees, but also of other individuals and entities associated with the organization. Therefore, the challenge facing an organization is how to successfully develop, sustain, review, and adapt its ethical standards and its commitment to socially responsible behavior.

Business Ethics

Business ethics is not a special set of ethical rules that differ from ethics in general. **Business ethics** is the application of the general ethical rules to business behavior. If a society deems dishonesty to be unethical and immoral, then anyone in business who is dishonest with employees, customers, creditors, stockholders, or competition is acting unethically and immorally.

Businesses pay attention to ethics because the public expects a business to exhibit high levels of ethical performance and social responsibility. Many ethical rules operate to protect society against various types of harm, and business is expected to observe these ethical principles. High ethical standards also protect the individuals who work in an organization. Employees resent invasions of privacy, being ordered to do something against their personal convictions, or working under hazardous conditions. Businesses that treat their employees with dignity and integrity reap many rewards in the form of high

Values
Relatively permanent and deeply held preferences upon which individuals form attitudes and personal choices.

Instrumental values
Standards of conduct or methods for attaining an end.

Terminal values
Goals an individual will ultimately strive to achieve.

Business ethics
The application of general ethics to business behavior.

morale and improved productivity. People feel good about working for an ethical company because they know they are protected along with the general public.

Pressures to Perform

In the past few years, the negative and questionable ethical practices of many public figures and corporations have attracted considerable media attention. White-collar crimes such as insider trading and money laundering appear to be on the increase. A recent *Business Week* article noted that white-collar crime drains billions of dollars a year from corporations and governments. This cost is ultimately borne by consumers and taxpayers. The rise in unethical behavior is blamed on the current emphasis on materialism as well as on economic and competitive pressures to perform.[33] In today's environment of intense competition, some have even questioned if ethics is a liability that limits an organization's ability to succeed.[34] Yet most would agree that good ethics makes good business sense. In fact, there are long-term costs to unethical behavior that can have very negative consequences for any organization.[35]

The pressures to perform are no more evident than in the sports industry. Coaches often feel pressure from demanding fans and/or owners—so much so that they are tempted to "bend the rules" to ensure a winning season. But according to Penn State head football coach Joe Paterno, that's just not necessary. Paterno, who is world renowned for winning football games, is also well-known for maintaining a highly principled football program. He is up front with all players about his personal commitment to do the right thing, in each and every circumstance. This commitment is well evidenced by the following quote:

> I wish I had known in those early days what I think I know today about coaching. I don't mean about techniques and play selection and strategies. I mean about coaching in its first and highest sense. A coach, above all other duties, is a teacher. Coaches have the same obligation as all teachers, except we may have more moral and life-shaping influence over our players than anyone else outside of their families.
>
> I think you have to demand ethical conduct. Number one, you don't say, "Well we're gonna try." You go in with the idea that you have certain convictions, certain beliefs, morals, and that they make good sense over the long run. Ethics and honesty are investments.

Coach Paterno's "investments" in a solid ethical environment in his football program have earned his teams tremendous respect from fans and others.

Managers must continually choose between maximizing the economic performance of the organization (as indicated by revenues, costs, profits, and so forth) and improving its social performance (as indicated by obligations to customers, employees, suppliers, and others). Most ethical trade-offs are conflicts between these two desirable ends—economic versus social performance.[36] Making decisions in such situations is not merely a matter of choosing between right and wrong, or between good and bad. Most of the alternatives are not so clear-cut. Individuals who effectively manage these ethical trade-offs have a clear sense of their own values and the values of their organization. They have developed their own internal set of universal, comprehensive, and consistent principles upon which to base their decisions.

MANAGERIAL GUIDELINES FOR ETHICAL DILEMMAS

Ethical dilemma
A situation in which a person must decide whether or not to do something that, although benefiting oneself or the organization, may be considered unethical and perhaps illegal.

An **ethical dilemma** is a situation in which a person must decide whether or not to do something that, although beneficial to oneself or the organization or both, may be considered unethical. Ethical dilemmas are common in the workplace. In fact, research suggests that managers encounter such dilemmas in their working relationships with superiors, subordinates, customers, competitors, suppliers, and regulators. Common issues underlying the dilemmas include honesty in communications and contracts, gifts and entertainment, kickbacks, pricing practices, and employee terminations.

Organizations need a set of guidelines for thinking about ethical dilemmas. These guidelines can help managers and employees identify the nature of the ethical problem and decide which course of action is the most likely to produce the most ethical results. The following three approaches—utility, human rights, and justice—provide managerial guidelines for handling ethical dilemmas.

Utility Approach

The **utility approach** emphasizes the overall amount of good that can be produced by an action or a decision. It judges actions, plans, and policies by their consequences. The primary objective of this approach is to provide the greatest good for the greatest number of people. It is often referred to as a *cost-benefit analysis* because it compares the costs and benefits of a decision, a policy, or an action. These costs and benefits can be economic (expressed in dollars), social (the effect on society at large), or human (usually a psychological or emotional impact). This type of results-oriented ethical reasoning tries to determine whether the overall outcome produces more good than harm—more utility or usefulness than negative results. The utility approach supports the ethical issues of profit maximization, self-interest, rewards based on abilities and achievements, sacrifice and hard work, and competition.[37]

The main drawback to the utility approach is the difficulty of accurately measuring both costs and benefits. For example, some things, such as goods produced, sales, payrolls, and profits, can be measured in monetary terms. Other items, such as employee morale, psychological satisfactions, and the worth of human life, do not easily lend themselves to monetary measurement. Another limitation of the utility approach is that those in the majority may override the rights of those in the minority.

Despite these limitations, cost-benefit analysis is widely used in business. If benefits (earnings) exceed costs, the organization makes a profit and is considered to be an economic success. Because this method uses economic and financial outcomes, managers sometimes rely on it to decide important ethical questions without being fully aware of its limitations or the availability of other approaches that may improve the ethical quality of decisions. One of these alternative approaches is the impact of the decisions on human rights.

Human Rights Approach

Human rights is a second method for handling ethical dilemmas. The **human rights approach** to ethics holds that human beings have certain moral entitlements that should be respected in all decisions. These entitlements guarantee an individual's most fundamental personal rights (life, freedom, health, privacy, and property, for example). These have been spelled out in such documents as the U.S. Bill of Rights and the United Nations Declaration of Human Rights.[38] A *right* means that a person or group is entitled to something or is entitled to be treated in a certain way. The most basic human rights are those claims or entitlements that enable a person to survive, make free choices, and realize his or her potential as a human being. Denying those rights to other persons and groups or failing to protect their rights is considered to be unethical. Respecting others, even those with whom we disagree or whom we dislike, is the essence of human rights, provided that others do the same for us.

The human rights approach to ethical dilemmas holds that individuals are to be treated as valuable ends in themselves simply because they are human beings. Using others for your own purposes is unethical if, at the same time, you deny them their rights to their own goals and purposes. For example, an organization that denies women employees an opportunity to bid for all jobs for which they are qualified is depriving them of some of their rights.

Utility approach
A situation in which decisions are based on an evaluation of the overall amount of good that will result.

Human rights approach
A situation in which decisions are made in light of the moral entitlements of human beings.

The main limitation on using the human rights approach as a basis for ethical decisions is the difficulty of balancing conflicting rights. For example, using a polygraph test to evaluate an employee's honesty to protect the organization's financial responsibilities may be at odds with the employee's right to privacy. Many difficult decisions have involved minorities and women who are competing with white men for the right to hold jobs in business and government. Rights also clash when U.S. multinational corporations move production to a foreign nation, causing job losses at home while creating new jobs abroad. In such cases, whose job rights should be protected?

The degree to which human rights are protected and promoted is an important ethical benchmark for judging the behavior of individuals and organizations. Most people would agree that the denial of a person's fundamental rights to life, freedom, privacy, growth, and human dignity is generally unethical. By defining the human condition and pointing the way to a realization of human potentialities, such rights become a kind of common denominator setting forth the essential conditions for ethical actions and decisions.

Justice Approach

Justice approach

A situation in which decisions are based on an equitable, fair, and impartial distribution of benefits and costs among individuals and groups.

A third method of ethical decision making concerns justice. Under the **justice approach,** decisions are based on an equitable, fair, and impartial distribution of benefits (rewards) and costs among individuals and groups. Justice is essentially a condition characterized by an equitable distribution of the benefits and burdens of working together. It exists when benefits and burdens are distributed equitably and according to some accepted rule. For society as a whole, social justice means that a society's income and wealth are distributed among the people in fair proportions.

A common question is, "Is it fair or just?" For example, employees want to know if pay scales are fair; consumers are interested in fair prices when they shop. When new tax laws are proposed, there is much debate about their fairness—where will the burden fall, and will all taxpayers pay their fair share? Using the justice approach, the organization considers who pays the costs and who gets the benefits. If the shares seem fair, then the action is probably just.

Determining what is just and unjust can be an explosive issue if the stakes are high. Since distributive rules usually grant privileges to some groups based on tradition and custom, sharp inequalities between groups can generate social tensions and clamorous demands for a change to a fairer system.

As with the utilitarian approach, a major limitation of the justice approach is the difficulty of measuring benefits and costs precisely. Another limitation is that many of society's benefits and burdens are intangible, emotional, and psychological. People unfairly deprived of life's opportunities may not willingly accept their condition. Few people, even those who are relatively well off, are ever entirely satisfied with their share of society's wealth. For these reasons, the use of the justice approach can be tricky. Although everyone is intensely interested in being treated fairly, many are skeptical that justice will ever be fully realized. In spite of these drawbacks, the justice approach to ethical dilemmas can still be applied in many business situations. Meeting the Challenge provides an opportunity for you to apply these decision-making approaches to several ethical dilemmas. How would you respond to these situations?

FOSTERING IMPROVED BUSINESS ETHICS

In recent years, many well-publicized and questionable business practices have brought business ethics to the forefront of concerns in the business community. Until the late 1980s, business ethics was little more than an obscure debate among some scholars. In the wake of many questionable events, however,

ARTHUR ANDERSEN & COMPANY

This video is part of a training program for employees at Arthur Andersen, a Big Six public accounting firm. If any professionals must have high ethical standards, certainly public accountants would be high on the list. After all, they certify the financial records of firms that people invest in. The video presents five situations that highlight specific ethical issues in the workplace. As you watch the five vignettes, think about how you might react.

- *Vignette 1: The High-Bid Dilemma.* A young assistant to the purchasing agent finds himself facing the "reality" of business when his boss, the company purchasing manager, prefers a high bid for bronze facing. The assistant recommends Metaltech, the low bidder, but the purchasing manager prefers Spin Cast Systems because the president of Spin Cast is a former fraternity brother and friend. The purchasing manager's advice: "If you take care of your suppliers, they'll take care of you."

- *Vignette 2: A Compensation Issue.* Discrimination is the source of contention when Sandy and Brenda start talking. Brenda, an African American, tells Sandy that she has discovered she is paid less than another secretary who started at the same time and has the same responsibilities. Brenda becomes annoyed when Sandy tries to find a logical reason for the difference in pay. Brenda's comment: "They expect me to be just the same as everyone else. Why can't they pay me the same?"

- *Vignette 3: Sexual Harassment.* Sexual harassment is against the law. Two types of conditions are classified as sexual harassment: (1) *quid pro quo,* or you do this and I'll do that; and (2) a hostile work environment. Shelly has a difficult time escaping the advances of Bill, who is described as "a very friendly fellow." She does not believe he treats other women the way he treats her and that she is being sexually harassed. She confides in Ginny, a co-worker, and asks, "What am I to do?"

- *Vignette 4: Competition or Revenge?* Is it fair to kick a person who is down and out? Phil, George, and Jean seem to think so. They resent the fact that Jack, a former co-worker who now works for another company, may be calling on their customers and cutting into their established business. To address the problem, Jean offers to spread false rumors about Jack. George tells him: "Survival is the name of the game."

- *Vignette 5: Creative Expense Reporting.* Jim and Ken are having a discussion about Jim's expense report. Jim lost his receipts and has filled out his expense report using ballpark figures, some of them debatable and some clearly not business expenses. Ken is not sure that what Jim is doing is appropriate, but Jim's comment is, "What's the difference?"

SOURCE: Adapted with permission of Arthur Andersen & Co.

businesses, business leaders, and academic institutions have placed greater emphasis on developing ethical standards and fostering an appreciation for adherence to ethical business behavior.[39] Unfortunately, many of these efforts have proved to be more image than substance. Part of the problem is that the sudden push for ethical standards has focused on addressing clear-cut ethical issues of good versus bad and right versus wrong. No one would question that pollution is bad, embezzlement is wrong, and honoring product warranties is right. But the advocates of business ethics have discovered that the real ethi-

At a meeting of the Security Council at the United Nations in September 1996, Arab and European foreign ministers told Prime Minister Benjamin Netanyahu that his policies made the latest burst of Middle East violence inevitable and were threatening peace in the region. Such actions help to foster ethical behavior at the international level.

© AP/Wide World Photos/David Karp

cal issues are not black and white, but gray and complex with no obvious solutions that enable everyone to win.

To foster improved business ethics in an organization, action must be directed at five levels: the international, societal, association, organizational, and individual levels. The most fundamental effort is directed at the individual.

Agreements among nations help to foster ethical behavior at the international level. Laws established by international governing bodies such the World Trade Organization and the United Nations help shape ethical behavior across nations.

Societal ethics are fostered to the extent that laws and regulations discourage unethical behavior and systems exist for recognizing and rewarding behaviors that epitomize strong ethical values. For example, the Foreign Corrupt Practices Act governs the actions of American firms engaged in international business activities. Award programs, such as the Business Ethics Award given annually by the Center for Business Ethics at Bentley College, help to reinforce the value of ethical behavior within our society.

At the association level, groups can join together and establish codes of ethics for their industry or profession and provide mechanisms for monitoring and disciplining members who violate the code. For example, the Society for Professional Journalists, an organization of 13,500 people involved in journalism, has developed a code of ethics that provides guidance for journalists across the globe. Not only has the association established such a code, but it invites on-line debate about proposed changes to the code. This debate has evolved to include discussions of both real and hypothetical ethical issues in the journalism profession.

At the organizational level, improving business ethics requires leaders who can model the expected ethical behavior, set realistic goals for workers, and encourage ethical behavior by providing an organizational environment that rewards such behavior and punishes violators. Leadership is perhaps the most important ingredient in developing an ethical organizational culture. According to Shirley Peterson, Vice President of Ethics and Business Conduct at Northrop Corporation, their value statement was drafted by the top twelve people in the organization. Why? Because at Northrop, management believes that ethics start at the top of the organization and filters through the organization from there.[40]

At the individual level, the challenge for organizations is to develop employees' awareness of business ethics (see Table 3.5) as well as to help them confront complex ethical issues. Employees find it helpful when their organization publicly announces what it believes in and expects in terms of employee

TABLE 3.5   Developing employee awareness of ethics

1. Enabling the ethical component of a decision to be recognized.
2. Legitimizing the consideration of ethics as part of decision making.
3. Avoiding variability in decision making caused by lack of awareness of rules or norms.
4. Avoiding ambivalence in decision making caused by an organizational reward system that psychologically pulls a person in opposite directions.
5. Avoiding ambivalence in decision making caused by confusion as to who is responsible for misdeeds, particularly when the employee has received an order from a superior.
6. Providing decision-making frameworks for analyzing ethical choices and helping employees to apply such frameworks.

SOURCE: S. J. Harrington, "What Corporate America Is Teaching about Ethics," *Academy of Management Executives,* 5, 1991, 21–29.

TABLE 3.6   Citicorp's Code of Conduct

The **Code of Conduct** provides a framework of Citicorp's values and ethical standards. The following principles must be applied in our day-to-day business.

- All decisions and actions must conform with all applicable laws, regulations and Corporate policies.
- Business must only be secured for Citicorp on the basis of our belief in competitve market systems and the appropriateness of earning a profit by providing our customers with efficient service.
- Economic substance alone is not justification for originating a transaction. It must be evaluated in the light of comprehensive knowledge of our customer's business and of the transaction's purpose.
- Individuals must be honest and trustworthy in all actions and relationships for, and in behalf of, Citicorp.
- Situations where personal interests conflict, or appear to conflict with the interests of Citicorp or its customers, must be avoided.

- The results of each action or decision must be fair and even-handed to all parties to the transaction or event, in both the short- and long-term.
- Each decision or act must be proper, in terms of both our own sense of integrity and the scrutiny of others. It should seem appropriate even if published in a major newspaper.
- Human dignity must be respected in all of our dealings with others.
- Communications must be honest and accurate. Confidentiality must be maintained where appropriate.
- Ethical conduct should be recognized and valued by all employees and agents of Citicorp.

SOURCE: *Code of Conduct & Ethical Policies,* Citicorp.

behavior.[41] Ultimately, though, ethical business behavior comes from the individual, not the organization.[42]

In the next section, we examine two of the most common ways in which organizations foster ethical behavior: (1) by creating codes of conduct, and (2) by developing ethics training programs. In general, such activities must reflect relevant employee concerns and must be tailored to specific needs and value statements.

Codes of Ethics

A **code of ethics** describes the general value system, ethical principles, and specific ethical rules that a company tries to apply. It can be an effective way to encourage ethical business behavior and raise an organization's standards of ethical performance. Such a document may be called a code of ethics, credo, declaration of business principles, statement of core values, or something similar. As an example, consider Citicorp's "Principles of Ethical Behavior," outlined in Table 3.6.

In response to the ethical problems that have been arising in the United States, many companies and professional societies are now publishing codes

Code of ethics
The general value system, principles, and specific rules that a company follows.

of conduct. In fact, about 90 percent of Fortune 500 firms and almost half of all other firms have ethics codes.[43] These organizations have likely determined that maintaining an ethical organization can be a strategic advantage.

Typically, a code of ethics covers a wide range of issues and potential problem areas that an organization and its members may encounter. It is a set of carefully articulated statements of ethical principles rooted in the organization's goals, objectives, organizational history, and traditions. A code contains explicit statements and precepts intended to guide both the organization and its employees in their professional behavior. A code helps employees know what is expected when they face uncertain ethical situations. It becomes the basis for establishing continuity and uniformity in managerial action and can be a unifying force that holds the organization together so that its employees can act in a cohesive and socially responsible manner.

An organization's code of ethics can serve several purposes. First, it creates employee awareness that ethical issues need to be considered in making business decisions. Second, it demonstrates that the organization is fully committed to stating its standards and incorporating them into daily activities. Third, a code can contribute to transforming an "us-them" relationship between the organization and its employees into an "us-us" relationship.[44] A code's impact on employee behavior is weakened if the code's purpose is primarily to make the company look good or if it is intended to give the company's top executives a legal defense when illegal or unethical acts are committed by lower-ranking employees.

A code of ethics can resemble a set of regulations ("Our employees will not . . ."), aspirations ("Our employees should . . ."), or factual statements ("Our organization is committed to . . ."), but all effective codes appear to share at least three characteristics:

1. They generally govern activities that cannot be supervised closely enough to assure compliance.
2. They ask more of employees than would otherwise be expected.
3. They can serve the long-term interest of the organization.

Johnson & Johnson has taken a unique approach to discussing and revising its code of ethics. It holds meetings in which new employees are challenged to explore whether the company ethics code is still valid. In this way employees can discuss the code in a nonthreatening, nonlecturing way and have an opportunity to bring up specific situations or cases.[45] These challenge sessions also acquaint employees with official company policy on ethical issues and show how those policies can be translated into the specifics of everyday decision making.

Given the rapid changes in the marketplace, some organizations have recognized that statements of ethical standards and socially responsible behavior have to be dynamic and provide a degree of flexibility. These organizations have found that a simple creed or policy statement is a more practical guideline for determining ethical practices and behaviors. McDonnell-Douglas Corporation governs its ethical practices with the simple creed that its employees are "honest and trustworthy in all relationships." JC Penney simply adopted the Golden Rule: "Do unto others as you would have them do unto you." Such statements serve more as a general reference point or an anchor that provides an ethical and socially responsible perspective while allowing flexibility of action in dealing with a wide variety of situations. Under these types of statements, individual managers or employees bear much of the responsibility for defining the ethical standards that they exercise within the prevailing corporate culture.

Ethics statements and social responsibility policies are not sufficient by themselves to cause people to behave in a socially responsible manner. A 20-

page policy statement by General Dynamics failed to prevent a widespread lapse in ethical conduct involving government contracts. The real challenge for top management is to create an environment that sustains, promotes, and develops ethical behavior and a commitment to social responsibility. The effort must begin at the highest levels of the organization. Unless top management, beginning with the CEO, provides leadership, commitment, and role modeling, no organization can hope to attain high ethical standards or consistently behave in a socially responsible manner. Top management must also ensure that the organization's expectations of ethical behavior and social responsibility are clearly conveyed to its employees and to all parties involved with the organization, that is, the stakeholders. This requires extensive communication among all parties and the establishment of systems within the organization to reinforce ethical behavior.[46]

Ethics Training Programs

Many organizations and associations have begun to provide ethics training for employees and members. In fact, a recent study by the Center for Business Ethics found that 45 percent of the 1,000 largest U.S. companies now provide some form of ethics training—up from 35 percent five years prior.[47]

The goals of ethics training vary widely from organization to organization. Some of the most prominent reasons include avoiding adverse publicity, potential lawsuits, illegal behavior, and monetary and criminal penalties. Many organizations also use ethics training to gain a strategic advantage, increase employee awareness of ethics in business decision making, and help employees be more attentive to ethical issues to which they may be exposed.[48]

Ethics training programs have been shown to help employees avoid rationalizations often used to legitimize unethical behavior. Among the rationalizations often advanced to justify organizational misconduct are believing that: (1) the activity is not really illegal or immoral; (2) it is in the individual's or the corporation's best interest; (3) it will never be found out; or (4) the company will condone it because it helps the company.

Ethics training programs can help managers clarify their ethical framework and practice self-discipline when making decisions in difficult circumstances. Allied Corporation, Martin Marietta, Arthur Andersen, McDonnell-Douglas, Hershey Foods, Pitney Bowes, and General Dynamics are among the prominent companies with training programs for managers, supervisors, and anyone else likely to encounter an ethical question at work.[49] Chemical Bank, one of the largest banks in the United States, has a very extensive ethics education program. All new employees must attend an orientation session at which they read and sign off on the bank's code of ethics.[50]

The content and approach of ethics training programs may differ depending on the organization's goals. Case studies, often specific to the business functions of the organization's audience, are the most widely used approach. Other popular approaches include presenting the rules or guidelines for deciding ethical issues (such as the Golden Rule or the utilitarian approach), using cognitive approaches that attempt to develop higher levels of ethical understanding, or developing a checklist such as the one shown in Table 3.7 to aid managers in making ethical decisions.[51]

The training approach at Boeing Corporation, where more than 145,000 employees have been exposed to the ethics value program, is a

The two most common ways in which organizations foster ethical behavior are by creating codes of conduct and by developing ethics training programs. Over half of all firms in the United States have ethics codes. And nearly half of the 1,000 largest U.S. companies provide some form of ethics training.

© Paul Chelsey/Tony Stone Images

TABLE 3.7   Checklist for managers to use when facing ethical dilemmas

1. Recognize and clarify the dilemma.
2. Get all possible facts.
3. List all your options.
4. Test each option by asking, "Is it legal? Is it right? Is it beneficial?"
5. Make your decision.
6. Double-check your decision by asking, "How would I feel if my family found out about this? How would I feel if my decision was printed in the local paper?"
7. Take action.

SOURCE: Developed in part from A. L. Otten, "Ethics on the Job: Companies Alert Employees to Potential Dilemmas," *The Wall Street Journal,* July 14, 1986, 17. Reprinted by permission of The Wall Street Journal, ©1986 Dow Jones & Company, Inc. All Rights Reserved Worldwide.

customized in-house program tailored to meet the organization's ethics goals. First, a division general manager delivers a message emphasizing ethical business practices. Next, employees receive a company-created pamphlet entitled "Business Conduct Guidelines," which stresses policies on ethics and standards of conduct and compliance. Hypothetical situations are presented, and a business ethics advisor in each division leads discussions. The training also stresses the procedures for discussing or reporting unethical behavior or infractions.

Whistleblowing

One method of monitoring the ethical conviction of the organization and its top management is to observe its approach to professional dissent or, as it is more commonly called, *whistleblowing.* Whistleblowing occurs when an insider reports alleged organizational misconduct to the public. A **whistleblower** is someone who exposes organizational wrongdoing in order to preserve ethical standards and protect against wasteful, harmful, or illegal acts.

Whistleblowing is becoming a staple on the front pages of newspapers and an all-too-frequent segment on *60 minutes* and other such news programs.[52] An employee—or, more often, a former employee—of a big corporation goes public with charges that the company has been playing dirty. The next step is a lawsuit that sets out the details of the misconduct and charges that the whistleblower was at best ignored and at worst harassed, demoted, or fired.

Doubtless, some whistleblower suits are brought by employees with an ax to grind. Others may be in search of a big payoff. For example, under the False Claims Act, whistleblowers can receive up to 25 percent of any money recovered by the government. Christopher M. Urda, for instance, was awarded $7.5 million in July 1992 for providing evidence that his employer, then a unit of Singer Corporation, bilked the Pentagon out of $77 million in the 1980s.[53]

Generally, employees are not free to speak out against their employers because there is a public interest in allowing organizations to operate without harassment from insiders. Organizations face countless ethical issues and internal conflicts in their daily operations. Choices must be made where there are many opinions. Mistakes are made, and waste does occur, but usually corrective action is taken.

Although whistleblowing typically exposes unethical practices, how it is done and how it is handled may also be ethically questionable. The costs of whistleblowing are high for both the company and the whistleblower. The company "gets a black eye" whether it wins or loses, which can create considerable internal conflict. The company spends much time and money defending itself and may damage general employee morale by seeming to be unsympathetic to legitimate concerns expressed by employees. The whistleblower also

Whistleblower
Someone who exposes organizational misconduct or wrongdoing to the public.

TABLE 3.8   A model whistleblower policy

- *Shout it from the rooftops.* Aggressively publicize a reporting policy that encourages employees to bring forward valid complaints of wrongdoing.
- *Face the fear factor.* Defuse fear by directing complaints to someone outside the whistleblower's chain of command.
- *Get right on it.* An independent group, either inside or outside the company, should investigate the company immediately.
- *Go public.* Show employees that complaints are taken seriously by publicizing the outcome of investigations whenever possible.

SOURCE: L. Driscoll, "A Better Way to Handle Whistle-Blowers: Let Them Speak," 36. Reprinted from July 27, 1992, issue of *Business Week* by special permission, copyright © 1992 by McGraw-Hill Companies, Inc.

suffers. Many times whistleblowers are subject to retaliatory action by disgruntled employers and often are blackballed for not being team players. Even if the whistleblower wins, the costs can be high: legal expenses, mental anguish, ostracism by former co-workers, a damaged career.

To avoid the costs for both the company and the employee, many companies have become more receptive to employee complaints. Some organizations have established regular procedures for professional dissent, such as hotlines that employees can use to report dangerous or questionable company practices or the use of ombudsmen who can act as neutral judges and negotiators when supervisors and employees disagree over a policy or practice. Confidential questionnaires are another device to encourage potential whistleblowers to report their concerns before they become a big issue. In these ways, progressive companies attempt to lessen the tensions between the company and its employees and maintain the confidence and trust between them.

Table 3.8 shows a model whistleblower policy developed by the Conference Board.[54] The policy can work in the real world if managers emphasize that ethics are more than fancy policy. Managers should ask employees whether they have confidence in the company's ethics system and make them believe that exposing internal wrongdoing is part of their job. Whistleblowers who raise real issues should be rewarded.[55] Whatever technique is used, it should permit individuals to expose unethical practices or lapses in socially responsible behavior without disrupting the organization.

MANAGERIAL IMPLICATIONS

Two approaches to addressing ethical issues have been identified—one proactive and one responsive. First, a manager can intervene to end unethical organizational practices by working against the persons and organizations behaving unethically. Second, the manager can initiate ethical organizational change by working with others and the organization. These approaches are not mutually exclusive. Depending on the individual, the organization, the relationships, and the situation, either or both approaches may be appropriate for addressing ethical issues.[56]

Achieving social responsibility and business ethics at an organizational level is a challenge that tomorrow's managers will face.[57] This challenge can be met when managers:

- Explore ways in which the organization can be more socially responsive.
- Recognize the effect of the organization's actions on its stakeholders.

- Create an environment in which employees commit to behaving in socially responsive and ethical ways.
- Make sure that a code of ethics is put in place and followed.
- Ensure that whistleblowing and ethical concerns procedures are established for internal problem solving.
- Involve line and staff employees in the identification of ethical issues to help them gain understanding and resolve issues.
- Determine the link between departments and issues affecting the company, and make them known to employees in the departments.
- Integrate ethical decision making into the performance appraisal process.
- Publicize, in employee communications and elsewhere, executive priorities and efforts related to ethical issues.

By following these guidelines, managers will be taking a major step toward achieving a high level of social responsibility in the organization and increasing employee awareness of ethical issues.

In this chapter we have explored the issues of social responsibility and business ethics. Managers of the future will be expected to address important social issues proactively and to maintain a high standard of ethical behavior.

Managerial Incident Resolution

ASTRA: POWER AND SEXUAL HARASSMENT

What happened at Astra? A *Business Week* cover story on the sexually harassing business environment at Astra USA appeared in May 1996. This story reported that investigators had identified dozens of women who claimed to have been either fondled or solicited for sexual favors by Bildman and other executives. Charges have been filed by many of these women; some out-of-court settlements have been made.

Shortly after learning of the impending *Business Week* article, the Swedish parent company, Astra AB, terminated CEO Lars Bildman. While Bildman had informed his superiors of the *Business Week* investigation months before, Carl-Gustav Johansson, a member of the parent company's executive committee, indicated that they had been unaware of the full scope of the allegations and that Bildman himself was the focus of some of the complaints. Johansson said that Lars Bildman was suspended because "we lost some trust in him."

Astra USA represents a bizarre case of an ethical culture gone bad. And why did sexual harassment permeate the entire organization? Because it emanated from the top. Astra provides a very disturbing example of how bad leadership can negatively affect an organization.

SUMMARY

- The concepts of social responsibility and ethics require an understanding of the stakeholder view of the organization. Whereas the traditional view of socially responsible behavior considers only the stockholders, contemporary theory recognizes a much broader group of constituents—stakeholders. Stakeholders include any individual or group that is affected by or can affect the organization.
- Corporate social responsibility has been the subject of much controversy and debate over the last several

decades. Although the concept defies precise definition, in a very general sense social responsibility refers to the interaction between business and the social environment in which it exists. The concept of social responsibility rests on two premises—social contract and moral agent.

- Three perspectives of corporate social responsibility have significant support from both practitioners and academics. The economic responsibility perspective suggests that the only social responsibility of business is to maximize profits within the "rules of the game." The public responsibility perspective argues that business has an obligation to act in a way that is consistent with society's overall expectations of business. Social responsiveness supporters suggest that it is the responsibility of business to act proactively to improve the welfare of society.

- There are four distinct strategies for responding to social issues. These strategies, which span a continuum ranging from "do nothing" to "do much," are (1) reaction, (2) defense, (3) accommodation, and (4) proaction. Although none of these strategies is appropriate for all organizations, the accommodation and proaction approaches to social responsibility are appropriate in most cases.

- As organizations consider a strategy for social responsibility, a number of "commandments" should be considered. In general, these commandments suggest that organizations should be observant of social issues, honest with their constituents, cooperative with stakeholders with regard to social concerns, and proactive in their efforts to fulfill their obligations to society.

- Values are the relatively permanent and deeply held desires of individuals or groups. They are the bases upon which attitudes and personal preferences are patterned. Values are among the most stable and enduring characteristics of individuals; they form the foundation of an individual's ethical behavior.

- Instrumental, or means-oriented, values describe desirable standards of conduct or methods for attaining an end. Terminal, or ends-oriented, values describe desirable ends or goals for the individual and reflect what a person is ultimately striving to achieve.

- There are three primary approaches for dealing with ethical dilemmas. The utility approach emphasizes the overall amount of good that can be produced by an action or a decision. The human rights approach holds that decisions should be consistent with fundamental rights and privileges such as those of life, freedom, health, privacy, and property. Under the justice approach, decisions are based on an equitable, fair, and impartial distribution of benefits (rewards) and costs among individuals and groups.

- Organizations often develop codes of ethics along with training programs to encourage and reinforce ethical business behavior. A code of ethics describes the organization's general value system, its ethical principles, and the specific ethical rules that it tries to apply.

- Several different approaches can be used in ethics training programs. These approaches include case studies, the presentation of rules or guidelines for deciding ethical issues, and cognitive approaches that attempt to develop higher levels of ethical understanding.

- A whistleblower is someone who exposes organizational wrongdoing in order to preserve ethical standards and protect against wasteful, harmful, or illegal acts. Organizations should develop and maintain policies and procedures that encourage reports of wrongful doing, yet discourage employees from making frivolous or unjustified allegations against others.

KEY TERMS

Stakeholders	Values	Human rights approach
Corporate social responsibility	Instrumental values	Justice approach
Social contract	Terminal values	Code of ethics
Moral agent	Business ethics	Whistleblower
Ethics	Ethical dilemma	
Ethical behavior	Utility approach	

REVIEW QUESTIONS

1. Describe the stakeholder view of the organization. How does the stakeholder view differ from the stockholder view, and what are the implications of these differences for the concept of corporate social responsibility?

2. Define the concept of corporate social responsibility. What are the two premises advanced by Bowen in his original definition of social responsibility and the three resulting perspectives?

3. Evaluate the four different strategies for social responsibility. Describe how these strategies differ and give an example of a company that has pursued each strategy.

4. What are the ten commandments of social responsibility? Which perspective of social responsibility (see Question 2) is most consistent with these commandments?

5. Explain why ethical behavior is considered to be individualistic.

6. What are values? Why are they the basis of an individual's ethical behavior?

7. Distinguish between terminal and instrumental values. Give an example of each.

8. Describe the utility, human rights, and justice approaches to ethical dilemmas, and explain how they differ.

9. What is a code of ethics? Describe the different goals an organization can have for developing a code of ethics.

10. What are the common approaches used in ethics training programs?

11. Explain what is meant by whistleblowing. What are the benefits that come from whistleblowing? What are some of the problems that might occur?

DISCUSSION QUESTIONS

Improving Critical Thinking

1. Consider the implications of self-regulation versus government-imposed regulation (refer to Commandments I and III). Why is it preferable for an industry to be self-regulated?

2. Describe an ethical dilemma you have experienced at work or as part of a business or social organization. What was your response? If you faced a similar dilemma now, would your response differ?

Enhancing Communication Skills

3. Select an organization with which you are familiar or that you are interested in researching. Evaluate the social responsibility strategy of that company with regard to the following social issues: (1) environmental protection, (2) worker health and safety, and (3) product safety. Has this company been in a reaction, defensive, accommodation, or proaction mode with regard to these social issues? Make an oral presentation of your findings to the class.

4. Using current business periodicals or newspapers, find an example of an organization that has faced an ethical problem. How did it solve the problem? Did the organization have a code of ethics? What actions did it take to resolve the problem? Write a summary of your findings as a way to demonstrate your understanding of the issue and practice your written communication skills.

5. Examine the policy your college or university has for handling academic dishonesty. How appropriate is the policy? Would you suggest any changes? Write up your suggestions and discuss them with a small group or your class.

Building Teamwork

6. In small groups, or as directed by your instructor, select a company that is considering relocating its major manufacturing plant from a domestic site to a country with lower labor costs. What are the social considerations that are most relevant for this company? Evaluate how this decision would be viewed by proponents of each of the three perspectives of social responsibility (economic responsibility, public responsibility, and social responsiveness).

7. As part of a small group, develop a code of ethics for an organization to which one or more of you belong, such as a fraternity, a sorority, a business association, or your college. What are the key issues that need to be addressed? Share your code with the class and the organization.

8. As part of a small group, develop an outline of an ethics training program for an organization to which one or more of you belong, such as a fraternity, sorority, or business association. What is the most appropriate approach? What key issues will you include?

INFORMATION TECHNOLOGY: Insights and Solutions

1. Using the Internet, locate information on the Society for Professional Journalists. Access the association's code of ethics. Review and analyze the code in a small group of students. Provide input on your assessment (good or bad) to the association using the Society's on-line mechanism for discussing ethical issues in the journalism profession.

2. Choose a social responsibility issue in which you have a particular interest (for example, environmental issues, health and safety issues, energy conservation issues, and the like). Using a research database in your library, identify an organization that is pursuing a reaction strategy and another organization that is pursuing a proaction strategy for dealing with that issue. Compare and contrast their strategies.

3. Use the Internet to identify companies with ethics training programs. Select one of those companies and, using e-mail, contact them to request their code of ethics and additional information about their ethics training program.

ETHICS: Take a Stand

Abbott Architecture has just received a commission to design an office building for a large multinational account that it has been trying to win for many years. Abbott could potentially make a substantial profit on the project as well as expand its influence into international circles. The only drawback is that the multinational customer is a developer doing business in China. The developer believes in human rights and equality and has assured Abbott that it supports the Chinese dissidents and their efforts for reform.

Nevertheless, Abbott cannot be assured that all the tenants of the building will advance these values. The partners/owners of Abbott feel strongly about fundamental human rights, but they also recognize that if they don't provide these services, someone else will. Abbott partners/owners must soon decide whether to accept the commission.

For Discussion
1. Divide the class into two groups. One group should take a stand for accepting the design job; the second group should take a stand against accepting the design job.
2. The members of each group should prepare arguments to support their position.
3. As a class, discuss the pros and cons of each viewpoint.
4. Take a poll to determine which side presented the more convincing arguments.

THINKING CRITICALLY: Debate the Issue

ECONOMIC RESPONSIBILITY VERSUS SOCIAL RESPONSIVENESS

Form teams with four to five students on each team. Half of the teams should prepare to argue the economic responsibility perspective of social responsibility. The other half of the teams should prepare to argue the social responsiveness perspective. Where possible, do some research to identify organizations that have behaved in ways prescribed by these perspectives and describe the outcomes of their behaviors. Your instructor will select two teams to present their findings to the class in a debate format.

Video Case

BANK OF ALMA

No Web Site Available

The Bank of Alma, Michigan, is a community bank with seven branches in central Michigan. The bank's customers reside primarily in small towns and rural areas. Business ethics is an important issue for both the bank and its customers. The bank asks its customers to be honest and forthcoming when disclosing financial information. Its customers, in turn, entrust the bank with their hard-earned money and expect the bank to safeguard their savings and keep their financial information confidential.

These issues weigh heavily on the minds of the employees of the Bank of Alma. The bank realizes that its reputation is its most important asset, and that any breach of ethics with its customers would be difficult to repair. As a result, the bank has a code of ethics based on the ethical principles of confidentiality, honesty, disclosure, and privacy. For example, the bank is very diligent in disclosing closing costs at the time of a loan application rather than waiting until the application is processed further. This practice helps the bank and its customers avoid any potential misunderstandings. The bank has also taken steps to reinforce the importance of maintaining a high level of ethical standards. Potential employees are administered a test that is designed to assess honesty. In addition, the managers of the bank have clearly articulated to their employees that certain breaches of ethics, such as disclosing a customer's financial information without proper approval, can result in the employee losing his or her job.

At the Bank of Alma, business ethics is more than a textbook term. It is a daily practice that determines the bank's reputation, creditability, and quality of relationship with its customers.

For Discussion
1. Discuss ways that the Bank of Alma demonstrates to its customers that business ethics is an important concern.
2. Discuss ways that the Bank of Alma encourages its employees to behave in an ethical manner.
3. If you were an employee of the Bank of Alma, would you find it easy or difficult to behave in an ethical manner? Discuss your answer.

CASE

FOOTBALL HERO OR CRIMINAL?

The National Football League (NFL) and college football are big business. Before Nebraska football star Lawrence Phillips dragged his ex-girlfriend by her hair and banged her head against a wall in September 1995; before he was suspended from the football team, then reinstated in time to help Nebraska win the national championship; before he was charged with drunken driving in June 1996 and signed a $5.6 million pro contract in July—before all that, things were much simpler for the teens of Lincoln, Nebraska.

Before, they knew Phillips as a hometown hero. He was a six-foot, 200-pound running back with an athletic "gift." But now as Phillips—who last year pleaded no contest to a misdemeanor assault charge and was placed on a year's probation—prepares for the professional football season, things are more complicated for Lincoln's teens. "I used to look up to him," says Ben Simtrek, 15, a nose guard on Lincoln High's football team. "I looked up to him after (University of Nebraska coach) Tom Osborne gave him another chance." But Phillips blew it with Simtrek with the drunken-driving arrest. "That did it. He is supposed to be a role model. Maybe as a superstar athlete he thinks he can get away with things, but that's not right."

Simtrek is not alone. A new *USA Weekend* poll shows that a majority of Americans want violent athletes kicked off their teams, suspended for an entire season, or even banned from pro sports for life. "We're telling kids there's a separate set of rules for different people," says Brian Wilcox, a Lincoln psychologist who is a national expert on the media and children. "It is very bad. Kids start to think there are different standards, and it destroys a real sense of right and wrong."

Such views are not unanimous. There are arguments made for giving sports stars the same chance as anyone else to rehabilitate themselves; letting the legal system, not coaches, penalize criminal behavior. Some argue that athletes shouldn't be punished twice—once by the courts and once by the coaches.

How important is winning? When *The Washington Post* reviewed the punishment given to 141 pro and college football players who were reported to police for violent behavior toward women from January 1989 to November 1994, it found that just one of these 141 men was disciplined by a team or league: a Philadelphia Eagles player who was denied re-entry into the NFL after serving 33 months in prison for rape.

The pressure to win is often overwhelming. Cornhusker (Nebraska University) football is big business, contributing $22 million annually to the school. The decision to allow Phillips to play again after his suspension was made by Joan Leitzel, Nebraska's interim chancellor; Coach Osborne; the director of athletics; and the vice chancellor for student affairs. Osborne points out that Phillips grew up "basically on his own" in an environment that was "largely confrontational and the toughest guy wins."

Whatever the final judgment of Nebraska football fans, Phillips's life moves on. In April 1996, St. Louis made him the NFL's number six draft pick. In June, he was arrested on the drunken-driving charge in California. Authorities said he was speeding with a flat tire and a blood-alcohol level about twice California's legal limit. A conviction of that charge would cause a probation hearing in Nebraska that could result in a prison sentence for a year.

Because of the uncertainty, Phillips's contract with the Rams forgoes the multimillion-dollar signing bonus, meaning no money up front. Phillips will have to stay out of legal trouble and prison—to get paid.[58]

For Discussion

1. Are athletes role models to young people in today's society?

2. Should athletes be held to a higher ethical standard than other individuals?

3. Do you think Phillips should be allowed to continue as a professional football player, given his legal problems?

EXPERIENTIAL EXERCISE 3.1

Observing and Reporting Unethical Behavior

For each of the following statements place an *O* on the line if you have observed someone doing this behavior. Place an *R* on the line if you reported this behavior within the organization.

O = Observed   R = Reported

1. _____ Coming to work late and getting paid for it.

2. _____ Leaving work early and getting paid for it.

3. _____ Taking long breaks or lunches and getting paid for them.

4. _____ Calling in sick when one is not ill.

5. _____ Using the company copier/fax for personal use.

6. _____ Using company postage for personal correspondence.

7. _____ Taking company supplies or merchandise for personal use at home.

8. _____ Accepting gifts, meals, or trips from customers or suppliers in exchange for giving them business.

9. _____ Filing for reimbursements or for other expenses that were not actually incurred.

10. _____ Using the company car for personal business.

11. _____ A student copying a friend's homework assignments.

12. _____ A student cheating on an exam.

13. _____ A student falsely passing off a term paper as his or her own work.

Complete the following questions either individually or in small groups as directed by your instructor.

1. From items 1 through 10, select the three behaviors that you consider the most unethical. Who is harmed and who benefits by these unethical behaviors?

2. Who is harmed and who benefits from the unethical behaviors in items 11 through 13? Who is responsible for changing these behaviors? Develop a realistic plan to accomplish this goal.

3. If you observed unethical behavior but didn't report it, why didn't you? If you did report the behavior, why did you? What was the result?

4. What other behaviors that you consider unethical have you observed or reported?

EXPERIENTIAL EXERCISE 3.2

What Good Is an Honor System?

Working in a small group of three to five individuals, read the following scenario and then answer the questions that follow. Try to come to a consensus with your group members about your responses. Report your answers to your instructor or to the whole class.

I went to a small liberal arts college where they had a very strict honor system. For example, if you saw another student cheating, you were supposed to turn that student in to the authorities. In reality, some students did cheat, but only rarely did other students report the problem. There seemed to be several reasons for this: (1) it was a hassle to get involved because you had to go to meetings, fill out forms, and answer numerous questions; (2) nobody wanted to be considered a "tattletale"; and (3) even if you were sure the person had cheated, you had to have very specific evidence to support the charge.

Ten years later, I am out of college and law school and practice law with a large firm. We have an honor sys-

tem here, too, but bringing a complaint against another professional is difficult: (1) it takes time and energy to get involved; (2) no one trusts or likes a person who turns in a peer; and (3) evidence to support a complaint is often poor or difficult to obtain.

For Discussion

1. What are the ethical dilemmas students face while going to college? What examples can you provide from your own or others' experience to support this?

2. Discuss the ethical dilemmas lawyers face in performing their jobs. Give some specific examples (consider recent news reports or stories from current television shows).

3. Discuss ethical dilemmas faced by other professional groups such as accountants, professors, engineers, and psychologists.

4. Discuss the pros and cons of an honor system.

ENDNOTES

1. M. Maremont, "Abuse of Power," *Business Week,* May 13, 1996, 85-98.

2. A. B. Carroll, *Business & Society: Ethics and Stakeholder Management* (Cincinnati: South-Western, 1989).

3. Ibid., 60.

4. See, for example, B. Harvey, ed., *European Perspectives on Business Ethics* (New York: Prentice-Hall, 1994); G. McDonald and P. Pak, "It's All Fair in Love, War, and Business: Cognitive Philosophies in Ethical Decision Making," *Journal of Business Ethics,* 15, 1996, 973-96.

5. "Is It Rainforest Crunch Time?" *Business Week,* July 15, 1996, 70-71; J. J. Laabs, "Ben & Jerry's Caring Capitalism," *Personnel Journal,* November 1992, 50-57.

6. M. L. Pava, "The Talmudic Concept of 'Beyond the Letter of the Law': Relevance to Business Social Responsibilities," *Journal of Business Ethics,* 15, 1996, 941-50.

7. T. R. Mitchell and W. G. Scott, "America's Problems and Needed Reforms: Confronting the Ethic of Personal Advantage," *Academy of Management Executive,* 4, 1990, 23-33.

8. H. R. Bowen, *Social Responsibilities of the Businessman* (New York: Harper & Row, 1953), 6.

9. Most of this discussion comes from S. L. Wartick and P. L. Cochran, "The Evolution of the Corporate Social Performance Model," *Academy of Management Review,* 10, 1985, 758-69.

10. A. B. Carroll, *Business & Society,* 60.

11. C. Grant, "Friedman Fallacies," *Journal of Business Ethics,* 10, 1991, 907-14.

12. "A CEO Forum: What Corporate Social Responsibility Means to Me," *Business and Society Review,* Spring 1992.

13. L. E. Preston and J. E. Post, "Private Management and Public Policy," *California Management Review,* 23, 1991, 57.

14. D. R. Dalton and R. A. Cosier, "The Four Faces of Social Responsibility," *Business Horizons,* May/June 1982, 19-27.

15. A. B. Carroll, *Business & Society,* 60.

16. S. W. Gellerman, "Why 'Good' Managers Make Bad Ethical Choices," *Harvard Business Review,* July/August 1986, 85-90.

17. L. Alexander and W. F. Matthews, "The Ten Commandments of Corporate Social Responsibility," *Business and Society Review,* 50, 1984, 62-66.

18. S. Vyakarnam, "Social Responsibility: What Leading Companies Do," *Long Range Planning,* 25, 1992, 59-67.

19. L. Alexander and W. F. Matthews, "The Ten Commandments of Corporate Social Responsibility."

20. "A CEO Forum: What Corporate Social Responsibility Means to Me," *Business and Society Review,* 22, 1992, 88-89; "Corporations Going Green," *Business Ethics,* March/April 1992, 100; D. Bihler, "The Final Frontier," *Business Ethics,* March/April 1992, 31; "On Company Time: The New Volunteerism," *Business Ethics,* March/April 1992, 33.

21. M. Scott, "An Interview with Howard Schultz, CEO of Starbucks Coffee Co.," *Business Ethics,* November/December 1995.

22. L. Reynolds, "A New Social Agenda for the New Age," *Management Review,* January 1993, 39-41.

23. Ibid.

24. R. N. Sanyal and J. S. Neves, "The Valdez Principles: Implications for Corporate Social Responsibility," *Journal of Business Ethics,* 10, 1991, 883-90.

25. S. Butler, "Green Machine," *Fast Company,* June-July 1996, 112-15.

26. T. R. Mitchell and W. G. Scott, "America's Problems and Needed Reforms: Confronting the Ethic of Personal Advantage," *Academy of Management Executive,* 4, 1990, 23-33.

27. M. Lewis, *Liar's Poker: Rising Through the Wreckage on Wall Street* (New York: Norton, 1989); and M. Mayer, *Nightmare on Wall Street: Salomon Brothers and the Corruption of the Marketplace* (New York: Simon & Schuster, 1993).

28. D. Stipp, "I Stole to Get Even: Yet Another Charity Scam," *Fortune,* October 30, 1995, 24.

29. For an interesting discussion, see D. M. Messick, "Why Ethics Is Not the Only Thing That Matters," *Business Ethics Quarterly,* 6, 2, April 1996, 223-26; M. Velasquez, "Why Ethics Matter: A Defense of Ethics in Business Organization," *Business Ethics Quarterly,* 6, 2, 201-22.

30. S. J. Harrington, "What Corporate America Is Teaching about Ethics," *Academy of Management Executive,* 5, 1991, 21-29.

31. M. Rokeach, *The Nature of Human Values* (New York: Free Press, 1973).

32. G. F. Cavanaugh, *American Business Values in Transition* (Englewood Cliffs, N.J.: Prentice-Hall, 1980).

33. K. Andrews, "Ethics in Practice," *Harvard Business Review,* September/October 1989, 99-104.

34. See for example, N. Dornenburg, "Is Ethics a Liability in Turbulent Competitive Environments?" *Business Ethics Quarterly,* 6, 2, April 1996, 233-39.

35. See B. Schwab, "Do Good Ethics Always Make for Good Business?" *Strategic Management Journal,* 17, 6, 499-500; and L. T. Hosmer, "Response to 'Do Good Ethics Always Make for Good Business?'" *Strategic Management Journal,* 17, 1996, 501.

36. L. T. Hosmer, *The Ethics of Management* (Homewood, Ill.: Irwin, 1987).

37. R. Perloff, "Self-Interest and Personal Responsibility Redux," *American Psychologist,* 42, 1987, 3-11.

38. M. Velasquez, D. Moberg, and G. Cavanagh, "Organizational Statesmanship and Dirty Politics: Ethical Guidelines for the Organizational Politician," *Organizational Dynamics,* Autumn 1993, 65-80.

39. B. Hager, "What's Behind Business' Sudden Fervor for Ethics," *Business Week,* September 23, 1991, 65.

40. L. K. Trevino and K. A. Nelson, *Managing Business Ethics: Straight Talk about How to Do It Right* (New York: Wiley, 1995), 299.

41. D. Fritzsche and H. Becker, "Linking Management Behavior to Ethical Philosophy—An Empirical Investigation," *Academy of Management Journal*, 27, 1984, 166-75.

42. S. J. Harrington, "What Corporate America Is Teaching about Ethics."

43. C. Wiley, "The ABC's of Business Ethics: Definitions, Philosophies and Implementation," *Industrial Management*, 37, 1, January/February 1995, 22-27.

44. S. Modic, "Corporate Ethics: From Commandments to Commitment," *Industry Week*, December 1987, 33-36.

45. J. A. Byrne, "Businesses Are Signing Up for Ethics 101," *Business Week*, February 15, 1988, 56-57.

46. J. Huey, "Finding New Heroes for a New Era," *Fortune*, January 25, 1993, 62-69.

47. C. Wiley, "The ABC's of Business Ethics: Definitions, Philosophies and Implementation."

48. Center for Business Ethics at Bentley College, "Are Corporations Institutionalizing Ethics?" *Journal of Business Ethics*, 5, 1986, 86-91.

49. B. Hager, "What's Behind Business' Sudden Fervor for Ethics."

50. C. Wiley, "The ABCs of Business Ethics: Definitions, Philosophies and Implementation."

51. A. L. Otten, "Ethics on the Job: Companies Alert Employees to Potential Dilemmas," *The Wall Street Journal*, July 14, 1986, 17.

52. M. P. Miceli and J. P. Near, "Whistleblowing: Reaping the Benefits," *Academy of Management Executive*, 8, 3, 1994, 65-72.

53. L. Driscoll, "A Better Way to Handle Whistle-Blowers: Let Them Speak," *Business Week*, July 27, 1992, 36.

54. Ibid.

55. Ibid.

56. R. P. Nielsen, "Changing Unethical Organizational Behavior," *Academy of Management Executive*, 3, 1989, 123-30.

57. J. Huey, "Finding New Heroes for a New Era."

58. "Victory, Violence and Values," Florida Today, *USA Weekend*, August 23-25, 1996, 4-6.

IBAX: A Company in Need of Leadership

INTEGRATIVE CASE FOR PART 1

As you will recall from the Managerial Incident/Resolution in Chapter 1, IBAX is a vendor of health care information systems software. The company began in 1983 as the Systems Division of Baxter Health Care Corporation, the world's largest supplier of hospital products. Over the first six years of its existence, Baxter's Systems Division grew through the acquisition of a number of small information systems companies. However, the division suffered from quality, customer satisfaction, and productivity problems that resulted in poor financial performance.

In 1990, Baxter reached an agreement with IBM to spin off the Systems Division and create a new company—IBAX. For IBM, the venture provided entry into the software side of the computer business. For Baxter, the partnership with IBM provided much-needed credibility in a computer-related business. There was great fanfare associated with the partnering of IBM and Baxter. Virtually everyone agreed that two highly successful companies like these would surely be able to make a mark in the health care information systems industry. Employees, customers, and even the trade press were tremendously enthusiastic about the future of the company.

Despite the favorable projections, IBAX got off to a very rocky start. Although the company was projected to break even in the first year of the partnership, it lost $11 million. The losses were a result of the same quality, customer satisfaction, and productivity problems that had plagued Baxter's Systems Division and had not been corrected since the formation of the partnership. As it became apparent that no significant improvements had been made in product quality or customer service, the trade press began to criticize the company harshly.

By late 1990, the principals in the partnership knew that a turnaround was imperative. The challenge was to find someone who could make that happen. In January of 1991, IBM and Baxter hired Jeff Goodman as the CEO of IBAX. Goodman, with a University of Virginia MBA, a General Electric background, and the successful turnaround of two other companies under his belt, had developed a reputation for his ability to turn poorly performing companies into highly efficient and effective organizations. The partners gave Goodman his orders—improve product quality, enhance customer satisfaction, and fix the financial profile of the company.

THE ASSESSMENT

As Goodman took the helm at IBAX, he assessed the management challenges he faced. Some of those challenges related to marketing issues, others to organizational and employee issues, and still others to financial issues. The paragraphs that follow describe what Goodman found when he evaluated IBAX at the beginning of 1991.

MARKETING ISSUES

In order to understand the marketing issues that were most relevant to turning IBAX around, you must understand the company's product line, its market position, and the efforts of its sales force.

The Products

IBAX's software products promised to provide high-quality, cost-effective methods of managing financial information, patient accounting information, and clinical information for its primary target market: hospitals located in the United States. The company maintains three core product lines:

- *Series 3000.* This software product serves hospitals of 100 beds or less. This product is a cost-effective information systems software package for small hospitals.
- *Series 4000.* This product is targeted at hospitals having 100–600 beds. The Series 4000 is appropriate for higher-capacity institutions that have unique requirements because of the breadth of services they offer.
- *Series 5000.* This product is targeted at major medical centers and teaching institutions. The Series 5000 software can be customized to meet the needs of larger health care institutions.

The Series 3000, 4000, and 5000 products provide three sources of revenue—software sales, installation and customization services, and ongoing software maintenance and support.

Unfortunately, there were significant problems with each of the core product lines. The customer base for the Series 3000 was eroding as a result of the changing nature of the hospital industry. Increasingly, small hospitals were unable to compete effectively because of size limitations. These institutions were being merged with or acquired by larger hospitals. The installed base for this product had declined from a high of 285 to 220 hospitals by early 1991.

The Series 4000 was the subject of a myriad of contract disputes between client hospitals and IBAX. The IBAX sales force had made commitments to the customers regarding such things as the disk capacity used by the system, response time, and the availability of product upgrades and add-ons. Unfortunately, such commitments had not been discussed with the developers of the products and were impossible to meet. The Series 4000 customers were angry about the unfulfilled promises of the sales force.

The company maintained a "hot list" of fifteen very large hospitals using the Series 5000 that were problem accounts. Because the IBM and Baxter names were so vulnerable in these hospitals, Goodman was instructed to do whatever it took to fix the problems quickly. In fact, he was required to report on the status of those accounts monthly to the IBAX partnership committee.

Beyond the core product lines, IBAX develops and markets department-based information systems to support functions such as pharmacy management, billing operations, and operating-room scheduling. In addition, it markets products that network physician offices to hospitals. The sales in these areas were not as significant as in the three primary product lines. Fortunately, neither were the problems.

Market Position

Interestingly, an assessment of IBAX's market position alone did not reflect the reality of the company's problems. As of 1991, the company had a 12 percent market share of the installed base in the United States. In other words, 600 of the 5,000 domestic hospitals used IBAX products. IBAX was, in fact, the market leader in the product segments in which it competed.

More relevant, however, was the fact that IBAX's market position was declining. The eroding base for the Series 3000, coupled with the company's problems with product quality and customer service, was resulting in a deteriorating customer base. Even those who still used IBAX products were hesitant to purchase add-on products because of their dissatisfaction with the company as a whole.

Sales Force

The morale of the sales force at IBAX was very poor. They were, as one IBAX employee said, "being hammered by the customers, the IBM and Baxter partners, and the trade press." The customers were perpetually unhappy because the products did not meet their expectations and did not perform as promised. Baxter blamed IBAX for giving the company a bad reputation in the hospitals it served; IBM thought IBAX's sales efforts were "amateurish" and were impeding IBM's efforts to secure hardware sales in hospitals. The trade press was continually criticizing the company and its products. Needless to say, the IBAX sales force was discouraged and was described as "wandering around leaderless, making very little progress in the field."

ORGANIZATIONAL AND EMPLOYEE ISSUES

From an organizational and employee perspective, IBAX was in a very poor position. As noted earlier, the company had developed through the acquisition of a number of small information systems software companies. As a result, it was geographically dispersed. Corporate headquarters was in Long Island, New York. There was a big operating facility in Orlando, Florida; a service center in Ohio; another business unit in Rhode Island; one in Illinois; and a major project staff in California. Employees in these various locations felt little need to cooperate with employees elsewhere in the organization. Consequently, it was difficult to develop and implement consistent product, marketing, and financial strategies.

Even more detrimental than IBAX's geographic fragmentation was the fact that there was no homogeneous culture within the company. Employee commitment to the company was very weak and there were no evolved corporate values.

Morale was extremely low and the employees were described as "generally miserable." The management style at IBAX was authoritative and directive. Employees felt disfranchised, as they were not involved in decision making and had little influence over what happened within the organization. The structure of the company was highly bureaucratic, and company policies and procedures were rigid and inflexible.

Intraorganizational communication at IBAX was so poor that the employees didn't even know how badly the company was performing. Some described their relationship with customers as "adversarial," and many employees didn't seem to understand why such a relationship was detrimental. The company had few performance standards and made little effort to hold employees accountable for their efforts.

Operationally, the company was very inefficient. The company had 750 employees and was well on its way to growing to 800. In an industry where labor costs represent a high proportion of total costs (60 percent), IBAX was heavily overstaffed. The sales of the company were simply not high enough to justify an employee base of that size.

Finally, there was a general void in the senior-level management team. Within two months after Goodman's arrival, the only senior staff at IBAX were Goodman, an attorney, and a human resource executive. Although the deficiency presented an immediate problem in that many functions were devoid of leadership, Goodman would have an opportunity to build an entirely new management team.

FINANCIAL ISSUES

The IBAX partnership was formed with an initial capital base of $80 million. It was a 50/50 partnership in that both IBM and Baxter contributed $40 million in a combination of assets and cash to the partnership. There was no debt in the initial capital structure and there was approximately $20 million in cash. Further, no losses were projected, and IBAX was forecasted to break even during the first year.

As we know, IBAX did not break even in the first year of the partnership. In fact, the company had operating losses in excess of $11 million in 1989 and $14 million in 1990. A total of $40 million was borrowed from the parent companies to support cash-flow losses of approximately $30 million per year for the first two years of the partnership. It was clear that the company could not continue as a viable entity unless its financial position greatly improved.

AFTER THE ASSESSMENT

Goodman's assessment of IBAX's current position was discouraging. The partners had been very clear in their expectations—he was to improve product quality, resolve the customer satisfaction problems, and fix the financial position of the company. Goodman suspected, however, that the partners had greatly underestimated the problems at IBAX. IBAX was ill-prepared to compete effectively in the highly competitive health care information systems industry.

As Goodman sat at his desk and contemplated the situation, he realized that he would need a plan. That plan would have to include (1) building a new team at the executive level, (2) educating the employees as to the severity of the company's problems, (3) improving productivity and efficiency at the operating level, (4) establishing and communicating standards for quality and performance, and (5) developing an organizational culture that provided employee empowerment, a focus on quality, and a commitment to do whatever necessary to meet the needs of the customer.

As you work your way through this book, you will learn about the modern management tools and techniques that were used to turn IBAX around. By watching the video that accompanies this case, you will have the opportunity to meet the senior-level executives and employees who were responsible for the turnaround. They will explain how they applied contemporary management theories and practices to resolve the problems faced by IBAX. The IBAX story provides a unique opportunity to observe a company that avoided failure and achieved success through innovative and effective management.

For Discussion
1. Why do you think IBAX performed so poorly before Goodman's arrival?
2. Why do you think Goodman felt that he had a realistic chance of turning the company around?
3. If you were Goodman, what is the first thing you would do to begin the turnaround?

P A R T

PART 2

PLANNING CHALLENGES IN THE 21ST CENTURY

Planning in the Contemporary Organization

■ CHAPTER OVERVIEW

Planning is one of the most important responsibilities of managers today. Plans provide a foundation for coordinating and directing the activities of the organization so that goals can be achieved. Through planning, managers prepare their organizations to achieve success in both the long term and the short term. Given the highly competitive nature of the business environment today, effective planning has never been more important.

In this chapter, we focus on planning in the contemporary organization. The planning function is explored, and special attention is given to understanding the planning process at both the strategic and the operational levels. We will also examine methods for encouraging, supporting, and rewarding effective planning.

■ LEARNING OBJECTIVES

When you have finished studying this chapter, you should be able to:

- Describe the managerial function of planning and explain why managers should plan.
- Discuss three approaches for initiating the planning process.
- Define strategic planning and describe the three levels of strategic planning.
- Discuss how quality can be achieved through strategic planning.
- Define operational planning and distinguish between standing and single-use plans.
- Describe a management-by-objectives program and discuss the advantages and disadvantages of this system of planning.
- Define contingency planning and identify the circumstances under which contingency planning would be appropriate.
- Discuss how advances in information technology have affected the planning function.
- Describe the common barriers to effective planning and explain ways to reduce these barriers.
- Discuss how tomorrow's managers can achieve success through planning.

C H A P T E R

Managerial Incident

FIRST UNION: PLANNING FOR THE FUTURE

Few industries have undergone as dramatic and radical change in the last decade as has the banking industry. Some banks have responded to the challenges very successfully; others have fallen away, actually disappearing from the industry all together. The leaders at First Union knew that the future would be challenging, but they planned to meet those challenges successfully.

The leadership team at First Union had some ideas about the changes that were on the horizon for banking organizations. These changes would dramatically affect the competitive structure of the entire banking industry. The following changes were forecast:

- industry consolidation driven by the need for greater economies of scale and scope;
- more intense competition around product quality and price;
- technological advances that would dramatically affect banking operations.

First Union needed to develop a plan for coping with the changes that would undoubtedly occur in the banking industry over the next decade. From the broadest level of corporate strategy to the most detailed of operational plans, the company needed a plan that would ensure its long-term success in the highly competitive banking environment of the 21st century.[1]

INTRODUCTION

First Union faced many challenges associated with competing in the rapidly changing banking industry. The company's success would depend upon the development of a plan for responding to those challenges. Without such a plan, First Union would likely experience significant competitive and operational difficulties in the years to come.

Planning provides a foundation for all organizational activities. Through planning, managers coordinate organizational activities so that the goals of the organization can be achieved. Organizational success is dependent upon the ability of managers to develop a plan that brings together, in a logical way, the diverse set of tasks that occur within the organization. In its simplest form, planning involves understanding where you are, knowing where you want to go, and devising the means to get there.

In this chapter, we explore the managerial function of planning. We begin by addressing a number of important questions about the nature of planning. With that information as a foundation, we discuss the two primary types of planning that occur within organizations—strategic and operational planning. Next, the concept of contingency planning is explored. The chapter concludes with a discussion of the barriers to planning, methods for overcoming those barriers, and the planning implications for tomorrow's managers.

MANAGERIAL PLANNING

Planning is an essential, but potentially complex, managerial function. To gain a better understanding of the planning function, let's start by answering a few key questions—what is planning, why should managers plan, and where should the planning process begin?

WHAT IS PLANNING?

Planning is the process of outlining the activities that are necessary to achieve the goals of the organization. Through planning, managers determine how organizational resources are to be allocated and how the activities of the organization will be assigned to individuals and work groups. The output of the planning process is the plan. A **plan** is a blueprint for action; it prescribes the activities necessary for the organization to realize its goals.[2]

The purpose of planning is simple—to ensure that the organization is both effective and efficient in its activities. In a broad sense, an organization must develop a plan that ensures that the appropriate products and services are offered to its customers. More specifically, planning gives guidance and direction to the members of the organization as to their role in delivering those products and services.[3]

Critical to understanding the planning process is an understanding of the relationships among goals, plans, and controls (see Figure 4.1). In general, **goals** represent the desired position of the organization. From the highest-level goal of maximizing shareholder wealth down to the goals of first-line operating managers, these targets for achievement are important determinants of the plans that an organization will develop. Plans establish the means for achieving the organization's goals. Through planning, managers outline the activities necessary to ensure that the goals of the organization are achieved. **Controls** monitor the extent to which goals have been achieved and ensure that the organization is moving in the direction suggested by its plans. Goals, plans, and controls are inextricably intertwined and must be well integrated if the planning process is to be successful.[4]

WHY SHOULD MANAGERS PLAN?

Planning is a critical managerial function for any organization that strives for success. In fact, it has often been said that "failing to plan is planning to fail." Yet most experienced managers recognize that there are both benefits and costs to planning.

Benefits of Planning

Theoretically, planning leads to superior performance for the organization. From a very general perspective, the planning process offers four primary benefits: (1) better coordination, (2) a focus on forward thinking, (3) a participatory work environment, and (4) more effective control systems.

Better Coordination   Planning provides a much needed foundation for the coordination of a broad range of organizational activities. Most organizations are comprised of multiple work groups, each of which is responsible for contributing to the accomplishment of the goals of the organization. A plan helps both to define the responsibilities of these work groups and to coordinate their

Planning
Setting goals and defining the actions necessary to achieve those goals.

Plan
A blueprint for action that prescribes the activities necessary for the organization to realize its goals.

Goals
The results that an organization seeks to achieve.

Controls
The mechanisms used to monitor the organization's performance relative to its goals and plans.

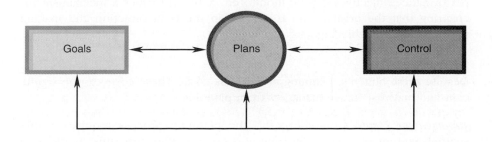

FIGURE 4.1
Planning as a linking mechanism

activities. Without such a mechanism for coordination, it would be difficult to direct the efforts of organizational members and groups toward common organizational goals.

Consider, for example, First Union's plan for coping with the changes in the banking industry. The plan would involve many people in many different departments—operations, information systems, personnel, and many others. Planning provides a mechanism for coordinating the activities of these diverse groups so that their efforts are consistent and synergistic.

Focus on Forward Thinking   The planning function forces managers to think ahead and consider resource needs and potential opportunities or threats that the organization may face in the future. While the identification of organizational problems and solutions is an important by-product of the planning process, its overriding focus should be on preparing the organization to perform more effectively and efficiently in the future than in the past.

The founder and CEO of Dell Computer, Michael Dell, says he focuses on the future because, "in my business, the life cycle of a product is six months, and so there are two types of people, the quick and the dead." Through forward thinking and a focus on understanding and responding to customer needs, Dell has become one of the computer industry's most respected competitors.[5]

First Union was most certainly looking ahead when it recognized the changes that would dramatically effect the banking industry. Today, 25 of the banks that were among the 50 largest banks ten years ago have disappeared, either through bankruptcy or acquisition by other banking institutions. Forward thinking led to First Union being the acquirer rather than the acquired when the industry began to consolidate.

Participatory Work Environment   The successful development and implementation of organizational plans requires the participation of a wide range of organizational members. As a consequence, a more participatory work environment typically evolves. Participatory work environments provide two important benefits to the organization.

First, the organization benefits from having access to a broad base of expertise and knowledge in developing its plans. This is particularly true in organizations with diverse groups of employees. Participatory planning usually leads to a more fully developed plan that reflects the multiple, diverse, and sometimes contradictory issues faced by the organization. Volvo, for example, found that involving employees in its plans to improve manufacturing quality contributed greatly to the success of that initiative.[6]

Second, organizational members are more likely to "buy in" to a plan that they have helped to develop. Employees who have participated in the planning process will typically be more committed to and supportive of their organization and its goals than those who have not been involved.[7]

More Effective Control Systems   As we will discuss later, an organization's plan provides a foundation for control. The implementation of the activities prescribed by the plan can be evaluated, and progress toward the achievement of performance objectives can be monitored. A plan provides a mechanism for ensuring that the organization is moving in the right direction and making progress toward achieving its goals.[8]

Costs of Planning

Despite these benefits, planning also entails costs. These costs can be significant and may discourage managers from planning.

Management Time   Done properly, the planning process requires a substantial amount of managerial time and energy. Managers must work with their employees to evaluate existing resources, identify opportunities to improve the operations of the work group, and establish organizational goals. Some work groups may find that planning requires an assessment of external information related to the products, prices, and strategies of competing firms. The collection, analysis, and interpretation of such information can be very costly.

Organizations that participate in the global business environment often find that planning is more complex and time-consuming than it is for purely domestic firms. International firms must analyze multiple economies, market forces, customer profiles, and other such variables. Consider, for example, the experience of Whirlpool as the company moved into the European and Asian markets. According to David Whitman, CEO of Whirlpool, planning the move into these new markets presented many challenges and was extremely time-consuming. It involved the analysis of several very different market environments and required significant product adaptation.[9] Nevertheless, Whitman would be the first to say that the time spent planning was time well spent and that effective planning was key to the company's success in the international marketplace.

Delay in Decision Making Another potential cost of planning is that it may delay decision making. Some managers argue that planning directs the focus toward evaluating rather than doing. This can delay the organization's response to changes in the industry, marketplace, or internal operations. The delay can be particularly detrimental when an organization's success is dependent upon its ability to respond to change quickly.

In the business environment of the 21st century, speed in response time is critical for success in most industries. Nimble competitors will seize opportunities that are missed by those who are too slow at the planning process. According to Barbara Kux, vice-president of Switzerland's Nestlé S.A., global managers have to be able to analyze, plan, and execute quickly to stay on top in the international marketplace. As she explains, "The first trait of a global manager is to be nimble. Move fast, but don't hipshoot. Do some analysis, but not too much analysis, and then act . . . it's better to be 70 percent right and move fast than to be perfect and wait. Speed is a plus in a global business."[10]

When you weigh the potential benefits of planning against the potential costs, it is clear that planning pays. There are many examples of firms on the brink of failure that have recovered through effective planning. Consider the experience of Continental Airlines, for example. Through effective planning, CEO Gordon Bethune pulled the airline out of its tailspin and restored its profitability. His plans, which included getting out of the short-haul business, cutting unprofitable routes, and expanding in non-U.S. markets, affected virtually every aspect of the company's operations.[11]

Planning benefits entrepreneurial companies just as it does large companies. Consider the experience of the entrepreneurs that recently purchased the ailing Lionel Trains. As you will read in Entrepreneurial Approach, the two entrepreneurs who acquired the small-time toymaker must develop an effective plan to restore the company's market share and profitability.

In the final analysis, managers plan because planning leads to better performance. In today's highly competitive business environment, planning can help managers cope with the challenges they face. For example, many organizations have found that achieving quality through effective planning is key to ensuring their competitiveness.[13] As we saw in Chapter 1, quality doesn't just happen—it requires planning from the top of the organization down to the front line. With the spotlight on quality in nearly every industry across the globe, effective planning has become critical for success.

Entrepreneurial Approach

LIONEL TRAINS IS BACK ON TRACK

Train sets today are about as hot as hula hoops—in other words, they're not very hot. Kids once pieced together elaborate train track configurations with their dads, now they are pounding away on Nintendo, mesmerized by computer games, or hanging out at video arcades. Kids today want high-tech stuff; train set technology seems to have stopped advancing sometime in the 1950s. This left toymaker Lionel Trains largely out of the market for high-tech toys.

But rock star Neil Young, a longtime model-train freak, is convinced that he can breathe some life back into Lionel Trains. How? His plan is to introduce computer technology into the old trains to capture the attention of the high-tech kids of the 21st century. The first step in implementing his plan was identifying the right resources and people for the job. His financial partner and part owner of the toy company is Martin Davis, ex-CEO of Paramount. Davis is an expert in acquiring turnaround companies. On the technical side, Young turned to Silicon Valley heavy Nolan Bushnell, founder of Atari and Chuck E. Cheese's Pizza Time Theatre, as well as to two well-known Silicon Valley engineers.

With his team in place, Young was ready to execute his plan. The first product out of the box was a remote control called the CAB-1. Driven by a computer chip, the remote control moves trains, switches, and accessories, and controls authentic audio sounds recorded live by Young and his crew at Norfolk and Southern train company. The technology can be applied to other model train products as well.

Young's team has put Lionel Trains back on track. As Young told *Micro-Times,* a northern California computer magazine: "[Lionel's] technology is now the leading technology in toys. We have other companies coming to us wanting to use our technology. The overall goal is to make an advanced toy that brings families together in a way that video games don't."

As a result of good planning, the future of Lionel Trains looks very bright indeed.[12]

WHERE SHOULD THE PLANNING BEGIN?

Assuming that organizations should plan, the question then becomes, "Who should initiate the planning process?" Planning is carried out at various levels of the organization and for various departments, work groups, and individuals at each level. Although a broad range of organizational members should be involved in the planning process, the process must be initiated and coordinated at some specific point in the organizational hierarchy. At what organizational level should planning begin?

Traditionally, there have been two basic approaches to planning, depending on where in the organizational hierarchy the planning function is initiated—the top-down approach and the bottom-up approach. Table 4.1 illustrates some of the differences between these two approaches. Today, however, many organizations take a more integrated approach that combines aspects of both top-down and bottom-up planning.

With a top-down planning approach, planning efforts begin with the board of directors and the top executives of the organization. They determine the general direction of the organization and establish a master plan to achieve its overall goals. The master plan establishes the parameters within which the work groups of the organization develop their plans. Managers develop plans for their work groups based on what their units must accomplish to support the master plan.

TABLE 4.1   Top-down versus bottom-up planning

	TOP-DOWN	BOTTOM-UP
Level at which initiated	Board of directors, top executive level	Individuals closest to product, service, or customer
Role of organizational units	As the plan moves down the hierarchy, units determine actions that will support the plan	Units develop their own goals and plans. As these plans move up the hierarchy, they are evaluated and adjusted for accuracy and feasibility
Specificity of plan	Begins as broad, becomes more specific as it moves down the hierarchy	Begins as very fragmented and specific, becomes cohesive and integrated
Advantages	Plans are driven by top management who are most knowledgeable about all factors affecting the organization	Those closest to customers, suppliers, and operating systems provide focus of plans
Disadvantages	Top managers are often far removed from the front line	Lower-level managers may lack understanding of all factors affecting the organization
Appropriateness	When the organization's success is dependent on quick response to external pressure and threats	When an organization's success is dependent on its ability to respond quickly to changes in operational systems

In contrast, bottom-up planning is initiated at the lowest levels of the organizational hierarchy—with those individuals who are most directly involved in the delivery of the organization's products and services and who are closest to the customers or suppliers of the organization. The managers and employees at the operational level of the organization begin the planning process by estimating sales potential, describing needed product and service modifications or new product and service developments, and identifying potential problems or opportunities in the supply of input resources. As these plans move up through the organization, they are developed further, refined, and evaluated for accurateness and feasibility. Finally, the board of directors and top-level executives bring together all the plans of the organization's work groups to develop a cohesive and well-integrated master plan that establishes the overall direction of the organization.[14]

Both the top-down and bottom-up approaches to planning have advantages and disadvantages. The primary advantage of top-down planning is that the top managers, who presumably are most knowledgeable about the organization as a whole, drive the development of the plan. Although one might argue that the people at the lowest level of the organization know the most about how the organization actually operates, top-level management has a more comprehensive understanding of the wide variety of internal and external factors that affect the overall success of the organization.

A determination of whether to use top-down or bottom-up planning depends on the specific circumstances facing an organization. A pharmaceutical company, for example, might choose a top-down approach because it must respond to FDA directives and other regulatory issues. Also, the two planning modes are not mutually exclusive, and flexible managers can benefit from both approaches.

© Mark Richards/PhotoEdit

Yet having those closest to the operating system, customers, and suppliers provide the focus for the planning process also offers advantages. These individuals may have a better understanding of the competitive and operational challenges faced by the organization than would the board of directors and top executives, who are far removed from the front line of the organization.

Which approach is better? The answer to that question depends on the specific circumstances facing the organization. Where success is largely a function of the organization's ability to respond quickly and effectively to changes in its operating system, customer focus, or supplier relationships, bottom-up planning may be more appropriate. When success is dependent upon the ability to make high-level organizational changes in response to more general external threats and pressures (such as industry consolidation via mergers and acquisitions, changes in the regulatory environment, or demographic trends), a top-down planning approach may be more appropriate. For example, a pharmaceutical company such as Eli-Lilly, which must respond to Food and Drug Administration (FDA) directives and other regulatory issues, might benefit from a top-down approach. In contrast, a computer firm such as Hewlett-Packard may find that a bottom-up planning approach supports its efforts to be sensitive to the technological needs of its customers in designing new products.

Further, and perhaps most important, these planning modes are not mutually exclusive. Many organizations use a bottom-up approach to formulate plans in one area (such as marketing) but develop plans in other areas (such as finance) from a top-down perspective. In fact, by being flexible, managers can capitalize on the benefits of both approaches.

Now that we have sketched out the managerial function of planning in general, let's examine the two primary types of planning that occur in most organizations—strategic and operational planning.

STRATEGIC VERSUS OPERATIONAL PLANNING

In general, most organizations engage in both strategic and operational planning. Although strategic and operational planning differ in a number of ways, they are also interrelated. Let's explore both of these important planning processes.

STRATEGIC PLANNING

Strategic planning
The process by which an organization makes decisions and takes actions to enhance its long-run performance.

Strategic plan
A plan that identifies the markets in which an organization competes, as well as the ways in which it competes in those markets.

Planning that is strategic in nature focuses on enhancing the competitive position and overall performance of the organization in the long term.[15] In other words, **strategic planning** is the process by which an organization makes decisions and takes actions that affect its long-run performance. A **strategic plan** is the output of the strategic planning process. Strategic plans define both the markets in which the organization competes and the way in which it competes in those markets.[16]

The purpose of strategic planning is to move the organization from where it is to where it wants to be and, in the process, to develop and maintain a sus-

CBS: Moving from Strategic Turmoil to Strategic Focus

Everyone knows that the media/entertainment business is highly competitive and rapidly changing—an all-around tough business. Characterized in recent years by mega-mergers such as Disney/ABC and Viacom/Paramount, the industry has suffered from both fickle audiences and fickle investors. While some media/entertainment companies have fared quite well through the chaos, others have not. Why? It has to do with strategic planning. As an illustration, consider the historical evolution of longtime industry giant CBS.

CBS, founded in 1925 and bought by William Paley in 1928, began as a radio network. Paley, who was 26 years old at the time, proceeded to change the face of broadcasting in this country, setting the standard in network television and building CBS into a first-class organization.

But today, things are not quite so bright at CBS. After Paley's death in 1990, Larry Tisch took the reins of the company. Under Tisch's leadership, the strategic focus once enjoyed by CBS became more like strategic turmoil. Tisch, who was extremely cost-conscious, refused to pay the price for football (causing the NFL's move to the Fox network), curbed spending on news, and worst of all, failed to move into cable as did NBC, ABC, and Fox. CBS lost 33 percent of its young audience in 1994 and 1995, falling behind Fox in market share for this segment of the market. As of 1996, the once-proud network generated fewer advertising dollars per hour of prime time than NBC, ABC or Fox.

Tisch left CBS in 1996 under pressure from institutional investors. His replacement, Leslie Moonves, faces the challenge of bringing strategic focus back to CBS. Moonves has developed a plan for doing so, which includes refocusing on CBS's traditional market segment and leaving the MTV crowd for other networks to chase. Industry analysts are watching CBS carefully, but most agree that if a turnaround is possible, Moonves is the man for the job. Only time will tell if CBS can refocus its strategy and regain its position as a leader in the media/entertainment industry.[17]

tainable competitive advantage within the industries in which it competes.[18] A **competitive advantage** is any aspect of an organization's operations that distinguishes it from its competitors in a positive way.[19] For example, most would point to Compaq's reputation for quality and service as being a key competitive advantage, while Gateway Computer's competitive advantage rests on its ability to provide computers differentiated on the basis of price. Apple Computer has distinguished itself through its innovative and user-friendly system designs, while a reputation for technologically advanced scientific computing equipment has given Hewlett-Packard its competitive edge. Through their strategies, each of these firms has developed a distinct competitive advantage and leadership position in the computer industry.[20]

Competitive advantage
Any aspect of an organization that distinguishes it from its competitors in a positive way.

You don't have to look far to find an organization that attributes its success to its strategy.[21] Similarly, there are numerous examples of companies that would attribute their failure or the failure of a given product, service, or project to the absence of an effective strategic plan.[22] Managing for Excellence illustrates how one-time industry giant CBS Entertainment evolved from a company with a strong strategic direction to a company suffering from the lack of a strategic plan. Today, CBS is struggling to regain its strategic focus and its leadership position in the media/entertainment industry.

Levels of Strategic Planning
Strategic planning occurs at three primary levels within the organization: the corporate, business, and functional levels.[23] Each level can be distinguished by

TABLE 4.2   Levels of strategic planning

	FOCUS	SPECIFICITY	PARTICIPANTS	TIME HORIZON
Corporate strategy	To develop a mix of business units that meets the company's long-term growth and profitability goals	• Broad	• Board of directors • Top-level executives	5–10 years
Business strategy	To develop and maintain a distinctive competitive advantage that will ensure long-term profitability	• More specific than the corporate strategy	• Top-level executives • Managers within the business unit	1–5 years
Functional strategy	To develop action plans that ensure that corporate and business strategies are implemented	• Very specific	• Middle-level managers • Lower-level managers	1–2 years

the focus of the strategic planning process, the participants in the process, the specificity of the strategy, and the time horizon of the plan. Table 4.2 summarizes the key differences in these three levels of strategic planning, and the discussion that follows elaborates on each.

Corporate Strategic Planning   Strategic planning that occurs at the corporate level of the organization focuses on developing corporate strategy. **Corporate strategy** addresses the question, "What business should we be in?" and is most relevant for organizations that operate in multiple lines of business. Corporate strategic planning involves assessing the organization's portfolio of business to determine whether an appropriate mix exists.[24] The objective is to develop a mix of business units that meet the long-term growth and profitability goals of the organization.

For example, consider media giant Time Warner. Time Warner operates in nearly every segment of the media industry and is the second largest entertainment and information business in the world (Disney is number one). The company operates three primary business units: (1) Time Inc. operates the company's news and information businesses, delivering products such as *Sports Illustrated, Time,* and *Entertainment Weekly;* (2) Time Warner Entertainment conducts various recording, movie, and TV businesses such as the HBO movie channel and other pay television channels; and (3) Time Warner Cable leads the company's telecommunications operations, with about 11.7 million cable television subscribers in the United States.[25] At the corporate level, managers must determine whether this particular mix of businesses positions the organization well for long-term success.

Diversification is often at the core of corporate strategy.[26] Diversification occurs when an organization chooses to add a new business unit to its portfolio of businesses. A company may pursue a strategy of diversification if it wishes to reduce its dependence on its existing business units or to capitalize on its core competencies by expanding into another business. Philip Morris, for example, embarked on a fairly aggressive strategy of diversification to lessen its dependence on the slow-growing and highly threatened tobacco industry. The acquisition of Kraft Foods and Miller Brewing was intended to diversify Philip Morris's revenue base.[27] In contrast, Xerox, which originally sold only copy machines, acquired numerous firms in the office products industry (such as makers of printers, fax machines, and scanners) in an effort to expand its product lines and capitalize on its name recognition in the copier business. Diversifying was a desirable option for both firms, although for very different reasons.

Because corporate strategy defines the very nature of the organization, it is formulated by the organization's board of directors and top-level executives.

Corporate strategy
Decisions and actions that define the portfolio of business units that an organization maintains.

In developing their strategic plans, however, these individuals rely to a great extent on information provided by middle- and lower-level managers.

Corporate strategy is relatively broad and general in nature and may extend as far as five to ten years into the future. While many would argue that it is impossible to formulate strategy ten years into the future in today's rapidly changing business environment,[28] it is important for corporate leaders to have a strategy for the long-term future of the organization—even if that strategy has to be adapted and adjusted in light of environmental and competitive changes that occur over the years.

Business Strategic Planning   The product of the strategic planning process at the business level is business strategy. **Business strategy** defines how each business unit in the organization's corporate portfolio will operate in its market arena. Strategy formulated at this level addresses the question, "How do we compete in our existing lines of business?" The primary focus of business strategic planning is to develop and maintain a distinct competitive advantage that will lead to long-term profitability.

Consider the various business strategies that must be developed for Philip Morris's portfolio of businesses. The tobacco segment of the business must have a strategy for dealing with the proposed increases in regulation and competing with the other tobacco companies both at home and abroad; Kraft must have a strategy for new product development, as well as for marketing its existing products across the globe; and Miller's strategy must focus on competing with the United States's leading brewer, Anheuser-Busch, as well as with the many other brewers that compete for market share in this "dog-eat-dog" industry.

Business strategy should be formulated by those individuals who are most familiar with the operations of the business unit. Consequently, the board of directors and corporate executives are typically not involved with strategy formulation at the business level. Instead, this responsibility lies with the top-level executives and managers within the specific business units. For example, the CEO and top management teams at Philip Morris's tobacco company, Kraft Foods, and Miller Brewing will be most instrumental in formulating business strategy for their respective units.

Business strategy is more specific than corporate strategy and spans a more limited time frame (one to five years). For example, given the improvements in artificial-intelligence technology in recent years, Hewlett-Packard may pursue a business-level strategy aimed at developing new products based on that technology. This strategy would position Hewlett-Packard to capitalize on potential market opportunities over the next several years.

Functional Strategic Planning   Functional strategic planning leads to the development of functional strategy. **Functional strategy** specifies the operations, research and development, financial, human resource management, and marketing activities necessary to implement the organization's corporate and business strategies. Table 4.3 lists some of the areas where functional planning occurs and gives examples of functional strategies in each area.

Strategy formulation at the functional level addresses the question, "How do we implement our corporate and business strategies?" While an organization's corporate and business strategies address what should be done, functional strategy focuses on how things will get done. In other words, corporate and business strategies deal with "doing the right thing," while functional strategy deals with "doing things right."

Consider, for example, the functional strategies necessary to implement Hewlett-Packard's product development strategy as described earlier. The research and development department would have to prepare product specifications and prototypes; the operations department would have to design a pro-

Business strategy
Defines how each business unit in the firm's corporate portfolio will operate in its market arena.

Functional strategy
Specifies the operations, research and development, financial, human resource management, and marketing activities necessary to implement the organization's corporate and business strategies.

TABLE 4.3   Examples of functional strategies

Human resource strategies:
- Recruit for management positions.
- Design commission structure.
- Develop training program.
- Design benefit package.

Marketing strategies:
- Develop market research study.
- Identify additional distribution channels.
- Create promotional program.
- Evaluate pricing structure.

Finance strategies:
- Secure debt financing.
- Evaluate capital structure.
- Initiate and manage budget process.
- Review and revise credit policies.

Operations strategies:
- Evaluate robotics system.
- Redesign quality control processes.
- Locate alternative sources of supply.
- Develop inventory management system.

duction system to manufacture the product; and the marketing department would have to develop a pricing, promotion, and distribution plan to bring the product to market. Each of these activities represents functional strategy.

Functional strategic planning is carried out by middle- and lower-level managers, who develop functional strategies to ensure that their units are supporting the corporate and business strategies of the organization. Strategic planning at the functional level is more specific than corporate and business strategic planning, and functional strategies typically span a shorter time frame, usually one or two years at most.

Achieving Quality through Strategic Planning

As the competitive environment of most industries continues to globalize and intensify, many organizations are searching for ways to achieve and maintain a competitive advantage. Increasingly, they are looking toward quality improvement as a means of establishing such an advantage.[29] As you will recall from Chapter 1, improving quality can lead to reduced costs, increased sales, and greater customer satisfaction.[30] Providing the highest-quality product or service has become the strategic challenge of the 1990s and will continue to be a key determinant of competitive success long into the future.[31] Firms such as Federal Express, Xerox, and Motorola claim that their success is inextricably linked to their strategic focus on quality.[32]

Achieving quality has become a primary objective of the strategic planning process in many organizations. In fact, total quality management programs have become an integral part of the strategic plans of many companies. The term **total quality management (TQM)** is widely used to describe organizational efforts to enhance product, service, process, and operational quality. As C. Jackson Grayson, a national expert in the area of quality, suggests, TQM stands for:

- *Total.* Managing all people, functions, customers, and suppliers.
- *Quality.* Meaning not just products, but processes, reliability, and quality of work life.

Total quality management (TQM)
A systematic approach for enhancing products, services, processes, and operational quality control.

TABLE 4.4   Developing a plan for total quality management

Establish a foundation:
- Set strategic objectives.
- Define a vision statement.

Build an infrastructure:
- Establish a TQM council.
- Appoint a TQM executive.
- Establish subordinate support committees.

Educate the work force:
- Conduct employee surveys.
- Hold executive workshops.
- Train management.
- Train other personnel.

Initiate process improvement:
- Identify candidate processes.
- Establish benchmarks.

Establish communication channels:
- Publish letters to employees.
- Establish other TQM media techniques.

Establish control system:
- Identify quantifiable indicators of quality improvement.
- Monitor indicators.

SOURCE: Adapted from A. C. Fenwick, "Five Easy Lessons," *Quality Progress,* December 1991, 63–66. © 1991 American Society for Quality Control. Reprinted with permission.

- *Management.* Meaning senior management strategy, goal setting, organizational structure, compensation, and profits.[33]

TQM does not stand alone as an organizational activity; it is not simply an additive to the customer service function; and it does not involve a discrete set of organizational members.[34] It is not a "quick fix."[35] Rather, TQM is an unwavering strategic commitment to enhancing the quality of an organization's output through continuous improvement by all members of the organization.[36] Further, quality-oriented strategies are appropriate for organizations of all sizes and types and across all industries.[37]

So how does a focus on quality affect the strategic planning process? Customer satisfaction becomes a driving force for the strategic plan. The strategic planning process focuses on identifying the needs and expectations of the customer and is driven by a commitment to meet those needs and exceed customer expectations.[38] Implementing the strategy of the organization focuses on empowering employees to do whatever is necessary to ensure customer satisfaction.[39] Table 4.4 illustrates a detailed plan for achieving TQM.[40]

Strategic planning is the focus of the next chapter. In Chapter 5 we will explore the process of strategic planning and the activities associated with each stage of that process. For now, let's turn our attention to the second type of planning—operational planning.

OPERATIONAL PLANNING

Operational planning focuses on determining the day-to-day activities that are necessary to achieve the long-term goals of the organization. **Operational plans** outline the tactical activities that must occur to support and implement

Operational planning
The process of determining the day-to-day activities that are necessary to achieve the long-term goals of the organization.

Operational plans
An outline of the tactical activities necessary to support and implement the strategic plans of the organization.

A great deal of operational planning was necessary for Disney to enter the European market with its Disneyland Paris theme park. Operational planning focuses on determining the day-to-day activities that are necessary to achieve the long-term goals of the organization.

©/AP/Wide World Photos

Standing plans
Plans that deal with organizational issues and problems that recur frequently.

Policies
General guidelines for decision making within the organization.

the strategic initiatives of the organization. Operational plans are more specific than strategic plans, address shorter-term issues, and are formulated by the mid- and lower-level managers who are responsible for the work groups in the organization.

Consider, for example, the comprehensive operational plans that were necessary to support Walt Disney Company's strategy to enter the European market with a new theme park—Disneyland Paris. From site location to construction to food service, from human resource management to marketing, operational plans had to be formulated, coordinated, and implemented (see Global Perspective). Today, one of Disney's strategies is to develop a "Broadway" presence. Having acquired the turn-of-the-century New Amsterdam Theatre, CEO Michael Eisner has made a commitment to restore the historical site, transforming it into the showplace of Broadway.[41] Implementing this strategy will require extensive operational planning—planning that will be carried out by many lower- and mid-level managers that reside far below Michael Eisner in the organizational hierarchy.

In general, plans can be categorized as standing or single-use plans, depending on whether they address recurring issues or are specific to a given set of circumstances. Most organizations maintain both standing and single-use plans, as both are applicable to a broad range of organizational situations.

While standing and single-use plans are usually developed for work groups within the organization, operational planning can also occur for individual organizational members. This individualized planning is called *management by objectives.*

Standing Plans

Standing plans are designed to deal with organizational issues or problems that recur frequently. By using standing plans, management avoids the need to "reinvent the wheel" every time a particular situation arises. In addition, such plans ensure that recurring situations are handled consistently over time. This may be particularly important for an organization with a highly diverse work force. Individuals from different cultural and social backgrounds may react to certain situations differently. Standing plans ensure that such situations will be handled in prescribed ways. In fact, some organizations such as BankAmerica, British Airways, and Nintendo boast of the intricacy of their standing plans and the level of control that is maintained as a result of these plans.[42]

Standing plans can, however, limit employees' flexibility and make it more difficult to respond to the needs of the customer. Given the customer focus of most successful businesses today, rigid constraints on employee behavior could have a negative effect on the performance of the organization. Therefore managers should carefully consider how standing plans can be used most effectively before they design and implement such plans.

Standing plans include: (1) policies, (2) procedures, and (3) rules. Each provides guidance in a different way.

Policies   **Policies** are general guidelines that govern how certain organizational situations will be addressed. Policies provide guidance to managers who must make decisions about circumstances that occur frequently within the organization. Most organizational units establish policies to provide direction for decision making.

For example, human resource management departments maintain policies that govern sick leave, vacation leave, and benefit options. Production departments establish policies for procurement, inventory management, and quality control. A university's administration maintains policies about admittance to certain academic programs, grade appeals, and permissible course waivers or substitutions. These policies provide a framework for decision making that elim-

DISNEY: FROM PARIS TO BROADWAY

The initial staffing of Disneyland Paris, a $4.4 billion theme park located in Paris, France, was no easy task. The staffing plan, which took well over a year to develop and implement, was based on Disney's recruiting experiences at other parks and in light of the unique employment market in France.

The company calculated that in order to hire the 12,000 employees it needed to open the park, it would have to attract approximately 120,000 applicants. One of the first things the human resource managers at Euro Disney learned was that Disney theme parks were not well known in France. To lure prospective employees, Disney launched an extensive advertising campaign that was intended to educate the French about the company's theme parks. The process of educating future workers continued as they waited in line to be interviewed. At the Disney casting center, applicants watched a five-minute video of Disney employees performing various jobs at the company's California theme park. Then applicants gathered in a theater to view a fifteen-minute video. The video stressed the importance of reliable transportation, appearance standards, and the necessity of working holidays and weekends. At the end of this video, applicants had an opportunity to leave if they were no longer interested in the job. Those who stayed went through a seven-minute interview. Based on the results of that interview, the best candidates were invited to further explore employment opportunities at Disney. Through its well-developed recruiting plan, Euro Disney was able to attract the employees necessary to open the park. It was a managerial challenge that required extensive planning and careful execution.[43]

Today, Disney's latest venture is a domestic one. The company plans to open a new theater and entertainment complex on Broadway in New York. As the human resource department prepares to staff this venture, it must once again establish a recruiting and hiring plan. How do you think the staffing process in New York might differ from the one used in Paris?

Global Perspective

inates the need to evaluate the specific circumstances surrounding each individual case.

Procedures   **Procedures** are a second type of standing plan. Procedures are more specific and action-oriented than policies and are designed to give explicit instructions on how to complete a recurring task. Most companies maintain some sort of procedures manual to provide guidance for certain recurring activities. Many use a standard operating procedures (SOPs) manual to outline the basic operating methods of the organization.

Most units of the organization will have procedures as well as policies. For example, human resource management departments develop procedures for filing benefit claims, documenting the reasons for sick leave, and requesting vacation time. Production departments establish procedures for identifying and evaluating suppliers and ordering supplies, operating a given inventory management system, and identifying and implementing specific quality-control criteria. A university will maintain specific procedures for registering for admittance to certain programs, appealing grades, and applying for course waivers and/or substitutions.

Procedures
Instructions on how to complete recurring tasks.

Meeting the Challenge

EVALUATING STANDING PLANS

Choose an organization with which you are familiar. This can be a company for whom you work or have worked, a social organization with which you are associated (such as a church, sorority, or fraternity), or even your university. Identify three policies, procedures, and rules that exist within that organization. Evaluate the purpose and effect of each.

Would you change the plan in some way? If so, indicate your proposed change and explain the effect that you feel it would have on the functioning of the organization. A format similar to the following can be used to summarize your assessment.

Policy	Purpose	Effect	Proposed Change	Effect
1.				
2.				
3.				

Procedure	Purpose	Effect	Proposed Change	Effect
1.				
2.				
3.				

Rule	Purpose	Effect	Proposed Change	Effect
1.				
2.				
3.				

Rules
Detailed and specific regulations for action.

Rules   **Rules** are the strictest type of standing plan found in organizations. Rules are not intended to serve as guidelines for making organizational decisions; instead, they provide detailed and specific regulations for action.

For example, a human resource management department may have rules governing the number of sick days an employee may take with pay, the months in which vacation time can be scheduled, and the lengthh of time an organizational member must be employed before qualifying for benefits. The production department may have rules governing the percentage of supplies that can be purchased from a single supplier, the method in which inventory must be accounted for, and the way in which products of substandard quality are handled. A university may have rules to govern the minimum grade point average necessary for admission to a given academic program, the period in which a grade can be appealed after a course is completed, and the specific courses that may be substituted for one another.

Meeting the Challenge provides an opportunity for you to evaluate and adapt standing plans for an organization with which you are familiar. Based on this exercise, you should see the potential value of establishing standing plans to cope with recurring organizational situations.

Single-Use Plans

Single-use plans
Plans that address specific organizational situations that typically do not recur.

Single-use plans are developed to address a specific organizational situation. Such plans are typically used only once because the specific situation to which they apply does not recur. Consider, for example, Disney's plan to renovate the New Amsterdam Theatre on Broadway. This would be a single-use plan, as Disney would be unlikely to acquire another building with the specific renovation requirements of this particular theater.

On an even larger scale, consider a plan developed to support the merger of two banking institutions. In response to the consolidation trends in the banking industry, First Union acquired First Fidelity Bancorporation in 1996—a bank with 680 branches in the northeastern United States. Merging the operations of these two banks and ensuring a successful transition for the employees and customers of both organizations required a detailed and well-developed plan. This plan was, however, a single-use plan. Once the plan had been implemented, it was of little use to First Union. In the event that First Union acquires another bank at some future date, it is unlikely that the specifics of that acquisition (such as number and location of branches, personnel, operating policies, and so forth) would be similar enough to the First Fidelity Bancorporation acquisition to justify the use of the same plan.

There are three primary types of single-use plans: (1) programs, (2) projects, and (3) budgets. Each offers a different degree of comprehensiveness and detail. Programs are the most comprehensive plans; projects have a narrower scope and, in fact, are often undertaken as a part of a program; and budgets are developed to support programs or projects.

Programs   **Programs** are single-use plans that govern a relatively comprehensive set of activities that are designed to accomplish a particular set of goals. Such plans outline the major steps and specific actions necessary to implement the activities prescribed by the program. The timing and sequencing of the efforts of individuals and units are also articulated in the plan.

Many organizations today have implemented diversity programs. Such programs are designed to recruit and hire a more diverse work force, as well as to educate employees on issues related to diverse work environments. Olive Garden, for example, took very proactive steps to recruit minority candidates for management positions and to provide diversity training for managers and employees at all levels of the organization. This program was developed to meet Olive Garden's goal of having a productive and diverse work force that reflects the company's customer base.

Projects   **Projects** direct the efforts of individuals or work groups toward the achievement of specific, well-defined objectives. Projects are typically less comprehensive and narrower in focus than programs and usually have predetermined target dates for completion. Many projects are designed to collect and analyze information for decision-making purposes or to support more comprehensive planning efforts, such as programs.

For example, the human resource management department at Olive Garden might be asked to research methods for attracting minority job applicants. This project has a narrower scope than the overall diversity program and would be undertaken to support Olive Garden's efforts to create a more diverse employee base. Similarly, the training and development department might be asked to take on the project of identifying and evaluating outside consulting firms that might provide diversity training for the organization.

Budgets   **Budgets** are the final form of single-use plans. Budgets are often undertaken as a part of other planning efforts because they specify the financial resource requirements associated with other plans (such as programs and projects). In addition, budgets serve as a mechanism for controlling the financial aspects of implementing the plan.[44]

Olive Garden would undoubtedly provide a budget to support its diversity initiatives. In fact, the size of that budget might provide some insight as to the importance of the project to the organization. The budget would be established to support the implementation of the diversity plan and to ensure that it is carried out in an effective and efficient manner.

Programs
Single-use plans that govern a comprehensive set of activities designed to accomplish a particular set of goals.

Projects
Single-use plans that direct the efforts of individuals or work groups toward the achievement of a specific goal.

Budgets
Single-use plans that specify how financial resources should be allocated.

Although all the types of standing and single-use plans discussed here can be used for very specialized planning purposes, they are often interrelated. For example, projects are often subcomponents of more comprehensive programs or are undertaken in an effort to develop or implement policies, procedures, and rules. In fact, most organizations will engage in all of these forms of planning over time.

Management by Objectives

Management by objectives (MBO)

A method for developing individualized plans that guide the activities of individual members of an organization.

A special planning technique, **management by objectives (MBO),** provides a method for developing personalized plans that guide the activities of individual members of the organization. The MBO approach to planning helps managers balance conflicting demands by focusing the attention of the manager and the employee on the tasks to be completed and the performance to be achieved at an individual level.[45]

MBO Process   Figure 4.2 outlines the primary steps in an MBO program. As the figure illustrates, MBO programs are circular and self-renewing in nature. The process begins when employees, in conjunction with their managers, establish a set of goals that serve as the foundation for the development of their work plans. Once a set of mutually agreeable goals has been determined, criteria for assessing work performance are identified. Next, employees formulate and implement the action plans necessary to achieve their goals and review their progress with their managers on an intermittent basis. At the end of the MBO period, the performance of the employees is compared to the goals established at the beginning of the period. Performance rewards should be based on the extent to which the goals have been achieved. Once the MBO cycle is complete, employees begin formulating goals to drive the next MBO planning period.[46]

Benefits of MBO   As originally conceived, MBO programs provide three primary benefits:

- MBO programs provide a foundation for a more integrated and system-oriented approach to planning. Establishing goals and action plans for indi-

FIGURE 4.2

Management by objectives: the cycle

SOURCE: K. Davis and J. Newstrom, *Human Behavior at Work: Organizational Behavior,* (New York: McGraw-Hill, 1989), 209. Reproduced with permission of McGraw-Hill.

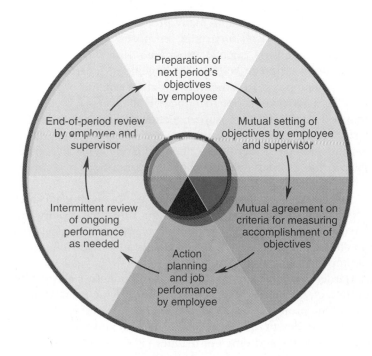

vidual employees forces managers to examine how the activities of each individual in their work group contribute to the achievement of the overall goals of the group. As an MBO system works its way up the hierarchy of the organization, it provides a mechanism for ensuring systemwide coordination of work efforts.

- The MBO approach to planning requires communication between employees and their managers since they must agree on the performance goals outlined in the plan. This increased communication often serves to build stronger relationships between managers and their employees.
- MBO systems lead to more participatory work environments where employees feel they have a voice and can have input into how their jobs should be designed and what their performance targets should be. Further, employees gain a greater understanding of their organization when they are forced to plan their activities in line with the organization's overall goals.[47]

In addition to these general benefits, MBO systems offer the more specific advantages listed in Table 4.5.[48] These benefits include such things as higher overall performance levels, prioritized goals, and greater opportunities for career development for both managers and employees.[49]

Disadvantages of MBO   At the same time, however, a number of disadvantages are associated with the use of MBO systems (see Table 4.5). These systems require a significant commitment on the part of management and, as a result,

---

TABLE 4.5   Advantages and disadvantages of an MBO system

Advantages
- Results in better overall management and the achievement of higher performance levels.
- Provides an effective overall planning system.
- Forces managers to establish priorities and measurable targets or standards of performance.
- Clarifies the specific role, responsibilities, and authority of personnel.
- Encourages the participation of individual employees and managers in establishing objectives.
- Facilitates the process of control.
- Provides a golden opportunity for career development for managers and employees.
- Lets individuals know what is expected of them.
- Provides a more objective and tangible basis for performance appraisal and salary decisions.
- Improves communications within the organization.
- Helps identify promotable managers and employees.
- Facilitates the organization's ability to change.
- Increases motivation and commitment of employees.

Disadvantages
- Requires time and commitment of top management, diverting their activities away from other important activities.
- May require excessive paperwork, thus complicating administrative processes.
- May create a tendency to focus on short-term versus long-term planning.
- Can be difficult to establish and put into operation.

SOURCE: Adapted from J. Gordon, *Management and Organizational Behavior* (Boston: Allyn & Bacon, 1990), 129–32.

may divert attention away from other important activities. Many systems require excessive paperwork that complicates the administrative processes within the organization. Further, some argue that MBO programs focus attention on short-run problems rather than on issues that are relevant to the long-term success of the organization. Finally, goals may be difficult to establish and put into operation in some cases. At a consequence, MBO systems may not be suitable for all job designs.[50]

In addition, the increasing diversity of the work force has created new challenges for those involved in MBO programs. While MBO systems work quite well for many employees from the United States, people from other cultures may not adapt well to this type of planning. The MBO concept is predicated on an employee's desire to be reasonably independent and his willingness to work toward predetermined goals—both of which are relatively common characteristics of workers in the United States. In many other cultures, however, such attitudes toward work are not common. MBO programs may be far less effective when used with individuals from such cultures.[51] Consequently, managers must be sensitive to the diversity of their work teams and may need to modify the MBO concept to suit different individuals.

In general, MBO systems are considered an effective tool. Although they can be cumbersome if implemented throughout every unit of an organization, these programs can be beneficial to the planning process when used selectively. Monsanto is an example of a firm that has embraced the MBO approach to planning. Corporate executives credit this system for the high level of commitment of Monsanto employees to the overall plans and strategy of the firm.[52]

THE RELATIONSHIP BETWEEN STRATEGIC AND OPERATIONAL PLANNING

Thus far, our examination of strategic and operational planning has highlighted their differences. Despite these differences, however, strategic and operational plans cannot be developed in isolation. In fact, both types of plans must be developed from an integrative perspective. Regardless of whether the organization uses a top-down or a bottom-up planning approach, in the end it must develop a single, well-integrated master plan. The operational plans of the various work units within the organizational system must be supportive of the organization's overall strategic plan.

Whenever the strategic and operational plans of an organization are inconsistent, problems are certain to result. A classic example of the problems that can result from an inconsistency in strategic and operational planning can be found in Hershey Foods's acquisition of Friendly's Restaurants. When Hershey Foods acquired Friendly's, the parent company applied its manufacturing mentality to the new subsidiary. Such a mentality was inconsistent with the service nature of Friendly's business. As a consequence, Friendly's suffered severe operational problems that resulted in a significant loss of market share.[53]

CONTINGENCY PLANNING ▬▬▬▬▬▬ FOR CHANGING ENVIRONMENTS

Contingency planning
Development of two or more plans based on different strategic operating conditions.

Contingency planning is an approach that has become very popular in today's rapidly changing business environment. Organizations that face strategic or operating conditions that are subject to significant change may choose to employ a contingency approach in their planning process. This approach is particularly useful when the organization's effectiveness is highly dependent on a particular set of business conditions.

Contingency planning requires the development of two or more plans, each of which is based on a different set of strategic or operating conditions that could occur. The plan that is implemented is determined by the specific circumstances that come to pass.[54] For example, while an organization may plan to begin production at a new plant facility in June 1997, managers should develop a contingency plan that ensures uninterrupted production in the event that the plant opening is delayed for some reason.

Where strategic and operating conditions change rapidly and in unpredictable ways, it is often necessary to engage in contingency planning. Consider the airline industry, for example. Herb Kelleher, the CEO of Southwest Airlines, says that it is virtually impossible to employ traditional long-range planning in the airline industry. Things change too much and too quickly—schedules change, routes change, competitors change, and fares change continually.[55] Under such conditions, contingency planning to gain a tactical advantage is critical.

Organizations often fail to develop contingency plans, which can create significant difficulties in the long term. One well-known drugstore chain, Revco, was caught recently without a contingency plan. Revco, assuming that an acquisition by longtime rival Rite Aid Corporation would be approved, developed a plan for consolidation that essentially dissolved the current organization. But the merger didn't materialize. Rite Aid withdrew its offer at the last minute, bowing to complaints by the Federal Trade Commission that the merger would limit competition in a nine-state area. Suddenly, Revco found itself back in business with no contingency plan for growth. Time will tell if the chain can turn out a new plan quickly enough to satisfy its customers and stockholders.[56]

THE IMPACT OF INFORMATION TECHNOLOGY ON PLANNING

Advances in information technology have significantly affected the managerial function of planning. From the establishment of corporate- and business-level goals and strategies to the development of functional strategies and operational plans, information technology can be used to improve the effectiveness and efficiency of the planning process. Since strategic planning is the focus of the next chapter, let's focus our attention here on how information technology can be used to support operational planning.

As we have learned, operational plans include standing plans such as policies, procedures, and rules. Advances in information technology in recent years have supported the more efficient development of such plans, as well as more effective implementation. Consider, for example, how a university might use information systems to communicate policies, streamline procedures, and monitor compliance with rules. Policies related to such things as admission to certain programs, grade appeals, permissible course waivers and substitution can be communicated to students via the Internet or a campus local area network. This enables students to have on-line, real-time access to important information rather than having to wait for the next year's catalog to be distributed. Class registration procedures have also been improved through the

Recent advances in information technology have led to more efficient development and more effective implementation of operational plans. University policies can be communicated to students via the Internet or a campus local-area network, giving students real-time access to important information.

© Jeff Greenberg/PhotoEdit

use of information technology. At many universities, students can register by telephone without ever coming to campus. This is a dramatic improvement over the long registration lines of days gone by. Monitoring compliance with rules such as minimum grade point average, prerequisite completion, and course substitution is also more efficient through the use of information technology. Database systems that maintain individual student records allow university administrators to readily identify students who are in violation of university rules.

The development and implementation of single-use plans can also be improved through the use of information technology. For example, project management software systems allow managers to track their progress on completing specific projects; spreadsheet software allows the monitoring of programs and project budgets.

First Union found information technology to be a critical factor in the successful implementation of its acquisition plan. Merging the computer operating systems of First Fidelity Bancorporation and First Union was not easy, but it was very important to the success of the merger. Today, all branches share a common operating system that enables customers to do their banking in the very same way in any branch from Florida to Connecticut. Internally, employees use the same systems as well. Consider, for example, First Union's recently developed Call Management System. This information management system, which allows managers to better quantify business development activity in their area, is used throughout the entire organization.

FACILITATING THE PLANNING PROCESS

Presuming that one accepts the proposition that planning is a critical organizational activity, it is important to examine ways to facilitate the planning process. While most managers would admit that they need to plan, many would also admit that they do much less planning than they should. This situation is a result of a number of barriers to planning.

BARRIERS TO EFFECTIVE PLANNING

Why do some managers fail to plan effectively? There are a number of potential causes—all of which may be overcome by developing an organizational culture that encourages and supports the planning process. Doing so, however, requires a clear understanding of the main reasons why managers fail to plan effectively.

Demands on the Manager's Time
Some managers may simply be too busy "putting out fires" to take the time to plan properly. Managers often feel as though they face a continuous stream of problems from the time they arrive at work until they leave. Although this constant troubleshooting may seem to leave few opportunities for planning, the hectic nature of the manager's day in itself suggests that planning is very much needed. Through better planning (such as policies, rules, and the like), managers can develop operational systems that are more effective and less problematic and demanding of their time.

Ambiguous and Uncertain Operating Environments
Environmental complexity and volatility are other commonly cited reasons for not planning. Managers who are uncomfortable with ambiguity may find it difficult and frustrating to plan under conditions of uncertainty. Yet while it may

be difficult to develop plans under such circumstances, effective managers make an effort to do so. Organizations that operate in rapidly changing and complex environments often find that planning provides a mechanism for coping with such conditions.

Resistance to Change

Finally, managers may hesitate to plan because they are resistant to change. Organizational members may associate planning with a need to change the way they do their jobs. Their hesitancy to change may discourage them from initiating the planning process.[57] Given the current focus on quality and continuous improvement, resistance to change can have very detrimental results for the organization in the long term.

OVERCOMING THE BARRIERS TO PLANNING

As discussed previously, achieving success through planning requires the participation of a broad range of organizational members. Consequently, organizations must develop and maintain a culture that encourages planning and rewards those who plan effectively. To do so, managers must involve employees in decision-making processes, tolerate a diversity of views, and encourage strategic thinking.

Involve Employees in Decision Making

Employee involvement in the planning process is essential for its success.[58] Regardless of whether a top-down or bottom-up approach is used, input from all levels of the organization is essential to the success of the organization's planning system. Managers should solicit the opinions and views of their employees when formulating plans, and they should maintain an open-door policy that encourages individual members of the organization to initiate communication about the planning efforts of the unit and the firm. Discouraging employees from sharing information that might be very important to the planning process (see Figure 4.3) will result in less effective organizational plans.[59]

Tolerate a Diversity of Views

Managers who are intolerant of a diversity of views within their unit eliminate one of the primary benefits associated with a participatory planning system.

In order to be successful in planning, an organization must involve a cross-section of its members, encouraging planning and rewarding those who plan effectively.

© Walter Hodges/Tony Stone Images

FIGURE 4.3

FRANK & ERNEST reprinted by permission of
Newspaper Enterprise Association, Inc.

Diverse views and perspectives lead to a broader assessment and evaluation of organizational problems and opportunities. In fact, this is one of the primary benefits of maintaining a diverse work force.[60] Organizations that encourage a wide range of different ideas and views are more likely to produce plans that are comprehensive and fully developed.

Encourage Strategic Thinking

Developing an organizational culture that encourages strategic and results-oriented thinking will lead to more effective planning. Thinking is a skill and, as is the case with most skills, it can be developed through training and practice.[61] Employees should be provided with the training necessary to develop strategic thinking skills and given the opportunity to practice those skills in their work environment. Further, individuals should be rewarded for thinking strategically when developing their plans.[62]

MANAGERIAL IMPLICATIONS

Tomorrow's manager will face many challenges in developing effective strategic and operational plans. Planning has become increasingly difficult as the pace of change in the business environment has accelerated. While change makes the planning process more difficult, it also makes planning more critical. Managers of the future must be forward thinking and focused on achieving the goals of their work groups and their organizations through effective planning.

The ultimate objective of the planning process is the development of good plans. Plans are good if they can be implemented successfully and result in the accomplishment of the goals for which they were designed. Managers are more likely to develop good plans when they:

- Recognize and communicate the importance of planning in achieving organizational success.
- Understand and appreciate the relationship between strategic and operational planning.
- Involve those responsible for implementing the plan in the planning process.
- Remove the barriers to planning at the work group and individual level.
- Reward those who think strategically and follow through with operational planning.
- Look to contingency planning as a means of maintaining flexibility in rapidly changing business environments.

In this chapter, we have examined the managerial function of planning. Our focus, at both the strategic and operational levels, has been on achieving organizational success through planning. The process of strategic planning is examined in much greater detail in the next chapter, where we discuss strategy as a tool for achieving competitive success in the 21st century.

FIRST UNION: PLANNING FOR THE FUTURE

By virtually all measures, First Union's plan for the future has been a success. In an effort to expand its markets into the northeast and to achieve the economies of scale and scope that have become so important in the banking industry, First Union acquired First Fidelity Bancorporation and its 680 branches in 1995. Merging the operations of these two banks was not easy—it required extensive and comprehensive planning by virtually every department in both institutions. But the merger, which was a tremendous success, made First Union the sixth largest bank in the United States. The newly expanded First Union now stretches 1,400 miles from north to south, covering the eastern United States from Connecticut to Florida. The company operates approximately 2,000 ATMs and 2,000 banks that provide services to more than 11 million customers.

First Union has also responded to the need for broader variety and higher-quality products and services. It has been proactive in investing in new and expanded product areas that provide added value to the customer and additional sources of revenue for the company. First Union customers can now choose from more financial products and services than ever before. Developing and delivering these new products and services required planning based on thorough analysis of the market demands.

Finally, First Union has been and remains committed to capitalizing on advanced technology to meet the needs of its customers. The leaders at First Union are focused on building what they call the "transitional bank"—the bridge to the financial services delivery channels of the future. While they admit that the future for delivery of banking services is unclear, the company stands ready to use the latest technology to meet the needs of its customers in the most effective and efficient manner.

First Union recognizes the importance of planning. Its leaders are committed to planning their future in light of the changes that will shape the banking industry of the 21st century.

SUMMARY

- Planning is an important managerial function through which managers outline the activities necessary to achieve the goals of the organization. The purpose of planning is to ensure organizational effectiveness and efficiency in both the short term and the long term.

- Traditionally, organizations used either a top-down or a bottom-up approach to planning. Most organizations today plan from an integrative perspective, using a top-down approach in some areas of the organization and a bottom-up approach in others.

- Strategic planning is the process by which an organization makes decisions and takes actions that affect its long-run performance. Strategy is the output of the strategic planning process. Corporate, business, and functional strategies vary with respect to focus, specificity, time horizon, and the participants in the planning process.

- Many organizations today are striving to achieve quality through strategic planning. Planning for qual-

ity requires a commitment to meeting customer needs and exceeding customer expectations, a willingness to empower employees, and a focus on continuous improvement in every aspect of the organization's operations.

- Operational planning determines the day-to-day activities that are necessary to achieve the long-term goals of the organization. Standing plans, which include policies, procedures, and rules, are developed to address issues that recur frequently in the organization. Single-use plans address a specific issue or problem that the organization experiences only once. Single-use plans include programs, projects, and budgets.

- Management by objectives (MBO) is a specialized approach to operational planning that occurs at the level of the individual organizational member. While MBO systems can be time-consuming and complex, employing this approach to plan the work activities of individual employees can be beneficial.

- Contingency planning involves the development of a set of plans that are designed for the varied strategic or operating conditions that the firm might face. Contingency planning is most appropriate for organizations that operate in environments that are subject to frequent or significant change.

- Advances in information technology have improved both the effectiveness and efficiency of the planning function. Information technology can be used to establish and implement the strategic and operational plans of an organization.

- The three common barriers to planning are demands on the manager's time, ambiguous and uncertain environmental conditions, and resistance to change. Overcoming the barriers to planning requires the development of an organizational culture that supports and encourages planning.

- The highly competitive, rapidly changing nature of the business environment will create many planning challenges for tomorrow's managers. Managers of the future must not only develop their own planning skills but must also create a work environment in which effective planning is encouraged and rewarded.

KEY TERMS

Planning	Business strategy	Rules
Plan	Functional strategy	Single-use plans
Goals	Total quality management (TQM)	Programs
Controls	Operational planning	Projects
Strategic planning	Operational plans	Budgets
Strategic plan	Standing plans	Management by objectives (MBO)
Competitive advantage	Policies	Contingency planning
Corporate strategy	Procedures	

REVIEW QUESTIONS

1. Describe the managerial function of planning, explaining what it is and why managers should plan.

2. At what levels of the organization can planning start? What are the advantages and disadvantages associated with the various approaches to planning?

3. Define strategic planning. What are the three levels at which strategy is formulated, and how do they differ in terms of: (a) focus, (b) participants, (c) specificity, and (d) time horizon?

4. Why and how are firms seeking to achieve quality through strategic planning?

5. What is operational planning and how does it differ from strategic planning? Describe standing and single-use plans and identify the various types of plans that fall into these two categories.

6. Describe an MBO program. What are the advantages and disadvantages of this type of planning?

7. What is contingency planning? Under what circumstances would it be most appropriate to use a contingency approach to planning?

8. How have advances in information technology affected the planning function?

9. What are the common barriers to planning? What might a manager do to reduce the barriers to planning?

10. How can tomorrow's manager achieve excellence through planning?

DISCUSSION QUESTIONS

Improving Critical Thinking

1. Evaluate the benefits of an MBO as an employer and as an employee. Would you want to participate in an MBO program? Why or why not?

2. As an employee of an organization, would you prefer a top-down or bottom-up approach to planning? What would you consider to be the advantages and disadvantages of each from an employee's perspective?

Enhancing Communication Skills

3. Consider an organization with which you have been fairly closely affiliated as an employee or a member (such as a business, church, sorority, and the like). Describe the planning system of this organization.

Was it effective? If not, why? What might the managers of the organization have done to ensure better planning? To improve your oral communication skills, present your analysis of this situation to the class.

4. How might the planning process for a new business venture differ from the process in an established business? How would it differ for small versus large businesses? To practice your written communication skills, prepare a one-page written summary of your response.

Building Teamwork

5. We know that planning occurs at the strategic and operational levels. Is it more important to plan at one level than at the other? Why or why not? Discuss this question in teams of four to five students and develop a position that you can present to the class.

6. Evaluate some of the standing plans at your university or college that directly affect you as a student. Are the policies, procedures, or rules that you identified meant to benefit or hinder the students? Why do you think that the administration at your school feels that it is necessary to have well-defined standing plans? What would happen if none of the plans that you identified existed? Form teams of four to five students, answer the preceding questions, and present your responses to the class.

---

1. Select a large, public company in which you have an interest. Using the Internet, locate an e-mail address for the company. Use e-mail to contact the firm and request information regarding their strategic plan. Present the information you obtain to your class.

2. Identify a local company that has a large marketing or sales department. Interview a manager in that department to find out how information technology has affected the planning function in their organization. In particular, ask how computer software is being used to monitor and track the company's customers.

3. Choose a university or college (other than your own) in which you have an interest. Using the Internet, find information about the policies, procedures and rules of the institution as they relate to admission.

INFORMATION TECHNOLOGY: Insights and Solutions

ETHICS: Take a Stand

Smart Toy Company is a subsidiary of a large corporation that owns a number of diversified businesses. The company, which employs about 500 workers, manufactures high-quality toys for preschool children. Smart Toy prides itself on its safety and employee satisfaction records. The company values the opinions of its workers and encourages a participatory planning process.

Recently, Smart Toy's market share has fallen dramatically as a result of the increasing demand for high-tech toys such as video games and remote-control cars. The effect of this loss in market share has been a significant reduction in the profitability of the subsidiary. Corporate headquarters has expressed its displeasure at the current situation at Smart Toy and has given the company six months to reverse the decline in profitability. If profitability cannot be restored within this time frame, the subsidiary will be shut down, and the employees will lose their jobs.

While Smart Toy's management feels that they can turn the business around within the next two years, the six-month time frame presents a significant problem. To achieve the profitability goals set by the parent company within the next six months, costs would have to be reduced significantly. To do so, the company would have to buy lower-quality materials, reduce its quality-control efforts, and eliminate its production safety programs. Top management is very concerned about the impact of such decisions on the quality and safety of Smart

Toy's products, as well as on the safety of production employees. Yet the only other alternative is to allow the company to be dissolved.

For Discussion

1. How do you feel about the demands corporate headquarters has imposed on Smart Toy Company?
2. Which of the two alternatives outlined above would you choose?
3. How might you address the issues presented in the case using planning techniques?

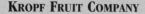

THINKING CRITICALLY: Debate the Issue

TOP-DOWN VERSUS BOTTOM-UP PLANNING

As was mentioned in the chapter, planning can begin at the top of the organization and flow downward or start at the bottom of the organization and move upward. Certain advantages and disadvantages are associated with each method.

Form teams of four to five students as directed by your instructor. Half of the teams should prepare to argue the benefits of top-down planning, while the other teams should prepare to argue the benefits of bottom-up planning. When developing your arguments you should draw from the experiences of real managers with whom you are familiar. Your instructor will choose two teams to present their findings to the class in a debate format.

Video Case

KROPF FRUIT COMPANY

Home Page **{http://www.kropf-inc.com/}**

In the early 1990s, the owners of Kropf Fruit Company faced a critical decision. Changing market conditions favored large fruit processors over medium-sized processors like Kropf. This trend resulted from a consolidation in the grocery store industry. As a result, the owners of Kropf were left with two options: (1) remain a medium-sized processor, or (2) expand and become a major player. Remaining a medium-sized processor meant that the company would continue to face unfavorable market conditions and some of the family members might eventually be forced to leave the business. Becoming a major player involved risk, but would allow the company to compete with other large growers and processors for major grocery store accounts.

The owners of Kropf decided to expand, but only within the parameters of carefully developed strategic and operational plans and clearly articulated goals. The plans were developed after the owners considered the strengths and weaknesses of the company along with the opportunities and threats in the firm's business environment. During the planning process, the owners also remained open to suggestions from their growers, creditors, customers, and employees. In the end, the company's strategic and operational plans represented a thoughtful analysis of what Kropf needed to do to remain competitive in its business environment today and in the future.

The expansion has been successful, although the owners of Kropf have worked long and hard and the firm has suffered some growing pains. Growth has provided the company access to some of the country's major grocery store chains and other new markets that are developing. A constant challenge has been developing short-term operating plans that adequately support the longer-term strategic plan. The owners of Kropf have found that communication between the company and its stakeholders is a critical step toward working out any difficulties. At this point, the owners of Kropf are satisfied with their expansion efforts. They are also convinced that both strategic and operational planning have been instrumental in their success.

For Discussion

1. Who initiated the planning process at Kropf? Was the planning process something that the owners resisted, or did they embrace planning as a management technique?

2. Describe how Kropf has used both strategic and operational planning to achieve business success.

3. If the owners of Kropf had not developed a strategic and operational plan, do you believe that their expansion effort would have been as successful? Why or why not?

CASE

MORGAN CHEMICAL

When Kenneth J. Morgan began peddling his industrial-strength cleanser to local businesses, he was 26 years old and full of dreams and ambitions that seemed far-fetched by most standards. However, the young entrepreneur from Ann Arbor, Michigan, eventually proved everyone wrong. From its meager beginnings, the company he founded grew to have more than $45 million in sales and operating facilities across the nation. Morgan's products now include an entire line of industrial cleansers primarily for hotels, restaurants, office buildings, and recreation centers. Amazingly, the company has remained more than 80 percent family owned throughout its history.

Now Bob Morgan is sitting in his Detroit headquarters looking out over the bay and thinking about how successful and well-focused his grandfather, Kenneth Morgan, had been. Even though Bob earned an MBA from Northwestern, at 31 years of age he knows that filling his grandfather's shoes will be difficult. Unfortunately, Morgan Chemical has been without skilled leadership since his grandfather's death almost seven years ago. Providing a new direction is Bob's first priority as a fledgling CEO.

As Bob attempts to develop a plan for the company, he finds the complexity of his task overwhelming. Morgan has 23 sales offices in the United States and manufacturing plants in three different states. In addition to the need to institute more formalized planning, the company faces several serious problems. The North Carolina plant has had to shut down production because of a misunderstanding with the local labor union. The industry is entering the mature stage of the life cycle, and many of Mor-

gan's larger competitors are beginning to merge to achieve better economies of scale. In addition, much of Bob's information about the internal operations of the firm is unreliable due to an ineffective and out-of-date management information system. Profits and sales have been declining over the last three years, and it has been more than five years since the company introduced a new product.

Bob doesn't know where to begin. How can he develop a plan that will put Morgan Chemical back on track?

For Discussion

1. How is the changing environment posing problems for Morgan Chemical? Do the changes present greater planning difficulties for Bob? Why or why not?
2. Would a top-down or bottom-up approach be better in this case? Why?
3. How would you advise Bob to begin developing a system for planning?

EXPERIENTIAL EXERCISE 4.1

Planning Your Career

Consider your own career plan. Have you developed a plan for your education and career? If you haven't developed a plan, consider the following questions in developing your plan. If you have, use your plan to respond to these questions.

1. What are your goals and objectives?

2. What must you do to achieve those goals and objectives?
   a. What resources will you require?
   b. What actions must you take?
3. What control mechanisms can you put in place to monitor your progress in achieving your plan?
4. What could happen to derail your plans? Do you have contingency plans that address those factors?

ENDNOTES

1. First Union Corporation, *1995 Summary Annual Report,* 1–30.
2. A. P. DeGeus, "Planning as Learning," *Harvard Business Review,* March/April 1988, 70–74.
3. P. F. Drucker, *Managing for Results* (New York: Harper & Row, 1964); Drucker, *The Effective Executive* (New York: Harper & Row, 1967).
4. C. Perrow, "The Analysis of Goals in Complex Organizations," *American Sociological Review,* 26, 1961, 854.
5. C. Farkas and P. DeBacker, *Maximum Leadership: The World's Leading CEOs Share Their Five Strategies for Success* (New York: Henry Holt, 1996).
6. E. E. Lawler III, "Total Quality Management and Employee Involvement: Are They Compatible?" *Academy of Management Executive,* 9, 1, 1995, 34–38.
7. J. A. Pearce II and W. A. Randolph, "Improving Strategy Formulation Pedagogues by Recognizing Behavioral Aspects," *Exchange,* December 1980, 7–10.

8. R. Michaels, "Planning: An Effective Management Tool or Corporate Pastime?" *Journal of Marketing Management,* Spring 1986, 259.
9. W. Taylor and A. Webber, *Going Global: Four Entrepreneurs Map the New World Marketplace* (New York: Viking, 1996).
10. Ibid.
11. J. Martin, "Tomorrow's CEOs," *Fortune,* June 24, 1996, 76–90.
12. A. E. Serwer, "An Odd Couple Aims to Put Lionel on the Fast Track," *Fortune,* October 30, 1995, 21.
13. B. M. Cook, "Quality: The Pioneers Survey the Landscape," *Industry Week,* October 21, 1993, 68–73; P. B. Crosby, "The Next Effort," *Management Review,* 81, 2, February 1992, 64; R. Jacob, "TQM: More Than a Dying Fad?" *Fortune,* October 18, 1992, 66–72.
14. W. H. Brickner and D. M. Cope, *The Planning Process* (Boston: Winthrop Publishers, 1977), 52–56.

15. R. Evered, "So What Is Strategy?" *Long Range Planning,* 16, 1983, 57-72.

16. M. Leontiades, "The Confusing Words of Business Policy," *Academy of Management Review,* 7, 1982, 45-48.

17. M. Gunther, "Turnaround Time for CBS," *Fortune,* August 19, 1996, 65-70.

18. A. Ginsberg, "Operationalizing Organizational Strategy: Toward an Integrative Framework," *Academy of Management Review,* 9, 3, 1984, 548-57.

19. C. C. Snow and L. G. Hrebiniak, "Strategy, Distinctive Competence and Organizational Performance," *Administrative Science Quarterly,* 25, 1980, 317-36.

20. D. A. Aaker, "How to Select a Business Strategy," *California Management Review,* Spring 1984, 167-75.

21. S. S. Thune and R. J. House, "Where Long-Range Planning Pays Off," *Business Horizons,* 14, 1970, 81-87; L. C. Rhyne, "The Relationship of Strategic Planning to Financial Performance," *Strategic Management Journal,* 5, 1986, 423-36; Z. A. Malik and D. W. Karger, "Does Long-Range Planning Improve Company Performance?" *Management Review,* 64, 1975, 27-31; R. Rumelt, *Strategy, Structure, and Economic Performance* (Boston: Graduate School of Business Administration, Harvard University, 1974).

22. A. D. Chandler, *Strategy and Structure: Chapters in the History of the American Industrial Enterprise* (Cambridge, Mass.: MIT Press, 1962).

23. S. C. Wheelwright, "Strategy, Management, and Strategic Planning Approaches," *Interfaces,* 14, 1984, 19-33.

24. M. Porter, "From Competitive Advantage to Corporate Strategy," *Harvard Business Review,* May-June 1987, 43-59.

25. Time Warner, *1996 Annual Report.*

26. H. Ansoff, "Critique of Henry Mintzberg's 'The Design School: Reconsidering the Basic Premises of Strategic Management,'" *Strategic Management Journal,* 12, February 1991, 449-61.

27. Phillip Morris, *1995 Annual Report.*

28. R. A. Burgelman and A. S. Grove, "Strategic Dissonance," *California Management Review,* 38, 2, 1996, 8-28.

29. *International Quality Study: The Definitive Study of the Best International Quality Management Practices* (joint project of Ernst & Young and American Quality Foundation, 1991), 1.

30. P. B. Crosby, "The Next Effort."

31. K. Bertrand, "In Service, Perception Counts," *Business Marketing,* April 1989, 44.

32. G. Labovitz, Y. Change, and V. Rosansky, *Making Quality Work* (New York: HarperBusiness, 1993).

33. B. M. Cook, "Quality: The Pioneers Survey the Landscape," *Industry Week,* October 21, 1991, 68-73.

34. R. Jacob, "TQM: More Than a Dying Fad?"

35. J. Neal and C. Tromley, "From Incremental Change to Retrofit: Creating High-Performance Work Systems," *Academy of Management Executive,* 9, 1, 1995, 42-54.

36. L. L. Axline, "TQM: A Look in the Mirror," *Management Review,* 80, 7, July 1991.

37. M. Barrier, "Small Firms Put Quality First," *Nation's Business,* May 1992, 22-32.

38. J. M. Juran, "Acing the Quality Quiz," *Across the Board,* July/August 1992, 58.

39. D. A. Garvin, "How the Baldridge Award Really Works," *Harvard Business Review,* November/December 1991, 80-93.

40. A. C. Fenwick, "Five Easy Lessons," *Quality Progress,* December 1991, 63-66.

41. F. Rose, "Can Disney Tame 42nd Street," *Fortune,* June 24, 1996, 95-104.

42. C. Farkas and P. DeBacker, *Maximum Leadership.*

43. V. Vaughn, "Disney Begins Massive Hiring Task," *Orlando Sentinel,* October 20, 1991, D1.

44. P. Drucker, *The Practice of Management* (New York: Harper, 1954).

45. K. Davis and J. Newstrom, *Human Behavior at Work in Organizational Behavior* (New York: McGraw-Hill, 1989), 209.

46. J. L. Mendelson, "Goal Setting: An Important Management Tool," in *Executive Skills: A Management by Objectives Approach* (Dubuque, Iowa: Brown, 1980).

47. Ibid.

48. J. Gordon, *Management and Organizational Behavior* (Boston: Allyn & Bacon, 1990), 129-32.

49. W. B. Werther and W. Heinz, "Refining MBO through Negotiations," in *Executive Skills: A Management by Objectives Approach* (Dubuque, Iowa: Brown, 1980).

50. J. N. Kondrasuk, "Studies in MBO Effectiveness," *Academy of Management Review,* 6, 1981, 419-30.

51. G. Hofstede, "Motivation, Leadership, and Organization: Do American Theories Apply Abroad?" *Organizational Dynamics,* Summer 1980, 55.

52. A. S. Smith and A. P. Houser, *Personnel Management* (Reading, Mass.: Addison-Wesley, 1986).

53. H. Dawley, "Friendly Makeover Completed: Company Moves Ailing Chain in New Direction—Maybe," *Restaurant Business,* April 10, 1992, 36.

54. D. D. McConkey, "Planning for Uncertainty," *Business Horizons,* January/February 1987, 40-43.

55. C. Farkas and P. DeBacker, *Maximum Leadership.*

56. "Revco: It's Great to Be Alive, Sort Of," *Business Week,* May 13, 1996, 46.

57. L. V. Gerstner, "Can Strategic Planning Payoff?" in *Perspectives on Strategic Marketing Management* (Boston: Allyn & Bacon, 1980).

58. "Strategic Planning Is Back," *Business Week,* August 25, 1996, 25-30.

59. J. Rosenzweig, F. Kast, and T. R. Mitchell, *The Frank and Ernest Manager* (Los Altos, Calif.: Crisp Publications, 1991).

60. See, for example, J. P. Fernandez and M. Barr, *The Diversity Advantage: How American Business Can Outperform Japanese and European Companies in the Global Marketplace* (New York: Lexington Books, 1993), M. D. Gentile, ed., *Differences That Work: Organizational Ex-*

cellence through Diversity (Boston: Harvard Business School Press, 1994).

61. See, for example, E. DeBono, *Six Thinking Hats* (Boston: Little Brown, 1985); K. Albrecht, *Brain Power: Learn to Improve Your Thinking Skills* (Englewood Cliffs, N.J.: Prentice-Hall, 1990).

62. J. Martin, "Business Planning: The Gap between Theory and Practice," *Long Range Planning,* 1979, 48.

Strategic Planning in a Global Environment

■ CHAPTER OVERVIEW

The development of effective strategy is essential for survival in today's business world. Organizations don't just happen to be successful—rather they develop and implement strategies that are designed to ensure their long-term success. Through strategic planning, managers initiate the actions necessary to get the organization from where it is to where it wants to be. Developing a competitive advantage is the primary purpose of the strategic planning process.

This chapter examines strategic planning as a managerial process. This process involves four primary activities: (1) strategic analysis, (2) strategy formulation, (3) strategy implementation, and (4) strategic control. Special emphasis is given to strategic planning and strategy as a competitive tool for contemporary organizations operating in an increasingly competitive global environment.

■ LEARNING OBJECTIVES

When you have finished studying this chapter, you should be able to:

- Define strategic planning and describe its purpose and benefits.
- Describe strategic analysis as a part of the strategic planning process.
- Discuss how strategy is formulated at the corporate and business levels.
- Describe strategy in terms of grand strategy, generic strategy, and international strategy.
- Explain the role of strategy implementation in the strategic planning process.
- Describe strategic control systems.
- Explain how advances in information technology have affected strategic planning.
- Discuss how tomorrow's manager can achieve success through strategic planning.

C   H   A   P   T   E

Whirlpool: Achieving a Global Competitive Advantage

Whirlpool entered the decade of the 1990s as a highly successful domestic company. With a dominant market share in the United States, the company had provided strong returns to its stockholders for many years. But CEO David Whitwam saw clouds on the horizon. Whirlpool's success was in a slow-growth, mature industry dominated by a few large players—General Electric, Maytag, Frigidaire, and Whirlpool. Together, these four companies accounted for 90 percent of the 40 million appliances sold each year in the United States. The four competitors slugged it out based on price year after year, looking for places to squeeze out costs and improve the margins ever so slightly. Appliances had become a slow-growth, low-margin business.

Recognizing the problems in the industry, the leaders at Whirlpool considered a number of strategic alternatives for the future. These alternatives included acquisitions in the United States, financial restructuring, diversification, and international expansion. As they considered the options, they concluded that targeting international markets was the best alternative. While the market for appliances in the United States was growing only at about 2 to 3 percent annually, the markets in other parts of the world were growing at 7 to 8 percent per year. Further, there were indications that the appliance preferences of consumers around the world were beginning to converge, providing an opportunity for standardizing product features. The closer Whirlpool leaders looked, the more they thought, "This is becoming a global industry. One of these days someone is going to figure that out and build lots of competitive advantage. That someone should be us."

Easily said . . . not as easily done. Becoming a global competitor would require a well-developed strategy. Developing and implementing that strategy was the managerial challenge at Whirlpool for the decade of the 1990s.[1]

INTRODUCTION

One might not expect to find a global pioneer in the seemingly stable and traditional market for dishwashers, refrigerators, and washing machines. In fact, as of 1995, the appliance industry did not yet appear to be fully "globalized" in the true sense of the word. Yet David Whitwam, CEO of Whirlpool, felt certain that appliances would eventually become a global business. Whitwam was committed to putting Whirlpool out in front and shaping the globalization of the industry rather than waiting for the competitors to make it happen. Doing so would require a thorough analysis of the global marketplace and the development of a comprehensive strategic plan for penetrating specific international markets.

Organizational strategy has been a topic of great interest for academics and practitioners for the last several decades.[2] Few managerial topics have received more attention in recent years than strategic planning. Effective strategic planning has been touted as a key solution to the reactive behavior that has characterized many U.S. corporations during the last several decades. In fact, most experts would agree that achieving a long-term competitive advantage in the business environment of the 21st century requires highly effective strategy.[3]

In this chapter, we examine the process of strategic planning as well as the result of that process: the strategic plan. Special attention is given to each of the four stages of the strategic planning process—strategic analysis, strategy formulation, strategy implementation, and strategic control. We will also explore how strategy can serve as a tool for meeting the business challenges of the 21st century.

THE IMPORTANCE OF STRATEGIC PLANNING ▬▬▬▬▬

As you may recall from Chapter 4, **strategic planning** is the process by which an organization makes decisions and takes actions that affect its long-run performance. A **strategic plan** is the output of the strategic planning process.[4] An organization's strategic plan provides direction by defining its strategic approach to business.[5]

Central to the concept of strategic planning is the notion of competitive advantage. As we noted in Chapter 4, the fundamental purpose of strategic planning is to move the organization from where it is to where it wants to be and, in the process, to develop a sustainable competitive advantage in its industry. Through strategic planning, managers develop strategies for achieving a competitive advantage over other organizations in their industry.

Yet today many experts question the ability of any organization to develop a *sustainable* competitive advantage. In fact, most would agree that in today's rapidly changing business environment, successful organizations must continually redefine their competitive advantage. Products and services are only temporary solutions to customers' problems; eventually someone always comes up with a better solution. Organizations that focus on finding the better solution will be those that maintain their competitive advantage. Doing so requires effective strategic planning throughout the ranks of the organization.

THE BENEFITS OF STRATEGIC PLANNING

Strategic planning requires a great deal of managerial time, energy, and commitment. To justify the associated costs, strategic planning must also produce tangible benefits.[6] Research suggests that the benefits of strategic planning are both economic and behavioral.[7]

From an economic perspective, a number of studies suggest that organizations that plan strategically outperform those that do not. Researchers have examined organizations in such industries as petroleum, food, drugs, steel, chemicals, and machinery and have focused on a variety of financial measures including return on investment, return on equity, and earnings per share. Their findings suggest that there are financial benefits associated with strategic planning.

The process of strategic planning can also produce behavioral benefits. Since effective planning requires the involvement of a broad base of organizational members, the benefits associated with participatory management are typically associated with strategic planning. These include:

- An increased likelihood of identifying organizational and environmental conditions that may create problems in the long run.
- Better decisions as a result of the group decision-making process.
- More successful implementation of the organization's strategy because organizational members who participated in the planning process understand the plan and are more willing to change.[8]

Given the potential benefits of strategic planning and the potential costs of the failure to plan, most organizations recognize that strategic planning is essential. In fact, many organizations stress that being a strategist is an important part of being a manager.[9]

STRATEGIC PLANNING AS A PROCESS

Strategic planning can be thought of as a process.[10] Figure 5.1 illustrates a process-driven strategic planning model that is simple, straightforward, and applicable to a wide variety of organizational situations. While the level of so-

Strategic planning
The process by which an organization makes decisions and takes actions to enhance its long-run performance.

Strategic plan
A plan that identifies the markets in which an organization competes, as well as the ways in which it competes in those markets.

phistication and formality of the strategic planning process will differ among organizations, the process itself should be similar across all organizations.[11]

As Figure 5.1 indicates, the strategic planning process is carried out in four stages, each of which raises an important question that must be addressed when developing a strategic plan.[12] Further, the feedback lines in the model suggest that the strategic planning process is interactive and self-renewing, continually evolving as changes in the business environment create a need for revised strategic plans.[13]

Strategic analysis

An assessment of the internal and external conditions of the firm.

The **strategic analysis** phase of the strategic planning process addresses the question, "What is the current position of the organization?" Accordingly, the internal and external conditions faced by the organization are evaluated during this phase of the process. The information gathered during strategic analysis serves as a foundation for the formulation of the organization's strategic plan.

Strategy formulation

The establishment of strategic goals for the organization and the development of corporate- and business-level strategies.

Strategy formulation answers the question, "Where does the firm want to be?" The intent of strategy formulation is to establish a mission, goals, and overall strategic direction for the organization. Corporate and business strategies are developed with the intention of bridging the gap between the current and desired position of the organization.

Strategy implementation

The actions required to ensure that the corporate- and business-level strategy of the organization is put into place.

Strategy implementation answers the question, "How can the organization get to where it wants to be?" This phase of the process involves doing whatever is necessary to ensure that the strategy of the organization is implemented effectively. Functional strategies are developed during the strategy implementation stage and organizational systems are adapted and modified to support the implementation of the organization's strategy.

Strategic control

The methods by which the performance of the organization is monitored.

The final stage of the strategic planning process, **strategic control,** answers the question, "How will the organization know when it has arrived?" This phase of strategic planning is designed to monitor the organization's progress toward implementing its plans and achieving its goals. Strategic control mechanisms identify deviations between actual and planned results so that managers can make the adjustments necessary to ensure that organizational goals can be achieved in the long term.[14]

The strategic planning process is the focus of the remainder of this chapter. The specific activities associated with each stage of the process are discussed in the following sections.

STRATEGIC ANALYSIS: ASSESSMENT IN A GLOBAL ENVIRONMENT

The first stage of the strategic planning process is strategic analysis. The purpose of strategic analysis is to evaluate the present situation of the organization.[15] Until you understand the current position of the organization, it is im-

FIGURE 5 1

The process of strategic planning

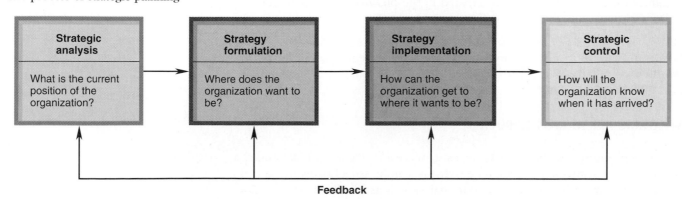

Feedback

possible to determine where it could and should be.[16] Strategic analysis requires two primary activities: (1) internal analysis and (2) environmental analysis.

CONDUCTING AN INTERNAL ANALYSIS

Strategic analysis requires a thorough evaluation of the internal operations of the organization. The purpose of internal analysis is to identify assets, resources, skills, and processes that represent either strengths or weaknesses for the organization. *Strengths* are aspects of the organization's operations that represent potential competitive advantages or distinctive competencies,[17] while *weaknesses* are areas that are in need of improvement.

Several areas of the organization's operations should be examined in an internal analysis. Key areas to be assessed include the marketing, financial, research and development, production operations, and general management capabilities of the organization. These areas are typically evaluated in terms of the extent to which they support the competitive advantage sought by the organization. Table 5.1 lists a number of variables in each key area that should be evaluated when conducting an internal analysis.[18]

One of the most important aspects of an organization's internal environment is its human resources. In fact, some management scholars suggest that the only thing that truly distinguishes one organization from another is its people. The human resources of the organization, from top management down to frontline workers, are what determine the ability of the organization to achieve a competitive advantage in its industry. The quality of an organization will never exceed the quality of the people within the organization. Southwest Airlines, Wal-Mart, and Tyson Foods are examples of organizations that view their human resources to be their most significant competitive strength. None of these companies enjoy a real advantage over their competitors—they simply utilize the power of their work force more fully than their competitors.[19]

TABLE 5.1   Internal organizational factors

MARKETING CAPABILITIES	FINANCIAL CAPABILITIES	GENERAL MANAGEMENT CAPABILITIES	RESEARCH AND DEVELOPMENT CAPABILITIES	PRODUCTION AND OPERATIONS CAPABILITIES
Product mix	Liquidity	Employee relations	Basic and applied product research competencies	Purchasing system
Market share position	Leverage	Organizational structure		Capacity (plant & equipment)
Market research capabilities	Efficiency/asset utilization	Compensation system	Process research competencies	Location of facilities
Distribution systems	Profitability	Rules, policies, and procedures	Physical facilities (i.e., laboratory)	Inventory management system
Sales organizations	Earnings per share	Quality of top management	Organization of R & D unit	Maintenance system
Customer goodwill, and brand loyalty	Trend analysis	Planning capabilities	Communication within the organization	Use of economies of scale
Promotion strategies			Quality of technological forecasting	Use of modern technologies (i.e., robotics)
Pricing strategies			Success ratio of new product innovations to products brought to market	

SOURCE: J. Montanari, C. Morgan, and J. Bracker, *Strategic Management: A Choice Approach* (Chicago: Dryden Press, 1990), 81–85.

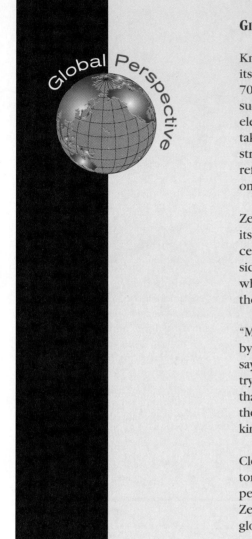

GILLETTE: INTERNATIONAL MANAGERIAL TALENT IS THE KEY TO THE FUTURE

Known best for its stalwart blade business, Gillette is well recognized for its success both at home and abroad. While razor blades make up about 70 percent of the company's profits, Gillette also distributes products such as Paper Mate and Waterman pens, Liquid Paper, Right Guard, Braun electric shavers, and Oral-B toothbrushes. After battling off four hostile takeover attempts in the late 1980s, CEO Al Zeien decided to follow a strategy that made the company as invulnerable as possible. The company refocused its efforts on global growth. The objective—to be the number one player in every product and market in which it competes.

Zeien believes that the company's success hinges on its ability to expand its corps of experienced international managers. At present, about 70 percent of Gillette's $6 billion annual revenues are generated from sales outside the United States. Yet only about 350 of Gillette's employees are what he would consider international managers, willing to move around the world for the corporation.

"More than any other factor, our growth rate in the future will be controlled by our ability to increase the number of expatriates from 350 to 700," Zeien says. "It won't be finances that make us grow. It won't be capital. We could try to *hire* the best and the brightest, but it's the *experience* with Gillette that we need. About half of our expats [international managers] are now on their fourth country. *That* kind of experience. It takes ten years to make the kind of Gillette manager I'm talking about—ten years at the base."

Clearly Zeien sees international human resources to be a key strategic factor for Gillette's success. That is why he spends a great deal of his time personally identifying and developing international managers. From Zeien's perspective, international management expertise will provide a global competitive advantage for Gillette in the future.[20]

Gillette is another company that considers its human resources to be its key competitive strength—on an international basis. As you read Global Perspective, the CEO of Gillette, Al Zeien, feels that the future success of the company depends upon its ability to recruit, develop, and retain a global work force who can support the company's international strategy. This is why he spends so much of his own time on building and developing a global management team.

Another important human resource issue relates to the increasing diversity in the U.S. work force. Capitalizing on workplace diversity presents a potential strategic advantage for many organizations.[21] Developing a diverse employee base is not about abiding by regulations or meeting organizational quotas. Diversity is not a problem to be solved, but an opportunity to be embraced.[22] To the extent that managers are prepared to capitalize on the breadth of thought and experience that is inherent in a diverse work force, they can formulate more creative strategies and plans.

EVALUATING THE EXTERNAL ENVIRONMENT

The second area to be assessed in a strategic analysis is the external environment of the organization. The purpose of an external analysis is to identify those aspects of the environment that represent either an opportunity or a threat for the organization. *Opportunities* are those environmental trends on which the organization can capitalize and improve its competitive position. External *threats* are conditions that jeopardize the organization's ability to prosper in the long term.

Figure 5.2 illustrates the primary dimensions of a global external environment. The external environment is divided into two major components—the general environment and the task environment. The **general environment** includes environmental forces that are beyond the influence of the organization and over which it has no control. Forces in the **task environment** are within the organization's operating environment and may be influenced to some degree.

General Environment

The general component of an organization's external environment includes economic, sociocultural, technological, and political-legal factors. The analysis must consider the global dimensions of all of these factors as well as their domestic effects. Table 5.2 lists examples of trends in each of these areas that might affect an organization's strategic plans.[23]

Economic Environment   The economic component of the general environment is represented by the general state of both the domestic and the world economy. The health of the domestic economy is reflected by variables such as total gross domestic product (GDP), growth in the GDP, interest rates, the inflation rate, the consumer price index, and unemployment rates. Similar measures can be used to evaluate the world economy. World trade and foreign direct investment trends are also useful for such an analysis.

Although a favorable economic climate generally represents opportunities for growth, this is not the case for all businesses. The alcoholic beverage industry, for example, has traditionally fared well during times of economic downturn. Mobile homes, bologna, and car repair services are other examples of products and services that are in greater demand during poor economic times.

General environment
Those environmental forces that are beyond a firm's influence and over which it has no control.

Task environment
Those environmental forces that are within the firm's operating environment and over which the firm has some degree of control.

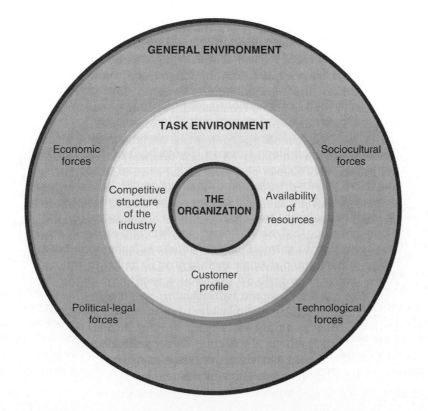

FIGURE 5.2
Dimensions of the global external environment

TABLE 5.2   Sample issues in the general environment

SOCIOCULTURAL	ECONOMIC	TECHNOLOGICAL	POLITICAL-LEGAL
Lifestyle changes	GNP trends	Total federal spending for R & D	Antitrust regulations
Career expectations	Interest rates		Environmental protection laws
Consumer activism	Money supply	Total industry spending for R & D	Tax laws
Rate of family formation	Inflation rates		Special incentives
Growth rate of population	Unemployment levels	Focus of technological efforts	Foreign trade regulations
Regional shifts in population	Wage/price controls	Patent protection	Attitudes toward foreign companies
Life expectancies	Devaluation/revaluation	New products	
Birth rates	Energy availability and cost	New developments in technology transfer from lab to marketplace	Laws on hiring and promotion
	Disposable and discretionary income	Productivity improvements through automation	Stability of government

SOURCE: T. Wheelen and J. D. Hunger, *Strategic Management* (Reading, Mass.: Addison-Wesley, 1990), 100.

Regardless of the direction of the effect, the economy is generally considered to be a strong determinant of the demand for goods and services. Consequently, forecasts of economic activity will influence the strategic plans of most organizations.

Sociocultural Environment   The sociocultural component of the general environment is represented by the attitudes, behavior patterns, and lifestyles of the individuals who ultimately purchase the products or services of the organization. In addition, the analysis must also consider demographic conditions and trends. As these aspects of the sociocultural environment change, so must the strategy of organizations that are affected by such changes.

Although some sociocultural trends cross national boundaries (such as the popularity of jeans among young people), not all developments occur on a global basis. In fact, many aspects of the sociocultural environment are specific to certain nations or groups of nations. Consequently, organizations that operate internationally often must cope with multiple heterogeneous sociocultural environments and therefore must develop strategies to deal with different environmental conditions.

One of the most important sociocultural trends in this country (and others) in the last several decades has been the increasing number of women entering the work force. Consider, for example, the effect of this trend on the demand for such products and services as convenience appliances, professional apparel, child care, and housekeeping services. Further, many businesses have adapted their products and services to respond to the slightly different needs of the female business consumer. For example, briefcases now come in sleeker and lighter designs, women's shoes can be purchased in more sensible styles, and room accommodations with special services for female patrons are available at a number of hotel chains. Even the sporting goods industry has benefited from women becoming more active in exercise. Reebok made its entry into the athletic-shoe business by targeting the women's market that had been overlooked by Nike.[24]

The "graying of America" is a demographic trend that will have significant impact for organizations with products that appeal to an older target market. As the baby boomers slip into their 50s, companies will want to look for ways to meet the needs of this large and aging segment of the population. Campbell Soup, for example, recognizes that older consumers eat more soup than their younger counterparts and are prepared to take advantage of this demographic trend.[25] CBS, which was highlighted in Chapter 4, is refocusing on its traditional market of older viewers—a timely strategy given the maturing of the baby boomers.[26]

Technological Environment   Technological forces are the third component of the general environment. They include changes in technology that affect the way organizations operate or the products and services they provide. To keep abreast of technological trends, many organizations engage in *technology forecasting*. Such forecasts identify trends in technology that require adaptation on the part of the organization.

The success of many organizations is dependent upon their ability to identify and respond to technological changes. IBM, General Motors, and Federal Express are just a few examples of firms that must keep abreast of technological changes if they hope to remain successful in the long term.

One of the most significant technological trends of the last several decades has been the increasing availability and affordability of management information systems. Through these systems, managers have access to information that can improve the way they operate and manage their businesses. The grocery store industry, for example, has been transformed by the introduction of scanner technology. Not only have scanners improved the efficiency of the grocery checkout process, but they also provide important inventory management information to support procurement and warehousing efforts. Grocery stores that were slow to take advantage of such technology were at a competitive disadvantage.

From a more creative perspective, consider how improvements in technology have affected the entertainment industry. Managing for Excellence describes a "digital convergence" of Hollywood and Silicon Valley—the product of which was Disney's blockbuster film *Toy Story*. *Toy Story* is more than just a kid's movie; it is an example of how technology has dramatically changed the economics of animated productions. And who was behind the development of this new technology? None other than Steve Jobs, founder of Apple Computer.

The sociocultural component of the general environment consists of the attitudes, behavior patterns, and lifestyles of the individuals who ultimately purchase products or services. As baby boomers reach age 50, companies will find new ways to meet the needs of this large segment of the population.

© Don Smetzer/Tony Stone Images

TOY STORY: TECHNOLOGY BREATHES NEW LIFE INTO ANIMATION

Managing for Excellence

The decade of the 1990s has brought advancements in technology that have affected nearly every industry in this country. One industry in which such effects are readily apparent is the entertainment industry. Computer technology has, for example, dramatically affected the production efficiency and quality of motion pictures. A recent and impressive product of what some have called the "digital convergence" of Hollywood and Silicon Valley is the Disney hit movie *Toy Story*.

Toy Story is a spectacular 3-D phenomenon that makes the animated productions of days gone by look antiquated and archaic. The technology that has breathed new life into traditional animated productions was developed by Pixar, a Bay Area computer graphics company founded by none other than Steve Jobs, the original entrepreneur behind Apple Computer. Pixar's animation technology is a cinematic milestone in that it makes possible for the first time the stockpiling of digital characters, sets, props, and even scenes. Stored in the computer, they can be used over and over again for other entertainment purposes such as sequel films, TV shows, and CD-ROM games. The technology developed by Pixar has so reduced the manual labor required for animation that the cost of creating animated products has fallen dramatically.

What does that mean for us as consumers? *Toy Story II,* perhaps?

Entrepreneurial Approach	

DEREGULATION IN THE EUROPEAN UNION CREATES OPPORTUNITIES FOR AIRLINE START-UPS

With the planned integration of Western Europe, many firms are looking for opportunities that might arise as national boundaries become less rigid. It seems that there are a number of such opportunities emerging as the airline industry in Europe moves toward full deregulation.

According to the planned deregulation, as of April 1, 1997, any European Union carrier can fly anywhere in the European Union irrespective of its nationality. In response to these changes, a number of startup airlines are taking to the skies. In Italy, for example, upstart Air One is causing big trouble for national carrier Alitalia. Air One has driven prices down so far that Alitalia is scrambling to sell seats on its planes. Alitalia will soon face another ambitious startup named Alpi Eagles, backed in part by the Benetton clothing family. Similar situations are playing out in Germany, France, and Britain.

The result is sure to be downward pressure on ticket prices all across Europe. In fact, American Express predicts that prices on some major national routes such as Paris-Marseilles and Berlin-Munich will fall by as much as 33 percent over the next couple of years. "Consumers are going to save billions of dollars," predicts Bob Harrell, airline consultant to American Express.

The question remains as to whether or not these new airline ventures will survive and prosper in the long term. If the deregulation experience of the U.S. airline industry is any indication, few of these new airlines will be around in five years. But one thing is for sure—as long as they're around, the competitive battle in the skies over Europe is going to get hotter and hotter.[27]

Political-Legal Environment   The final component of an organization's general environment is its political-legal environment. The political-legal environment includes the regulatory parameters within which the organization must operate. Tax policy, trade regulations, minimum-wage legislation, and pollution standards are just a few kinds of political-legal issues that can affect the strategic plans of an organization. Consider, for example, the bill recently signed by President Clinton that raises the minimum wage in the United States. How do you think McDonald's and other fast-food restaurants will be affected by such an increase? These companies will likely look for ways to maximize the efficiency of their human resources. In addition, new pricing strategies might be necessary in light of increased labor costs.

Like the sociocultural environment, the political-legal environment often varies dramatically from nation to nation. As a consequence, organizations that operate internationally must develop a strategy for dealing with multiple political-legal systems. An excellent example of international political-legal issues can be found in the deregulation of the airline industry in the European Union. Slated for 1997, this change is having a tremendous impact on the strategic plans of European airlines such as Germany's Lufthansa, Italy's Alitalia, and Great Britain's British Airways. In fact, as is described in Entrepreneurial Approach, deregulation is leading to the establishment of new airline ventures that are driving ticket prices down across Europe.

Task Environment

In addition to general environmental issues, organizations must also be aware of trends in the task environment. Recall that these forces are within the organization's operating arena, and may be influenced to some degree by the organization. Critical task environmental variables include the competition in an industry, the profiles of the targeted customer base, and the availability of resources.

Competition   Over the last decade, competition has been heating up across the board. In fact, some have gone so far as to use the term *hypercompetition* to describe the competitive environment of the 1990s.[28] In such an environment, success goes to organizations that have a clear understanding of the mission, strategies and competitive advantages of their competitors.[29] This is why competitive analysis is so important in today's business environment.

Consider, for example, the degree of competitive analysis that takes place between Coke and Pepsi, Burger King and McDonald's, or Nike and Reebok. These companies make it their business to know as much about their competitors as they know about themselves. In doing so, they are better able to anticipate what their competitors might do and how it might influence the marketplace.

In assessing the competition in a given industry, it is important to evaluate both individual competitors and the way they interact. Where possible, competitors should be evaluated using a common set of characteristics. For example, each competitor might be assessed in light of its market share, marketing strategy, product mix, product quality, and financial strength. Such information provides managers with a better understanding of how their organization compares to its competitors, as well as with a general sense of the roles that each plays within the industry. One can rest assured that IBM, Compaq, Apple, and Hewlett-Packard maintain sophisticated systems for tracking and evaluating the strategic moves of all the competitors in the computer industry.

Competitive analysis has become increasingly complex as more and more industries have globalized. Some organizations simply overlook important international competitors because they are "hard to see."[30] Even if such competitors are easily identified, it is often difficult to obtain information about them, as few international firms are subject to the same disclosure regulations as U.S. companies. Nevertheless, competitive analysis is an essential aspect of the strategic planning process, and managers must commit the time and energy necessary to gain a clear understanding of their competitors both domestically and globally.

Customer Profiles   Customer profiles must also be assessed as part of the strategic analysis. At a time when the "the customer is king" philosophy has been embraced by organizations across the globe, and a quality orientation has become essential to the success of most organizations, it is imperative to have an in-depth understanding of the characteristics, needs, and expectations of the organization's customers.

An organization's customer may be another firm in the production chain, or it may be the ultimate consumer. When an organization's customers are mainly industrial or wholesale clients, it needs information about the types of organizations that are using its products and services, their specific needs and expectations, their financial health, and the extent to which they are dependent upon the organization's products and services.

When an organization's customers are consumers, their demographic and psychographic characteristics, as well as their specific needs and expectations, are the most relevant dimensions for analysis. Relevant demographic characteristics include average age, income levels, gender, and marital status. Psychographic characteristics relating to the consumer's lifestyle and personality may also be critical determinants of buying behavior.

American Express has learned the hard way that understanding your customer is essential for success in fast-changing, highly competitive markets. The company seemed to turn a deaf ear to consumers who wanted more innovative product features and retailers who wanted better rates. As a result, American Express lost market share to its two largest competitors, MasterCard and

Visa, and is now scrambling to develop new products that are more attractive to today's demanding consumers.[31]

Again, as with competitive analysis, the globalization of the marketplace has complicated the process of customer analysis. With customers spread across the globe, the relevant dimensions for analysis are more difficult to identify, evaluate, and predict. Therefore, managers in international organizations must take special care to ensure that they have a clear understanding of their customers in each national market served.

Resource Availability   Resource availability is the final component of the organization's task environment. The term *resource* can be applied to a broad range of inputs and may refer to raw materials, personnel or labor, and capital. To the extent that high-quality, low-cost resources are available to the organization, opportunities exist to create marketable products or services. When any resource is constrained, the organization faces a threat to its operations. Thus, strategic plans will be affected by the availability of the resources needed both domestically and globally, to produce goods and services.

Consider, for example, the labor strife experienced by the National Basketball Association just prior to beginning the 1996 season. A group of star players, including Michael Jordan and Patrick Ewing, tried to decertify their own union to block a new contract deal. This labor resource problem created a real threat to the viability of the organization. Had NBA commissioner David Stern not been able to negotiate a deal that was acceptable to the players, the NBA would have had to delay the start of the season, much to the grave disappointment of owners and fans alike.[32]

Strategic analysis provides important information about the organization's existing situation. Recall that the purpose of this stage of the strategic planning process is to answer the question, "What is the current position of the organization?" By examining the internal and external environment of the organization, this question can be answered and the organization can begin to define its competitive advantage.

It is important to remember, however, that in rapidly changing business environments, the results of a strategic analysis can change quickly. For example, as we noted earlier, internal strengths form the basis of competitive advantage for most firms. But changes in external environmental conditions can affect the value of any particular organizational strength. Consider, for example, how General Electric's capabilities in transistor technology was devalued with the introduction of semiconductors; how American Airlines's relationship with the Civil Aeronautics Board became less valuable when the airline industry was deregulated; and how the advent and growth of the personal computer devalued IBM's capability in the mainframe computer business. While internal strengths are clearly an important source of competitive advantage, organizations must be sensitive to the ways in which changing external environmental conditions might affect the relative value of any particular strength.[33]

STRATEGY FORMULATION: ACHIEVING A COMPETITIVE ADVANTAGE

Once the strategic analysis is completed and the current position of the organization has been assessed, corporate and business strategy can be formulated. Recall that strategy formulation addresses the question, "Where does the organization want to be?" Answering that question requires: (1) establishing the mission of the organization, (2) setting strategic goals, (3) identifying strategic alternatives, and (4) evaluating and choosing the strategy that provides a competitive advantage and optimizes the performance of the organization in the long term.

ESTABLISHING AN ORGANIZATIONAL MISSION

Based on the information derived from the strategic analysis, an organizational mission can be developed. An **organizational mission** defines the reason(s) for which the organization exists and provides strategic direction for the members of the organization.[34] It is a statement of the overall purpose of the organization and describes the attributes that distinguish it from other organizations of its type.[35]

A mission statement should be more than words on a piece of paper. It should be a living, breathing document that provides both information and inspiration for the members of the organization. Such documents should reflect the strategic vision of the leaders of the organization with regard to what the organization is and what it can become. A mission statement provides focus for the organization by getting its members to work together in the pursuit of common goals.[36]

Although mission statements will vary greatly among firms, every mission statement should describe three primary aspects of the organization: (1) its primary products or services, (2) its distinctive competitive advantage(s), and (3) its overall strategy for ensuring long-term success. This information serves as the foundation upon which corporate and business strategy is built. If, for example, the mission of your university is to meet the educational needs of individuals in your state by offering innovative programs in the arts, science, business, engineering, and health care, the strategy of the university should be developed to fulfill that mission.

Figure 5.3 contains the mission statements for Whirlpool.[37] As you can see in the mission statement, Whirlpool considers their customer to be the global marketplace. Now that you have an understanding of how important a mission statement can be, evaluate the mission statement of an organization with which you are familiar, as explained in Meeting the Challenge.

Organizational mission
The reasons for which the organization exists; it provides strategic direction for the members of the organization.

SETTING STRATEGIC GOALS

Once the mission of the organization has been developed, strategic goals can be established. **Strategic goals** are very broad statements of the results that an organization wishes to achieve in the long term. Such goals relate to the mission of the organization and specify the level of performance that it desires to achieve.

Most organizations establish their goals to reflect their perception of success. In many organizations, managers look to profit as an indicator of success, and maximizing profit becomes their primary strategic goal. However, Peter Drucker, a prominent management theorist, warns against focusing solely on profit as a measure of success. He suggests that a preoccupation with profits alone can lead to short-term thinking and reactive management behavior. Rather, success should be operationalized more broadly and should include such things as market standing, innovation, productivity, physical and financial resources, profitability, managerial performance and development, worker performance and attitudes, and public responsibility.[38]

Strategic goals
The results that an organization seeks to achieve in the long-term.

Whirlpool, in its chosen lines of business, will grow with new opportunities and be the leader in an ever-changing global market. We will be driven by our commitment to continuous quality improvement and to exceeding all of our customers' expectations. We will gain competitive advantage through this, and by building on our existing strengths and developing new competencies. We will be market-driven, efficient and profitable. Our success will make Whirlpool a company that worldwide customers, employees and other stakeholders can depend on.

FIGURE 5.3
Whirlpool corporation mission statement

SOURCE: J. Abrahams, *The Mission Statement Book: 301 Corporate Mission Statements from America's Top Companies* (Berkeley, CA: Ten Speed Press, 1995), p. 518.

Meeting the Challenge

MAKING A MISSION STATEMENT WORK

The following exercise can help you develop your skills at evaluating mission statements. Choose a mission statement to evaluate from an organization in which you have an interest. Evaluate the mission statement by responding to each of the following questions. Use a scale of 1 (not at all) to 5 (to a high degree) to indicate how well the mission statement meets each of the criteria. Place the number that corresponds to your response on the line to the left of each statement.

1._____ To what degree does the mission statement discuss the organization's primary products or services?

2._____ To what degree does the mission statement consider the organization's competitive advantage(s)?

3._____ To what degree does the mission statement describe the attributes of the organization that distinguish it from others of its type?

4._____ To what degree does the mission statement reflect the strategic vision of the organization's leaders?

5._____ To what degree does the mission statement discuss the organization's overall strategy for long-term success?

_____ Total

Add the numbers to obtain the total score. Scores can range from a low of 5 to a high of 25. If the mission statement you examined scored lower than 20, how would you revise the statement so that it would meet the criteria of an effective mission?

Further, it is important to recognize that strategic success can vary greatly across organizations and between industries. Two organizations may measure and evaluate success in dramatically different ways. For example, a growth-oriented firm such as Blockbuster Video may stress market share gains, whereas an organization that operates in a mature, slow-growth industry, such as General Foods, may place its emphasis on maximizing bottom-line profitability.

Several characteristics are associated with effective strategic goals. Because the goals established during the planning process serve as a benchmark by which the organization will eventually evaluate its performance, it is important that they be: (1) specific, (2) measurable, (3) time linked, and (4) realistic, but challenging. Table 5.3 provides some guidance on how to develop goals that meet these criteria.

IDENTIFYING STRATEGIC ALTERNATIVES

The third stage of the strategy formulation process involves identifying strategic alternatives. These alternatives should be developed in light of the strengths, weaknesses, opportunities, and threats facing the organization, its mission, and its strategic goals. Strategic alternatives should focus on optimizing organizational performance in the long term.[39]

Strategy can be defined in a variety of ways. The following sections describe three ways to define strategic alternatives.

Grand Strategy

Many organizations define their strategic alternatives in terms of grand strategies. A **grand strategy** is a comprehensive, general approach for achieving the

Grand strategy
A comprehensive, general approach for achieving the strategic goals of an organization.

TABLE 5.3   Criteria for effective goals

Effective goals should meet the following criteria:

- *Specific goals* relate to a particular and easily defined performance area. For example, setting a goal of increasing productivity by 40 percent is not meaningful if "productivity" is not defined. Will productivity be measured by sales per employee? Sales per square foot? Cost per unit? Effective goals must be specific as to what will be evaluated.
- *Measurable goals* are usually expressed in quantitative terms. For example, increasing sales by 20 percent and reducing costs by 15 percent are examples of quantitative goals. Sometimes, however, it is necessary to express goals in qualitative terms. For example, an organization might establish a goal of being more socially responsive. While this goal cannot be expressed quantitatively, it is an important qualitative goal against which the organization will eventually evaluate its performance. Where possible, however, goals should be established in clearly measurable, quantitative terms.
- *Time-linked goals* are to be achieved within a specified time period. For example, an organization might establish a goal of increasing market share by 3 percent by 1998. Because the goal is time linked, it provides the organization with a deadline for achieving its target performance.
- *Realistic, but challenging goals* provide a challenge for those who must meet them, but the challenge should not be so great that the goal cannot be achieved. People don't strive to achieve goals that are set unrealistically high. On the other hand, a goal that is set too low is not motivating. Finding the balance between challenge and realism is important in setting goals.

strategic goals of an organization.[40] Grand strategies, which can be applied at both the corporate and business levels, fall into three broad categories: stability, growth, and retrenchment strategies.

Stability Strategies   Stability strategies are intended to ensure continuity in the operations and performance of the organization. At the corporate level, stability implies that the organization will remain in the same line(s) of business as it has in the past. No new businesses are added; no businesses are eliminated. The organization maintains a stable and unchanged corporate portfolio. Wendy's is an example of a firm that began as and continues to be a chain of fast-food restaurants. Like Wendy's, Wrigley Gum has pursued a strategy of stability from inception, focusing only on gum products.

At the business level, stability strategies require very little, if any, change in the organization's product, service, or market focus. Organizations that pursue stability strategies continue to offer the same products and services to the same target markets as in the past. They may, however, attempt to capture a larger share of their existing market through market penetration.

Growth Strategies   Growth strategies are designed to increase the sales and profits of the organization. At the corporate level, growth strategies imply the addition of one or more new businesses to the corporate portfolio. This may be accomplished by adding a business that has synergistic potential with an existing business unit or by adding a business that is unrelated to the firm's existing businesses. General Mills, for

Wendy's is a firm that began as and continues to be a chain of fast-food restaurants, representing a corporate strategy of stability. Such a strategy requires little, if any, change in the organization's product, service, or market focus.
© Mark Richards/PhotoEdit

example, at one time pursued an aggressive strategy of growth at the corporate level. The company acquired and developed several businesses that were unrelated to its core food-products business (for example, Monet Jewelry and Talbots mail order) as well as several restaurants that were synergistically related (for example, Red Lobster, Darryl's, and Casa Gallardo).

At the business level, growth strategies involve the development of new products for new or existing markets or the entry into new markets with existing products. The purpose of growth strategies is to increase the sales and profits of the organization in the long term and to position the organization as a market leader within its industry.

In many cases, growth strategies focus on being innovative, seeking out new opportunities, and taking risks. Such strategies are suitable for organizations that operate in dynamic, growing environments where creativity and organizational responsiveness are often more important than efficiency. Sony is an example of a firm that offers a steady stream of innovative product alternatives—many of them displace the firm's existing products, but contribute to the organization's growth in sales and profits.

Owens Corning is another company that has maintained its leadership position in its industry by pursuing growth strategies based on innovation. Most recently, the company developed an innovative new Fiberglas product, Miraflex, that will generate $20 million in sales during its first year on the market and $500 million in year five.

Retrenchment Strategies   The purpose of a retrenchment strategy is to reverse negative sales and profitability trends. At the corporate level, retrenchment often requires the elimination of one or more business units either through divestment (the sale of the unit as an ongoing concern) or through liquidation (the sale of assets of the business unit). The cash generated from the elimination of a business unit is often used to acquire other business units, build more promising units, or reduce corporate debt.

At the business level, retrenchment strategy focuses on streamlining the operations of the organization by reducing costs and assets. Such reductions may require plant closings, the sale of plants and equipment, spending cuts, or a reduction in the work force of the organization. Further, new systems, processes, and procedures must be designed to support the new, leaner organization. If the retrenchment strategy is successful, stability or growth strategies may be considered in the long term.

In recent years, we have seen many firms pursuing retrenchment strategies, including one-time giants Kodak, IBM, General Motors, Sears, and Digital.[41] Kodak's turnaround story is particularly interesting, as it required both corporate- and business-level turnaround strategies. Appointed in December 1993, Kodak's CEO, Bob Fisher, inherited a poorly performing company with a very dispirited work force. The company had undergone a total of five restructurings in the previous three years—restructurings that had destroyed 40,000 jobs. In 1996, after selling off unrelated businesses acquired during earlier corporate diversification strategies, instituting improvements in quality and efficiency, and investing in new product development, the company is back on track and profitable once again.

Generic Strategy

While no two strategies are exactly alike, the strategies of some organizations do have common characteristics. Michael Porter, a well-known Harvard professor of industrial economics, has identified three **generic strategies** that describe the strategy of most organizations.[42] Generic strategies reflect the primary way in which an organization competes in its market. They are commonly referred to as: (1) cost leadership, (2) differentiation, and (3) focus.

Generic strategies
The fundamental way in which an organization competes in the marketplace.

Porter defines the generic strategies along two primary dimensions—the competitive advantage provided by the strategy and the competitive scope of the strategy. Competitive advantage is achieved by offering customers superior value either through a lower price or through a differentiated product or service that justifies a higher price. Competitive scope refers to the breadth of the market targeted by the organization. Some organizations target their products and services to very broad markets, while others identify a relatively narrow segment of the market.

The matrix in Figure 5.4 identifies the three generic strategies based on competitive advantage and competitive scope.[43] As you will note, the focus strategy has been broken into two separate strategies depending on whether the competitive advantage sought is cost leadership or differentiation.

Cost Leadership   Organizations that pursue a **cost leadership strategy** compete on the basis of price. To do so, the organization must be highly efficient so that it can achieve a low-cost position in the industry. Costs may be minimized by maximizing capacity utilization, achieving size advantages (economies of scale), capitalizing on technology improvements, or employing a more experienced work force.

Numerous organizations and products have succeeded based on cost leadership. Examples include Bic pens, Timex watches, Budget motels, and Food Lion grocery stores. Each has concentrated on maximizing the efficiency of its production and delivery systems, achieving a lower cost structure than its competitors, and passing the benefit of lower costs on to the consumer in the form of lower prices.

Differentiation   Organizations that pursue a **differentiation strategy** compete by offering products or services that are differentiated from those of their competitors in some way. The company charges a higher price based on the differentiated product or service feature. Distinctive characteristics may include exceptional customer service, quality, dependability, availability, innovation, or image.

Many organizations pursue a differentiation strategy. Examples of products that have succeeded through such a strategy include Cross pens, Seiko watches, and Maytag appliances. Consider Volvo cars for a moment. What is the differentiating characteristic of these vehicles? Has this differentiation strategy been successful for Volvo?

Cost leadership strategy
A strategy for competing on the basis of price.

Differentiation strategy
A strategy for competing by offering products or services that are differentiated from those of competitors.

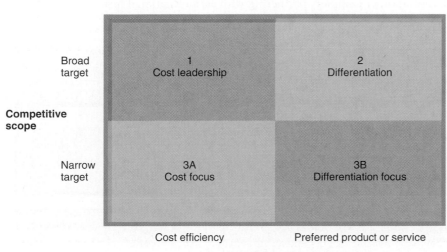

FIGURE 5.4

Generic strategies matrix

SOURCE: Adapted with permission of The Free Press, a Division of Simon & Schuster from *Competitive Advantage: Creating and Sustaining Superior Performance* by Michael E. Porter. Copyright © 1985 by Michael E. Porter.

Focus strategy
A strategy for competing by targeting a specific and narrow segment of the market.

Focus   The final generic strategy identified by Porter is a focus strategy. A **focus strategy** occurs when an organization targets a specific, narrow segment of the market and thereby avoids competing with other competitors that target a broader segment of the market. Further, companies that pursue a focus strategy may compete in their niche market with either a cost leadership or a differentiation strategy. Therefore, the focus strategy appears in two boxes of the matrix in Figure 5.4. If the market segment is very narrow and competition is extremely limited, however, neither competitive advantage may be necessary.

Examples of products that have succeeded based on a focus strategy include BMW motorcycles, A&W root beer, and White Castle hamburgers. A prime example of an organization that has used such a strategy within the grocery store industry is Fiesta Mart, a Texas-based grocery store chain that caters to Hispanic consumers.

International Strategy

Organizations choose to engage in international business activity for a variety of reasons.[44] Many are trying to improve production efficiency by taking advantage of lower labor costs or better access to raw material. Others may be seeking new market opportunities. Regardless of the motive, an organization that pursues an international strategy must make decisions about both its mode of entry into international markets and the focus of its strategy.

Mode of Entry   An organization can enter an international market in several different ways. Each mode of entry offers certain advantages and disadvantages and requires a different level of commitment. Commitment may be thought of as a loss of flexibility to withdraw from a market. In other words, once a strategic decision has been made to enter a particular international market, the entry mode selected will determine how easily the organization can rescind its decision and cease operations in that market.

As illustrated in Figure 5.5, entry modes range from informal agreements with export management companies, to contractual obligations with overseas licensees, contractors, or franchisors, to actual investment in foreign assets via strategic alliances or wholly owned subsidiaries. Obviously, the more attractive the market identified and the more experience the organization has with international business activities, the more willing management may be to make a strong commitment to that market.

Strategic alliances, in particular, seem to be one of the most attractive methods for moving into the international marketplace today. Everywhere you turn, you see another company partnering with an international firm to gain entrance

FIGURE 5.5
International strategies and commitment

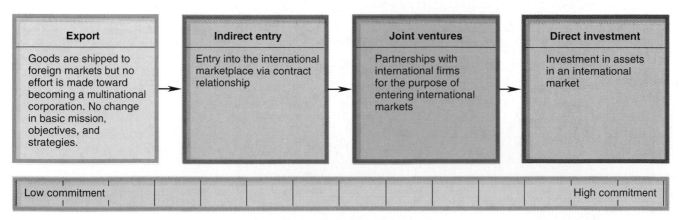

Degree of commitment

to their national market. For example, General Motors has built a worldwide presence through strategic alliances with companies across the globe; Sterling Drug partnered with Sanofi, a French pharmaceutical company, to gain access to distribution channels in Europe; and AT&T joined with Italy's Italtel to build a telecommunications infrastructure to support the economic development of that country.

Yet research shows that many international strategic alliances fail. Consider for example, the strategic alliance between Northwest Airlines in the United States and KLM in The Netherlands. While the alliance is actually reasonably profitable, the culture clash between the partners has resulted in such severe problems that the partnership will undoubtedly be dissolved in the near future.[45]

Multidomestic versus Global Strategic Focus A second dimension of international strategy relates to the focus of the strategy, which may be either multidomestic or global. An organization pursues a **multidomestic strategy** when it operates in multiple international markets and follows an independent strategy in each market. Essentially, the organization views each nation in which it operates as a distinct host country market. There is not a conscious attempt to transport products, services, technology, managerial skills, or other resources across national boundaries. Consequently, the organization recognizes few economies of scale or operating efficiencies associated with the integration of its overseas units. An international organization that pursues a multidomestic strategy can offer products or services tailored to meet differing market demands. Many cosmetics, food, and entertainment companies pursue multidomestic strategies. When Whirlpool entered the international marketplace with its appliance products, it pursued a multidomestic strategy, adapting products for specific international markets.

With a **global strategy,** the organization pursues an integrated strategy in multiple national markets. National boundaries no longer define the firm's competitive spheres; competitive boundaries are represented simply by the world marketplace. Where possible, efficiency and standardization serve as the driving forces for strategy. Product differences are minimized. The transfer of resources, technology, and managerial skills is critical to the implementation of the strategy.

Multidomestic strategy
A strategy for competing in multiple international markets by tailoring products and services to meet the specific needs of each host country market.

Global strategy
A strategy for competing in multiple international markets with a standard line of products and services.

Sony has pursued a global strategy rather than a multidomestic strategy in the international marketplace. It markets relatively standardized products to the world market.
© Jeff Greenberg/Unicorn Stock Photos

IBM and Sony are examples of firms that have pursued a global strategy effectively. Both of these organizations market relatively standardized products to high-volume world markets. While Whirlpool entered the international marketplace with a multidomestic strategic orientation, CEO David Whitwam believed that the market for appliances would eventually become global in nature. Thus, Whirlpool will eventually adopt a global strategic orientation.

EVALUATING AND CHOOSING STRATEGY

Designing strategy can be a very challenging task. When determining an optimal strategy for the organization, managers can draw upon a variety of tools and techniques to generate, evaluate, and choose among strategic alternatives. Among the most popular evaluation and decision-making techniques are portfolio assessment models and decision matrices.

Portfolio assessment models provide a mechanism for evaluating an organization's portfolio of businesses, products, or services. These models classify the organization's portfolio of holdings into categories based on certain important criteria (such as growth rate or competitive position). Based on that classification, the organization's portfolio is assessed as to the appropriateness of the mix of business units, products, or services. The optimal strategy for each business unit, product, or service may vary according to its position in the portfolio. Popular portfolio assessment models include the BCG growth-share matrix and the General Electric industry attractiveness/business strength matrix. Both of these portfolio assessment models are discussed in Chapter 7.

Decision matrices help managers choose among strategic alternatives. A decision matrix provides a method for evaluating alternative strategies according to the criteria that the organization's managers consider most important (such as contribution toward sales growth, market share growth, profitability, and the like). Managers rate strategic alternatives according to the established criteria and select the alternative that has the best overall rating. Chapter 7 also provides a detailed discussion of decision matrices that can be used to make strategic choices.

Once the strategy formulation stage of the strategic planning process is complete, it is time to begin implementing the strategy. Strategy implementation is a critical and complex component of the strategic planning process.

STRATEGY IMPLEMENTATION: FOCUSING ON RESULTS

The importance of strategy implementation should never be underestimated, for the best-formulated strategy is worthless if it cannot be implemented effectively. If an organization is to achieve the best results from its strategic planning efforts, it must ensure that its strategy is put into action.

Few managers find it difficult to formulate competitive strategy. When it comes time to execute the plan, however, many experience difficulty. Why is that so? Many managers simply underestimate and undermanage the strategy implementation process. Organizations that achieve strategic success commit a tremendous amount of time, energy, and effort to making sure that the strategy is implemented effectively.[46]

Recall that strategy implementation addresses the question, "How can the organization get to where it wants to be?" Answering that question requires two primary activities. First, functional strategy must be developed. Second, various aspects of the organizational system must be designed to ensure that the selected strategy can be institutionalized.[47]

FORMULATING FUNCTIONAL STRATEGY

Recall from Chapter 4 that functional strategy provides an action plan for strategy implementation at the level of the work group and individual. It puts corporate and business strategy into operation by defining the activities needed for implementation.

Depending on the specific strategy to be implemented, functional strategy may need to be formulated by a variety of work groups within the organization. Consider, for example, the functional strategies that would be necessary if Coca-Cola decided to develop a new line of fruit juices. The research and development department would have to develop a formula; the marketing department would have to conduct taste tests, develop promotional campaigns, and identify the appropriate distribution channels; and the production department would have to purchase new equipment and perhaps build new facilities to produce the fruit juice line. Table 5.4 outlines just a few of the functional strategies necessary to introduce a new line of fruit juices.

The most significant challenge lies in coordinating the activities of the various work groups that must work together to implement the strategy. The strategies must be consistent both within each functional area of the business (such as the marketing department) and between functional areas (such as the marketing department and the production department).[48] For example, if Coca-Cola's new fruit juice line is to be priced at a premium level, it must be promoted to buyers who desire a premium product and distributed through channels that reach those buyers. These marketing decisions must be consistent. Further, the production department must purchase high-quality raw materials and produce a product that is worthy of a premium price. Without consistency within and between the work groups of the organization, the implementation process is sure to fail.

TABLE 5.4   Examples of functional strategies needed to implement a new product development strategy

Marketing:
- Coordinate with R&D for formula development
- Conduct market research with consumers
- Develop a pricing strategy
- Design promotional materials
- Identify and negotiate with potential distributors
- Coordinate with Production as to product specifications
- Coordinate with Human Resources regarding personnel needs

Production:
- Identify suppliers of input materials
- Negotiate purchasing agreements
- Arrange for storage facilities for both raw materials and finished goods
- Design and/or purchase new production equipment
- Coordinate with Human Resources regarding personnel needs

Human Resources:
- Work with Production to assess human resource needs
- Work with Marketing to assess human resource needs
- Identify potential candidates for new positions
- Develop compensation and benefits packages for new employees
- Design and provide training for new employees

INSTITUTIONALIZING STRATEGY

While functional strategies are essential to the strategy implementation process, it is also important that the strategy be institutionalized within the organization. Institutionalizing a strategy means that every member, work group, department, and division of the organization subscribes to and supports the organization's strategy with its plans and actions. Theory suggests that a fit must exist between the strategy of the organization and its structure, culture, and leadership if the strategy is to be institutionalized. Each of these topics will be examined in much greater detail in a subsequent chapter (organizational structure in Chapter 9, culture in Chapter 11, and leadership in Chapter 13), but here we will briefly discuss their relationship to strategy.

Organizational Structure

Organizational structure

The primary reporting relationships that exist within an organization.

Organizational structure, most commonly associated with the organizational chart, defines the primary reporting relationships that exist within an organization.[49] The structure of an organization establishes its chain of command and its hierarchy of responsibility, authority, and accountability.[50]

Departmentalization of organizational activities is the focus of the structuring process. Organizing work responsibilities into departments requires grouping individuals on the basis of the tasks they perform. If, for example, work units are structured so that all production tasks are grouped together, all marketing tasks are grouped together, and all finance tasks are grouped together, then the departments are organized on the basis of function. Similarly, if work units are structured so that all tasks related to serving the U.S. market are grouped together, all tasks for the European market are grouped together, and all tasks for the Asian market are grouped together, then organizational members are grouped according to the geographic market served.

Alfred Chandler, one of the earliest researchers in the area of strategy, originally advanced the idea that "structure follows strategy."[51] In essence, Chandler's findings indicate that an organization's strategy should influence its choice of organizational structure. For example, organizations that pursue growth through product development may benefit from a structure that is departmentalized by products. In contrast, those that pursue a geographic market development strategy may find an area-based structure to be most suitable. Furthermore, when an organization fails to change its structure in response to changes in its strategy, it will most likely experience operational problems that will eventually result in declining performance.[52] Since Chandler's classic research, a significant body of research has developed that suggests that organizations should develop structures that are appropriate for and supportive of their strategies. In fact, several studies have successfully linked a strategy-structure fit to superior financial performance.[53]

In Chapter 9, a number of organizational structures will be identified and discussed. In addition, we will examine the advantages and disadvantages of the different structures as well as their suitability for varying strategic conditions.

Organizational Culture

Organizational culture

The system of shared beliefs and values that develops with an organization. In simple terms, organizational culture is the personality of the organization.

The second organizational component that should be in alignment with an organization's strategy is organizational culture. **Organizational culture** refers to the system of shared beliefs and values that develops within an organization. It guides the behavior of and gives meaning to the members of the organization.[54]

Peters and Waterman's classic survey of America's best-managed companies has drawn attention to the contribution of organizational culture to strategic success. Peters and Waterman attributed the success of such firms as Procter & Gamble, General Electric, and 3M, in large part, to an organizational culture that supports their strategic initiatives.[55] Many organizations that wished to emulate the success of these companies began to look to changes in organizational culture as a means of doing so.

In an organization with an effective culture, employees are convinced that top management is committed to the implementation of its strategy. Further, employees believe that they will receive the support necessary to implement the plans of the organization. For example, 3M, which maintains a culture that values innovation, supports its "champions" of new product designs by removing bureaucratic impediments, giving them access to whatever resources they need, and providing executive support for their efforts. Individuals who champion new product concepts are confident that they will get the support necessary to bring their ideas to fruition.[56]

Reward systems are also a critical component of the organization's culture. Employees must know not only that they will be supported, but that they will be rewarded for taking the actions necessary to implement the organization's strategy. While financial rewards will always be important to some degree, other types of rewards can be useful as well. For example, a manager of one of IBM's sales offices rented Meadowlands Stadium, home of the New York Giants, to stage a special tribute to the salespeople in his office. He invited family, friends, and colleagues of his sales personnel to attend the ceremony and had each salesperson run through the players' tunnel to be recognized for his or her outstanding sales achievements.

Developing a strong, pervasive organizational culture has become more challenging as the work force in the United States has become more culturally diverse. As we mentioned in Chapter 1, people with different backgrounds, from different nations, or with different cultural frames of references often have very diverse views about organizations and how they should function. Reaching agreement can be more difficult in such groups—both in establishing common goals and in determining methods for achieving those goals. Managers must be prepared to work harder and more creatively to ensure that a strong organizational culture exists within culturally diverse organizations.

Organizational Leadership

Leadership is the third organizational component that should be in alignment with the strategy of the organization. If an organization is to implement its strategy effectively, it must have the appropriate leadership.[57] Without effective leadership, it is unlikely that the organization will realize the benefits of its selected strategy. This is particularly true when a quality orientation is a key aspect of its strategy.[58]

At the top of organization must be the visionary leader. Such leaders can envision the future, communicate their vision to those around them, empower the people of the organization to make the vision happen, and reward them when it becomes a reality.[59] Bill Gates of Microsoft has often been described as a visionary leader. Gates saw an opportunity to redefine the market for personal computing operating systems and made that vision a reality with the introduction of Microsoft Windows. The effective implementation of that strategy has made Microsoft one of the most successful organizations in the United States.

Equally important to strategy implementation is effective leadership in the ranks of managers. In today's organizations, they may be team leaders, coaches, or champions rather than tra-

Bill Gates of Microsoft, shown here after making a gift of $10.5 million to the Brooklyn Public Library, is often described as a visionary leader. He envisioned the future, communicated his vision to his employees, empowered them to fulfill the vision, and rewarded them when it became a reality with the introduction of Microsoft Windows.

© Florent Flipper/Unicorn Stock Photos

ditional middle managers, but the idea is the same. These individuals must do whatever is necessary to ensure that their work groups are making a contribution toward fulfilling the mission of the organization, achieving its goals, and implementing its strategy. Canon, the $19 billion maker of cameras, copiers, printers, and fax machines, attributes its success to strong leadership throughout the organization. Leadership is discussed in Chapter 13, where we examine the relationship between leadership and strategy in greater detail.

It is essential for an organization to develop the systems necessary to support its strategy. Structure, culture, and leadership are among the aspects of an organization's system that are particularly relevant for effective strategy implementation. When a strategy is being implemented, it is also very important to monitor both the success of the implementation process and the effectiveness of the strategy. Strategic control provides the mechanism for doing just that.

STRATEGIC CONTROL: ENSURING QUALITY AND EFFECTIVENESS

The last stage of the strategic planning process is strategic control. Strategic control involves monitoring the implementation of the strategic plan and ensuring quality and effectiveness in terms of organizational performance. An effective control system identifies problems and signals the organization that a change may be needed.

Achieving strategic control in organizations that are heavily involved in the international marketplace can be particularly difficult. When operating units are in geographically dispersed locations, differences in time, language, and culture complicate the control process. Acquiring information is more difficult when the scope of the organization's operations is broad, and processing and interpreting information from such diverse sources can be challenging. Consequently, organizations that pursue international strategies must often maintain very sophisticated control systems.

In general, control mechanisms can be either feedforward or feedback controls. Let's examine what each involves.

FEEDFORWARD CONTROLS

Feedforward controls
Controls designed to identify changes in the external environment or the internal operations of the organization that may affect its ability to fulfill its mission and achieve its strategic goals.

Feedforward controls are designed to identify changes in the external environment or the internal operations of the organization that may affect its ability to fulfill its mission and meet its strategic goals. Premise controls are one of the most common feedforward controls. Premise controls are designed to identify changes in any condition, internal or external, upon which the strategy of the organization was based.

Consider, for example, a large construction company that plans to develop 500,000 acres of residential property over the next three years. By the end of the first year of the company's plan, the economy begins to deteriorate, and interest rates, inflation, and unemployment begin to rise. If premise controls are in place and are designed to detect changes in the economic conditions upon which the construction company's plan is based, the company will know to adapt its strategy to the changing economic conditions.

FEEDBACK CONTROLS

Feedback controls
Controls that compare the actual performance of the organization to its planned performance.

Feedback controls compare the actual performance of the organization to its planned performance. These controls usually target the goals established in the organization's strategic and operational plans. One of the primary benefits of feedback control is that it focuses the attention of managers on the results for which they are responsible in the organization's plan. This may discourage managers from spending too much time on situations and issues that are unrelated to the overall goals of the organization. Often feedback controls evaluate financial results, such as revenues, profitability, stock price, and budget variances. Other feedback controls monitor nonfinancial results such as customer relations, product and service quality, productivity, and employee turnover.

Organizations should maintain both feedforward and feedback controls. Relying on only one type of control could be a mistake, because these controls focus on different issues that could affect the organization's plans. Just as organizations establish different goals and pursue different strategies, they should develop control systems to meet their specific strategic needs. An organization's control system must be in alignment with its strategic initiatives.[60]

For example, an organization pursuing a growth strategy is unlikely to develop the same control system as one that is pursuing a retrenchment strategy. The growth-oriented firm would monitor such variables as forecasts for demand, sales levels, sales growth, increases in market share, and brand awareness. In contrast, the organization pursuing retrenchment would monitor such variables as supply costs, productivity, sales per employee, sales to assets, gross and net margins, and other indicators of efficiency and bottom-line profitability.

INFORMATION TECHNOLOGY AND STRATEGIC PLANNING

The increasing availability and sophistication of information technology have had a tremendous impact on the ability of organizations to develop effective strategic plans. Such technology has made both internal and external sources of information more readily available to managers who are responsible for strategic planning. For example, tracking the sales of individual products in specific regions and at various price levels is much simpler given the information technology available today. Similarly, information regarding such things as market share fluctuations, profitability, and productivity measures is more readily available; operational activities such as purchasing, inventory management, and human resource management are more easily monitored as well. A well-designed management information system can provide accurate, timely information to managers throughout the organization.

Unfortunately, many organizations fail to use the information made available by management information systems to ensure effective strategic planning.[61] Given the increasing competitiveness in most industries, however, many organizations are searching for ways to improve their strategic planning processes. More effective use of information technology will provide a solution for many such organizations.

Strategic planning is a critical organizational activity that will affect the long-term performance of most organizations. We conclude by exploring the implications of strategic planning for the manager of tomorrow.

MANAGERIAL IMPLICATIONS

At several points so far in this book, we have suggested that the business environment is in a state of constant change. These changes will present special challenges for those who must plan strategically. Table 5.5 presents today's frame of reference for developing strategy, as well as one person's view of the frame of reference for tomorrow's managers.[62]

TABLE 5.5   A frame of reference for tomorrow's manager

TODAY'S FRAME OF REFERENCE	A NEW FRAME OF REFERENCE
Long-term future is predictable to some extent.	Long-term future is unknowable.
Visions and plans are central to strategic management.	Dynamic agendas of strategic issues are central to effective strategic management.
Vision—a single shared organizationwide intention. A picture of a future state.	Challenge—multiple aspirations, stretching and ambiguous. Arising out of current ill-structured and conflicting issues with long-term consequences.
Strongly shared cultures.	Contradictory countercultures.
Cohesive teams of managers operating in a state of consensus.	Learning groups of managers, surfacing conflict, engaging in dialogue, publicly testing assertions.
Decision making as a purely logical, analytical process.	Decision making as an exploratory, experimental process based on intuition and reasoning by analogy.
Long-term control and development as the monitoring of progress against plan milestones. Constraints provided by rules, systems, and rational argument.	Control and development in open-ended situations as a political process. Constraints provided by the need to build and sustain support. Control as self-policing learning.
Strategy as the realization of prior intent.	Strategy as spontaneously emerging from the chaos of challenge and contradiction, through a process of real-time learning and politics.
Top management drives and controls strategic direction.	Top management creates favorable conditions for complex learning and politics.
General mental models and prescriptions for many specific situations.	New mental models are required for each new strategic situation.
Adaptive equilibrium with the environment.	Nonequilibrium, creative interaction with the environment.

SOURCE: R. Stacey, "Strategy as Order Emerging from Chaos," Reprinted from *Long Range Planning*, 26, February 1993, 10–17, © 1993, with kind permission of Elsevier Science Ltd., The Boulevard, Langford Land, Kidlington OX51GB, UK.

While the future of the business environment remains uncertain, it is important for you, as a manager of the future, to recognize the changing nature of the environment and the implications of those changes for strategic planning. As you engage in strategic planning, you may want to keep the following tips in mind:

- Use a participatory approach to planning where possible.
- Recognize the importance of a thorough and accurate assessment of the current situation of the organization. A plan will be only as good as the analysis on which it is based.
- Make sure your mission statement is a working document that provides direction for the members of the organization.
- Strategic goals serve as targets for achievement. Make sure they are measurable, specific, and realistic.
- Strategy should be designed to provide the organization with a distinctive competitive advantage in the long term. Never lose sight of that imperative.

- Strategy is meaningless if it is not implemented well. Ensure that you plan for implementation all along the way.
- Never underestimate the importance of strategic control. It is the only means of ensuring that the company is on track.

In this chapter, you have learned about the process of strategic planning. This process provides a strong foundation for the development and implementation of effective strategy. Although strategic planning creates many challenges for managers, it is essential for those organizations that strive to achieve excellence in the highly competitive business environment of today and tomorrow.

WHIRLPOOL: ACHIEVING A GLOBAL COMPETITIVE ADVANTAGE

Managerial
Incident
Resolution

By virtually all measures of performance, Whirlpool's strategy for penetrating the international marketplace has been a tremendous success. The company is the only global player in its industry, a strategic innovator whose rivals are struggling to keep pace.

Less than ten years ago, Whirlpool was a purely domestic company—producing and selling all of its products in the United States. Today, Whirlpool builds products in eleven countries and sells them across the globe. It is the largest appliance manufacturer in the world and the only company that has a presence in all five of the world's major markets—North America, South America, Central America and the Caribbean, Europe, and Asia. The company currently maintains a multidomestic strategic orientation with a different strategy for each region, but is moving toward a more global orientation in its markets.

The results speak for themselves. Total sales at Whirlpool have more than doubled since the initiation of its international strategy and currently stand at $8 billion annually. The company employs over 40,000 people across the globe. In 1990, the company's shares traded at under $25 and its total stock market value was $1.6 billion. Five years later Whirlpool shares were trading as high as $70 and its total market value was more than $5 billion.

The story of Whirlpool under David Whitwam is a story about strategy, technology, and competitiveness. But most of all, it is a story about change in the new global economy and how a firm used strategic planning to get out in front of that change and take a leadership position on a global level.

SUMMARY

- Strategic planning is the process by which an organization makes decisions and takes actions that affect its long-run performance. The purpose of strategic planning is to move the organization from where it is to where it wants to be. Both economic and behavioral benefits are associated with strategic planning.
- The strategic planning process consists of four primary stages: (1) strategic analysis, (2) strategy formulation, (3) strategy implementation, and (4) strategic control.
- Strategic analysis involves identifying the organization's internal strengths and weaknesses and external opportunities and threats, and assessing their strategic implications.

- Strategy formulation follows strategic analysis and results in the development of strategy at the corporate and business levels. Strategy formulation requires the development of an organizational mission, the determination of strategic goals, the identification of strategic alternatives, and the evaluation and selection of an appropriate strategy.
- Strategies can be thought of as grand strategies, generic strategies, or international strategies. Grand strategies include stability, growth, and retrenchment strategies. The three generic strategies that can be formulated are cost leadership, differentiation, and focus. International strategy relates both to the mode of entry and to the focus of the strategy.

- Strategy implementation puts the strategy of the organization into effect. It is the action phase of the strategic planning process. Strategy implementation requires two primary activities: (1) functional strategy must be developed, and (2) the organizational system must be designed to ensure effective institutionalization.

- Strategic control involves monitoring the organization's progress toward fulfilling its mission, achieving its strategic goals, and implementing its strategic plans. In general, control mechanisms can be either feedforward or feedback controls.

- Information technology can be used to improve the strategic planning efforts of most organizations. From data collection to support strategic analysis to the monitoring of performance indicators, management information systems can provide managers with data that can enhance the effectiveness of the strategic planning process.

- The rapidly changing business environment creates many challenges for managers who must plan strategically. Managers of the future must remember the basic principles of strategic planning as they attempt to ensure the competitiveness of their organizations through the development of effective strategy.

KEY TERMS

Strategic planning	Task environment	Focus strategy
Strategic plan	Organizational mission	Multidomestic strategy
Strategic analysis	Strategic goals	Global strategy
Strategy formulation	Grand strategy	Organizational structure
Strategy implementation	Generic strategies	Organizational culture
Strategic control	Cost leadership strategy	Feedforward controls
General environment	Differentiation strategy	Feedback controls

REVIEW QUESTIONS

1. Why is it important for organizations to engage in strategic planning? What are the benefits of the strategic planning process?

2. What are the three organizational levels at which strategy must be formulated? How do they differ with respect to: (a) focus, (b) participants, (c) specificity, and (d) time horizon?

3. Describe the process of strategic planning. How are the four stages of the process interrelated?

4. What is the purpose of strategic analysis?

5. What is involved in: (a) developing an organizational mission, (b) assessing managerial values and attitudes, (c) identifying the strengths and weaknesses of the firm, and (d) identifying the opportunities and threats facing the organization?

6. What is grand strategy? What are the three broad categories of grand strategy?

7. What are the three generic strategies developed by Michael Porter? Give examples of organizations or products that have pursued each strategy.

8. What role does strategy implementation play in the strategic planning process?

9. What are functional strategies? What aspects of a firm's organizational system need to be in alignment with its strategy?

10. Describe the elements of strategic control.

11. How has information technology affected the strategic planning process in contemporary organizations?

DISCUSSION QUESTIONS

Improving Critical Thinking

1. What are some of the changes in the business environment in the last 20 years that have increased the need for strategic planning for many businesses?

2. How has the emergence of a global marketplace complicated the process of strategic analysis for many organizations?

Enhancing Communication Skills

3. Consider an organization that you have worked for at some time or that you currently work for. Would you classify that organization as having a stability, growth, or retrenchment strategy? Do the organization's culture, leadership, and control systems match its strategy? To improve your oral communication skills, prepare a brief presentation for the class.

4. Under what conditions might an organization choose to shift from a cost leadership strategy to a product differentiation strategy? Would this be a difficult adjustment for most organizations? To practice your written communication skills, write a one-page summary of your response.

Building Teamwork

5. Describe the effect each of the following would have on an organization.

  a. Ineffective implementation of a good strategy.

  b. Effective implementation of a poor strategy.

  c. Ineffective implementation of a poor strategy.

  Discuss this with a group of four or five students.

6. Form teams of four or five students. For each of the following strategies, identify an organization (beyond those cited in the text) that can be characterized as pursuing each strategy: (1) cost leadership, (2) differentiation, and (3) focus. Why did you choose these particular organizations? Be prepared to discuss your selections with the class.

---

1. Select an industry in which you have a particular interest (such as banking, restaurant, or sporting goods). Using the Internet, identify the three or four top competitors in that industry. Also using the Internet, research the strategy of each of these firms and categorize them according to the generic strategies advanced by Michael Porter.

2. Select an organization in which you have a particular interest. Use the Internet to locate an e-mail address for this organization. Contact them via e-mail and request a copy of their mission statement. Evaluate the mission statement utilizing the format provided in Meeting the Challenge.

3. Select a particular country in which you are interested. Research that country using an electronic database system (several should be available in your library). Focus specifically on learning more about the components of the general external environment (such as the economic system, political-legal system, and so on). Use presentation software such as PowerPoint to develop a presentation for your class.

> INFORMATION TECHNOLOGY: Insights and Solutions

> ETHICS: Take a Stand

PRIMO IN ROHANDA: IS IT "BLACK MARKETING"?

Freshly promoted to international tobacco products manager for U.S. Tobacco, Suzanne Thompson finds herself at the cutting edge of the firm's growth strategy for the next decade. Faced with declining sales and increasing taxes on tobacco products in the United States, U.S. Tobacco (UST) has turned to the international marketplace to achieve organizational growth. Further, the prestige image of American cigarettes in many foreign markets permits higher prices and margins on tobacco products. This is particularly true of the Primo brand, whose symbol of a sophisticated, urban professional male is recognized virtually worldwide.

In Rohanda, UST's plans have run afoul of a government policy that formally bans the import of cigarette products. While the health ministry supports the ban, the major beneficiaries of the policy are the government-owned cigarette monopoly and the country's tobacco farmers. The monopoly is required to buy the crop from these farmers at above-market prices.

Intense pressure from U.S. tobacco companies and the U.S. Department of Commerce has failed to convince the government of Rohanda to repeal the ban on cigarette imports. Ironically, American brands have traditionally controlled about 20 percent of Rohanda's cigarette market as a result of black-market sales by established distributors in neighboring Kalanda. Rohanda's government has not enforced the ban in the past, nor has it made any effort to stop UST from spending $8 million a year to advertise Primo. Apparently the government is convinced that the high prices for black-market cigarettes are sufficient protection for the brands offered by their monopoly.

Disgusted by what he considers a duplicitous policy, Suppakorn Rachinda, Primo brand manager in Southast Asia, has submitted to Suzanne his first-ever strategic plan for Rohanda. He proposes to double the advertising budget in Rohanda to $16 million and increase prices to Kalanda distributors by 20 percent. He argues that this plan will allow UST to capitalize on its premium position in Rohanda and share in the lucrative black-market profits. He asserts further that the plan will not produce higher prices in Kalanda since the struggling distributors will not have to raise prices, thus assuring that the nonsmuggling distributors will be unable to do so. Finally, he maintains that the plan is consistent with established practice of Rohanda's government, if not its formal policy.

Suppakorn's proposed marketing plan is now on Suzanne's desk, awaiting her approval for implementation in the coming year.[63]

For Discussion

1. Is there any difference between the letter and the spirit of the law in this case?

2. If the Rohanda government is not concerned with the smuggling operation, should UST be concerned?

3. What are the implications of Suzanne's decision if she accepts the strategic plan?

THINKING CRITICALLY: Debate the Issue

MULTIDOMESTIC VERSUS GLOBAL STRATEGY

Form teams of four or five students per team. Half of the teams in the class should prepare to argue the benefits of multidomestic strategy, while the other half should prepare to argue the benefits of global strategy. Use the experiences of real companies in preparing your arguments. Your instructor will select two teams to present their findings to the class in a debate format.

Video Case

SONIC

Home Page: {http://www.sonicdrivein.com/}

Imagine yourself cruising down the road in your convertible and thinking to yourself, "Boy, am I hungry!" The only thing that will satisfy you is a hamburger, french fries, and a root beer float. Further imagine parking your car and ordering your meal through your own personal drive-in window. After a few minutes, a carhop delivers your meal. You are amazed when you notice that your carhop delivered your meal wearing roller skates.

Is this scene possible only in your imagination? Not if you are familiar with Sonic, the fastest-growing fast-food chain in the United States. Sonic is a traditional drive-in, with window service, carhops, onion rings, root beer, and cherry limeade. The company started in the early 1950s, when entrepreneur Troy Smith purchased a steak house on a piece of property that also included a root beer stand. To make a little extra money, Smith decided to sell hot dogs and root beer to any customer that drove onto his lot. The root beer stand turned out to be more profitable than the steak house, and the seeds for Sonic were sown.

Sonic, which refers to "Service with the Speed of Sound," grew steadily until the early 1980s, when a poor economy and inconsistent management caused the company to experience a period of rapid decline. In 1981 and 1982, sales plummeted and 300 restaurants closed. In 1983 C. Steven Lynn, an experienced franchising and fast-food executive, was brought in to turn the company around. Lynn immediately urged Sonic's franchisees to go back to the basics and stick to the company's unique market niche. In addition, he rekindled a spirit of cooperation among Sonic's 1,400 restaurants, which has resulted in cost savings through joint advertising and volume purchasing.

Today, Sonic is flourishing again by pursuing a focus strategy within a clearly defined market niche. The company is continuing to expand in the southwestern and southeastern portions of the United States, and has 1,400 restaurants in 25 states. At the same time, sales have been increasing at a 14.4 percent annual compounded rate. Sonic is cautious, however, and is growing at a measured pace. The company is not trying to be all things to all people. It is content to grow within its market niche, which seems to suit its customers just fine.

For Discussion

1. Discuss the advantages of a focus strategy for Sonic.
2. Describe Sonic's market niche. Will this market niche continue to grow or decline over time?

CASE

FASTENERS, INC., FACES COMPETITION PRESSURES

Mr. Palladino leaned back in his chair and stared at the ceiling. What in the world could be going wrong with his company? Fasteners, Inc., had been in business for nearly ten years, and up until two years ago, the firm had commanded a strong market share in the fastener industry. Since then, however, the company had been experiencing declining sales and profits as a result of some competitive changes that had redefined the market for fasteners.

The industry had become driven by costs and price. Standardized fasteners had become the norm, and Fasteners, Inc., had no way to distinguish itself from its competitors. Further, the company had no cost advantage over its competitors; in fact, it seemed to have a slightly higher cost structure than its two biggest competitors. It was time for a new strategic plan.

As Mr. Palladino considered his situation, he wondered where to begin. Obviously, he was going to have to rely on his top managers to help develop a new strategy. As he prepared to draft a memo notifying this group

of a strategic planning meeting, he thought about the meeting agenda. He knew that he needed to organize the meeting so that the management group could make the most of their strategic planning time.

For Discussion

1. How might Mr. Palladino and his managers have avoided their current declining position?
2. Develop an agenda for Mr. Palladino's planning meeting. Where should the managers begin in their efforts to develop a new strategy for Fasteners, Inc.?

EXPERIENTIAL EXERCISE 5.1

Developing a Strategic Plan

Form a team with at least four other people. As a group, assume that you are the executive committee for the college of business administration at your university. Develop a strategic plan for your college through the year 2000. In doing so, address the following:

1. Develop a mission statement for the college.
2. Evaluate the dean's office with respect to its current strategic orientation.
3. Identify the strengths and weaknesses of the college.
4. Identify the opportunities and threats facing the college.

5. Develop a mission statement for the college.
6. Develop a set of strategic alternatives.
7. Establish strategic goals for the college.
8. Select a strategy.
9. Develop implementation and control plans.

Make a presentation to the class of your analysis, your strategic decision, and your implementation plans. How does your plan compare to the plans of other groups in your class? How did the assumptions you made about the internal and external environment of the college affect your strategic plan?

ENDNOTES

1. W. Taylor and A. Webber, *Going Global: Four Entrepreneurs Map the New World Marketplace* (New York: Viking, 1996).

2. H. Mintzberg, *The Rise and Fall of Strategic Planning* (New York: Free Press, 1994).

3. J. A. Byrne, "Strategic Planning: It's Back," *Business Week*, August 26, 1996, 46-53.

4. R. Evered, "So What Is Strategy?" *Long Range Planning*, 16, 1983, 57-72; A. Ginsberg, "Operationalizing Organizational Strategy: Toward an Integrative Framework," *Academy of Management Review*, 9, 1984, 548-57.

5. M. Leontiades, "The Confusing Words of Business Policy," *Academy of Management Review*, 7, 1982, 45-48.

6. M. Thankur and L. M. R. Calingo, "Strategic Thinking Is Hip, But Does It Make a Difference," *Business Horizons*, September/October 1992, 47-54.

7. For example, see J. A. Pearce, E. B. Freeman, and R. B. Robinson, "The Tenuous Link between Formal Strategic Planning and Financial Performance," *Academy of Management Review*, 12, 1987, 658-75; S. Schoeffler, R. D. Buzzell, and D. F. Heany, "Impact of Strategic Planning on

Profit Performance," *Harvard Business Review*, March/April 1974, 137-45; D. M. Herold, "Long-Range Planning and Organizational Performance: A Cross-Valuation Study," *Academy of Management Journal*, March 1972, 91-102.

8. J. A. Pearce II and W. A. Randolph, "Improving Strategy Formulation Pedagogies by Recognizing Behavioral Aspects," *Exchange*, December 1980, 7-10.

9. H. H. Hinterhuber and W. Popp, "Are You a Strategist or Just a Manager?" *Harvard Business Review*, January/February 1992, 105-14.

10. H. Mintzberg, "Crafting Strategy," *Harvard Business Review*, July-August 1987, 66-75.

11. R. Evered, "So What Is Strategy?" *Long Range Planning*, 16, 1983, 57-72.

12. S. R. Baldwin and M. McConnell, "Strategic Planning: Process and Plan Go Hand in Hand," *Management Solution*, June 1988, 29-37.

13. Ibid.

14. M. Goold and J. Quinn, "The Paradox of Strategic Control," *Strategic Management Journal*, 11, 1990, 43-57.

15. P. J. H. Schoemaker, "How to Link Strategic Vision to Core Capabilities," *Sloan Management Review,* Fall 1992, 67–81.

16. H. Mintzberg, "Crafting Strategy."

17. C. C. Snow and L. G. Hrebiniak, "Strategy, Distinctive Competence, and Organizational Performance," *Administrative Science Quarterly,* 25, June 1980, 317–37.

18. J. Montanari, C. Morgan, and J. Bracker, *Strategic Management: A Choice Approach* (Chicago: Dryden Press, 1990), 81–85.

19. J. P. Pfeffer, *Competitive Advantage through People: Unleashing the Power of the Work Force* (Boston: Harvard Business School Press, 1994).

20. C. Farkas and P. DeBacker, *Maximum Leadership: The World's Leading CEOs Share Their Five Strategies for Success* (New York: Henry Holt, 1996).

21. J. P. Fernandez and M. Barr, *The Diversity Advantage: How American Business Can Outperform Japanese and European Companies in the Global Marketplace* (New York: Lexington Books, 1993).

22. M. D. Gentile, ed., *Differences That Work: Organizational Excellence through Diversity* (Boston: Harvard Business School Press, 1994).

23. T. Wheelen and D. J. Hunger, *Strategic Management* (Reading, Mass.: Addison-Wesley, 1990), 100.

24. K. Labich, "Nike vs. Reebok: A Battle for the Hearts, Minds and Feet," *Fortune,* September 18, 1995, 90–106.

25. L. Grant, "Stirring It Up at Campbell," *Fortune,* May 13, 1996, 80–86.

26. M. Gunther, "Turnaround Time for CBS," *Fortune,* August 19, 1996, 65–70.

27. S. Toy, "Dogfight over London—and Paris, Rome, Madrid . . . ," *Business Week,* August 12, 1996, 48.

28. R. A. D'Aveni, "Coping with Hypercompetition: Utilizing the New 7S's Framework," *Academy of Management Executive,* 9, 3, 1995, 45–60.

29. M. A. Hitt, B. B. Tyler, C. Hardee, and D. Park, "Understanding Strategic Intent in the Global Marketplace," *Academy of Management Executive,* 9, 2, 1995, 12–19.

30. S. A. Zahra and S. S. Chaples, "Blind Spots in Competitive Analysis," *Academy of Management Executive,* 7, 2, 1993, 7–28.

31. L. Grant, "Why Warren Buffett's Betting Big on American Express," *Fortune,* October 30, 1995, 70–84.

32. K. Labich, "NBA's David Stern: Still a Gamer," *Fortune,* October 30, 1995, 28.

33. J. Barney, "Looking Inside for Competitive Advantage," *Academy of Management Executive,* 9, 4, 1995, 49–61.

34. S. F. Stershirc, "Mission Statements Can Be a Field of Dreams," *Marketing News,* February 1, 1993, 7ff.

35. J. A. Pearce and F. David, "Corporate Mission Statements: The Bottom Line," *Academy of Management Executive,* 1, 1987, 109–116.

36. D. L. Calfee, "Get Your Mission Statement Working," *Management Review,* January 1993, 54–57.

37. Whirlpool, *1995 Annual Report.*

38. R. B. Robinson, "Planned Patterns of Strategic Behavior and Their Relationship to Business-Unit Performance," *Strategic Management Journal,* 9, 1988, 43–60.

39. J. A. Pearce, K. Robbins, and R. Robinson, "The Impact of Grand Strategy and Planning Formality on Financial Performance," *Strategic Management Journal,* 8, 1987, 125–34.

40. R. B. Robinson, "Planned Patterns of Strategic Behavior."

41. "A Whole New Set of Glitches for Digital's Robert Palmer," *Fortune,* August 19, 1996, 193–94.

42. Adapted from M. Porter, *Competitive Advantage: Creating and Sustaining Superior Performance* (New York: Free Press, 1985).

43. P. Wright, "Strategic Options of Least-Cost, Differentiation, and Niche," *Readings in Strategic Management,* March/April 1986, 21–26.

44. G. M. Feiger, "Managing the New Global Enterprise," *The McKinsey Quarterly,* Summer 1988, 25–38.

45. S. Tully, "Northwest and KLM: The Alliance from Hell," *Fortune,* June 24, 1996, 64–72.

46. L. A. Huston, "Using Total Quality to Put Strategic Intent into Motion," *Conference Executive Summary,* September/October 1992, 21–23.

47. A. Ginsberg, "Operationalizing Organizational Strategy."

48. For example, see R. Hayes and S. Wheelwright, *Restoring Our Competitive Edge: Competing through Manufacturing* (New York: Wiley, 1984).

49. A. D. Chandler, *Strategy and Structure: Chapters in the History of the American Industrial Enterprise* (Cambridge, Mass.: MIT Press, 1962).

50. R. Rumelt, *Strategy, Structure, and Economic Performance* (Boston: Graduate School of Business Administration, Harvard University, 1974).

51. A. Chandler, *Strategy and Structure.*

52. For example, see C. Bartlett, "How Multinational Organizations Evolve," *Journal of Business Strategy,* 3, Summer 1982, 20–32; R. Drazin and P. Howard, "Strategy Implementation: A Technique for Organizational Design," *Columbia Journal of World Business,* 19, Summer 1984, 40–54; J. R. Galbraith and R. K. Kazanjian, *Strategy Implementation: Structure Systems and Process* (St. Paul, Minn.: West Publishing, 1978).

53. For example, see D. Miller, "Configurations of Strategy and Structure: Towards a Synthesis," *Strategic Management Journal,* 7, 1986, 233–49; D. Miller, "Strategy Making and Structure: Analysis and Implications for Performance," *Academy of Management Journal,* 30, 1987, 7–32; D. Miller, "Relating Porter's Business Strategies to Environment and Structure: Analysis and Performance Implications," *Academy of Management Journal,* 31, 1988, 280–308.

54. J. S. Ott, *The Organizational Culture Perspective* (Monterey, Calif.: Brooks Cole, 1989).

55. T. J. Peters and R. H. Waterman, *In Search of Excellence: Lessons from America's Best-Run Companies,* (New York: Harper & Row, 1982).

56. 3M, *1995 Annual Report;* "Master of Innovation," *Business Week,* April 1990, 58–63.

57. A. K. Gupta and B. Govindarajan, "Business Unit Strategy, Management Characteristics, and Business Unit Effectiveness at Strategy Implementation," *Academy of Management Journal,* 27, March 1984, 25-41.

58. J. M. Juran, "Acing the Quality Quiz," *Across the Board,* July/August 1992, 58.

59. F. Westley and H. Mintzberg, "Visionary Leadership and Strategic Management," *Strategic Management Journal,* 1989, 10, special issue, 17.

60. P. Lorange and D. Murphy, "Considerations Implementing Strategic Control," *Journal of Business Strategy,* 4, Spring 1984, 27-35.

61. M. Goold and J. Quinn, "The Paradox of Strategic Controls," *Strategic Management Journal,* 11, 1990, 43-57.

62. R. Stacey, "Strategy as Order Emerging from Chaos," *Long Range Planning,* 26, February 1993, 10.

63. This case was prepared by Fred L. Miller, associate professor of marketing at Murray State University, for use in the 1992 *Business Ethics Program* of Arthur Anderson and Company.

Effective Managerial Decision Making

■ CHAPTER OVERVIEW

Consider all the decisions necessary to carry out any major effort—from launching a space satellite to marketing and producing a new line of automobiles. The managers responsible for these decisions rely on good decision-making skills.

A manager's responsibility as a decision maker is very important. While all managers are called upon to make decisions, the kinds of decisions that are required will vary with their level of authority and type of assignment. Poor decisions can be disastrous to a department and an organization. Good decisions help work to flow and enable the organization to achieve its goals.

This chapter introduces concepts and models that focus on the demands of managerial decision making. Managers may not always make the right decision, but they can use their knowledge of appropriate decision-making processes to increase the odds of success. Skill as a decision maker is a distinguishing characteristic of most successful managers.[1] We will explore how managers in organizations make decisions by discussing the seven steps in the decision-making process and examining two commonly used models of decision behavior. Since managers are frequently involved with groups and teams, we focus on the participative model of group decision making by looking at techniques that managers can use to improve this process.

■ LEARNING OBJECTIVES

When you have finished studying this chapter, you should be able to:

- Explain the steps in the decision-making process.
- Examine some of the ethical dilemmas managers face in decision making.
- Describe the rational-economic model of decision making.
- Discuss the behavioral decision model.
- Illustrate the participation model of decision making.
- Recognize the advantages and disadvantages of group decision making.
- Explain the various techniques used to improve group decision making.
- Discuss the implications of effective decision making for future managers.

C H A P T E

Managerial Incident

THE CENTENNIAL OLYMPICS: QUICK DECISIONS REQUIRED

As the host city for the Centennial edition of the modern Olympic games, Atlanta had captured the world's attention in July 1996. Local officials had gone all out to showcase the city's charm and hospitality, and at the same time present to the world the most memorable Olympic games. The International Olympic Committee and the Atlanta Committee for the Olympic Games had worked hard to prepare venues for the various athletic events, as well as an infrastructure to accommodate the millions of visitors the city would welcome. In the midst of downtown Atlanta, Centennial Olympic Park was created to serve as a gathering point and entertainment center for spectators and visitors. After a glorious opening ceremony, the command was made to "let the games begin." Things ran relatively smoothly through the first week of the two-week event. Granted, there were occasional problems and complaints, such as buses that either broke down or did not run on time, bus drivers who did not know how to get to their destinations, traffic paralysis on the subway, and a computer system that suffered seemingly interminable delays in reporting results. There was even a somewhat humorous report that on one occasion, a group of British, Polish, and Ukrainian rowers found it necessary to hijack a bus to get them to their rowing site 55 miles from downtown Atlanta. But all this pales in comparison to what was about to happen at the midpoint of the games.

At 1:25 A.M. on Saturday, July 27, 1996, in the midst of a crowd of reveling visitors and locals, a terrorist bomb exploded with a deafening roar in Centennial Park, killing one person and injuring more than 100 others. Almost immediately Olympic and local officials, along with the Federal Bureau of Investigation and the Georgia Bureau of Investigation, would be forced to make several critical decisions. Would the games continue on schedule, or would there be postponements and cancellations? If continued, would spectators be allowed full access to places where they had previously been admitted? Would there be changes in the security measures at the athletic venues? Would the public gathering places be closed? These are but a few of the decisions that officials faced, and they needed to be made very quickly, for in less than eight hours athletic events were scheduled to resume.[2]

INTRODUCTION

In Atlanta local and Olympic officials, in concert with the FBI, had several critical decisions that needed to be made in a hurry. No one wanted to bow to terrorist activities, so outright cancellation of the games was an alternative that was not particularly attractive to anyone involved. However, postponement of scheduled events was certainly an option, as security checks and "sanitizing sweeps" of the various venues could cause delays. Even if security could be assured rather quickly, there was still the issue of insensitivity to the dead and injured if the games continued on schedule as if nothing had happened. And, if the security checks were not thorough due to haste, there was always the possibility of further personal tragedy if any additional explosive devices were in the area.

Some decisions, like those made by officials in Atlanta, are critical and can have a major impact on personal and organizational lives. Other decisions are more routine, but still require that we select an appropriate course of action.

This chapter introduces concepts and models that focus on the demands of managerial decision making. **Decision making** is the process through which managers identify and resolve problems and capitalize on opportunities. Here the focus is on how managers in organizations make decisions. First, we ex-

Decision making
The process through which managers identify and resolve problems and capitalize on opportunities.

plore how individuals make decisions by examining the seven steps in the decision-making process, ethical dilemmas in decision making, and two models of decision behavior. Since managers are often involved with groups and teams, we discuss group considerations in decision making. Finally, we look at techniques that managers can use to improve group decision making and the implications of achieving excellence in the decision-making process.

STEPS IN THE DECISION-MAKING PROCESS

Good decision making is important at all levels in the organization. It begins with recognition or awareness of problems and opportunities, and concludes with an assessment of the results of actions taken to solve those problems. Before we begin to examine these steps in greater detail, think about how you make decisions. How skilled a decision maker are you?

Take a few minutes to complete the decision-making process questionnaire (DMPQ) in Meeting the Challenge. The DMPQ evaluates your current level of decision-making ability.[3] As we progress through the chapter, you will learn more about sharpening these skills, which are an important part of most managerial experiences.

An effective decision-making process generally includes the seven steps shown in Figure 6.1. Although the figure shows the steps proceeding in a log-

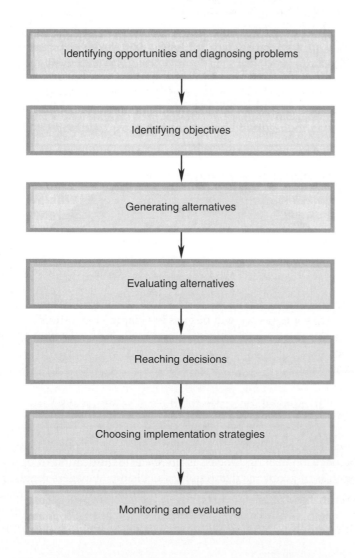

FIGURE 6.1
Seven steps in the decision-making process

Meeting the Challenge

ASSESSING YOUR DECISION-MAKING SKILLS

This decision-making process questionnaire (DMPQ) evaluates your current decision-making skills. These behaviors are part of most managerial experiences, but you will find that the questions are applicable to your own experience even if you are not yet a manager. If you do not have experience in a management-level position, consider a group you have worked with either in the classroom or in an organization such as a fraternity, sorority, club, church, or service group.

Use the following scale to rate the frequency with which you perform the behaviors described in each statement. Place the appropriate number (1–7) in the blank preceding the statement.

Rarely	Irregularly	Occasionally	Usually	Frequently	Almost Always	Consistently/ Always
1	2	3	4	5	6	7

_____ **1.** I review data about the performance of my work and/or my group's work.

_____ **2.** I seek outside information, such as articles in business magazines and newspapers, to help me evaluate my performance.

_____ **3.** When examining data, I allow for sufficient time to identify problems.

_____ **4.** Based on the data, I identify problem areas needing action.

_____ **5.** To generate alternative solutions, I review problems from different perspectives.

_____ **6.** I list many possible ways of reaching a solution for an identified problem.

_____ **7.** I research methods that have been used to solve similar problems.

_____ **8.** When generating alternative courses of action, I seek the opinions of others.

_____ **9.** I explicitly state the criteria I will use for judging alternative courses of action.

_____**10.** I list both positive and negative aspects of alternative decisions.

---

ical, sequential order, managerial decision making often unfolds in a quite disorderly and complex manner. Keep in mind that managers are influenced at each step in the decision-making process by their individual personalities, attitudes, and behaviors (as we will discuss in Chapter 14), ethics and values (as discussed in Chapter 3), and culture, as we will discuss later in the chapter. First, though, we will briefly examine each of the seven steps in managerial decision making.

IDENTIFYING OPPORTUNITIES AND DIAGNOSING PROBLEMS

Decision makers must know where action is required. Consequently, the first step in the decision-making process is the clear identification of opportunities or the diagnosis of problems that require a decision. Managers regularly review data related to their areas of responsibility, including both outside information and reports and information from within the organization. Discrepancies between actual and desired conditions alert a manager to a potential opportunity

_____**11.** I consider how possible decisions could affect others.

_____**12.** I estimate the probabilities of the possible outcomes of each alternative.

_____**13.** I study information about problems that require my decisions.

_____**14.** I determine if I need additional data in light of my objectives and the urgency of the situation.

_____**15.** To reach a decision, I rely on my judgment and experience as well as on the available data.

_____**16.** I support my choices with facts.

_____**17.** Before finally accepting a decision, I evaluate possible ways to implement it.

_____**18.** I choose the simplest and least costly methods of putting my decisions into effect.

_____**19.** I select resources and establish time frames as part of my implementation strategy.

_____**20.** I choose implementation strategies that help achieve my objectives.

Enter your score for each category in the following table, and sum the five category scores to obtain your total score. Enter that total score in the space indicated. Scores can range from a low of 4 to a high of 28 in each skill category. Total scores can range from a low of 20 to a high of 140. Your instructor will have further information on your scores.

SKILL AREA	STATEMENTS	SCORE
Diagnosing the problem	1, 2, 3, 4	_____
Generating alternatives	5, 6, 7, 8	_____
Evaluating alternatives	9, 10, 11, 12	_____
Reaching decisions	13, 14, 15, 16	_____
Choosing implementation strategies	17, 18, 19, 20	_____
Total score		_____

or problem. Identifying opportunities and problems is not always easy, considering human behavior in organizations. Sometimes the origins of a problem may be deeply rooted in an individual's past experience, in the complex structure of the organization, or some combination of individual and organizational factors. Therefore, a manager must pay particular attention to ensure that problems and opportunities are assessed as accurately as possible. Other times the problem may be so obvious that it is easily recognized, even by the casual observer. This was certainly true in the case of the Centennial Olympic Park incident described in the opening Managerial Incident. The entire world was immediately and painfully made aware of its existence.

The assessment of opportunities and problems will be only as accurate as the information on which it is based. Therefore, managers put a premium on obtaining accurate, reliable information. Poor-quality or inaccurate information can waste time and lead a manager to miss the underlying causes of a situation.[4] This basic principle is well understood by U.S. business managers, who spend millions of dollars each year on market research to identify trends in consumer preferences and buying decisions. Nevertheless, sometimes crucial information is overlooked. For example, in developing the new Coke, Coca-Cola conducted exhaustive taste tests, but failed to assess one crucial factor: brand loyalty. The unveiling of the new Coke was one of the most spectacular marketing flops of all time.[5]

Even when quality information is collected, it may be misinterpreted. Sometimes, misinterpretations accumulate over time as information is consistently misunderstood or problematic events are unrecognized.[6] Most major disasters or accidents turn out to have had long incubation periods in which warning signs were misunderstood or overlooked. Consider the following regarding some 1996 news headline–grabbing events: Months before ValuJet Flight 592 crashed into the Florida Everglades, killing all 110 people on board, the Federal Aviation Administration had the safety data it later used to ground the airline. Unfortunately, this information was stored in warehouses out of sight of the FAA's key decision makers. In Saudi Arabia, U.S. authorities wanted to widen the security zone that surrounded the complex that housed U.S. troups, but the Saudis denied the request. It wasn't until four days after a terrorist bomb killed nineteen Americans that Defense Secretary William Perry learned about the denial.[7] And none of us is likely to soon forget how misinterpreted information regarding O-ring safety led to the space shuttle *Challenger* disaster, in which all seven crew members perished.[8]

To complicate matters further, even when managers have accurate information and interpret it correctly, factors beyond their control may affect the identification of opportunities and problems. Nevertheless, by insisting on high-quality information and interpreting it carefully, managers will improve their chances of making good decisions.

IDENTIFYING OBJECTIVES

Objectives
The desired results to be attained.

Objectives reflect the results the organization wants to attain. Both the quantity and quality of the desired results should be specified, for these aspects of the objectives will ultimately guide the decision maker in selecting the appropriate course of action. In the opening Managerial Incident, the objective of officials was to maintain the integrity of the Olympic games, but at the same time ensure the personal safety of the athletes and spectators.

As you will recall from Chapters 4 and 5, objectives are often referred to as targets, standards, and ends. They may be measured along a variety of dimensions. For example, profit or cost objectives are measured in monetary units, productivity objectives may be measured in units of output per labor hour, and quality objectives may be measured in defects per million units produced.

Objectives can be expressed for long spans of time (years or decades) or for short spans of time (hours, days, or months). Long-range objectives usually direct much of the strategic decision making of the organization, while short-range objectives usually guide operational decision making. Regardless of the time frame, the objectives will guide the ensuing decision-making process.

GENERATING ALTERNATIVES

Once an opportunity has been identified or a problem diagnosed correctly, a manager develops various ways to achieve objectives and solve the problem. This step requires creativity and imagination. In generating alternatives, the manager must keep in mind the goals and objectives that he or she is trying to achieve. Ideally, several different alternatives will emerge. In this way, the manager increases the likelihood that many good alternative courses of action will be considered and evaluated.

Customer focus groups and employee sessions provide the manager with a means of viewing a problem or opportunity from varying perspectives and coming up with several good alternative courses of action for consideration and evaluation.

© Charles Gupton/Tony Stone Images

Managers may rely on their training, personal experience, education, and knowledge of the situation to generate alternatives. Viewing the problem from varying perspectives often requires input from other people such as peers, employees, supervisors, and groups within the organization. For example, consumer product companies such as Procter & Gamble often use customer focus groups to supply information that can be used in this stage of decision making.

The alternatives can be standard and obvious as well as innovative and unique. Standard solutions often include options that the organization has used in the past. Innovative approaches may be developed through such strategies as brainstorming, nominal group technique, and the Delphi technique. These strategies, which encourage consideration of multiple alternatives, will be discussed in more detail later in the chapter as methods for enhancing group decision making.

EVALUATING ALTERNATIVES

The fourth step in the decision-making process involves determining the value or adequacy of the alternatives generated. Which solution is the "best"? Fundamental to this step is the ability to assess the value or relative advantages and disadvantages of each alternative under consideration. Predetermined decision criteria such as the quality desired, anticipated costs, benefits, uncertainties, and risks of each alternative may be used in the evaluation process. The result should be a ranking of the alternatives. For example, the manager might ask, "Will this alternative help achieve our quality objective? What is the anticipated cost of this alternative? What are the uncertainties and risks associated with this alternative?" We more thoroughly examine the tools used by managers to evaluate alternatives in Chapter 7.

REACHING DECISIONS

Decision making is commonly associated with making a final choice. Reaching the decision is really only one step in the process, however. Although choosing an alternative would seem to be a straightforward proposition—simply consider all the alternatives and select the one that best solves the problem—in

When he took no quick action after becoming CEO of IBM corporation in 1993, Lou Gerstner was criticized for being indecisive. But, after carefully studying IBM strategy during the previous twenty years, he began reshaping IBM's corporate culture during 1994 and early 1995. He cut $6 billion in expenses and IBM's stock prices doubled.

© /AP/Wide World Photos

reality, the choice is rarely clear-cut. Because the best decisions are often based on careful judgments, making a good decision involves carefully examining all the facts, determining whether sufficient information is available, and finally selecting the best alternative.[9]

Lou Gerstner exhibited such cautious restraint when, in 1993, he took over as CEO of IBM corporation, which was losing its stronghold in the computer industry. Wall Street expected Gerstner to take quick and bold action. When he took no action that Wall Street could see in his first year, he came under fire for being indecisive. But Gerstner was doing his homework, reviewing every IBM planning document that had been written since the late 1970s. Then, during 1994 and early 1995, Gerstner removed many ingrained operating procedures as he began reshaping IBM's corporate culture. Six billion dollars in expenses were cut, and stock prices doubled as IBM had its first profitable year since 1990.[10]

CHOOSING IMPLEMENTATION STRATEGIES

The bridge between reaching a decision and evaluating the results is the implementation phase of the decision-making process. When decisions involve taking action or making changes, choosing ways to put these actions or changes into effect becomes an essential managerial task. The keys to effective implementation are (1) sensitivity to those who will be affected by the decision, and (2) proper planning and consideration of the resources necessary to carry out the decision. Those who will be affected by the decision must understand the choice and why it was made; that is, the decision must be accepted and supported by the people who are responsible for its implementation. These needs can be met by involving employees in the early stages of the decision process so that they will be motivated and committed to its successful implementation.

According to recent research, senior executives frequently complain that middle and operating managers fail to take actions necessary to implement decisions. Implementation problems often occur as a result of poor understanding and lack of commitment to decisions on the part of middle management.[11] However, this was certainly not the case for the Saturn Motor Company as described in Managing for Excellence. Notice how thoroughly prepared the implementation strategy was for the automobile recall decision made by Saturn. After Saturn made the decision to recall all affected automobiles, a very extensive plan was put into effect to insure that all affected Saturn owners would be serviced.

The planning process is a key to effective implementation. Without proper planning, the decision may not be accepted by others in the organization, cost overruns may occur, needed resources may not be available, and the objectives may not be accomplished on schedule. To plan properly for implementation, managers need to perform the following activities:

- Determine how things will look when the decision is fully operational.
- Draw up a chronological schedule of the activities and tasks that must be carried out to make the decision fully operational.
- List the resources and activities required to implement each activity or task.
- Estimate the time needed for each activity or task.
- Assign responsibility for each activity or task to specific individuals.

MONITORING AND EVALUATING

No decision-making process is complete until the impact of the decision has been evaluated. Managers must observe the impact of the decision as objectively as possible and take further corrective action if it becomes necessary.

THE SATURN MOTOR COMPANY: TOTAL RECALL

In its first few years of operation, Saturn became a modern-day success story for General Motors, which had been beset by heavy financial losses and image problems in its other carmaking operations. A market research survey revealed that Saturn ranked behind only the Lexus and Infiniti (two high-priced Japanese luxury automobiles) in customer satisfaction. But in August 1993, Saturn's top managers faced a problem that required an immediate decision. Over 380,000 cars manufactured during 1991, 1992, and the first four months of 1993 had a wiring problem in the alternator that could potentially ignite an engine fire. Saturn's response to the wiring problem was swift and decisive. Despite the fact that only 34 fires had been reported, indicating that the odds were less than one in 10,000 that a fire might occur, Saturn decided on a total recall.

A media blitz announced Saturn's intention to recall the more than 380,000 affected automobiles and make the necessary repairs. Radio and television news programs carried the story, as did all newspapers. To ensure that all affected Saturn owners were informed, notices were mailed to them with instructions to call their dealership to make an appointment for repairs. Richard Lefauve, president of Saturn corporation, was a guest on NBC's *Today Show,* where he explained that Saturn's decision was prompted by its commitment to its customers. Saturn was going to do whatever was necessary to demonstrate that commitment. In fact, Lefauve said that any Saturn owner who did not come in for repairs would receive a phone call from his or her dealer to ensure that the owner knew of the problem. Saturn dealers canceled vacation plans, extended service department hours, and provided customers with snacks in an attempt to turn the recall into a campaign of reassurance that Saturn's service was superior. Saturn's swift and decisive response to the problem proved to be a good decision. Surveys of affected Saturn owners and dealers revealed that customer response was positive. The recall effort simply confirmed most Saturn owners' belief that they had made the correct choice when they purchased their automobiles.[12]

Quantifiable objectives can be established even before the solution to the problem is put into effect. For example, 3M recently began a five-year program dubbed "Challenge '95" to increase quality control and reduce manufacturing costs by 35 percent. The company must constantly monitor its efforts to determine whether it is making progress toward those goals.

Monitoring the decision is useful whether the feedback is positive or negative. Positive feedback indicates that the decision is working and that it should be continued and perhaps applied elsewhere in the organization. Negative feedback indicates either that the implementation requires more time, resources, effort, or planning than originally thought, or that the decision was a poor one and needs to be re-examined.

The importance of assessing the success or failure of a decision cannot be overstated. Evaluation of past decisions as well as other information should drive future decision making as part of an ongoing decision-making feedback loop.

Thus far we have explored how managers in organizations make decisions by examining the seven steps in the decision-making process. The process starts when the organization recognizes a problem or becomes aware that an opportunity exists. The process concludes with an assessment of the results. As we have stressed, the ability to make effective decisions is a distinguishing characteristic of most successful managers.[13] In the next section, we discuss two models of decision behavior.

INFORMATION TECHNOLOGY AND THE DECISION-MAKING PROCESS

While timely and accurate information is useful in virtually every state of the decision-making process, it is especially critical at the first and last steps. Problems are identified when information reveals that some aspect of performance is less than desirable. The sooner accurate performance information can be placed in the hands of the decision makers, the sooner problems can be corrected, lessening the potentially undesirable or costly consequences to the organization. When a decision is finally made and implemented, the follow-up monitoring and evaluating process is performed to ensure that desirable results are again being achieved. Once again, timeliness and accuracy in performance feedback are critical, for if the selected decision alternative was not a good one, undesirable consequences will continue to be suffered. The quantum leaps that are being made in the processing and distribution of information are providing managers with greatly improved capabilities for problem recognition and successful solution as they engage in the decision-making process.

MODELS OF DECISION MAKING

Many models of the decision-making process can be found in the management literature. Although these models vary in scope, assumptions, and applicability, they are similar in that each focuses on the complexity of decision-making processes. In this section, we examine two decision-making models: the rational-economic model and the behavioral model. Our goal is to demonstrate the variations in how decision making is perceived and interpreted.[14]

RATIONAL-ECONOMIC DECISION MODEL

Rational-economic decision model
A prescriptive framework of how a decision should be made that assumes managers have completely accurate information.

The **rational-economic decision model** is prescriptive rather than descriptive; that is, it concentrates on how decisions should be made, not on how they actually are made. Such models, which focus on how a decision maker should behave, are said to be *normative*. The model makes several important assumptions about the manager and the decision-making process:

- The manager is assumed to have "perfect"—completely accurate—information and to have all the information that is relevant to the situation.
- The model assumes that the decision maker operates to accomplish objectives that are known and agreed upon and has an extensive list of alternatives from which to choose.
- As the model's name implies, it assumes that the manager will be rational, systematic, and logical in assessing each alternative and its associated probabilities.
- The model assumes that the manager will work in the best interests of the organization.

Also implicit in the model is the assumption that ethical dilemmas do not arise in the decision-making process.

As these assumptions suggest, the rational-economic decision model does not address the influences that affect the decision environment or describe how managers actually make decisions; instead, it provides guidelines to help the organization or group reach an ideal outcome. As a consequence, in practice the model may not always be a realistic depiction of managerial behavior. For example, the model portrays decision making as a straightforward process. In reality, making a decision is rarely that simple. First, people hardly ever have access to complete and perfect information. Second, even if information about all possible alternatives were available, individuals are limited in their ability to comprehend and process vast amounts of information. Third, decision makers seldom have adequate knowledge about the future consequences of alternatives. Furthermore, in most decision-making situations, personal factors such as fatigue or individual personalities, emotions, attitudes, motives, or behaviors are likely to intervene to prevent a manager from always acting in a completely rational manner. In addition, an individual's culture and ethical values will influence the decision process.

From a global perspective, it is especially important to be sensitive to how culture influences decision making. Individuals from different backgrounds and cultures will have different experiences, values, and behaviors, which in turn will influence the way they process information and make decisions. For example, Japanese managers follow a unique consensual decision-making process in which subordinates are involved in considering the future direction of their companies. Individuals and groups who have ideas for improvement or change discuss them extensively with a large number of peers and managers. During this lengthy information communication process, some agreements are hammered out. At this point, a formal document is drafted and circulated for the signature or personalized stamp of every manager who is considered relevant to the decision. Only after all the relevant managers have put their seals on the proposal is the idea or suggestion implemented.[15]

Managerial decision making is also influenced by the individual's ethics and values. As we discussed in Chapter 3, managers have power by virtue of their positions to make decisions that affect people's lives and well-being; consequently the potential for ethical dilemmas is always present.[16] In an **ethical dilemma,** managers must decide whether or not to do something that will benefit themselves or the organization but may be considered unethical and perhaps illegal.

Several recent publications have suggested that ethical dilemmas are going to occur more and more frequently in the future as a result of the dramatic changes the business environment is undergoing. For example, managers may have to answer questions such as the following: What do companies owe employees who are let go after 30 years of service? Is it right to cancel a contract with a loyal distributor when a cheaper supplier becomes available? Is it proper to develop condominiums on land that is an unofficial wildlife refuge?

The following questions may help you when you face a situation that has ethical implications:[17]

- Have you accurately assessed the problem?
- Do you have all the necessary information?
- Where are your loyalties?
- Have you generated a list of possible alternatives and considered how each will affect the other parties involved?
- Have you tested each alternative by asking whether it is legal, fair, and just to all parties involved?
- Would your decision change if you were to disclose it to your family, your boss, or society as a whole?
- Does your decision have any symbolic potential? Could it be misunderstood?

Ethical dilemma
A situation in which a person must decide whether or not to do something that, although benefiting oneself or the organization, may be considered unethical and perhaps illegal.

Managers should encourage ethical decision making throughout the organization by providing subordinates with clear guidelines for making decisions and establishing rules for enforcing the guidelines. Both the guidelines and the rules should be communicated to subordinates on a regular basis.

BEHAVIORAL DECISION MODEL

Behavioral decision model
A descriptive framework for understanding that a person's cognitive ability to process information is limited.

Unlike the rational-economic model, the **behavioral decision model** acknowledges human limitations that make rational decisions difficult to achieve. The behavioral decision model is descriptive and provides a framework for understanding the process that managers actually use when selecting from among alternatives.

The behavioral decision model suggests that a person's cognitive ability to process information is limited. In other words, a human being can handle only so much information before overload occurs. Even if complete information were available to decision makers, these cognitive limitations would impede them from making completely rational decisions.

Applying this assumption to managerial decision making, the model suggests that managers usually attempt to behave rationally within their limited perception of a situation. But most organizational situations are so complex that managers are forced to view problems within sharply restricted bounds. They frequently try to compensate for their limited ability to cope with the information demands of complex problems by developing simple models. Thus, the managers' behavior can be considered rational, but only in terms of their simplified view of the problem.

The behavioral decision model introduces several concepts that are important to understanding how we make decisions. These concepts include bounded rationality, intuition, satisficing, and escalation of commitment.

Bounded Rationality

Bounded rationality
Recognizes that people are limited by such organizational constraints as time, information, resources, and their own mental capacities.

The notion of **bounded rationality** recognizes that people cannot know everything; they are limited by such organizational constraints as time, information, resources, and their own mental capacities.[18] Bounded rationality is a useful concept because it explains why different individuals with exactly the same information may make different decisions.

Bounded rationality affects several key aspects of the decision-making process. First, decision makers do not search out all possible alternatives and then select the best. Rather, they identify and evaluate alternatives only until an acceptable solution is found. Having found a satisfactory alternative, the decision maker stops searching for additional solutions. Other, and potentially better, alternatives may exist, but will not be identified or considered because the first workable solution has been accepted. Therefore, only a fraction of the available alternatives may be considered due to the decision maker's information processing limitations.

Intuition

Intuition
An unconscious analysis based on past experience.

Intuition has been described as everything from an unconscious analysis based on past experience to a paranormal ability called a "sixth sense."[19] Several theories have attempted to explain intuition, but none has been proved. We do know that intuition is based on the individual's years of practice and experience. For example, a decision maker who detects similarities between the current situation and one encountered previously will select or modify actions that proved effective in that situation in the past.[20] Managers use intuition to obtain a quick understanding of a situation and to identify solutions without go-

HEWLETT-PACKARD: PC MAKER REALIZES A DREAM

In August 1994, Hewlett-Packard executive Webb McKinney's life changed when his boss informed him that (1) he was going to lead H-P's venture into the home personal computer business, and (2) he had better have a product on store shelves in one year. This was a tall order considering that McKinney had no employees, H-P had no experience selling home PCs, and it did not have a product in the works. Up to that point the company's main experience with PCs was in the business market. It had started selling PCs to businesses in the 1980s, and by 1994 had become one of the leaders in the business PC market. But the home market was sure to present challenges to H-P. After all, the company had built its fortune selling expensive equipment to scientists, engineers, and businesses, not to cost-conscious consumers. Despite this, H-P would have two things working in its favor when it eventually marketed its new product. Hewlett-Packard had a strong reputation with consumers through its calculators, printers, and fax machines. It also had very good relationships with retailers, which would certainly facilitate getting shelf space.

In August 1995, Hewlett-Packard's Pavilion line of home computers hit the market, and it has become one of the industry's hottest brands. These machines have received strong accolades from the trade press, which ranks them among the best home PCs in terms of price, quality, and service. Pavilion is designed for the entire family, and is quite user friendly, with color-coded cables and a "Personal Page" to guide users through the PC's software. Within just eight months H-P has captured 5.5 percent of the U.S. home market, just slightly behind the 7 percent share of Apple, which holds the third-largest share of the market. With figures like these, H-P's goal to be one of the three biggest PC makers in the United States by 1998 certainly seems well within reach.[21]

ing through extensive analysis. Many critics feel that many U.S. corporations place too much emphasis on decision analysis and suggest that managers should trust their feelings and experience more often.[22]

Satisficing

Satisficing means searching for and accepting something that is satisfactory rather than insisting on the perfect or optimal. Satisficers do not try to find optimal solutions to problems, but search until they find an acceptable or satisfactory solution and then adopt it. In short, managers tend to satisfice rather than optimize in considering and selecting alternatives. Some satisficing behavior is unavoidable because managers do not have access to all possible contingencies in making decisions. To a large extent Hewlett-Packard's decision to venture into the home personal computer business, described in Entrepreneurial Approach, was a satisficing decision. With a goal of simply being one of the top three competitors in this market, Hewlett-Packard management had identified a level of performance that would be satisfactory, but certainly not perfect.

Satisficing
The search and acceptance of something that is satisfactory rather than perfect or optimal.

Escalation of Commitment

When managers face evidence that an initial decision is not working, they frequently react by committing more resources, even when feedback indicates the action is wrong.[23] This **escalation of commitment** phenomenon is the tendency to commit more to a previously selected course of action than would be expected if the manager followed an effective decision-making process.[24] One reason for escalation of commitment is that individuals feel responsible

Escalation of commitment
The tendency to increase commitment to a previously selected course of action beyond the level that would be expected if the manager followed an effective decision-making process.

When he introduced ZapMail, a satellite-based network that was to provide two-hour document delivery service, Fred Smith of FedEx failed to anticipate the impact of fax machines, and FedEx lost over $300 million in the first year after ZapMail was introduced. Rather than escalating his commitment, Smith disbanded Zap-Mail in order to cut the company's losses.

© UPI/Corbis-Bettmann

Vigilance
The concern for and attention to the process of making a decision that occurs when the decision maker considers seven critical procedures.

for negative consequences and try to justify their previous decisions. Managers may also stay with a course of action simply because they believe consistency is a desirable behavior. In addition, managers may worry that if they change course, others may regard the original decision as a mistake or a failure.

In contrast, consider how Fred Smith, the CEO of Federal Express, changed course and cut the company's losses on ZapMail. ZapMail was a satellite-based network that was to provide two-hour document delivery service. Believing Federal Express's hard-copy delivery services would be severely eroded by the burgeoning electronic mail market, Smith decided to invest heavily in ZapMail. Unfortunately, he failed to anticipate the impact of low-cost fax machines, and Federal Express lost over $300 million in the first year alone. Smith admits that making the decision to disband ZapMail after the organization had committed so many resources to the concept and the technology was difficult.

WHAT MAKES A QUALITY DECISION?

How can managers tell whether they have made the best possible decision? One way is to wait until the results are in, but that can take a long time. In the meantime, managers can focus on the decision-making process. Although nothing can guarantee a perfect decision, using vigilance can make a good decision more likely. **Vigilance** means being concerned for and attentive to the correct decision-making procedures. Vigilant decision makers use the following procedures:[25]

- Survey the full range of objectives to be fulfilled and identify the values and qualities implicated by the choices.
- Thoroughly canvass a wide range of alternative courses of action. This is the idea-gathering process, which should be quite separate from idea evaluation.
- Carefully weigh whatever they know about the costs and risks of both the negative and positive consequences that could flow from each alternative.
- Intensively search for new high-quality information relevant to further evaluation of the alternatives.
- Assimilate and take into account any new advice or information to which they are exposed, even when the information or advice does not support the course of action initially preferred.
- Re-examine all the possible consequences of all known alternatives before making a final choice, including those originally regarded as unacceptable.
- Make detailed provisions for implementing or executing the chosen course of action and give special attention to contingency plans that might be required if various known risks materialize.

While vigilance will not guarantee perfect decisions every time, this approach can help managers be confident they have followed procedures that will yield the best possible decision under the circumstances. Spending more time at this stage can save time later in the decision process.

GROUP CONSIDERATIONS
IN DECISION MAKING

So far in this chapter we have been examining how managers make decisions individually. In practice, managers often work with their employees and peers in the company and may need to solicit input from them. Decision making is frequently entrusted to a group—a board, standing committee, ad hoc committee, or task force. Group decision making is becoming more common as organizations focus on improving customer service through quality management and push decision making to lower levels.[26] Accordingly, this section examines some of the issues related to using groups to make decisions.

PARTICIPATIVE DECISION MAKING

Participative decision making is not a single technique that can be applied to all situations. As we will see, managers can use a variety of techniques to involve the members of the organization in decision making. The appropriate level of subordinate participation in decision making depends on the manager, the employees, the organization, and the nature of the decision itself.

Participative Models

Vroom and Yetton developed a model for participation in decision making that helps managers determine when group decision making is appropriate.[27] According to this participative model, the effectiveness of a group decision is governed by both its quality and its acceptance (the degree to which group members are committed to the decision they have made). Updated by Vroom and Jago to reflect the decision-making environment of managers more adequately, this model expands the three basic decision-making methods (individual, consultative, and group) into five styles of possible decision participation.[28] To arrive at the best decision, a manager needs to analyze the situation and then choose one of the five decision-making styles.

As Table 6.1 shows, the five styles can be arranged along a continuum. The decision methods become progressively more participative as one moves from the highly autocratic style (AI), in which the manager decides alone, to the consultative style (CI), where the manager consults with the group before deciding, to the group style (GII), where the manager allows the group to decide.[29]

According to Vroom and Jago, the nature of the decision itself determines the appropriate degree of participation, and they provide diagnostic questions to help managers select the appropriate level. Figure 6.2 shows how these questions can be used in a decision tree format to arrive at the appropriate decision style. (The structure and use of decision trees will be discussed in more detail in Chapter 7.) For the sake of simplicity, the decision tree in Figure 6.2 treats each question as having only two answers, yes or no. By starting at the left and answering the questions, managers can follow the tree to arrive at one of the decision styles described in Table 6.1.

In general, a participative decision style is desirable when subordinates have useful information and share the organization's goals, when subordinates' commitment to the decision is essential, when timeliness is not crucial, and when conflict is unlikely. At the same time, group decision making is more complex than decision making by individuals, but good communication and conflict management skills can overcome this difficulty.[30]

It is important to note that inappropriate use of either group or individual decision making can be costly. Using groups ineffectively wastes organizational

TABLE 6.1   Decision styles

	DECISION STYLE	DESCRIPTION
Highly autocratic ↑	AI	The manager solves the decision problem alone using information available at the time.
	AII	The manager solves the decision problem alone after obtaining necessary information from subordinates.
	CI	The manager solves the decision problem after obtaining ideas and suggestions from subordinates individually. The decision may or may not reflect their counsel.
	CII	The manager solves the decision problem after obtaining ideas and suggestions from subordinates as a group. The decision may or may not reflect their counsel.
↓ **Highly democratic**	GII	The group analyzes the problem, identifies and evaluates alternatives, and makes a decision. The manager acts as coordinator of the group of subordinates and accepts and implements any solution that has the support of the group.

NOTE: A = autocratic; C = consultative; G = group.

SOURCE: V. H. Vroom, "A New Look at Managerial Decision Making," 69–70. Reprinted, by permission of the publisher, from *Organizational Dynamics* (Spring 1973). © 1973, American Management Association, New York. All rights reserved.

resources because the participants' time could have been spent on other tasks; it also leads to boredom and reduces motivation because participants feel that their time has been wasted. Making decisions individually that would have been better made by groups can lead to poor coordination among organization members, less commitment to quality, and little emphasis on creativity, as well as to poor decisions.[31]

Group Size

In deciding whether a participative model of decision making is appropriate, a manager must also consider the size of the group. In general, as group size increases, the following changes in the decision-making process are likely to be observed:[32]

- The demands on the leader's time and attention are greater, and the leader is more psychologically distant from the other members. This becomes much more of a problem in self-managing teams, where several individuals can take on leadership roles.
- The group's tolerance of direction from the leader is greater, and the team's decision making becomes more centralized.
- The atmosphere is less friendly, actions are less personal, more subgroups form, and in general, members are less satisfied.
- Rules and procedures become more formalized.

As our discussion thus far suggests, both group and individual decision making offer potential advantages and disadvantages. These are examined in the next sections. Then we turn our attention to structured techniques managers can use to improve group decision making.

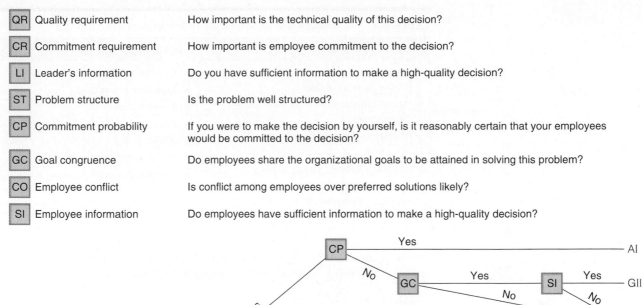

	QR	Quality requirement	How important is the technical quality of this decision?

QR | Quality requirement | How important is the technical quality of this decision?

CR | Commitment requirement | How important is employee commitment to the decision?

LI | Leader's information | Do you have sufficient information to make a high-quality decision?

ST | Problem structure | Is the problem well structured?

CP | Commitment probability | If you were to make the decision by yourself, is it reasonably certain that your employees would be committed to the decision?

GC | Goal congruence | Do employees share the organizational goals to be attained in solving this problem?

CO | Employee conflict | Is conflict among employees over preferred solutions likely?

SI | Employee information | Do employees have sufficient information to make a high-quality decision?

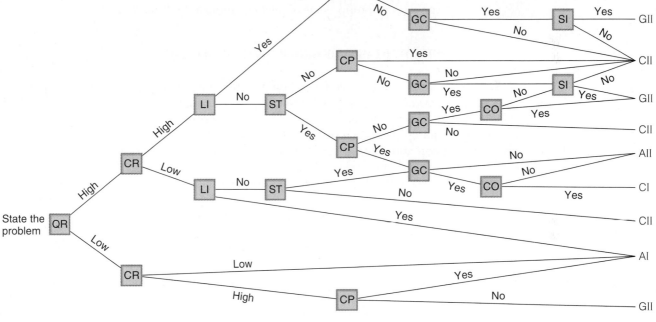

ADVANTAGES OF GROUP DECISION MAKING

Committees, task forces, and ad hoc groups are frequently assigned to identify and recommend decision alternatives or, in some cases, to actually make important decisions. In essence, a group is a tool that can focus the experience and expertise of several people on a particular problem or situation. Thus, a group offers the advantage of greater total knowledge. Groups accumulate more information, knowledge, and facts than individuals and often consider more alternatives. Each person in the group is able to draw on his or her unique education, experience, insights, and other resources and contribute those to the group. The varied backgrounds, training levels, and expertise of group members also help overcome tunnel vision by enabling the group to view the problem in more than one way.

Participation in group decision making usually leads to higher member satisfaction. People tend to accept a decision more readily and to be better satisfied with it when they have participated in making that decision. In addition, people will better understand and be more committed to a decision in which they have had a say than to a decision made for them. As a result, such a de-

FIGURE 6.2
Vroom and Jago decision tree

SOURCE: Reprinted from V. H. Vroom and A. G. Jago, *The New Leadership: Managing Participation in Organizations* 1988, Upper Saddle River, NJ: Prentice Hall. Copyright 1988 by V. H. Vroom and A. G. Jago. Used with permission of the authors.

TABLE 6.2   Advantages and disadvantages of group decision making

ADVANTAGES	DISADVANTAGES
• Experience and expertise of several individuals available	• Greater time requirement
• More information, data, and facts accumulated	• Minority domination
	• Compromise
• Problems viewed from several perspectives	• Concern for individual rather than group goals
• Higher member satisfaction	• Social pressure to conform
• Greater acceptance and commitment to decisions	• Groupthink

cision is more likely to be implemented successfully. A summary of the advantages of group decision making appears in Table 6.2.

DISADVANTAGES OF GROUP DECISION MAKING

While groups have many potential benefits, we all know that they can also be frustrating. In fact, the traditional interacting group is prone to a variety of difficulties. One obvious disadvantage of group decision making is the time required to make a decision (see Table 6.2). The time needed for group discussion and the associated compromising and selecting of a decision alternative can be considerable. Time costs money, so a waste of time becomes a disadvantage if a decision made by a group could have been made just as effectively by an individual working alone. Consequently, group decisions should be avoided when speed and efficiency are the primary considerations.

A second disadvantage is that the group discussion may be dominated by an individual or subgroup. Effectiveness can be reduced if one individual, such as the group leader, dominates the discussion by talking too much or being closed to other points of view. Some leaders try to control the group and provide the major input. Such dominance can stifle other group members' willingness to participate and could cause decision alternatives to be ignored or overlooked. All group members need to be encouraged and permitted to contribute.

Another disadvantage of group decision making is that members may be less concerned with the group's goals than with their own personal goals. They may become so sidetracked in trying to win an argument that they forget about group performance. On the other hand, a group may try too hard to compromise and consequently may not make optimal decisions. Sometimes this stems from the desire to maintain friendships and avoid disagreements. Often groups exert tremendous social pressure on individuals to conform to established or expected patterns of behavior. Especially when they are dealing with important and controversial issues, interacting groups may be prone to a phenomenon called *groupthink*.[33]

Groupthink
An agreement-at-any-cost mentality that results in ineffective group decision making.

Groupthink is an agreement-at-any-cost mentality that results in ineffective group decision making. It occurs when groups are highly cohesive, have highly directive leaders, are insulated so they have no clear ways to get objective information, and, because they lack outside information, have little hope that a better solution might be found than the one proposed by the leader or other influential group members.[34] These conditions foster the illusion that the group is invulnerable, right, and more moral than outsiders. They also encourage the development of self-appointed "mind guards" who bring pressure on dissenters.

In such situations, decisions, often important decisions, are made without consideration of alternative frames or alternative options. It is difficult to imagine conditions more conducive to poor decision making and wrong decisions.

Recent research indicates that groupthink may also result when group members have preconceived ideas about how a problem should be solved.[35] Under these conditions the team may not examine a full range of decision alternatives or they may discount or avoid information that threatens the team's preconceived choice.

Irving Janis, who coined the term *groupthink,* focused his research on high-level governmental policy groups faced with difficult problems in complex and dynamic environments. The groupthink phenomenon has been used to explain numerous group decisions that have resulted in serious fiascoes. Examples of such decisions include the Bay of Pigs invasion, the Watergate coverup, and NASA's decision to launch the space shuttle *Challenger.*[36] Of course, group decision making is quite common in all types of organizations, so it is possible that groupthink exists in private-sector organizations as well as in those in the public sector. Table 6.3 summarizes the characteristics of groupthink and the types of defective decision making that will likely result.

Groupthink is common in tightly knit groups that believe in what they are doing: citizen groups who censor book acquisitions for the local library, environmental groups who will save us from ourselves at any price, business leaders who presume that they control other people's economic destinies, or government functionaries who think that they know better than the voters what is in the national interest. None of the decisions made by these groups is necessarily wrong, but that is not the point. Rather, it is the single-mindedness of the decision process, the narrow framing, and limited deliberation that are of concern.[37] In Global Perspective, Compaq executives displayed groupthink tendencies when they favored maintaining the status quo in hopes that consumers would eventually return to Compaq's higher-priced models.

TECHNIQUES FOR QUALITY IN GROUP DECISION MAKING

Managers can use several structured techniques to foster quality in group decision making.[39] Here we will briefly explore brainstorming, the nominal group technique, the Delphi technique, devil's advocacy, and dialectical inquiry.

Brainstorming
Brainstorming is a technique that encourages group members to generate as many novel ideas as possible on a given topic without evaluating them. As a

Brainstorming
A technique used to enhance creativity that encourages group members to generate as many novel ideas as possible on a given topic without evaluating them.

TABLE 6.3   Characteristics of groupthink and the types of defective decisions that may result

CHARACTERISTICS OF GROUPTHINK	TYPES OF DEFECTIVE DECISIONS
• Illusion of invulnerability	• Incomplete survey of alternatives
• Collective rationalization	• Incomplete survey of goals
• Belief in the morality of group decisions	• Failure to examine risks of preferred decisions
• Self-censorship	• Poor information search
• Illusion of unanimity in decision making	• Failure to reappraise alternatives
• Pressure on members who express arguments	• Failure to develop contingency plans

Global Perspective

COMPAQ: MEETING YET ANOTHER CHALLENGE

Challenges were nothing new to the Compaq Computer Corporation. While still in its infancy in the mid-1980s, Compaq's dominance of the portable-computer market was about to be threatened by IBM's impending new product introduction. But, with the timely development and introduction of more powerful and lower-priced desktop computers, Compaq was able to deflect that threat. In the early 1990s disaster was at the doorstep again when Compaq began to post losses. In increasing numbers, consumers were shying away from Compaq's expensive models and purchasing less costly clones. Compaq executives were slow to react to this changing climate, complaining that they would not be able to deliver a new, low-priced model until early 1993, and at the same time reassuring themselves that the consumers would eventually return to their own high-end models.

This didn't sit well with Benjamin Rosen, Compaq's chairman. He secretly recruited two middle managers to evaluate how long it would take to introduce a competitive, low-priced model. They determined that components already existed that would allow Compaq to begin producing such machines almost immediately. Rosen reacted by firing Compaq's chief executive and embarking on the path toward new, low-cost models. Within the year, several models with prices under $1,000 were introduced. By the end of 1994, Compaq's sales had risen to over $10 billion, and the company had regained its position as the number one U.S. seller of desktop computers, shipping more than 4.8 million personal computers worldwide.[38]

group process, brainstorming can enhance creativity by overcoming pressures for conformity that can retard the development of creative decision making. Brainstorming primarily focuses on generating ideas rather than on choosing an alternative. The members of the group, usually five to twelve people, are encouraged to generate ideas during a specific time period while withholding criticism and focusing on nonevaluative presentation.[40] In this way, individuals who may be concerned about being ridiculed or criticized feel more free to offer truly novel ideas.

The following rules should guide the brainstorming process:[41]

- Freewheeling is encouraged. Group members are free to offer any suggestions to the facilitator, who lists ideas as people speak.
- Group members will not criticize ideas as they are being generated. Consider any and all ideas. No idea can be rejected initially.
- Quantity is encouraged. Write down all the ideas.
- The wilder the ideas the better.
- Piggyback on or combine previously stated ideas.
- No ideas are evaluated until after all alternatives are generated.

Brainstorming enhances creativity and reduces the tendency of groups to satisfice in considering alternatives. One advocate of brainstorming is Bill Gates, the CEO of Microsoft. He often joins programmers in the brainstorming sessions that give birth to new products. According to Gates, it is very important to him and to those who work with him at Microsoft to encourage creative group decision making.[42]

Nominal Group Technique

The **nominal group technique (NGT)** is a structured process designed to stimulate creative group decision making where agreement is lacking or the members have incomplete knowledge of the nature of the problem.[43] It is a means of enhancing creativity and decision making that integrates both individual work and group interaction with certain basic guidelines. NGT was developed to foster individual as well as group creativity and further overcome the tendency of group members to criticize ideas when they are offered.

NGT is used in situations where group members must pool their judgments to solve the problem and determine a satisfactory course of action. First, individual members independently list their ideas on the specific problem. Next, each member presents his or her ideas one at a time without discussion. As with brainstorming, members are asked to generate ideas without direct comment, but the idea-generation phase of NGT is more confined than it is with brainstorming because group members present ideas in a round-robin manner rather than through freewheeling. Members' ideas are recorded so everyone can see them. After all the members' ideas are presented, the group discusses the ideas to clarify and evaluate them. Finally, members vote on the ideas independently, using a rank-ordering or rating procedure. The final outcome is determined by the pooled individual votes and is thus mathematically derived.

NGT may be most effective when decisions are complex or where the group is experiencing blockages or problems, such as a few dominating members. NGT is generally effective in generating large numbers of creative alternatives while maintaining group satisfaction.[44]

Delphi Technique

The **Delphi technique** was originally developed by the Rand Corporation to enable groups to consult experts and use their predictions and forecasts about future events.[45] Using survey instruments or questionnaires, a group leader solicits and collects written, expert opinions on a topic. The leader collates and summarizes the information before distributing it to the participants. This process continues until the experts' predictions are systematically refined through feedback and a consensus emerges.

Like NGT, the Delphi technique can be used to define problems and to consider and select alternatives. The Delphi technique is also best used under special circumstances. The primary difference between NGT and the Delphi technique is that with the Delphi technique participants do not meet face to face.

A significant advantage of the Delphi technique is that it completely avoids group interaction effects. Even NGT is not completely immune to social facilitating pressure that results from having an important person in the same room. With Delphi, participant experts can be thousands of miles apart.

Devil's Advocacy Approach

The last two techniques to enhance group decision making, devil's advocacy and dialectical inquiry, were developed to deal with complex, strategic decisions. Both techniques encourage intense, heated debate among group members. A recent study found that disagreement in structured settings like meetings can lead to better decision making.[46] Disagreement is particularly useful for organizations operating in uncertain environments.

The **devil's advocacy** approach appoints an individual or subgroup to critique a proposed course of action. One or more individuals are assigned the role of devil's advocate to make sure that the negative aspects of any attractive decision alternatives are considered.[47] The usefulness of the devil's advocacy technique was demonstrated several years ago by Irving Janis in his discussion of famous fiascoes attributed to groupthink. Janis recommends that everyone in the group assume the role of devil's advocate and question the as-

Nominal group technique (NGT)
A structured process designed to stimulate creative group decision making where agreement is lacking or where the members have incomplete knowledge concerning the nature of the problem.

Delphi technique
Uses experts to make predictions and forecasts about future events without meeting face to face.

Devil's advocacy
An individual or subgroup is appointed to critique a proposed course of action and identify problems to consider before the decision is final.

sumptions underlying the popular choice. An individual or subgroup can be formally designated as the devil's advocate to present critiques of the proposed decision. Using this technique avoids the tendency of groups to allow their desire to agree to interfere with decision making. Potential pitfalls are identified and considered before the decision is final.

Dialectical Inquiry

Dialectical inquiry
Approaches a decision from two opposite points and structures a debate between conflicting views.

With **dialectical inquiry,** a decision situation is approached from two opposite points, and advocates of the conflicting views conduct a debate, presenting arguments in support of their positions. Each decision possibility is developed and assumptions are identified. The technique forces the group to confront the implications of their assumptions in the decision process.[48] Bausch and Lomb successfully uses this technique by establishing "tiger teams" composed of scientists from different disciplines. Team members are encouraged to bring up divergent ideas and offer different points of view. Xerox uses round-table discussions composed of various functional experts to encourage divergent and innovative decision making.

MANAGERIAL IMPLICATIONS ▬▬▬▬▬▬▬▬▬▬▬▬▬▬▬▬▬▬▬

The most important characteristic of successful decision makers is that they do not approach decisions unprepared. Responsibility for decision making comes only to those who have earned it. Responsibility is earned by decision makers who demonstrate both a record of success and an understanding of their organization. As a manager, you need to realize that successful decision making means understanding the organization's basic beliefs and culture, its goals and vision, and its activities and the plans that guide them.[49]

How will changes in the managerial role in the next decade affect the decision making of tomorrow's manager? The following guidelines, developed by Robert Denhardt in his recent book *The Pursuit of Significance,* reflect current thinking about managerial techniques that foster quality decision making:[50]

- Be committed to the decision-making process; use it, and let data, not emotions, drive decisions.
- Seek employees' input before you make key decisions.
- Believe in, foster, and support group decision making in the organization.
- Believe that the best way to improve the quality of decisions is to ask and listen to employees who are doing the work.
- Seek and use high-quality information.
- Avoid "top-down" power oriented decision making wherever possible.
- Encourage decision-making creativity through risk taking, and be tolerant of honest mistakes.
- Develop an open atmosphere that encourages organization members to offer and accept feedback.

In this chapter we have set forth some fundamentals of how managers in organizations make decisions. We examined the steps in the decision-making process, issues related to ethical decision dilemmas, and two models of decision behavior. Since managers are often involved with groups, we discussed group decision-making concerns and techniques that managers can use to improve the group decision process. In Chapter 7 we will build on these fundamentals by presenting quantitative tools for making better decisions.

THE CENTENNIAL OLYMPICS: QUICK DECISIONS MADE

In the aftermath of the bombing in Atlanta's Centennial Olympic Park, actions were quick and decisive on the part of both government and Olympic officials. As the wounded were being removed for medical attention, Federal Bureau of Investigation and Georgia Bureau of Investigation agents immediately sealed off the area to begin the arduous task of evidence gathering. The existing Olympic security force of 30,000 police, military, and private guards, 1,000 bomb experts, and 40 bomb-sniffing dogs, immediately began the task of "sweeping and sanitizing" the area. Athletic venues were thoroughly checked and sealed.

Meanwhile, Juan Antonio Samaranch, president of the International Olympic Committee, was alerted to the blast, and, after conferring with the full committee, a decision was made and ratified by 2:00 A.M. The local organizing committee and the White House approved it before it was made public. At dawn on that same Saturday, Francois Carrard, the IOC's director general, announced to the press in no uncertain terms: "The games will go on. I repeat: The games will go on. Buses are rolling, the athletes have been notified—the games will go on." It was also decided that Olympic flags would be lowered to half staff, and a moment of silence would be observed before each athletic event in honor of and respect for the dead and injured. All volunteers were asked to report to their stations on the morning after the bombing to assist with security as spectators began arriving at the various athletic venues. Security was set at a heightened level, and all spectators were required to open packages and purses and submit them to inspection. To allow for complete evidence gathering, Olympic Centennial Park was not scheduled to reopen until Tuesday, at which time security would be doubled. Although the spirit and mood was dampened for many, the Centennial edition of the modern Olympic games continued with no delays.[51]

SUMMARY

- The decision-making process includes seven steps: (1) identifying and diagnosing the problem, (2) identifying objectives, (3) generating alternatives, (4) evaluating alternatives, (5) reaching decisions, (6) choosing implementation strategies, and (7) monitoring and evaluating.

- Ethical dilemmas often occur as alternatives are being evaluated. An ethical dilemma is a situation in which the decision makers must decide whether or not to do something that will benefit themselves or the organization but may be considered unethical and perhaps illegal.

- The rational-economic decision model assumes that the manager has completely accurate information and an extensive list of alternatives from which to choose; it also assumes that he or she will be rational and systematic in assessing each alternative and will work in the best interests of the organization.

- The behavioral decision model acknowledges human limitations to decision making and addresses the issues of bounded rationality, intuition, satisficing, and escalation of commitment. Bounded rationality recog-

nizes that people cannot know everything and are limited by such organizational constraints as time, information, resources, and their own mental capacities. Intuition has been described as everything from an unconscious analysis based on past experience to a paranormal ability called a "sixth sense." Satisficing means searching for and accepting something that is satisfactory rather than optimal. Escalation of commitment is the tendency to commit more resources to a previously selected course of action than would be expected if the manager followed an effective decision-making process.

- The increased involvement of groups and teams in management actions requires that managers understand group considerations in decision making. The participation model of group decision making provides guidelines for the appropriate level of subordinate participation in decision making.

- A manager must consider both the advantages and disadvantages to group decision making. The advantages include greater experience and expertise, more information, higher satisfaction, and greater acceptance of and commitment to the decisions. The disadvantages are that group decisions take more time, one member or subgroup may dominate, individual goals may supplant group goals, social pressure to conform may be brought to bear on members, and groupthink may develop.

- Managers can use several structured techniques to aid in group decision making. These include brainstorming, the nominal group technique, the Delphi technique, devil's advocacy, and dialectical inquiry.

KEY TERMS

Decision making
Objectives
Rational-economic decision model
Ethical dilemma
Behavioral decision model
Bounded rationality

Intuition
Satisficing
Escalation of commitment
Vigilance
Groupthink
Brainstorming

Nominal group technique (NGT)
Delphi technique
Devil's advocacy
Dialectical inquiry

REVIEW QUESTIONS

1. Define decision making.
2. Explain the steps a manager can use to handle ethical dilemmas in decision making.
3. How does bounded rationality affect the decision-making process?
4. What are the seven steps of the decision-making process? Which step is most important?
5. Under what conditions would a manager use a group to make a decision?
6. Describe the advantages and disadvantages of group decision making compared to individual decision making. Provide specific examples to demonstrate your understanding.
7. What is groupthink? What are the signs a manager should look for to recognize groupthink?
8. What are the key guidelines for brainstorming?
9. How can brainstorming be used to improve group decision making?
10. What are the three basic categories of decision making in the Vroom-Jago participation model?

DISCUSSION QUESTIONS

Improving Critical Thinking

1. Is the rational-economic model of decision making so unrealistic that it is of no value to a decision maker? Why or why not?
2. Describe a situation in which you satisficed when making a decision.

Enhancing Communication Skills

3. What types of ethical dilemmas do you think future managers will face? How can you prepare yourself to handle ethical dilemmas? To develop your written communication skills, find some recent examples in current business publications and write a short paper on this subject.
4. Consider a recent decision that you have made, such as choosing a major or buying a car. How vigilant were you in making your decision? To practice your oral communication skills, be prepared to present your decision process to the class or a small group as directed by your instructor.

Building Teamwork

5. Interview a manager in a local business. Ask the manager to describe a business decision that she recently made and to explain the process that led to that decision. Analyze the manager's decision with regard to the two models of decision making described in the chapter. Form small groups and share the results of your interview with the team. Did the team members find any issues in common among all the managers interviewed?
6. Think about a group decision with which you have been involved. Did the group experience any signs of groupthink? Why or why not? Form small groups and look for common problems that members have experienced. Summarize your findings and be prepared to report them to the class.

1. Use the Internet to locate information on automobile manufacturers that have made the decision to recall any of their cars during the last twelve months. Then arrange this information in an electronic spreadsheet that will allow you to provide four lists. The first list will use manufacturer for the primary sort. The second list will use model name for the primary sort. The third list will use model year for the primary sort. The fourth list will use cause of problem (that is, part or component of the car) for the primary sort.

2. Using presentation software, develop a slide show to present your automobile recall findings to your classmates.

3. Using database software, store your automobile recall data in a fashion that would allow you to add more information as additional recalls occur. The structure of your database should also allow you to retrieve information on manufacturers, month and year of recalls, automobile models, or the particular component of the car that required repair or replacement.

ETHICS: Take a Stand

Harry was a senior member of the outside auditing team of a public company. Among his many responsibilities was the accurate and complete reporting of all financial information and transactions that could affect potential and current investors in the company. Inadvertently, a copy of a private memo from the company's controller to members of top management was placed in Harry's mail. The memo dealt with an acquisition that was about to take place, but the controller had not mentioned the acquisition to Harry. Harry therefore asked the controller about the acquisition when he returned the memo.

The controller seemed disturbed that Harry had received the memo. She grabbed the memo from Harry's hand and said that the acquisition was only under consideration. Thus, it should not be reported in the financial statements. She also said that if Harry mentioned the situation to anyone, he would look foolish because the transaction did not have to be reported under "generally accepted accounting principles."

Harry was taken aback by the controller's reaction. The memo provided significant detail about the transaction, and he was sure that the deal was final. In accordance with his firm's policy, Harry decided to bring the situation to the attention of the manager in charge of the auditing job. The manager said that he knew of the acquisition, but because the deal was not final when he completed his field work, he had decided to ignore it at the request of the chief financial officer. The partner on the job agreed with the decision.

Harry was certain that the acquisition would be very important to potential and current investors in the company. He was not comfortable with the way the problem had been handled and felt that some serious ethical issues were involved. He knew his next decision would be critical.

For Discussion
1. If you were Harry, what would you do?
2. What criteria would you use in taking action?
3. Develop a plan for Harry based on the steps of the decision-making process outlined in the chapter.

THINKING CRITICALLY: Debate the Issue

WHO SHOULD MAKE THE DECISION?

Form teams as directed by your instructor. Half of the teams should take the position that group decision making leads to high-quality decisions and high organizational performance. The other teams should take the position that group decision making impedes organizational performance and that decisions should not be made by groups. Research the topic using current business publications to provide support for your team's position. Your instructor will select two teams to present your arguments in a debate format.

Video Case

NEXT DOOR FOOD STORE

Related Web Site: {http://multimag.com/bus/imperialoil/}

Store Location Map:
{http://multimag.com/bus/imperialoil/storemap.html}

Next Door Food Store is a chain of 30 convenience stores and gas stations located throughout central Michigan. Similar to other convenience-store chains, the purpose of Next Door Food Store is to provide gasoline and convenience-store items to people who are in a hurry. Decision making in the corporate headquarters and at each individual store is an ongoing activity. The convenience-store industry is very competitive and the managers of Next Door Food Store are continually challenged to respond to routine problems and emerging industry trends.

Two of the key considerations that face the managers at Next Door Food Store are how to manage their distribution channels and how to select the items that are offered in their stores. Rather than building their own warehouse, to date the company has decided to use vendors to stock their stores on a just-in-time basis. The vendors have proved to be an invaluable resource in providing the company important marketing and product-mix information. As a result, the company strives to maintain an excellent relationship with its vendors and is less persuaded to build its own warehouse. In regard to the company's relationship with its vendors, one of the managers of Next Door Food Store remarked, "We can always get a better price (from a vendor), but that might not mean better service."

Selecting items to sell in the stores is an ongoing challenge. There are literally hundreds of items to choose from, and some suppliers are very aggressive. For instance, on one occasion the company accepted a cash payment from Coca-Cola in exchange for a commitment to sell only Coca-Cola soft-drink products. This decision angered many of the company's loyal Pepsi drinkers, and the agreement with Coca-Cola was hastily canceled. On a more routine basis, it is difficult for the managers of Next Door Food Store to know whether an emerging market trend represents a promising opportunity or is just a passing fad. An example is bottled water and health-conscious fruit drinks. Early on, the managers of Next Door Food Store decided to dedicate a generous amount of cooler space to these products. The decision to stock bottled water and fruit drinks was risky at the time, but has proven to be very profitable. Both of these lines of products have shown consistent sales growth since they were originally stocked at Next Door Food Store's 30 outlets.

Decision making at Next Door Food Store is an important part of each manager's job. In particular, the decisions that are made regarding distribution channels, product mix, and other critical areas play an important role in determining the company's present and future profitability.

For Discussion
1. Review the seven steps in the decision-making process provided in the chapter. Which steps are utilized by the managers of Next Door Food Store? Which steps appear to be the most critical for the convenience-store industry?
2. Are the managers of Next Door Food Store affected by bounded rationality? If so, provide an example from the case that illustrates this concept.

CYPROS COMPUTER DESIGN: A CASE OF MIXED BLESSINGS

CASE

As manufacturing vice-president for Cypros Computer Design, Jessica Okaty ponders the problem she faces. Cypros's management is always searching for ways to increase efficiency and recently installed new equipment (robots) along with a new simplified work system. To the surprise of everyone, including Jessica, the expected increase in productivity has not materialized. In fact, production has begun to drop, quality has fallen off, and employee turnover has risen.

Jessica does not believe that there is anything wrong with the new equipment. She has obtained reports from other companies that are using the robots, and they confirm this opinion. In addition, representatives from the firm that designed the equipment have inspected it and report that it is operating at peak efficiency.

Jessica suspects that some aspects of the new work system may be responsible for the declining productivity, but this view is not shared by her immediate subordinates—four unit supervisors, each in charge of a section, and her supply manager. They attribute the drop in production to insufficient training of the robot operators, lack of an adequate system of financial incentives, and poor morale. Clearly, this issue is arousing considerable feeling and is a source of potential disagreement among Jessica's subordinates.

This morning Jessica received a phone call from her division manager. He had just received her production figures for the last six months and was calling to express his concern. He said that the problem was hers to solve as she thought best, but that he would like to know within a week what steps she was planning to take.

Jessica shares her division manager's concern about the falling productivity and knows that her subordinates are also concerned. Her task is to decide what steps to take to rectify the situation.

For Discussion

1. Using the Vroom-Jago participation model of decision making in Figure 6.2, decide upon the appropriate decision style for Jessica to use. Support your answer.

2. Form groups of three to five people and repeat the process from Question 1. Try to achieve a consensus. Pick a spokesperson to report your group's solution to the class.

3. How much agreement was there within the group and within the class about the appropriate decision style for the case? Why?

4. Even though the Vroom-Jago model seems clear-cut, people often offer different answers to the diagnostic questions (in Figure 6.2) about the situation. What factors may account for differences in the way managers diagnose decision situations?

EXPERIENTIAL EXERCISE 6.1

Brainstorming: Creative Group Decision Making

Step 1 Form small groups as directed by your instructor. Each group will have an opportunity to develop some creative solutions to problems that typically arise on a college campus. Before beginning the exercise, review the rules for brainstorming discussed in the chapter.

Step 2 From a current campus newspaper, select a problem or issue that needs to be solved on your campus. Possible issues might include student apathy about elections, the need for recycling programs, or the lack of funding for student programs.

Step 3 You have 10 minutes after the words "Begin brainstorming" to generate ideas. Have one person write down all the alternatives. Remember, do not evaluate ideas.

Step 4 You have 10–15 minutes to discuss and evaluate the ideas that were generated in Step 3.

Step 5 You have 5 minutes to decide on the final solution that you will present to the class.

Step 6 Discuss as a class what happened in your group. How did your ideas emerge? Did you experience frustrations? What did you find most difficult about trying to use the brainstorming process?

EXPERIENTIAL EXERCISE 6.2

Examining Decision Making: An Organizational View

Examine current issues of business periodicals such as *Business Week, The Wall Street Journal,* or *Fortune,* and identify a significant decision recently made by a major company. Choose a company located in your city or state or one that you are familiar with. Possible decisions include the decision to expand into international markets, restructure, or hire a new CEO.

1. In the decision you identified, did the manager or managers appear to use good decision-making skills?

2. Did they follow the decision-making steps?

3. How successful was the company in implementing its decision?

4. Was the decision made by a group or an individual?

5. If you were advising the managers who made the decision, what criteria would you use?

SOURCE: Adapted from P. Fandt, *Management Skills: Practice and Experience* (St. Paul, Minn.: West Publishing, 1994).

ENDNOTES

1. H. Mintzberg, "The Manager's Job: Folklore and Fact," *Harvard Business Review,* March/April 1990, 163-76.

2. Based on "Blast Rocks Atlanta," *Orlando Sentinel,* July 28, 1996, A1; D. Eyring and R. Roy, "Explosion Shatters Good Will in Moment," *Orlando Sentinel,* July 28, 1996, A1; "Traffic Woes Spark Mutiny and Frustration," *Orlando Sentinel,* July 23, 1996, A1; K. Brandon and J. Coates, "IBM Defends Ballyhooed Olympic Computer System," *Orlando Sentinel,* July 23, 1996, A5.

3. P. Fandt, *Management Skills: Practice and Experience* (St. Paul, Minn.: West Publishing, 1994).

4. C. O'Reilly, "Variations in Decision Makers' Use of Information Sources," *Academy of Management Journal,* 25, 1982, 756-71; C. O'Reilly, "The Use of Information in Organizational Decision Making: A Model and Some Propositions," in B. Staw and L. Cummings, eds., *Research in Organizational Behavior,* Vol. 5 (Greenwich, Conn.: JAI Press, 1983), 103-39.

5. "Coke's Brand-Loyalty Lesson," *Fortune,* August 5, 1985, 44-46.

6. D. Vaughan, "Autonomy, Interdependence, and Social Control: NASA and the Space Shuttle Challenger," *Administrative Science Quarterly,* 35, 1990, 225-57.

7. D. Jones and E. Neuborne, "Fate, Fortune Ride on Flow of Critical Data," *USA Today,* July 2, 1996, pp. B1-2.

8. D. Vaughan, "Autonomy, Interdependence, and Social Control: NASA and the Space Shuttle Challenger."

9. K. Eisenhardt, "Making Fast Strategic Decisions in High-Velocity Environments," *Academy of Management Journal,* 32, 1989, 543-76.

10. M. A. Verespej, "Gutsy Decisions of 1994: Gerstner Looked before Leaping," *Industry Week,* January 23, 1995, 36.

11. S. W. Floyd and B. Wooldridge, "Managing the Strategic Consensus: The Foundation of Effective Implementation," *Academy of Management Executive,* 6, 1992, 27-39.

12. A. Adler, "Saturn Recalls All Cars Made before April '93 for Fire Risk," *The Columbia SC State,* August 11, 1993, A1; B. Meier, "Engine Fires Prompt G.M. to Issue Recall of 80% of Saturns," *New York Times,* August 11, 1993, A1; O. Suris, "Recall by Saturn Could Tarnish Its Reputation," *The Wall Street Journal,* August 11, 1993, A3; R. Truett, "Calls Swamp Saturn Dealers since Recall," *Orlando Sentinel,* August 11, 1993, A1.

13. H. Mintzberg, "The Manager's Job."

14. J. G. March, "Decision Making Perspective," in A. H. Van de Ven and W. S. Joyce, eds., *Perspectives on Organization Design and Behavior* (New York: Wiley, 1981).

15. N. J. Adler, *International Dimensions of Organizational Behavior,* 2d ed. (Boston: PWS-Kent Publishing, 1991); P. Sethi, N. Maniki, and C. Swanson, *The False Promise of the Japanese Miracle* (Marshfield, Mass.: Pitman, 1984).

16. F. N. Brady, *Ethical Managing: Rules and Results* (New York: Macmillan, 1990).

17. Adapted from S. W. Gellerman, "Why 'Good' Managers Make Bad Ethical Choices," *Harvard Business Review,* July/August 1986, 85-90; K. H. Blanchard and N. V. Peale, *The Power of Ethical Management* (Homewood, Ill.: Irwin, 1987).

18. H. A. Simon, *Model of Man* (New York: Wiley, 1957).

19. O. Behling and N. L. Eckel, "Making Sense out of Intuition," *Academy of Management Executive,* 5, 1991, 46-54.

20. R. Rowen, *The Intuitive Manager* (Boston: Little, Brown, 1986).

21. J. Schmit, "PC Maker Realizes a Dream," *USA Today,* July 17, 1996, B4.

22. O. Behling and N. L. Eckel, "Making Sense out of Intuition."

23. C. R. Schwenk, "Information, Cognitive Biases, and Commitment to a Course of Action," *Academy of Management Review,* 11, 1986, 298-310.

24. M. H. Bazerman, *Judgment in Managerial Decision Making* (New York: Wiley, 1986).

25. I. Janis and L. Mann, *Decision Making: A Psychological Analysis of Conflict, Choice, and Commitment* (New York: Free Press, 1977).

26. D. Ciampa, *Total Quality* (Reading, Mass.: Addison-Wesley, 1992).

27. V. H. Vroom and P. W. Yetton, *Leadership and Decision Making* (Pittsburgh, Penn.: University of Pittsburgh, 1973).

28. V. H. Vroom and A. G. Jago, *The New Leadership: Managing Participation in Organizations* (Upper Saddle River, N.J.: Prentice-Hall, 1988).

29. V. H. Vroom, "A New Look at Managerial Decision Making," *Organizational Dynamics,* Spring 1973, 69-70.

30. V. H. Vroom and A. G. Jago, *The New Leadership.*

31. R. A. Cooke and J. A. Kernagan, "Estimating the Difference between Group versus Individual Performance on Problem-Solving Tasks," *Group and Organization Studies,* 12, 1987, 319-42.

32. W. L. Ury, J. M. Brett, and S. B. Goldberg, *Getting Disputes Resolved* (San Francisco: Jossey-Bass, 1989).

33. I. L. Janis, *Victims of Groupthink* (Boston: Houghton Mifflin, 1972).

34. L. R. Beach, *Making the Right Decision: Organizational Culture, Vision, and Planning* (Upper Saddle River, N.J.: Prentice Hall, 1993).

35. Whyte, "Groupthink Reconsidered," *Academy of Management Journal,* 14, 1989, 40-55.

36. Adapted from C. R. Schwenk and R. A. Cosier, "Effect of the Expert, Devil's Advocate, and Dialectic Inquiry Methods on Prediction Performance," *Organizational Behavior and Human Performance,* 1, 1980, 409-24.

37. Beach, *Making the Right Decision.*

38. Based on "Compaq Storms the PC Heights from Its Factory Floor," *The New York Times,* November 13, 1994, 1; "Compaq Plans to Begin Selling PCs by Mail," *The Wall Street Journal,* December 9, 1992, B4; "Compaq Expects

to Be No. 1," *Dallas Morning News,* December 1, 1994, 30; M. Allen, "Bottom Fishing: Developing New Line of Low-Priced PCs Shakes Up Compaq," *The Wall Street Journal,* June 15, 1992, A1; K. Damore, "Volatile Desktop Market Comes to a Close," *Computer Reseller News,* December 12, 1994, 35–38; "Compaq Slimline," *USA Today,* July 3, 1996, A11; "Compaq Virtual Office," *USA Today,* June 27, 1996, B11.

39. D. M. Schweiger, W. R. Sandberg, and J. W. Ragan, "Group Approaches for Improving Strategic Decision Making: Analysis of Dialectical Inquiry, Devil's Advocacy, and Consensus," *Academy of Management Journal,* 29, 1986, 51–71.

40. A. F. Osborn, *Applied Imagination,* rev. ed. (New York: Scribner, 1957).

41. Ibid.

42. B. Schlender, "How Bill Gates Keeps the Magic Going," *Fortune,* June 18, 1990, 82–89.

43. A. Delbecq, A. Van de Ven, and D. Gustafson, "Guidelines for Conducting NGT Meetings," in *Group Techniques for Program Planning* (Glenview, Ill.: Scott Foresman, 1975).

44. R. DeStephen and R. Hirokawa, "Small Group Consensus: Stability of Group Support of the Decision, Task Process,

and Group Relationships," *Small Group Behavior,* 19, 1988, 227–39.

45. D. M. Hegedus and R. V. Rasmussen, "Task Effectiveness and Interaction Process of a Modified Nominal Group Technique in Solving an Evaluation Problem," *Journal of Management,* 12, 1986, 545–60.

46. R. Cosier and C. Schwenk, "Agreement and Thinking Alike: Ingredients for Poor Decisions," *Academy of Management Executive,* 4, 1990, 69–74.

47. C. R. Schwenk and R. A. Cosier, "Effect of the Expert, Devil's Advocate, and Dialectic Inquiry Methods on Prediction Performance."

48. Ibid.

49. L. R. Beach, *Making the Right Decision,* 6.

50. Developed from D. C. Couper and S. H. Lobitz, *Quality Policing: The Madison Experience* (Washington, D.C.: Police Executive Research Forum, 1991); R. B. Denhardt, *The Pursuit of Significance* (Belmont, Calif.: Wadsworth, 1992).

51. Based on P. Hersh, "Decision Came Quickly that Games Would Go On," *Orlando Sentinel,* July 28, 1996, A15; "Blast Rocks Atlanta"; D. Eyring and R. Roy, "Explosion Shatters Good Will in Moment."

Decision-Making Tools and Techniques

■ CHAPTER OVERVIEW

As we saw in Chapter 6, every day managers face situations where they must make a decision. Many times a decision is needed because a problem has arisen. Other times a decision is needed because an opportunity has presented itself. Regardless of the reason, when a decision is needed, successful managers will be ready to leap into action and make the decision to avoid losing ground in the increasingly competitive marketplace. We also learned from Chapter 6 that decision making is a multistep process, and that tomorrow's managers must possess decision-making skills.

Merely understanding the steps in the decision-making process is not enough, however. Many quantitative tools and techniques can be used to evaluate alternative courses of action prior to making a decision. Tomorrow's managers must be equipped with these analytical tools, for their proper use will help managers improve the quality of their decision making.

Organizational decisions are often categorized as either long-range strategic decisions or short-range operational decisions. Analytical tools and techniques have evolved to help managers make better decisions in both of these areas. This chapter focuses on the methodologies, procedures, and applications for some of the more prominent decision-making aids.

■ LEARNING OBJECTIVES

When you have finished studying this chapter, you should be able to:

- Discuss the different classifications for managerial decisions.
- Recognize the difference between strategic decision making and operational decision making.
- Describe the strategic decision-making matrix approach for strategy selection.
- Identify the differences between the growth-share matrix and the industry attractiveness/business strength matrix approaches for evaluating business portfolios.
- Discuss the differences between decision making under certainty, risk, and uncertainty.
- Describe the solution approaches that would be taken for risk and uncertainty situations.
- Explain the structure of and use of decision trees.
- Discuss the basics of breakeven analysis, linear programming, and PERT analysis.

Managerial Incident

GE APPLIANCE PARK: ANTIQUATED RELIC OR GOLDEN OPPORTUNITY?

Appliance Park, General Electric's five-factory complex near Louisville, Kentucky, was in trouble. Three other aging and ailing GE appliance plants had ceased operation during the early 1990s, and Appliance Park seemed destined to follow. This would be a particularly sad ending, for Appliance Park was once the showcase for GE's most innovative appliances and manufacturing technology. But the 40-year-old factories at Appliance Park had become outdated, losing both money and market share. In 1992 alone its losses were close to $50 million.

What to do with Appliance Park was a question that haunted GE chairman John Welch. This decision would be particularly difficult, for it would affect corporate profits or losses, the livelihoods of thousands of workers, and to some extent the health and vitality of the local community. Furthermore, making matters worse, in 1992 the federal government announced new energy standards for washing machines that would take effect in 1994. With less than two years until this deadline, Welch set his focus on the washing machine division and weighed his options. He could turn GE's washing machine production over to an outside contractor, which would result in the loss of 1,500 jobs, and would endanger the long-run survivability of Appliance Park. Or he could risk an investment of upwards of $70 million to overhaul the antiquated washing machine factories.[1]

INTRODUCTION

In the opening Managerial Incident, we saw that GE's chairman John Welch faced a dilemma. One GE executive argued that it made no business sense to invest in an aging and antiquated facility that was losing money. However, simply closing the facility would have a devastating impact on the lives of many workers and their families. But if problems could be solved, perhaps Appliance Park could be returned to a profitable state.

In Chapter 6 we saw that any person or organization faced with a decision has a rather straightforward task at hand. By following a systematic set of steps, the decision maker can select a course of action (the decision) from a set of many potential alternatives. After implementing the decision, follow-up monitoring will enable the decision maker to assess whether the chosen alternative has been producing desirable results. As routine as the decision-making process may seem, however, it requires considerable preparation to assemble and analyze all available information.

We begin this chapter with a discussion of the different categories of decision-making situations and then distinguish between strategic decision making and operational decision making. Several analytical tools and techniques have been developed to aid in making both strategic decisions and operational decisions, and we will examine them here. Much of the material that you will encounter in this chapter is a direct outgrowth of the quantitative perspective on management that was described in Chapter 2.

MANAGERIAL DECISION SITUATIONS

Before examining specific tools and techniques for decision making, let's review the conditions under which a decision situation might arise and the different ways of classifying those situations.

SOURCES OF ORGANIZATIONAL AND ENTREPRENEURIAL DECISIONS

Managers are faced with decisions when a problem occurs or when an opportunity arises. A **problem** occurs when some aspect of organizational performance is less than desirable. This definition is purposely broad so that it will cover any aspect of organizational performance, such as overall bottom-line profits, market share, output productivity, quality of output, or worker satisfaction and harmony, to name just a few of the countless possibilities. When such unsatisfactory results have occurred, the successful manager will both recognize the problem and find a solution for it.[2] The decision that GE wold eventually make in regard to Appliance Park would be in response to a problem or problems, the symptoms of which were operating losses and loss of market share. Think back to the decision by Saturn to recall its cars, as described in Managing for Excellence in Chapter 6. That decision was also made in response to a problem: in this case, the wiring problem and its potential to cause engine fires.

Problem
A situation where some aspect of organizational performance is less than desirable.

Managers do not always make decisions in response to problem situations. Often decisions are made because an opportunity arises. An **opportunity** is any situation that has the potential to provide additional beneficial outcomes. When an opportunity presents itself, success will be achieved by those who recognize the potential benefits and then embark upon a course of action to achieve them. For example, consider Pepsi-Cola's decision to add a freshness date on its beverage containers.[3] This decision was precipitated by a perceived opportunity to capture additional market share by offering something that Pepsi's competitors were not offering. Not to be outdone in the never-ending cola wars, Coca-Cola soon followed with freshness dates on its own products. The cola wars have soared to dizzying heights, both figuratively and literally. In trying to capitalize on an opportunity to have its products prominently displayed, Pepsi has sponsored the Russian space station *Mir*, while Coke was flying a spaceship version of a soda fountain as an experiment aboard the space shuttle *Endeavour*.[4] The cola competition may have reached its height (or depth, depending on your perspective) at the 1996 Olympic games in Atlanta. At the opening ceremonies, the song "Georgia on My Mind" was sung by Gladys Knight. Most observers had expected to see Ray Charles perform that number,

Opportunity
A situation which has the potential to provide additional beneficial outcomes.

Competition between the cola giants reached from the dizzying heights of outer space to the playing fields of the 1996 Olympic games in Atlanta.
© Florent Flipper/Unicorn Stock Photos

Managing for
Excellence

3M: CLEANING UP WITH NEW PRODUCT DEVELOPMENT

The 3M Corporation has always had a strong reputation for innovation. With a staff of some 8,000 researchers, the company routinely spends 6 to 7 percent of its revenue on research and development, which is nearly double the industry average. In fact, researchers spend about 15 percent of their time brainstorming and working on projects of their own choosing. When Livio De-Simone assumed the CEO position in 1991, 3M's annual revenue was at the $14 billion level. But DeSimone was troubled by the lack of freshness in the company's recent accomplishments. Most were variations on old ideas, leading to stagnation in 3M's growth.

DeSimone determined that the company's innovative spirit needed to be rejuvenated. He set a goal of capturing 30 percent of annual revenues from products less than four years old. He then embarked on a major reorganization effort. Cross-functional teams were created, and marketing personnel were moved closer to scientists. Open lines of dialogue were established with potential customers so that their preferences could be assessed at each stage of a product's development. DeSimone also initiated a program in which managers were requested to focus on the most promising ideas, and then rush them from the lab to the market.

DeSimone's moves paid off handsomely. One of the most successful products that came out of this effort was Scotch-Brite Never Rust scour pads, an environmentally friendly product that is manufactured from recycled plastic beverage bottles. Unlike traditional steel wool pads, Scotch-Brite pads will never leave rust stains on the sink or tiny steel splinters in consumers' hands. Within a year and a half of its introduction, the Scotch-Brite pad had captured 22 percent of the $100-million-per-year U.S. market. Because of the success of this and other new products, 3M's net profits in 1994 increased 5 percent to $1.3 billion. Furthermore, $1 billion of 3M's 1994 revenue was derived from products introduced during the year. Expectations are that improvements like this will continue in the foreseeable future.[5]

---

for it is arguably his signature song. But Ray Charles is a spokesperson for Pepsi, and the Coca-Cola Company, the most prominent of all Olympic sponsors, did not want him to perform in front of the worldwide audience. Hence, the substitution.[6]

Much like the freshness dating situation for soft drinks, there are numerous other illustrations of companies following the lead of their competitors to cash in on an opportunity. In the battery wars, Duracell first introduced the concept of a battery tester contained in the packaging. However, in 1996 the Energizer Bunny topped that by introducing batteries with the test mechanism designed as an integral part of the battery. One need only push the buttons and the LCD display on the battery indicates whether it is good or bad. And let's not forget about the breakfast cereal wars. When Post cut its prices in mid-1996, the remaining members of the "Big Four" began to lose market share. In rapid order, Kellogg, General Mills, and finally Quaker Oats reduced the prices of their breakfast cereals.[7]

From an entrepreneurial perspective, a good example of a successful response to an opportunity is the founding of Big Bob's Used Carpet Shops of America. After replacing the carpeting in his home, David Elyacher placed a classified ad in the Sunday newspaper offering his old carpet for sale. He received 50 phone calls on the day of the ad and sold the carpet that same day. When would-be buyers continued to call, Elyacher ran another ad offering to buy used carpet and told local carpet installers that he was interested in buying any carpeting they had replaced. He then leased warehouse space and opened a store. Within nine months he had opened a second store, and three more followed within the next few years, all in the greater Kansas City area. Big Bob's now has stores in seven states and has signed contracts for outlets in several others.[8]

Finding opportunities is a key function of the research and development scientists of 3M, described in Managing for Excellence. Here we see how the establishment of cross-functional teams and a customer focus rejuvenated the company's innovative spirit.

Regardless of whether a decision is precipitated by a problem, an opportunity, or both, it is important to understand the nature of the decision situation. Accordingly, we turn our attention to methods of classifying decision situations.

CLASSIFICATION OF DECISION SITUATIONS

On a very basic level, Herbert Simon, a management scholar and prolific researcher in the area of decision making, proposed that decisions can be classified as either programmed or nonprogrammed.[9] When the decision situation is one that has occurred in the past and the response is routine, the decision is referred to as a **programmed decision.** Identifying alternative courses of action in such situations is usually routine, for the alternatives are quite familiar to the decision maker. As an example of a programmed decision, consider the customer assistance operator for the Charleswood Company, a manufacturer of kits of unassembled furniture. If a customer discovers that a component or hardware item is missing from her kit, she can call an 800 number for assistance. The operator routinely obtains the missing part number from the customer, and then authorizes immediate UPS shipping of that part.

When a decision is made in response to a situation that is unique, unstructured, or poorly defined, it is called a **nonprogrammed decision.** These decisions often require considerable creativity, cleverness, and innovation to elicit a list of reasonable alternative courses of action. The investment group that took control of the Schwinn Bicycle Company, described in Entrepreneurial Approach, made nonprogrammed decisions as they tried to reverse the slide that Schwinn had been in for years. After internal restructuring, a shift to a customer focus, and the development of some hot new models, Schwinn rolled back to its former prominence in the industry.

The changing nature of today's business environment presents an interesting dilemma for decision makers. On the one hand, the rapidly changing, global business environment creates a need for more nonprogrammed decisions than ever before. With quality and continuous improvement as major strategic initiatives, organizations are constantly being challenged to find creative and innovative solutions to unique new problems and opportunities. At the same time, the changing composition of the work force suggests that more programmed decisions might be beneficial. Today's work force is constantly becoming more diverse in racial, ethnic, and gender composition. Workers with diverse backgrounds and cultural values often have different perceptions of appropriate organizational goals and objectives and therefore respond differently to the same decision situation. In such circumstances, the more programmed the decision responses can be, the more likely that workers will make consistent, quality decisions.

Whatever the type of decision situation, managers can use certain tools and techniques to achieve excellence in the decision-making process. We will first examine tools that aid in making long-range strategic decisions and then shift our attention to tools and techniques that are useful for making shorter-range operational decisions.

Programmed decision
Decisions made in response to routine situations that have occurred in the past.

Nonprogrammed decision
Decisions made in response to situations that are unique, unstructured, or poorly defined.

SCHWINN: ROLLING BACK ON TRACK

In recent years Schwinn, that venerable old company that had been providing children with bicycles for almost a century, found its fortunes declining so dramatically that it was forced to file for Chapter 11 bankruptcy protection in late 1992. Schwinn's share of the domestic bicycle market had fallen from its 1950s level of 25 percent to a meager 7 percent when bankruptcy proceedings started. Schwinn had failed to recognize that the customers of the 1990s were interested in something different than were the customers of the 1950s. While Schwinn continued to sell its products out of small bike shops, other companies, such as Huffy and Murray, were sapping Schwinn's market share by selling less costly, child-oriented bikes through large discounters like K-Mart, Wal-Mart, and Toys R Us. In addition, Schwinn was slow to react to the growing popularity of road and mountain bikes. Perhaps the most devastating blow to Schwinn was that it was losing its name recognition with the younger generation.

Despite this gloomy picture, Schwinn managed to rise from the depths with a completely new image, thanks to the entrepreneurial spirit of a group of investors named the Scott Sports Group. Scott purchased Schwinn's name and its assets, and then moved its operations to Colorado, which happens to be the capital of mountain biking. Scott then completely restructured the marketing, product development, and operations management systems. Schwinn then assumed a customer focus. In an attempt to give the customers what they wanted, Schwinn developed several radical new models that have won praise from industry analysts. The new leadership group has brought Schwinn back to its former prominence in the bicycle industry.[10]

STRATEGIC DECISION-MAKING TOOLS

Strategic decision making occurs at the highest levels in organizations. As we saw in Chapter 5, this type of decision making involves the selection of a strategy that will define the long-term direction of the firm. Two important areas for strategic decision making are in strategy selection and evaluation of portfolios.

STRATEGY SELECTION: THE STRATEGIC DECISION-MAKING MATRIX

Many times, organizations find that there is not one clear-cut, obvious strategy that should be pursued. Instead, several potentially attractive alternatives may exist. The task for management is to select the strategy that will best facilitate the achievement of the multiple objectives of the organization. A tool that can be helpful in such cases is the **strategic decision-making matrix.**[11]

Strategic decision-making matrix
A two-dimensional grid used to select the best strategic alternative in light of multiple organizational objectives.

When management faces several strategic alternatives and multiple objectives, it is helpful to organize these factors into a two-dimensional decision-making matrix.[12] To illustrate, let's consider the case of an organization that has established a goal of strong growth and has implemented that goal by specifying three objectives: increased profit, increased market share, and increased production output. Suppose management has determined that three alternative growth strategies are reasonable options for the organization—product development, horizontal integration, and a joint venture. To form the strategic decision-making matrix, the alternative strategies are listed along the side of the matrix, while the objectives are listed along the top, as in Table 7.1.[13]

Since the objectives of the organization won't always be equally important, different weights can be assigned to them. Management usually assigns the

TABLE 7.1   Strategic decision-making matrix

	OBJECTIVES			
	INCREASED PROFIT	INCREASED MARKET SHARE	INCREASED PRODUCTION OUTPUT	TOTAL WEIGHTED SCORE
ALTERNATIVE STRATEGIES	.5	.3	.2	
Product Development	2	2	3	.5(2) + .3(2) + .2(3) = 2.2
Horizontal Integration	4	2	2	.5(4) + .3(2) + .2(2) = 3.0
Joint Venture	5	3	3	.5(5) + .3(3) + .2(3) = 4.0

weights based upon its subjective assessment of the importance of each objective. The weights are shown directly below the objectives in Table 7.1. In this example, increased profit is the most important objective; therefore it has received the highest weight. Note that the sum of the weights must equal 1.0.

To use the matrix, management must first rate each alternative strategy on its potential to contribute to the achievement of each objective. A 1-to-5 rating scale is used, with 1 indicating little or no potential for achieving an objective and 5 indicating maximum potential. Once an alternative strategy has been rated for each objective, the strategy's total weighted score can be computed by multiplying its rating for each objective by the corresponding weight of the objective, and then summing across all objectives, as shown in the last column in Table 7.1. The decision maker can then select the strategy with the highest weighted score. In this example, the joint venture strategy is the most desirable alternative, because it will allow the organization to achieve the best combination of profitability, market share, and production output.

EVALUATION OF PORTFOLIOS

Whenever an organization becomes involved in several businesses and industries or with several products and services, it becomes necessary to make decisions about the role each business line will play in the organization and the manner in which resources will be allocated among these business lines. Although this discussion of the portfolio approaches focuses on the evaluation of multiple business lines, these approaches can also be used at the product or service level. This is done by replacing business lines on the matrix with products or services. The most popular technique for assessing the balance of the mix of business lines in an organization is portfolio matrix analysis. A **business portfolio matrix** is a two-dimensional grid that compares the strategic positions of each of the organization's businesses.

A portfolio matrix can be constructed using any reasonable pair of indicators of a firm's strategic position. As we will see, usually one dimension of the matrix relates to the attractiveness of the industry environment and the other to the strength of a business within its industry.[14] The two most frequently used portfolio matrices are the growth-share matrix and the industry attractiveness/business strength matrix.

Business portfolio matrix
A two-dimensional grid that compares the strategic positions of each of the organization's businesses.

The Growth-Share Matrix
The earliest business portfolio approach to be widely used for corporate strategy formulation is the growth-share matrix. This technique was developed by the Boston Consulting Group (BCG), a leading management consulting firm. Figure 7.1 illustrates a BCG matrix.[15]

FIGURE 7.1
The BCG growth-share matrix

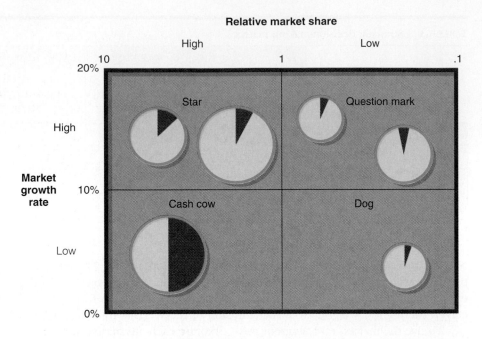

BCG matrix
Business portfolio matrix that uses market growth rate and relative market share as the indicators of the firm's strategic position.

Market growth rate
A measure of the annual growth percentage of the market in which the business operates.

Relative market share
The firm's market share divided by the market share of its largest competitor.

Stars
Businesses that fall into the high market growth/high market share cell of a BCG matrix.

Cash cows
Businesses that fall into the low market growth/high market share cell of a BCG matrix.

The **BCG matrix** is constructed using *market growth rate* and *relative market share* as the indicators of the firm's strategic position. Each of these indicators is divided into two levels (high and low), so that the matrix contains four cells. The rows of the matrix show the market growth rate, while the columns show the relative market share. **Market growth rate** is the percentage at which the market in which the business operates is growing annually. In the BCG matrix, 10 percent is generally considered the dividing line between a low rate and a high rate of market growth. **Relative market share** is computed by dividing the firm's market share by the market share of its largest competitor. For example, a relative market share of 0.4 means that the sales volume of the business is only 40 percent of the market leader's sales volume. In the BCG matrix, a relative market share of 1.0 is usually set as the dividing line between high and low relative market share.

To use the BCG matrix, each of the organization's businesses is plotted in the matrix according to its market growth rate and relative market share. Figure 7.1 illustrates a BCG matrix for an organization with six businesses. Each circle represents a business unit. The size of a circle reflects the proportion of corporate revenue generated by that business, and the pie slice indicates the proportion of corporate profits generated by that business.[16] Note that each cell in the BCG matrix has a descriptive label; these labels reflect the roles that the businesses in the cells play in the overall strategy of the firm.

Stars   Businesses that fall into the high market growth/high market share cell are referred to as **stars.** These businesses offer attractive profit and growth opportunities. However, they also require a great deal of money to keep up with the market's rate of growth. Consequently, in the short term they are often cash-using rather than cash-generating units, but usually this situation reverses in time. BCG analysis advocates retaining stars in the corporate portfolio.

Cash Cows   Businesses that fall into the low market growth/high market share cell are referred to as **cash cows.** These businesses generate substantial cash surpluses over what they need for reinvestment and growth. Cash cows are generally yesterday's stars whose industries have matured. Although not attractive from a growth standpoint, they are quite valuable, for the cash surpluses they generate can be used to pay bills, cover dividends, provide funds

Meeting the
Challenge

DEVELOPING A BCG MATRIX FOR YOUR COLLEGE

To get experience in developing a BCG matrix, examine the various academic departments of your business school. Consider that the total market consists of your university's school of business and its three geographically closest competing business schools. The academic departments in your school will be the "business units" being analyzed. Construct a BCG matrix using the following guidelines:

- Allow the market growth rate axis to reflect a unit's average annual growth.
- Allow the relative market share axis to reflect the ratio of a particular department's student enrollment to the enrollment of that department's largest competitor (from among the four schools being studied).

Use a circle to plot each department on the BCG matrix. The size of the circle can represent the proportion of the total business school enrollment generated by students majoring in that department's curriculum. The circle's pie slice can reflect the percentage of the total business school faculty assigned to that department.

Even though this is a nonprofit organization, the location of the circles on the matrix will be some indication of the stature of the different departments. Some departments may have large student enrollments with low faculty staffing levels, while others may have relatively small student enrollments but high faculty staffing levels. This analysis can then be used in allocating resources to individual departments or in making expansion and contraction decisions about individual departments.

SOURCE: Adapted with the permission of Prentice Hall from *Strategic Management*, 6th ed. by F. R. David. Copyright © 1996 by Prentice-Hall, Inc.

for investment, or support struggling businesses (such as the question marks described in a following section). BCG analysis also views cash cows favorably and advocates keeping them in the corporate portfolio.

Dogs   Businesses that fall into the low market growth/low market share cell are known as **dogs.** These businesses typically generate low profits, and in some cases they may even lose money. They also frequently consume more management time than they are worth. Unless there is some compelling reason to hold onto a dog (such as an expected turnaround in market growth rate), BCG analysis suggests that such businesses be removed from the portfolio.

Question Marks   Businesses that fall into the high market growth/low market share cell are referred to as **question marks.** The rapid market growth makes these businesses look attractive from an industry standpoint. Unfortunately, their low market share makes their profit potential uncertain. Question-mark businesses are often called *cash hogs* because they require large infusions of resources to keep up with the rapid growth and product development of the market. BCG analysis suggests that the organization must very carefully consider whether continued funding for a question mark is worthwhile. Management must consider the question mark's potential to gain market share and move into the star category.

BCG portfolio analysis can be used in both for-profit and not-for-profit organizations and in manufacturing and service organizations. Turn your attention, for the moment, to Meeting the Challenge.[17] Here is an opportunity for

Dogs
Businesses that fall into the low market growth/low market share cell of a BCG matrix.

Question marks
Businesses that fall into the high market growth/low market share cell of a BCG matrix.

Red Lobster and Olive Garden, both operated by Darden Restaurants, represent an example of a service organization balancing its portfolio. Red Lobster is a cash cow—a mature chain in a mature segment of the restaurant industry whose growth rate has subsided; Olive Garden is a star, and will continue to grow significantly for several years to come.

© Jeff Greenberg/Unicorn Stock Photos

you to gain hands-on experience in developing a BCG matrix using your own business school as the industry and the various academic departments as the business units.

The BCG business portfolio matrix makes valuable contributions in the area of strategic decision making. It enables a corporation to highlight the flow of cash resources among the units in its portfolio, and it provides a sound rationalization for resource allocation, investment, expansion, and contraction decisions. It also enables management to assess the balance among the units within its portfolio. A balanced portfolio should contain units in several cells. The status of individual business units can shift over time. For example, question marks can move into the star category, and stars will eventually evolve into cash cows. For these reasons, it is important to have question marks "waiting in the wings" to replace stars, and stars waiting to replace any cash cows that might slip into the dog category.

Darden Restaurants, a division of General Mills, provides a classic example of a service organization that tries to balance its portfolio to ensure its long-term success. The restaurant group currently operates two familiar restaurant chains: Red Lobster and Olive Garden. Each chain is in a different stage of development and occupies a different position on the BCG matrix. Red Lobster is a mature chain in a mature segment of the restaurant industry. Although Red Lobster still has opportunities for expansion, its growth rate has subsided from the early 1980s, when units were popping up everywhere. Olive Garden, General Mills Restaurants's entry into the Italian dinnerhouse segment, was started in 1980. The intention was to build this chain into a leader in its segment by penetrating the domestic market. And while Olive Garden has already achieved this leadership position, it is still in the early growth stage and will continue to enjoy significant growth for several years to come.[18] Placing these restaurant chains on a BCG matrix, we find that Red Lobster is a cash cow and Olive Garden is a star.

It is interesting to note that in the prior edition of this book, we talked about a third chain, China Coast, that had just begun operations. With only 51 restaurants and a short track record, China Coast was categorized as a question mark. The questions about China Coast were answered when Darden abruptly closed all China Coast restaurants in 1995.[19] As a potential replacement in the portfolio, Darden is testing a Caribbean concept restaurant, Bahama Breeze. Time will tell whether this venture will become successful, but for now it replaces China Coast as the question mark in Darden's BCG matrix. As long as Darden Restaurants continues to generate new concepts as the older concepts mature and saturate their relevant markets, the company is destined for long-term success.

The BCG business portfolio matrix approach is not without its shortcomings. Some critics have argued that the four-cell classification scheme is overly simplistic. Others contend that accurately measuring market share and growth rate can be difficult. Furthermore, when the analysis is based on just these two factors, other important variables may be overlooked.[20] In an attempt to overcome some of the limitations of the BCG approach, more refined models have been proposed. One of the early refinements of the BCG approach is the General Electric model, which attempts to overcome some of the BCG shortcomings.

The Industry Attractiveness/Business Strength Matrix

General Electric (GE) developed a nine-cell business portfolio matrix that overcomes some of the limitations of the BCG matrix. The **GE matrix** uses several

GE matrix
A business portfolio matrix that uses industry attractiveness and business strength as the indicators of the firm's strategic position.

factors to assess industry attractiveness and business strength. Table 7.2 lists
the various factors that can contribute to industry attractiveness and business
strength.[21] Furthermore, the GE approach allows for three levels of industry
attractiveness and business strength, resulting in its nine-cell structure.

To use the GE matrix, each of the organization's businesses is rated as to
industry attractiveness and business strength. To measure the attractiveness
of an industry, the decision maker first selects from Table 7.2 those factors

TABLE 7.2   Factors contributing to industry attractiveness and business strength

INDUSTRY ATTRACTIVENESS	BUSINESS STRENGTH
MARKET FORCES	
Size (dollars, units, or both)	Your share (in equivalent terms)
Size of key segments	Your share of key segments
Growth rate per year:	Your annual growth rate:
Total	Total
Segments	Segments
Diversity of market	Diversity of your participation
Sensitivity to price, service, features, and external factors	Your influence on the market
Cyclicality	Lags or leads in your sales
Seasonality	
Bargaining power of upstream suppliers	Bargaining power of your suppliers
Bargaining power of downstream suppliers	Bargaining power of your customers
COMPETITION	
Types of competitors	Where you fit, how you compare in terms of products,
Degree of concentration	marketing capability, service, production strength,
Changes in type and mix	financial strength, and management
Entries and exits	Segments you have entered or left
Changes in share	Your relative share change
Substitution by new technology	Your vulnerability to new technology
Degrees and types of integration	Your own level of integration
FINANCIAL AND ECONOMIC FACTORS	
Contribution margins	Your margins
Leveraging factors, such as economies of scale and experience	Your scale and experience
Barriers to entry or exit (both financial and nonfinancial)	Barriers to your entry or exit (both financial and nonfinancial)
Capacity utilization	Your capacity utilization
TECHNOLOGICAL FACTORS	
Maturity and volatility	Your ability to cope with change
Complexity	Depths of your skills
Differentiation	Types of your technological skills
Patents and copyrights	Your patent protection
Manufacturing process technology required	Your manufacturing technology
SOCIOPOLITICAL FACTORS IN YOUR ENVIRONMENT	
Social attitudes and trends	Your company's responsiveness and flexibility
Laws and government agency regulations	Your company's ability to cope
Influence with pressure groups and government representatives	Your company's aggressiveness
Human factors, such as unionization and community acceptance	Your company's relationships

SOURCE: Derek F. Abell and John S. Hammond, *Strategic Market Planning: Problems & Analytical Approaches,* © 1979, p. 214. Adapted by permission of Prentice-Hall, Englewood Cliffs, New Jersey.

that are likely to contribute to the attractiveness of the industry in question. Each factor is assigned a weight based upon its perceived importance. These weights must sum to 1.0. The industry is then assigned a rating for each of these factors using some uniform scale (for example, a 1-to-5 rating scale). Finally, a weighted score is obtained by multiplying weights by factor scores, and then adding to obtain a total weighted value. To arrive at a measure of business strength, each business is rated using the same procedure as for industry attractiveness. Table 7.3 illustrates these calculations for a hypothetical business in a corporation's portfolio.[22]

The total weighted scores for industry attractiveness and business strength are used to locate the business on the nine-cell matrix. Figure 7.2 illustrates a GE business portfolio matrix that contains eight businesses, with each circle reflecting one business.[23] The area of a circle is proportional to the size of the entire industry, while the pie slice within the circle represents the business's share of that market.

The GE matrix provides the decision maker with rationalization for resource allocation, investment, expansion, and contraction decisions within different cells, in much the same way as the BCG matrix. Businesses that fall into the three green cells at the upper left of the GE matrix are given top investment priority. These are the combinations of industry attractiveness and business strength that are most favorable. The strategic prescription for businesses located in these three cells is to invest and grow. Businesses positioned in the three blue cells are next in priority. These businesses deserve selective reinvestment to maintain and protect their industry positions. Finally, businesses

TABLE 7.3   Illustration of industry attractiveness and business strength computations

INDUSTRY ATTRACTIVENESS	WEIGHT	RATING (1–5)	VALUE
Overall market size	0.20	4.00	0.80
Annual market growth rate	0.20	5.00	1.00
Historical profit margin	0.15	4.00	0.60
Competitive intensity	0.15	2.00	0.30
Technological requirements	0.15	3.00	0.45
Inflationary vulnerability	0.05	3.00	0.15
Energy requirements	0.05	2.00	0.10
Environmental impact	0.05	1.00	0.05
Social/political/legal	Must be acceptable		
	1.00		3.45

BUSINESS STRENGTH	WEIGHT	RATING (1–5)	VALUE
Market share	0.10	4.00	0.40
Share growth	0.15	4.00	0.60
Product quality	0.10	4.00	0.40
Brand reputation	0.10	5.00	0.50
Distribution network	0.05	4.00	0.20
Promotional effectiveness	0.05	5.00	0.25
Productive capacity	0.05	3.00	0.15
Productive efficiency	0.05	2.00	0.10
Unit costs	0.15	3.00	0.45
Material supplies	0.05	5.00	0.25
R&D performance	0.10	4.00	0.20
Managerial personnel	0.05	4.00	0.20
	1.00		4.30

SOURCE: La Rue T. Hosmer, *Strategic Management: Text and Cases on Business Policy,* © 1982, p. 310. Adapted by permission of Prentice-Hall, Upper Saddle River, New Jersey.

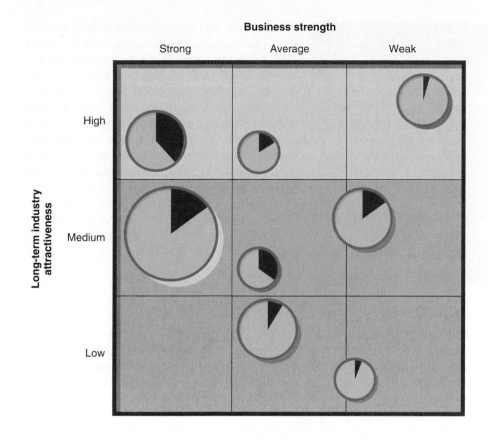

Business strength

FIGURE 7.2

The GE industry
attractiveness/business strength
matrix

positioned in the three pink cells at the lower right of the matrix are serious candidates for divestiture due to their low overall strength.[24]

Although similar to the BCG approach, the GE matrix offers several improvements. For one thing, it allows for intermediate rankings between high and low and between weak and strong, yielding nine rather than four cells. A second improvement is that it incorporates a much wider variety of strategically relevant variables. Whereas the BCG matrix considers only two factors (industry growth rate and relative market share), the GE matrix takes many factors into consideration (see again Table 7.2) to determine industry attractiveness and business strength. Finally, and perhaps most importantly, the GE approach emphasizes allocating corporate resources to businesses with the greatest chance of achieving competitive advantage and superior performance.[25]

Despite these improvements, the GE matrix does have its critics. Like the BCG matrix, it prescribes only a general strategic posture and provides no real guidance on the specifics of the business strategy. Another criticism of the GE approach (and the BCG approach, for that matter) is that they are static. They portray businesses as they are at one point in time and do not take into account that businesses evolve over time. Consequently, these approaches do not detect businesses that are about to become winners because their industries are entering the takeoff stage or businesses that are about to become losers as their industries enter the decline stage.[26]

OPERATIONAL DECISION MAKING

The strategic decision making just examined is typically conducted at high levels within the organization and covers long time horizons. Operational deci-

Saturn's decision to recall 380,000 automobiles due to faulty wiring is an example of an operational decision, but one that received the attention of the highest levels of management.

sion making, on the other hand, relates to decision situations that cover much shorter spans of time. While these decisions are typically made at lower levels within the organization, this need not always be the case. In Chapter 6 you learned about Saturn's decision to recall 380,000 automobiles due to faulty wiring. Whether or not to recall is by no means a long-term strategic decision. This decision applied to the immediate short-term future. Nevertheless, you can be sure that it received the full attention of top management. In the next sections, we will introduce structure to the operational decision-making process. Once that structure is in place, a variety of computational decision-making techniques can be applied.

APPLYING STRUCTURE TO THE DECISION-MAKING PROCESS

Several basic elements of decision making can be identified in the decision-making steps described in Chapter 6. They are referred to as alternative courses of action, states of nature, and payoffs. These elements can often be conveniently arranged into a structured array to aid in the decision analysis. Such an array is called a *payoff matrix*.

Alternative Courses of Action

Alternative courses of action
Strategies that might be implemented in a decision-making situation.

The **alternative courses of action** in a decision-making situation are the strategies that the decision maker might implement to solve the problem or respond to the opportunity. To make quality decisions, the decision maker must first identify viable and potentially attractive alternative courses of action. In the opening Managerial Incident, GE officials had two alternative courses of action from which to choose. One alternative was to simply close Appliance Park and cut their losses. The other alternative was to identify causes of poor performance and then correct them.

States of Nature

States of nature
Conditions over which the decision maker has little or no control.

States of nature are future conditions that can occur. They will affect the outcome of the decision, yet the decision maker has little or no control over them.[27] For example, corporate financial officers must often decide how to invest surplus funds. Future interest rates are a state of nature that will affect the outcome of their decisions. States of nature can reflect any type of future event that is likely to affect the outcome of a decision, including such events as weather, competitor behavior, economic conditions, political events, new laws, and consumer behavior. The more certain the decision maker is about the likelihood of various states of nature, the easier will be the decision making. Unfortunately, as we will see later, decision makers are rarely able to foresee future events with complete certainty. The degree of certainty that the decision maker possesses will affect the decision-making process.

Payoffs

The interaction of each alternative course of action with each state of nature will result in a decision outcome. Each combination of alternative and state of nature will produce a separate outcome. Suppose that a company can choose to invest surplus funds in fixed-rate certificates of deposit (CDs) or in a money market account. If the company invests in CDs and interest rates rise, the yield will not be as great as it would have been if the money had been invested in a money market account. Outcomes of decision situations are often referred to as **payoffs** since the objective in many business decisions can be measured in units of monetary value.

Payoff Tables

By properly organizing these elements, a systematic decision analysis can be undertaken. In decision theory, payoffs are called *conditional values* because each payoff is conditional upon a particular alternative course of action having first been selected and a particular state of nature having subsequently occurred. Whenever a decision situation is to be analyzed, the basic elements of the situation can be arranged in a matrix called a **payoff table** or a *conditional value matrix,* due to the conditional nature of the payoffs.[28] The alternative courses of action form the rows of the table, and the states of nature form the columns, as in Table 7.4.[29] Then each cell in the table contains the outcome, or payoff, for a particular combination of an alternative course of action and state of nature. Organizing the decision-making elements in this structured format allows for the systematic analysis of the decision problem and the eventual selection of an appropriate course of action.

If you compare the payoff table for operational decision making with the strategic decision-making matrix discussed earlier, you will see some similarity. Both use a two-dimensional matrix with decision alternatives arranged along the left side. But here the similarity ends. The strategic decision-making matrix employs multiple objectives and arranges them across the top of the matrix. The payoff table uses a single objective, whose measurements appear within the cells of the matrix. External factors (that is, states of nature) affecting the outcomes of the decisions are arranged across the top of the payoff table.

TECHNIQUES THAT ENHANCE QUALITY IN DECISION MAKING

The manner in which the information in the payoff table is analyzed is a function of the decision-making environment. At a basic level of analysis, three different decision-making environments are generally identified, depending on the amount of knowledge that exists about future conditions that might occur: (1) decision making under certainty, (2) decision making under risk, and (3) decision making under uncertainty.[30] The more information the decision maker has about future conditions, the easier will be the selection of an alternative course of action. As the future becomes more clouded, it becomes more difficult to identify one best tool for analyzing the decision. As a result, in such cases decision makers tend to have less confidence in the alternative they select for implementation.

Payoffs
The outcomes of decision situations.

Payoff table
A matrix that organizes the alternative courses of action, states of nature, and payoffs for a decision situation.

TABLE 7.4   Structure of a payoff table

ALTERNATIVE COURSES OF ACTION	STATES OF NATURE		
	S_1	S_2	S_3
A_1	O_{11}	O_{12}	O_{13}
A_2	O_{21}	O_{22}	O_{23}
A_3	O_{31}	O_{32}	O_{33}
A_4	O_{41}	O_{42}	O_{43}

NOTE: A_i = alternative courses of action; S_j = states of nature; O_{ij} = outcome associated with alternative i and state of nature j.

Decision Making under Certainty

In decision making under certainty, the decision maker knows with certainty what conditions will subsequently occur and affect the decision outcomes. Hence, the decision maker knows what the outcome will be for each alternative course of action. In such a situation, a rational decision maker will logically select the alternative with the most desirable outcome. For example, suppose you have $1,000 that you would like to place in your neighborhood bank for one year. Suppose further that your alternatives are limited to depositing the money in a savings account that yields 5 percent annual interest or a CD that yields 6 percent annual interest. If both investments are equally secure, you will not need access to this money during the year, and your objective is to maximize your monetary payoff, then you would choose the CD.

Decision Making under Risk

Decision makers, however, seldom encounter conditions of certainty. In most instances decision makers do not know with certainty which future state of nature will occur and subsequently influence the decision outcome. In many cases, however, the decision maker may have a reasonable idea of the chances, or probability, of each state of nature occurring. Consider the financial officer's decision on investing surplus funds. Examination of economic forecasts might provide the officer with the likelihood, or probability, that future interest rates will reach certain levels. When such probabilities are present, the process is referred to as decision making under risk. In decision making under risk, the probabilities are used to obtain expected values of outcomes for each decision alternative. The decision maker then selects the alternative that maximizes the expected outcome, assuming that the outcomes in the payoff table are attractive (for example, profits). If the outcomes in the payoff table represent an undesirable parameter (such as cost), then, of course, the decision maker should select the alternative that minimizes the expected outcome.

Table 7.5 shows the structure of a decision situation that has been scaled down for ease of illustration.[31] In this situation, an organization has a surplus of $100,000 available for short-term (one-year) investment. The financial officer is considering three simple investment alternatives: the stock market, bonds, or a money market account. In this example, the gain to be realized after one year will depend upon the economic conditions that prevail during that year. For simplicity, assume that the economy might rise, remain stationary, or fall. The conditional payoffs for each combination of alternative and state of nature are shown in the payoff table of Table 7.5. Notice that in one cell the return is a negative number, indicating a loss if the money is invested in the stock market and the economy subsequently falls.

Expected value
The product of a payoff and its probability of occurrence.

Expected monetary value (EMV)
The sum of each expected value for an alternative.

Expected Monetary Value   An **expected value** is the product of a conditional value and the probability of its occurrence. In a decision-making matrix, each alternative strategy has a total **expected monetary value (EMV),** which is the sum of each expected value for that alternative.[32] In Table 7.6, probabilities have

TABLE 7.5   Payoff table for sample illustration: conditional value matrix

ALTERNATIVES	STATES OF NATURE		
	RISING ECONOMY	STATIONARY ECONOMY	FALLING ECONOMY
Stock Market	$20,000	$5,000	−$8,000
Bonds	$ 5,000	$5,000	$5,000
Money Market	$10,000	$7,000	$4,000

TABLE 7.6   Calculation of expected monetary values: expected value matrix

	STATES OF NATURE			
Probability	.3	.5	.2	
ALTERNATIVES	RISING ECONOMY	STATIONARY ECONOMY	FALLING ECONOMY	Expected Monetary Value
Stock Market	$6,000	$2,500	−$1,600	$6,900
Bonds	$1,500	$2,500	$1,000	$5,000
Money Market	$3,000	$3,500	$ 800	$7,300

Maximum expected monetary value = $7,300, associated with the money market alternative.

been assigned to each state of nature.[33] The decision maker would have estimated these probabilities after careful analysis of various economic indicators.

The matrix of Table 7.6 illustrates the calculation of the EMVs for each alternative course of action. This is referred to as an *expected value matrix*.
The expected values within Table 7.6 are obtained by multiplying the conditional values in Table 7.5 by their probabilities of occurrence. The figures indicate that the most desirable alternative is the money market option, which
yields $7,300, the highest expected monetary value. This highest EMV of
$7,300 is an interesting figure. You might mistakenly conclude that the money
market will generate a return of $7,300, but in fact this can never happen. If
the money market account is the selected alternative, the conditional values,
as shown in Table 7.5, indicate that the only possible returns are $10,000,
$7,000, or $4,000. Then what does the $7,300 figure reflect? The $7,300 value
is the long-run average return that would occur if the decision maker faced
this situation repeatedly and selected the money market alternative each time.
On some occasions the return would be $10,000 (30 percent of the time, as-

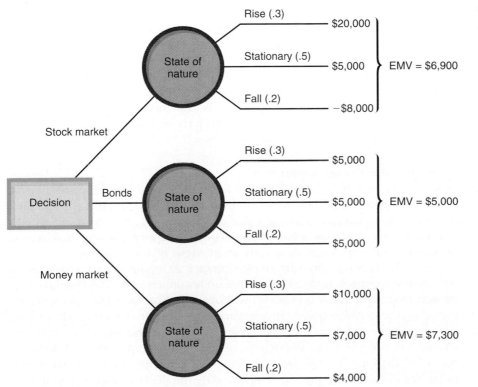

FIGURE 7.3
Decision tree

suming that the probabilities reflect long-run frequencies for different economic conditions). Furthermore, 50 percent of the time, the return would be $7,000, and 20 percent of the time, a return of $4,000 would be realized. Averaging the returns from repeated decisions over a long period of time gives the $7,300 figure.

Decision tree
A branching diagram that illustrates the alternatives and states of nature for a decision situation.

Decision Trees   As we have just seen, the payoff matrix is a convenient way to analyze alternatives in decision making under risk situations. Our investment example might also have been structured in a **decision tree** format, with various tree branches and junctions (or nodes) depicting the same decision scenario.[34] Figure 7.3 displays this problem in a decision tree format.

In this tree diagram, the box represents a decision point, with alternatives emanating from it. Circles represent points in time after the potential decision has been made when states of nature (future events) are about to occur. Each circle in this diagram has the three states of nature emanating from it. Each state of nature is followed by its probability of occurrence. Finally, payoffs are shown at the termination of each state-of-nature branch. Each payoff is still a conditional value. The events the payoffs are conditional upon can be found by tracing from the decision point to the payoff. For example, if the money market alternative is selected and the economy remains stationary (with a .5 probability), the payoff will be $7,000. The tree can be used to compute expected monetary values and will give the same results as the payoff table, as Figure 7.3 shows. Although a decision tree can be used for simple problems such as this, this approach is most useful for situations where sequential decisions must be made over time. In such cases an alternative-choice branch will be followed by a state-of-nature branch, which may be followed by another decision point with more branches emanating from it. With such a complex series of interrelated decisions, decision trees are the only recourse for obtaining a solution.

A decision tree approach proved to be quite helpful to the United States Postal Service (USPS) in the early 1980s, when it began to explore the possibility of expanding the five-digit ZIP Code. The USPS viewed the developmental study as a two-phase decision process. Phase I focused on information dissemination and the acquisition of automated equipment for pilot testing. Phase II dealt with the continuation of the postal automation strategy. Six alternatives were included in this phase (one of which was to cancel Phase II and terminate the expanded ZIP Code concept). We all know through our daily dealings with the USPS that the expanded ZIP Code concept (called ZIP+4) was adopted. What we probably didn't know is that this decision was prompted by an extensive decision tree analysis of the alternatives based on internal rate of return and net present value of cash flows.[35]

Decision Making under Uncertainty

In some cases a decision maker cannot assess the probability of occurrence for the various states of nature. When no probabilities are available, the situation is referred to as decision making under uncertainty. In such situations the decision maker can choose among several possible approaches for making the decision. Each approach takes a different view of the likelihood of future events.[36] To illustrate two extremes, consider an optimistic approach and a pessimistic approach to decision making under uncertainty. The optimistic approach assumes that the best payoff will occur regardless of the alternative selected by the decision maker. If you were an optimistic decision maker facing the investment decision described earlier, you would choose the stock market alternative, because it has the highest of the optimistic payoffs ($20,000). On the other extreme, a pessimistic approach assumes that the worst payoff will occur regardless of the alternative selected by the decision maker. If you were a pessimistic decision maker facing the same investment decision, you would choose the bond alternative, because it has the highest of the pessimistic pay-offs ($5,000).

Different decision makers will have different perceptions about which future events are likely to occur and different levels of aversion to risky ventures; both will influence their decision making. To accommodate these differences, several uncertainty approaches have been developed. Although the details will not be covered here, we can note that these approaches generally fall between the optimistic and pessimistic extremes described earlier. None of these approaches can be described as the "best" approach, for there is no one best uncertainty approach. Each has utility for different decision makers, since different people often have different ways of looking at a problem.[37]

ETHICAL AND SOCIAL IMPLICATIONS IN DECISION MAKING

The treatment of decision making presented thus far may leave the impression that all managers need to do is plug in the numbers to generate the best choice of an alternative. However, managers must also be careful to consider more than just the numbers. Often they will have to look beyond the numbers and consider the ethical and social implications of their decisions. In addition to the profits and losses of the situation, GE executives had to concern themselves with the fate of some 1,500 workers as they considered what to do with Appliance Park, described in the opening Managerial Incident.

The city of Orlando, Florida, thinks along these lines when it hires workers for a new expressway project. The Orlando/Orange County Expressway Authority made hiring the homeless a condition for contractors bidding on highway landscaping and maintenance contracts worth millions of dollars. The intent was to provide the homeless with basic on-the-job training, an opportunity to move into better jobs, and a chance to break out of their endless cycle of poverty.[38] In the same vein is a heartwarming announcement made just before Christmas 1995 by Aaron Feuerstein, president of Malden Mills Industries of Methuen, Massachusetts. When a devastating December fire destroyed a large portion of the textile mill, Feuerstein decided to continue to pay wages and health insurance benefits to 800 out-of-work employees while trying to get the mill running again.[39]

In Global Perspective, GM and Saturn officials had to balance economics and social implications in their decisions surrounding the introduction of a larger model. Outsourcing would certainly facilitate cost reduction, but the advantages of total outsourcing would have to be weighed against the impact on current GM workers and workers in related supply industries.

QUANTITATIVE DECISION-MAKING AIDS

Many quantitative models, tools, and techniques are available that can aid in various types of decision-making situations. Although a detailed presentation of these models is beyond the scope of this book, it is important to have some awareness of these tools and techniques. The next sections provide a brief overview of some of the more important models.

Breakeven Analysis
Breakeven analysis is a quantitative technique that allows managers to examine the relationships between output levels, revenues, and costs. By analyzing these factors, managers can determine the level of output at which the firm will break even (that is, where total revenue equals total cost; at this point

Aaron Feuerstein continued paying 800 of the Malden Mills' 3,200 employees who remained out of work for three consecutive months due to a fire that occurred just before Christmas in 1995.

©/AP/Wide World Photos

Breakeven analysis
A graphical display of the relationship among volume of output, revenue, and costs.

SATURN: NEW MODEL GOES GLOBAL FOR PARTS

Since it started as a semiautonomous company in 1990, Saturn has built reliable small cars that have lured import buyers back to General Motors. The Saturn division has won countless customer service awards and boundless customer loyalty. However, for years Saturn dealers have wished for a larger car to offer customers who have simply outgrown Saturn's limited lineup of small cars. Concurrently, CEO Jack Smith has pushed GM to develop cars that can be built in the United States and Europe on the same basic platform, saving billions of dollars in product development costs. These two goals will come together in Innovate, code name for the next-generation Saturn. In 1994 developers decided that the European Opel Vectra, which was a year away from being overhauled, would serve as the ideal platform. Innovate should be ready to go on sale in the United States in 1999.

Unlike current models of Saturn, which are built in the Spring Hills, Tennessee, plant, the Innovate will be built elsewhere. Current plans call for the use of a GM plant in Wilmington, Delaware, which was scheduled to close down in late 1996. The project will be a crucial test of Smith's ambitious goal to globalize the automative giant's manufacturing operations. Most of the major parts for Innovate will be made by outside suppliers, many not organized by the United Auto Workers Union. The number of European- and Asian-manufactured parts will be double that of Saturn's popular SL2 model, while the number of Mexican- and Canadian-manufactured parts will be five times that of the SL2.[40]

the firm makes no profit, but incurs no loss). Furthermore, managers can project the profit or loss associated with any level of output. For a familiar example, consider the situation faced by the promoter of a rock concert. Revenue generated by the concert will be determined largely by the price charged per ticket and the number of tickets sold. (In some cases concession and souvenir sales might add to this revenue.) Expenses, for the most part, will consist of the contracted fee negotiated with the rock act, concert hall rental charges, and other personnel services (such as ticket takers and security guards). The promoter can use breakeven analysis to help determine ticket prices and the number of tickets that must be sold to break even or, more important to the promoter, to generate varying levels of profit.

Breakeven analysis depicts the output, revenue, and cost relationships in a graphical format, as illustrated in Figure 7.4.[41] In this format, output volume (in units of product) is represented on the horizontal axis of the graph, while the vertical axis indicates the levels of costs and revenues (in dollars).

Seven elements can be defined and illustrated on the breakeven graph.[42]

1. Fixed cost. Fixed cost includes those costs that remain constant regardless of the volume of output. Fixed cost comprises such items as overhead, administrative salaries, rent, and mortgage payments. It is shown by a horizontal line on the graph.

2. Total variable cost. This reflects the costs that increase as the volume of output rises. Variable costs include such items as raw material cost, direct

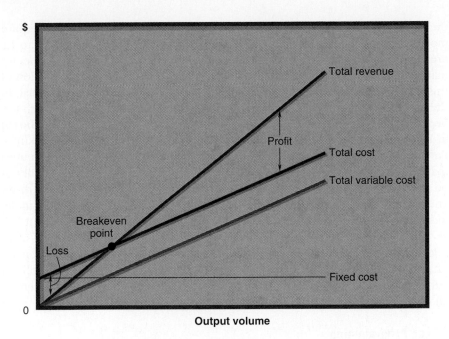

FIGURE 7.4
Breakeven analysis

labor cost, and the cost of energy consumed in the manufacture of the product. Total variable cost is obtained by multiplying the output level by the variable cost per unit (that is, the material, labor, and energy costs consumed per unit of output). On the graph, the total variable cost is zero when there is no output, but increases as the output level rises.

3. Total cost. The sum of fixed cost and total variable cost is the total cost. It is represented by a line that is parallel to the total variable cost line, but shifted upward due to the addition of the fixed cost.

4. Total revenue. This is the total dollars received from the sale of the output. Total revenue is obtained by multiplying the per-unit selling price by the output level. On the graph, revenue is zero when there is no output, but increases as the output level rises.

5. Breakeven point. On the graph, there is one level of output where total cost equals total revenue. This is defined as the breakeven point, for it is here that the organization will realize no profit, but incur no loss.

6. Profit. Profit is the amount by which total revenue exceeds total cost on the graph. Profit will be realized at all output levels to the right of the breakeven point.

7. Loss. Loss is the amount by which total cost exceeds total revenue. On the graph, a loss will be incurred at all output levels to the left of the breakeven point.

Breakeven analysis is a useful tool for analyzing the costs, revenues, profits, and losses at various levels of output. The simple linear structure displayed here does have its limitations, though. Often fixed cost does not remain constant through all levels of output. For example, to exceed some critical volume of output, it may be necessary for the organization to expand its plant, thereby incurring a sudden increase in its overhead, administrative expenses, and other contributors to fixed cost. A situation like this would be reflected as a step increase in the fixed cost line.

Similarly, price and unit variable cost may change as output volume changes. Higher levels of output may result in quantity discounts in the purchase of raw materials. Lower raw material costs would lead to a decrease in the slope of the variable cost line. Higher levels of output may also require more overtime from workers. The higher cost of labor would lead to an increase in the slope of the variable cost line. If higher levels of output occur, management must often reduce the selling price to encourage consumption of this additional output. Lowering the selling price would lead to a decrease in the slope of the revenue line. When situations such as these occur, the breakeven graph will not display the crisp, uniform, linear relationships shown in Figure 7.4. Instead, the lines may contain bends, curves, breaks, and kinks. Furthermore, these lines generally represent estimates of costs and revenues that will occur in the future. Since estimates are rarely exact, the lines will not be precise and sharp. Instead, the actual values might be above or below those lines. Consequently, the breakeven point should be regarded not as a single, indisputable value, but as an indication of an approximate range of output levels where breakeven is most likely to occur. Regardless of the amount of irregularity in these graphs, however, the fundamental relationships will remain intact. Profit will occur when total revenue exceeds total cost, losses will occur when total cost exceeds total revenue, and breakeven will occur when total cost equals total revenue.

Linear Programming

Often managers are faced with the decision of how to allocate limited resources among competing users in a manner that optimizes some objective. These resources can be as diverse as materials, machines, money, energy, employees, and the like. Linear programming is a powerful tool that can help the manager solve such allocation problems.

Although the linear programming computations are quite technical, desktop computer software for solving this type of problem is available. Nevertheless, managers need to be familiar with the basic structure of a linear programming problem. After all, they will be responsible for recognizing these allocation situations and will have to structure the linear programming formulation for the decision situation before the computer can take over and perform the calculations.

To develop a linear programming formulation, the decision maker must structure two basic components: the objective function and a set of constraints.[43] An **objective function** is a symbolic, quantitative representation of the primary goal that the decision maker is seeking to optimize. **Constraints** are algebraic statements, in equation form, that reflect any restrictions on the decision maker's flexibility in making decision choices. Before developing these two components, the decision maker must have a clear understanding of the decision variables in the problem. **Decision variables** represent the factors that the decision maker can manipulate, that is, the decisions that must be made. Table 7.7 illustrates a simple production decision where two products (bookcases and compact disc racks) are to be manufactured from three raw materials (wood, plastic laminate, and glue) whose supplies are limited. The data in the table indicate the amount of each raw material used in making each product, the amount of each raw material available, and the profit contribution for each product. The decision maker must decide how much of each product to manufacture to maximize profit, while at the same time being careful not to exceed the available supplies of each raw material. Steps 1 to 4 at the bottom of Table 7.7 show how the decision maker would define algebraic symbols to represent the number of units of each product to make (the decision variables) and the subsequent objective function and constraints that would have been formulated. This linear programming model is now ready for desktop computer solution.

The linear programming situation illustrated in Table 7.7 was kept exceedingly simple for illustration purposes. In reality, managers often face re-

Objective function
A symbolic, quantitative representation of the primary goal that the decision maker is seeking to optimize.

Constraints
Algebraic statements, in equation form, that reflect any restrictions on the decision maker's flexibility in making decision choices.

Decision variables
The factors that the decision maker can manipulate.

TABLE 7.7   Linear programming

PRODUCT INFORMATION			
Raw Material	BOOKCASES	COMPACT DISC RACKS	**Raw Material Available**
Lumber	8	5	400
Plastic Laminate	4	2	120
Glue	1	2	60
Profit per unit	$15	$10	

Step 1. Definition of decision variables:
   Let X_1 = the number of book cases manufactured.
   Let X_2 = the number of CD racks manufactured.
Step 2. Establish objective function:
   Maximize profit, or MAX $15X_1 + 10X_2$.
Step 3. Establish constraints:
   Resource constraints: Amount of each raw material used must be less than or
      equal to the amount available.
   Lumber constraint: $8X_1 + 5X_2 \leq 400$.
   Plastic laminate constraint: $4X_1 + 2X_2 \leq 120$.
   Glue constraint: $1X_1 + 2X_2 \leq 60$.
   Nonnegativity constraints: You cannot make a negative number of bookcases
   or CD racks.

$$X_1 \quad 0$$
$$X_2 \quad 0$$

Step 4. Summarize problem:
   MAX $15X_1 + 10X_2$
subject to: $8X_1 + 5X_2 \leq 400$
         $4X_1 + 2X_2 \leq 120$
         $1X_1 + 2X_2 \leq 60$
         $X_1 \quad 0$
         $X_2 \quad 0$
   (Solution: $X_1 = 20$; $X_2 = 20$; profit = $500)

source allocation problems consisting of hundreds or even thousands of decision variables and similar numbers of constraint equations. Linear programming has seen some very diverse applications over the years. For example, Owens Corning Fiberglas uses it to develop multiproduct production schedules, American Airlines uses it for scheduling flight crews and aircraft, and Major League Baseball uses it to assign umpires to baseball games.[44]

PERT

Organizations must often undertake large, unique projects that involve many highly interrelated work activities. In such cases, managers must be prepared to schedule all of those activities and the resources they consume so that the project can be completed in a timely fashion. General Motors had to coordinate thousands of activities as the Saturn project moved from the concept stage to a working factory producing automobiles.

   PERT (Program Evaluation and Review Technique) is a technique designed to aid in scheduling project activities. The PERT approach uses a network diagram to arrange and visually display project activities. Such a diagram can help managers to plan far in advance, pinpoint potential bottlenecks and trouble spots, and determine whether resources should be reallocated among activities.

PERT (Program Evaluation and Review Technique)
A network approach for scheduling project activities.

In the PERT approach, four preliminary steps must be performed before the project analysis can begin: (1) activity identification, (2) precedence identification, (3) activity time estimation, and (4) network construction.[45] Activity identification requires that managers determine all of the elements of work (activities) that must be performed for the project to be completed. To establish the activity precedence relationships, managers must determine which activities can be conducted simultaneously and which must be performed sequentially. It is also necessary to estimate the amount of time each activity will consume so that a time schedule can eventually be developed for the project activities. Finally, all of this information must be assembled into a network model to facilitate the analysis.

Figure 7.5 shows a network model for a very simple project, consisting of only five activities. In this project, a team of fraternity brothers will build a bicycle shed for the fraternity house. The arrows in the PERT diagram represent the activities, while the circles (nodes) represent events. The amount of time each activity will take is indicated on the appropriate arrow. The nodes (events)

FIGURE 7.5

PERT analysis

Data generated in preliminary analysis of project:

Activity	Description	Immediate Predecessors	Activity Time (Days)
A	Design dimensions of shed	—	2
B	Set forms for concrete slab	A	1
C	Cut lumber for shed to proper dimensions	A	2
D	Pour concrete slab and allow to cure	B	4
E	Assemble shed	C, D	3

Resulting project network generated:

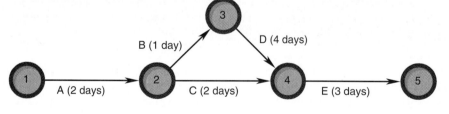

Identification of critical path:

Path	Time	
ABDE	10 days	(critical path)
ACE	7 days	

Earliest start (ES), earliest finish (EF), latest start (LS), and latest finish (LF) time estimates:

Activity	ES	EF	LS	LF	
A	0	2	4	6	ES for first activity = 0, or today's calendar date.
B	2	3	6	7	ES for other activities = largest EF of activity's immediate predecessors.
C	2	4	9	11	EF for activity = its ES + its activity time.
D	3	7	7	11	LF for last activity = some target completion time (14 days here).
E	7	10	11	14	LF for other activities = smallest LS of activity's immediate successors. LS for activity = its LF − its activity time.

represent points in time. For example, at node 2, activity A (design the dimensions of the shed) has been completed, and activities B and C (set the forms for the concrete slab and cut the lumber for the shed) are ready to be started. Furthermore, precedence relationships can be recognized immediately from the diagram. For example, setting the forms for the concrete slab (activity B) and cutting the lumber for the shed (activity C) cannot begin until after the shed has been designed and its dimensions are known (activity A). Also, activities B and C (setting forms and cutting lumber) can be conducted simultaneously, since no precedence relationship exists between them.

Once the preliminary PERT steps have been performed, the network can be analyzed to determine reasonable start and finish times for each activity and a likely project duration. Project duration is determined from the network's critical path. A path is any sequence of activities that extends from the beginning to the end of the project. In our simple illustration, two paths extend from the beginning to the end of the project (path A-B-D-E and path A-C-E). The most time-consuming path in the network is the critical path. The critical path dictates the minimum amount of time in which the project can be completed and also indicates which activities are most critical to getting the project completed on time. In this example, the critical path is path A-B-D-E (10 days). Any delays on these activities will lengthen the duration of the project. We have assumed in this example that the fraternity brothers' main concern is finishing the project in fourteen days, so that it will be completed when the other brothers return for the fall semester. Figure 7.5 summarizes the results from all the calculations of start and finish times for each of the project's activities.

This overview of PERT has described the technique in its most basic form. By expanding this form, managers can deal with situations where the time required for activities is uncertain or where resources can be reallocated among activities to alter a project's completion time and cost. British Airways successfully used PERT to analyze the necessary activities in a program to create a new image for the corporation.[46]

INFORMATION TECHNOLOGY AND DECISION-MAKING TOOLS

In Chapter 6 we were introduced to a seven-step decision-making process, and focused on how timely and accurate information is extremely beneficial in the first step (problem identification) and the last step (monitoring and evaluating). The tools and techniques that we have introduced in this chapter are quantitative models that enable us to assess the promise of various alternative courses of action. Consequently, these tools and techniques have their biggest impact on the midsection of the decision-making process, where alternatives are evaluated and decisions reached. When we use quantitative models of this type, the old axiom rings true: Garbage in, garbage out. Regardless of how sophisticated these analytical tools are, their output (decision recommendations) will be worthless if the information being processed is suspect. Once again, the huge advances in information gathering, processing, and dissemination technology serve to make this aspect of the decision-making process more reliable. The confidence we can place in our decisions will only increase as the technological advances in information handling continue.

MANAGERIAL IMPLICATIONS

Decision making has always been one of the primary activities of managers. As the global business economy continues to expand and change dramatically, the level of managerial decision making can only be expected to increase in the future. If they are to make quality decisions, managers will have to become thoroughly familiar with the structure of decision making and at the same time must equip themselves with the tools and techniques that can aid in the decision-making process. This means that tomorrow's managers should:

- Be able to recognize quickly problems and opportunities that call for a decision.
- Be able to recognize the different time frames and scopes of strategic decisions versus operational decisions.
- Be equipped with all the tools and techniques that can aid in making strategic decisions.
- Be familiar with the framework for operational decision making as well as the structural components for displaying operational decisions.
- Be able to recognize the different decision-making environments under which their operational decisions will be made.
- Have an awareness and understanding of the various quantitative tools that can aid in making operational decisions.

This chapter has presented several quantitative tools and techniques that can aid in making both strategic and operational decisions. These tools and techniques are quite analytical, suggesting that we need only "plug in the numbers" to select the best alternative. As we saw several times in our discussions, however, decision making cannot always go entirely by the numbers. Many times, experience, good judgment, and even intuition are valuable commodities when making decisions about future courses of action, especially since we can never be entirely certain about what the future holds in store for us.

**Managerial
Incident
Resolution**

GE APPLIANCE PARK: A REMARKABLE TURNAROUND

In attacking the Appliance Park decision, GE Chairman John Welch and his high-level executives had to first search for the basic problems that were leading to such symptoms as loss of market share and financial loss. Then it would be necessary to judge whether performance could be brought into line with corporate goals by addressing the problems. After detailed study by the executive team, problems were found in three areas: labor relations, inventory/manufacturing costs, and product design.

To improve poor labor relations, an agreement was struck with the local Electronics Workers Union. Labor and management agreed to move away from the historically "antagonistic and confrontational" patterns of the past. A program was implemented in which work teams with strong voices in operational decisions were created. The number of job classifications was drastically reduced, providing teams with flexibility in their work assignments. Inventory requirements were reduced and inventory turnover rates were more than doubled, freeing up almost $500 million in working capital. This working-capital savings was put to use in the area of new product design. In 1994 and 1995 GE planned to introduce between 300 and 400 new appliance models. Through niche marketing, these new models were to be targeted to specific groups of consumers.

Instead of the feared loss of 1,500 jobs through closure, GE actually hired close to 700 new employees at Appliance Park to handle the increased business. The loss of nearly $50 million in 1992 changed to a profit of $40 million in 1994 and close to $80 million in 1995—a remarkable turnaround, indeed.[47]

SUMMARY

- Programmed decisions are routine responses to decision situations that may have occurred in the past or with which the decision maker is quite familiar. Nonprogrammed decisions are responses to situations that are unique, unstructured, or poorly defined.

- Strategic decision making occurs from a very broad perspective and is performed at the highest levels within organizations. It involves the selection of a corporate-level strategy and the choice of competitive strategies to be pursued by the various business units of the organization. Strategic decision making is most often nonroutine by nature. Operational decision making pervades all levels in the organization and is usually concerned with routine day-to-day decisions.

- Selection of a business strategy can be facilitated by means of the strategic decision-making matrix approach. This tool allows the decision maker to evaluate a variety of potential strategies in conjunction with several objectives. Objectives are ranked by their importance, and strategies are rated by their likelihood of achieving those objectives. This method ultimately allows for the ranking of alternative strategies.

- Two popular matrix approaches for evaluating a business portfolio are the BCG growth-share matrix and the GE industry attractiveness/business strength matrix. Although both have two dimensions, they measure different factors and include a different number of levels for each factor. The two factors in the BCG matrix are market growth rate and relative market share. With two levels for each factor, a four-cell matrix results. The GE matrix uses industry attractiveness and business strength as its factors. Three levels for each factor are defined, resulting in a nine-cell matrix. In both approaches, an organization's business units are placed in the appropriate cell; then prescriptions for strategic decision making are made relative to the cell occupied by the business unit.

- In decision making under certainty, the decision maker knows exactly which future state of nature will occur. In decision making under risk, the decision maker is not sure which state of nature will occur, but can assess the probability, or likelihood, of each occurring. In decision making under uncertainty, the decision maker not only is not sure which state of nature will occur, but has no estimate of the probability that each will occur.

- Various computational criteria exist for analyzing decision making under conditions of certainty, risk, and uncertainty. When risk conditions prevail, payoff tables can be used in conjunction with state-of-nature probabilities to arrive at expected payoffs for each alternative. The alternative with the best expected payoff will then be selected. When uncertainty conditions prevail, decision makers must assess their degree of optimism about the likely occurrence of future events in order to make a choice.

- Decision trees provide another format for assessing decision making under risk situations. Alternative courses of action and states of nature are laid out in a tree diagram rather than in a matrix. Decision trees are particularly useful when the decision maker faces a sequence of interrelated decisions that occur over time.

- Breakeven analysis is a quantitative technique that allows managers to graphically examine the relationships between output levels, revenue, and costs. Linear programming is a technique that allows managers to determine how to best allocate limited resources among competing users in a manner that optimizes some objective. PERT is a network technique that allows managers to schedule a complex set of interrelated activities that must be performed to complete large, unique projects.

KEY TERMS

Problem	Stars	Expected value
Opportunity	Cash cows	Expected monetary value (EMV)
Programmed decision	Dogs	Decision tree
Nonprogrammed decision	Question marks	Breakeven analysis
Strategic decision-making matrix	GE matrix	Objective function
Business portfolio matrix	Alternative courses of action	Constraints
BCG matrix	States of nature	Decision variables
Market growth rate	Payoffs	PERT (Program Evaluation and
Relative market share	Payoff table	Review Technique)

REVIEW QUESTIONS

1. Identify the two situations that are likely to result in a business decision being made.

2. Describe the strategic decision-making matrix technique for selecting from among strategy alternatives. In what way is this approach similar to the format for decision making under risk for operational decision making?

3. Describe the structure, purpose, and approach of the four-cell BCG matrix.

4. Describe the structure, purpose, and approach of the nine-cell GE matrix.

5. What is a state of nature?

6. What is the difference between a conditional value and an expected value?

7. Describe how decision making under certainty, risk, and uncertainty differ.

8. What are decision trees, and where are they most useful?

DISCUSSION QUESTIONS

Improving Critical Thinking

1. Discuss the pros and cons associated with the two business portfolio matrix techniques described in this chapter. Which, if any, do you find more appealing? Why?

2. Assume that you are about to prepare for an examination in one of your business courses and have several alternatives as to the amount of studying that you can do. The exam can have several possible degrees of difficulty (depending upon how tough your professor decides to make it!). Discuss how this situation could be cast into a decision-making matrix format. What would you use as a measure of payoffs for this situation?

3. Refer back to Question 2. Think for a moment about your own personal feelings and premonitions as to how difficult the exam might be. Using these premonitions on exam difficulty and the payoffs you described in Question 2, which alternative would you select and why?

Enhancing Communication Skills

4. Assume that you are employed as a counter attendant in a fast-food restaurant. What are two requests that a customer might make that would require a routine decision? Two requests that would require a nonroutine decision? To enhance your oral communication skills, prepare a short (10-15 minute) presentation for the class in which you describe these requests and explain why you classified them in this way.

5. Think of some task, project, or endeavor that you have recently faced that required you to make a series of interrelated decisions. Thoroughly describe that situation and the decisions you made. Then convert this verbal description into a decision tree diagram that displays these interrelationships. To enhance your written communication skills, write a short (1-2 page) essay describing this endeavor, the decisions you faced, and the tree diagram displaying these interrelationships.

Building Teamwork

6. Put yourself in the position of a student member of your campus homecoming committee. One of your committee's duties is to book a successful comedian (fee $10,000) for one of your homecoming events, and develop a plan to conduct that event. To refine your teamwork skills, meet with a small group of students who have been given this same assignment. Assign each team member some aspect of this endeavor to research in order to determine the costs you are likely to incur, potential sources of revenue, available concert halls or auditoriums, and any other pertinent information. Then, use breakeven analysis to develop a thorough plan for staging this entertainment event. Finally, select a spokesperson to present the details of your plan to the rest of the class.

7. List several objectives with different units of payoff measure that might be encountered in various business decisions. To refine your teamwork skills, meet with a small group of students who have been given the same assignment. Compare your lists for common items, then consolidate your ideas into a single list. Select a spokesperson to present to the rest of the class your list of payoff measures and where they might be encountered.

1. Use the Internet to locate information and generate a list of all products introduced by 3M during the most recent calendar year. Place these products into appropriate categories (such as office supplies, household items, and so on) and store the information in an electronic spreadsheet that can be sorted by category.

2. Use the Internet to locate information on GE's Profile line of kitchen appliances. Generate a list of all refrigerators in that line. Information should include configuration (for example, side-by-side, top freezer, and so on), colors, sizes, special features, and prices. Arrange this information into an electronic spreadsheet that can be sorted by any of these aspects of the refrigerators.

3. Use the Internet to locate information on the Coca-Cola Company and the Pepsi-Cola Company. Use a word-processing package to prepare a brief synopsis of what's new in the cola wars for your classmates.

> INFORMATION TECHNOLOGY: Insights and Solutions

ETHICS: Take a Stand

Pennsylvania's largest health insurer, Pennsylvania Blue Shield, has invested almost $10 million since 1986 in Philip Morris, Inc., the world's largest cigarette manufacturer. The money represents about 0.5 percent of Blue Shield's total investment in stocks and bonds, according to financial reports filed with the Pennsylvania State Insurance Department. In 1992 alone, Blue Shield bought 1.8 million shares of Philip Morris stock. Currently, the insurer has a total of more than $4.3 million invested in Philip Morris.[48]

For Discussion

1. Discuss the ethics of the health insurer's decision to invest in an industry that arguably has a negative impact on human health.

2. Can this investment be justified on the basis of Blue Shield's obligation to generate sufficient cash to service claims by policyholders?

3. Does the fact that the investment is less than 1 percent of Blue Shield's total portfolio have any bearing in this matter?

THINKING CRITICALLY: Debate the Issue

BCG ANALYSIS—GOOD OR BAD?

Form teams of four or five students as directed by your instructor. Research the use of the BCG growth-share matrix for business portfolio analysis. In particular, try to ascertain and understand both the positive and negative aspects of this approach. Prepare to debate either the positive or the negative aspects of the BCG approach. When it is time to debate this issue in front of the class, your instructor will tell you which position you will take.

Video Case

KING SYSTEMS

Home Page: {http://www.iquest.net/kingsystems/cor.htm}

King Systems Corporation, located in Noblesville, Indiana, is a family-owned business that specializes in the precision design and manufacturing of anesthesia and respiratory care products. Observing that doctors often put lip balm on the surgical masks of children to provide a pleasant aroma and calm the childrens' fears, the company came up with a line of "scented" masks that are used on patients' faces when anesthetics are administered. The scented masks are brightly colored, and are available in the flavors of strawberry, cherry, and bubble gum. They are also adjustable to provide maximum comfort, and are available in infant, toddler, and child sizes.

Just four years after the company started, one of King Systems's original partners left the firm to begin a competing business. The partner that left was in charge of marketing and customer development, so the remaining partners had very little knowledge of their customers' needs. Some confusion existed for a period of time, until the company decided to take a fresh approach to market development. The fresh approach, according to Kevin Burrow, a member of the family that owned the company and vice-president of sales and marketing, was to ask each customer, "What do you need to better do your job?" This approach led the company to develop a number of new products, some of which are customized for each individual physician's needs. As a result, today the company has over 3,500 different configurations of a single anesthesia product. In addition, the company has an improved rapport with its many customers.

King Systems Corporation is now on firm financial ground, and is recognized as a major manufacturer of anesthesia care products. Sales and profit growth have been excellent. The employees of the company share a bonus of 1 percent of gross sales every month. When asked to describe the essence of the success of his business, King Systems CEO and President Flois Burrow indicated that it all boils down to caring—for the customers, employees, and vendors.

For Discussion

1. What kind of quantitative decision-making tools could be used by the managers of King Systems to assist them in their decision making?
2. Shortly after the marketing and customer development partner left the firm, what decision-making tool or tools could the remaining partners have used to access the relative strength of each of their product lines?
3. Due to the critical nature of their profession, physicians prefer to make as many of their decisions as possible under conditions of certainty rather than under conditions of risk. What role does King Systems play in helping physicians make decisions under certainty rather than under risk?

WORD PROCESSING 'R ME

Ann Houser was lying on the beach in Clearwater, Florida, enjoying the last weeks of the summer vacation before her senior year in college. As she lay there, she was trying to think of a way to earn extra money during the school year. "Why not take advantage of my excellent typing skills?" she thought. "I could type term papers and reports for my classmates. There is sure to be plenty of work." The more she thought about it, the more she liked the idea. She rolled off her beach blanket, picked up a small piece of driftwood, and began scrawling a decision plan in the sand.

Ann thought aloud: "I must lease hardware right now for one semester and will have to choose between a simple word-processing machine and a more sophisticated personal computer with word-processing software and a laser printer. Then I will see how much work comes in. At the end of the fall semester, I will have to decide what I will do during the spring semester, which will be my last semester in this business venture. At that time I must decide whether to change equipment or continue with what I originally leased. If I originally leased a word processor, I might be approaching my capacity, so I'll have to decide whether to continue with the word processor or trade up to a microcomputer. If I originally leased a microcomputer, I might have too much firepower, so I'll have to decide whether to continue with the microcomputer or trade down to a word processor. Of course, my decision will be influenced by the demand for my services during the fall semester. But regardless of whether demand was high or low during the fall, it could change during the spring. It seems to me that the profit I realize will depend upon the type of hardware I lease coupled with the demand level that occurs."

At the end of all this musing, Ann realized that she had developed a tree diagram that reflected the sequence of decisions she was facing over the next academic year. The diagram put everything into perspective for her, and as she folded up her blanket she had a very good feeling about her new venture.

For Discussion
1. Try to develop a diagram like the one Ann scratched into the sand, showing the sequence of decisions, alternatives, and states of nature that she would be facing during the upcoming academic year.
2. Discuss the additional information that Ann will have to obtain or estimate if she is to use her diagram to systematically analyze the sequence of decisions that she faces.

EXPERIENTIAL EXERCISE 7.1

Decision Making under Risk

Purpose: To gain experience in the analysis of a risk decision situation through the use of payoff tables.

Procedure: Review the conditional values provided in the accompanying payoff table. Then, assuming that the probabilities for the states of nature are .2, .2, and .6 for S_1, S_2, and S_3, respectively, perform the analysis requested.

	STATES OF NATURE		
ALTERNATIVES	S_1	S_2	S_3
A_1	32	25	19
A_2	21	28	29
A_3	18	20	26

Step 1 Use the conditional values and the probabilities to derive an expected value matrix.

Step 2 Calculate the total expected value for each alternative.

Step 3 Select the best alternative and provide an interpretation for its total expected value.

EXPERIENTIAL EXERCISE 7.2

Using Decision Trees in Everyday Life

Purpose: To gain a better appreciation for the fact that many everyday decision situations are composed of a sequence of interrelated decisions that could be displayed as a decision tree.

Procedure: Think about the decisions you make each semester before registering for your college courses. Your course selections are no doubt driven to a large extent by the requirements for your program of study. Your selection of specific class sections, however, is probably influenced by such factors as the instructor, the time of day and days of the week the class meets, conflicts with other classes, conflicts with work schedules, and conflicts with sleep schedules. Your decision process probably has some sequential elements to it, for example, "If I schedule this class at this time, then these classes cannot be scheduled because . . ." Develop a tree diagram to illustrate the sequential decision aspects of the class scheduling process that you went through in a recent semester.

ENDNOTES

1. Based on J. R. Norman, "A Very Nimble Elephant," *Forbes,* October 10, 1994, 88–92; Z. Schiller, "If You Can't Stand the Heat, Upgrade the Kitchen," *Business Week,* April 25, 1994, 35; Z. Schiller, "GE's Appliance Park: Rewire or Pull the Plug?" *Business Week,* February 8, 1993, 30.

2. M. J. Hicks, *Problem Solving in Business and Management* (London: Chapman & Hall, 1991).

3. "Pepsi Puts Freshness Dates on Diet Soda Bottles, Cans," *Orlando Sentinel,* March 31, 1994, B5.

4. S. Borenstein, "Not Just for the Taste of It: Colas Use Space for Ads," *Orlando Sentinel,* May 1, 1996, A1*ff.*

5. Based on S. Tully, "Why to Go for Stretch Targets," *Fortune,* November 14, 1994, 148–50; "The Mass Production of Ideas, and Other Impossibilities," *The Economist,* March 18, 1995, 72.

6. "Coke Rules," *Orlando Sentinel,* July 25, 1996, B1.

7. "Cereal Wars," *USA Today,* June 27, 1996, B1.

8. "Big Bob's Used Carpet Shops of America," in *Real World Lessons for America's Small Businesses: Insights from the Blue Chip Initiative* (*Nation's Business,* on behalf of Connecticut Mutual Life Insurance Company and the U.S. Chamber of Commerce, 1992), 92–93.

9. H. A. Simon, *The New Science of Management* (Englewood Cliffs, N.J.: Prentice-Hall, 1977), 47.

10. Based on Z. Espinosa, "The Comeback Rig—Schwinn Bounces Back with a Hot New Suspension Bike," *Mountain Bike,* February 1995, 50–52; G. Strauss, "Schwinn Files for Chapter 11," *USA Today,* October 9, 1992, B1.

11. J. M. Kopf, J. G. Krevze, and H. H. Beam, "Using a Strategic Planning Matrix to Improve a Firm's Competitive Position," *Journal of Accountancy,* 175, July 1993, 97–101.

12. F. R. David, "The Strategic Planning Matrix—A Quantitative Approach," *Long Range Planning,* 19, October 1986, 102.

13. F. R. David, *Strategic Management,* 4th ed. (New York: Macmillan, 1993), 234.

14. A. A. Thompson Jr. and A. J. Strickland III, *Strategic Management: Concepts and Cases* (Homewood, Ill.: Irwin, 1992), 193.

15. J. A. Pearce III and R. B. Robinson Jr., *Strategic Management: Formulation, Implementation, and Control,* 4th ed. (Homewood, Ill.: Irwin, 1991), 263.

16. F. R. David, *Strategic Management,* 225–27.

17. Adapted from F. R. David, *Strategic Management,* 251–52.

18. Personal interview with Blain Sweat, Olive Garden Restaurants, April 20, 1994.

19. J. DeSimone, "Darden Shuts Door on China Coast," *Orlando Sentinel,* August 23, 1995, B1*ff.*

20. P. Haspeslagh, "Portfolio Planning: Uses and Limitations," *Harvard Business Review,* 60, January/February 1982, 58–73.

21. D. F. Abell and J. S. Hammond, *Strategic Market Planning: Problems & Analytical Approaches* (Englewood Cliffs, N.J.: Prentice-Hall, 1979).

22. P. Kotler, *Marketing Management: Analysis, Planning, and Control,* 6th ed. (Englewood Cliffs, N.J.: Prentice-Hall, 1988).

23. A. A. Thompson Jr. and A. J. Strickland III, *Strategic Management.*

24. S. C. Certo and J. P. Peter, *Strategic Management: Concepts and Applications,* 2d ed. (New York: McGraw-Hill, 1991), 107–10.

25. J. A. Pearce III and R. B. Robinson Jr., *Strategic Management,* 267–72.

26. C. W. Hofer and D. Schendel, *Strategy Formulation: Analytical Concepts* (St. Paul, Minn.: West Publishing, 1978), 33.

27. T. M. Cook and R. A. Russell, *Introduction to Management Science,* 3d ed. (Englewood Cliffs, N.J.: Prentice-Hall, 1985), 399–402.

28. D. W. Miller and M. K. Starr, *The Structure of Human Decisions* (Englewood Cliffs, N.J.: Prentice-Hall, 1967), 106.

29. B. Render and R. M. Stair Jr., *Introduction to Management Science* (Boston: Allyn & Bacon, 1992), 598.

30. E. F. Harrison, *The Managerial Decision-Making Process* (Boston: Houghton Mifflin, 1975), 151–58.

31. B. Render and R. M. Stair Jr., *Introduction to Management Science,* 598.

32. D. Samson, *Managerial Decision Analysis* (Homewood, Ill.: Irwin, 1988), 148–51.

33. B. Render and R. M. Stair Jr., *Introduction to Management Science,* 600.

34. D. Samson, *Managerial Decision Analysis,* 23–32.

35. "Decision Tree Analysis in the United States Postal Service," *Interfaces,* March/April 1987, 35–41.

36. T. M. Cook and R. A. Russell, *Introduction to Management Science,* 402–4.

37. J. Sengupta, *Decision Models in Stochastic Programming: Operational Methods of Decision Making under Uncertainty* (New York: North Holland, 1982).

38. R. Roy, "Expressway Not a Dead End for Homeless—Program Will Give Them Jobs," *Orlando Sentinel,* April 21, 1993, 1ff.

39. Cable News Network, December 17, 1995.

40. Based on M. Maynard, "New Saturn Is Heavy on Outsourcing," *USA Today,* July 5, 1996, B1; M. Maynard, "Innovate: New GM Car Is Equipped with Challenge," *USA Today,* July 5, 1996, B3; "Saturn Says Demand Tops Production," *Orlando Sentinel,* July 26, 1996, B5; R. Blumenstein, "GM Confirms Plan for Midsize Saturn, Available by 1999," *Wall Street Journal,* August 7, 1996, C18.

41. L. J. Krajewski and L. P. Ritzman, *Operations Management: Strategy and Analysis,* 3d ed. (Reading, Mass.: Addison-Wesley, 1993), 45.

42. Ibid., 44–46.

43. B. Render and R. M. Stair Jr., *Introduction to Management Science,* Chap. 2.

44. Ibid., Chaps. 2, 4, 6.

45. Ibid., Chap. 9.

46. Ibid.

47. Based on J. R. Norman, "A Very Nimble Elephant"; Z. Schiller, "If You Can't Stand the Heat, Upgrade the Kitchen"; Z. Schiller, "GE's Appliance Park: Rewire or Pull the Plug?"

48. "Health Insurer Holds Stock in Cigarette Maker," *Orlando Sentinel,* March 31, 1993, C5.

IBAX: PUTTING A RETRENCHMENT STRATEGY INTO ACTION

Recall the situation at IBAX—the IBM and Baxter partnership that provides health care information systems software. The company, which had been projected to break even in the first year of the partnership (1989), lost more than $25 million over its first two years of operation. Poor product quality and customer service had led to widespread customer dissatisfaction. Coupled with internal productivity problems, these difficulties had resulted in a very unfavorable financial position for IBAX.

Jeff Goodman, who was hired as CEO of IBAX at the beginning of 1991, was faced with the challenge of turning IBAX around. Based on his assessment of the situation, Goodman knew that this would not be an easy task. He needed a strategic plan.

DEVELOPING THE PLAN

In developing the strategic plan for IBAX, Goodman worked his way through the strategic planning process. He conducted a strategic analysis, formulated a strategy, developed implementation plans, and established strategic control mechanisms (see Chapters 4 and 5 for a discussion of the process of strategic planning).

STRATEGIC ANALYSIS

Goodman began by conducting a strategic analysis of IBAX. The information provided in the section of the Part 1 integrative case titled "The Assessment" details much of the information that was evaluated during the strategic analysis. This information is summarized in Table 1, which outlines the major strengths, weaknesses, opportunities, and threats that Goodman identified. It is apparent from Table 1 that the internal analysis revealed few strengths and many weaknesses, which would have serious implications for the long-term performance of the company. Further, while the external environmental analysis revealed some very significant threats, there were also opportunities that the company could capitalize on in the long term. It was clear from strategic analysis, however, that the first priority at IBAX had to be on overcoming its many weaknesses.

STRATEGY FORMULATION

Once the strategic analysis was completed, a strategy had to be formulated. This involved assessing the mission of the company, establishing strategic goals, identifying and evaluating strategic alternatives, and choosing a strategy.

The mission of IBAX was fairly clear: to be a leading provider of high-quality information systems software to health care organizations. The mission

TABLE 1   SWOT analysis for IBAX

STRENGTHS
• Relatively large installed base • Qualified employees • Partners' (IBM's and Baxter's) commitment to the company
WEAKNESSES
• Poor product quality • High cost structure as a result of overstaffing • Low customer satisfaction • No senior management team • No homogeneous corporate culture/no evolved values • Low employee morale • Ineffective sales force • No performance standards • Ineffective organizational structure
OPPORTUNITIES
• Health care reform focused on improved efficiency • Growth in alternative methods of delivering health care
THREATS
• Economic recession of 1990–1991 • Strong competition in the health care information systems industry • Stagnant market in terms of hospital growth • Small hospitals merging with larger hospitals • Fast pace of technology change making products obsolete • Health care regulatory reform creating an uncertain future

didn't need to be changed; rather, IBAX needed to fulfill its mission more effectively. The strategic goals of the organization were equally clear and had been established by the partners from the outset—improve product quality, customer satisfaction, and the financial position of the company.

IBAX appeared to have only one feasible strategic alternative—retrenchment/turnaround. The retrenchment strategy would require IBAX to reduce its assets and costs to become more efficient, as well as to develop an entirely new organizational system including such things as organizational structure, culture, product quality standards, performance standards, and reward systems.

STRATEGY IMPLEMENTATION

Implementing the retrenchment strategy began early in 1991 and continued throughout the year and into the next. The company's organizational design underwent a radical transformation, and the way employees were managed with regard to communication, motivation, and leadership also changed. Since subsequent cases will discuss each of these aspects of the turnaround in greater detail, just a brief overview of the changes that were made at IBAX will be provided here.

It was clear that IBAX was operationally inefficient. To improve efficiency, geographically dispersed units would have to be merged, and employees would have to be released. Goodman started by closing and consolidating locations. By 1991, IBAX had only two main locations—one in Orlando, Florida, where approximately 75 percent of the organization was housed, and the other in New York, where a technology development center was located.

After consolidating facilities, Goodman looked for other ways to improve efficiency. Based on the benchmarks of other companies in the industry, IBAX should have been generating $125,000 in revenue per employee. The company was far below that target, which seemed to indicate that it was heavily over-staffed. Goodman cut $15 million of labor costs from the company's cost structure by reducing the work force from 750 employees to 580.

Once facilities had been closed and the employee base had been reduced, it was time to change the internal functioning of the organization. Goodman moved the company from a functionally based organizational structure to a structure based on product lines. Self-managed teams were created as the primary unit within each product-based group, and decision making was pushed down to the lowest levels of the organization. To support this new structure, many changes were made in the human resource management function and the culture of the organization.

Goodman put a priority on developing a strong leadership team within the company. Then he enlisted that team to help him deliver the message regarding the need for change. He knew that employees had to really understand the problems facing IBAX before they could be persuaded to change their behaviors. He implemented what he called "open-book management"—that is, the financial statements were open and accessible to all employees. Where necessary, Goodman taught employees how to read and understand financial statements so they would be better informed.

Once the employees were convinced that radical and dramatic changes were needed, Goodman set about getting their input on what needed to be changed and how to make those changes. He set up a motivation and reward system that encouraged broad-based participation in the turnaround. He was committed to doing everything he could to help the employees feel ownership of IBAX and to empower them to do whatever was necessary to make the company a success.

STRATEGIC CONTROL

The final phase of Goodman's strategic planning efforts related to establishing strategic controls. Developing and implementing clear performance standards were crucial to the success of the retrenchment strategy. Each business unit engaged in a benchmarking process to establish financial and product quality standards that it would be held accountable for meeting. These control measures ensured that the company was making progress toward achieving both its strategic and operational goals.

THE RESULTS

As you will learn as you work your way through the IBAX case, Goodman's plan was a success. Product quality began to improve, customer satisfaction began to rise, and the company began to recover financially—all areas of significant weakness for the company at the outset. Through the retrenchment strategy, IBAX was able to meet the strategic goals set by the IBM and Baxter partners. The integrative cases that follow will provide additional details on how the retrenchment strategy was actually put into place.

For Discussion

1. What were the benefits to Goodman of following a systematic model of strategic planning?

2. Do you think Goodman could have chosen any strategic alternatives other than retrenchment? If so, what were they?

3. What steps did Goodman take to ensure successful implementation of the strategy?

Organizing for Quality, Productivity, and Job Satisfaction

■ ## CHAPTER OVERVIEW

This chapter, and the three that follow, focus on the managerial function of organizing. Increasingly, organizations are finding that their long-term success is dependent upon their ability to organize activities effectively, efficiently, and with a priority on quality. Management theory clearly recognizes the importance of organizing to support the strategic and operational needs of the contemporary organization.

This chapter describes organizing as a process and focuses on the first stage of that process. Special attention is given to contemporary approaches to organizing that support delegation and employee empowerment, and improving the organization's ability to respond to environmental change.

■ ## LEARNING OBJECTIVES

When you have finished studying this chapter, you should be able to:

- Explain why organizing is an important managerial function.
- Describe the process of organizing and outline the primary stages of the process.
- Discuss the concept of job design and identify the core job dimensions that define a job.
- Describe the evolution of job design theory.
- Describe reengineering as a management tool and discuss the effect of reengineering programs on job design.
- Identify the concepts related to developing effective organizational relationships, including chain of command, span of control, line versus staff personnel, and delegation.
- Discuss why it is important for managers to delegate.
- Explain why managers often fail to delegate and suggest methods for improving delegation skills.

C H A P T E R

Managerial
Incident

LEVI STRAUSS & COMPANY: REDESIGNING THE ORGANIZATION

Levi Strauss & Company has an enviable history. Record sales, record profits, committed workers, great brands . . . these are the things that characterize Levi's past. In 1995, the company generated record sales of nearly $7 billion and profits of more than $700 million. Levi's market value was an estimated $10 billion, four times its value when it went private in 1985.

So what's the problem? Despite Levi's indisputable past successes, the company was facing an uncertain future. Retail customers were becoming increasingly demanding, suppliers more numerous and dispersed, and consumers more fickle. What's more, Levi's management had discovered that its service was substandard. It was slow to fill orders, taking as long as 30 days to restock a store. It was unreliable as well. The company shipped less than 40 percent of its orders when it said it would. In fact, one of Levi's biggest customers had remarked, "We trust many of your competitors implicitly. We sample their deliveries. We *open* all Levi's deliveries." Another said, "Your lead times are the worst. If you weren't Levi, you'd be a goner." Those were powerful statements that got the attention of Levi's top management.

The closer they looked, the more Levi's management realized how deepseated the problems were. They involved the entire supply chain, from product inception to delivery of the product to the retailer. From beginning to end, the company needed a complete redesign of its jobs and its processes. This was the challenge for Levi's management team.[1]

INTRODUCTION

Levi has an excellent product that is in great demand by consumers around the globe. As a consequence, the company's retail customers had been willing to tolerate substandard performance in the delivery of products and servicing of their accounts. But just how long would they be willing to put up with Levi's poor customer service? Levi needed to make some significant operational improvements if it was to have satisfied retail customers. This required a reassessment of the way in which jobs at Levi were structured and operational processes were designed. This was Levi's managerial challenge as the company approached the 21st century.

As you will recall, all organizations exist to fulfill a specific mission and achieve a specific set of goals. If an organization is to fulfill its mission and achieve its goals, certain activities must occur. When an organization is small and relatively simple, those activities may be defined and coordinated fairly easily. As organizations become larger and more complex, however, organizational activities may be more difficult to define and coordinate. In general, the challenges associated with organizing activities and allocating resources among those activities become greater as the size and complexity of the organization increase. Nevertheless, organizing is an important managerial function in organizations of all sizes and types.

This chapter focuses on the managerial function of organizing. It begins by defining the concept of organizing and outlining the primary stages of the organizing process. That process includes determining tasks, designing jobs, and defining working relationships. Accordingly, we will discuss each of these topics as they relate to the job of the contemporary manager. Special attention is given to the trend toward greater employee participation in designing jobs and coordinating the activities of the organization.

WHAT IS ORGANIZING?

Organizing refers to the process of determining the tasks to be done, who will do them, and how those tasks will be managed and coordinated. It is an interactive and ongoing process that occurs throughout the life of the organization. As an organization develops and matures, so must its organizational system. Many times firms must adapt their organizational systems to cope with changes that occur in their competitive environment. For example, the CEO of Royal Insurance's U.S. operations found that a fairly radical redesign of the organization was necessary for the company to remain competitive in the rapidly changing insurance industry. Managing for Excellence describes the organizational changes made at Royal Insurance.

As Figure 8.1 shows, the process of organizing can be divided into two primary stages. In the first stage, the foundation of the organizational system is developed. Work activities are determined and assigned to specific job positions, and working relationships between individuals and work groups are defined. This chapter will focus specifically on these aspects of the organizing process. The second stage of the organizing process involves developing an organizational design that supports the strategic and operational plans of the firm. This requires grouping organizational members into work units, developing integrating mechanisms to coordinate the efforts of diverse work groups, and determining the extent to which decision making in the organization is centralized or decentralized. These aspects of organizing will be addressed in Chapter 9.

Organizing
The process of determining the tasks to be done, who will do them, and how those tasks will be managed and coordinated.

JOB DESIGN

As we noted, the first stage of the organizing process involves outlining the tasks and activities to be completed and assigning them to individuals and groups within the organization. Before managers can design specific jobs, they need to identify the work that must be done to achieve the organization's strategic and operational goals.

Consider, for example, an organization that manufactures and distributes small appliances. In order to fulfill its mission and achieve its goals, the orga-

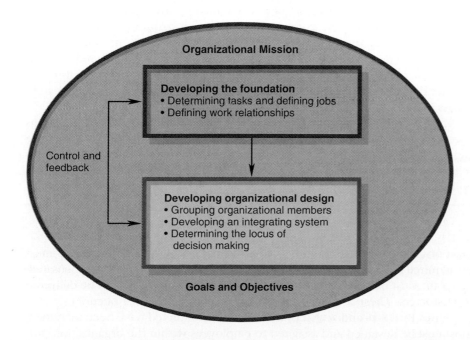

FIGURE 8.1
The process of organizing

Managing for Excellence

REMAKING ROYAL: REDESIGNING AN ORGANIZATION FOR IMPROVED RESPONSIVENESS

Robert Mendelsohn, CEO of the U.S. operations of 150-year-old Royal Insurance, wanted his organization to be a leader in its industry. But he knew that there would have to be some radical changes in the design of the organization if it was to achieve that goal.

Royal Insurance was like so many other U.S. firms in the early 1990s—structured hierarchically, with centralized decision making that limited the organization's ability to efficiently respond to customers. Mendelsohn was committed to transforming that traditional organizational design to a more contemporary model that would enable the firm to meet the challenges of the 21st century.

Mendelsohn knew that Royal had good people, yet they were not organized to use their talents effectively. All decisions were controlled from the center of the organization—corporate headquarters. Policies were adopted on a national level and applied all across the country, without any consideration of the regional markets that Royal served. The people who dealt with the customers had no authority to design products or services to meet the needs of those customers. Further, employees had to go to corporate headquarters for guidance on all decisions, making response time to customers extremely long.

But all that changed when Mendelsohn began his efforts to redesign the organization. According to Mendelsohn, "What we wanted to do was design a system that would deliver for the customers and producers very quick service and innovative products." To do that, the organizational chart was redesigned with the customer and producer in the center; the closer the employees to that center, the more authority they have to make decisions regarding product and service design and delivery. Underwriters have more autonomy and authority in their roles, relying on corporate-level underwriter experts to provide coaching and counseling on risky situations rather than make the final decision, as they had in the past. Cross-functional teams were established both at corporate headquarters and in regional offices. While employees used to have to go up a rigid chain of command to get decision-making information, now they go to the cross-functional support teams for answers to their questions.

Along with the decentralization of decision making came a commitment to technology. Royal had fallen behind in technology investments, but Mendelsohn knew that had to be corrected if the new organizational design was to be effective. Local area networks were put in place throughout branch offices across the country, enabling better communication within local and regional markets. In addition, videoconferencing capabilities were put in place throughout the organization. This provided an opportunity for better communication across branch offices throughout the country.

According to Mendelsohn, the new organizational design is a tremendous success. In his words, "I will say I think that the organizational structure we came up with is very innovative and seems to be working. The marketplace is telling us it's working." Time will tell if Royal's new decentralized structure will enable the company to reach its goals.[2]

---

nization must complete a number of tasks and activities. Raw materials must be acquired and inventoried; people must be hired, trained, and compensated; the plant must be managed and maintained; and the product must be delivered to customers. These are just a few of the activities that must occur.

Once the tasks and activities that must be completed have been identified, jobs must be designed and assigned to employees within the organization. **Job**

TABLE 8.1   Job description of an office manager

- Serves as general office manager of the department. Duties include supervising all administrative functions necessary for the operation of the department. These duties involve interviewing applicants, selecting new assistants, and training assistants. Also supervises assistants' daily work assignments and coordinates their assignments.
- Keeps accurate payroll records, payroll certifications, and personnel action forms on all department employees. Coordinates maintenance of leave records for all employees and management. Sends weekly reports to payroll departments. Distributes paychecks to department personnel. Prepares all recruiting and hiring records for the department.
- Prepares all travel requests, travel reimbursement requests, short invoices, requisitions, work orders, and purchase orders. Orders all appropriate materials and supplies for employees and management on a quarterly basis.
- Sets up as needed and maintains all office records and files, including administrative files, forms, memos, and correspondence. Coordinates scheduling and duplicating of reports and correspondence. Assigns workloads and priorities so that deadlines are met in a timely fashion. Supervises the security of all files, including personnel files of employees.
- Opens and closes the four offices used. Responsible for the security of each office, the maintenance of telephone coverage, and the routing of messages and visitors. Supervises the distribution of incoming and outgoing mail including fax and priority mailings. Responsible for annual and quarterly reports, promotion papers, and employee evaluations.
- Handles replies to routine inquiries from employees, customers, and the community. Refers nonroutine items to appropriate persons or manager. This includes telephone responses as well as initiating correspondence for manager's signature.

design refers to the set of tasks and activities that are grouped together to constitute a particular job position. The importance of effective job design should not be underestimated, as the overall productivity of the organization will be affected by the way jobs are designed.[3] While managers commonly blame an employee's poor performance on his or her lackluster efforts, in many cases the real problem is poor job design.[4]

The design of a job can be assessed, to a degree, by reviewing the associated job description. A **job description** details the responsibilities and tasks associated with a given position. Table 8.1 provides a job description for an office manager position. This job description is intended to provide the job holder, as well as other organizational members, with an understanding of the responsibilities associated with the job of an office manager.

Although job descriptions are commonly used to describe how jobs are designed, some relevant job characteristics may not be evident from a job description. Before we go on to discuss the various job design models that have evolved over the years, it is important to examine the fundamental characteristics that can be used to describe most jobs.

Job design
The set of tasks and activities that are grouped together to define a particular job.

Job description
An outline of the responsibilities and tasks associated with a given job.

CORE JOB DIMENSIONS

A number of core job dimensions can be used to characterize any job: (1) skill variety, (2) task identity, (3) task significance, (4) autonomy, and (5) feedback.[5] Each of these core job dimensions can significantly affect the satisfaction and performance of the individual who occupies the job. As Table 8.2 illustrates, these dimensions affect the degree to which employees find their work meaningful, feel responsibility for the outcomes of their job, and understand the re-

TABLE 8.2   The core dimensions of a job

CORE JOB DIMENSIONS	EFFECT OF DIMENSION
• Skill variety • Task identity → • Task significance	Meaningfulness of the work
• Autonomy →	Responsibility for outcomes of the work
• Feedback →	Knowledge of results of the work activities

SOURCE: Adapted from J. R. Hackman, G. Oldham, R. Janson, and K. Purdy, "A New Strategy for Job Enrichment." Copyright © 1975 by The Regents of the University of California. Reprinted from *California Management Review*, 17, 4. By permission of The Regents.

sults of their work activities. More specifically, skill variety, task identity, and task significance can affect the degree to which employees find their work meaningful; autonomy can affect the extent to which employees feel responsible for the outcomes of their jobs; and feedback can affect the degree to which employees understand the results of their work activities.[6] Let's explore these relationships in more detail.

Skill Variety

Skill variety
The degree to which a job challenges the job holder to use various skills and abilities.

The first of the job dimensions, **skill variety,** refers to the degree to which a job challenges the job holder to use his or her skills and abilities. When a variety of skills are necessary to complete a task and those skills are perceived to be of value to the organization, employees find their work to be more meaningful.

Consider, for example, how a production manager and a mailroom clerk might feel about the meaningfulness of their work. The production manager's job requires the use of a relatively diverse and highly valued set of skills and abilities, and he or she may therefore perceive the job to be quite meaningful. The job of the mailroom clerk, in contrast, is narrower in terms of skill variety and of less perceived value to the organization than the production manager's job. As a result, the mailroom clerk is likely to feel that his job is less meaningful.

Task Identity

Task identity
The degree to which a job requires the completion of an identifiable piece of work.

Task identity, the second dimension, refers to the degree to which the job requires the completion of an identifiable piece of work—a tangible outcome which can be attributed to the employee's efforts. For example, individuals who build entire computers will likely find their jobs to be more meaningful than employees who simply slide a chip into place on the circuit board of the computer.

Task Significance

Task significance
The degree to which a job contributes to the overall efforts of the organization.

The third job dimension, **task significance,** relates to the degree to which the job contributes to the overall efforts of the organization or to the world at large. Where task significance is high, the work will be more meaningful. For example, civil engineers who design an entire highway system will likely find their jobs to be more meaningful than assembly-line workers who are responsible for producing a component that goes into other products. This is particularly true when the employees don't know what the end product is, what it does, or who uses it.

AMP, Inc., a leader in the connector market, found a way to improve job satisfaction by increasing task significance for the individuals who make the components the company sells. Sales engineers from companies who use AMP's products met with the workers and talked with them about their customers and their products. Some of the salespeople even brought along end products, such as power tools, took them apart, and showed the AMP workers how the components they built fit in. One worker summed up the reaction by saying: "I sometimes felt that we made millions of these parts and they simply dumped them in the ocean after we shipped them out. Now I know where most of them go." The jobs of these workers had greater task significance as a result of this experience.[7]

Autonomy

The fourth job dimension, **autonomy,** reflects the degree to which job holders have freedom, independence, and decision-making authority in

their jobs. When employees are highly autonomous in their work roles, their success is dependent upon their own capabilities and their desire to complete the task. Therefore, they tend to feel greater responsibility for the success or failure of their efforts, and in general, greater job satisfaction.[8] When there is low autonomy, employees are less likely to feel accountable for the outcome of their work.

Consider, for example, organizational trainers who teach a seminar that prepares participants to pass a national certification exam. These trainers may have little latitude in selecting the material to be covered in the course and often must employ a course design that is prescribed by the testing agency. They have little autonomy in conducting their jobs. In contrast, consider trainers who teach a management development seminar that is intended to help participants learn more about their own management style. These trainers are free to determine both the material to be covered and the methods by which it should be delivered. They are likely to feel more personal responsibility for their work than will the trainers who deliver a prepackaged training seminar.

Home Depot, the highly successful retailer of hardware and home improvement materials, provides a great deal of autonomy to its employees. In fact, management makes it clear to employees that they have the autonomy to do whatever is necessary to meet the needs of their customers. As a consequence, Home Depot has many satisfied employees who view their work as a career rather than simply a job.[9]

Feedback

The final dimension of job design is **feedback,** or the extent to which job holders are provided information about the effectiveness of their efforts. When feedback is frequent and constructive, employees develop a better understanding of the relationship between their efforts and the outcomes of their work. Where feedback is insufficient, employees have little understanding of the value of their efforts.[10]

Although feedback typically comes from the employee's supervisor, some organizations have begun to use customer feedback to motivate employees to be more customer oriented in their

This architect using blueprints to create 3-D images on a computer experiences a high degree of task significance, and a resulting feeling of job satisfaction.
© Jeff Greenberg/Unicorn Stock Photos

Autonomy
The degree to which job holders have freedom, independence, and decision-making authority.

Feedback
Information about the status and performance of a given effort or system.

Employees who are highly autonomous in their work roles, like this Home Depot employee, experience a great deal of job satisfaction because they know that their success depends on their own abilities and their desire to do a good job.
© Michael Newman/PhotoEdit

work. Caterpillar, for example, provides regular customer feedback to employees to focus their attention on the need for quality in all aspects of the business.[11]

Chaparral Steel is another company that has employed very innovative approaches to providing feedback to employees. Not only are employees advised of customer feedback, but they are also given time off annually to visit the plants of competitors. This provides employees with an opportunity to compare their efforts to those of their competitors.[12] Monsanto uses a similar technique to help its employees understand their customers better.[13]

Because the core dimensions of job design affect the extent to which job holders find their work meaningful, feel responsibility for their efforts, and understand the relationship between their activities and the results of those activities, they have a significant effect on the job holders' attitude.[14] Motivation, quality of work performance, **job satisfaction,** absenteeism, and turnover will all be a function of the core job dimensions to some degree. Consequently, managers should consider the effect of various job designs on each core dimension as they assign tasks and work activities to individuals within the organization.

The increasing diversity of the work force has made the assessment of job design more complicated. Individuals from diverse cultural backgrounds may view certain job characteristics differently. For example, while many people from an American culture may perceive a job with low autonomy negatively, people from other cultures may perceive low autonomy favorably. Similarly, managers who work in the international environment must also consider how perceptions of job design may differ among diverse cultures. As a general rule of thumb, managers should avoid making broad generalizations about employees' perceptions of specific job characteristics. Rather, where possible, managers should assess their employees' suitability for a particular job on an individual basis.

How does your job stack up with regard to these job characteristics? Meeting the Challenge provides an opportunity for you to assess a past or present position you've held in an organization (such as a business, church, social club, or student organization) in terms of skill variety, task identity, task significance,

Job satisfaction
The degree to which an individual feels positively or negatively about their job.

TABLE 8.3   Job design theory evolution

THEORY	CORE JOB DIMENSIONS	EFFECT*
Classical theory/scientific management (mechanistic approaches)	Skill variety	Negative
	Task identity	Negative
	Task significance	Negative
	Autonomy	Negative
	Feedback	Negative
Human relations (behavioral approaches)	Skill variety	Positive
	Task identity	None
	Task significance	None
	Autonomy	Positive
	Feedback	None
Contemporary management (participatory approaches)	Skill variety	None
	Task identity	Positive
	Task significance	None
	Autonomy	Positive
	Feedback	Positive

*None = no appreciable effect.

JOB ASSESSMENT AND REDESIGN

This exercise enables you to assess a job that you currently hold or have held in the past in terms of the five core job dimensions and to make recommendations for improving its design.

Part A: Using the following scales, rate the job you are assessing in terms of its skill variety, task identity, task significance, autonomy, and feedback.

|___|___|___|___|___|___|___|___|___|
High   Skill variety   Low

|___|___|___|___|___|___|___|___|___|
High   Task identity   Low

|___|___|___|___|___|___|___|___|___|
High   Task significance   Low

|___|___|___|___|___|___|___|___|___|
High   Autonomy   Low

|___|___|___|___|___|___|___|___|___|
High   Feedback   Low

To the extent that your responses fall toward the left end of the scales, you probably find the job to be meaningful and challenging. To the extent that your responses fall toward the right end of the scales, the job could probably be redesigned to improve job satisfaction and enhance productivity.

Part B: Based on your responses to Part A, how might you redesign your job to improve each of the five core job dimensions? Would any of the participatory approaches to job redesign be appropriate? If so, which one(s)? Why do you feel it (they) would be appropriate?

autonomy, and feedback. At this point, you are prepared to complete the assessment aspect (Part A) of the exercise. After reading the next section, you'll be prepared to suggest ways in which the job could be redesigned to improve job satisfaction (Part B).

It is interesting to examine how the principles of job design have evolved over time and, more specifically, how changes in design theory have affected the five core job dimensions. Table 8.3 outlines how job theory has evolved, the major job design approaches that have resulted from each school of thought, and how each approach affects core job dimensions. The discussion that follows provides a rationale for the evolution of job design theory.

THE EVOLUTION OF JOB DESIGN THEORY

As management theory has evolved, so have many of the basic principles of job design. As we discussed in Chapter 2, classical management theory and scientific management supported the concepts of division of labor and specialization. These early theories of management gave rise to a mechanistic approach to job design, in which jobs are highly structured and rigidly defined. The movement toward the human relations school of thought, however, introduced other job design variables, most of which dealt with human behavior. As a result, more behavioral approaches to job design gained acceptance. Contemporary management thought is now affecting how jobs are designed, and participatory approaches are gaining popularity today. Let's examine how each of these approaches has affected the concept of job design, as well as the core job dimensions.

Mechanistic Approaches: Focus on Efficiency

As you should recall from Chapter 2, scientific management theorists emphasized the benefits of division of work and specialization. Productivity and efficiency were the driving forces for job design. Repetition, skill simplification, and time and motion efficiency were the primary focus of job design efforts. The result was highly specialized jobs that were routine, repetitive, and highly efficient.

One need only recall the classic example of a pinmaking operation in Adam Smith's *Wealth of Nations* to understand the potential efficiencies of division of labor and highly specialized work roles. Smith suggested that the productivity of ten pinmakers could be greatly improved by applying these concepts. One pinmaker performing all the tasks necessary to make a pin could make only 10 pins per day. The total productivity of ten pinmakers making pins in this fashion would be 100 pins per day. But if the ten pinmakers organized the activities of the group so that one pinmaker drew the wire, another straightened it, a third cut it, and a fourth sharpened it to a point, while others were performing the operations necessary to complete the head of the pin and prepare the final product, the group could produce 48,000 pins per day—an average of 4,800 pins per pinmaker per day. Obviously, the productivity of the group improved dramatically when jobs were redesigned to be highly specialized.

The benefits of specialization are easy to identify (see Table 8.4). Specialized tasks are considered to be more efficient because work activities are broken down into routine, repetitive actions. Further, such actions can be mastered readily by individual workers and require less training than more complex tasks. Additionally, when tasks are highly specialized, workers may be selected based on specific characteristics that make them uniquely qualified to perform the task effectively and efficiently.

Specialization also has disadvantages, however (see Table 8.4). Often, the skill variety, task identity, and task significance associated with such tasks are low. Further, job holders typically have less autonomy and may receive no feedback or feedback that is inconsequential. To the extent that these conditions exist, job holders will find little challenge in their work and may lose interest in their jobs.

In cases where excessive specialization has created jobs that are perceived to be unrewarding and uninteresting, it is difficult to motivate workers to perform well. Absenteeism and turnover are often greater, and even when employees are on the job, they may take frequent and lengthy breaks or socialize with other employees excessively. In some cases, the benefits of specialization may be offset by the loss of productivity associated with job dissatisfaction and nonproductive work time.

Historically, many manufacturing firms have sought the benefits of specialization in designing jobs. The assembly-line production scheme is founded

TABLE 8.4   Potential advantages and disadvantages of job specialization

ADVANTAGES	DISADVANTAGES
• Greater efficiency due to repetition	• Low skill variety, task identity, and task significance
• Tasks are easier to master and require little training	• Little autonomy and feedback, resulting in low interest and motivation
• May select workers based on specific qualifications	• Lower productivity due to high absenteeism and frequent breaks

on the concept of highly routine and specialized tasks. Consider, for example, the traditional automobile manufacturing plant. As the chassis of the car flows through the assembly line, workers perform a series of highly specialized tasks that contribute in some way to the production of the final product. While any given worker may do little more than attach a specific component or insert and tighten several screws, the result of the combined efforts of all the participants in the assembly process is a complete and fully functioning vehicle.

Today, there are fewer highly specialized jobs in the United States than in the past. Robotics technology has replaced many specialized jobs, particularly in the manufacturing environment. In addition, many organizations that require low-skilled labor have moved their operations overseas, where there is access to less expensive labor. Finally, other organizations have found alternative job design options that overcome some of the negative aspects of highly specialized jobs.

The human relations theorists were the first to suggest alternate job design methods. As we will discuss next, the emphasis moved from division of labor and specialization toward job designs with greater breadth, depth, and challenge.

Behavioral Approaches: Focus on Motivation, Satisfaction, and Productivity

Behavioral approaches to job design became popular during the movement toward the human relations school of thought. When the human relations theories of management began to emerge, the net benefits of specialized job design became the subject of some controversy. As concerns about the disadvantages of highly specialized job designs continued to mount, managers began to explore methods for enhancing the ways jobs were structured. Such efforts led to the development of more innovative approaches to job design, including job enlargement, job enrichment, and job rotation programs.

Job Enlargement   To understand job enlargement programs, one must understand the concept of job scope. **Job scope** refers to the number of different activities that a specific job requires and the frequency with which each activity is performed. Jobs that involve many different activities have broader scope than jobs that are limited to a few activities. Jobs with broad scope typically rate more favorably in terms of skill variety, task identity, and task significance than do jobs with a narrower scope. As a consequence, jobs with broad scope are often more meaningful for job holders than jobs with narrow scope.

Job scope
The number of different activities required in a job and the frequency with which each activity is performed.

Consider, for example, how the job scope of an office manager and a typist in a clerical pool might differ. The office manager's job will involve a relatively broad set of tasks and thus will have relatively wide scope. In any given day, the office manager may take dictation, type a letter, complete and sign time cards, make travel arrangements, schedule appointments, and interview, hire, or fire office staff. The typist's job, in contrast, is much narrower in that it involves only typing documents.

Job enlargement programs are designed to broaden the scope of a specific job. The intent of job enlargement is to increase the horizontal tasks and responsibilities associated with a given work position to reduce the monotony of the job and provide greater challenge for the employee. For example, to enlarge the job of a typist, the office manager might require her to assume additional job responsibilities such as answering the phones, processing payroll forms, and providing copying services. The typist would be responsible for a greater variety of tasks and might be less bored and more highly satisfied with her job.

Job enlargement
Programs designed to broaden job scope.

While many companies have implemented job enlargement programs in an effort to redesign highly specialized and routine jobs, many other firms have been forced to enlarge jobs in response to changes in their strategy. In recent years, we have seen industries consolidate, companies merge, and organizations downsize and streamline to remain competitive. Such strategic initiatives often require changes in the way jobs are designed.

Aetna Life and Casualty Company is one organization that has found job enlargement to be necessary to increase the timeliness and quality of its service. Initially, the tasks associated with processing an insurance application were separated into highly specialized, mind-numbing tasks. One person entered the application on a log sheet, another calculated the premium, another typed it up, and another sent it out to the customer. The delay in moving the application from person to person resulted in a 26-minute process taking 28 days to complete. Through a job enlargement program, Aetna consolidated the tasks into a single job completed by a "customer account manager." This new process, called "one and done," has resulted in two major benefits to the company: (1) it has reduced the time for processing insurance applications, and (2) direct contact with customers has made employees more sensitive to the need for quality customer service.[15]

Job depth
The degree of control given to a job holder to perform the job.

Job Enrichment   Central to the concept of job enrichment is the notion of **job depth,** which refers to the degree of control that individuals have over the jobs they perform. Job depth is high when the planning, doing, and controlling aspects of the job are the responsibility of the job holder. When one or more of these aspects is the responsibility of some other organization member, job depth is low. Jobs that have high job depth typically rate more favorably on the core job dimensions of skill variety, task identity, and autonomy than jobs with low job depth.

Just as specialization has led to jobs with a narrow job scope, highly specialized jobs often lack depth. In such cases, the planning and controlling aspects of a job are often separate from the doing aspect of the job. For example, the manager of a clerical pool may assume responsibility for receiving work to be typed, clarifying instructions with the originator of the work, setting priorities for scheduling work orders, checking the final document for typographical errors and neatness, delivering the completed work to the individual who brought the document in to be typed and communicating with that individual about the acceptability of the work. When the manager assumes these responsibilities, the actual typing of the document is all that is left for the typist to do. Clearly, the job depth of the typist's position is quite low.

Job enrichment
Programs designed to increase job depth.

Job enrichment programs are designed to increase the depth of individual jobs and to close the gap between planning, doing, and controlling a particular set of activities.[16] Through *vertical loading,* the job holder may be given greater discretion in setting schedules and planning work activities, determining appropriate methods for completing the task, and monitoring the quality of the output from the work process. For example, the job depth of the typist would be increased if he assumed responsibility for accepting and logging in the work, scheduling work orders, and communicating with the originator of the work about its acceptability.

Just as downsizing has led to enlarged jobs, such efforts have also led to enriched jobs. When a layer of management is eliminated, the group of employees above and below that management level must assume greater responsibility. This creates a situation of vertical loading of job responsibilities and leads to jobs with greater job depth. For example, U.S. West increased the job depth associated with many positions when layers of management were eliminated as part of its "Winning in the '90s" reorganization program.[17]

In addition, quality-management programs have also created greater job depth in some organizations. Individual accountability for contributing to the goals of the organization increases in quality-oriented companies, and with that accountability often comes greater job depth. Caterpillar, for example, in an effort to ensure high-quality products, has redesigned jobs so that individual employees (rather than inspectors at the end of the line) are accountable for the quality of the product at each stage of the manufacturing process. As part of this new system, employees participate in both the planning and control aspects of the manufacturing process.[18]

Job Rotation   Job rotation is a third method of reducing the level of specialization associated with a given job. **Job rotation** involves shifting individuals from one position to another once they have mastered their original job. Employees rotate through a number of job positions that are at approximately the same level and have similar skill requirements. For example, an individual who works in a bank might rotate between being a teller, a customer service representative, a loan processor, a proof operator, and a safe deposit box attendant. At a higher organizational level, a financial manager who works for a multinational firm might rotate among positions at various foreign subsidiaries to gain international business experience.

Job rotation
Assigning individuals to a variety of job positions.

Job rotation offers several advantages. Organizations that use job rotation typically have more flexibility in developing work schedules, making work assignments, and filling vacancies within the company quickly. In addition, employees are often more challenged and less bored with their jobs and usually have a better understanding of the organization as a whole. In fact, at the level of the individual employee, job rotation has been found to have a positive effect on both promotion rates and salary growth.[19] Yet job rotation can also be disruptive to the organization. More time and resources must be spent on training, and optimal performance in any given job may be difficult to achieve on a consistent basis.

Today, a new form of job rotation is emerging in response to downsizing. Since many organizations have reduced their work force in recent years, employees have far fewer internal career opportunities available. With fewer promotions to hand out, some companies are trying to motivate employees by shifting them sideways instead of up. American Greetings has found lateral moves to be very effective in rejuvenating employees who have become bored in their present positions. Nabisco Foods, Corning, Inc., and Eastman Kodak are other companies that are looking to lateral job moves as a method of motivating employees whose career progression has been stymied by the restructuring efforts of the organization.[20] This new form of job rotation may have long-term promise for organizations that hope to retain good employees by providing greater challenge in their jobs.

Job enlargement, enrichment, and rotation programs represent methods of redesigning specialized jobs to increase the motivation, job satisfaction and, in some cases, productivity of employees. Such efforts often have a very positive effect on overcoming the disadvantages of more mechanistic approaches to job design. Many managers who are concerned with maintaining a quality orientation in their work units have embraced these programs as one way to do so. In addition, some managers have turned toward more participatory approaches to job design.

Participatory Approaches: Focus on Quality
In recent years, both management theorists and practitioners have been rethinking the traditional approaches to job design.[21] Efforts to develop more innovative and effective approaches to job design have been inspired by increasing competitive pressures in many industries.[22] ALCOA, for example, attempted to restore its competitive position in the world marketplace though the use of innovative approaches to job design.[23]

Several participatory approaches to designing jobs have emerged in recent years and have begun to gain fairly widespread acceptance. The benefits of such approaches are similar to the benefits associated with participatory decision making discussed in Chapter 6. Jobs that are designed with the involvement of the affected individuals often provide greater satisfaction for the job holder and lead to greater productivity.

Participatory approaches to job design are not intended to replace previous methods of job design, but rather to supplement both the mechanistic and the behavioral theories of job design. The most popular participatory approaches, and the ones that will be discussed here, include employee-centered work redesign programs and self-managed teams.

Employee-centered work redesign
An approach whereby employees design their work roles to benefit the organization and satisfy their individual goals.

Employee-Centered Work Redesign   **Employee-centered work redesign** is an innovative approach to job design that presents a practical solution to the one of the most significant challenges of job design—bridging the gap between the individual and the organization. This method of job design links the mission of the organization with the needs of the individual by allowing employees to design their work roles to benefit the organization as well as themselves. The unique aspect of this job design approach is that employees are accountable for justifying how their job will support the mission of the organization as well as improving their productivity and job satisfaction.[24]

A number of benefits are associated with employee-centered work redesign programs. Because jobs are designed by the job holder, these programs tend to favorably affect the core job dimensions that are most relevant to the individual employee. Studies suggest that very tangible improvements in both productivity and job satisfaction result from employee-centered work redesign efforts. Further, such programs foster an organizational climate that supports cooperative efforts between individuals and work groups. Finally, employee-centered work redesign programs are consistent with the quality improvement efforts of many companies. Because the employees of an organization are in the best position to know where quality improvements can be achieved, jobs can be designed so quality problems can be identified and resolved more quickly.[25]

Table 8.5 outlines some of the factors that are critical to the success of an employee-centered work redesign program, as well as some of the anticipated benefits for both the employee and the organization.[26] Table 8.6 outlines the

TABLE 8.5   Employee-centered work redesign

CRITICAL FACTORS	EMPLOYEE BENEFITS	ORGANIZATIONAL BENEFITS
• Strong commitment from management to the program to ensure success • Teamwork between employees and managers to redesign work roles • Organizational benefits in work productivity, work quality, and cost containment • Demonstrate positive impact on staff and existing systems • Hands-on problem-solving format	• Career and professional growth opportunities realized within the organization • Increased job satisfaction • Gain insights into the organization • Opportunity to contribute to organizational goals • Learn to communicate needs, concerns, and interests • Broaden organization perspective • Career growth opportunities enhanced • Access to information • Critical skills identified	• Greater use of employees • Taps into employee skills, knowledge, and creativity • Increased productivity and improved quality • Reduced employee turnover • Employees become stakeholders, not job holders, in the organization • Increased accountability leads to cost-effective behavior • Promotes positive work attitude to discourage employee grievances • Supports cooperative teamwork between employees and management

SOURCE: Excerpts from "Employees Redesign Their Jobs" by S. L. Perlman, copyright November 1990. Reprinted with the permission of *Personnel Journal*, ACC Communications, Inc., Costa Mesa, California; all rights reserved.

TABLE 8.6   How to execute an employee-centered work redesign program

Employee-centered work redesign programs focus on treating employees as part-ners rather than subordinates. To execute such a system, the following steps must be taken:

- Teach employees about the mission and goals of the organization and their de-partment.

- Have employees complete a needs assessment survey to help them identify per-sonal job satisfaction and professional development goals. These should be con-sistent with the mission and goals of the department and the organization.

- Conduct an exercise to help employees learn to recognize possible obstacles to achieving their goals and identify methods for eliminating or minimizing such barriers.

- Ask employees to prepare an inventory of their existing work responsibilities. This inventory should be broken into three distinct categories: work that will be retained, work that will be modified, and work that will be eliminated. Em-ployees should also identify new work that should be added to their current job.

- Employees should outline methods for accomplishing all modified and new tasks in the inventory. This process increases the employees' sense of account-ability for their newly designed jobs.

- Finally, a careful review of the proposal by management should be followed by implementation on a trial basis. This provides for monitoring of the new job de-sign and allows for corrections to be made quickly and easily.

SOURCE: Excerpts from "Employees Redesign Their Jobs," by S. L. Perlman, copyright Novem-ber 1990. Reprinted with the permission of *Personnel Journal*, ACC Communications, Inc., Costa Mesa, California; all rights reserved.

process that one would follow in implementing an employee-centered work redesign program.[27]

Amoco Oil Company is an excellent example of a firm that uses an em-ployee-centered work redesign program to support its strategic goals. This com-pany offered detailed training sessions to help employees at its Yorktown, Vir-ginia, refinery to identify their roles in pursuing the company's mission. The benefits of involving employees in this process have been tremendous, and the company plans to implement a similar program in other refineries.[28]

Self-Managed Teams   All of the approaches to job design discussed so far have focused on designing the jobs of individual organizational members. The **self-managed team** approach to job design shifts the focus from the individual to a work group (recall the discussion of self-managed teams in Chapter 1). In-stead of managers dictating a set of narrowly defined tasks to each individual employee, responsibility for a substantial portion of the organization's activi-ties is assigned to a team of individuals who must determine the best way to fulfill those responsibilities. Today, self-managed teams exist in organizations of all sizes and types and in and across departments within those organiza-tions.[29] Entrepreneurial Approach describes how one relatively small organi-zation has moved to self-managed teams in an effort to improve the quality of its customer service.

The distinguishing feature of the self-managed team approach to job de-sign is that the group is completely independent. The team must justify its choice of work methods only in terms of strong productivity and contribution to the overall effort of the firm. As with employee-centered work redesign pro-grams, jobs that are designed by self-managed teams tend to reflect the core job dimensions that are most relevant to the individual employees of the work group.

Self-managed teams
Groups of employees who design their jobs and work responsibilities to achieve the self-determined goals and objectives of the team.

ARMELLINI EXPRESS LINES: THE MOVE TOWARD SELF-MANAGED TEAMS

Headquartered in Palm City, Florida, Armellini Express Lines is the largest independent carrier of fresh cut flowers in the United States. Founded in 1945 by Joseph Armellini, the company has grown from having a single truck on the road to having 160 trucks in operation in 1996. Among the company's 625 employees are six of the seven Armellini family members. Led by father Jules Armellini, the company grossed over $50 million in revenues in 1995.

Despite the company's history of success, the family recognized that they could improve performance by improving the efficiency of their operations. The office was organized into isolated departments based on function. Communication between the departments was very limited, hindering the effective integration of activities across departments. Decision making was highly centralized, with the Armellinis making most of the decisions in the firm.

To counteract these problems, Armellini redesigned the organization based on self-managed teams. They moved away from the classic departmental structure based on tasks, to interdependent work teams. In order to facilitate cooperation and interaction between team members, employees are encouraged to communicate more freely. This has meant literally removing some of the walls that separate departments. E-mail communication is on the rise as well. Decision making is being pushed down in the organizational hierarchy, enabling employees on the line to make important decisions that affect the quality of customer service provided by the company. To support this decentralization effort, employees are being given access to important financial and performance-related information.

The Armenellis believe that their new organizational system will improve their customer service and the overall performance of the firm. All indications are that their self-managed work teams will be a tremendous success at Armenelli Express Lines.

While research has suggested that self-managed teams can achieve higher productivity and deliver better quality products and services with lower relative costs,[30] a number of situational factors appear to influence the effectiveness of such groups. These factors include the personalities of the group members, the ability of the group to exercise control and assume responsibility, and the nature of the tasks to be completed.[31] Therefore, the success of a self-managed team will depend upon the particular individuals involved and the nature of the job responsibilities.

Organizations that have designed very narrow, highly specialized jobs in an effort to maximize efficiency may find self-managed teams to be advantageous. The team approach has been credited with improving overall organizational effectiveness,[32] in ways such as avoiding redundant efforts, increasing cooperation between organizational members, spawning new ideas, generating solutions to problems, maintaining motivation, improving product quality, and increasing profits.[33] In fact, using a team approach rather than the traditional assembly-line approach to manufacturing has worked successfully for many organizations.[34] Few would dispute the success of the team concept at NUMMI (New United Motors Manufacturing, Inc.), the joint venture between General Motors and Toyota. This facility is organized around self-managed teams that establish their own work standards, work flow, production process, tools to be used, and work schedules. The significant improvements in productivity and quality experienced by NUMMI can be attributed, in large part, to its team orientation.[35] There are many other organizations that have successfully im-

OTICON: AN ORGANIZATIONAL REVOLUTION

Ars Kolind, the CEO of Denmark's Oticon, has taken organizational redesign to a new level—organizational revolution.

Oticon makes hearing aids, hardly an industry in which one would expect
to find a company with radical ideas about organizational design. But Oticon's design could be clearly labeled "radical." Kolind's idea of a renovation of Oticon's organizational structure was a complete "dis-organization"
of the company. The idea began in 1988, when Kolind arrived at a financially troubled Oticon. Kolind realized that more than cost cuts and increased productivity would be needed to revive the company. So in 1990,
he announced the revolutionary plan that changed the internal design of
the company in fairly radical ways.

The plan allows employees to organize into work groups according to
projects. Today at Oticon, teams form, disband, and form again as the
work requires. This is radically different from the previous structure,
which organized employees into departments or functions. When a project begins, and a corresponding work group is formed, the employees actually move their office into the designated area. According to Kolind, this
process allows the employees to "become more creative, action-
oriented, and efficient."

Although Oticon employs only 150 people at its headquarters in Denmark, hundreds of projects may be going on at one time. Most people
work on several projects at once, creating a "free market" in work. Project leaders create ideas and compete to attract resources and people to
deliver products. "We want each project to feel like a company, and the
project leader to feel like a CEO," Kolind says. When the company appears to begin organizing, Kolind makes sure to step in and "dis-organize"
it again. Last year the company began to show signs of organization while
working on a potential breakthrough product. Kolind responded by "ex-
ploding the organization." Within three hours, over a hundred people had
relocated within the building. Kolind's advice is, "To keep a company
alive, one of the jobs of top management is to keep it dis-organized."

If the economic performance of Oticon is an indication of the effectiveness of the new organization, then most would agree that it's working.
Since 1990, Oticon has more than doubled in size and operating profits
are nearly ten times their 1990 level.

Global Perspective

plemented self-managed teams, such as Xerox, Chrysler, and British Telecom.
As you will read in the Managerial Resolution at the close of this chapter, teams
became an integral part of Levi's new organization design. For an especially interesting story of teamwork in action, read how Oticon, a Scandinavian manufacturer of hearing aids, has created an organizational "revolution" in order
to make the team concept work in Global Perspective.

Service organizations have found much success with the team concept
as well. GTE, for example, found that it could respond more quickly and efficiently to customers' requests for repairs and service by creating teams of
technicians in the field. The company eliminated several supervisory positions and reorganized the technicians into teams based on geographic areas.

Together, the team assumes responsibility for dispatching, service delivery, and reporting. Armed with cellular phones and laptop computers, the technicians work as a team to manage the workload within their geographic territory.[36]

Perhaps the most challenging yet rewarding teams are those that are interfunctional in nature. Many self-managed teams include engineers, financial managers, marketing managers, and production managers—all of whom must work together toward common goals and objectives. General Foods, a strong proponent of the team approach, claims that organizing the company into interfunctional work teams has been, in general, the most critical factor in creating a work environment that supports peak performance.[37] In fact, some would argue that the effective use of interfunctional work teams is the key to achieving a quality orientation within an organization.[38]

REENGINEERING AND JOB DESIGN

As we know, quality has become the key competitive weapon of the 1990s. Few organizations will prosper in today's environment without a focus on quality and continuous improvement. Corporations across the globe have implemented quality improvement programs in an effort to reduce costs, improve customer satisfaction, increase market share, and last but not least, improve the bottom line.

Closely related to the quality movement, though separate and distinct in some very important ways, is another important management tool—business process reengineering. For organizations that compete on the basis of quality, achieving simplicity, speed, and flexibility within the organizational system can be crucial. And, according to some experts, the way to achieve those qualities is through business process reengineering.[39]

Reengineering
Radically changing the organizational processes for delivering products and services.

During **reengineering,** an organization seeks out and implements radical change in the processes that it uses to produce and deliver its products and services. Every manager and employee becomes involved in the process of assessing every aspect of the company's operations and rebuilding the organizational system with a focus on improving efficiency, identifying redundancies, and eliminating waste in every way possible.

Reengineering is not easy or cheap, but the results have been remarkable for some companies. Consider the following: through reengineering, Union Carbide reduced its fixed costs by $400 million in three years; GTE expects to double its revenues and reduce its costs by half in its telephone division as a result of reengineering; and AlliedSignal's vice-president for materials management estimates that reengineering his unit will save the company $100 million a year.[40] Even small companies can benefit from such programs. Shelby Die Casting Company, a small manufacturer of aluminum castings, avoided closing a plant in Shelby, Mississippi, by involving its workers in redesigning the way the plant functioned.

Reengineering efforts have a significant effect on the way jobs are designed.[41] Any reengineering project will raise critical questions about how work and work processes can be optimally configured. Answering such questions will require managers to look for creative approaches to job design—approaches that maintain or improve the effectiveness and efficiency of the organization. Table 8.7 outlines one method for reengineering that will help to identify appropriate job design.[42]

Now that we have concluded our discussion of job design, take a moment to go back to Part B of Meeting the Challenge. How might you redesign the position you evaluated to improve job satisfaction? Would a participatory ap-

TABLE 8.7   Steps in process engineering

1. *Seize control of the process.* Many processes vitally important to a firm's success "just happen." The sequence of activities that count the most usually require interventions from many organization units. Good ideas for new products dissipate in the path from one unit to another. Seizing control of a process means giving it an owner who has authority to break through the departmental walls.

2. *Map it out.* Most companies are organized in ways that make it difficult to identify key processes. Reengineering can only be accomplished if the organization is mapped out, usually graphically, so as to provide a step-by-step description of how the process works. Then, by carefully identifying and eliminating problem areas, a more streamlined operation can be reengineered.

3. *Eliminate sources of friction.* One method of eliminating organizational friction is to devise an alternative to the traditional passing of work down the established hierarchy. Many companies have set up coordinating "brand management" or "czar" positions to keep things moving along. Other methods include streamlining administrative processes (purchasing, billing, etc.), minimizing handoffs by having as few units processing transactions as possible, creating new, higher-paying positions with greater authority, and time compression through responsibility expansion.

4. *Close the loop.* Becoming a fast-cycle company involves mind-set change as well as technique adoption. In reengineered businesses, the most common phrase you hear is "Life is short." This is not so much a philosophical justification as a plea to get on with it. Reengineering studies can create volumes of paperwork and creative and colorful flowcharts. But the only studies worth doing are those that make change happen.

5. *Don't drop the ball.* The only studies whose changes will stick are those done with eyes wide open about the transitory nature of improvement programs. Few improvements last indefinitely. Technologies will change, allowing for further enhancements in speed. Also, superior approaches will be developed for common problems. Knowing that the results of this year's reengineering will need reengineering at some point is essential to making any effort successful.

SOURCE: R. M. Tomasko, "Intelligent Resizing: View from the Bottom Up (Part II)," 18–23. Reprinted by permission of publisher, from *Management Review,* June 1993. © 1993, American Management Association, New York. All rights reserved.

proach to job design be appropriate? Why or why not? How could you redesign the job to support improved quality in the organization?

Thus far, we have explored how managers determine the work to be done and assign that work to individual employees or work groups. Equally important, however, is the process of defining the working relationships, both vertical and horizontal, that exist within the organization. The next section examines how working relationships can be established to ensure that the organization fulfills its mission and achieves its goals.

ORGANIZATIONAL RELATIONSHIPS

The working relationships that exist within an organization will affect how its activities are accomplished and coordinated. Consequently, it is essential to understand both the vertical and horizontal associations that exist between individuals and work groups within the organization. Relevant to this topic are: (1) chain of command, (2) span of control, (3) line and staff responsibilities, and (4) delegation.

CHAIN OF COMMAND

Chain of command
The line of authority and responsibility that flows throughout the organization.

Unity of command
A principle that each employee in the organization is accountable to one, and only one, supervisor.

The vertical relationships that exist within an organization are defined by its chain of command. The **chain of command** delineates the line of authority and responsibility that flows throughout the organization and defines the supervisor and subordinate relationships that govern decision making.

One of the most basic principles of organizing, unity of command, is used in defining vertical relationships. The **unity of command** principle suggests that each employee in the organization should be accountable to one, and only one, superior. When individual employees must report to more than one superior, they may be forced to prioritize their work assignments and resolve conflicting demands on their time.

As you will recall from Chapter 2, the concept of a well-defined chain of command was originally advanced by the classical management theorists. In its purest form, the concept is consistent with the bureaucratic organizational system. Although contemporary managers still embrace the idea of a chain of command, the flexibility of the organization to respond quickly and proactively to change may be severely limited when decision making is rigidly tied to the official hierarchy. For that reason, organizations that operate in very dynamic environments may prefer to maintain flexibility in their chain of command so that they can respond more effectively to change. Eastman Kodak is an example of an organization that has been experimenting with a complex but relatively flexible chain of command in an effort to improve its responsiveness to changing business conditions. While efforts to date have been largely within the information systems department, the structure holds promise for other divisions of Kodak's business.[43] Consider also how Royal Insurance used cross-functional support teams to overcome the burden of what had traditionally been a very rigid chain of command (see Managing for Excellence earlier in the chapter).

SPAN OF CONTROL

Span of control
The number of employees reporting to a particular manager.

A second important aspect of working relationships is **span of control,** which refers to the number of employees that report to a single manager. At one time it was thought that there was a universally appropriate span of control (for example, six employees should report to each manager), but managers now recognize that span of control will vary in accordance with a number of variables. Organizational characteristics such as task complexity, the volatility of the competitive environment, and the capabilities of both the employees and the manager will influence the appropriate span of control.

As an example of how certain conditions might affect span of control, consider the job characteristic of task complexity. In theory, when tasks are very complex, span of control should be relatively narrow. This allows the manager to spend more time with each individual subordinate to help him or her deal with the complexity of the job. In contrast, where jobs are highly standardized and routine (low complexity), a manager will not need to spend as much time supporting individual subordinates, and span of control may be larger.

Which comes first—job design or span of control? That depends. Although one typically thinks of jobs being designed first and span of control being determined by the nature of the job, the reverse can happen. Jobs may be designed to support a company's preferred span of control. For example, in an effort to cut costs, Ameritech recently reduced management levels, consolidated staff functions, and increased the average span of control. To do so, the company had to create common internal operating systems that standardized and simplified job design.[44]

Span of control is a critical organizational variable for a number of reasons. It defines the layers of management that exist within the company. An organization that maintains a relatively narrow span of control will have more hierarchical levels than an organization with the same number of employees but a wider span of control. As Figure 8.2 illustrates, the span of control and the resulting layers of management determine whether the organization maintains a tall or a flat structure.[45]

In general, tall structures are associated with a long chain of command and bureaucratic controls. Consequently, they are often thought to be ineffective in rapidly changing environments. On the other hand, managers in tall structures have fewer subordinates to supervise and are less likely to be overcommitted and overburdened. Free from the burden of excessive numbers of subordinates, such managers may have more time to analyze situations, make effective decisions, and execute the actions associated with their decisions. Consequently, they may be more effective than managers in flat organizations.

Managers in flat organizations, by contrast, have greater demands in terms of direct supervision because they have wider spans of control. They may feel hassled, frustrated, and incapable of coping effectively with the nonsupervisory demands of their job. Yet flat structures are often thought to facilitate decentralized decision making, participatory management, and responsiveness to the challenges inherent in highly competitive environments. Wide spans of control suggest a need for greater self-direction and initiative on the part of individual employees and may result in more effective employee development. As will be discussed in the Managerial Resolution at the close of the chapter, Levi's effort to reorganize led to wider spans of control and more opportunities for employees.

FIGURE 8.2

Tall versus flat structure

SOURCE: Adapted from *The Structuring of Organizations* by Mintzberg, ©1991. Adapted by permission of Prentice-Hall, Inc., Upper Saddle River, NJ.

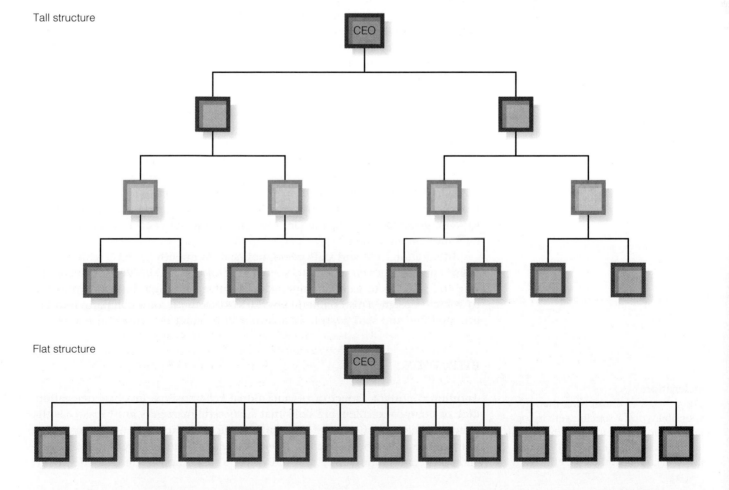

Tall structure

Flat structure

Clearly, advantages and disadvantages are associated with both tall and flat structures. Therefore, organizations must choose a span of control that supports their particular strategic and operational goals. For example, many global firms may find they need a relatively small span of control at the upper levels of the organization. The challenges of managing geographically dispersed and culturally diverse operating units may require a narrower span of control.

General Electric has changed its span of control as a part of a major restructuring program. Ten years ago, managers supervised six people on average; today they supervise twelve. The reasons for the change are many. GE wanted to improve its products, get closer to its customers, and trim costs. Some say that GE's greatest challenge was convincing managers that they did not need to have complete control over every aspect of their operation. They had to learn to rely on the individuals in their work groups to make the decisions necessary to achieve the goals of the unit.[46]

LINE AND STAFF RESPONSIBILITIES

The third aspect of organizational relationships is that of line and staff responsibilities. Line and staff positions exist within virtually all organizations, but the individuals who occupy these positions play very different roles within the organization.

Line personnel
Those organizational members that are directly involved in delivering the products and services of the organization.

Staff personnel
Those organizational members that are not directly involved in delivering the products and services of the organization, but provide support for line personnel.

Line personnel are directly involved in delivering the product or service of the organization. The individuals and work groups that have formal authority for decisions that affect the core production efforts of the firm are the line personnel. **Staff personnel,** in contrast, are not part of the product or service delivery system chain of command, but rather provide support to line personnel. Line personnel or work groups may call upon staff personnel to provide expert advice or perform specific support services. Staff personnel do not have authority or responsibility for decisions that relate to the core delivery system of the organization.

As organizations experiment with less rigid hierarchical structures and team-oriented approaches, the distinction between line and staff responsibilities is blurring. U.S. West, for example, has moved away from making distinctions between line and staff, preferring to call employees either supervising managers or individual contributors. This is consistent with the quality management movement, which suggests that all members of the organization must contribute to fulfilling the mission and achieving the goals of the organization. The differences in the way employees contribute is far less important than the commonality inherent in working to achieve the same organizational goals. As a consequence, the distinction between line and staff has become less important.

In addition, line and staff personnel now frequently coexist within work teams that collectively pursue a specific set of tasks. Consider, for example, Chrysler's efforts to gain a competitive advantage through the team approach to vehicle design. This company provides an example of a company that has grouped line and staff personnel together in product development teams.[47]

DELEGATION

Delegation
The process of transferring the responsibility for a specific activity or task to another member of the organization and empowering that individual to accomplish the task effectively.

Another important aspect of organizational relationships involves delegation. One of the most challenging skills that successful managers must master is the ability to delegate effectively. **Delegation** refers to the process of transferring the responsibility for a specific activity or task to another member of the organization and empowering that individual to accomplish the task effectively.

Traditionally, supervisors delegate tasks to those in their work group. The **scalar principle** of management suggests that a clear line of authority should run through the organization (chain of command) so that all persons in the organization understand to whom they can delegate and from whom they should accept delegated tasks.[48]

The Process of Delegation

To delegate effectively, managers must understand that delegation involves three distinct but highly related activities: (1) assignment of responsibility, (2) granting of authority, and (3) establishing accountability. All are essential to the success of the delegation process.[49]

Assignment of Responsibility   The delegation process begins when a manager assigns a subordinate the responsibility for a specific task or set of tasks. **Responsibility** refers to the employee's obligation to complete the activities that he or she has been assigned. Clear communication of the specific activities for which the employee is responsible is essential if the task is to be delegated successfully.

Granting of Authority   Managers must give their employees the authority to accomplish their work successfully.[50] **Authority** is the formal right of an employee to marshal the resources and make the decisions necessary to fulfill her or his work responsibilities. Without sufficient authority, it is unlikely that employees will complete delegated tasks successfully.

Consider, for example, a restaurant manager who has to leave early one evening and says to one of the waiters: "Make sure all the employees complete their closing duties." Assuming that the statement is made only to the waiter and not to the other employees, the manager has put the waiter in a very difficult position. She has just delegated the responsibility for ensuring that closing activities are completed properly without giving the waiter the authority he needs to succeed at that task. The other employees are unlikely to feel compelled to cooperate with the waiter so that he can fulfill his responsibility to the restaurant manager. To complete any task successfully, one must be given the authority necessary to carry out that task.

Establishing Accountability   Managers must hold their employees accountable for completing the tasks for which they assume responsibility and are given the necessary authority. When there is **accountability** for performance, employees understand that they must justify their decisions and actions with regard to the tasks for which they have assumed responsibility. Delegating decision-making responsibility without the associated accountability will compromise the overall benefits of the delegation process.

As Figure 8.3 illustrates, delegation can be thought of as a triangle, with each of these elements representing a point. Should one element be missing, the delegation process will be ineffective. To delegate successfully, managers must clearly communicate the responsibilities they are delegating, provide their employees with the formal authority necessary to fulfill those responsibilities, and develop the necessary control and feedback mechanisms to ensure that the employee is held accountable for successfully completing the delegated task.[51]

The Benefits of Delegation and Empowerment

Delegation offers a number of advantages. When used properly, delegation can lead to a more involved and empowered work force.[52] As we discussed in Chapter 1, empowerment can lead to heightened productivity and quality, reduced costs, more innovation, improved customer service, and greater commitment from the employees of the organization.[53] Delegation involves empowering em-

---

Scalar principle
A clear line of authority must run throughout the organization.

Responsibility
An obligation on the part of an employee to complete assigned activities.

Authority
The formal right of an employee to marshal resources and make decisions necessary to fulfill work responsibilities.

Accountability
Employees must justify their decisions and actions with regard to the task they have been assigned.

FIGURE 8.3

The delegation triangle

SOURCE: C. O. Longnecker, "The Delegation Dilemma," *Supervision*, 52, February 1991, 3–5. Reprinted by permission of © National Research Bureau, P.O. Box 1, Burlington, Iowa 52601-0001.

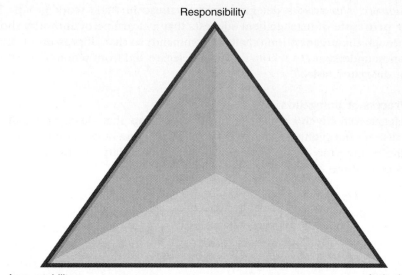

Delegation, as demonstrated by Federal Express, can lead to a more empowered work force and resulting heightened productivity and quality, reduced costs, more innovation, improved customer service, and greater commitment from employees.

© Terry Farmer/Tony Stone Images

ployees at all levels to make decisions, determine priorities, and improve the way work is done.[54]

Delegating decisions and activities to individuals lower in the organizational hierarchy often leads to better decision making. Those who are closest to the actual problem to be solved or the customer to be served may be in the best position to make the most effective decisions. In addition, response time may be improved since information and decisions need not be passed up and down the hierarchy. This will be particularly critical in organizations where delays in decision making can make the difference between success and failure. At Hewlett-Packard, for example, decision making has traditionally taken place at the top levels of the organization. Recently, however, top management realized that the delegation of decision making to the lower ranks of the organization was the only way to function effectively in an industry that was rapidly changing and highly competitive.[55]

Additionally, delegation is beneficial from an employee development perspective. By delegating tasks and decision-making responsibility to their employees, managers provide an opportunity for the development of analytical and problem-solving skills. The employees are forced to accept responsibility, exercise judgment, and be accountable for their actions. The development of such skills will benefit the organization in the long term.

Finally, through delegation and empowerment, managers magnify their accomplishments. By delegating tasks that their employees have the ability to complete, managers can use their time to accomplish more complicated, difficult, or important tasks. This can lead to a more creative and productive work group as a whole.[56]

Many organizations have benefited from empowering employees through delegation. Xerox, the American Society for Quality Control, and Federal Express are a few examples of organizations that have claimed significant success from employee empowerment. As we saw in Managing for Excellence, delegation and empowerment at Royal Insurance had a very positive effect on the quality of its product and the efficiency of its production process. By forcing decision making to the lowest levels of the organizational hierarchy, Royal Insurance personnel empowered its employees to do what was necessary to improve the operations of the company.

Managers should be cautioned about the potentially negative perceptions that ineffective delegation can create. Delegation must never be used to avoid work responsibilities that should legitimately be assumed by the manager. Delegation is not a way to "pass the buck," but rather a method for enhancing the overall productivity of the work group. If employees perceive the delegation as a way to reduce the manager's responsibilities and increase their own, their respect for the manager will undoubtedly deteriorate. This may be particularly problematic in diverse work groups where perceptions of delegation may vary. In such situations, it may be appropriate for managers to explain to their employees how delegation benefits the entire work group.

In general, effective delegation is a vital skill for successful managers. Yet it is a skill that many managers lack. Why? There are a number of reasons why managers fail to delegate.[57]

Reasons for Failing to Delegate

Delegation requires planning—and planning takes time.[58] How often have you heard someone say, "By the time I explain this task to someone, I could do it myself"? This is a common excuse for maintaining responsibility for tasks rather than delegating them.[59] In some cases, such a decision may make sense. However, when tasks are recurring and would warrant the time to train someone who could assume responsibility for the work, such a decision would not be appropriate. The Experiential Exercise at the end of this chapter provides a tool for managers to use in determining whether a task is appropriate for delegation.

Second, managers may simply lack confidence in the abilities of their subordinates. Such a situation fosters the attitude, "If you want it done well, do it yourself." This problem is particularly difficult to overcome when the manager feels pressure for high-level performance in a relatively short time frame. The manager simply refuses to delegate, preferring to retain responsibility for tasks to ensure that they are completed properly.

As a further complication, managers experience dual accountability. Managers are accountable for their own actions and the actions of their subordinates. If a subordinate fails to perform a certain task or does so poorly, it is the manager who is ultimately responsible for the subordinate's failure. Therefore, when the stakes are high, managers may prefer to perform certain tasks themselves.[60]

Finally, managers may refrain from delegating because they are insecure about their value to the organization.[61] Such managers may refuse to share the information necessary to complete a given task or set of tasks because they fear they will be considered expendable to the organization.

Learning to Delegate Effectively

Despite the perceived disadvantages of delegation, the reality is that managers can improve the performance of their work groups by empowering their employees through effective delegation. So how do managers learn to delegate effectively? They apply the basic principles of delegation.

Principle 1: Match the Employee to the Task   Managers should carefully consider the employees to whom they delegate.[62] The individual selected should possess the skills and capabilities needed to complete the task and, where possible, should stand to benefit from the experience. Further, managers should delegate duties that challenge employees somewhat, but which they can complete successfully.[63] There is no substitute for success when it comes to getting an employee to assume responsibility for more challenging assignments in the future.

Implicit in this principle is an acceptance of an *incremental learning* philosophy. This philosophy suggests that as employees prove their ability to perform effectively in a given job, they should be given tasks that are more complex and challenging. In addition to employee development benefits, such a strategy will be beneficial for the overall performance of the work group.[64]

Principle 2: Be Organized and Communicate Clearly   Most cases of failed delegation can be attributed to either poor organization or poor communication. When managers or employees do not clearly understand what is expected, the delegation process is sure to fail. The manager must have a clear understanding of what needs to be done, what deadlines exist, and what special skills will be required.[65] Delegation is a consultative process whereby managers and employees gain a clear understanding of the scope of their responsibilities and how their efforts relate to the overall efforts of the group or organization.[66]

Further, managers must be capable of communicating their instructions effectively if their subordinates are to perform up to the managers' expectations.[67] Effective communication about delegated tasks is particularly important in diverse work groups. As we know, people from different cultures may have different frames of reference and may interpret messages differently. Consequently, managers should be sure to clarify their instructions very carefully if they have any reason to believe that they may not be understood.

Principle 3: Transfer Authority and Accountability with the Task   The delegation process is doomed to failure if the individual to whom the task is delegated is not given the authority to succeed at accomplishing the task and is not held accountable for the results. The manager must expect employees to carry the ball and let them do so.[68] This means providing employees with the necessary resources and power to succeed, giving them timely feedback on their progress, and holding them fully accountable for the results of their efforts.

Principle 4: Choose the Level of Delegation Carefully   Delegation does not mean that the manager can walk away from the task or the person to whom the task is delegated. The manager may maintain some control of both the process and the results of the delegated activities. Depending upon the confidence the manager has in the subordinate and the importance of the task, the manager can choose to delegate at several levels (see Figure 8.4).[69]

Many good managers find it difficult to delegate. Yet few managers have been successful in the long term without learning to delegate effectively.[70] This

Managers can delegate in degrees. Consider the following alternative levels of delegation.

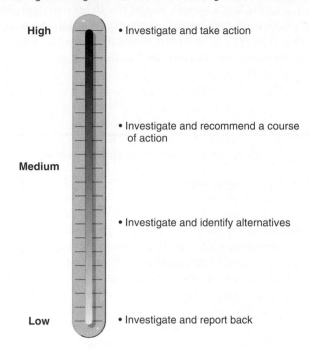

High • Investigate and take action

• Investigate and recommend a course
  of action

Medium

• Investigate and identify alternatives

Low • Investigate and report back

FIGURE 8.4

Degree of delegation

SOURCE: Adapted from M. E. Haynes, "Delegation: There's More to It than Letting Someone Else Do It!", 9–15. Reprinted, by permission of publisher, from *Supervisory Management*, January 1980. © 1980, American Management Association, New York. All rights reserved.

is particularly true in situations where growth and expansion are critical. For example, consider the experience of Debi Fields, the successful entrepreneur who created Mrs. Fields' Cookies. To support the growth goals of her company, Mrs. Fields had to abandon her hands-on, control-oriented leadership style for a more participative, delegation-oriented style.[71]

MANAGERIAL IMPLICATIONS

In this chapter, we have learned how jobs are designed and organizational relationships are determined. As a future manager, you should keep the following organizing tips in mind:

• Identify the tasks and activities that must be completed in order for the goals of the organization to be achieved.

• Design jobs so that job holders will find their jobs interesting and challenging.

• Look for ways to use participatory approaches to job design as a means of improving quality.

• Consider reengineering business processes as a means of improving organizational performance.

• Don't be trapped by traditional hierarchical organizational relationships. More flexible and adaptable organizational designs are appropriate in many situations.

• Remember—all successful managers delegate. Develop a system of delegation that works for you and your work group.

This chapter has focused on some of the foundation principles of organization theory and, more specifically, on the first stage of the organizing process. The next chapter will address the second stage of the process and the concept of organizational design. The design of an organization defines the way organizational members are configured or grouped together; the types of mechanisms used to integrate and coordinate the flow of information, resources, or tasks between organizational members; and the degree of centralization or decentralization of decision making within the organization. An understanding of these organizing concepts, along with those discussed in this chapter, is essential for understanding the managerial function of organizing.

Managerial Incident Resolution	## LEVI STRAUSS & COMPANY: REDESIGNING THE ORGANIZATION

Thomas Kasten, a Levi's vice-president and member of the company's U.S. Leadership Team, was given the responsibility for redesigning every aspect of the Levi's organization to ensure its competitiveness in the 21st century. Kasten, with a team of hundreds—many of whom were drawn from the middle ranks of management—hatched a plan to totally redesign the company, with new business processes, systems, and facilities. Thousands of new jobs were created, complete with formal job descriptions, qualifications, and titles. A staffing process that required current employees to apply for those jobs was also developed.

The redesign of jobs created whole new categories of jobs with new responsibilities, qualifications, and titles. A look at their customer fulfillment organization, for example, reveals jobs like process leader, performance consultant, source relations manager, and system relationship coordinator. Those jobs have never existed before. And they require new skills and new behaviors. Current employees had to apply for those jobs and demonstrate they possessed the appropriate competencies.

As one might guess, the remaking of Levi did not come without significant stress on the part of employees who were being asked to change. But Levi tried to minimize that stress by providing tools for its employees who desired to take personal responsibility for making the necessary changes. Some of those tools included:

- "The Little Blue Book"—a handbook to help people prepare for the organizational changes. *Individual Readiness for a Changing Environment* is an informal, 145-page binder full of self-assessment tools and self-improvement resources. One section, called "Knowing Myself," contains diagnostics that measure personal values, interests, talents, and attitudes. Another section, "Taking Action," offers advice on upgrading skills. A final section, "Marketing Myself," presents a refresher course on resumes and interviews.

- "The Lunch Box"—a collection of materials, formally known as *Mapping Your Future*, describes the new Levi and the process for staffing it. It contains booklets outlining the design principles behind the new company, posters tracing the interview and evaluation process, and a career planning workbook. This became the most important self-help tool in the change process.

- "Graphic Gameplan"—a process manual for helping employees learn to work in teams, which was an important dimension of Levi's new design. The Gameplan process requires teams to develop a team portrait, critical success factors, key obstacles, and major work categories.

Levi has been redesigned for the 21st century. To date, it looks as though the changes have been successful. Time will tell whether or not the company's design will ensure its success in the future.

SUMMARY

- The managerial function of organizing is critical for all managers and all organizations. The activities of the organization must be organized so that it can fulfill its mission and achieve its goals.

- Organizing is a two-stage process. The first stage involves delineating the work that needs to be done, assigning that work to specific job holders, and creating the work relationships necessary to support the product and service delivery system of the organization. The second stage involves assigning organizational members to work groups, developing an integrating system to coordinate the work of those groups, and defining the locus of decision making in the organization.

- Job design issues relate to the first stage of the organizing process. Job design refers to the way tasks and activities are grouped to constitute a particular job. Core job dimensions that can be used to describe a job include: (1) skill variety, (2) task identity, (3) task significance, (4) autonomy, and (5) feedback. The first three dimensions determine the meaningfulness of jobs; the fourth dimension, autonomy, determines the degree to which individuals feel responsible for their work; and the final dimension, feedback, relates to the extent to which job holders understand the outcome of their jobs.

- Job design principles have evolved along with management theory. Classical management theory and scientific management theory suggested relatively mechanistic approaches to designing jobs. The human relations school of thought supported behavioral approaches to job design. Job enlargement, enrichment, and rotation programs became accepted methods of increasing the motivation, job satisfaction, and overall productivity of job holders. Contemporary management theory prescribes more participatory approaches to job design. Employee-centered work redesign programs and self-managed teams are two examples of job design programs that are participatory in nature.

- Reengineering involves a search for and implementation of radical change in the processes by which the organization produces and delivers its products and services. Through this process, organizations redesign the ways work is done with a focus on improving efficiency, identifying redundancies, and eliminating waste in everything the company does. Reengineering has a significant impact on the way jobs are designed.

- Organizational work relationships are defined by the concepts of: (1) chain of command, (2) span of control, (3) line versus staff personnel, and (4) delegation. The chain of command defines the vertical relationships that exist within the organization. Span of control refers to the number of subordinates who report to any supervisor. Line personnel are individuals or work groups that have direct responsibility for the delivery of the organization's product or service, while staff personnel provide an advisory or support function to the line personnel. Delegation refers to the process of transferring the responsibility for a specific activity or task to another member of the organization and empowering them to accomplish it effectively.

- Effective delegation requires the assignment of responsibility for a task, the granting of the authority necessary to complete the task, and the transfer of accountability to the individual to whom the task has been delegated.

- Effective delegation is essential for successful managers. Managers often fail to delegate because of a failure to plan, a lack of confidence in their subordinates, hesitancy to assume dual accountability for the actions of those to whom they delegate, or insecurity about their own value to the organization. Effective delegation requires matching the employee to the task, clearly communicating task responsibilities, giving authority to and imposing accountability on the person to whom the task is delegated, and choosing the appropriate level of delegation.

KEY TERMS

Organizing	Job scope	Unity of command
Job design	Job enlargement	Span of control
Job description	Job depth	Line personnel
Skill variety	Job enrichment	Staff personnel
Task identity	Job rotation	Delegation
Task significance	Employee-centered work redesign	Scalar principle
Autonomy	Self-managed teams	Responsibility
Feedback	Reengineering	Authority
Job satisfaction	Chain of command	Accountability

REVIEW QUESTIONS

1. Why is organizing an important managerial function?
2. Describe the process of organizing. What does each stage in the process entail?
3. Define job design. What are the core job dimensions that define a specific job?
4. How has job design theory evolved? What do the mechanistic, behavioral, and participatory approaches to job design prescribe, and how does each affect the core job dimensions?
5. What is reengineering? How will reengineering programs affect the ways jobs are designed?
6. Discuss the following concepts: (1) chain of command, (2) span of control, and (3) line versus staff personnel.
7. What is delegation and why is it important to delegate?
8. Why might managers find it difficult to delegate? How might they improve their delegation skills?

DISCUSSION QUESTIONS

Improving Critical Thinking

1. Consider an organization that you have either worked for or been affiliated with in some way. How might you redesign the jobs that must be done in that organization to achieve: (a) increased efficiency, (b) enhanced quality of the product or service, and (c) improved employee satisfaction? Are these objectives mutually exclusive? Could you design the jobs so that all of these objectives could be achieved?

2. The concept of self-managed teams has gained popularity in recent years. Consider moving toward that type of job design in a job you have held or hold currently. What would be the advantages and disadvantages to this approach?

Enhancing Communication Skills

3. Certain advantages and disadvantages are associated with having a fairly rigid chain of command. What are they? Can you identify certain business conditions and/or organizations where a rigid chain of command would be appropriate? What conditions and/or organizations would benefit from the use of a more flexible chain of command? Present your conclusions to the class orally.

4. Consider the job design of the following grocery store positions: (a) cashier, (b) produce manager, and (c) general manager. How would these jobs differ with regard to the core job dimensions discussed in this chapter? How would these jobs rate in terms of meaningfulness, the responsibility the job holder feels for outcomes, and the job holder's understanding of the results of work activities? To practice writing, develop a written summary of your response.

Building Teamwork

5. The competitive pressures of today's business climate (such as stronger global competition, weakened economic conditions, greater demands from consumers) have forced many firms to reconsider how they might operate more efficiently and effectively. Form a team with four or five fellow students. As a group, identify and research at least three firms that have responded to such pressures by reassessing and adjusting their organizational system. Have their efforts been effective?

6. Your boss is a terrible delegator. She rarely delegates tasks, preferring to retain the responsibility for the efforts of your entire work unit rather than take a risk by assigning the task to a member of the group. Even when she does delegate a meaningful task, she rarely gives the authority necessary to complete the task successfully. Form a team of four to five fellow students and discuss ways to encourage your boss to delegate more.

INFORMATION TECHNOLOGY: Insights and Solutions

1. Using a library database system, research the concept of self-managed teams. Identify several companies that are using self-managed teams. Try to identify both manufacturing and service firms. Report on the companies' success with this job design. Do manufacturing and service organizations differ with regard to their success with the team approach? Speculate as to why such differences do or do not exist.

2. Select one of the companies profiled in the chapter that has undergone a major reengineering or reorganization effort (Royal Insurance or Oticon might be particularly interesting). Use the Internet to learn more about this company. What caused this firm to need to change? Has the performance of the firm improved since the organizational changes have been implemented?

3. Identify a firm in which you have a particular interest from a career perspective. Using e-mail, attempt to contact a human resource specialist who could provide you information about an entry-level job in which you would be interested. Ask that person to help you assess the core job dimensions of that particular job. Are you still interested in starting your career in such a position? Why or why not?

ETHICS: Take a Stand

Playtime Toys recently restructured its operations in an effort to achieve a stronger competitive position within its industry. The competitiveness of the toy industry had intensified in the last two years, and more efficient, low-priced competitors had begun to chip away at Playtime's market share. If Playtime's restructuring plan was not successful at driving down costs, the company would likely not survive the next year.

Playtime's restructuring plan included the elimination of an entire layer of management, as well as the selective elimination of certain job positions. As a result, the job responsibilities of a number of individuals throughout the organization had changed dramatically over the last month.

Susan Pilcher was one of those individuals. Susan was one of two managers on the production lines for baby swings. When the other production line manager's job was eliminated in the restructuring, Susan's span of control doubled. Where she originally supervised 15 employees on one line, she now supervised 30 employees working on two production lines. Managing the two lines effectively was very difficult. Yet Susan was determined to maintain productivity goals. Otherwise she felt certain that she would be the next supervisor eliminated.

Unfortunately, the pressure to maintain productivity was affecting the quality of the company's products. Playtime was a small operation, and production managers performed quality checks as part of their normal job responsibilities. Like Susan, many of the company's production managers had been forced to assume increased responsibilities, leaving little time to perform regular quality checks.

Susan was particularly aware of this issue, as the company had received two customer complaints about weak straps on baby swings that she knew had not been checked. But pressure to perform had left her in a quandary as to how to resolve this problem. Thus far, no serious incidents had occurred, but what if a child was hurt next time? On the other hand, if she complained about this problem, how would upper management view her ability to supervise, and how would this affect her future in the company?

For Discussion
1. Why was Susan experiencing this dilemma?
2. What would you do if you were Susan?

THINKING CRITICALLY: Debate the Issue

Form teams of four to five students. Half of the teams should prepare to argue the benefits of job specialization. The other half of the teams should prepare to argue the benefits of job enlargement. Your instructor will select two teams to present their arguments to the class in a debate format.

Video Case

RHEACO, INC.

Related Web Site: `{http://www.tmac.org/reports/casestdy/`
`cas-rhea.htm}`

Rheaco, Inc., of Grand Prairie, Texas, was in trouble. Its primary business was to sell fabricated sheet metal to defense contractors, but the defense industry was shrinking. In addition, the company was delinquent on 50 percent of its deliveries and had received complaints about its product quality from a number of its customers. To add to Rheaco's problems, many of its customers were following a national trend of reducing the number of suppliers that they maintained in an effort to improve their own product quality.

As a result of these difficulties, Rheaco sought help from the Automation Robotics and Research Institute at the University of Texas. The institute assisted Rheaco in developing a program to completely revise its organizational structure, operations, and company culture. The first priority was revising Rheaco's manner of organizing and its factory layout. As a first step, the company's job shops were broken up into cells, with each cell producing a different family of parts. This design improved the efficiency of Rheaco's operations, to the point where one Rheaco employee remarked, "Material flowed like water and people moved to the work instead of work to the people." This step corrected an old nemesis at Rheaco, which was inefficient work flow. Human resource management at the plant was also improved. Employees were assigned to work cells according to their interests and skills. Members of the work unit of each cell had responsibility for a part, figuratively speaking, "from cradle to grave." That meant providing the employees with responsibility and accountability in a number of areas, including scheduling, quality, purchasing, and maintenance. In addition, each cell assumed responsibility for its output, and could easily determine whether it was meeting its daily and monthly objectives.

Additional changes were made, including the implementation of just-in-time inventory control, total quality management, employee empowerment, and cellular manufacturing. A number of changes at the managerial level were also made, simplifying the movement of information throughout the company. Today, Rheaco appears to have a bright future. Manufacturing capacity is up 300 percent, and the company is solidifying its customer relationships. New customers are also being sought, as the company proceeds with its new manner of organizing.

For Discussion

1. Discuss the importance of organizing at Rheaco. How does proper organizing translate into improved firm performance?
2. Beyond creating a more efficient workplace, what is it about Rheaco's new methods of organizing that provides an enhanced potential for employee motivation, satisfaction, and productivity?

MAJOR APPLIANCES SCALES DOWN

Recently, customer service problems and employee morale problems surfaced at Major Appliances. The problems, precipitated by recent downsizing of the organization, put a damper on management's enthusiasm for the benefits of their new organizational design.

Six months ago, the company had downsized to cope with the increasingly competitive global environment. The growth of the company in the early 1980s had led to expansion of the work force at all ranks within the company. However, growth had stabilized, and sales were expected to remain flat for the next several years. In addition, the company had recently installed a new computer system that performed many functions previously accomplished by employees. These two factors influenced the decision to downsize to improve the efficiency of the organization. As Dave Fick, CEO, told the key management group, "The purpose of the restructuring plan is to remain competitive in the increasingly mature appliance industry. We need to stretch the capabilities of each employee to achieve this goal."

The impact of the downsizing efforts seemed to be particularly negative for the Accounting Support Department. Originally, three people worked in this department, with one assigned to each of the following jobs: accounts payable, accounts receivable, and payroll. Management felt that, given the new computer system, one person should be able to perform all three functions. Consequently, management terminated two workers and shifted the responsibility for all three jobs to the remaining person—Mr. Matsuda.

Initially, Mr. Matsuda was excited about his additional responsibilities and the opportunity to expand his role in the company. But he soon became disillusioned. He found it nearly impossible to fulfill his responsibilities in a timely fashion. Bills were not paid on time, errors were made in employee paychecks, and Mr. Matsuda was falling further and further behind in all of his duties. He was working every Saturday but was still unable to catch up with his work. While the company had to pay additional overtime costs, the problems continued. Customers and suppliers had begun to complain, and so had employees. Something needed to be done to correct the situation.

For Discussion

1. What was the management at Major Appliances trying to accomplish by redesigning the way work was done in the Accounting Support Department?
2. Using the terms introduced in this chapter, describe what happened to Mr. Matsuda's job. How were the five core job dimensions affected by the changes in his job design?
3. Was his reaction to his new job design what you would expect? Why or why not?
4. How could the problems in the Accounting Support Department have been avoided?

EXPERIENTIAL EXERCISE 8.1

Assuring Positive Delegation

Using either your present job or a past job as an example, think about a task that you would like to delegate. Answer the following questions about the task and the existing situation. Based on your answers, decide if the task should have been delegated.

1. *Precise task.* Could I specify in writing the precise task I'm going to delegate? In other words, could I specify what it is, how much of it needs to be done, and within what time frame?

2. *Benefits.* Could I specify in writing why delegating this particular task to this particular individual is good for her, good for the organization, and good for me?

3. *Measure of results.* Could I specify in writing how I will know: (a) whether the task has been done, and (b) how well it has been done?

4. *Competence.* Is the person to whom I intend to delegate this task: (a) competent to do it, or (b) in need of step-by-step instructions or supervision?

5. *Motivation.* Is there any evidence in my past relationship with this person that he wants, needs, or is motivated to do work outside the customary job?

6. *Measure of cost.* If the person makes an error, specifically what would be the dollar costs? The human costs?

7. *Check performance.* Is it possible for me to oversee or measure the employee's performance on the task without interfering with his work?

8. *Correct mistakes.* If problems arise, can we correct mistakes quickly without great cost or difficulty?

9. *Clearance.* Do I need to check this delegation with my boss?

10. *Rewards.* What are the rewards, both formal and informal, that I can give this person if the delegated task is done well? Do I need to tell the person what these rewards are?

11. *Next tasks.* If the person masters the task that has been delegated, what are the specific subsequent tasks that should be delegated to her?

12. *Responsibility and authority.* Can I, in delegating this task, delegate both the responsibility and the authority to this person?[72]

ENDNOTES

1. D. Sheff, "Levi's Changes Everything: An Inside Account of the Most Dramatic Change Program in American Business," *Fast Company*, June-July 1996, 65-74.

2. M. A. Hoffmann, "Remaking Royal: An Insider's View," *Business Insurance*, September 18, 1995, 3-7.

3. P. C. Grant, "Managing the Downside of Top Performance," *Supervisory Management*, November 1989, 25-27.

4. M. A. Campion and P. W. Thayer, "How Do You Design a Job?" *Personnel Journal*, 68, January 1989, 43-46.

5. J. R. Hackman, G. R. Oldham, R. Janson, and K. Purdy, "A New Strategy for Job Enrichment," *California Management Review*, 17, Summer 1975, 57-71.

6. Ibid., 58.

7. C. L. Fowler, "ASQC/Fortune Special Report," *Fortune*, 1992.

8. N. Dodd and D. Ganster, "The Interactive Effects of Variety, Autonomy, and Feedback on Attitudes and Performance," *Journal of Organizational Behavior*, 17, 1996, 329-47.

9. M. Hammer, *Beyond Reengineering* (New York: Harper-Collins, 1996), 50.

10. See, for example, T. J. Galpin, *The Human Side of Change* (San Francisco: Jossey-Bass, 1996).

11. Caterpillar, Inc., *1991 Annual Report.*

12. T. Peters, "Thriving on Chaos," *Working Woman*, Sept. 1993, 42-48.

13. M. Hammer, *Beyond Reengineering*, 47.

14. See, for example, J. W. Dean Jr. and S. A. Snell, "Integrated Manufacturing and Job Design: Moderating Effects of Organizational Inertia," *Academy of Management Journal*, 34, 1991, 776-804; G. Johns, J. L. Xie, and F. Yongqing, "Mediating and Moderating Effects in Job Design," *Journal of Management*, 18, 1992, 657-76.

15. M. Hammer, *Beyond Reeingineering*, 28.

16. J. B. Cunningham and T. Eberle, "A Guide to Job Enrichment and Redesign," *Personnel*, 67, February 1990, 56-61.

17. R. Lynch, "A Baby Bell Reexamines Itself," *Journal of Business Strategy*, September/October 1991, 8-11.

18. Caterpillar, Inc., *1990 Annual Report*, 8.

19. M. A. Campion, L. Cheraskin, and M. J. Stevens, "Career-Related Antecedents and Outcomes of Job Rotation," *Academy of Management Journal*, 37, 6, 1994, 1518-42; S. Stites-Doe, "The New Story about Job Rotation," *Academy of Management Executive*, 10, 6, 86-87.

20. J. E. Rigdon, "Using Lateral Moves to Spur Employees," *The Wall Street Journal*, May 26, 1992, PB1(W), PB1(E), col. 3, B1.

21. See, for example, I. Mitroff, R. O. Mason, and C. M. Pearson, "Radical Surgery: What Will Tomorrow's Organiza-

tions Look Like?" *Academy of Management Executive,* 8, 1994, 11–21; S. Caudron, "Integrated Workplace Paradox," *Personnel Journal,* August 1996, 75, 8, 68–71.

22. M. H. Safizadeh, "The Case of Workgroups in Manufacturing Operations," *California Management Review,* 33, Summer 1991, 61–82.

23. R. Jacob, "Thriving in a Lame Economy," *Fortune,* October 5, 1992, 44–54.

24. S. L. Perlman, "Employees Redesign Their Jobs," *Personnel Journal,* 67, November 1990, 37–40.

25. See, for example, J. A. Neal and C. L. Tromley, "From Incremental Change to Retrofit: Creating High-Performance Work Systems," *Academy of Management Executive,* 9, 1995, 42–54.

26. Ibid.

27. Ibid.

28. Amoco Corporation, *1990 Annual Report,* 12.

29. See, for example, P. J. Keating and S. F. Jablonsky, "Get Your Financial Organization Close to the Business," *Financial Executive,* May/June 1991, 44–50; M. H. Safizadeh, "The Case of Workgroups in Manufacturing Operations."

30. See, for example, M. A. Campion and A. C. Higgs, "Design Work Teams to Increase Productivity and Satisfaction," *HR Magazine,* October 1995, 101–7.

31. P. Chance, "Great Experiments in Team Chemistry," *Across the Board,* May 1989, 18–25.

32. See, for example, M. A. Campion, G. J. Medsker, and A. C. Higgs, "Relations between Work Group Characteristics and Effectiveness: Implications for Designing Effective Work Groups," *Personnel Psychology,* 46, 1993, 823–45; M. A. Campion, E. Papper, and G. J. Medsker, "Relations between Work Team Characteristics and Effectiveness: A Replication and Extension," *Personnel Psychology,* 49, 1996, 429–52.

33. Ibid.

34. T. R. Horton, "Delegation and Team Building: No Solo Acts Please," *Management Review,* November 1989, 25–27.

35. Ibid.

36. M. Hammer, *Beyond Reengineering,* 159–62.

37. M. Bassin, "Teamwork at General Foods: New & Improved," *Personnel Journal,* May 1988, 67, 5, 62–70.

38. See, for example, E. E. Lawler III, "Total Quality Management and Employee Involvement: Are They Compatible?" *Academy of Management Executive,* 1994, 8, 1, 68–76.

39. M. Hammer, *Beyond Reeingineering,* 28.

40. A. K. Naj, "AlliedSignal's Chairman Outlines Strategy for Growth," *The Wall Street Journal,* August 17, 1993, PB4(W), PB4(E), col. 3.

41. J. Oberle, "Quality Gurus: The Men and Their Message," *Training,* January 1990, 47–52.

42. R. M. Tomasko, "Intelligent Resizing: View from the Bottom Up (Part II)," *Management Review,* June 1993, 18–23.

43. A. Laplante, "Kodak Experiments with Local Support," *Computerworld,* December 1990, 24, 50, 90(1).

44. Ameritech, *1992 Annual Report.*

45. H. Mintzberg, *The Structuring of Organization* (Upper Saddle River, N.J.: Prentice Hall, 1979), 136.

46. J. S. McClenahen, "Managing More People in the '90s," *Industry Week,* March 20, 1989, 31–38.

47. Chrysler Corporation, *1990 Annual Report.*

48. S. C. Bushardt, D. L. Duhon, and A. R. Fowler Jr., "Management Delegation Myths and the Paradox of Task Assignment," *Business Horizons,* March/April 1991, 34, 37–43.

49. Chrysler Corporation, *1990 Annual Report.*

50. M. E. Douglas, "How to Delegate Safely," *Training and Development Journal,* February 1987, 8.

51. C. O. Longnecker, "The Delegation Dilemma," *Supervision,* 52, February 1991, 3–5.

52. J. D. O'Brian, "Empowering Your Front-Line Employees to Handle Problems," *Supervisory Management,* 38, 1, January 1993, 10(1).

53. D. Vinton, "Delegation for Employee Development," *Training and Development Journal,* January 1987, 65–67.

54. M. C. Dennis, "Only Superman Didn't Delegate," *Business Credit,* February 1993, 41.

55. T. Peters, "Letting Go of Controls," *Across the Board,* June 1991, 14–18.

56. M. Yate, "Delegation: The Key to Empowerment," *Training and Development Journal,* April 1991, 23–24.

57. J. H. Carter, "Minimizing the Risks from Delegation," *Supervisory Management,* February 1992, 1–2.

58. J. Lawrie, "Turning Around Attitudes about Delegation," *Supervisory Management,* 35, December 1990, 1–2.

59. R. Wilkinson, "Eight Supervisory Tips," *Supervision,* July 1991, 52, 7, 12–15.

60. J. Lawrie, "Turning Around Attitudes about Delegation."

61. R. Rohrer, "Does the Buck Ever Really Stop?" *Supervision,* 52, July 1991, 7–8.

62. J. T. Straub, "Do You Choose the Best Person for the Task?" *Supervisory Management,* October 1992, 7.

63. D. Vinton, "Delegation for Employee Development."

64. M. E. Douglas, "How to Delegate Safely."

65. M. Yate, "Delegation: The Key to Empowerment."

66. D. Vinton, "Delegation for Employee Development."

67. R. Wilkinson, "Think before You Open Your Mouth!" *Supervision,* 52, May 1991, 17–19.

68. M. Townsend, "Let the Employees Carry the Ball," *Personnel Journal,* 69, October 1990, 30–31.

69. M. E. Haynes, "Delegation: There's More to It than Letting Someone Else Do It," *Supervisory Management,* 25, January 1980, 9–15.

70. T. R. Horton, "Delegation and Team Building: No Solo Acts Please," *Management Review,* September 1992, 58–61.

71. A. Prendergast, "Learning to Let Go," *Working Woman,* January 1992, 42–45.

72. J. Lawrie, "Turning around Attitudes about Delegation," Reprinted by permission of publisher from Supervisory Management, December 1990, American Management Association, New York. All rights reserved.

Designing the Contemporary Organization

■ CHAPTER OVERVIEW

Developing an organizational design that supports the strategic and operational goals of an organization can be a very challenging managerial task. This is particularly true today, as many organizations struggle to find that delicate balance between organizational responsiveness and operational efficiency. Achieving success will depend, to a large degree, on the ability of managers to develop an effective and flexible organizational design.

This chapter focuses on a number of issues related to organizational design. Special attention is given to the effect of various strategic orientations on the structure of organizations, the impact of interdependence between operating units on the integration needs of organizations, and the extent to which environmental stability or volatility affects how decision making occurs within organizations.

■ LEARNING OBJECTIVES

When you have finished studying this chapter, you should be able to:

- Explain why organizational design is important for organizational success.
- Identify the three major components of organizational design.
- Discuss the four types of organizational structure and the strategic conditions under which each might be appropriate.
- Describe the factors that affect an organization's need for coordination and explain how integrating mechanisms can be used to coordinate organizational activities.
- Explain the concept of locus of decision making and the advantages and disadvantages of centralized and decentralized decision making.
- Describe organic and mechanistic organizational systems and discuss the relationships between these systems and environmental stability.
- Describe an adaptive organizational design.

BIG BLUE: DEVELOPING AN ORGANIZATIONAL DESIGN THAT WORKS

Few companies have enjoyed such great success as International Business Machines (IBM). "Big Blue," as it is affectionately called by many, built a worldwide reputation for the delivery of high-quality, advanced information technology for use by organizations across the globe. Its aggressive growth strategies earned it a place at the top of the highly volatile and rapidly changing computer industry year after year.

Surprisingly, however, the company's competitive edge began to deteriorate significantly in the early 1990s. In fact, due to a number of factors (a sluggish world economy, a general slowdown in the computer industry, and intensified competition), IBM experienced a substantial decline in revenues and profits in 1991 and 1992. The company's problems eventually resulted in the ousting of Jim Akers, who had been the CEO for many years. When Lou Gerstner took the helm as CEO, restoring IBM's profitability was his first priority.

One aspect of the company that received significant scrutiny was its organizational design. Many criticized IBM's excessively bureaucratic organizational system, suggesting that it hampered decision making and stifled creativity. Such a design was likely inappropriate for an organization operating in a dynamic industry where innovation is critical to long-term success.

The management at IBM considered a number of possible changes in the organizational design. Among the options under consideration were the elimination of middle levels of management, the decentralization of decision making, and the regrouping of work activities along product lines. Complicating the situation, however, was the fact that IBM's organizational design had been in existence for a very long time. It was deeply rooted and would be difficult to change. Nevertheless, the long-term success of this firm would depend, to some degree, on its ability to make the necessary changes in its organizational design.[1]

INTRODUCTION

In the early 1990s, management at all levels of IBM was concerned about the company's declining competitive position. The company's organizational design seemed inappropriate for the industry in which it operated. Burdened with excessive layers of management that complicated and delayed decision making, IBM found itself incapable of competing effectively with its more flexible and proactive competitors. A major restructuring of the firm's organizational design was imperative.

Organizational design is an important aspect of management. The way in which an organization is designed will determine how efficiently and effectively its activities are carried out. Organizations must be designed so that the mission of the organization can be fulfilled and its goals can be achieved. Increasingly, managers are looking to organizational design as a method for competing more effectively in global markets and achieving a quality orientation across the organization as a whole.[2]

This chapter begins with a discussion of the concept of organizational design from a contingency perspective. The primary components of organizational design are identified, and the role that each plays in the overall design of the organization is examined. The implications of various organizational and environmental variables (such as strategy, interdependence, and external environmental pressures) will be evaluated for each organizational design component. Finally, the chapter concludes with a discussion of adaptive organizations and offers some guidelines for managers who must design their organizations for the business environment of the future.

ORGANIZATIONAL DESIGN FROM ▆▆▆▆▆▆▆▆▆▆▆▆▆▆▆▆ A CONTINGENCY PERSPECTIVE

Organizational design is a plan for arranging and coordinating the activities of an organization for the purpose of fulfilling its mission and achieving its goals. More specifically, design defines (1) the configuration of organizational members, (2) the types of mechanisms used to integrate and coordinate the flow of information, resources, and tasks between organizational members, and (3) the locus of decision making—the level of the organizational hierarchy at which most decision making occurs. The ultimate success of an organization will depend, in part, on the ability of its managers to develop an organizational design that supports its strategic and operational goals.

Design provides a mechanism for coping with the complexity that results from managing multiple tasks, functions, products, markets, or technologies. Although organizational design issues are important to all organizations, the more complex an organization's operations, the more sophisticated its design must be.

For example, a small organization that produces a single product with a small work force will likely find it easier to organize and coordinate its organizational members than will a multinational organization with multiple product lines, operating facilities spread across the globe, and a highly diverse work force. Further, growth-oriented organizations will find that effective design is a key to managing the complexity that results from developing new products, entering new geographic markets, or pursuing new customer groups. In sum, all organizations (small, large, and growing) must maintain an organizational design that is appropriate for the level of complexity they face.

There is no universal design that is appropriate for all organizations. In fact, the contingency approach to organizing suggests that organizational design must be consistent with a fairly broad range of variables that are largely a function of the organization's strategy (such as size, level of development, product diversity, geographic coverage, and customer base).[3] Consequently, just as strategy varies among organizations, so will organizational design.

The 1990s have been characterized by a need for corporate redesign. Nearly everywhere you look, another company is struggling to find an alignment between its strategy and structure. The highly volatile and competitive business environment that has existed during this decade has forced many companies to reconsider their strategic focus, and consequently, the way in which their organizations are designed. Consider, for example, the experiences of such companies as Xerox, Sears, Kodak, and American Express—just to name a few. The leaders of these organizations continue to struggle to define both an effective strategy and an organizational design that supports that strategy. In contrast, however, consider Rubbermaid, Chrysler, Ford, and Harley-Davidson. These organizations have reformulated their strategies in light of the competitive challenges they face and have redesigned their organizations to support those strategies. The result is that they are achieving a much higher level of success than those companies that have not.[4]

Most experts agree that the highly competitive business environment of the future will force organizations to seek new strategies, and with them new forms of organizational design.[5] In fact, success will go to those who continue to innovate and experiment with ways to design their organizations to enhance their competitiveness.[6]

Organizational design
The way in which the activities of an organization are arranged and coordinated so that its mission can be fulfilled and its goals achieved.

COMPONENTS OF ORGANIZATIONAL DESIGN

As noted earlier and illustrated in Figure 9.1, an organization's overall design is defined by three primary components: (1) organization structure, (2) integrating mechanisms, and (3) locus of decision making. As a system, these components enable the members of the organization to fulfill its mission and work toward the achievement of its goals. Each of these components will vary with the overall strategy of the organization.

ORGANIZATIONAL STRUCTURE

Organizational structure
The primary reporting relationships that exist within an organization.

Organization structure is the first component of organizational design. **Organizational structure** refers to the primary reporting relationships that exist within an organization. The chain of command and hierarchy of responsibility, authority, and accountability are established through organizational structure and are often illustrated in an organizational chart.

The structuring process involves creating departments by grouping tasks on the basis of some common characteristic such as function, product, or geographic market. If, for example, work units are created by grouping all production tasks together, all marketing tasks together, and all finance tasks together, then the units are organized by function. In contrast, if work units are formed by grouping together all tasks related to serving a specific region of the U.S. market (such as northeast, southeast, central, or west), then the geographic market served is the basis for departmentalization.

An organization's strategy has significant implications for its structure.[7] Organizations group their members along that aspect of their operations that is most complex. For example, an organization with significant product diversity will likely find a structure departmentalized by product to be most suitable for managing its broad range of products. If, in contrast, a firm has a relatively narrow product line but serves a wide geographic market, it might find a geographically based structure to be most appropriate.

In general, four types of organizational structure are predominant in organizations today. Three of these—the functional, divisional, and matrix structures—are traditional organizational forms that have been used by U.S. corpo-

FIGURE 9.1
Dimensions of organizational design

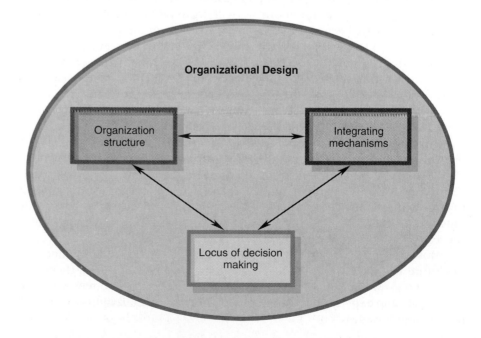

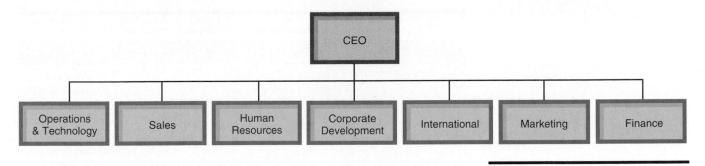

FIGURE 9.2
Functional structure: Coors Brewing
Company

rations for decades. The last structure, the network structure, has emerged more recently and represents a contemporary approach for meeting the challenges of today's business environment. In the next several sections, we will describe each structural alternative, suggest some strategic conditions for which each might be appropriate, and outline some of the major advantages and disadvantages associated with each structure.

Functional Structure: Enhancing Operational Efficiency

Functional structures are the most commonly used organizational form today.[8] The **functional structure** groups organizational members according to the particular function that they perform within the organization and the set of resources that they draw upon to perform their tasks. Figure 9.2 illustrates a functional organizational chart for Coors Brewing Company. As the chart shows, this firm structures its activities according to the functions of operations and technology, sales, human resources, corporate development, international, marketing, and finance.[9]

When an organization's greatest source of complexity comes from the diverse tasks and responsibilities that must be performed, rather than from its products, geographic markets or customer groups, a functional structure may be appropriate. Entrepreneurial organizations or organizations that are in the early stages of the organizational life cycle often have limited product diversity and geographic scope. Task diversity may represent the organization's greatest source of complexity, and as a consequence, a functional structure may be most suitable.

Table 9.1 outlines the major advantages and disadvantages associated with the functional structure. On the positive side, functional structures support task specialization and may help employees develop better job-related skills. In addition, work groups may be more cohesive because employees work with individuals with similar skills and interests and the group's leader has a common functional orientation with the group members. Finally, this structure supports tight, centralized control and may result in greater operational efficiency.

But this structure has disadvantages as well. Most of these disadvantages stem from the problems associated with coordinating diverse work groups. Work groups organized along functional lines are often insulated from the activities of other departments and may not truly understand the priorities and initiatives of other work groups. Further, the functional structure leads to the development of specialized managers rather than generalists who may be more appropriate for top-level management positions. Finally, profit centers usually do not exist in a functionally structured organization. Therefore only top-level corporate executives can be held clearly accountable for bottom-line profitability.

Divisional Structures: Providing Focus

A second common form of organizational structure is the divisional structure. In most cases, a **divisional structure** is designed so that members of the organization are grouped on the basis of common products or services, geo-

Functional structure
Members of the organization are grouped according to the function they perform within the organization.

Divisional structure
Members of the organization are grouped on the basis of common products, geographic markets, or customers served.

TABLE 9.1   Advantages and disadvantages of traditional organizational structures

	ADVANTAGES	DISADVANTAGES
Functional	• Facilitates specialization • Cohesive work groups • Improved operational efficiency	• Focus on departmental versus organizational issues • Difficult to develop generalists needed for top management • Only top management held accountable for profitability
Product divisional	• Enhanced coordination • Better assessment of manager performance and responsibility • Development of generalist managers	• Managers may lack expertise to operate in wide geographic regions • Duplication of resources
Geographic divisional	• Allows focus on specific new markets • Good structure for growth along geographic lines • Adaptable to local needs	• Duplication of product or product/technology efforts • Coordination and integration are difficult • May be difficult to manage diverse product lines
Matrix	• Can achieve simultaneous objectives • Managers focus on two organizational dimensions, resulting in more specific job skills	• Complex, leading to difficulties in implementation • Behavioral difficulties from "two bosses" • Time-consuming from a planning/coordination perspective
Network	• Maximizes the effectiveness of the core unit • Can do more with fewer resources • Flexibility	• Fragmentation makes it difficult to develop control systems • Success is dependent on ability to locate sources • Difficult to develop employee loyalty

graphic markets, or customers served. The primary advantage of a divisional structure is the focus it provides in supporting the strategic goals of the organization. The primary disadvantage is that resources and efforts may be duplicated across divisions (see Table 9.1)

Product divisional structure
A structure in which the activities of the organization are grouped according to specific products or product lines.

Product Divisions   In a **product divisional structure,** product managers assume responsibility for the production and distribution of a specific product or product line to all the geographic and customer markets served by the organization. These managers coordinate all functional tasks (finance, marketing, production, and so on) related to their product line. Product divisional structures can be based on services as well as products. As an example of such a structure, consider the civil engineering firm Bowyer Singleton & Associates. As illustrated in Figure 9.3, this company operates with a product divisional structure organized along its primary service segments—land development planning and design, transportation planning and design, survey and mapping, and environmental sciences services. In fact, as you will read in Entrepreneurial Approach, the leaders at Bowyer Singleton & Associates found that this structure was essential for the implementation of their growth-oriented product development strategy.

BOWYER SINGLETON & ASSOCIATES: A NEW STRATEGY CALLS FOR A NEW STRUCTURE

Bowyer Singleton & Associates (BSA), a civil engineering firm, has experienced significant success since its inception in 1972. By 1995, BSA was generating $8 million in sales and employing more than 90 people. The company's original service, land development engineering and transportation engineering, had provided the foundation of its success. They also provided the foundation of the firm's organizational structure as the firm's operations were organized into two primary departments that corresponded with those services. While BSA also offered limited survey and mapping and environmental sciences services, both were subsumed under the land development and transportation departments.

In 1995, founder and CEO Jim Bowyer decided to pursue a formal strategic planning process. He knew that bold new strategies would be necessary to ensure the firm's long-term success in the highly competitive business environment of the future. As a result of the planning process, BSA decided to fully expand its survey and mapping and environmental sciences services. The objective was to generate a significant portion of the firm's total revenues from these two service areas.

To support this new strategy, the organizational structure of BSA was changed. No longer did the company operate with only two departments that subsumed the firm's survey and mapping and environmental sciences efforts. Rather they expanded the structure by adding two new departments that corresponded with their new service areas. Leaders for these departments were identified, action plans were established, and monitoring and control mechanisms were put in place. By the end of the first year, both departments had exceeded the revenue goals established for them in the strategic plan. The new organizational structure facilitated the implementation of the plan by grouping together the people and resources that were necessary to implement BSA's service expansion strategy.

BSA continues to pursue its service expansion strategy today—and it has the organizational structure to make it work![10]

Product divisional structures are considered most appropriate for organizations with relatively diverse product lines that require specialized efforts to achieve high product quality. When products are targeted to different, distinct groups; require varied technologies for production; or are delivered through diverse distribution systems, a product-based structure may be suitable. For example, consider IBM's move to create autonomous operating divisions based on the firm's distinct product lines. Recognizing the importance of a product orientation to IBM's overall success, top management believed that a product divisional structure would provide the product focus necessary to regain their competitive edge.[11]

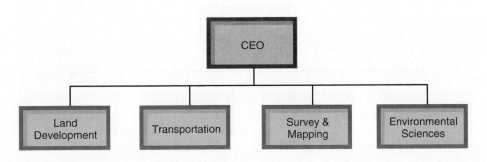

FIGURE 9.3
Product divisional structure: Bowyer Singleton and Company

Geographic divisional structure
A structure in which the activities of the organization are grouped according to the geographic markets served.

Kellogg maintains a geographic divisional structure, focusing primarily on its breakfast food products and marketing to a broad geographic market composed of four regions: North America, Europe, Latin America, and Asia-Pacific.

© Michael Newman/PhotoEdit

Customer divisional structure
A structure in which the tasks of the organization are grouped according to customer segments.

Many large organizations not only have diverse product lines, but actually operate several diverse and distinct businesses. In such cases, the product divisional structure actually takes the form of an SBU (strategic business unit) divisional structure, in which each business unit is maintained as a separate and autonomous operating division. PepsiCo, Inc., provides an excellent example of a company organized around its primary businesses—soft drink, snack foods, and restaurants. Interestingly, PepsiCo uses a variety of structural alternatives within each business unit. The restaurant SBU, for example, is organized primarily along product lines (Kentucky Fried Chicken, Pizza Hut, Taco Bell), whereas the soft-drink SBU is organized by geographic region.[12]

Geographic Divisions   The **geographic divisional structure** groups the activities of the organization along geographic lines. Each geographic division is responsible for distributing products or services within a specific geographic region.

A geographic divisional structure is appropriate for organizations of varying strategic conditions. In general, this structure is most appropriate for organizations with limited product lines that either have wide geographic coverage or desire to grow through geographic expansion. This structure permits organizations to concentrate their efforts and allocate their resources toward penetrating multiple regional markets with products and services that are, when necessary, adapted to meet local needs and preferences.[13]

Organizations pursuing international strategies often choose a geographically based structure.[14] Companies with relatively narrow, mature product lines may find that their primary growth opportunities are in the international marketplace. Entering those markets effectively often requires a strong understanding of local market conditions and customer preferences. A geographic divisional structure provides a mechanism for learning more about local markets and making the necessary adaptations to the company's products and services. Multinational organizations in the food, beverage, and cosmetics industries have found that this organizational structure supports their efforts to respond to local market demands.

Kellogg provides an excellent example of a firm that maintains a geographic divisional structure. As the world's leading ready-to-eat cereal producer, Kellogg focuses almost exclusively on its cereals and other breakfast food products. Because of this product focus, Kellogg's primary source of complexity comes from the broad geographic markets it serves, many of which are international. Thus, a geographic divisional structure is ideal for this company. As illustrated in Figure 9.4, Kellogg's operations are structured around four main geographic regions—North America, Europe, Latin America and Asia-Pacific.[15]

Customer Divisions   A **customer divisional structure** groups tasks according to different customers. Each customer-based unit focuses on meeting the needs of a specific group of the organization's customers. CIGNA Property & Casualty is an example of a company that uses a customer divisional structure. CIGNA

FIGURE 9.4
Geographic divisional structure: Kellogg Company

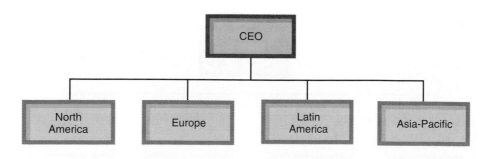

abandoned a product-based structure in 1990 in favor of a structure organized around customer business segments. The company feels that this change will provide the strong customer focus that is essential in the insurance industry.[16]

A customer-based structure is appropriate for organizations that have separate customer groups with very specific and distinct needs. With the quality movement in full swing, and the emphasis on meeting the needs of the customer first and foremost, this structure is highly appropriate for organizations that must adapt their products and services for different customer groups. It may also be suitable for organizations that wish to grow by targeting new and distinct customer groups. Resources can be allocated to support the customer groups with the greatest growth potential.

Matrix Structure: An International or Project Perspective

The organizational structures discussed so far have grouped activities along a specific, single dimension of the organization's operations (function, product, geographic region, or customer base). Rather than focusing on a single dimension of the organization's operations, a **matrix structure** defines work groups on the basis of two dimensions simultaneously (such as product/function, product/geographic region, and so on). Davis and Lawrence defined a matrix structure as one that "employs a multiple command system that includes not only a multiple command structure but also related support mechanisms and an associated organizational culture and behavior patterns."[17] In other words, the distinguishing characteristic of the matrix structure is its dual chain of command.[18]

For illustrative purposes, consider the organizational chart in Figure 9.5. The chart is for PGP, Inc., a fictitious multinational company that distributes a relatively broad range of health and beauty products. The vice-presidents of the product and geographic divisions report directly to PGP's CEO and assume full responsibility for the operations of their respective divisions. For example, the vice-president for South America is ultimately responsible for the distribution of all products (hair care, nail care, cosmetics, skin care) to the South

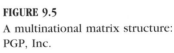

Matrix structure

A structure in which the tasks of the organization are grouped along two organizing dimensions simultaneously (such as product/geographic market, product/function).

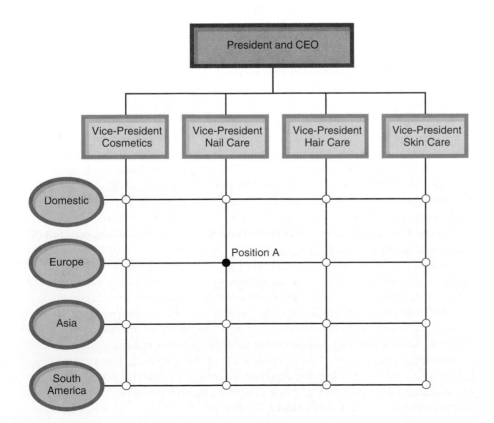

FIGURE 9.5
A multinational matrix structure: PGP, Inc.

American market. In contrast, the vice-president of the nail care division assumes responsibility for the distribution of nail care products worldwide. Theoretically, these vice-presidents have equal organizational power.

The dual chain of command is illustrated at the next level of the hierarchy. Consider the manager occupying position A. What are this person's job responsibilities? Who is her boss? Is it the vice-president of nail care products or the vice-president for Europe? The person who occupies position A on PGP's organizational chart is responsible for distributing nail care products in Europe. Therefore, this manager has both a product and area focus to her job, and as a result, she can develop more specific job skills. In addition, this manager has two bosses to whom she is equally accountable—the vice-president of nail care products and the vice-president for Europe.

The matrix structure provides PGP with a viable way to focus on both specific products and geographic markets, thereby enabling the company to achieve simultaneous objectives. If forced to organize around only one organizational dimension, PGP would forgo the benefits associated with the other dimension. The matrix structure enables many global organizations to focus both on enhancing the quality of their products through the product dimension and on achieving greater penetration of discrete national or regional markets through the geographic dimension of the structure.

Despite the obvious advantages of the matrix structure, it also has a number of disadvantages (see Table 9.1). Most notable is the complexity inherent in a dual chain of command. Managing within this structure requires extraordinary planning and coordination between work groups.[19]

Global Perspective describes the organizational structure at Asea Brown Boveri (ABB), a joint venture between AB of Sweden and BBC Brown Boveri of Switzerland. By penetrating worldwide markets through an international matrix structure, ABB has become the world's leading electrical engineering firm. As you will read, ABB's efforts were so successful that its overall organizational design earned a new label—the transnational organization.

Network Structures: The Key to Flexibility

For decades, organizations have aspired to be large. Growth was considered to be synonymous with success, and the "bigger is better" syndrome governed the strategic decision making of most companies.[20] This is not so today. Organizations are finding that being lean and flexible is often preferable to being big.[21] This is particularly true for companies that operate within rapidly changing industries or face intense global competition.[22]

In response to these changes, a number of successful organizations have abandoned the traditional organizational structures of the past and have moved toward a more contemporary form of organizational structure—the network structure.[23] Some experts believe that the flexibility inherent in strategic network structures will be critical for competitive success in the 21st century.[24]

Network structure
A contemporary organizational structure that is founded on a set of alliances with other organizations that serve a wide variety of functions.

At the foundation of the **network structure** is a sophisticated product delivery system that is built around alliances with other groups. These groups perform some of the activities necessary to deliver the products and services of the organization.[25] They may be independent, market-driven internal work units, or in many cases, they may be outside the organization.

For example, the central organization may coordinate the production, marketing, financing, and distribution activities necessary to market a particular product without owning a single manufacturing plant, creating a single line of advertising copy, or even taking possession of the product. The central organization simply coordinates the activities of others so that the product reaches the ultimate consumer in the most efficient method possible.[26] Figure 9.6 illustrates the network organizational structure.[27]

ASEA BROWN BOVERI: ACHIEVING GLOBAL-SCALE EFFICIENCY AND LOCAL-MARKET SENSITIVITY

Global Perspective

Percy Barnevik, CEO of Asea Brown Boveri, doesn't think that traditional unidimensional organizational structures are appropriate for today's highly competitive global marketplace. Instead, Barnevik claims, global companies have to look for ways to achieve multiple objectives simultaneously—objectives such as capturing global-scale efficiency while being highly sensitive to local-market needs. And that's why Barnevik thinks that the dual-dimensional matrix structure is appropriate for his organization.

ABB is organized along both regional and product dimensions. Regions include countries across the globe; products include power generation, industrial and building systems, and rail transportation. Operating managers at the country level are accountable to both regional- and product-based executive vice-presidents. For example, the operating manager of the power generation company in Switzerland reports up through a chain of command to the executive vice-president of power generation, who oversees power generation businesses across the globe. But that same operating manager also reports up the line to the executive vice-president of Europe, who is responsible for all business activity in that region of the world.

Interestingly, Barnevik credits sophisticated information technology with much of the success of the structure. ABB's system, ABACUS, provides the ongoing information required for the supervision and complex decision-making that must occur in an organization like ABB.

Barnevik believes that the matrix structure has been key to achieving a global leadership position in the industries in which ABB operates, and thus has enabled ABB to become the world's leading electrical engineering company. In fact, ABB's structure has been so innovative and effective that Harvard professors Chris Bartlett and Sumantra Ghashal have given a new label to ABB's organizational design—the transnational organization.

Three primary types of network structures are found in organizations today—internal, stable, and dynamic networks.[28] These structures vary in terms of their commitment to outsourcing. Recall from Chapter 4 that outsourcing occurs when one organization contracts with another organization to perform some aspect of its operations.

An **internal network** exists in organizations that choose to avoid outsourcing, but wish to develop internal entrepreneurial ventures that are driven by market forces and thus are competitive with alternative sources of supply. These internal units operate independently and negotiate with the central unit like any outside vendor. Each unit functions as a profit center that specializes in a particular aspect of the organization's product delivery system.

The component business of General Motors serves as an excellent example of an internal network structure. GM's component business maintains eight independent divisions that specialize in the production of some aspect of the automotive system (such as AC spark plugs). These divisions are encouraged to conduct business on the open market, yet they cooperate with the central

Internal network
A network structure that relies on internally developed units to provide services to a core organizational unit.

FIGURE 9.6
Network structure

SOURCE: R. E. Miles and C. C. Snow, "Organizations: New Concepts for New Forms," 62–73. Copyright © 1986 by The Regents of the University of California. Reprinted from *California Management Review*, 28, 3. By permission of The Regents.

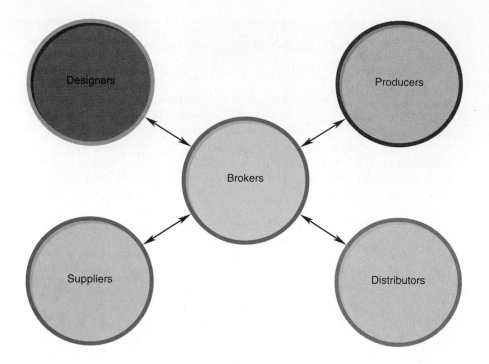

Stable network
A network structure that utilizes external alliances selectively as a mechanism for gaining strategic flexibility.

Dynamic network
A network structure that makes extensive use of outsourcing through alliances with outside organizations.

unit of GM's component business whenever appropriate. The net result is greater effectiveness for the corporation as a whole.[29]

Organizations that maintain a **stable network** rely to some degree on outsourcing to add flexibility to their product delivery system. The central organization contracts with outside vendors to provide certain products and services that are essential to its product delivery system. Although these vendors are independent of the central organization, they are typically highly committed to the core firm.

BMW is an example of a company that has adopted a stable network structure. Somewhere between 55 and 75 percent of BMW's production comes from outsourcing. Partnerships with vendors serve a critical function in the company's product delivery system. Although BMW does not own its vendor firms outright (as GM does), it does maintain stable relationships with them and may even make a financial investment in these organizations where appropriate.[30]

A **dynamic network** differs from internal and stable networks in that organizations with this structure make extensive use of outsourcing to support their operations. Partnerships with vendors are less frequent, and less emphasis is placed on finding organizations to service the central organization only. Typically, the central organization focuses on some core skill and contracts for most other functions. For example, Motorola capitalizes on its manufacturing strengths, Reebok on its design strengths, and Dell Computer on its design and assembly strengths; in each case, the company prefers to outsource most other aspects of its product delivery system.[31]

A number of advantages and disadvantages are associated with the network structure (see Table 9.1).[32] The effectiveness and efficiency of the core unit are maximized by the use of a network structure. The organization can do more with less because it is using others' resources. Flexibility is an inherent benefit of this organizational form, because the core unit can change vendors quickly should product changes be necessary. Many international firms have found that the network structure provides them with the speed and flexibility necessary to compete effectively in highly competitive global markets.[33] In fact, some multinationals are abandoning the matrix structure in favor of the more adaptable network form.[34]

The primary disadvantage of a network structure is that because operations are fragmented, it may be difficult to develop a control system that effectively monitors all aspects of the product delivery system.[35] However, advanced information technology can be utilized to better monitor the activities
of networked companies. In fact, systems that address the unique needs of the
network organization are being developed and refined today.[36]

It is not uncommon for an organization to use some type of network structure to get into a specific market very quickly and then adopt a more traditional structure later. IBM, for example, utilized a dynamic network structure
to enter the personal computer market. Lagging the competition in this market, IBM assembled a network of suppliers, designers, and marketers to bring
its product to market very quickly. Once the company had established itself in
the personal computer arena, it reintegrated many of these functions into its
central operating system.[37]

We have examined the four basic types of structures that are commonly used
in organizations today. These structures define how the work groups of the organization are structured and specify reporting relationships within the organizational hierarchy. Meeting the Challenge gives you an opportunity to assess the
organizational structure of an organization with which you are familiar. Take
some time to work through the exercise before moving on to learn about the
second component of organizational design—integrating mechanisms.

MANAGING COMPLEXITY THROUGH INTEGRATION

Integrating the activities of an organization involves controlling and coordinating the flow of information, resources, and tasks among organizational members and work groups. Whereas structure serves to segregate organizational
members into different work units, the goal of the integration component of
organizational design is to coordinate the work of these distinct groups. An organization's many and diverse work groups are linked together through integrating mechanisms. As we will soon learn, integrating mechanisms include
such things as management information systems, liaison personnel, and interfunctional work teams.

The complexity of an organization's operations will affect its need for integration. For example, a purely domestic firm with a narrow product line and
a single manufacturing facility will find the integration of its work groups to
be more manageable than will a multinational corporation with broad product
lines and manufacturing facilities spread across the globe. In general, the more
complex an organization's operations, the more sophisticated its coordinating
mechanisms must be.

FIGURE 9.7
Levels of work group
interdependence

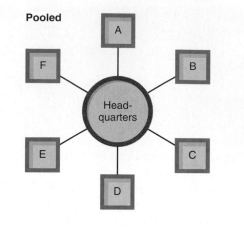

Interdependence
The degree to which work groups are interrelated.

Pooled interdependence
Occurs when organizational units have a common resource but no interrelationship with one another.

Sequential interdependence
Occurs when organizational units must coordinate the flow of information, resources, and tasks from one unit to another.

A local bank with branch offices around the city provides an example of pooled versus sequential or reciprocal interdependence. While all branches work together with the central office, each branch has only limited interaction with the other branches. The success of each branch contributes to the overall success of the organization.

In general, an organization's integration needs will vary with the level of interdependence that exists among work groups.[38] In organizations where work groups must closely coordinate their activities to achieve organizational goals, integration needs will be high. In contrast, where work groups exist relatively independently and without significant interaction, integration needs are low. Before we discuss specific integrating mechanisms that might be used to coordinate the activities of an organization, let's examine the various levels of interdependence that may exist in an organization and how that interdependence affects its integration needs.

Interdependence and Integration Needs

Central to the discussion of integration is the concept of interdependence. **Interdependence** refers to the degree to which work groups are interrelated and the extent to which they depend upon one another to complete their work. The level of interdependence between work groups will affect the need for integrating mechanisms.[39] Figure 9.7 illustrates the three primary levels of work group interdependence, and the following discussion describes each in greater detail.

Pooled Interdependence **Pooled interdependence** occurs when organizational units have a common source of resources, but have no interrelationship with one another. Consider, for example, a local bank with branch offices spread around the city. Though all branches must coordinate their efforts with the central office, they have very limited interaction with one another. They have little need to cooperate and coordinate with one another to achieve their goals. Managers work independently to achieve the goals of their own work group, which, in turn, contributes to the overall performance of the organization.

Sequential Interdependence **Sequential interdependence** exists when work groups must coordinate the flow of information, resources, or tasks from one unit to another. Sequential interdependence is associated with a typical manufacturing assembly line. The output of one unit becomes the input for another unit. Organizations with sequentially interdependent units have greater coordination needs than organizations with units that have pooled interdependence.

Reciprocal Interdependence   **Reciprocal interdependence** represents the greatest level of interrelatedness between work groups, in that work is passed back and forth between work units. The final product requires the input of a number of different departments at varying times during the production process. Consider a university system, in which students' registration materials must be shuffled from one administrative unit to another and back. These work groups are interrelated, and the effective functioning of the system requires a high level of integration among the groups.

The higher the level of interdependence of an organization's work groups, the greater its needs for coordination. The sophistication of an integrating system should be in alignment with its specific coordination needs. For example, an organization with pooled interdependence between its work groups may be able to function effectively with a few relatively simple integrating mechanisms. In contrast, an organization with reciprocal interdependence between work groups will require more sophisticated integrating mechanisms.

Integrating mechanisms are not without costs. As we will discuss, many of the tools for coordinating the activities of the organization have human or financial costs that are tangible and measurable. Therefore, organizations must carefully evaluate their coordination needs so that they can develop integrating mechanisms that are cost-effective and in line with those needs.

Integrating Mechanisms

At the foundation of an organization's ability to coordinate the activities of its subunits is its information processing capacity. Effective coordination is dependent upon the flow of information between the individual units of the organization so that work can be scheduled, resources shared and transferred, and conflicting objectives resolved. Toward this end, organizations develop integrating mechanisms that enhance their information processing capacity and support their need for coordination. **Integrating mechanisms** are methods for managing the flow of information, resources, and tasks throughout the organization.

Many different mechanisms can be used to process information and coordinate the activities of interdependent work units. Some of these mechanisms are characteristic of general management systems. Others are developed specifically to increase the coordination potential of the organization. Still others are designed to reduce the organization's need for coordination. Figure 9.8 illustrates the three major categories of integrating mechanisms, each of which is discussed below.[40]

General Management Systems   Some coordination of work units may be achieved through the development of general management systems such as the managerial hierarchy, basic rules and procedures, and plans and goals. Such mechanisms form the foundation of an organization's integration system.

As we have discussed, an organization's managerial hierarchy is established by its organizational structure. Recall that organizational structure defines work

Reciprocal interdependence
Occurs when information, resources, and tasks must be passed back and forth between work groups.

Integrating mechanisms
Methods for managing the flow of information, resources, and tasks within the organization.

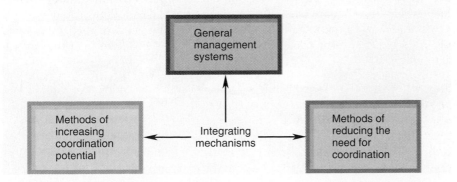

FIGURE 9.8
Integrating mechanisms

SOURCE: Adapted by permission, J. R. Galbraith. "Organizational Design: An Information Processing View," *Interfaces*, 4, May 1974, 3. Copyright 1974, The Institute of Management Sciences and the Operations Research Society of America (currently INFORMS), 2 Charles Street, Suite 300, Providence, RI 02904 USA.

groups on the basis of the task characteristic that presents the greatest source of diversity (that is, function, product, geographic, market, or customer). By grouping organizational members in this fashion, coordination within the groups is enhanced.

Similarly, most organizations develop basic rules and procedures that govern the behavior of their members. Organizations that make extensive use of rules and procedures are often thought to be bureaucratic, highly formalized, and closely governed. In contrast, organizations that use fewer rules and procedures are considered to be more flexible, less formal, and participatory in nature.

Most universities make extensive use of rules and procedures to coordinate the activities of their colleges and departments. Student records must be processed according to specific guidelines; overrides into classes must be handled systematically; and parking tickets and overdue library books must be dealt with before the registration process can be completed. These rules and procedures are mechanisms that ensure that the activities of the various units of the university are well coordinated.

The development of plans and goals can also serve as a means of integrating the operations of an organization. Plans that require implementation by multiple work groups provide a foundation for action by those units. A well-developed business plan will detail the activities of specific departments within an organization, thereby providing guidance about how those activities are to be coordinated. Similarly, certain behaviors are implied by specific achievement-based goals.

Quality-management programs serve as an excellent integrating mechanism for many companies. The plans that result from such programs provide a foundation for integrating and coordinating the activities of diverse groups toward common quality-oriented goals.

Increasing Coordination Potential   For most organizations, general management systems do not provide sufficient coordination potential. Additional integrating mechanisms are needed to coordinate the organization's activities effectively. Information systems and lateral relationships are two of the most common mechanisms for increasing coordination potential both vertically and horizontally within the organization.

Information systems such as computer and telecommunication networks enable companies to coordinate efforts on a worldwide scale. In addition to facilitating the flow of information, information systems can provide control mechanisms to help identify and solve coordination problems.

© Cindy Charles/PhotoEdit

Information systems facilitate the flow of information up and down the traditional chain of command and across organizational units. Management information systems have become increasingly important mechanisms for implementing strategy[41] and increasing coordination potential in recent years.[42] The computerized transfer of important information and data provides a powerful tool for coordinating diverse departments or operating units.[43] Additionally, information technology can provide control mechanisms that ensure that coordination problems are identified and resolved in a timely fashion.[44] In fact, some have argued that information technology has advanced organizational coordination to the same magnitude that mass-production technologies advanced manufacturing in the Industrial Revolution.[45]

Many multinational corporations have developed sophisticated management information systems to support their global operations. With the advent of more sophisticated and affordable computer technology, decision-making data can be transmitted almost simultaneously from division to division around the globe. Computer and telecommunication networks provide the infrastructure for coordinating operations on a worldwide scale. Electronic mail, teleconferencing, and high-speed data systems are a few of the mechanisms used by multinational companies. Look back at the Global Perspective for a moment. The information technology system at Asea Brown Boveri, ABACUS, is considered to be critical for coordinating a diverse set of businesses across the globe.

The second important method for increasing coordination potential is to establish lateral relationships. Such relationships exist across horizontal work units and serve as mechanisms for exchanging decision-making information. In general, lateral relationships can be thought of as **boundary-spanning roles.** The primary purpose of the boundary-spanning function is to develop an understanding of the activities of units outside the boundaries of one's own work group. Such knowledge helps employees and work groups understand how their actions and performance affect others within the organization, as well as the organization as a whole.

The boundary-spanning function can be served through a number of different relationships that vary in formality and level of commitment to the coordinating function. Integrating relationships include liaisons, committees and task forces, and integrating positions and interfunctional work teams.

When two or more work units have a recurring need to communicate with each other, it may be beneficial to establish a liaison position to support their communication needs. People who occupy such positions retain their association with their primary unit, but also assume responsibility for interacting with other work groups. For example, the marketing department of an organization might identify an individual to act as a formal liaison with the company's engineering department. Although this individual remains in his marketing role, he also serves as the primary contact point for the interaction between the marketing department and the engineering department.

When the effective management of multiple interdependent units is critical to the success of the organization, it may be appropriate to establish a committee (a permanent group) or a task force (a temporary group) to facilitate communication between the groups. The committee or task force would be made up of representatives from each of the work groups involved. As was the case with the formal liaison position, the committee or task force assignment is only a part of each representative's job—their primary job responsibilities remain with the unit they represent.[46] Multinational corporations, for example, often use committees or councils composed of corporate executives and representatives from both domestic and foreign subsidiaries. This council assumes responsibility for both assimilating and disseminating critical information needed by the operating units of the company.

Boundary-spanning roles
Lateral relationships that help to integrate and coordinate the activities of the organization (that is, liaisons, committees, task forces, integrating positions, and interfunctional work teams).

When an organization has very high integration needs, it may become necessary to establish a standing integrating position or interfunctional work teams. The primary responsibility of individuals serving in integrating positions is to facilitate communication between work groups. Such individuals do not represent a specific operating unit and thus are not formally associated with any of the work groups with which they work. Their full-time work responsibilities are associated with managing the interdependence between work units. Interfunctional work teams are a more radical approach to integration, in that members from various functional groups are permanently assigned to a team that is given responsibility for completing a particular set of tasks (see the discussions of self-managed teams in Chapters 1 and 8).

Although integrating mechanisms designed to increase coordination potential can be quite costly, they may be warranted when strategic effectiveness requires close coordination and cooperation between organizational subunits. IBM, for example, has established interfunctional work teams that focus on issues of product and service quality throughout the organizational system.[47] These teams provide the integration and coordination necessary to support IBM's efforts to improve quality.

Philip Morris has developed formal lateral relationships in an effort to integrate the activities of its various subunits more effectively. Through an extensive network of committees, task forces, and other lateral associations, this company has developed a sophisticated information processing system that supports its strategic and operational goals.

Reducing the Need for Coordination   The third and final method of integration is to reduce or eliminate the need for coordination between work groups. In essence, the organization creates "slack resources" that reduce the interdependence of the work groups and, as a result, the need for integrating mechanisms. For example, the organization might establish longer lead times for sequentially interdependent work to be completed, or maintain larger inventories of work in progress. Both measures would reduce the need for tight coordination between units. Although this is an effective way to reduce the need for coordination, it is not necessarily the most efficient. Creating slack resources in this way is inconsistent with recent trends toward quality management and improved productivity and efficiency. As a result, such a practice may lead to suboptimal organizational performance.

Another way organizations can reduce the need for coordination is to create work units that have only pooled interdependence. By doing so, the need for integration is minimized. One benefit of interfunctional work teams is that work groups are relatively independent, thereby reducing the need for integration between diverse functional units. However, forming interfunctional teams simply to reduce integration needs may not be appropriate if it results in redundant resource utilization. In general, independent units should be formed only when there are other strategic reasons to do so.

Matching Integrating Mechanisms with Coordination Needs

As mentioned previously, integrating mechanisms have costs. The hardware and software support for management information systems have very tangible costs. So do the personnel who must manage the information system. Integrating positions have clearly identifiable costs as well. While not as easily measured, the management time and energy that go into developing effective management systems (managerial hierarchy, rules and procedures, plans and goals) and acting in lateral relationship roles (liaisons, committees and task forces, integrating positions) also have costs. Therefore, it is important for an organization to develop a cost-effective integration system that satisfies its coordination needs while minimizing the financial and managerial resources required to maintain the system.

LOCUS OF DECISION MAKING

The third component of organizational design involves the locus of decision making within the organization. Essentially, **locus of decision making** refers to whether the organization's decision making is centralized or decentralized. This may be determined by examining how decision-making authority is divided between corporate headquarters and the operating units or between top management of an operating unit and the departmental work groups.[48]

If, for example, an organization's decision-making authority rests with corporate headquarters or the top levels of management of an operating facility, its organizational design is centralized. An organization that maintains its locus of decision making at lower levels (for example, at the subsidiary or departmental level) is decentralized. IBM's plan to restructure into autonomous operating units, for example, was an attempt to decentralize by pushing decision-making authority down to the lower levels of the organizational hierarchy.

It is helpful to think of centralized and decentralized decision making as two ends of a continuum. Most organizations' locus of decision making will fall somewhere between those two extremes. In addition, the locus of decision making in most organizations is mixed, with decisions in some areas (such as finance) being relatively centralized, while decisions in other areas (such as marketing) may be relatively decentralized.

Centralized versus Decentralized Decision Making

Certain advantages and disadvantages are associated with both centralized and decentralized decision making. Their respective advantages and disadvantages are nearly mirror images of each other.

In general, centralized decision making gives top management more control than does decentralized decision making. This may be appropriate when work groups are highly interdependent or when maximizing the efficient use of resources is essential to the success of the organization. The primary disadvantage of centralized decision making is that it may limit the organization's ability to respond quickly and effectively to changes in its environment.

In contrast, the primary advantage of decentralized decision making is that organizations can respond to environmental changes more rapidly and effectively when decisions are being made by the people closest to the situation.[49] In addition, many proponents of quality management would argue that the individuals who are closest to the customers and suppliers are best prepared to make many decisions. Coordination between units may be hindered by decentralized decision making, however, and achieving efficiency through standardization may be more difficult to accomplish. Further, the growing diversity of the work force has increased the variance in decision-making styles.

Organizations must determine their locus of decision making in light of the advantages they seek, as well as the specific strategic and operational conditions they face. There are many examples of firms that have used each form of decision making very successfully. Consider, for example, the rather unstable history of Apple Computer. A shift to a more centralized organizational design rescued Apple when it was floundering in the mid-1980s. John Sculley, who replaced Steven Jobs as the CEO of Apple, concluded that the decentralized system of the past had resulted in organizational inefficiencies that were unacceptable in an industry that had become highly competitive and, to a significant degree, efficiency driven. As a result, Sculley decided to centralize decision making, consolidate manufacturing facilities, reduce overhead by eliminating redundant activities among work units, and adopt a more consistent marketing focus across product lines. These efforts to centralize and standardize the company's activities enabled Apple to increase its efficiency and

Locus of decision making
The degree to which decision making is centralized versus decentralized.

regain its position as an industry leader. By the late 1980s, Apple was enjoying a sales growth rate twice that of the industry, and profit margins that tripled since Sculley had taken the helm.[50] Of course, Apple has suffered a tumultuous history since John Sculley left the company in 1993. CEO Gilbert Amelio, who took office in 1996, is now working to stabilize the company's performance.

Mechanistic versus Organic Systems

An organization's locus of decision making will determine the extent to which it is mechanistic or organic.[51] This typology, originally advanced by Tom Burns and Gene Stalker, describes organizations according to the level of centralization or decentralization in their decision-making process.

Mechanistic systems are associated with highly centralized organizations where decision-making authority rests with the top levels of management. Tasks are highly specialized, and work procedures are governed by detailed rules and guidelines. Interorganizational communication flows primarily from superior to subordinate, and hierarchical relationships serve as the foundation for authority, responsibility, and control. Mechanistic systems are usually designed to maximize specialization and improve efficiency. However, organizations with this design may find it difficult to respond quickly and effectively to changes that affect their operations.

Organic systems, in contrast, are designed to enhance an organization's ability to respond to environmental change by decentralizing decision making to those in the organization who are closer to customers, suppliers, and other external constituents. Organizational members are not only permitted to participate in decision making, but are encouraged to do so. Tasks are often broader and are more interdependent than in mechanistic systems. Rules and guidelines are far less prevalent and may exist only to provide the parameters within which organizational members can make decisions. The patterns of communication are far more intricate, and horizontal communication is common. While a vertical hierarchy typically exists, extensive use of teams and other lateral relationships facilitates communication and decision making across vertical lines. An organic system may be less efficient than a mechanistic system, however.

Saturn provides an excellent example of a company that has developed an organic design in an industry that is characterized by mechanistic organizations. As you will in read in Managing for Excellence, Saturn's consensus-based approach to decision making epitomizes a more organic organizational design.

The need for organic systems has escalated in the last two decades with the increasing predominance of knowledge companies and knowledge workers. What is knowledge work? **Knowledge work** has been defined as "a set of activities using individual and external knowledge to product outputs characterized by information content."[53] That is a pretty fancy way of saying that knowledge work is work that requires the acquisition, creation, packaging, or application of knowledge. Knowledge work includes such activities as research and product development, advertising, education, and professional services such as law, accounting, and consulting.[54]

By their very nature, organic systems are more appropriate for knowledge companies and workers. Knowledge workers tend to enjoy higher levels of freedom in how and when they perform their work responsibilities, and thus experience more discretion and autonomy in their jobs. Thus, day-to-day task controls that are typically imposed on administrative or operational workers cannot be imposed on knowledge workers. Rather, their activities must be monitored on a much broader level, with a focus on ensuring that they are contributing to the strategic goals of the organization. This management system is consistent with that of an organic organizational design.[55]

Mechanistic systems
Highly centralized organizations in which decision-making authority rests with top management.

Organic systems
Decentralized organizations that push decision making to the lowest levels of the organization in an effort to respond more effectively to environmental change.

Knowledge work
Work that requires the acquisition, creation, packaging, or application of knowledge.

SATURN: DECISION MAKING BY CONSENSUS

The automobile industry, characterized by assembly lines and mass production, would seem to be a strange place to find an organization with decentralized decision making. But that is exactly what you'll find at Saturn Corporation, a subsidiary of General Motors. Saturn has introduced two revolutionary ideas for organizations in the automobile industry: (1) an organizational structure that amounts to a virtual democracy at all levels, and (2) a partnership between management and labor that gives more power to the workers.

In contrast to the pyramidal hierarchies you'll find in most automobile manufacturers, Saturn is structured in a series of concentric circles that permit all employees to have a say in decision making. At the core of the structure is the "Work Unit." A Work Unit consists of about fifteen team members and a "Work Unit Counselor." Counselors have some management functions such as managing daily production, leading the teams in establishing priorities and goals, and monitoring training, budget, quality, and safety issues. Yet the Counselor's role is more that of an executor working for the unit than of a manager working for upper management. In fact, the Work Unit team members make all the decisions for the group—with consensus and without the help of a formal leader. They plan their own work and define their own jobs. They keep their own records and control their own materials.

There is a structure at Saturn—Work Units combine to become a Work Unit Module; Work Unit Modules combine to become Business Units. So while there is some system of rank, the system is composed more of overlapping units than hierarchical layers of superior/subordinate work groups.

At Saturn, there is a commitment to taking employee and management perspectives into account in every decision. The result is that virtually every decision involving the design, manufacture, and marketing of the Saturn is reached by a consensus of employees and management. Management by consensus is not always the fastest method, but it usually pays off, according to Saturn vice-president Jim Lewandowski. "In a traditional plant, [decisions] probably would have been made a lot sooner. But decision by consensus, by our own people, holds a clear and definite advantage: Once a decision is made, our people are committed to it. They are committed because they were directly involved in the process."[52]

You may want to stop at this point and take a look at Experiential Exercise 9.2, which appears at the end of the chapter. This exercise provides an assessment instrument that can be used to evaluate the degree to which an organization demonstrates mechanistic versus organic characteristics. Think of an organization with which you have been associated. How does it rate according to this assessment instrument?

The Impact of Environmental Stability

Which system is better—a mechanistic system that enhances efficiency or an organic system that enhances responsiveness? There is no simple answer to that question. The most effective system for any organization will vary as a function of the specific circumstances that the organization faces. More specifically, the stability of the environment in which the organization operates will have a significant impact on the effectiveness of either system.

The external environment for any given organization can be characterized along a continuum ranging from stable to turbulent. In general, **stable environments** experience relatively little change, or the change is of low impact

Stable environments
Environments that experience little change.

to the organization. Product life cycles are long and enduring; marketing strategies remain relatively constant; and economic and political factors have little influence on the strategic or operational aspects of the firm. Competitive pressures are manageable and changes in buyers' needs are minimal. Although few industries would fit this description, some organizations do face relatively stable environments. For example, manufacturers of staple items such as detergents, cleaning supplies, and paper products enjoy relatively stable environmental conditions.

Turbulent environments, in contrast, are characterized by rapid and significant change. An organization that faces turbulent environmental conditions must cope with shorter decision windows, changing buyer patterns, fragmented markets, greater risk of resource and product obsolescence, and a general lack of long-term control.[56] Such conditions intensify the pressure for organizations to respond effectively to change. IBM, for example, faces a relatively turbulent environment in which technological change creates competitive pressures for all industry players. The key to success in such an environment lies in developing an organizational design that allows managers to identify and respond to the opportunities and threats facing the organization.[57]

In general, organizations that operate in stable external environments find the mechanistic system to be advantageous. This system provides a level of efficiency that enhances the long-term performance of organizations that enjoy relatively stable operating environments. In contrast, organizations that operate in volatile and frequently changing environments are more likely to find that an organic system provides the greatest benefits. This system allows the organization to respond to environmental change more proactively.

ORGANIZATIONAL DESIGN FOR A CHANGING ENVIRONMENT

While many organizations have been coping with changing environmental conditions and intense competition for decades, others are just beginning to feel the effects of escalating rates of technological change and an increasingly competitive global marketplace. Such business conditions will continue to affect a wide variety of organizations and industries in the future. As this occurs, organizations will continue to seek innovative organizational designs to cope with the challenges of the business environment.

Although most organizations will maintain traditional hierarchical structures to some degree, many will increasingly make use of alliances among people and organizations. Surrounding the conventional chain of command will be a complex network of committees, task forces, interfunctional teams, partnerships, and other informal relationships that will provide a forum for creativity and innovation. As Raymond Gilmartin, CEO of the high-tech medical equipment manufacturer Becton Dickinson, says, "Forget structures invented by the guys at the top. You've got to let the task form the organization."[57]

This new model of organizational design goes by a number of names; two of the most common are the **adaptive organization** and the **horizontal corporation.**[58] The purpose of this design is to reduce the bureaucracy that stifles employee creativity and puts an unacceptable distance between the customer and the decision makers in the organization. Such organizations will pull out all the stops to capitalize on their human resources, develop partnerships with other organizations with common objectives, and let the needs of the customer drive the actions of the organization. Doing this effectively may be the

Turbulent environments
Environments that are characterized by rapid and significant change.

Adaptive organization (horizontal corporation)
An organization that eliminates bureaucracy that limits employee creativity and brings the decision makers of the organization closer to the customer.

TABLE 9.2   McKinsey's 10-point plan for developing an adaptive organization

- Organize primarily around process, not task.
- Flatten the hierarchy by minimizing subdivision of processes.
- Give senior leaders responsibility for processes and process performance.
- Line performance objectives and evaluation of all activities to customer satisfaction.
- Make teams, not individuals, the focus of organization performance and design.
- Combine managerial and non-managerial activities as often as possible.
- Emphasize that each employee should develop several competencies.
- Inform and train people on a just-in-time, need-to-perform basis.
- Maximize supplier and customer contact with everyone in the organization.
- Reward individual skill development and team performance instead of individual performance alone.

key to success for the organization of the future. Table 9.2 describes McKinsey & Co.'s ten-point blueprint for developing an organizational design that is appropriate for the organization of the future.

MANAGERIAL IMPLICATIONS

The manager of tomorrow must be aware of the importance of organizational design to the long-term performance of his or her company. The increasing availability and sophistication of technology will change the way organizations are designed and coordinated. Further, the ever-increasing demands for quality will create additional pressures for achieving maximum efficiency and effectiveness in every aspect of an organization's operations. And as more and more industries globalize, organizations will be faced with the challenge of coordinating their efforts across different nations and among diverse people. In preparing to meet these challenges, managers must:

- Remember that organizational design provides an important mechanism for achieving the strategic and operational goals of the organization.
- Structure their organizations to cope with the source of greatest complexity.
- Consider ways that partnerships between members of the organization, as well as alliances with other organizations, can create synergy and improve organizational performance.
- Look for ways to increase the integration potential of the organization or to reduce the need for integration.
- Evaluate the advantages and disadvantages associated with centralized versus decentralized decision making, given the specific circumstances of the organization.
- Strive to develop an adaptive organization that is prepared to meet the challenges of the 21st century.

Managers must create an organizational design that is adaptable, flexible, and supportive of the strategy of their organizations. Doing so will be one of the major challenges of the 21st century.

Big Blue: Developing an Organizational Design that Works

Top management at IBM faced significant challenges as they prepared to re-design their organizational system. Yet given the changes in the competitive structure of the computer industry, it seemed imperative for the company to realign the components of its organizational design.

IBM began by reducing its work force by more than 20,000 people. While layoffs were avoided, the company offered buyout packages and early retirement to middle managers throughout the organization. In addition, IBM developed six independent and highly autonomous business units that were based on its primary product lines. This new structure provided the strong product focus that management felt was essential for success. Further, in an attempt to decentralize decision making, top management gave these product divisions significant latitude with respect to their strategic and operational activities. Along with this increased decision-making authority came the associated accountability. Each division is responsible for producing its own financial statements at year end and is evaluated on the basis of its individual performance. IBM, according to Sam Albert, a computer industry consultant and former IBM executive, was "very creatively and judiciously looking for anything and everything to eliminate bureaucracy to speed up the process and to do things on economy of scale."

The evidence to date would suggest that IBM has been successful in its efforts to turn the company around. According to a recent reports, IBM is "raking in new business, its stock is roaring, and it's regaining the respect of Corporate America."[59] Sales in 1996 were about $58.3 billion—a healthy 8 percent increase from the previous year. The company is gaining momentum, but the turnaround is still a work in progress. Nevertheless, the future looks bright for the newly redesigned IBM.

SUMMARY

- Organizing is an important managerial function that leads to the development of organizational design. An organization's design serves as a mechanism for managing its tasks, functions, products, markets, and technologies effectively.

- Organizational design determines the configuration of organizational members (structure); the flow of information, resources, and tasks throughout the organizational system (integration); and the centralization or decentralization of decision-making authority (locus of decision making).

- Organizations structure their activities by grouping certain tasks and responsibilities into work units. The four primary forms found in organizations today are functional, divisional, matrix, and network structures. Certain strategic conditions imply certain organizational structures. In general, organizations should employ a structure that enables them to cope with their greatest source of complexity (such as function, product, diversity, or geographic market diversity).

- Integrating mechanisms help to coordinate the flow of information, resources, and tasks between work groups. The level of interdependence among the subunits of an organization will determine, to a large degree, the organization's need for integrating mechanisms. Integrating mechanisms include general management systems (managerial hierarchy, rules and procedures, plans and goals), methods for increasing coordination potential (information systems and lateral relationships), and methods for reducing the need for coordination (creation of slack resources and independent work units).

- The extent to which an organization centralizes or decentralizes decision-making authority will determine its locus of decision making. While centralized decision making gives top management more control, decentralized decision making provides for faster and more effective responses to change.

- An organization can be described as mechanistic or organic, depending on its locus of decision making. Mechanistic systems maintain a centralized locus of decision making and are most suitable for organizations that operate in mature, stable environments. Organic systems maintain a decentralized locus of decision making and are most appropriate for firms operating in dynamic, rapidly changing environments.

- Many organizations will implement an adaptive organizational design in the future. Adaptive organizations rely on teams, lateral relationships, and alliances to supplement the traditional hierarchy. This network of relationships is designed to foster creativity and support proactive responses to environmental changes that affect the organization.

KEY TERMS

Organizational design
Organizational structure
Functional structure
Divisional structure
Product divisional structure
Geographic divisional structure
Customer divisional structure
Matrix structure
Network structure

Internal network
Stable network
Dynamic network
Interdependence
Pooled interdependence
Sequential interdependence
Reciprocal interdependence
Integrating mechanisms
Boundary-spanning roles

Locus of decision making
Mechanistic systems
Organic systems
Knowledge work
Stable environments
Turbulent environments
Adaptive organization (horizontal
    corporation)

REVIEW QUESTIONS

1. What is organizational design? Why is it important for an organization to develop an effective design?

2. What are the three primary components of organizational design?

3. Identify and describe each of the four types of organizational structure discussed in the chapter.

4. How does interdependence affect the need for coordination and integration?

5. Outline the three major categories of integrating mechanisms.

6. Explain the concept of locus of decision making. Under what strategic conditions would a centralized locus of decision making be appropriate? A decentralized locus of decision making?

7. What are the differences between mechanistic and organic organizational systems? What effect would the environment have on an organization's choice of a mechanistic versus an organic system?

8. How is organizational design likely to change in the future?

DISCUSSION QUESTIONS

Improving Critical Thinking

1. How might the organizational design of a research and development firm in the pharmaceutical industry differ from the organizational design of a consumer food products manufacturer?

2. Consider the organization you currently work for or one that you worked for in the past. Would you characterize that organization as centralized or decentralized? What are the advantages and disadvantages associated with the locus of decision making in that organization? If you had the power to change the locus of decision making in that organization, what would you do?

Enhancing Communication Skills

3. Suppose the dean of the College of Business Administration hired you to coordinate the efforts of five different student organizations, each of which was affiliated with a different functional department within the college. What integrating mechanisms might you use? To practice your oral communication skills, make a brief presentation of your ideas to the class.

4. Develop a plan to redesign an organization with which you are familiar using McKinsey & Co.'s blueprint for developing an adaptive organizational design (see Table 9.2). Develop a written draft of the plan for your instructor to review.

Building Teamwork

5. Think of several different businesses that might be started on your campus to serve the needs of students. Select one of those business concepts and, with a team of students, discuss how that business might be developed using a dynamic network system.

6. With a group of fellow students, identify a set of organizations that maintain relatively mechanistic organizational systems. Also develop a list of organizations that are more organic. Share your lists with the class, as well as your rationale for classifying these organizations as you did.

INFORMATION TECHNOLOGY: Insights and Solutions

1. Identify a firm in which you have a specific interest and about which you have some knowledge. Using one or more of the database sources in your library, locate an organizational chart for the company. Based on what you know of the industry in which the firm operates and its strategy, answer the questions in Meeting the Challenge. Report your findings and conclusions to the class.

2. Identify an international organization in which you have an interest. Research the ways in which the organization uses technology to support its international operations. Report your findings to the class.

3. Choose two companies to research: one which operates in a stable environment and another that operates in a turbulent environment. Using e-mail, contact someone in each organization. Ask them to describe the level of decentralization/centralization that exists within their organization. Compare and contrast the two organizations.

ETHICS: Take a Stand

At Dobbs Electronics Manufacturing Company, there is an important need for open communication between the production department and the sales department. The success of the salespeople often depends on whether they can promise timely shipment to their customers, and the production department has to be able to fulfill those promises. To be competitive in the industry, Dobbs's sales representatives frequently promise customers earlier shipping dates than the production department can comfortably meet. In the past, the production department has attempted to meet these earlier dates, even though it meant rushing jobs, working overtime, and reducing machine downtime for scheduled maintenance. Production has tired of the situation, however. The relationship between the two departments has deteriorated dramatically in recent months and, at this point, communication between the groups has literally come to a halt.

The top management at Dobbs has recognized the problem and knows that they need to take steps to reestablish communication channels between the two groups. They decided to appoint a formal liaison for both departments. These liaisons will meet and set reasonable production/sales schedules that will work for both departments and will be in the best interest of the organization as a whole.

Tom Short, who has been appointed the liaison for the production department, is faced with a tough situation. The manager of production, with the support of most of the employees within the department, has insisted that Tom add three weeks to the production schedule he negotiates with the sales department. While everyone in production knows they could deliver the product in a much shorter time frame, they are determined to allow more than enough time to complete their tasks. In addition, some members of the group feel strongly that the department should "show those people in sales that we won't be pushed around."

Tom is very uncomfortable about this situation. He feels as though his department is pressuring him to lie to his counterpart in the sales department.

To complicate things further, Tom believes that to delay the production schedule would not be in the best interest of the company as a whole. Yet if he
doesn't comply with the wishes of his department, he stands to be heavily criticized by both his boss and his peers.

For Discussion

1. How would you feel if you were in Tom's situation?
2. What actions would you recommend for Tom?
3. Can you think of other organizational relationships or situations that
   might lead to similar problems?

THINKING CRITICALLY: Debate the Issue

Form teams of four to five students. Half of the teams should prepare to argue
for the benefits of a dynamic network structure. The other half of the teams
should prepare to argue the disadvantages of such a structure. Where possible, identify companies that have adopted a dynamic network structure and assess their performance as related to this structural form. Choose two teams to
present their arguments in a debate format.

A. C. PETERSEN FARMS, INC.

No Web Site Available

A. C. Petersen Farms started as a horse-and-wagon milk delivery business
in 1914. The West Hartford, Connecticut, firm expanded over the years,
making ice cream and running restaurants.

In the early 1980s, the firm ran into some difficulty trying to compete
with fast-food restaurant chains and trying to manufacture ice cream products with outdated equipment. As a result, the company's milk processing
facility and six of its thirteen family restaurants were sold. The mid-1980s
were not good to A. C. Petersen Farms. The restaurant chain continued to
dwindle until there were only five restaurants left. The company was still
involved in ice cream wholesaling, but revenues and profits were disappointing. Employee morale plummeted. Key personnel left, making industry observers wonder if the company would survive.

Then a series of changes gave the company a new lease on life. In 1992, a
new generation of Petersens took over leadership of the firm. Allen C. Petersen became president and his cousin, Raymond E. Petersen Jr., became
executive vice president. The two cousins made wholesale changes. The
ice cream processing plant was bought back. A team approach was implemented in the plant, customer service was given a new emphasis in the
restaurants, and a lighthearted company newsletter, named the Monthly
Moos, was produced. Special events were staged to attract attention and
improve employee morale. For instance, the company produced the
world's largest ice cream sandwich, partly as a means of drawing attention to the ice cream sandwiches the company sells.

The new management team reorganized the company into two separate
areas. Allen Petersen took control of the manufacturing end of the com-

Video Case

pany, and Raymond Petersen took control of the restaurants. In 1993 A. C. Petersen Farms became the first Connecticut restaurant chain to ban smoking. This new policy may have cost the company some patrons, but it gained others and gave the company statewide visibility.

Today, A. C. Petersen Farms is growing again. The company seems to be on the right track, thanks to new management, a new organizational structure, and a lot of new ideas.

For Discussion

1. What type of organizational structure makes the most sense for A. C. Petersen Farms at this time? Explain your answer.

2. What are the advantages and disadvantages of centralized decision making for a firm like A. C. Petersen Farms?

CASE

CHOCOLATE AND MUCH MORE

David Troy addressed the executive board of Chocolate and Much More at their planning meeting. "As you know, our company has developed a relatively diverse product line over the past 30 years. We began as a small chocolate manufacturer operating in San Francisco. Opportunities arose, and we moved into assorted other candies and became a major player in the U.S. market. Our next endeavor was to move into specialty cookies and candy in the German market and, as you know, we achieved great success in that market as well.

"Our strategic plan is now focused on expanding into Europe, Southeast Asia, and Japan. We recognize that these markets are very different culturally and, consequently, have different preferences for candy and cookies. In addition, the impending unification of Europe has resulted in increased competition and regulation for firms that wish to compete in that market. As we formulate our plan, let's consider the importance of competing on an international level and its impact on our product development and marketing strategies. Our success depends on our ability to remain flexible and react quickly to customer desires!"

For Discussion

1. As Chocolate and Much More attempts to formulate its strategic plan, what issues must it consider with respect to its organizational design?

2. Evaluate the repercussions of moving into new international markets without the appropriate organizational design.

3. What recommendations might you make to this company?

EXPERIENTIAL EXERCISE 9.1

Organizational Characteristics Questionnaire

This brief assessment instrument measures the degree to which five characteristics are present in a particular organization's structure. It can be used to examine any real organization.

Instructions: The ten questions that follow ask about certain organizational conditions. You must refer to a specific organization in order to respond to these questions. Give your best overall judgment about how well each statement actually describes conditions in the organization that you have in mind. There are no right or wrong answers, since the purpose is to describe an existing organization's conditions and characteristics.

	Completely	Mostly	Partly	Slightly	Not at All

1. Work roles in this organization are highly specialized; each person has clear-cut authority and responsibility.
2. The formal hierarchy in this organization is formal to the point of being rigid and inflexible.
3. In this organization people are selected and promoted on the basis of their demonstrated technical competence.
4. People in this organization often seem so concerned with conforming to rules and procedures that it interferes with their mental health.
5. Everyone in this organization expects to be subject to the same set of rules and controls; there are no favorites.
6. People in this organization are often so wrapped up in their own narrow specialties that they can't see that we all have common interests; this causes unnecessary conflicts.
7. The offices and positions in this organization are arranged in a clear and logical hierarchy.
8. Overall, this organization is a political bureaucracy, with a "managerial elite" who got where they are through political savvy.
9. Managers in this organization see themselves as being on a clear "career ladder" and expect to make regular progress in their career paths.
10. Many of the rules in this organization have either become ends in themselves, with no logical function, or have come to specify the minimum tolerable performance levels.

Scoring: To score your answers, use the following key. Add up the points for all ten questions to get your score. A high score indicates a "good" bureaucracy, while the lower the score, the less the organization is a good bureaucracy; it either lacks the right bureaucratic characteristics or goes far overboard on some. A score between 25 and 35 is about average; scores of about 35 are suggestive of a "good" bureaucratic structure. Scores from 18 to 24 are a cause for concern, and scores below 18 indicate serious problems: either overbureaucratic rigidity or underbureaucratic chaos.

	RESPONSE				
QUESTION NUMBERS	COMPLETELY	MOSTLY	PARTLY	SLIGHTLY	NOT AT ALL
1, 3, 5, 7, 9	5 points	4 points	3 points	2 points	1 point
2, 4, 6, 8, 10	1 point	2 points	3 points	4 points	5 points

EXPERIENTIAL EXERCISE 9.2

ORGMECH Survey

This assessment instrument places an organization along the organic-mechanistic dimension first defined by Tom Burns and Gene Stalker. The mechanistic end of the dimension approximates the classic highly formalized bureaucracy, while the organic end can be used to describe a more participatory type of organization.

Instructions: Consider an organization with which you are familiar. Indicate the extent to which each of the following ten statements is true of or accurately characterizes the organization in question.

	To a Very Great Extent	To a Considerable Extent	To a Moderate Extent	To a Slight Extent	To Almost No Extent
1. This organization has clear rules and regulations that everyone is expected to follow closely.	____	____	____	____	____
2. Policies in this organization are reviewed by the people they affect before being implemented.	____	____	____	____	____
3. In this organization a major concern is that all employees be allowed to develop their talents and abilities.	____	____	____	____	____
4. Everyone in this organization knows who is his or her immediate supervisor is; reporting relationships are clearly defined.	____	____	____	____	____
5. Jobs in this organization are clearly defined; everyone knows exactly what is expected in any specific job position.	____	____	____	____	____
6. Work groups are typically temporary and change often in this organization.	____	____	____	____	____
7. All decisions in this organization must be reviewed and approved by upper-level management.	____	____	____	____	____
8. In this organization the emphasis is on adapting effectively to constant environmental change.	____	____	____	____	____
9. Jobs in this organization are usually broken down into highly specialized, smaller tasks.	____	____	____	____	____
10. Standard activities in this organization are always covered by clearly outlined procedures that everyone is expected to follow.	____	____	____	____	____

Scoring: On the scoring grid, note the number that corresponds to your response to each of the ten questions. Enter the numbers in the boxes, then add up all the numbers in the boxes. This is the organization's ORGMECH score.

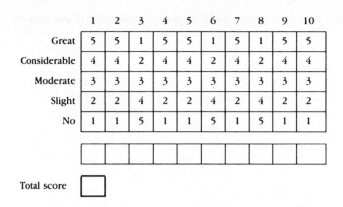

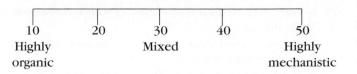

	1	2	3	4	5	6	7	8	9	10
Great	5	5	1	5	5	1	5	1	5	5
Considerable	4	4	2	4	4	2	4	2	4	4
Moderate	3	3	3	3	3	3	3	3	3	3
Slight	2	2	4	2	2	4	2	4	2	2
No	1	1	5	1	1	5	1	5	1	1

Total score

Interpretation: High scores indicate high degrees of mechanistic/bureaucratic organizational characteristics. Low scores are associated with adaptive/organic organizational characteristics.

10	20	30	40	50
Highly organic		Mixed		Highly mechanistic

For Discussion

- How would you feel (or how do you feel) about working in a mechanistic organization?
- How would you feel (or how do you feel) about working in a organic organization?
- Is it desirable to have as low a score as possible? Why or why not?
- Are certain characteristics of the organization you describe inconsistent with one another? What effects does this have?

ENDNOTES

1. S. Fatsis, "Restructuring Revives IBM PC's," *Orlando Sentinel,* May 23, 1993, F1.

2. See, for example, A. P. Carnevale, *America and the New Economy* (American Society for Training and Development and the U.S. Department of Labor Employment and Training Administration, 1993); W. Kiechel, "How We Will Work in the Year 2000: Six Trends Reshaping the Workplace," *Fortune,* May 17, 1993, 38-41.

3. See, for example, R. K. Kazanjian and R. Drazine, "Implementing Internal Diversification: Contingency Factors for Organization Design Choices," *Academy of Management Review,* 12, 2, 1987, 342-54; D. Miller, "The Genesis of Configuration," *Academy of Management Review,* 12, 4, 1987, 686-701; L. M. Kikulis, T. Slack, and C. R. Hinings, "Sector-Specific Patterns of Organizational Design Change," *Journal of Management Studies,* 32, January 1995, 67-100.

4. I. I. Mitroff, R. O. Mason, and C. M. Pearson, "Radical Surgery: What Will Tomorrow's Organizations Look Like?" *Academy of Management Executive,* 8, 2, 1994, 11-21.

5. Ibid.

6. N. Nohria and J. D. Berkley, "An Action Perspective: The Crux of the New Management," *California Management Review,* Summer 1994, 70-92.

7. D. Miller, "Relating Porter's Business Strategies to Environment and Structure: Analysis and Performance Implications," *Academy of Management Journal,* 31, 1988, 280-308; D. Miller, C. Droge, and J. M. Toulouse, "Strategic Process and Content as Mediator between Organizational Context and Structure," *Academy of Management Journal,* 31, 1988, 544-69.

8. R. B. Duncan, "What Is the Right Organization Structure?" *Organizational Dynamics,* Winter 1978, 59-80.

9. Coors Brewing Company, *1995 Annual Report.*

10. From interviews with Jim Bowyer, CEO of Bowyer Singleton & Associates, August 1995.

11. M. W. Miller and L. Hays, "Gerstner's Nonvision for IBM Raises a Management Issue," *The Wall Street Journal,* July 29, 1993, B1.

12. PepsiCo, *1996 Annual Report.*

13. R. Sookdeo, "The New Global Consumer," *Fortune,* Autumn/Winter 1993, 68-77.

14. P. S. Lewis and P. M. Fandt, "The Strategy-Structure Fit in Multinational Corporations: A Revised Model," *International Journal of Management,* June 1990, 137-46.

15. Kellogg Company, *1996 Annual Report.*

16. C. L. Fowler, "Focusing Expertise at CIGNA, ASQC/Fortune Special Report," *Fortune,* 1992.

17. M. Davis and P. R. Lawrence, *Matrix* (Reading, Mass: Addison-Wesley, 1977), 3.

18. J. R. Galbraith, "Matrix Organization Designs: How to Combine Functional and Project Forms," *Business Horizons,* February 1971, 29-40.

19. E. W. Larson, and D. H. Gobeli, "Matrix Management: Contradictions and Insights," *California Management Review,* Summer 1987, 126-38.

20. J. A. Byrne, "Is Your Compnay Too Big?" *Business Week,* March 27, 1989, 84-94.

21. W. Kiechel, "How We Will Work in the Year 2000."

22. A. P. Carnavale, *America and the New Economy.* (San Francisco: Jossey, Bass, 1991).

23. R. E. Miles and C. C. Snow, "Organizations: New Concepts for New Forms," *California Management Review,* 28, Spring 1986, 62-71.

24. H. H. Hinterhuber and B. M. Levin, "Strategic Networks—The Organization of the Future," *Long Range Planning,* 27, 3, 1994, 43-53.

25. S. Tully, "The Modular Corporation," *Fortune,* February 8, 1993, 106–14.

26. J. A. Byrne, "The Virtual Corporation," *Business Week,* February 8, 1993, 98–103.

27. R. E. Miles and C. C. Snow, "Organizations: New Concepts for New Forms."

28. C. C. Snow, R. E. Miles, and H. J. Coleman Jr., "Managing 21st Century Network Organizations," *Organizational Dynamics,* 10, February 1992, 5–20.

29. Ibid.

30. Ibid.

31. Ibid.

32. R. E. Miles, "Adapting to Technology and Competition: A New Industrial Relations System for the 21st Century," *California Management Review,* 31, Winter 1989, 9–28.

33. R. Charan, "How Networks Reshape Organizations—For Results," *Harvard Business Review,* September/October 1991, 104–15.

34. F. V. Guterl, "Goodbye, Old Matrix," *Business Month,* February 1989, 32–38.

35. J. B. Bush and A. L. Frohman, "Communication in a 'Network' Organization," *Organization Dynamics,* 20, 2, 1991, 23–36.

36. C. Ching, C. W. Holsapple, and A. B. Whinston, "Toward IT Support for Coordination in Network Organizations," *Information & Management,* 30, 1996, 179–199.

37. R. E. Miles and C. C. Snow, "Managing 21st Century Network Organizations."

38. See, for example, J. L. Chency, "Interdependence and Coordination in Organizations: A Role-System Analysis," *Academy of Management Journal,* 26, 1983, 156–62; J. K. Ito and R. B. Peterson, "Effects of Task Difficulty and Interunit Interdependence on Information Processing Systems," *Academy of Management Journal,* 4, 1986, 139–49; J. E. McCann and D. L. Ferry, "An Approach for Assessing and Managing Inter-Unit Interdependence," *Academy of Management Review,* 4, 1979, 113–20.

39. J. D. Thompson, *Organizations in Action* (New York: McGraw-Hill, 1967).

40. J. R. Galbraith, "Organizational Design: An Information Processing View," *Interfaces,* 4, May 1974, 3.

41. P. W. Yetton, K. D. Johnston, and J. F. Craig, "Computer-Aided Architects: A Case Study of IT and Strategic Change," *Sloan Management Review,* 35, 4, 1994, 57–68.

42. T. W. Malone, M. S. S. Morton, and R. R. Halperin, "Organizing for the 21st Century," *Strategy & Leadership,* July/August 1996, 7–10.

43. P. G. Keen, "Redesigning the Organization through Information Technology," *Planning Review,* May/June 1991,

4–9; A. B. Shani and J. A. Sena, "Information Technology and the Integration of Change: Sociotechnical System Approach," *Journal of Applied Behavioral Science,* 30, 2, June 1994, 247–70.

44. R. Leifer and P. K. Mills, "An Information Processing Approach for Deciding upon Control Strategies and Reducing Control Loss in Emerging Organizations," *Journal of Management,* 22, 1, 1996, 113–37.

45. S. P. Bradley, J. A. Hausman, and R. L. Nolan, eds., *Globalization, Technology, and Competition* (Boston, Mass.: Harvard Business School Press, 1993).

46. W. J. Altier, "Task Forces: An Effective Management Tool," *Management Review,* February 1987, 52–57.

47. M. Hardaker and B. K. Ward, "How to Make a Team Work," *Harvard Business Review,* November/December 1987, 112–20.

48. G. Garnier, "Context and Decision Making Autonomy in Foreign Affiliates of U.S. Multinational Corporations," *Academy of Management Journal,* 25, 1982, 893–908.

49. T. Peters, "Letting Go of Controls," *Across the Board,* June 1991, 15–18.

50. See, for example, B. R. Schlender, "Yet Another Strategy for Apple," *Fortune,* 122, 10, 1990, 81. and J. Sculley, *Odyssey: Pepsi to Apple—A Journey of Adventure Ideas for the Future* (New York: Harper & Row, 1987).

51. T. Burns and G. Stalker, *The Management of Innovation* (London: Tavistock, 1961), 119–22.

52. "Winning Team Plays," *Supervisory Management,* 39, 8, August 1994, 8–9.

53. G. Davis, "Conceptual Model for Research on Knowledge Work," (Minneapolis, Minn.: University of Minnesota, MISRC working paper, MISRC-WP-91-10, 1991).

54. T. H. Davenport, S. L. Jarvenpaa, and M. C. Beers, "Improving Knowledge Work Processes," *Sloan Management Review,* Summer 1996, 53–65.

55. Ibid.

56. See, for example, R. Hayes and W. Abernathy, "Managing Our Way to Economic Decline," *Harvard Business Review,* 58, July/August 1980, 67–77; H. Stevenson and D. Gumpert, "The Heart of Entrepreneurship," *Harvard Business Review,* 63, March/April 1985, 85–94; H. H. Stevenson, M. J. Roberts, and D. E. Grousbeck, *New Business Ventures and the Entrepreneur* (Homewood, Ill.: Irwin, 1989).

57. B. Dumain, "The Bureaucracy Busters," *Fortune,* June 17, 1991, 36–50.

58. J. Byrne, "The Horizontal Corporation," *Business Week,* December 20, 1993, 76–81.

59. I. Sager, "How IBM Became a Growth Company Again," *Business Week,* Dec. 9, 1996, 154.

Managing Human Resources

■ CHAPTER OVERVIEW

At McDonald's Corporation, there is a Vice-President for Individuality. At Carson Pirie Scott & Company, there is a Vice-President of Customer Satisfaction through People Involvement. Although the titles are very different, both positions involve the same managerial function—the management of people in organizations. Increasingly, top-performing organizations invest much time, attention, and energy into their human resources. They have found that these resources are the organization's most critical assets. Effective management of human resources leads to greater productivity, quality, and organizational performance.

In the two previous chapters, we considered the organizing function as it related to designing the organization to achieve its goals and objectives. In this chapter, we continue our discussion of the organizing function by examining how organizations acquire and develop human resources. We focus on the human resource planning process as it occurs within organizations, including rigorous recruiting, screening, and selection of the best candidates; training; evaluating; and compensating fairly and appropriately for the positions. Legal human resource issues, including discrimination concerns and affirmative action programs, are also considered. Finally, we explore some emerging issues that are affecting human resource management today.

■ LEARNING OBJECTIVES

When you have finished studying this chapter, you should be able to:

- Describe the legal environment of human resource management.
- Discuss the human resources planning process.
- Describe different recruiting techniques used by organizations.
- Explain the four major selection methods.
- Describe the problems inherent in performance appraisals.
- Demonstrate how managers use performance appraisal information.
- Explain how compensation and benefits are used in organizations.
- Define and discuss labor-management relations.
- Explain the influences of information technology on human resources.
- Discuss current issues in human resource management.

C H A P T E R

10

Managerial Incident

CORNING: IT SIMPLY MAKES GOOD BUSINESS SENSE

Corning, Inc., is best known for popular consumer products, such as Corningware, Corelle, and Pyrex brands of housewares. More recently, Corning has earned a reputation as one of the most quality-oriented companies in the world by creating a work environment that supports and rewards a quality orientation in everything the company does.

Much of the credit for the changes at Corning is attributed to James R. Houghton, the founder's great-great-grandson, who took over as chair and chief executive officer in 1983. Houghton had three major goals for Corning: total quality, high return on equity, and improved human resource management systems. For the challenges to be met, new partnerships had to be formed with employees, and human resources had to be better utilized.

Revising the human resource management system required extensive planning. Work-force diversity programs, teamwork and group-based tasks, performance-based incentives and reward systems, intense training and development programs, and strategies for continuous improvement were all intensively studied, designed, and implemented. The company wanted to create an environment in which all employees could realize their potential and contribute effectively to the goals of the organization. Individual differences were to be valued and celebrated, not simply tolerated.

The issue of work-force diversity became a top priority for Houghton. He believed that Corning's work force should more closely mirror the company's customer base. This meant changing many of the traditional human resource management practices. The company had higher attrition rates for minorities and women than for white men, which suggested that recruiting, selecting, training, and development programs were ineffective. Talented women and blacks joined the company only to plateau or resign. Few reached upper-management levels, and no one could say exactly why. Reversing this trend represented a significant management challenge for Corning.[1]

INTRODUCTION

As managers at Corning realized, achieving the goals of the organization requires effective human resource management. Corning's reputation for quality was a function, to a large degree, of its highly effective human resource management system. Nevertheless, continued success will be dependent upon the company's ability to maintain a work environment that encourages and rewards a quality orientation among employees and meets the needs of a more diverse work force.

Human resource management (HRM) involves the management of the organization's employees. HRM consists of all the activities required to enhance the effectiveness of an organization's work force and to achieve organizational goals and objectives. In today's highly competitive marketplace, human resource management has become critical to improving the competitiveness of many firms. It is particularly important in industries where success is dependent upon achieving the highest possible product and service quality. For example, the corporate philosophy at Southwest Airlines, a service-driven organization that has turned a profit for 23 consecutive years, is "Employees are Number 1. The way you treat your employees is the way they will treat your customers. It's difficult to change someone's attitude, so hire for attitude and train for skill."[2]

Besides competitiveness, HRM must deal at the same time with changing legal requirements and changes in the work force. These critical issues have

Human resource management (HRM)

The management of the employees of the organization consisting of all the activities required to enhance the effectiveness of an organization's work force and to achieve organizational goals and objectives.

forced human resource managers to recognize and respond to a multitude of external environmental forces.

The focus of this chapter is on the role of human resource managers and the activities that are involved in the HRM function. Because of the increasing importance of legal issues, we begin by examining those aspects of the legal environment that affect HRM practices, focusing on the major legislation regulating employment practices and affirmative-action programs. Next, we explore the major HRM activities that help the organization attract, retain, and develop the quality and quantity of employees needed to meet organizational goals. More specifically, we examine HRM planning and job analysis, staffing, training, performance appraisal, compensation, and labor relations. In the last part of the chapter, we turn our attention to information technology influences and some current issues affecting HRM, including international HRM, work-force diversity, sexual harassment, and health concerns in the work environment.

LEGAL ENVIRONMENT OF HUMAN RESOURCE MANAGEMENT

One factor that has contributed to the increased importance of human resource managers is the number and complexity of legal issues faced by organizations. Federal and state laws that specify required, acceptable, and prohibited employment practices place many constraints on recruitment, selection, placement, training, and other human resource activities. For example, Xerox sets recruitment and representation goals in accordance with federal guidelines and reviews them continually to make sure that they reflect work-force demographics. While all companies with federal contracts are required to make this effort, Xerox extends the guidelines by setting diversity goals for its upper-level jobs and holding division and group managers accountable for reaching those goals.[3]

EQUAL EMPLOYMENT OPPORTUNITY LEGISLATION

In an effort to reduce employment discrimination based on racial bigotry and sexual stereotypes, Congress passed several laws that directly address the problem of employee discrimination.[4] The Civil Rights Act of 1964, the Civil Rights Restoration Act of 1988, and the Civil Rights Act of 1991 are equal employment opportunity (EEO) laws that prohibit the consideration of race, color, religion, national origin, or gender in employment decision making. Other legislation, such as the Americans with Disabilities Act of 1990 and the Age Discrimination in Employment Act of 1967, prohibits employment decisions based on biases against the handicapped and the elderly. In general, the purpose of EEO legislation is to ensure that unemployment decisions are based on job-related criteria only. Toward that end, a substantial amount of legislation deals with various forms of employee protection. Table 10.1 summarizes the major federal laws and regulations that affect the management of human resources.

The most current piece of legislation to take effect is the Family and Medical Leave Act (FMLA), which allows individuals to take up to twelve weeks of unpaid leave per year for the birth or adoption of a baby or the illness of a family member. Some companies have been slow to inform employees of their right under this act because of the disruption that they perceive will happen in the workplace. How much do you know about the FMLA? Since it is your responsibility to be well informed, take a few minutes to examine Table 10.2, which presents some of the highlights of the FMLA.

TABLE 10.1   Major federal laws protecting employees

LAW OR REGULATION	YEAR	DESCRIPTION
Fair Labor Standards Act	1938	Established minimum wages paid to employees and the 40-hour workweek: regulates child labor.
Social Security Act	1935	Established the Social Security system.
Equal Pay Act	1963	Requires that men and women receive equal pay for equal work.
Title VII of Civil Rights Act	1964 (amended in 1972)	Makes it illegal to discriminate on the basis of race, color, religion, national origin, or gender.
Age Discrimination in Employment Act	1967 (amended in 1986)	Prevents age discrimination in employment against persons between 40 and 70 years of age.
Occupational Safety and Health Act	1970	Requires organizations to provide safe, nonhazardous working conditions for employees.
Pregnancy Discrimination Act	1978	Broadens discrimination to include pregnancy, childbirth, and related conditions.
Americans with Disabilities Act	1990	Prohibits discrimination in employment against persons with physical or mental disabilities or those who are chronically ill.
Civil Rights Act	1991	Amends and clarifies Title VII, Americans with Disabilities Act, and other EEO laws.

TABLE 10.2   The family and medical leave act

YOU SHOULD KNOW THAT	BUT REMEMBER
• It protects workers who want to take time off to care for a new baby, a seriously ill family member, or themselves. • Workers can take as much as twelve weeks leave per year, and it doesn't have to be taken at one time. • It applies to all public agencies, including schools. • The worker's health insurance continues throughout the length of the leave. Upon returning to work, he or she must be returned to the original job or given an equivalent position.	• It doesn't cover leaves to care for siblings, unmarried partners, or nontraditional family members. • The leave is an unpaid one. • It applies to only those employers with 50 or more employees within a 75-mile radius. • Only about half of all workers are covered. Employees must have worked at the company for at least one year. The right can be denied to so-called key workers, or those considered most critical to the organization.

SOURCE: *Self,* "News Flash," June 1996, 121. Copyright ©1996 by the Condé Nast Publications, Inc.
NOTE: More information is available from the Women's Legal Defense Fund's *Guide to the Family and Medical Leave Act,* 1875 Connecticut Ave. NW, #710, Washington, DC 20009.

The Civil Rights Act of 1964 established the Equal Employment Opportunity Commission (EEOC). This organization is responsible for enforcing federal laws related to job discrimination. Although the EEOC can prosecute an organization that violates the law, the commission usually tries to persuade offending organizations to change their policies and pay damages to anyone who has encountered discrimination. To help organizations comply with federal employment regulations, the EEOC also publishes written guidelines that clarify the law and instruct organizations on their legal obligations and responsibilities. Current federal law prohibits discrimination on the basis of gender, age, physical or mental disability, military experience, religion, race, ethnic origin, color, or national origin.[5]

AFFIRMATIVE-ACTION PROGRAMS

Affirmative action refers to the legal requirement that employers must actively recruit, hire, and promote members of minority groups and other protected classes, if such individuals are underrepresented in the organization. Individuals who fall within a group identified for protection under equal employment laws and regulations are a **protected class.** That is, if the qualified labor pool in a community is 20 percent African American and 5 percent Hispanic American, then 20 percent and 5 percent of the labor force of an organization operating in that community should be African American and Hispanic American, respectively.

Organizations often have patterns of employment in which protected groups are underrepresented relative to the number of group members who have appropriate credentials in the marketplace. To correct imbalance in their work force, organizations may adopt affirmative-action programs. An affirmative-action program is a written, systematic plan that specifies goals and a timetable for hiring, training, promoting, and retaining groups protected by federal EEO laws and regulations. While affirmative action is not synonymous with quotas, under federal regulations all companies with federal contracts greater than $50,000 and with 50 employees or more are required to establish annual plans in the form of numerical goals or timetables for increasing employment of women and minorities.

During the last few years, there has been vocal opposition to affirmative-action plans across the United States. In the November 1996 elections, California voters overwhelmingly supported the dismantling of the state's affirmative-action programs by passing Proposition 209. This proposition bans race and gender preferences in public hiring, contracting, and education. Supporters said the goal was to create a color-blind society and eliminate gender preference in hiring. Opponents branded it a very negative attack on diversity and the needed affirmative-action programs.[6]

Protected class
Composed of individuals who fall within a group identified for protection under equal employment laws and regulations.

Affirmative action plans have met with vocal opposition across the United States during the last few years. California voters passed Proposition 209 by a wide margin, banning race and gender preferences in public hiring, contracting, and education.
© Michael Newman/PhotoEdit

Many organizations have found that simply dictating affirmative action in hiring cannot change an organization's culture. It takes more than simply hiring members of protected classes. Education and management development are often necessary to encourage the general work force to appreciate individuals of a different gender, race, or ethnic background.

Monsanto, the St. Louis–based maker of chemicals and drugs, serves as an excellent example of an organization that tries to encourage workplace diversity. The company began by conducting exit interviews with minorities and women who left the organization. Based on information obtained from the interviews, the company developed a series of diversity management programs to help it retain such employees. One program, called "Consulting Pairs," trains employees throughout the company to serve as in-house consultants (working in race- or gender-matched pairs) on race and gender issues.[7] Another example of a proactive affirmative-action plan is the efforts of Avon Products to maintain a more diverse work force.[8] This company wanted its work force to reflect its customer base and developed a program that took a bottom-up approach to achieving diversity in the workplace.

Perhaps more than any other area of management, the HRM process is affected by the legal environment.[9] Moreover, due to societal and political forces, the legal landscape of HRM is constantly changing. Therefore, it is important for managers to keep abreast of which employment practices are permissible and which are prohibited. For example, many organizations have appearance and grooming rules and guidelines for employees, especially those who deal with the public. Although there have been cases of "appearance" discrimination, businesses generally retain the right to require their employees to meet appearance standards. In contrast, there is growing pressure to prohibit employment decisions based on sexual preference. Because of such trends, human resource managers are becoming increasingly important members of the organization.

HUMAN RESOURCE PLANNING

Have you ever wondered why some organizations, such as Corning, have been successful so consistently? Or why some college and professional sports teams consistently win championships? As we know from Chapters 4 and 5, planning is one ingredient for achieving the goals and objectives of the organization. It would be unthinkable for a company not to plan for its future material needs, plant capacity, or financing. Similarly, organizations must plan for their human resource needs.

Human resource planning is the process of determining future human resource needs relative to an organization's strategic plan and taking actions necessary to meet those needs in a timely manner. The planning process is shown in Figure 10.1. In planning to meet human resource requirements, managers must be familiar with both the organization's job requirements and labor demand and supply issues; they must also know how to reconcile supply and demand through recruitment, selection, training, performance appraisal, and compensation programs. We will discuss each of these aspects of human resource planning in the following sections.

JOB ANALYSIS

Job analysis involves assimilating all of the information about a particular job. Job analysis information, in turn, is used to develop two important documents: the job description and job specifications. As we know from Chapter 8, a **job**

Human resource planning
The process of determining future human resource needs relative to an organization's strategic plan and taking the actions necessary to meet those needs in a timely manner.

Job analysis
Assimilating all of the information about a particular job, including job descriptions and job specifications.

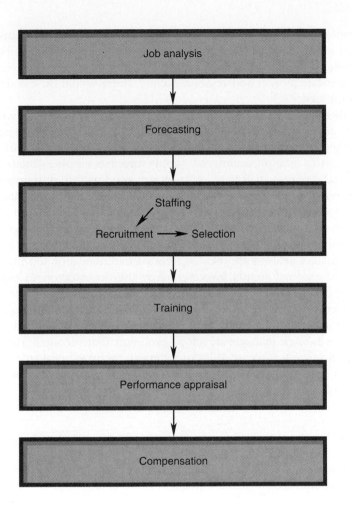

FIGURE 10.1
Human resource planning process

description details the responsibilities and tasks associated with a given position. **Job specifications** identify the knowledge, skills, abilities, and other employee characteristics needed to perform the job. Taken together, job descriptions and job specifications provide the human resource manager with a foundation for forecasting the supply of and demand for labor within the organization and developing programs to meet the company's human resource requirements. Job descriptions and job specifications also help the organization comply with EEO laws by ensuring that HRM decisions are based on job-related information.

Job description
An outline of the responsibilities and tasks associated with a given job.

Job specifications
The identification of the knowledge, skills, abilities, and other employee characteristics needed to perform the job.

FORECASTING

An important aspect of human resource planning is forecasting the supply of and demand for human resources for both short-term planning (one to two years) and long-term planning (three to five years). Both types of forecasts require looking into the future.

Demand forecasting involves determining the number of employees that the organization will need at some point in the future as well as the knowledge, skills, and abilities that these employees must possess. The organization's external and internal environments are the major determinants of the demand for human resources. For example, changes in the economy may affect the demand for a product or service and, thus, affect the need for certain types of employees. In addition, demand is based on the organization's strategic goals and plans and internal work-force changes, such as retirements, resignations,

Demand forecasting—the type a manager employs when planning the opening of additional stores, for example—involves determining the number of employees that will be needed at some point in the future as well as the knowledge, skills, and abilities that those employees must possess.

© Bonnie Kamin/PhotoEdit

Staffing
Bringing in or placing people into the organization and making sure they serve as productive members of the work force.

Recruitment
The process of finding and attracting job candidates who are qualified to fill job vacancies.

terminations, and leaves of absence. If Wal-Mart, for example, plans to open three new stores two years from today, its human resource managers must begin planning now to staff those facilities. Likewise, if the company intends to close or relocate a branch or regional facility, there would be less demand for certain employees.

Supply forecasting involves determining what human resources will be available, both inside and outside the organization. Internal programs such as promotions, transfers, training, and pay incentives are designed to meet demand through existing employees. Internal supply forecasts simply estimate the effect that internal programs will have on turnover, termination, retirement, promotion, and transfer rates.[10] For example, monetary incentives are often used to induce employees to accept transfers or obtain the training needed for promotion. To meet human resource demand, most organizations must rely on some extent on bringing in employees from the outside. Human resource professionals and labor market analysis are used to forecast external labor supply. Together, internal and external supply forecasts allow the organization to estimate the number of people who will enter and leave various organizational jobs, as well as the effects of HRM programs on employee skills and productivity.[11]

After estimating the demand for and potential supplies of human resources, the human resource manager develops programs that reconcile the two forecasts. If a shortage is forecast, HRM programs to increase employee hiring, promotions, transfers, and training are devised. If an excess is predicted, workforce reduction programs must be implemented.

STAFFING

The **staffing** function has two primary components: recruitment and selection. We will examine each of these aspects in more detail.

Recruitment

Recruitment is the process of finding and attracting job candidates who are qualified to fill job vacancies. Job descriptions and job specifications, both discussed earlier, are important in the recruiting process because they specify the nature of the job and the qualifications required of candidates.

Recruitment, or the search process, can occur in a variety of settings, both inside and outside the organization. Both internal and external recruitment have certain advantages and disadvantages.[12] These are summarized in Table 10.3 and discussed in more detail in the next paragraphs.

Most vacant positions in organizations are filled through internal recruitment. Internal recruitment involves identifying potential internal candidates and encouraging them to apply for and be willing to accept organizational jobs that are vacant. Methods of internal recruitment include job banks, employee referral systems, job postings, and advertisements in company newsletters. Every organization represents an internal labor market to some degree. Many employees, both entry-level and upper-level, aspire to move up the ranks through promotion. Promotion from within becomes more feasible when companies invest in training and development activities. At higher levels, transfers can be an important development tool for acquiring additional job knowledge, as well as a means of creating new job ladders for upward mobility. Both promotion and transfer policies can create a favorable climate for attracting qualified employees and retaining valued ones.

External recruitment involves advertising for and soliciting applicants from outside the company. If internal sources do not produce an acceptable candidate, a wide variety of external sources are available. These sources differ in terms of ease of use, costs, and the quality of applicants obtained.

TABLE 10.3   Internal versus external recruitment

	ADVANTAGES	DISADVANTAGES
Internal Recruitment	• Helps morale of promotee • Better assessment of abilities • Lower cost for some jobs • Motivator for good performance • Causes a succession of promotions • Have to hire only at entry level	• Inbreeding • Possible morale problems of those not promoted • Political infighting for promotions • Strong management development program needed
External Recruitment	• New blood and new perspectives • Cheaper than training a professional • No group of political supporters in the organization already • May bring new ideas, creativity, and insights	• May not select someone who will fit • May cause morale problems for internal candidates not promoted • Longer adjustment or orientation time needed

External sources include walk-ins, public employment agencies, temporary-help agencies, labor unions, educational institutions, referrals from current and past employees, competitive sources, and newspaper and trade publications. The source used will depend upon the job skills required and the current availability of those skills in the labor market. For example, organizations frequently use external placement firms and private employment agencies to find applicants for upper-level managerial positions, but look to educational institutions for candidates for entry-level managerial positions. As technology develops, human resource managers are increasingly using computerized databases as well as the Internet and list servers in the recruitment task.

Finding and hiring the best people is a top priority for many organizations. For example, Microsoft Corporation has devised and refined recruiting techniques to hire the very brightest software developers. Bill Gates, CEO, insists that only the very brightest candidates are recruited and considered, even though the company receives over 120,000 résumés each year. New software developers at Microsoft need to possess not merely extremely high intelligence, creativity, and technical expertise, but also, the capacity to acquire quickly whatever skills might be needed in the future.[13]

Selection

Once applicants have been recruited, the organization must select the right person for the job. **Selection** is the process of evaluating and choosing the best-qualified candidate from the pool of applicants recruited for the position. It entails the exchange of accurate information between employers and job candidates to optimize the person-job match. Although organizations usually make these decisions, applicants also select organizations to meet their economic and occupational needs.

The procedure of selecting and matching applicants to jobs begins after an adequate number of applicants have been recruited. At the heart of the selection process is the prediction of whether or not a particular applicant is capable of performing the job tasks associated with the position for which he or she is being considered.

Selection
The process of evaluating and choosing the best qualified candidate from the pool of applicants recruited for the position.

Careful selection procedures can be time-consuming and costly. However, a wrong decision can also be costly when it results in litigation, lost time, or wrongful-discharge complaints. Some organizations are now using expensive selection procedures, even for positions that historically would have been filled without much screening. For example, when Toyota Motor Corporation wanted to fill positions at its new automobile assembly plant in Kentucky, it received 90,000 applications from 120 countries for its 2,700 production positions, and thousands more for the 300 office jobs. To select workers who would conform to the Japanese emphasis on teamwork, loyalty, and versatility, Toyota required applicants to spend approximately 25 hours completing written tests, workplace simulations, and interviews. The tests examined not only literacy and technical knowledge, but also interpersonal skills and attitudes toward work. In addition, each person took a physical examination and a drug test.[14] This process enabled Toyota to select those candidates who had the greatest likelihood of succeeding in their jobs.

During the selection process, managers must determine the extent to which job candidates have the skills, abilities, and knowledge required to perform effectively in the positions for which they are being considered. To make such judgments, managers and human resource professionals rely on various tools and techniques for selection, including application forms, employment tests, interviews, and assessment centers.

Application Forms   The application form is the first source of information about a potential employee. It records the applicant's desired position, serves as a prescreening device to help determine whether an applicant meets the minimum requirements of a position, and allows preliminary comparisons with the credentials of other candidates.

The application form contains a series of inquiries about job-related qualifications and experience, such as an applicant's educational background, previous job experience, physical health, and other information that may be useful in assessing an individual's ability to perform a job. If you currently hold a job or have ever looked for one, chances are that you have completed an application form for employment.

In collecting information on a candidate's background and current status, the application form should ask only questions pertaining to the applicant's ability to perform the job. If the information helps the employer select more qualified candidates, then it is job related. In nearly all instances, questions regarding gender, age, race, or national origin are not predictive of future employment success and should be avoided.

Employment Tests   Any instrument, device, or information used to make an employment decision is considered a test by the EEOC's Uniform Guidelines on Employee Selection. An **employment test** is a means of assessing a job applicant's knowledge, skills, and abilities through written responses (such as a math test) or simulated exercises (such as a motor skills test). The major types of tests used in the selection process are intelligence tests, job aptitude and knowledge tests, personality inventories, and job performance tests.

Interviews   Interviews are relatively formal, in-depth conversations conducted for the purpose of assessing a candidate's knowledge, skills, and abilities, as well as providing information to the candidate about the organization and potential jobs. They are used with more than 90 percent of all people hired for industrial positions.

Interviews permit a two-way exchange of information. Most interview questions are straightforward inquiries about the candidate's experience or education. At Microsoft, however, prospective employees are asked questions that

Employment test
Any instrument, device, or information used to make an employment decision is considered a test by the EEOC's Uniform Guidelines of Employee Selection.

indicate a candidate's capabilities of grasping new knowledge extremely quickly and generating acute questions on the spot; of possessing such familiarity with programming structures that a quick glance is sufficient for them to understand a long printout of code; and of having photographic recall of code they had written. In other words, Microsoft is testing how an applicant thinks.[15]

If interviews are used, managers should take steps to maximize their effectiveness. Typically, a structured interview format works best. A specific list of topics and the order in which they will be covered should be determined in advance. When managers are responsible for interviewing potential candidates, they need to keep the following points in mind:

- Ask precise, specific questions that are job related.
- Probe for details and be a careful listener.
- Avoid biases such as making snap judgments, stereotyping, or looking only for negative information.
- Be careful to avoid prohibited discriminatory questions.
- Keep written records of the interview.
- Use multiple interviewers.
- Keep in mind that candidates from diverse backgrounds and cultures may interpret questions differently. Be sure that the candidate understands your questions.

Interviews should never be the sole basis for selecting a candidate. Instead, they should be used along with other selection devices to provide additional information on candidates' strengths and weaknesses. Chase Manhattan Bank, for example, developed an analytical interview because of its interest in the thought processes of its future employees. According to vice-president Stanley Burns, Chase's college recruiting efforts generally include several types of interviews. An initial interview, either on campus or in New York, determines whether the candidate's overall abilities, motivation, and interpersonal skills seem to fit the bank's requirements. Candidates are subsequently interviewed by a human resource specialist who informs the candidate about Chase's organizational structure and career opportunities and determines whether the candidate meets the general criteria for a specific business unit. Finally, the candidate is interviewed by managers who assess very specific analytical skills. In describing the analytical interview, Burns notes that Chase is looking at the specific mental abilities required for successful performance in both its training program and its management jobs.

When formulating the analytical interview, the company recognized that while many job requirements varied depending on the specific business unit, certain mental abilities were needed for strong analytical skills to develop. Consequently, Chase studied the content and structure of its training program and its entry-level management jobs to identify critical mental abilities. Six abilities were determined to be necessary: memory, learning speed, logical reasoning, divergent thinking, convergent thinking, and an affinity for numbers. The bank then developed a series of cases that could be used in a structured interview to focus on these six mental abilities. The cases, along with probing interviewer questions, are used to see if the candidate has the basic problem-solving capabilities necessary for success at Chase Manhattan.[16]

Although it is illegal to ask job applicants questions that violate EEO law, a recent study by New York's Hanigan Consulting Group found that managers ask for information that could be considered prohibitive in nearly 70 percent of all interviews.[17] Most managers do this because they are uninformed. Some managers, however, knowingly ask questions that put the interviewee in a position of revealing information prohibited by EEO law. What would you do if you were asked such a question? Table 10.4 provides some examples of "loaded" ques-

Meeting the Challenge

MAKE THE FIRST INTERVIEW SAVVY: KNOW WHAT TO ASK AND WHAT TO AVOID

Whether you are able to land the job you want may depend on the questions you ask in your next interview. Those questions reveal a lot about you, possibly more than you realize. It is inappropriate to ask about pay before the company actually offers you a job. Regardless of your experience, education, or rank, all job applicants should adhere to this rule. Asking about compensation and benefits is usually viewed as a selfish question and is not going to help you get a job. That question should be set aside until a job offer is actually made.

In a recent poll of 1,000 U.S. employers, a lengthy list of questions were compiled from applicants turned down for everything from entry-level professional jobs to clerical and administrative positions. The following questions were the questions most frequently asked:

1. What does your company do?
2. What are your psychiatric benefits?
3. Who gets the frequent flier miles?
4. Can you tell me about your retirement plan?
5. The job description mentions weekend work. Do I really have to do that?
6. What does your company consider a good absenteeism record?
7. Do you have free parking?

Many people really don't know what to ask when they go on an interview. HR managers indicate that individuals who ask good questions are more likely to be considered "winners." These individuals are interested in the company, what role they can play with the organization, and how they can make a contribution. The "losers," by contrast, ask few or no questions, or ask bad ones. They are also almost entirely focused on the bottom line

tions and possible responses.[18] Refer now to Meeting the Challenge to gain some critical information on what to ask and what to avoid in the interview.

Assessment center
A controlled environment used to predict the probable success of job applicants based on their behaviors in simulated situations.

Assessment Centers   Many organizations approach the employee selection process very systematically through an assessment center that combines a variety of procedures. An **assessment center** is a controlled environment used to predict the probable success of job applicants based on their behaviors in simulated situations. Assessment centers are most often used for selecting candidates for managerial positions and sales personnel. Some organizations, however, use them to evaluate current nonmanagerial employees for supervisory training and advancement and to select college graduates for entry-level supervisory positions.

The situations or exercises in the assessment center are essentially performance tests that reflect the type of work done in managerial positions, such as decision making, writing, speaking, managing time, giving feedback, and completing leadership tasks. Presumably, simulations provide a good indication of how well the individual will do on the job. Assessment ratings of candidates are provided by trained observers who are usually human resource managers.

Although assessment centers are costly, virtually every study has found that they are better predictors of employee performance than other selection approaches. Further, employees typically report that assessment centers have given them a fair chance to show their abilities. AT&T, the pioneer of this technique, is perhaps the best-known user, but more than 2,000 organizations have assessment-center programs in operation.[19]

(their own) and generally ask about money and benefits instead of the company's future, its goals, and the role they are likely to play.

What are some good questions to ask? First, savvy applicants should show an interest in the reality of life on the job. Second, make it plain that you are not clueless as to what that reality might be. The following queries would be appropriate ways to convey that.

- It's in the nature of the industry and the nature of the job that there are going to be some really intense periods with long days and tight deadlines. Still, could you describe what a typical week or month on the job might be like?

- I realize it's important to have a good overview of the company as a whole. At my level, what type of working relationship would I have with people from other areas of the firm?

- Could you tell me how this position came to be open? Is this position available because of growth in the company or has someone recently left the position?

- Why is the position we are discussing important to the firm?

- Can you tell me how your career has developed at the company? You seem so excited about the firm, I would love to hear about it.

- You explained to me earlier what the formal reporting relationships are at the company. Do managers tend to hold tight reins on their subordinates or is the relationship more flexible?

These questions are just a starting point. Since most successful professionals keep current with happenings in their industry and since they recognize that business doesn't occur in a vacuum, professionals should ask about the industry. These questions show that you have done some research and are thinking about the potential challenges that confront decision makers throughout the industry.

Regardless of the selection method used, the organization must be able to demonstrate that its selection methods are valid and do not illegally discriminate against employee classes protected by EEO legislation. **Validity** means that a test actually measures what it says it measures and refers to inferences about tests. It may be valid to infer that college admission test scores predict college academic performance, but it is probably invalid to infer that those same test scores predict athletic performance. To validate their tests, organizations must show that test performance is related to subsequent job performance. If not, then use of the tests may adversely affect protected employees and could result in legal problems for the organization. Employment selection tests that were unrelated to job performance and excluded women and minorities were the catalyst for much of the legislation that affects the HRM function today. The EEOC publishes comprehensive guidelines on test validation and employee selection. Currently, most organizations make great efforts to use valid selection methods and to make selection decisions based upon anticipated job performance.

Validity
A relationship between what a test proposes to measure and what is actually measured.

TRAINING

Training is a planned effort to assist employees in learning job-related behaviors that will improve their performance. The primary reason that organizations train new employees is to prepare them to work toward achieving the goals and objectives of the organization. At the same time, effective training should

Training
A planned effort to assist employees in learning job-related behaviors in order to improve performance.

TABLE 10.4   How to handle loaded interview questions

Here's a sampling of what interviewers *shouldn't*, but might ask:

- *What they ask:*   "Our division is spread out over several floors. Is that OK?"
- *What they mean:*   We spend a lot of our day running up and down the stairs, but in that wheelchair you might have difficulties.
- *How to answer:*   "Getting from place to place is not a problem for me."

Note: Under the Americans with Disabilities Act, the employer must make stairways more accessible.

- *What they ask:*   "Will it be a problem for you to work long hours?"
- *What they mean:*   Do you have to get home every night to young children?
- *How to answer:*   "I value my personal life, but I can make myself available when necessary."

- *What they ask:*   "Does your family mind you traveling?"
- *What they mean:*   Are you a single parent with child-care concerns?
- *How to answer:*   "Will travel be part of my job responsibilities?"

- *What they ask:*   "What were the dates of employment for your past jobs?"
- *What they mean:*   How old are you?
- *How to answer:*   "Give them the dates and say, "As you see from the longevity of my employment, I'm very dependable."

Note: Anyone over 40 is protected from age discrimination.

- *What they ask:*   "As a consulting firm, we must be responsive to our clients. Will you be readily available?"
- *What they mean:*   Are you going to be taking off a lot of religious holidays?
- *How to answer:*   "My attendance record is exemplary."

- *What they ask:*   "We are looking for people who have a long-term commitment to the company. Is that what you have in mind?"
- *What they mean:*   You're a young woman with a wedding ring. Will you get pregnant and leave?
- *How to answer:*   "I like this company. Maybe you can tell me what it takes to move up here."

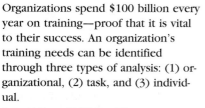

Organizations spend $100 billion every year on training—proof that it is vital to their success. An organization's training needs can be identified through three types of analysis: (1) organizational, (2) task, and (3) individual.

© David Young-Wolff/PhotoEdit

help trainees bring their skills, knowledge, and abilities up to the level required for satisfactory performance. As employees continue on the job, additional training provides them with the opportunity to acquire new knowledge and skills and improve their effectiveness on the job.

Training is vital to the success of modern organizations, both large and small. This is evidenced by the fact that organizations spend $100 billion every year on training.[20] Rapidly changing technology requires that employees possess the knowledge, skills, and abilities needed to cope with new processes and production techniques. Further, changes in management philosophy create a need for management development as well. For example, when faced with a tough global challenge, Xerox and Motorola increased their investment in employee training.[21] Training has helped Xerox regain market share from Japan. At Motorola, training gave the company the edge to grow in the face of strong Japanese competition in cellular phones and semiconductors.

An organization's training needs can be identified through three types of analysis: (1) organizational, (2) task, and (3) individual.[22] Organizational analysis uses the company's strategic plan to identify the knowledge, skills, and abilities that will be needed in the future as jobs and the organization change. Task analysis uses job descriptions and job specifications to compare present job requirements with employee knowledge, skills, and abilities. Finally, individual training needs can be determined by focusing on how individuals perform their jobs. Performance appraisal information is often used to identify performance weaknesses that may be overcome with training.

Types of Training Programs

Once the training needs of the organization have been assessed, training programs must be designed and developed. Here we examine a few of the various kinds of training programs that typically exist in organizations.

The first step in the training process is to get new employees off to a good start. This is generally accomplished through an orientation program. **Orientation** is the formal process of familiarizing new employees with the organization, their job, and their work unit. Orientation procedures vary widely from company to company. Generally, their purpose is to enable new employees to fit in so that they become productive members of the organization. The newcomer may need several hours, several weeks, or several months of work with other employees to become completely familiar with the organization. In recent years, many companies have realized that the socialization process begins in orientation and can make a significant difference to new employees. For example, one division of Intel revised its orientation program and experienced significant decreases in turnover and increases in employees mastering their jobs.[23]

Technical training programs are designed to provide nonmanagerial employees with specialized skills and knowledge in the methods, processes, and techniques associated with their job or trade. In union settings, apprenticeship training programs are common for skilled occupations. With advances in training technology, many organizations are using computer-assisted instruction and interactive video training for their nonmanagerial employees. However, approximately 90 percent of technical training programs still use on-the-job training methods.[24]

On-the-job training is conducted while employees perform job-related tasks. This type of training is the most direct approach and offers employers the quickest return in terms of improved performance. This emphasis on training may be driven by the entrepreneurial spirit of a company's CEO, as you will see in Entrepreneurial Approach as you read about Israel's high-tech pioneer, Uzia Galil. Galil places a very high priority on recruiting the best candidates and then training individuals in ways that he feels are appropriate to bring out their entrepreneurship behaviors.

Management development programs are designed to improve the technical, interpersonal, and conceptual skills of supervisors, managers, and executives. On-the-job training for managers might include rotating through a variety of positions, regular coaching and mentoring by a supervisor, committee assignments to involve individuals in decision-making activities, and staff meetings to help managers become acquainted with the thinking of other managers and with activities outside their immediate area. Most of these on-the-job training methods are used to help managers broaden their organizational knowledge and experience. Some popular off-the-job training techniques include classroom training, simulations, role playing, and case discussion groups.

Training and Quality Management

Organizations that implement aggressive quality-improvement programs often find that additional training and employee development are essential to the success of the program. Through quality-oriented training programs, organizations

Orientation
The process of familiarizing new employees with the organization, their job, and their work unit, which enables them to become productive members of the organization.

Entrepreneurial Approach

HIGH-TECH PIONEER FINDS SUCCESS IN RECRUITING ONLY HIGH-ENERGY INDIVIDUALS

Israel has always been known for being an agrarian, inward-looking society. Now it is a hotbed of high-technology entrepreneurship, thanks to the inspiration of Uzia Galil and his transformational leadership. How did Uzia Galil build a $1.2 billion empire?

After spending many years studying in the United States and witnessing the continuous flow of information between universities and business, Galil saw the opportunities for Israel to be a leader. In the United States, the inspiration for new ideas and the creation of technology came from creative and risk-taking individuals and the entrepreneurial styles they had. The opposite was true in Israel, where Galil found no value placed on entrepreneurship.

Galil was determined to build a high-tech industry and boost the country's economy by transferring the model from the United States to Israel. This meant not only securing funding for young companies, but also recruiting individuals who possessed the energy and spirit of adventure that an entrepreneur needs to be successful.

Galil considers himself a builder and has taken many small entrepreneurial teams and incubated them in-house. He's trained and coached would-be entrepreneurs until they have developed the skills necessary to create and secure a company and turn a profit.

The 71-year-old entrepreneur recruits high-energy individuals like himself to lead companies. Israel's high-tech pioneer has built a $1.2 billion empire by nurturing young companies and young people. According to Galil, "It all depends on the people."

SOURCE: T. Stein, K. Callan, D. Menaker, and C. Brown-Humes, "The World's Greatest Entrepreneurs," *Success,* June 1996, 35–46.

---

ensure that employees know the quality goals of the organization, understand how their jobs relate to achieving those goals, and possess the skills and abilities necessary to contribute effectively.

In the search for quality over quantity, many companies are finding that they must modify their training techniques. Companies in the service industry, such as Fed Ex, Bell Canada, USAA, and Northwest Airlines, have found that some types of training actually hinder customer service and increase employee stress and job dissatisfaction as well.[25]

In developing training programs to support a quality orientation in the organization, HRM professionals must be aware of the economic, social, and political forces that have implications for training.[26] For example:

- Increased global and domestic competition has led to greater need for competitive strategies that often require extensive training.
- Rapid advances in technology have created an acute need for people with specialized technical skills.
- Widespread mergers, acquisitions, and divestitures have created a need to redesign many jobs. As a result, new training programs and reward systems may be necessary.
- A better-educated work force that values self-development and personal growth has an enormous desire for learning and a growing need for new forms of participation at work.
- As some occupations become obsolete and new occupations emerge due to the changing nature of the business environment, flexible training policies are needed to prevent increased turnover and lower productivity.

PERFORMANCE APPRAISAL

After employees have been trained and have settled into their jobs, managers usually begin to evaluate their performance. **Performance appraisal** is a systematic process of evaluating each employee's job-related achievements, strengths, and weaknesses, as well as determining ways to improve performance.

Performance is almost never one dimensional—there are always several dimensions to job performance. For example, the leading home-run hitter on a baseball team may not be the best fielder or have the highest batting average. Consider that students evaluate university professors on one dimension of their performance—teaching. But, for most professors, their job has at least two other important dimensions—research and professional service.

Performance appraisals are invaluable aids in making many HRM decisions and are essential for distinguishing between good and poor performers. Managers can use performance appraisal information in four ways:

1. *Motivation.* Organizations try to motivate employees by basing pay, bonuses, and other financial rewards on performance. Since performance is frequently a basis for rewards, it is important to evaluate performance so that those rewards can be provided fairly and serve as a motivator for future performance. Merit-pay plans, for example, are designed to compensate people according to their job performance.

2. *Personnel movement.* Performance appraisal information helps managers develop an inventory of people appropriate for personnel movement. In other words, performance appraisals can be used to determine who should receive a promotion, transfer, or demotion, and who should be dismissed.

3. *Training.* By identifying areas of poor performance, performance appraisals help the manager suggest training or other programs to improve certain skills or behaviors.

4. *Feedback.* Performance appraisals provide a mechanism for giving employees feedback about their work performance. If employees are to do their jobs better in the future, they need to know how well they have done them in the past so that they can adjust their work patterns as necessary.

Rating Performance

Effective performance appraisals usually consider various dimensions of a job. A variety of methods are available, but the most widely used approaches evaluate either behaviors or performance results.[27]

Behavior-Oriented Approaches   Behavior-oriented approaches to performance appraisal focus on assessing employee behavior. Two commonly used methods are graphic rating scales and behavioral-anchored rating scales.

When graphic rating scales are used to assess performance, employees are evaluated on a series of performance dimensions, such as initiative, tardiness, and accuracy of work, using a five- or seven-point scale. For example, a typical rating scale ranges from 1 to 5, with 1 representing poor performance and 5 representing outstanding performance. The rater evaluates the employee on each performance dimension by checking the appropriate place on the scale.

Performance dimensions on a graphic rating scale tend to be fairly general, and as a result the scales are relatively flexible and can be used to evaluate individuals in a number of different jobs. But because the graphic rating scale is general, considerable interpretation is needed to apply it to specific jobs. As a result, the scale sometimes produces inconsistent and inaccurate ratings of employees. In general, the more clearly and specifically the scales and performance dimensions are defined, the more effective the evaluation system.

Performance appraisal
A systematic process of evaluating employee job-related achievements, strengths, and weaknesses, as well as determining ways to improve performance.

To define various aspects of an employee's job more clearly, some organizations use behavioral-anchored rating scales (BARSs). BARSs are similar to graphic rating scales, but use more detailed examples of job behaviors to represent different levels of performance. The BARS approach relies on job analysis information to describe a range of desirable and undesirable behaviors for each performance dimension. Each of these behavioral descriptors is used as an anchor to distinguish between high, moderate, and low performance. Using BARS reduces subjective interpretation of performance because they are based on clearly stated job-related activities. They are costly to construct, however, and both subordinates and supervisors require training in their use.[28]

Results-Oriented Approach   An alternative to the behavior-oriented approaches to performance appraisal is a results-oriented method. One of the most common results-oriented performance appraisal systems is management by objectives (MBO). As you will recall from Chapter 4, MBO is a system of guided self-appraisal that is useful in evaluating an employee's performance. Through the MBO process, specific goals are set for individual members of the organization. Employees are evaluated on the basis of how well they have achieved the results specified by their goals.

Because results-oriented approaches to performance appraisal use objective performance criteria, there is less bias in the evaluation process. Such approaches are not very useful for training purposes, however, because they provide little information that can be used to improve performance. Results can also be contaminated by factors beyond the employee's control. Equipment breakdowns, economic changes, and the availability and quality of supplies are just a few of the factors that can affect performance. When using this approach, organizations must also guard against encouraging a "results at any cost" mentality among their employees.

Problems with Performance Appraisal

While we would like to believe that every manager carefully assesses each employee's performance, most people who have given or received a performance appraisal are aware of the subjective nature of the process. This subjectivity can lead to the following common problems.

Halo Effect   The *halo effect* occurs when a manager rates an employee high or low on all items because of one characteristic. For example, a worker who has few absences might receive high ratings in all other areas of work, including quantity and quality of output. The manager may not really think about the employee's other characteristics separately. While an employee may perform at the same level across all dimensions, most people do some things better than others. Thus, the ratings should differ from one dimension to another.

Rater Patterns   Students are well aware that some professors tend to grade easier or harder than others. Likewise, a manager may develop a rating pattern. For example, some managers have a problem with central tendency. *Central tendency* occurs when the rater judges all employees as average, even though their performance varies. Managers with wide spans of control and, thus, many subordinates may have less opportunity to observe the behavior of individual employees. Such managers are more likely to play it safe and rate most of them in the middle of the scale rather than high or low.

Another common rater pattern is the leniency-severity error. A *leniency error* occurs when the rater evaluates some in a group higher than they should be or when the rater is unjustifiably easy in evaluating performance. In contrast, a *severity error* occurs when a rater tends to be unjustifiably harsh in evaluating employee performance.

Contrast Error A *contrast error* is the tendency to rate employees relative to each other rather than to performance standards. If almost everyone in a group is doing a mediocre job, then a person performing somewhat better may be rated as excellent because of the contrast effect. But, in a higher-performing group, the same person might have received only an average rating. Although it may be appropriate to compare people at times, performance appraisal ratings should evaluate performance against job requirements rather than against other employees.

There is no simple way to eliminate the problems associated with performance appraisal. However, making raters aware of the potential problems through training programs is beneficial in overcoming the errors and the problems that result.

COMPENSATION

Compensation consists of wages paid directly for time worked, incentives for better performance, and indirect benefits that employees receive as part of their employment relationship with the organization. Together, these elements make up the compensation that employees receive for the work they do for the organization.

Direct Compensation: Base Pay and Incentives
Base pay refers to wages and salaries employees receive in exchange for performing their jobs. Base pay rates are determined by economic forces in the labor market, by competitor wages, and, in unionized firms, by negotiation. In most noncommission jobs, base pay represents the majority of the compensation an employee receives.

To attract, retain, and motivate employees, however, many organizations offer compensation beyond base pay in the form of *incentives* such as bonuses, commissions, and profit-sharing plans. These incentives are designed to encourage employees to produce results beyond expected performance norms. Today, in an effort to improve the quality of products and services, many organizations are experimenting with various incentive plans to reward employees who contribute toward meeting the quality goals of the organization.

An example of a particularly creative approach to improving service quality can be found at E.T.C. Carpet Mills in Santa Ana, California. This company has successfully used incentives to encourage its employees to provide better customer service. Since customers often had to wait more than an hour for an order at competing firms, E.T.C. established a goal of ten-minutes-or-less waiting period for customers. When an order is finished within ten minutes, the company puts $1 into a bonus fund. Every three months the balance of the fund is divided evenly among the company's ten employees. As a result, employees often receive bonuses of $600 each, and the company has developed a reputation for superior customer service.[29]

Indirect Compensation: Benefits
Benefits, a more indirect type of compensation, are payments beyond wages or salaries that are given to employees as a reward for organizational membership. Benefits can be categorized into several types: required and voluntary security, retirement, time-off, insurance and financial, and social and recreational. Examples of the benefits an organization can provide are listed in Table 10.5.[30]

Organizations commonly provide health, dental, disability, and life insurance coverage for employees and sometimes for their families. The costs of these plans may be paid entirely by the company or shared with the employee.

Compensation
Wages paid directly for time worked (base pay), incentives for better performance, and indirect benefits that employees receive as part of their employment relationship with the organization.

TABLE 10.5   Examples of different benefits by category

REQUIRED SECURITY	VOLUNTARY SECURITY	RETIREMENT	TIME-OFF	INSURANCE	FINANCIAL	SOCIAL AND RECREATIONAL
• Worker's compensation • Unemployment compensation • Old age, survivors', and disability insurance • State disability insurance • Medicare hospital benefits	• Severance pay • Supplemental unemployment benefits • Leave of absence	• Social Security • Pension fund • Early retirement • Preretirement counseling • Retirement gratuity • Retirement annuity • Disability retirement benefits	• Vacation time • Company-subsidized travel • Holidays • Sick pay • Military reserve pay • Social-service sabbatical	• Medical • Dental • Travel accident insurance • Group insurance rates • Disability insurance • Life insurance • Auto insurance	• Credit union • Profit sharing • Company-provided housing or car • Legal services • Purchase discounts • Stock plans • Financial counseling • Moving expenses • Tuition assistance/reimbursement • Relocation planning and assistance	• Recreational facilities • Company publications • Professional memberships • Counseling • Company-sponsored events • Child-care services • Food services • Wellness and health services/facilities • Service awards

Also, employees usually receive some pay for time that they don't work, such as vacations, sick days, and holidays. Retirement programs are also a common benefit.

Some companies even provide benefits such as counseling, wellness programs, credit unions, legal advice, and tuition reimbursement for educational expenses. For example, RJR Nabisco pays for the educational expenses of its employees. It has committed $5 million annually to help employees and their children attend college or job-training programs. The company offers a wide range of financial assistance for high school graduates, including scholarships to college, trade, or vocational schools. While RJR Nabisco can't pay the full college bill, the company's goal is to ensure that nobody is denied a postsecondary education for financial reasons. This focus on education is part of a benefits package that includes giving workers time off for parent-teacher conferences and even for a child's first day of school.[31] Herman Miller, Inc., the world's second-largest manufacturer of office furniture, developed an unusual benefit called the silver parachute. Managing for Excellence highlights this novel approach to protecting all 35,000 of the company's employees in the event of a hostile takeover.

A benefit package can represent a significant cost to an organization. In a recent survey of major U.S. manufacturing firms, benefits represented an average of 37.7 percent of the organizational payroll.[32] Although benefits represent a major cost to an organization, they are also a key factor in attracting and retaining employees.

Compensation programs reflect the overall culture, life-cycle stages, and strategic plans of the organization.[33] As shown in Table 10.6, for example, the compensation practices appropriate for a newly formed organization may be different than for a more mature organization.[34] For example, to encourage innovation, flexibility, and an entrepreneurial culture, a new organization might

HERMAN MILLER'S SILVER PARACHUTES

Herman Miller, Inc., the world's second-largest manufacturer of office furniture, developed a novel approach to severance pay called a "silver parachute." Unlike the "golden parachute" offered only to senior executives at firms likely to be targets of a takeover, the silver parachute extends to all 35,000 of the company's employees. The parachute would be activated in the event of a hostile takeover, and the ripcord would be pulled if a worker's job were eliminated, his salary reduced, or working conditions or benefits altered.

This unusual form of severance pay would be paid within ten days of termination. Those employees with between one and five years of service would receive twice their previous twelve-month compensation. Longer-service employees would receive two and one-half times their salary for the previous twelve months. Besides assuring employees of severance pay should they lose their jobs in a hostile takeover, this benefit makes the company a less attractive takeover target. If the silver parachute is not activated, it has no cost to the company.

Managing for
Excellence

offer stock-equity programs to encourage employees to participate in the growth and success of the company. In contrast, highly structured pay and benefit programs may be more appropriate for a large, stable organization.[35]

Designing Equitable Reward Systems

Most organizations attempt to develop a compensation system that carefully considers issues of equity or fairness. Compensation is often the prime reason an individual works. However, compensation usually has several meanings to employees. Compensation has economic meaning because it allows people to obtain the necessities and luxuries they need and want; compensation is symbolic because it is a means of "keeping score" and a measure of achievement; and an increase in compensation indicates growth because it reflects how well employees' performance and capabilities have grown.

In practice, developing an equitable or fair compensation system is quite challenging, primarily because most organizations have very complex compensation systems. Equity theory, discussed in Chapter 15, is the basis for designing fair pay plans. Compensation designers are concerned with three sources of fairness expectations: (1) external fairness, (2) internal fairness, and (3) employee fairness.[36] *External fairness* refers to expectations that the pay

TABLE 10.6   Matching compensation and organizational life cycles

COMPENSATION	ORGANIZATIONAL LIFE-CYCLE STAGE			
	INTRODUCTORY	GROWTH	MATURITY	DECLINE
Pay	Competitive, but conservative wages/salaries	Moderate wages/salaries	Above-market wages/salaries	High wages/salaries with pressure for reductions
Incentives	Stock-equity possibilties	Bonuses tied to objective; stock options	Bonuses, incentive plans, stock options	Reduced bonuses, cost-saving incentive plans
Benefits	Core benefits	Complete benefits at moderate level; limited executive perks	Comprehensive benefits; expanded executive perks	Cost-consciousness limits benefit costs; frozen executive perks

for a job in one organization is fair relative to the pay for the same job in other organizations. Wage surveys are used to compare the organization's pay rates with other organizations in the industry to ensure that the pay remains competitive. *Internal fairness* refers to expectations that the pay for the job the individual is performing within the organization is fair relative to the pay of higher- and lower-level jobs in the same organization. Job evaluation procedures use job specifications to determine the relative worth of jobs in the organization. *Employee fairness* refers to expectations that individuals on a given job are paid fairly relative to co-workers on the same job. Differences in pay among co-workers are acceptable if the variations are based on differences in performance or seniority. Because compensation can be so complex, many organizations have compensation specialists in the human resource department who develop, administer, and oversee the compensation system. They ensure that the organization provides compensation that is both competitive and equitable.

In many organizations, the human resource planning process that we have been examining is affected by labor-management relations. In the next part of the chapter, we examine the role of unions and the strategies organizations use in dealing with them.

LABOR-MANAGEMENT RELATIONS

Labor-management relations
The formal process through which employees and unions negotiate terms and conditions of employment including pay, hours of work, benefits, and other important aspects of the working environment.

The term **labor-management relations** refers to the formal process through which employees and unions negotiate terms and conditions of employment, including pay, hours of work, benefits, and other important aspects of the working environment. Unions are employee groups formed for the purpose of negotiating with management regarding the terms and conditions related to their work. Unions represent workers and seek to protect and promote their members' political, social, and economic interests through collective bargaining.

Given the turbulent history of labor-management relations, it should come as no surprise that the process of forming a union is closely regulated by the government. The National Labor Relations Board (NLRB) is the government agency that oversees this process in the private sector. It enforces the provisions of the Wagner Act of 1935 and the Taft-Hartley Act of 1947 (an amendment to the Wagner Act), two major laws governing labor-management relations. When recognized by the NLRB, unions have the legal right to negotiate with private employers over terms and conditions of employment and to help administer the resulting contract.

Unions have political power and use their lobbying efforts to support legislation that is in their own interests and the interests of all employees. They can also provide workers with an opportunity to participate in determining the conditions under which they work.

Management can pursue several different strategies in dealing with organized labor. With a conflict orientation, management refuses to "give in" to labor and recognizes the union only because it is required to do so by law.[37] This approach was exemplified by Frank Lorenzo's use of hardball tactics to cut labor costs at two airlines, Continental and Eastern. We can attribute the demise of both airlines and Lorenzo (personal bankruptcy and loss of credibility) as a result of many of these tactics. Although Continental Airlines did eventually reorganize, it has not accepted unionization. Other organizations use a more cooperative approach commonly associated with Japanese-style management practices. Each party recognizes that the other party is necessary for attaining their respective goals. Recognition of shared interests has led to labor-management relationships characterized by mutual trust and friendly attitudes.[38] Chrysler Corporation, Ford Motor Company, Cummins Engine Company, Bridgestone/Firestone, Inc., and others have established cooperative relations with unions in the hope that teamwork will boost productivity and quality and hold down costs.[39]

In general, management prefers that employees do not belong to unions. Why then do employees join unions? Unionization is attractive to employees who believe that employment conditions are deteriorating, and that as individuals they have little power to change those conditions.[40] Studies have shown that workers who are dissatisfied with various aspects of the workplace, such as wages, job security, benefits, unfair treatment, and workplace governance, are more likely to join a union if they believe that the union will be effective in remedying the situation.[41]

What is the future outlook for unions? Union membership has declined in the last decade for several reasons. One reason for this trend is that effective HRM in organizations has reduced the need for union protection. Other reasons include a decrease in union-organizing attempts, a decline in traditionally unionized industries, a decline in the economic well-being of companies (making it more difficult for unions to pressure for better wages and benefits), and effective management opposition to unions.

INFORMATION TECHNOLOGY INFLUENCES ON HUMAN RESOURCES

In our increasingly complex world, human resource managers will be required to function within the context of an incredible rate of change, coming in part from the overwhelming amount of information and technological advances headed their way.[42] As a functional area of an organization, HRM plays a key role in the flow of the physical resources throughout the firm. The rapidly expanding application and use of information technology has influenced HRM by providing access to current environmental elements and quality information resources. In turn, this information helps managers identify problems and understand them so that they can be solved.

Information technology has had a considerable impact on how HRM gathers, tracks, applies, distributes, and responds to data affecting the flow and utilization of personnel in organization. **Human resource information systems (HRISs)** make it possible to track and monitor economic forecasts, competitors, and legislation that influences long-range personnel planning; to produce models for salary forecasting, job analysis and evaluation, recruiting, employee training, and annual appraisal of employee performance; to provide benefits to current and retired employees; and to report EEO policies and practices, grievance records, and affirmative action to the government.

Other important influences of information technology on HRM are the availability of user-friendly software programs, especially databases, that are easily adapted to track employees and provide current profiles of employees.[43] Many companies now advertise and recruit using Web sites or have developed videoconferencing facilities on site. Korn/Ferry International, an executive recruiting firm, recently used videoconferencing to find a public relations director for the Hong Kong and Tokyo offices of a U.S. corporation. Additionally, training programs have proliferated as technology becomes less expensive and easier to use. For example, videoconferencing is used at United Technologies and Hewlett-Packard for engineers to participate in long-distance learning programs, such as accredited graduate-level engineering courses at various universities around the United States.

Human resource information systems (HRISs)
Used to track and monitor economic, legislative, and competitive changes and to support and provide organized information to solve complex HR problems.

CURRENT ISSUES IN HUMAN RESOURCE MANAGEMENT

We conclude our examination of HRM by discussing several current issues facing today's managers. These include HRM in the multinational corporation, work-force diversity, sexual harassment, and health concerns in the work environment.

HRM IN THE MULTINATIONAL CORPORATION

Effective management of human resources is of critical importance to multinational corporations that compete in the global marketplace. Multinational organizations face greater diversity in both their labor and managerial work force and, as a result, must develop an HRM system that is flexible and adaptable to a wide variety of cultural situations. As a result, the job of the HRM manager in a multinational organization is far more complex than that of his or her domestic counterpart.

Perhaps one of the most significant challenges associated with the HRM process in multinational organizations lies in managing expatriate personnel. An expatriate is an organizational member who is a citizen of the country in which the multinational is headquartered, but is assigned to a position in one of the company's foreign operating facilities. For example, if a French firm sends a French manager to oversee its plant in Australia, it has chosen to use an expatriate in that position.

Managing expatriates presents some unique challenges for human resource professionals in terms of selection, training, and compensation.[44] For example, expatriates must be selected based on a broader set of characteristics than domestic personnel. Situational factors such as stage of career development and family commitments become more important, as do personal characteristics such as flexibility, cultural empathy, and maturity.[45] Further, the training process is more complex for expatriate managers.[46] Language and cross-cultural training for both the expatriate and his or her family is essential. An expatriate's compensation package is also more complex than a domestic manager's compensation package. In addition to the traditional base salary, incentives, and benefits, expatriates may receive a cost-of-living adjustment, an overseas premium to compensate for the hardship of living in a foreign environment, and other perquisites such as membership in social clubs, transportation allowances, and home-leave expenses to make the overseas assignment more attractive.

Historically, many multinationals have experienced disappointing results from managers sent on overseas assignments. In general, U.S. multinationals have achieved much less success with expatriates than have most Japanese and many European firms.[47] The disappointing results of U.S.-based firms has been attributed, in large part, to ineffective HRM practices in many U.S. firms; but all indications are that American organizations are improving their international HRM systems tremendously.[48] It is clear that multinationals that employ careful selection procedures, require and administer effective training programs, and offer compensation packages that reward and motivate the expatriate will achieve greater success in the global environ-

Because of the greater diversity in both their labor and managerial work force, multinational organizations must develop an HRM system that is flexible and adaptable to a wide variety of cultural situations.
© Michael Newman/PhotoEdit

TRAINING MANAGERS IN JAPAN

The Japanese manager experiences a very different training protocol than the manager trained in the United States. Not only do the formal training programs differ, but we can also examine the variations in career paths, career breadth versus depth, formality, and age at which managers are considered "seasoned."

In Japan, the lack of formal business school training necessitates management training done on the job. Most junior levels of management start for individuals ten years after school, when they are 32 to 34 years old. Therefore, their 20s are spent learning the company by doing routine jobs, rotating to three or four different divisions.

Once Japanese managers do reach the bottom rung of the managerial ladder, they find themselves subjected to even more rigorous on-the-job training, supplemented by both in-house and external courses. Formal assessments take place as often as three times a year. Job rotation in Japan's big multinational companies tends to become more international at this stage in a manager's career. Managers' job descriptions are left vague. The Japanese feel that this allows trainees to broaden their responsibilities. Great emphasis is placed on group learning, which the Japanese feel produces organizational knowledge creation. Or, according to the Japanese, by sharing knowledge, the whole company learns.

In recent years, an increasing number of Japanese students have been applying for MBAs and executive courses in the United States. In addition, there is a growing number of Western-style business schools in Japan. Experts feel that the reason for this is that Japan will have a need for more entrepreneur-type managers to take Japanese firms into the next century, and that Western business schools can help them fill this need.

SOURCES: T. Stein, K. Callan, D. Menaker, and C. Brown-Humes, "The World's Greatest Entrepreneurs," *Success*, June 1996. 35–46; "Where East Meets West: Making Managers the Japanese Way," *The Economist*, March 2, 1993, 22–24.

Global Perspective

ment of today and tomorrow. Are there some lessons to be learned from the methods that Japanese firms use to train their managers? The Global Perspective points out some of the differences between U.S. and Japanese management training.[49]

WORK-FORCE DIVERSITY

The changing nature of the work force represents a challenge for many organizations. For example, the influx of women and minorities is having a tremendous impact on the workplace. Women accounted for 60 percent of the total growth of the U.S. work force between 1970 and 1985, and they are expected to make up a similar percentage of new entry-level employees between 1991 and 2000. Many of these women have children. In fact, one of the fastest-growing segments of the labor market is mothers with infants.[50] In addition, it is projected that a third of the newcomers into the work force between 1996 and the year 2000 will be minority-group members.[51]

Demographic changes in the work force have forced organizations to introduce new HRM programs and adapt existing programs and policies. For example, today's managers must be prepared to interact with people of different cultures as superiors, peers, and subordinates. Consequently, many organizations are developing training programs to enhance their managers' knowledge and awareness of cultural differences. Other organizations have found it necessary to offer language training to employees for whom English is a second language. Flexible work schedules and telecommuting are often used to accommodate the needs of mothers with infants, and maternity leave and child-care assistance programs are offered in more organizations.

Increases in the number of highly capable women and minorities in the work force have created a need for many organizations to review their promotion and compensation policies. Corporate America has been accused of maintaining attitudes and prejudices that have created a "glass ceiling" denying women access to managerial and executive positions.[52] As a result, women continue to occupy jobs that pay less than male-dominated jobs.

The increasing number of women has also forced organizations to examine work-family issues. In a recent poll of 500 companies, pay, advancement opportunities for women, child care, flexible hours and benefits, and resources provided for adoption aid and elder care were examined. The companies that ranked in the top ten as great places for women to work were (listed alphabetically):

1. Barnett Banks Inc., Jacksonville, Florida
2. Eli Lilly & Co., Indianapolis, Indiana
3. Hewlett-Packard Co., Palo Alto, California
4. IBM Corp., Armonk, New York, New York
5. Johnson & Johnson, New Brunswick, New Jersey
6. MBNAAmerican Bank, Wilmington, Delaware
7. Merck & Co., Whitehouse Station, New Jersey
8. National Bank Corp., Charlotte, North Carolina
9. Patagonia Inc., Ventura, California
10. Xerox Corp., Stamford, Connecticut

The historical earnings gap between men and women has led to calls for comparable-worth legislation. *Comparable worth* is the concept that people in jobs requiring comparable levels of knowledge, skills, and abilities should be paid similarly even if the job tasks and market rates are significantly different. To date, only a few states and local municipalities have passed laws mandating equal pay for comparable worth in public-sector jobs.[53] Although comparable-worth legislation affecting private employers is unlikely, organizations must continue to monitor the status of women and minorities and proactively work to remove the vestiges of non-job-related biases.

Throughout this textbook we have presented examples of organizations that are adapting to these changes successfully. Avon, Corning, Monsanto, IBM, and Du Pont are just a few of the organizations that have recognized the trend toward a more diverse work force and have developed plans for managing that diversity effectively.

SEXUAL HARASSMENT

Sexual harassment
Actions that are sexually directed, are unwanted, and subject a worker to adverse employment conditions.

Sexual harassment refers to actions that are sexually directed, are unwanted, and subject the worker to adverse employment conditions.[54] The Supreme Court and the EEOC recognize two major forms of sexual harassment.[55]

The first is *"quid pro quo"* harassment, in which sexual compliance is required for job-related benefits and opportunities such as pay and promotions.

TABLE 10.7   EEOC guideline suggestions for preventing sexual harassment

- Establish a policy on sexual harassment and distribute a copy of the policy to all employees. Such policies make a major contribution to the prevention and control of sexual harassment.
- Develop mechanisms for investigating complaints. The organization needs a system for complaints that ensures that they are satisfactorily investigated and acted upon. This will also deter fear of retaliation.
- Develop mechanisms for handling the accused so that they are assured of a fair and thorough investigation that protects their individual rights.
- Communicate to all employees, especially to supervisors and managers, concerns and regulations regarding sexual harassment and the importance of creating and maintaining a work environment free of sexual harassment.
- Discipline offenders by using organizational sanctions up to and including firing the offenders.
- Train all employees, especially supervisors and managers, about what constitutes sexual harassment, and alert employees to the issues and behaviors involved.

Harassment by supervisors and managers who expect sexual favors as a condition for a raise or promotion is inappropriate and unacceptable behavior in the work environment. The second form of sexual harassment has been termed "hostile environment" harassment. In this case, the victim does not suffer any tangible economic injury, but workplace conduct is sufficiently severe to create an abusive working environment. A pattern of lewd jokes and comments in one instance and sexually oriented graffiti and posters in another have been viewed by the courts as sexual harassment.[56]

Sexual harassment can occur between a manager and a subordinate, among co-workers, and among people outside the organization who have business contacts with employees. The vast majority of situations involve harassment of women by men. As a result of losing suits and appeals, companies are becoming more conscious of sexual harassment and are doing more to protect the rights of women. Training sessions, booklets, guidelines, and company policies regarding acceptable workplace behavior are some of the proactive methods for discouraging sexual harassment.[57] Some actions suggested by the EEOC guidelines are listed in Table 10.7.

HEALTH CONCERNS IN THE WORK ENVIRONMENT

Employee health problems are inevitable in any organization. These problems can range from simple illness, such as colds, to far more serious health problems. Some employees have emotional problems; others have drinking or drug problems; still others may have chronic illnesses that cause excessive absenteeism. All these difficulties may significantly affect the ability of employees to fulfill their job responsibilities. Many organizations are taking a proactive role to assist employees in dealing with these issues. Some of the more popular approaches are employee assistance programs and wellness programs.

Employee assistance programs (EAPs) are designed to help employees cope with physical, personal, and emotional problems. These problems may include substance abuse, alcoholism, stress, emotional illness, and family disturbances. In such programs, employers establish a liaison with a social service counseling agency. Employees who have problems may contact the agency voluntarily or by employer referral. The employer pays the counseling costs up to a predetermined limit.

Employee assistance programs (EAPs)
Designed to help employees cope with physical, personal, and emotional problems including substance abuse, alcoholism, stress, emotional illness, and family disturbances.

The growing interest in EAPs is due, in part, to an increase in the incidence of physical and emotional problems in the working population. In the long run, EAPs can save a company money. For example, alcoholism costs corporate America an estimated $86 billion a year due to employee health problems and poor performance. The expense of helping an alcoholic recover through an EAP is a fraction of the long-term potential cost.[58]

Unlike EAPs, which deal with problems after they have occurred, wellness programs are designed to maintain or improve employee health before problems arise. *Wellness programs* are activities that organizations engage in to promote good health habits, identify and correct health problems, direct lifestyle changes, and/or encourage a healthy work environment.

According to the Centers for Disease Control in Atlanta, Georgia, more than half of all deaths in the United States are directly related to lifestyle. Companies overwhelmed with medical costs are spending millions on wellness programs, an extremely popular addition to an organization's benefit program. These programs are a viable option when an employer desires to improve productivity, decrease absenteeism, and lower health-care costs. Estimates are that more than 50,000 U.S. firms provide some type of company-sponsored health promotion program.

U-Haul, Control Data, Southern California Edison, Adolph Coors, and Baker Hughes are companies that emphasize wellness by providing their employees with financial incentives to meet certain "wellness" criteria, such as not smoking and maintaining a normal weight. These incentives can be in the form of lower employee health insurance premiums or higher benefits. For example, Baker Hughes saves $2 million annually because nonsmoking employees are charged less for health insurance. Adolph Coors saves $3.2 million by offering its employees incentives to meet weight, smoking, blood pressure, cholesterol, and other health criteria.[59]

MANAGERIAL IMPLICATIONS

In this chapter you were introduced to the role of human resource management in today's organizations. As a manager, you will be called upon to make human resource decisions; therefore, it is important to remember the following points:

- Recognize that human resource planning is a critical element of the strategic planning process and is essential for long-term organizational success.
- Base all HRM decisions on job-related criteria and not on racial, gender-based, or other unjustified biases.
- Remember that job analysis is essential to effective human resource planning and the development of programs that satisfy the organization's human resource requirements.
- Carefully evaluate both internal and external sources of recruitment.
- Be innovative in scheduling work, designing jobs, and rewarding employees so that you can respond effectively to the changing composition and needs of the work force.
- To keep pace with rapid changes in technology, be sure to upgrade the knowledge and skill base of employees through training programs.
- Develop equitable pay systems, unbiased performance appraisals, and equal access to training opportunities, to avoid unionization.
- Take advantage of the increasing use of information technology to provide accurate and current information on the changing work force.

Many corporate public relations documents refer to people as "the most valuable resource" of the organization.[60] These organizations realize that human resources must be well managed to succeed in the business environment of today and tomorrow. A well-developed human resource management system results in a more productive work force, higher morale and job satisfaction, and a reputation for being a great place to work.

CORNING: IT SIMPLY MAKES GOOD BUSINESS SENSE

To break the cycle of high attrition rates for minorities and women, Corning established a human resource plan and goals that involved more than producing excellent products. First, the plan organized two quality-improvement teams headed by senior executives; one targeted black employees and the other targeted female employees. New selection and recruitment programs were developed, and Corning established a nationwide scholarship program that provided renewable grants in exchange for a summer of paid work at a Corning installation. The majority of program participants have come to work for Corning full-time after graduation, and very few have left the company so far. The company also expanded its summer intern program, with an emphasis on minorities and women, and established formal recruiting contacts with campus groups such as the Society of Women Engineers and the National Black MBA Association.

Corning also wanted to create a high-quality work environment for employees. Part of its plan included mandatory awareness training for some 76,000 salaried employees. One goal of the training was to identify unconscious company values that work against minorities and women. Corning made an effort to improve communications by printing regular stories and articles about the diverse work force in its in-house newspaper and by publicizing employee success stories that emphasized diversity. It worked hard to identify and publicize promotion criteria. Career planning systems were introduced for all employees.

At Corning, corporate staff is being cut; layers of management are being eliminated, and the number of employees is decreasing. What is left is a leaner and trimmer organization staffed by a more diverse group of employees who share power as they go about their daily tasks. All of these changes focused on the proper utilization of human resources. In the words of CEO James Houghton, "it simply makes good business sense."[61]

> **Managerial Incident Resolution**

SUMMARY

- A substantial amount of legislation deals with various forms of employee rights, including protection against discrimination, equal employment opportunity, and affirmative-action programs. These laws prohibit discrimination on the basis of gender, race, color, religion, or national origin in all areas of employment.

- Human resource planning is the process of determining future human resource needs relative to an organization's strategic plan and devising the steps necessary to meet those needs. It includes job analysis, forecasting, staffing, training, performance appraisal, and rewarding.

- During the process of selection, managers must determine the extent to which job candidates have the skills, abilities, and knowledge required to perform effectively in the positions for which they are being considered. The major selection methods—application forms, employment tests, interviews, and assessment centers—must be job related and have no discriminatory effects.

- Training is a planned effort to facilitate employee learning of job-related behaviors in order to improve performance. Organizations train new employees to help achieve the organization's objectives and help employees develop their skills, knowledge, and abilities.

- Performance appraisal is a systematic process of evaluating each employee's job-related achievements, strengths, and weaknesses, as well as determining ways to improve performance.

- Employees are rewarded with compensation, such as pay, incentives, and benefits. Most organizations attempt to develop a compensation system that carefully considers issues of equity or fairness.

- The term *labor-management relations* refers to the formal process through which employees and unions negotiate conditions of employment. Numerous government regulations define and regulate labor-management relations.

- The rapidly expanding application and use of information technology has influenced HRM by providing access to current environmental elements and quality information resources. These systems provide accurate and timely information that helps managers identify problems and understand them so that they can be solved. Additionally, information technology has influenced recruiting strategies and training programs.

- Some of the current issues facing today's managers include HRM in the multinational corporation, workforce diversity, sexual harassment, and health concerns in the work environment.

KEY TERMS

Human resource management
   (HRM)
Protected class
Human resource planning
Job analysis
Job description
Job specifications
Staffing

Recruitment
Selection
Employment test
Assessment center
Validity
Training
Orientation
Performance appraisal

Compensation
Labor-management relations
Human resource information
   systems (HRISs)
Sexual harassment
Employee assistance programs
   (EAPs)

REVIEW QUESTIONS

1. Describe the steps in the human resource planning process.
2. Distinguish between supply and demand forecasting.
3. Describe the different recruiting techniques used by organizations.
4. What are the different methods organizations use to select employees?
5. Distinguish between behavior- and results-oriented performance appraisal methods.
6. Explain ways in which interviewing can be improved.

7. What are some of the common problems inherent in performance appraisals?
8. When is it appropriate to use MBO?
9. Discuss the three key laws that address discrimination in employment.
10. Explain the various ways that managers can use performance appraisal information.
11. Discuss the ways that training has been affected by the use of information technology.
12. What are some of the current HRM issues facing managers in organizations today?

DISCUSSION QUESTIONS

Improving Critical Thinking

1. Evaluate the reward system of an organization with which you are familiar in terms of how equitable it is.
2. Look for a current article in a newspaper or magazine that describes sexual harassment. Why is this a problem for managers?
3. Describe an orientation program that you have attended. What suggestions would you make to improve the program?

4. Discuss why union membership is declining. Would you be interested in joining a union? Why or why not?

Enhancing Communication Skills

5. Write a report that describes an interview that you have had. Was it structured or unstructured? What was your impression of the interviewer? Of the organization? What could have been done to improve the interview? Present your experiences and suggestions for improvement to the class.

6. Obtain an application form from a local organization. Analyze the form and discuss the impact of any questions that could be discriminatory. Present the form and your analysis to the class.

Building Teamwork

7. Form small groups as directed by your instructor. Discuss the following issue: Organizations need to increase their focus on training to improve competitiveness.

8. Have you ever been the victim of illegal discrimination? Form a team of six to eight students. Exchange your experiences with members of your team. How do your experiences and reactions to discrimination compare with those of your team members? Do gender, race, or other characteristics affect the amount and type of experiences?

INFORMATION TECHNOLOGY: Insights and Solutions

1. Investigate the different ways in which organizations within the same industry are using information technology to recruit candidates. First select several well-known companies and, using the Internet, search for information about each organization and whether they are using electronic means for recruiting. Often they will offer to send you a video or request that you send a résumé. Develop a matrix and compare the different techniques. What impression do you form about the organization from the way the Web pages look? Describe the differences between these impressions and your impression of recruiting materials you may receive in person.

2. Another way to examine recruiting strategies is to see how colleges and universities are using their Web sites to attract interested students. Using a similar strategy to the one you used in Item 1, select a general category of college (for example, regional, large state, small private, large private). Compare the different techniques that college recruiting centers are using.

3. Talk to a human resource manager and find out the type of information kept in the organization's HRIS. Was the system written for the organization exclusively or was it a software program that was purchased? If you were interested in a career in HRM, what type of computer skills would you need?

ETHICS: Take a Stand

Seth had just been recognized by his law firm for his outstanding performance on the Donner case. He had masterfully convinced the jury of the innocence of his client. He had been thorough, well prepared, and persuasive. Linda, a partner in the firm, asked Seth to join her in a celebration lunch to discuss his "future with the firm."

During the course of the meal, the conversation took an unexpected turn. Linda began commenting on how attractive and sexy she thought Seth was and expressed a desire to spend more time with him. When Seth refused the advances, she reminded him of how much a partner could do to further his career at the firm and said the firm needed an "attractive" asset like Seth.

The working relationship between Linda and Seth quickly deteriorated after this encounter. Unwelcome innuendos became commonplace, and Linda would often rub her shoulder against his or put her hand on his arm when they were alone. Discussions about work often resulted in comments about "how new associates really got ahead in the firm." Because of these confrontations, Seth tried being rude to Linda or simply avoiding her whenever possible. He began to dread going to the office each day.

Although Seth was certain he was being subjected to sexual harassment, he was hesitant to pursue it any further. After all, shouldn't a man be immune to such behavior? He felt that making a formal complaint would irreparably damage his future in this firm or in any other law firm. After all, Linda was a prominent law partner and a well-known author. Seth was concerned that no one would believe him because her advances were made in private. Since he was the newest associate lawyer at the firm, he feared any complaints might hurt the chances of other new associates succeeding at the firm. Furthermore, he was afraid people would think he was "weak." After all, shouldn't he have been able to handle these verbal assaults on his own? How would he ever be able to deal with tough clients? If he did come forward, would people wonder why he had allowed things to escalate to this point? Because of his embarrassment, he had not revealed the situation to anyone. Although these questions weighed heavily on his mind, he also felt he had a responsibility to himself and other young associates in the workplace. Seth hoped he would make the right decision.

For Discussion

1. Discuss what action you think Seth should take.

2. What are the possible problems that Seth may face with his peers? With his supervisor?

3. Would the situation be any different if the advances had been made by a man toward a woman?

THINKING CRITICALLY: Debate the Issue

COMPENSATION—PUBLIC OR PRIVATE?

Form teams of four to five students as directed by your instructor. As assigned by your instructor, prepare to argue one side of the following issue: Compensation practices in the organization, including all employee/management salaries and benefits, should (or should not) be made public. Research your team's position, and be prepared with specific company examples, rules, and policies. Your instructor will select two teams to present their findings to the class in a debate format.

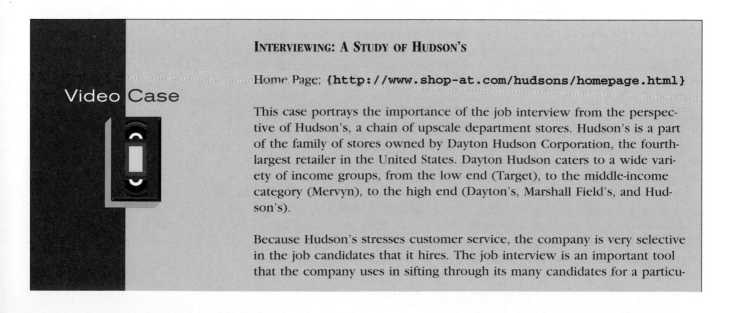

Video Case

INTERVIEWING: A STUDY OF HUDSON'S

Home Page: {http://www.shop-at.com/hudsons/homepage.html}

This case portrays the importance of the job interview from the perspective of Hudson's, a chain of upscale department stores. Hudson's is a part of the family of stores owned by Dayton Hudson Corporation, the fourth-largest retailer in the United States. Dayton Hudson caters to a wide variety of income groups, from the low end (Target), to the middle-income category (Mervyn), to the high end (Dayton's, Marshall Field's, and Hudson's).

Because Hudson's stresses customer service, the company is very selective in the job candidates that it hires. The job interview is an important tool that the company uses in sifting through its many candidates for a particular job. Specifically, the company is looking for people who enjoy responsibility, have strong leadership skills, thrive in a fast-paced environment, have a high energy level, and are enthusiastic about retail sales. The company also wants employees who can cope with customer demands in a friendly, even-tempered, and professional manner.

While interviewing a job applicant, the managers at Hudson's are looking for these and other specific skills and qualities. They are also observing how the applicant handles the interview itself. For example, if the applicant has difficulty answering a straightforward question, an interviewer may wonder if the applicant might have difficulty fielding routine customer inquiries. In an interview, an applicant makes a good impression by dressing in an appropriate manner, being well groomed, demonstrating good interpersonal skills, and showing a high degree of interest in the company. In addition, a job applicant makes a good impression by being prepared for the interview. That means knowing something about the company, its products, and the job itself. One manager in the case remarked that the biggest single problem that interviewees face is a lack of preparation. According to this manager, a job candidate should be able to tell an interviewer why he is a good choice for the job that is available, and how his personal goals fit with the company's goals.

An effective résumé is also an excellent complement to a good interview. One manager at Hudson's indicated that she looks for résumés that are well prepared, provide a good list of previous accomplishments, and are concise but thoughtful. Job candidates should also follow up on an interview to demonstrate to the company that they have a high degree of interest in the job. Along the same line, a Hudson manager featured in the case remarked, "I am always impressed by a thank-you note."

Good interviewing skills are important for landing a good job. This case provides many useful suggestions for effective interviewing at Hudson's or any other corporation.

For Discussion
1. What would be a good game plan for preparing for an interview with Hudson's? What would you do in the days following the interview?
2. How does Hudson's philosophy of employment interviews fit with its business strategy?

CASE

THE CAMPUS INTERVIEW

After four years of college, Courtney was excited and looking forward to pursuing a career as a CPA in one of the top accounting firms in New Orleans. During her four years in college, she had maintained a 3.7 grade point average in her accounting classes, had been president of the Student Accounting Association, was an active member of a business fraternity, and worked part-time for an accounting professor. She used the campus placement service to develop her résumé and prepare for interviews, and felt prepared to present herself to potential employers.

Her first interview was going quite well until the interviewer, Jon Hall, asked her, "Courtney, I see from your application materials that you have a five-year-old son, but I don't see a wedding ring. If you are a single parent, what are you going to do about him if you get the job and have to travel?" Courtney was caught off-guard by the question but responded, "Gee, Mr. Hall, do you mean I have to get rid of him if I get the job?" Jon's face turned red. He quickly thanked Courtney for her time and ended the interview.

As Courtney left the placement office, she wondered if she had handled the situation correctly. She also wondered if she should take any further action.

For Discussion

1. Discuss Courtney's handling of the interviewer's question. Are there any other ways she could have handled the situation?
2. Are there any general rules applicants can follow in dealing with potentially illegal questions asked either on an application form or in an interview?

EXPERIENTIAL EXERCISE 10.1

Career Stages Profile

Purpose: The Career Stages Profile (CSP) measures primary central activities and relationships and provides an understanding of your career stage.

Procedure: For each of the following statements, indicate how much you agree or disagree that the statement applies to you now in your current job. Use the following scale and place the appropriate number in the blank next to the statement.

Strongly Agree	Agree	Neither Agree Nor Disagree	Disagree	Strongly Disagree
5	4	3	2	1

_____ 1. My work involves assisting others and learning from the experience.

_____ 2. My work includes supportive work relationships with my peers.

_____ 3. My supervisor's responsibility is to provide me with challenging assignments that allow me opportunities to grow and learn.

_____ 4. I am involved in training possible successors who can perform my job.

_____ 5. I expect my supervisor to give me guidance, help me develop skills, and provide opportunities that will increase my level of understanding.

_____ 6. I depend on my supervisor to provide challenging assignments that will give me exposure to higher levels in the organization and increase my visibility.

_____ 7. One of my important roles is developing younger employees.

_____ 8. I am sometimes concerned that my career is over, worry about my identity outside work, and resent the idea of losing my influence over the organization's future.

_____ 9. I need feedback, coaching, and personal acceptance from my supervisor.

_____ 10. My supervisor respects my competence and knows she has my full personal commitment.

_____ 11. I am very concerned about not being able to achieve all the things I had hoped in both my work and my personal life.

_____ 12. My current work activities consist primarily of completing major long-term projects and assignments.

_____ 13. My major work responsibilities are to provide technical assistance and support to my supervisor.

_____ **14.** I am concerned about the number of important decisions I make on my own and about the conflicts between my work and my personal life.

_____ **15.** A lot of my time at work is spent training new people and handling special assignments.

_____ **16.** My most important work-related relationships center on professional involvements outside the organization.

_____ **17.** I often feel concerned about coping with organizational politics and the conflicting demands placed on me.

_____ **18.** Most of my current work is done independently and requires specialized technical contributions.

_____ **19.** My most important work relationships are with the younger employees I am mentoring.

_____ **20.** I expect my supervisor to provide me with a lot of freedom and autonomy.

Scoring: Transfer the values from the statements above to the following columns. Next, add up the points for each column. These are your scores on the Career Stages Profile.

Stage 1	Stage 2	Stage 3	Stage 4
1. _____	2. _____	3. _____	4. _____
5. _____	6. _____	7. _____	8. _____
9. _____	10. _____	11. _____	12. _____
13. _____	14. _____	15. _____	16. _____
17. _____	18. _____	19. _____	20. _____
Total _____	_____	_____	_____
Exploration and testing	Establishment and advancement	Maintenance	Withdrawal

Interpretation: Scores in each stage can range from a low of 5 to a high of 25. Scores of 20 or higher should indicate the stage of your career at the present time. Scores of 10 or less normally indicate that you have already passed or not yet started that stage.

ENDNOTES

1. J. Hoerr, "Sharpening Minds for a Competitive Edge," _Business Week,_ December 17, 1990, 72–78; R. R. Thomas, "From Affirmative Action to Affirming Diversity," _Harvard Business Review,_ March/April 1991, 107–17; T. A. Steward, "New Ways to Exercise Power," _Fortune,_ November 6, 1989, 52–64; and S. Sherman, "A Brave New Darwinian Workplace," _Fortune,_ January 25, 1993, 50–56.

2. K. Schwartz, "Southwest CEO Incorporates Fun into Airline's Financial Success," _The Associated Press,_ Chicago, November 26, 1996, B8; K. Frieberg and J. Frieberg, _Nuts! Southwest Airlines' Recipe for Business and Personal Success,_ forthcoming.

3. T. L. Leap and M. D. Crino, _Personnel/Human Resource Management_ (New York: Macmillan, 1993).

4. L. Joel III. _Every Employee's Guide to the Law_ (New York: Pantheon Books, 1994.)

5. Ibid.

6. H. O'Neill, "California Undoing Affirmative Action," _Los Angeles Times,_ November 17, 1996, C22.

7. J. E. Ellis, "Monsanto's New Challenge: Keeping Minority Workers," _Business Week,_ July 8, 1991, 60–61.

8. H. Keets, "Avon Calling-On Its Troops," _Business Week,_ July 8, 1991, 53; S. B. Garland, "How to Keep Women Managers on the Corporate Ladder," _Business Week,_ September 2, 1991, 64; N. J. Perry, "If You Can't Join 'Em, Beat 'Em," _Fortune,_ September 21, 1992, 58–59.

9. J. Ledvinka and V. G. Scarpello, _Federal Regulation of Personnel and Human Resource Management,_ 2nd ed. (Boston: PWS-Kent, 1991).

10. V. G. Scarpello and J. Ledvinka, _Personnel/Human Resource Management: Environments and Functions_ (Boston: PWS-Kent, 1994).

11. L. Dyer, "Human Resource Planning," in K. M. Rowland and G. R. Ferris, eds., _Personnel Management_ (Boston: Allyn & Bacon, 1992), 52–78.

12. Based in part on a discussion in R. L. Mathis and J. H. Jackson, _Personnel/Human Resource Management,_ 7th ed. (St. Paul, Minn.: West Publishing, 1994), 210.

13. R. Stross, _The Microsoft Way_ (New York: Addison-Wesley, 1996).

14. R. Koenig, "Toyota Takes Pains and Time Filling Jobs at Its Kentucky Plant," _The Wall Street Journal,_ December 1, 1987, 1.

15. R. Stross, _The Microsoft Way._

16. S. Burns, "From Student to Banker: Observations from the Chase Bank," paper presented at the Association of Amer-

ican Colleges and the National Endowment for the Humanities Conference, Princeton, New Jersey, April 1993.

17. M. Davids, "How to Handle Loaded Questions," *Working Woman,* July 1992, 12.

18. Based in part on a discussion in M. Davids, "How to Handle Loaded Questions."

19. G. M. McEvoy and R. W. Beatty, "Assessment Centers and Subordinates' Appraisals of Managers: A Seven-Year Examination of Predictive Validity," *Personnel Psychology,* 42, 1989, 37-52.

20. M. E. Grossman and M. Magnus, "The $5.3 Billion Tab for Training," *Personnel Journal,* 68, 1989, 54-56.

21. E. Lawler, S. Mohrman, and G. Ledford, *Employee Involvement and Total Quality Management* (San Francisco: Jossey-Bass, 1992).

22. R. L. Mathis and J. H. Jackson, *Personnel/Human Resource Management.*

23. M. Syers, "Breakthrough in Orientation Models," *Harvard Business Review,* July/August 1996, 110-117.

24. Bureau of National Affairs, *Planning the Training Program: Personnel Management,* (Washington, D.C.: BNA Books, 1975).

25. A. Berstein, "How to Motivate Workers: Don't Watch 'Em," *Business Week,* April 29, 1991, 56.

26. Adapted from Cassner-Lotto and Associates, *Successful Training Strategies* (San Francisco: Jossey-Bass, 1988).

27. W. F. Cascio, *Managing Human Resources,* 2d ed. (New York: McGraw-Hill, 1989).

28. For a review of BARS literature, see G. P. Latham and K. N. Wesley, *Increasing Productivity through Performance Appraisal* (Reading, Mass.: Addison-Wesley, 1981), 61-64.

29. "Motivation," *Inc.,* December 1986, 120.

30. For a more detailed discussion of benefits, see R. L. Mathis and J. H. Jackson, *Personnel/Human Resource Management,* 413-39.

31. M. A. Littell, "Family-Friendly Employee Benefits," *Good Housekeeping,* July 1992, 100.

32. J. R. Morris, *Employee Benefits* (Washington, D.C.: Chamber of Commerce of the United States, 1986).

33. L. L. Cummings, "Compensation, Culture, and Motivation: A System Perspective," *Organizational Dynamics,* Winter 1984, 33-44.

34. R. L. Mathis and J. H. Jackson, *Personnel/Human Resource Management,* 359.

35. A. C. Hax, "A New Competitive Lesson: The Human Resource Strategy," *Training and Development Journal,* May 1985, 76-82.

36. V. G. Scarpello and J. Ledvinka, *Personnel/Human Resource Management: Environments and Functions;* G. T. Milkovich and J. Newman, *Compensation* (Homewood, Ill.: BPI/Irwin, 1990).

37. R. E. Walton and R. B. McKersie, *A Behavioral Theory of Labor Negotiations: An Analysis of a Social Interaction System* (New York: McGraw-Hill, 1965).

38. Ibid.

39. A. Bernstein, "Busting Unions Can Backfire on the Bottom Line," *Business Week,* March 18, 1991, 108.

40. J. M. Brett, "Why Employees Want Unions," *Organizational Dynamics,* 8, 1980, 47-59.

41. W. C. Hammer and F. J. Smith, "Work Attitudes as Predictors of Unionization Activity," *Journal of Applied Psychology,* 63, 1978, 415-21; C. A. Schriesheim, "Job Satisfaction, Attitudes towards Unions and Voting in a Union Representation Election," *Journal of Applied Psychology,* 63, 1978, 548-52.

42. L. Holman, "Globalization in the Information Age," *Lessons in Leadership Newsletter,* October 1996, 3.

43. R. McLeod Jr., *Management Information Systems,* 6th ed. (Upper Saddle River, N.J.: Prentice-Hall, 1995).

44. M. E. Mendenhall, E. Dunbar, and G. R. Oddou, "Expatriate Selection, Training and Career-Pathing: A Review and Critique," *Human Resource Management,* 26, Fall 1987, 340.

45. M. G. Henry, "The Executive Family: An Overlooked Variable in International Assignments," *Columbia Journal of World Business,* Spring 1985, 84-92.

46. C. Lee, "Cross-Cultural Training: Don't Leave Home without It," *Training,* March 1993, 20-25.

47. M. A. Conway, "Reducing Expatriate Failure Rates," *Personnel Administrator,* July 1984, 31-38.

48. A. L. Hixon, "Why Corporations Make Haphazard Overseas Staffing Decisions," *Personnel Administrator,* March 1986, 91-95.

49. T. Stein, K. Callan, D. Menaker, and C. Brown-Humes, "The World's Greatest Entrepreneurs," *Success,* June 1996, 35-46; "Where East Meets West: Making Managers the Japanese Way, "*The Economist,* March 2, 1993, 22-24.

50. A. M. Morrison and M. A. Von Glinow, "Women and Minorities in Management," *American Psychologist,* 45, 1990, 200-208.

51. W. B. Johnson, "Global Workforce 2000: The New Labor Market," *Harvard Business Review,* March/April 1991, 115-19.

52. S. B. Garland, "Throwing Stones at the Glass Ceiling," *Business Week,* August 19, 1991, 64.

53. Ledvinka and Scarpello, Federal Regulation of Personnel and Human Resource Management.

54. G. N. Powell, "Sexual Harassment: Confronting the Issue of Definition," *Business Horizons,* July/August 1983, 24-28.

55. *Meritor Savings Bank v. Vinson,* 477 U.S. 57 (1986); EEOC, *Policy Guidance on Sexual Harassment,* March 1990.

56. *Robinson v. Jacksonville Shipyards,* USDC MFLA, No. 86-927-J-1 2 (1991); *Ellison v. Brady,* 54 FEP Case 1346 (1991).

57. For a more thorough discussion, see M. Galen, Z. Schiller, J. Hamilton, and K. Hammonds, "Ending Sexual Harassment: Business Is Getting the Message," *Business Week,* March 18, 1992, 98-100.

58. W. C. Symonds, "How to Confront and Help an Alcoholic Employee," *Business Week,* March 25, 1991, 78.

59. G. Koretz, "An Incentive a Day Can Keep Doctor Bills at Bay," *Business Week,* April 29, 1991, 22.

60. Perpetual Financial Corporation, *Profiles in Quality: Blueprints for Action from 50 Leading Companies* (Needham Heights, Mass.: Allyn & Bacon, 1991), 85-86.

61. J. Hoerr, "Sharpening Minds for a Competitive Edge."

Organizational Culture, Change, and Development

■ CHAPTER OVERVIEW

In today's highly competitive global marketplace, the whole notion of transformation and change threatens some and excites many. As we approach the beginning of a new century, we are entering the age where individuals and organizations must learn something new every day, or those individuals and organizations will decline. At all levels of operations, people must strive for quality, innovation, value, relationship building, and excellence in management practices. Managers recognize that to build viable organizations, change must be viewed as an integral rather than a peripheral responsibility. This means changing the concept of the hierarchical organization to the concept of the horizontal corporation. Many of the leading companies in the world—such as AT&T, Motorola, GE, Du Pont, Texas Instruments, and IBM—are making or have already made sweeping changes that are moving them closer to flattened, decentralized organizations. The traditional hierarchical and bureaucratic organization is being challenged as never before by new methods involving participation, involvement, flexibility, and entrepreneurial behavior. These issues reflect a fundamental challenge faced by organizations as they strive to produce quality products and services and learn to manage changing cultures, strategies, and practices.[1]

This chapter explores the issues associated with understanding and managing change. It is based upon the viewpoint that the important responsibility of managing change can best be undertaken and accomplished by first understanding an organization's culture and then by analyzing the forces that drive and resist change. Only when managers have this foundation will their change processes and interventions be successful.

■ LEARNING OBJECTIVES

When you have finished studying this chapter, you should be able to:

- Discuss the foundations of organizational culture.
- Describe two basic components of organizational culture.
- List and explain the three forms of organizational artifacts.
- Explain the impact of culture on an organization.
- Demonstrate an understanding of organizational change.
- Identify and describe the four targets of planned change.
- Describe the three-step process of planned change.

369

- Identify the six strategies for overcoming resistance to change.
- List and describe the people-focused approaches to organizational change.
- Discuss ethical issues in organizational change.
- Explain how information technology is influencing both culture and organizational changes.

Managerial Incident

MANAGING AN UNRULY ADOLESCENT: LANE LEARNS WHAT ADULTHOOD IS ALL ABOUT

Often referred to both internally and externally as the perpetual adolescent, Oracle is a $4 billion independent software company, second only to Microsoft, located in California's Silicon Valley. Until 1992, Oracle was led by founder Larry Ellison, who is often considered one of the most powerful men in the high-tech industry and certainly one of the most ruthless competitors.

Ellison's visionary style and entrepreneurial success created Oracle, the primary developer of critical databases. But his spirit and creativity also drove the company into near-failure. In the early 1990s, Oracle began suffering growing pains manifested by a wild culture perpetuated by entrepreneur Ellison. Disorganized and near bankruptcy, Ellison persuaded Ray Lane, an ex-IBM and ex-EDS administrator, to join Oracle.

Lane faced an organization that was founded on entrepreneurial culture, with renegade salespeople, runaway technology, little or no accountability, and employees with a love-hate relationship with the company. For example, Lane found out that a common joke Oracle employees liked to tell was, "What's the difference between Oracle and the Boy Scouts? The Boy Scouts are led by adults."

Ray Lane was faced with an organization of 20,000 employees, who still followed a communication practice left over from the startup days: taking problems straight to the top, to founder Ellison. Not long after Lane arrived, a McKinsey consulting report summed up the company's market position: customers loved the technology but hated dealing with Oracle employees. Customers often had as many as five Oracle employees salespeople calling on them. They could expect the hard sell, too; the high-velocity force more closely resembled boiler-room stock salespeople.

The culture at Oracle focused on beating customers into submission, competitor slamming, and inflated claims for Oracle's product specs. Lane found that consulting services were often neglected and salespeople were in the habit of giving away consulting services to close a deal.

Clearly Lane had to play the adult and take the leadership role to move Oracle into a competitive position for the challenges facing the company. His strengths and secrets of success were his ability to relate to all types of people and guide their thinking. But Lane was faced with the unruly adolescent and the challenge of restructuring Oracle. He had to devise a way of capturing energy, enthusiasm, and talent. How would Lane put Oracle back on track while accommodating its unique culture?[2]

INTRODUCTION

In today's breakneck global business environment, companies that survive accept change as a means of seeking new and better ways of doing business. For example, the Japanese concept of *kaizen,* or continuous improvement, has become much more than the phrase *du jour;* today, it is the imperative for success.[3] While too often change is driven by crisis, transition marked by patient but steady progress over a relatively lengthy period is often more substantial and impressive.

Transition involves changing the culture and is typically not linear. Transition involves a deliberate disturbance of the equilibrium and status quo and is a major event in the life of an organization. Most of the time, these events are drastic and intense, and such changes can be revolutionary and traumatic, as we saw in the Managerial Incident with Oracle. Cultural change involves a disruptive break with the past and substantial changes in the way leaders lead each other and the way employees lead themselves.

The contemporary manager faces extraordinary challenges.[4] As we have mentioned in previous chapters, today's dynamic, complex, and sometimes unpredictable environment demands that managers and organizations take a proactive role in keeping up with and responding to change.

Change is a pervasive, persistent, and permanent condition for all organizations. When organizations fail to change in necessary ways, the costs can be high. According to MIT professor David Birch, "For every corporation in the U.S., the best predictor of death is stability."[5] Innovation, flexibility, and the ability to change have become necessary business survival skills.

This chapter examines the issues associated with managing change, beginning with the organization's culture. We will explore the components of organizational culture by examining organizational artifacts and then will look at how culture affects the organization. Next, we turn our attention to the responsibility of managing change; as we will see, this can best be accomplished by analyzing the forces that drive and resist change. Finally, we examine the processes and interventions that can be used to manage change successfully.

FOUNDATIONS OF ORGANIZATIONAL CULTURE

Before we can understand the issues involved in organizational change, we need to examine the foundations of the organization, or its culture. Because culture guides the behavior of and gives meaning to organizational members, it has a direct and powerful influence on the change process.[6] We define **organizational culture** as the system of shared beliefs and values that develops within an organization. In simple terms, organizational culture is the personality of the organization.

Culture influences how people act in organizations; the ways people perform, view their jobs, work with colleagues, and look at the future are largely determined by cultural norms, values, and beliefs.[7] Just as no two individual personalities are the same, no two organizational cultures are identical.[8] For example, the organizational culture at 3M focuses on innovative thinking and creativity. Every employee at 3M is encouraged to call up any other employee and tap into that person's expertise. 3M wants as many people as possible talking to each other and sharing information. This internal best-practices system discourages territoriality, breaks down the walls between business units, and goes far to stimulate creativity.[9]

Cultures develop from a variety of factors. When a new organization is formed, the culture reflects the drive and imagination of the founding individual or group. Ray Kroc, the founder of McDonald's, espoused quality, service, cleanliness, and value, and these are still the corporate creed. Reward systems, policies, and procedures instituted within an organization also affect its culture by further specifying notions of appropriate behavior. The culture at Walt Disney Corporation has been influenced by its creative founder, Walt Disney, who created entertainment that was focused on family values and traditional beliefs.

Organizational culture
The system of shared beliefs and values that develops with an organization. In simple terms, organizational culture is the personality of the organization.

An organization's culture guides the behavior of and gives meaning to organizational members. Ray Kroc, founder of McDonald's, espoused quality, service, cleanliness, and value—still the corporate creed.
© UPI/Corbis-Bettmann

Cultures evolve and change over time in even the most stable periods.[10] In times of trouble, they may change rapidly because whatever else the culture may value, it prizes survival most of all. Economic crises, changes in laws or regulations, social developments, global competition, demographic trends, and other events influence what the organization must do to survive, and the culture tends to evolve accordingly.[11]

Cultures also change when an organization discovers, invents, or develops solutions to problems that it faces. Successful approaches to solving problems tend to become part of the culture and are used whenever the organization faces similar conditions. For example, as we read in the Managerial Incident, the culture at Oracle underwent a fundamental change when Ray Lane joined the company and instituted, for the first time, controls.[12]

COMPONENTS OF AN ORGANIZATION'S CULTURE

As Figure 11.1 shows, organizational culture has two basic components. These components can be visualized as an iceberg because what you see on the surface is based on a much deeper reality.[13] The visible elements are the routines (practices) that constitute the organization's culture. These are sustained by hidden ideologies, shared values, expectations, and norms that are at the deepest level or core of the organization. Managers must recognize that it may not be possible to change the surface without changing what lies below.[14]

EXAMINING CULTURE THROUGH ORGANIZATIONAL ARTIFACTS

Artifacts
Cultural routines that form the substance of public functions and events staged by the organization.

The visible elements in Figure 11.1 consist of a number of artifacts. **Artifacts** are cultural routines that form the substance of public functions and events staged by the organization. Artifacts support and reinforce the organization's hidden ideologies, shared value systems, and norms. The artifacts level of cul-

FIGURE 11.1
Components of organizational culture visualized as an iceberg

Artifacts

Ideologies

Shared values

Norms

Expectations

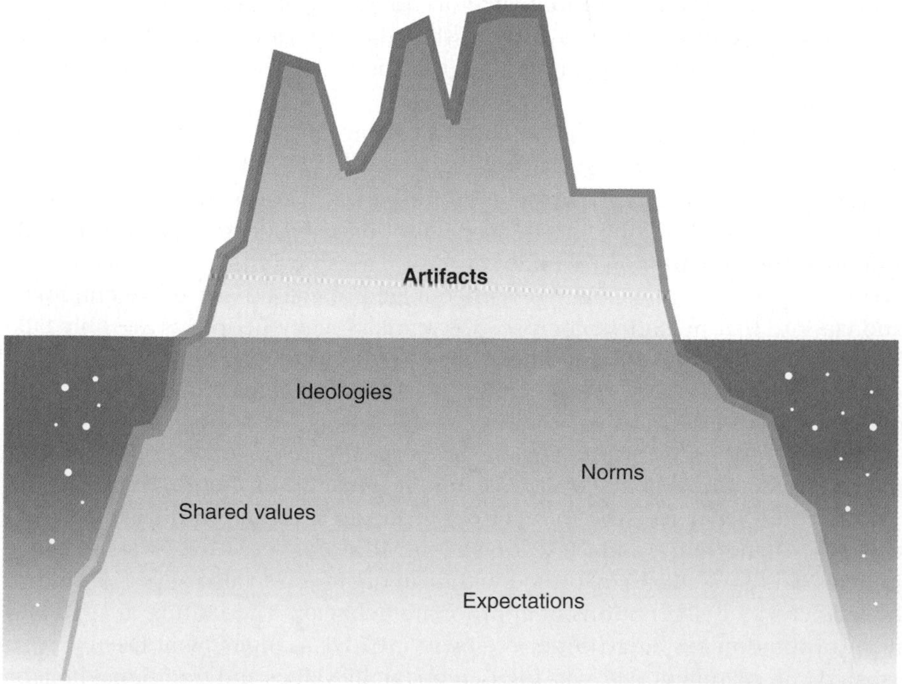

tural analysis is tricky because it is easy to obtain but hard to interpret. While we can often describe the behavior patterns that are evident within organizations, it is hard to explain why these patterns exist.

Symbolism of Rites, Rituals, and Ceremonies
Some of the most obvious displays of organizational culture are rites, rituals, and ceremonies.[15] **Rites** are a relatively dramatic, planned set of recurring activities used at special times to influence the behavior and understanding of organizational members.

Rituals and *ceremonies* are usually more elaborate systems of rites. Evaluation and reward procedures, farewell parties, award banquets, and product promotions are examples. They are carried out through social interaction and usually occur for the benefit of an audience.

Microsoft Corporation celebrated the successful introduction of its software package Windows with a gala party for 5,000 employees at the Seattle Kingdome. A red Corvette with the word *Windows* written on its door was placed onstage next to an Edsel emblazoned with *OS/2* (IBM's competing software). The employees chanted: "Windows, Windows, Windows." The climax of the evening came when ten leather-clad bikers led by President Bill Gates roared onstage riding Harley-Davidsons, while the song "Leader of the Pack" blared from the loudspeakers.[16] This celebration reflects Microsoft's unorthodox and creative management culture.

Through rituals and ceremonies, participants gain an understanding of and cement beliefs that are important to the organization's culture. Mary Kay Cosmetics schedules regular ceremonies to spotlight positive work achievements and reinforce high performance expectations. At the company's annual meeting, an affair marked by lavish pomp and intense drama, top employees are recognized and rewarded for high sales. The celebration goes beyond the fancy setting and presentation of pink Cadillacs to star salespeople. Members praise the opportunities provided to them by Mary Kay, the heroine of the company. The process gives all Mary Kay employees a sense of purpose—not merely to sell cosmetics, but to reach their full potential.

Language Systems and Metaphors
Language systems and metaphors are the way that organizational members typically express themselves and communicate with each other. Metaphors use familiar elements or objects to make behavior or other unfamiliar processes or actions comprehensible.[17] They include special terminology, abbreviations, jargon, slang, and gestures that are almost unintelligible to outsiders, but are used inside the organization to convey a sense of belonging or community. For example, Disney employees label anything positive a "good Mickey" and anything negative a "bad Mickey"; Levi Strauss management calls its open-door policy the "fifth freedom"; and Ruby Tuesday's shareowners (employees) firmly state the company's goal "to be our guests' first choice, a great place to work, and a great investment."

Stories, Sagas, and Myths
Organizations are rich with stories of winners, losers, successes, and failures. **Stories** are accounts based on true events; they often contain both truth and fiction. For a new employee, the organization is like a foreign culture—the per-

The rites, rituals, and ceremonies at Mary Kay Cosmetics give all Mary Kay employees a sense of purpose—not merely to sell cosmetics, but to reach their full potential.
© Nina Berman/Sipa Press

Rites
A relatively dramatic, planned set of recurring activities used at special times to influence the behavior and understanding of organizational members.

Language systems and metaphors
The way that organizational members typically express themselves and communicate with each other.

Stories
Accounts based on true events; they often contain both truth and fiction.

Entrepreneurial Approach

NEVER KILL A NEW PRODUCT IDEA AT 3M

Employees at 3M are encouraged to be entrepreneurs and to try out new ideas in the marketplace rather than putting their trust in market forecasts. The culture of 3M encourages all employees to pursue innovation. This is reflected in 3M's "eleventh commandment," "Thou shalt not kill a new product idea." Any idea that leads to product diversity—such as the worker safety mask, which was developed from a failed plastic-cup project for brassieres—is acceptable. 3M researchers are encouraged to spend 15 percent of their time pursuing pet projects that might have a payoff down the line. In 1990 more than one-fourth of 3M's worldwide sales came from new products—products that did not exist ten years ago.

This emphasis on innovation is supported by a story about the invention of transparent cellophane tape. According to the story, an employee accidentally invented the tape, but was unable to get his superiors to buy the idea. Marketing studies predicted a relatively small demand for the new material. Undaunted, the employee found a way to sneak into the boardroom and tape down the minutes of the upcoming executive meeting with his transparent tape. The board members were impressed enough with the novelty to give it a try, and the cellophane tape—Scotch tape—became an incredible success.

In essence, 3M's culture promotes an entrepreneurial environment based on the belief that failure can lead to success. Not only do such stories serve as symbols of the company's entrepreneurial orientation, but they help unify diverse organizational units as employees come to share the same values.

SOURCE: J. Martin, "Tomorrow's CEO's," *Fortune*, June 24, 1996, 84–88. ©1996 Time Inc. All rights reserved.

son has to learn how to fit in and avoid major blunders. Organizational stories tell new members the real mission of the organization, how it operates, what behavior is acceptable, and how individuals can fit into the organization. For example, managers at Semco, a Brazilian equipment producer, tell the story of how they changed the behavior of Ricardo Semier, the company's CEO. Semco tried to follow the example of his father, the company founder, when he took over lead of the company. He acted as a hard-driving disciplinarian and found that this style spawned workers and managers who didn't care, subsequently producing unsatisfactory performance. Managers took him on a "retreat" where they persuaded him to reorganize himself. He began to delegate, cut back on micromanaging, empowered his work force, and redesigned the organization. Since these changes, sales have increased 600 percent and employees consider the company a paradise to work in.[18]

Stories also serve as symbols of the organization's entrepreneurial orientation and promote values that unify employees from diverse organizational units. For example, Entrepreneurial Approach tells the story of the invention of Scotch tape—a favorite story at 3M.[19]

In many organizations, the members have a collection of stories that they tell repeatedly. Often one of the most important stories concerns the founding of the organization. Such stories may convey the lessons to be learned from the heroic efforts of an entrepreneur whose vision may still guide the organization. The founding story may become so embellished that it becomes a saga. *Sagas* are historical accounts describing the unique accomplishments of a group and its leaders or heroes. According to Peters and Waterman, members of "strong culture" companies are likely to have an enormous fund of sagas that tell about the exploits of the founder or other strong leaders.[20] At Hewlett-Packard (HP), sagas feature the legendary accomplishments of the founders,

Bill Hewlett and Dave Packard, and are used to communicate the unique way of doing things at HP to outsiders or newcomers.

Myths differ from stories and sagas in that they lack a factual basis. Even though myths are unproven beliefs, they are accepted uncritically and are used to justify current actions by communicating the practical benefits of certain techniques and behaviors. Old-timers' stories about how things were "in the good old days" are frequently examples of myths.

Myths
Unproven beliefs that are accepted uncritically and used to justify current actions by communicating the practical benefits of certain techniques and behaviors.

THE IMPACT OF CULTURE ON THE ORGANIZATION

In organizations with strong cultures, shared values and beliefs create a setting in which people are committed to one another and share an overriding sense of mission. This culture can be a source of competitive advantage. Unique, shared values can provide a strong corporate identity, enhance collective commitment, create a stable social system, and reduce the need for formal and bureaucratic controls.

A strong culture can be a double-edged sword, however. A strong culture and value system can reinforce a singular view of the organization and its environment. If dramatic changes are needed, it may be very difficult to change the organization. General Motors (GM), which has a strong culture, experienced enormous problems in adapting to a dynamic and highly competitive environment. GM found it necessary to establish a new division (and thus a new culture) to produce the Saturn automobile. At Harley-Davidson, a new senior management team had to replace virtually all of the company's middle managers to establish a new competitive culture. At what was once U.S. Steel, now USX, the problems with the old steel division were so ingrained in the culture that executives sold the division and purchased a series of divisions with strong, resilient cultures.

Many companies are striving to achieve high levels of quality, customer service, and satisfaction. For example, the U.S. automobile industry feels that quality is the key to competing effectively with the Japanese automobile industry. These companies are learning that to achieve this goal, they must provide new employee reward systems, organizational designs, and customer-service training that focuses on interpersonal skills for salespeople as well as dealers. Changes such as these can have dramatic effects on the organization's culture.[21]

Managers recognize that the world is changing at an unprecedented rate and everything is in constant flux, from the economy to markets. The workplace is beset by changes of all sorts from all sides. This is especially evident when we consider the influence of information technology on organizational culture and change.

INFORMATION TECHNOLOGY: THE IMPACT ON CULTURE AND CHANGE

Organizations can benefit from the dramatic changes that are already occurring in information technology. The heart of all these new technologies is the same: removing barriers of distance and time, lowering costs, and improving the overall ability of people to communicate their thoughts and needs.

The more technology an organization has in place, the more it removes barriers, and the less tolerant employees will be of ivory-tower, nonempowering, non-information-sharing management. These are the technologies that enable the empowerment buzzword, because they furnish lower layers of organizations with enough information to make intelligent decisions and then act on them.

Continuous information flows and instantaneous communication within and among businesses pulls together organizational layers, effectively if not literally flattening organizational charts. Managers can provide data that employees need, and employees can quickly resolve concerns with management. The phenomenon of e-mail alone has changed many organizations: anyone can send e-mail to the CEO, and an assistant usually can't intercept it.

People at the bottom of the traditional organizational chart were often the ones in contact with the customer or involved in the hands-on work of the factory. But these were the individuals least likely to have any information to assist them in making decisions. Technology changes that. For example, a Fed Ex employee who is able to access information on a customer's package can act on it immediately instead of waiting for information from a central office.

Neither organizations nor individuals can afford to ignore these new possibilities and cultural influences while all around them both competitors and colleagues build new relationships that will soon be as commonplace as the telephone.

CHANGING AN ORGANIZATION'S CULTURE

Changing an organization's culture can be very complicated. Well-known management expert Peter Drucker suggests that managers can modify the visible aspects of culture such as the language, stories, rites, rituals, and sagas. They can change the lessons to be drawn from common stories and even encourage employees to see a different reality. Because of their positions, senior managers can interpret situations in new ways and adjust the meanings attached to important organizational events. They can also create new rites and rituals. Modifying the culture in these ways takes time and enormous energy, but the long-run benefits can be positive.[22] At Oracle, Ray Lane reorganized the sales force, shifting the culture toward relationship building rather than beating customers into submission. The change has been positive, and during his four-year tenure the value of stock has grown almost tenfold to $33.12 per share.[23]

Top managers can set the tone for a culture and for cultural change. Throughout this book, we illustrate how managerial excellence is shaping the corporate landscape of the 1990s. In most of these incidents, we see that managers are building on the shared values in the culture of their organizations. Ray Lane of Oracle has focused on providing leadership and organizational savvy. Bill Gates, founder and CEO of Microsoft, focuses on his vision of a computer on every desk and in every home to bring new benefits to people's personal lives and business pursuits. Denny's, under attack a few years ago for being one of America's most racist companies, worked to make over its culture. As we see in Managing for Excellence, Denny's focused on changing the hierarchical environment, making diversity a performance criterion for all managers, opening up opportunities for diversity in the work force, and creating a culture to motivate employees.[24]

Anita Roddick, founder and managing director of The Body Shop, wants the organization to preserve its sense of being different while changing to be current. Her protests against animal testing builds on the shared values in the culture of her organization.

© /AP/Wide World Photos

DENNY'S: A MODEL FOR MAKING DIVERSITY PAY OFF

The day that Denny's settled a federal lawsuit in 1993 for discriminating against African American customers in California, six black Secret Service agents waited nearly an hour for breakfast at a Denny's location in Maryland. While their white colleagues finished their breakfast at a nearby table, the black agents were ignored. When the black agents went public with their treatment, Denny's became a national symbol of big business bigotry almost overnight.

In May 1994, Denny's settled two class-action lawsuits. By December 1995, the company paid $54 million to 295,000 aggrieved customers and their lawyers. In the consent decree it signed with the plaintiffs, Denny's promised to treat all customers equally in the future. The consent decree also mandated that the company publicize its nondiscriminatory policies and offer its employees training in diversity issues. An independent civil rights monitor was appointed to supervise Denny's for seven years and to investigate any additional discrimination charges. To its all-white management team, diversity was a foreign concept.

As if this wasn't enough, Denny's parent company had sagging financial performance. The debt laden company lost $55.2 million in 1995 on revenues of $2.6 billion. Facing stiff competition in the marketplace and an image problem, Denny's had a major challenge.

Denny's cultural renaissance began in 1995 with the arrival of its new CEO, Jim Adamson. Adamson's challenge was to make the necessary changes in the organization's culture to eliminate the entrenched prejudice and to turn the company into a model of organizational sensitivity and diversity. Adamson designed a four-step strategy to cultivate cultural diversity in the company. The first step was to loosen up the hierarchical environment. Second, diversity became a performance criterion for all managers. The third step required all employees to attend mandatory workshop training on racial sensitivity. And last, Adamson seized every opportunity to speak out on diversity.

Adamson's goal was to implant diversity as deeply in the new Flagstar/Denny's as racism was rooted in the old. Management training programs were created to provide minorities with entree into the executive ranks. The company also began a fast-track program to help minorities become Denny's franchisees. Every applicant who completed the training could buy a franchise with a loan guaranteed by Denny's. And to remedy the shortage of minority-owned suppliers, the company provided vendors with price lists and specs needed to get an order.

Adamson also assembled a dedicated team of professionals to help effect cultural change at the company. Minority employees now hold various executive positions such as Director of Minority Business Development, Director of Diversity Affairs, and VP of Human Resources. With the help of this team, a diversity training program was created for the company's employees. This training program reinforces the requirements of the consent degree forbidding discrimination, such as failure to seat blacks as quickly as whites. The legal points are combined with customer service guidelines; treating everyone equally is the best way to avoid complaints. Despite the progress it has made on diversity, Flagstar/Denny's profitability remains a problem. Interest payments of $230 million contributed to a loss of $55.2 million in 1995. Adamson's challenge is to raise profits enough to offset the high debt. To pull this off, he is rethinking everything from advertising to menu items and implementing long-term growth oriented strategic changes. Some of these strategic changes include divesting the company of all low-margin, non-restaurant businesses, and updating the company's information technology systems. Also, to spice up sales, Adamson is lowering prices and improving quality.

Adamson promised Flagstar's board of directors he would remain until the company's red ink disappears. "When I leave, I want it said that I made Flagstar a much more inclusive, user-friendly company", says Adamson. In other words, he wants diversity to pay off.

SOURCE: F. Rice, "Denny's Changes its Spots", *Fortune*, May 13, 1996, 133–142.

Managers who strive for quality products and services understand that they must involve the keepers and holders of the culture, build on what all organizational members share, and teach new members how to behave. Sometimes managers attempt to revitalize an organization by dictating minor changes rather than building on shared beliefs and values. While things may change a bit on the surface, a deeper look often finds whole departments and key people resisting change. To be successful, change must be consistent with important values in the culture and emerge from participants within the organization. Anita Roddick, founder and managing director of The Body Shop, has stressed that she wants the organization to preserve its sense of being different while changing to be current. Because success spurs change, culture is often difficult to maintain. Roddick believes that The Body Shop will never be just like every other company.[25]

THE CHALLENGE TO UNDERSTAND ORGANIZATIONAL CHANGE

Change is essential to an organization's survival. Change leads to new ideas, technology, innovation, and improvement. Therefore, it is important that organizations recognize the need for change and learn to manage the process effectively. For example, Bally Manufacturing Corporation was once the largest and most respected builder of slot machines. In the late 1980s, it lost its number one position to International Game Technology. Industry executives say that Bally's management failed to change with the times. They were reluctant to adopt the computer technology that addressed quality-control problems and revolutionized machines.[26]

Organizational change
Any alteration of activities in an organization that can be in the structure of the organization, the transfer of work tasks, introduction of a new product, or in attitudes among members.

Organizational change is any alteration of activities in an organization. Alterations can involve the structure of the organization; the transfer of work tasks; the introduction of a new product, system, or technology; or attitudes among members. According to Chad Holliday, executive vice-president of Du Pont and chair of Du Pont Asia Pacific, the change process is even more difficult in organizations with multiple facilities in several nations, as can be seen in Global Perspective. He contends that change can be a painful process for any organization that wants to be a high-performing competitor in the global marketplace.[27] Managers must learn to recognize not only when change is occurring in an organization, but also to select the right people.

TARGETS FOR CHANGE

A variety of elements in an organization can be changed. Which elements are chosen is partly determined by the manager's ability to diagnose the organization's problems or opportunities accurately. There are four primary targets for change. These include individual, group, organizational, and environmental targets.

Chad Holliday: Adjusting the Culture

Global Perspective

"For me to be knowledgeable about any single business decision is almost impossible. I have to try to put the right people in place," says Chad Holliday, a committed internationalist, executive vice-president of Du Pont and chair of Du Pont Asia Pacific.

Twenty-six years ago, Holliday turned a summer job at Du Pont into a full-time one and set in motion a career which has seen him rise through various plant-level supervisory jobs and executive positions to his current duties. Holliday now resides in Tokyo and is in charge of 7,000 employees and business totaling $3.5 billion in sales. He oversees Du Pont's business dealings in fifteen Far Eastern countries. Not surprisingly, he spends half his time on personnel decisions.

In the dynamic global environment of the late 1990s, foreign experience is no longer considered a backwater but rather a fast track to the top. However, Holliday changed the way international business had been conducted at Du Pont and stirred up concern in the traditional corporate headquarters.

He took a very different approach to running the Asia Pacific division. For example, in 1991, Holliday made a controversial decision to recruit local talent to head up Du Pont in Japan. Several of Du Pont's top managers back in the company's Wilmington, Delaware, corporate headquarters expressed worries about Holliday's decision. They were concerned because this was not in line with the culture of Du Pont. Change did not come easily for these traditionalists; they were worried about corporate loyalty and feared that valuable trade secrets might be stolen.

Despite the controversy, Holliday stood by his decision and chose Akira Imamichi as president of a joint venture between Du Pont and Mitsui Petrochemical. Imamichi worked out well. Earnings have been growing more than twice as fast since he took over, despite the Japanese economy being in a rut. And as Holliday had hoped, Imamichi has been able to eliminate some biases of Du Pont's American managers in Japan toward the local work force, which is 98 percent Japanese. Holliday was concerned that certain employees who spoke English well and exhibited "Western" traits such as taking personal credit for business success might receive favoritism. "Sure enough, Imamichi came in and made valuable personnel changes, says Holliday. "People we thought weren't very good he thought outstanding, and vice versa." Holliday has found that some business decisions, even when they disrupt the culture, are worth the risk.

At an individual level, organizations can target several areas. These changes fall under the general category of human resource changes and include changing the number and skills of the human resource component as well as improving levels of employee motivation and performance. Changes in these areas usually occur either as a result of new staffing strategies or because the company has embraced the strategic goal of recognizing and valuing diversity in the work force. Individual targets are accomplished through employee training or development programs.[28]

Managers may consider changing the nature of the relationships between managers and subordinates or the relationships within work groups. This might include change or redirection of management leadership styles, group composition, or decision-making procedures. For example, several months after Intel Corporation opened its DuPont, Washington, plant in 1996, the assembly teams proposed a change in production scheduling. Team leaders and the plant manager suggested compressed, alternating shifts so that all workers rotated and the distribution of work days would be more equitable.[29]

At the organizational level, managers can change (1) the basic goals and strategies of the organization; (2) the products, quality, or services offered; (3) the organizational structure; (4) the composition of work units; (5) organizational processes such as reward, communication, or information processing systems; and (6) the culture. For example, to survive in the global environment and avoid bankruptcy, Navistar International redesigned its organizational structure. By transforming its sluggish bureaucracy and becoming a streamlined, world-class manufacturer and innovator, Navistar was able to revitalize its competitive advantage.[30]

An organization can also work to change sectors of its environment. As we discussed in earlier chapters, sectors in the external environment can be influenced and changed in a number of ways. It is virtually impossible to change one aspect of an organization and not affect other aspects. Changes in products or services offered may require new technology or a new distribution system. Adopting new technology may necessitate hiring different types of employees or revamping the corporate training system. Once again, the interconnection of systems and subsystems makes the job of management extremely complex and challenging.

To understand the difficulties involved in identifying targets of change, take the time to complete Meeting the Challenge.

MANAGING ORGANIZATIONAL CHANGE

In recent years, a great deal of research and practical attention has focused on the necessity for change and the change process. If managers could design per-

FIGURE 11.2

Lewin's three phases of the planned change process

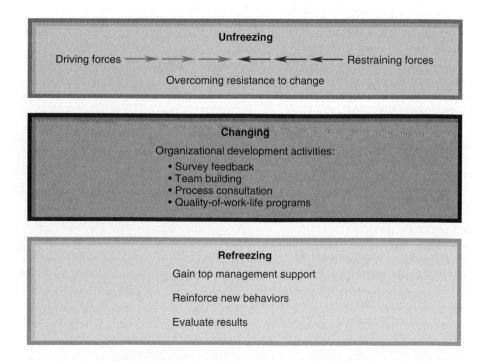

fect organizations and if the scientific, market, and technical environments were
stable and predictable, there would be no pressure for change. But such is not
the case. The statement that we live in the midst of constant change is a cliché,
but is relevant nevertheless. As you recall, Chapters 4 and 5 discussed change
at the strategic level. This chapter addresses change at the behavioral level.

   Not only is change a constant of the modern business environment, but it
is becoming more complex. According to Jack Welch, CEO of General Electric,
globalization compounds the problem of effectively managing change.[31] One
well-known business writer states that contemporary business organizations are
facing change that is more extensive, more far-reaching in its implications, and
more fundamental in its transforming quality than anything since the modern
industrial system took shape.[32] Popular literature, including best sellers, warns
that organizations' futures depend on their managers' ability to master change.

   Managers must recognize that the forces of change are significant and pervasive. Learning to recognize and manage change is one of the most important
skills a manager can develop. Change is natural, and managers must help their
organizations work with change, not against it. It seems reasonable to assert
that organizations must manage change in order to be responsive to changing
environments.[33]

Force-field analysis
A systematic process for examining
the pressures that are likely to support or resist a proposed change.

Unfreezing
Developing an initial awareness of the
need for change and the forces supporting and resisting change.

FIGURE 11.3
Driving and restraining forces

A FRAMEWORK FOR CHANGE

One useful tool for taking a systematic look at the forces in play around a proposed change is called force-field analysis.[34] While this may sound like something from a Steven Spielberg movie, a **force-field analysis** is really just a systematic process for examining the pressures that are likely to support or resist
a proposed change. This framework was proposed by the organizational researcher Kurt Lewin, who visualized change as the three-step process shown
in Figure 11.2. Lewin's approach recognizes that merely introducing a change
does not guarantee that the change will be successful. Let's take a closer look
at the three steps in the change process.

UNFREEZING

The first step, **unfreezing,** involves developing an initial awareness of the need
for change and the forces supporting and resisting change. Most people and
organizations prefer stability and the perpetuation of the status quo. In such a
state, forces for change are equally offset by forces that want to maintain the
status quo. Lewin called these driving forces and restraining forces, respectively. They are shown in Figure 11.3.

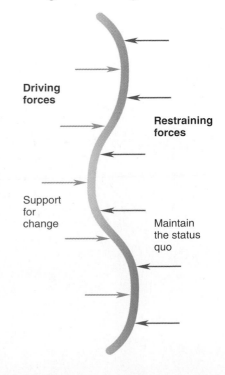

Driving forces

Restraining forces

Support for change

Maintain the status quo

External forces
Environmental factors that are fundamentally beyond the control of management.

Driving Forces

Driving forces for change are either internal or external. While **external forces** are fundamentally beyond the control of management, internal forces generally are within the control of management. Changes in one or more of the key environmental sectors discussed in Chapter 5 might be the external forces that provide the impetus for change in an organization. The environment includes many economic, technological, political, and social forces that can trigger the change process. For example, in the economic domain, changes in the inflation rate, interest rates, and the money supply can affect the ability of an organization's managers to get needed resources. New laws and regulations, trade tariffs, and court decisions emanating from the political domain can affect the way an organization conducts its business.

Internal forces
Inside factors that are generally within the control of management.

Change may also be initiated in response to **internal forces** at an organization.[35] For example, in a 1996 Work USA Survey, workers who were contacted complained that workplace changes had an adverse impact on their workload and morale (44 percent); their relationship with the company, such as satisfaction or commitment (37 percent); and the quality of the company's products and services (23 percent).[36] Recall from Managing for Excellence how the internal driving forces at Denny's jolted management out of their complacency and forced the organization to move from being one of America's most racist companies to a model of multicultural sensitivity.[37]

Managers must recognize that external and internal driving forces can be highly interrelated. Because organizations operate as open systems, external and internal driving forces will always be connected. For example, employees' attitudes toward work may change because of a new organizational policy or as a result of new legislation. Additionally, employees must cope with changes in their personal lives as well as changes in the organization.

Restraining forces
Promote organizational stability or the status quo and resist change.

Restraining Forces

While change is driven from one side, it is simultaneously resisted from another. Regardless of the pressure these driving forces exert, the **restraining forces** are clearly as threatening. People resist change for several reasons. First, they may genuinely believe, and could be right, that the change is not in their own best interests. Change can be threatening, and individuals may assess the consequences of the change in a totally different way from those who are initiating the change. It may represent a loss and threaten vested interests, such as power, responsibility, authority, control, and/or prestige. For example, a major obstacle to the successful introduction of personal computers in many organizations was middle managers' fear that they would become expendable, because upper-level managers could now monitor and control lower-level operations and direction.

People may resist change because they lack the abilities or skills to cope with it. Diversity in the work force may exacerbate this resistance. If proposed changes are going to require new skills, the organization has to include skill training as part of the planned change effort.

Finally, organizations have built-in resistance to change. Policies, rules, standard operating procedures, work methods, organizational charts, and job descriptions are examples of organizational infrastructure that serve to maintain the status quo. An organization's traditions, culture, and top-management philosophy also resist change because they are developed over a long period of time and are not easily cast aside by organizational leaders. As we saw in the Managerial Incident with Oracle, the organizational culture can have a major impact on the way an organization operates. Changes that seem to violate the accepted culture will be more difficult to implement successfully than changes that seem to emerge naturally out of the culture.

Strategies for Unfreezing

To be successful, any change process must overcome the status quo—by unfreezing old behaviors, processes, or structures. To call on a physics metaphor, unfreezing occurs only if the strength of the driving forces exceeds the strength of the restraining forces. If the restraining forces cannot be sufficiently reduced or the driving forces sufficiently increased, the change should not be attempted. If these forces can be managed, however, the next step is to design a strategy that will reduce resistance and stimulate support.

There are six general strategies for dealing with resistance to change. These are identified as (1) education and communication, (2) participation and involvement, (3) facilitation and support, (4) negotiation and agreement, (5) manipulation and co-optation, and (6) explicit and implicit coercion.[38] More details and the advantages and disadvantages of these six strategies are explained in Table 11.1.

Effective managers understand that resistance to change is something to be recognized and constructively addressed rather than feared. The presence of resistance typically suggests that something can be done to achieve a better fit among the change, the situation, and the people the change will affect. A manager needs to listen to such feedback and act accordingly.

CHANGING

The second step of the change process, **changing,** focuses on learning new required behaviors. Many changes that occur in an organization—new equip-

Changing
The second step in the change process, focusing on learning new required behaviors.

TABLE 11.1   Methods for dealing with resistance to change

APPROACH	COMMONLY USED	ADVANTAGES	DRAWBACKS
Education and communication	Where there is a lack of information or inaccurate information and analysis	Once persuaded, people will often help with the implementation of the change	Can be very time-consuming if lots of people are involved
Participation and involvement	Where the initiators do not have all the information they need to design the change, and where others have considerable power to resist	People who participate will be committed to implementing change, and any relevant information they have will be integrated into the change plan	Can be very time-consuming if participants design an inappropriate change
Facilitation and support	Where people are resisting because of adjustment problems	No other approach works as well with adjustment problems	Can be time-consuming and expensive and can still fail
Negotiation and agreement	Where someone or some group will clearly lose out in a change, and where that group has considerable power to resist	Sometimes it is a relatively easy way to avoid major resistance	Can be too expensive in many cases if it alerts others to negotiate for compliance
Manipulation and co-optation	Where other tactics will not work or are too expensive	It can be a relatively quick and inexpensive solution to resistance problems	Can lead to future problems if people feel manipulated
Explicit and implicit coercion	Where speed is essential, and the change initiators possess considerable power	It is speedy and can overcome any kind of resistance	Can be risky if it leaves people mad at the initiators

SOURCE: Reprinted by permission of the *Harvard Business Review.* Excerpt from "Choosing Strategies for Change" by John P. Kotter and Leonard A. Schlesinger, 57, March/April 1979, 111. Copyright © 1979 by the President and Fellows of Harvard College; all rights reserved.

ment, policies, or products—are relatively easy to implement in isolation. However, major difficulties can arise when dealing with human reactions to such organizational changes or attempting to change human actions and relationships directly. For example, organizational change that involves individuals directly or indirectly can require changes in roles, technical skills, interpersonal skills, or values and attitudes.

The primary tool for planned change is called organizational development. **Organizational development (OD)** is a process of planned change that uses behavioral science knowledge, theory, and technology to help an organization improve its capacity for effective change.[39]

In recent years, a number of OD intervention activities have emerged that can be useful in facilitating planned change. The most widely used approaches concentrate primarily on people-focused change. These approaches tend to rely a great deal on active involvement and participation by many members of the organization. If successful, people-focused approaches improve individual and group processes in such areas as decision making, problem identification and solving, communication, and interpersonal relationships. We will examine three popular and effective techniques of people-focused organizational change: survey feedback, team building, and process consultation.

Organizational development (OD)
A process of planning change in organizations that use behavioral science knowledge, theory, and technology to help an organization improve its capacity for effective change.

Survey feedback
A method of improving relationships among members of groups or departments that gather information, perceptions, and attitudes through a customized survey questionnaire and present the information to participants to discuss.

Survey Feedback   The primary objective of **survey feedback** is to improve relationships among the members of groups or between departments through the discussion of common problems.[40] As an organizationwide intervention, survey feedback requires the administration of standardized or customized survey questionnaires to appropriate managers and their employees. The intent is to anonymously gather accurate information, perceptions, and attitudes about various aspects of an organization, work unit, and individual managers. The information is then presented or "fed back" to participants as they engage in a collaborative process to discuss the meaning and explore possible interpretations of the findings.

Survey feedback requires that managers (1) encourage open and free discussion of the findings, probable causes of problems, and possible implications for performance; (2) propose and encourage suggestions for resolving problems; and (3) carry out agreed-upon changes as quickly as possible.[41] A major strength of survey feedback is that it deals with managers and employees in

In order for team building to be successful, four conditions must be present: (1) a lack of teamwork must be hindering the organization's effectiveness; (2) the culture of the organization must support a team approach; (3) the teams must be willing to undertake the team-building process; and (4) there must be adequate internal resources to support team building.
© Michael Newman/PhotoEdit

the context of their own jobs, problems, and work relationships. It helps to bring problems to the surface and clarifies issues.

Team Building   One possible result of the survey feedback process is an awareness that a manager and his or her work group are not functioning as a team. Through the team-building process, members of a work group can diagnose how they work together and plan changes to improve their effectiveness.[42]

Like survey feedback at the organizational level, **team building** involves some form of data collection and feedback. Teams may consist of members who work alongside one another daily or are together on a project for a short time. The key elements, however, are the collaborative assessment of the information by all members of the group and the achievement of a consensus about what might be done to improve group effectiveness. A series of activities and exercises is designed to solve problems, enhance communication among team members, and develop a sense of teamwork.[43]

The advantage of team building is that it can often provide a useful way to involve employees in an organizational change program and increase collaborative behavior. In order for team building to be an appropriate OD approach, however, several conditions must be present. First, a lack of effective teamwork must be seriously hindering organizational effectiveness. Second, the culture of the organization must support a team approach to getting work done. Third, the teams must be receptive to undertaking the team-building process. For example, the team must be willing to devote time and energy to team building. Also, the active support of the team leader and his superior is critical to success. Fourth, adequate resources must exist internally to support team building.[44]

Process Consultation   **Process consultation** is related to team building in that it involves structured activities designed to improve group functioning. Process consultation directs attention toward the key processes through which members of a group work with one another. Thus, this tactic has a more specific focus than team building. Process consultation helps a group function better on such things as group norms and roles, decision making, conflict resolution, communication, and task activities.

Process consultation is characterized by the use of a skilled third party or facilitator, such as an external consultant, a human resource professional, or a manager skilled in process activities. It is often effective in changing attitudes and group norms, improving interpersonal and decision-making skills, increasing group cohesiveness, and enlarging interactions and appreciation for team members.

REFREEZING THE CHANGE

The third and final step in the changing process, **refreezing,** centers on reinforcing new behaviors, usually by positive results, feelings of accomplishment, or rewards from others. Once management has implemented changes in organizational goals, products, processes, structures, or people, it cannot sit back and simply expect the change to be maintained over time. Laws of physics dictate that an object moved away from equilibrium will tend to return to the original equilibrium point unless new forces are present to prevent this. Lewin reminds managers that new goals, structures, behaviors, and attitudes must be solidified, or refrozen, if that change is to become the new status quo.

To make sure that change sticks, the manager or organization must undertake some additional activities. Let's look at three commonly employed approaches that are useful in accomplishing the refreezing step of the change process.

Team building
A process by which members of a work group diagnose how they work together and plan changes to improve their effectiveness.

Process consultation
Involves structured activities directed toward key "processes" through which members of a group work with one another on specific issues and activities.

Refreezing
The third step in the change process, which centers on reinforcing new behaviors, usually by positive results, feelings of accomplishment, or rewards from others.

Gain Top-Management Support

Formal or informal sponsorship of a change by top management gives legitimacy to new behaviors. If employees elsewhere in the organization see that top managers support and accept the change, they will more readily do so themselves. Thus, if a change involves the redesign of a communication or information processing system, top management must encourage the use of the new system by using it themselves.

Reinforce New Behaviors

Behaviors that are positively reinforced tend to be repeated. In designing a change, attention must be paid to how the new behaviors will be reinforced and rewarded. The reward systems should be carefully considered when planning change, and redesigned, if necessary. If the rewards or reinforcements inherent in the change fall short of employee expectations, the change will likely fail.

Evaluate the Change

Finally, an important and often overlooked step in the refreezing process is evaluation. Management needs to know if the change has had the intended effects. Too many managers install changes, undertake training programs, and redesign structures with the mistaken belief that simply because the change was made, it will be successful. In many cases, this assumption proves incorrect. This is particularly true when the change was unilateral or was made without those affected perceiving the need for change. Sabotage of changes imposed by management has been known to occur in such situations.

Evaluation is also beneficial because it forces the manager making the change to establish the criteria for judging its success before the change is instituted. Doing so provides additional guidance when planning the tactics for making the change. It also forces managers to give careful thought to how the results of the change will be measured at some point in the future.

ETHICAL ISSUES IN ORGANIZATIONAL CHANGE

Regardless of how carefully managed a change might be, it will usually raise ethical issues. Managers and employees need to be aware of potential ethical concerns during organizational change. Asking some of the following questions can serve as a guide for managing the change ethically.[45]

- Does the manager or OD consultant have any vested interests in using a particular technique? Do all the alternative techniques receive a fair hearing?
- Who will determine the target(s) of change? Which members of the organization will participate in diagnosing, planning, and implementing the change and to what degree?
- To what extent should the organization disclose all aspects of the change in advance?
- Whose values influence the adoption of goals and the methods chosen to accomplish them?
- Do employees feel manipulated? To what extent do employees have the right to participate in changes that affect them?

These are difficult questions that managers and employees can use as a basis for recognizing the potential ethical concerns involved in organizational change.[46] With these questions, informed choices can be made. A starting point is the need to be sensitive to the potential for ethical problems during planned change programs.

MANAGERIAL IMPLICATIONS

Current research suggests a number of activities that will help managers achieve effective organizational culture, change, and development:[47]

- Solicit input from those who will be affected by organizational change. Involvement is essential to accepting the need for change.
- Carefully formulate your message regarding the need for and nature of organizational change. The success of the change process will depend on effective communication.
- Assess your organizational environment and be sure that the tone and the tempo of the change fit the organization. Timing is everything.
- Serve as a role model for the behaviors sought by the organizational change. Actions speak louder than words.

This chapter has focused on the need for managers to understand the culture of their organization and the role that culture plays in managing change. Cultures themselves change through evolution in light of changes in activities, in response to changing internal and external events, or through revolution as the organization deals with major challenges. Yet change is especially difficult in today's business environment of global competitiveness, diverse work forces, and technological changes. It is part of the manager's job to help the organization and its members overcome resistance to needed changes in its culture. Doing this requires an understanding of both the organization as it currently exists and its vision of what it wants to become.

Managing an Unruly Adolescent: Lane Learns What Adulthood Is All About

Managerial Incident Resolution

Shortly after Larry Ellison, founder and billionaire CEO of Oracle, hired Ray Lane to run the organization, Lane set about putting the kinds of controls in place that a maturing high-tech company needed. He chose not to cramp Oracle's entrepreneurial culture, but at the same time saw that employees needed leadership and needed to know what was expected of them.

One of the first changes was a restructuring and organization along five business lines, thereby clarifying employees' roles and reporting relationships. He introduced a system of personnel evaluations, a first for Oracle.

Lane also put a program in place called "Vision and Values," spelling out how people should interact and communicate. With an employee base of over 20,000, Lane had to end the practice of taking problems straight to the top. Horizontal communication became the new norm; employees were required to discuss issues first with peers, and then, if necessary, to take them to the next step in the formal command chain.

Oracle has fared well during Lane's four-year tenure. He has brought about change that has preserved the positive aspects of Oracle's culture and increased the value of its stock almost tenfold. On the other hand, Larry Ellison has time to pursue his nemesis, Bill Gates, and "play in the lab with the kids," says Lane.

SUMMARY

- Organizational culture is the system of shared beliefs and values that develops within an organization and influences the way people act, perform their jobs, work with colleagues, and view the future.

- Culture can be viewed as an iceberg. The visible elements of an organization's culture consist of the practices or routines referred to as artifacts. These are sustained by hidden ideologies, shared values, expectations, and norms that are at the deepest level or core of the organization. By studying the artifacts, or visible elements, one can better understand an organization's culture. These artifacts are (1) rites, rituals, and ceremonies; (2) language systems and metaphors; and (3) stories, sagas, and myths.

- A strong culture can be a source of competitive advantage for an organization. It can provide a stable social system and reduce the need for formal and bureaucratic controls. Conversely, it can reinforce a singular view of the organization and its environment and make it difficult to change the organization.

- Information technology removes barriers and enables information to reach all levels of the organization. It can flatten organizational charts and provide data that employees need. Neither organizations nor individuals can afford to ignore these new possibilities while all around them both competitors and colleagues build new relationships that will soon be an commonplace as the telephone.

- A force-field analysis is a systematic process for examining the pressures that are likely to support or resist a proposed change. It involves three steps: unfreezing, changing, and refreezing.

- Six strategies for overcoming resistance to change have been identified: (1) education and communication, (2) participation and involvement, (3) facilitation and support, (4) negotiation and agreement, (5) manipulation and co-optation, and (6) explicit and implicit coercion. Each offers advantages and disadvantages and is appropriate under certain conditions.

- People-focused approaches to change tend to rely a great deal on active involvement and participation by many members of the organization. These methods include survey feedback, team building, and process consultation.

- Regardless of how carefully a change is managed, it usually raises ethical issues. Managers and employees need to be aware of potential ethical concerns during the organizational change process.

KEY TERMS

Organizational culture	Organizational change	Changing
Artifacts	Force-field analysis	Organizational development (OD)
Rites	Unfreezing	Survey feedback
Language systems and metaphors	External forces	Team building
Stories	Internal forces	Process consultation
Myths	Restraining forces	Refreezing

REVIEW QUESTIONS

1. Define organizational culture.
2. How does an organization's culture evolve?
3. Describe the two basic components of organizational culture.
4. List and explain three types of organizational artifacts. Give an example of each.
5. How can culture influence an organization's competitive advantage?

6. Define organizational change.
7. Identify and describe the targets of planned change.
8. Describe the three-step process of planned change.
9. Explain six strategies for overcoming resistance to change.
10. Explain how information technology can be either positive or negative to an organization.

DISCUSSION QUESTIONS

Improving Critical Thinking

1. Since managers cannot actually see an organizational culture, what aspects of the organization might allow them to make some guesses about the nature of the culture?
2. As a manager, which of the six strategies for overcoming resistance to change would you most like to be involved with?
3. What does the statement "You can't make just one

decision" mean in the context of organizational change?
4. Provide some examples of situations where resistance to change was positive.

Enhancing Communication Skills

5. Suggest ways in which a manager can maintain a culture. To practice your oral communication skills, prepare a presentation using some examples from current successful organizations.

6. Why do people resist change? Write a brief paper that gives some examples of this concept.

Building Teamwork

7. Describe the major differences between cultures in
   a. a high school and a college or university.
   b. different college or university classes.
   c. different campus organizations.
   d. a public college and a private college.
   e. a government (public) organization and a private organization.

   In a small group, discuss each of these settings and report your findings to the class.

8. Working in a small group, think of a recent change that has taken place at your college or university. Analyze the driving and restraining forces. Write down the key issues that should be considered and report your findings to the class or instructor.

INFORMATION TECHNOLOGY: Insights and Solutions

1. Form a small group as instructed by your professor. Each person in the group should select the same organization but use a different search engine on the Internet to collect information on the company. Compile the information and put together a report about the organization. How do the different search engines compare? How does the information you gathered differ? Use the knowledge gained from this exercise to better understand the power of the Internet.

2. Make a list of all forms of information technology available to you as a college student on campus. After completing your list, compare it with a partner in class. Are there items that have changed how you interact with others, pay bills, register, get advising, communicate, complete research? Are there individuals that you communicate with electronically but have never met personally? What types of technological changes have been difficulty for you to adjust to? Why?

3. Select an issue that you feels needs changing in your community, state, or country. This might be an issue involving literacy, education, the homeless, environment, labor laws, building codes, employment, and so on. Using the Internet, locate the resources and consumer groups who are already working on this issue. Contact the groups for information and get involved!

ETHICS: Take a Stand

As an administrative manager for Visystem, Inc., for over eight years, Jeri is very satisfied with the company and her work. The culture of the organization is one of the reasons she has been so happy. As she describes it, the company isn't really a company, it's a big family where members support and care about each other. Often, Jeri has seen ideas that looked good for the company voted down because they were bad for individual employees. Visystem is very decentralized, so Jeri makes decisions in her department without having to follow a lot of rigid rules or be closely supervised by top managers. Employee satisfaction is high, turnover is low, and a recent attitude survey found that 95 percent of the people said that they would recommend Visystem to a friend as a good place to work.

In Jeri's department, employees work in small project groups and are supportive and friendly. They celebrate weddings and birthdays together, support the local college football team, spend holidays together, and often help out when an employee has a personal problem. Although most of Jeri's subordinates are hourly workers, they strive to complete assignments, even if it means coming in on weekends or staying late.

James, a member of Jeri's department, is a very dedicated employee who has worked hard and been loyal to the company for 25 years. In addition to working at Visystem, he takes care of his family and attends a community college to earn some credits. In the last two years, virtually every possible disaster has happened to James: death of both parents, divorce, major physical problems, and personal problems with relatives. As a result, James got very sick. After his sick leave was used up, Jeri let him use vacation time until that was gone. Visystem has a system for this type of problem: its short-term disability program pays 80 percent of an employee's salary for a month and then two-thirds of the salary for a year. Jeri knew that James couldn't live on this limited income, however, so she gave him time off without docking his pay. James assured her that he would make up the time when things were straightened out at home.

Jeri felt she could adjust the disability policy because (1) the company believes in treating people differently, as long as the different treatment was not discriminatory, (2) the role of policy in the company is not clear, and (3) she reported her actions to the company president, who backed her decision.

For Discussion

1. Did Jeri's actions set a precedent that could erode respect for policies, rules, and procedures in the organization?
2. What kind of message did Jeri's actions send to people in the department? Was she a humane manager? Does her message say that this company really cares about its people?

THINKING CRITICALLY: Debate the Issue

VALUING CHANGE

Form small teams as directed by your instructor. Half of the teams should prepare to argue that organizational changes that incorporate downsizing and restructuring have valuable culture that cannot be measured or studied. The other half of the teams should take the perspective that culture can be measured and studied to understand how organizations function. Use current periodicals and organizational examples to strengthen your team's arguments. Your instructor will select two teams to present their findings to the class in a debate format.

Video Case

LANIER

Home Page {http://www.lanier.com/}

Recently, the managers of Lanier made a critical and far-reaching decision. Lanier, the largest distributor of office equipment in the world, would no longer behave as a "sales-driven" company, but would redefine itself as a "customer-driven" corporation. This decision represented a bold step for Lanier, a company with over 1,600 sales and service centers in more than 100 countries. The company, best known for its expertise in sourcing and distribution, would bet its future on customer service.

Lanier was founded in 1934 by Tommy Lanier, a distributor of Ediphone dictation machines. The company grew slowly until the 1960s, when it experienced rapid growth and became a national leader in office equipment sales. In the 1980s, Lanier became a subsidiary of the Harris Corporation. Today, Lanier is the largest distributor of office equipment in the world.

A focus on customer service is consistent with Lanier's business strategy. Lanier does not compete on price, but rather differentiates itself from its competitors on the basis of quality and service. The company has developed several programs to reinforce its emphasis on these attributes. These programs include: (1) Customer Vision, (2) The Performance Promise, (3) 100 Percent Sold, and (4) The Lanier Team Management Process. The idea behind the Customer Vision Program is that Lanier must see its business through the eyes of its customers and respond accordingly. This encourages the company to make its customers' priorities its priorities. Through the Performance Promise program, Lanier attempts to outdo its competitors by providing product guarantees, free loaners while repairs are being completed on Lanier products, and a 24-hour toll-free helpline. The 100 Percent Sold program has the ultimate goal of having every Lanier customer buy all of their office equipment from Lanier. Finally, The Lanier Team Management Process is a program that stresses a never-ending process of continuous improvement in quality, reliability, and performance in all things Lanier does at all levels in the company.

Lanier has coupled its new customer-service initiatives with extensive training for all of its employees. This has meant producing training materials in many different languages at considerable cost. In addition, the culture of the company is changing to reflect the new customer emphasis. At each level within the company, the employees are being asked to determine specifically, "Who is your customer?" In many cases, this process has helped employees realize that they have many internal as well as external customers to satisfy.

Lanier's emphasis on customer satisfaction is paying off. Sales remain strong and the company has received a number of "best supplier" awards. Culture change is never easy. However, the company's willingness to back up its culture change with concrete programs and training seems to be making the difference.

For Discussion

1. Why was a change in culture necessary at Lanier?

2. What steps has Lanier taken to ensure that its culture change will be taken seriously by its employees?

3. How important is a company's culture in your selection of a place to work? How will you determine what the culture is?

CASE

CHANGING THE SYSTEM AT SCLD

The Seminole County Library District (SCLD) has six branches and employs 42 full-time staff members, including 12 librarians. SCLD has an excellent reputation for community service, thanks to Charles Klee, the director who ran SCLD for 25 years until his recent retirement. Charles knew every staff member personally, having hired and indoctrinated (with his community service ideals) all 42. None of the 12 librarians has a college degree, but Charles trained all of them and promoted them into librarian positions. His approach to management was traditional, and he rarely delegated or involved the staff in policy making.

Upon Charles's retirement, Shannon Miller was hired as director. After two weeks on the job, Shannon discovered two major problems. First, the state library accreditation commission had put SCLD on probation, limiting the availability of state grants and funding sources if immediate action was not taken to raise standards. The level of computer use in cataloging, maintenance of reference sources, linkage with other resource centers, and tracking of borrowed materials was totally inadequate. Second, she was notified that the state university had dropped SCLD from the approved list of library systems for its graduate interns. Interns were an important source of inexpensive labor and a force for improvement and revitalization.

Shannon had experience with computerized library systems and was promised the resources and trained personnel to implement a new computer system. She called a staff meeting to discuss her concerns and objectives and explain the changes that needed to take place to put SCLD back on the approved internship program and have the computer system up and operational in one year. The staff members voiced suspicions about computers and suggested that the new system was an excuse to weed out unneeded personnel. Some argued that it would require people to learn extensive programming skills that they didn't have or weren't interested in learning. Still others felt it would dilute their efforts at delivering personal service. They made negative comments about the university internship program.

In the last two days, Shannon has received phone calls from fifteen community patrons who have heard that the new computer system would reduce personal service.

For Discussion

1. What are the possible targets of change? Use a force-field analysis to examine the pressures that are likely to support or resist a proposed change.
2. What approach should Shannon use for dealing with the resistance to change?

EXPERIENTIAL EXERCISE 11.1

Understanding the Culture of Your Organization

Purpose: To better understand and describe the culture of an organization. This can be done either individually or in a small group if several members of the class work in the same organization.

Procedure: Think about an organization with which you are familiar. It could be one in which you are employed, or a campus organization such as a fraternity/sorority or service club. How would you describe the organization's culture to a friend or new employee? Try to be objective in your analysis and identify examples of the artifacts in use. Answer each of the following questions. After you have completed the questions, share the information about the culture of your organization with a small group or the class.

1. What are the main norms (that is, the do's and don'ts)?

2. What are the main ceremonies and rituals and what purpose do they serve?

3. What metaphors and language dominate everyday conversations?

4. What kinds of beliefs and values dominate the organization (officially and unofficially)?

5. What are the images that people use to describe the organization?

6. What are the favorite topics of informal conversation?

7. What reward systems are in place? What messages do they send in terms of which activities or accomplishments are valued and which are not?

8. What are the dominant stories or sagas that people tell? What measures are they trying to convey?

9. Think of two influential people in the organization. In what ways do they symbolize the character of the organization?

ENDNOTES

1. For a more thorough discussion of change and the impact on leadership see H. Sims and C. Manz, *Company of Heroes* (New York: Wiley, 1996).

2. J. Martin, "Tomorrow's CEO," *Fortune,* June 24, 1996, 76–90; J. Malawian, "Larry Ellison Is Captain Ahab and Bill Gates is Moby Dick," *Fortune,* October 28, 1996, 119–22.

3. T. Peters, "Perpetual Job Insecurity," in *Lessons in Leadership;* and T. Peters, "Crazy Times Call for Crazy Organizations" in *Lessons in Leadership* (Provo, Utah: Covey Leadership Center, 1996).

4. For a thorough discussion of challenges, see J. Kouzes and B. Posner, *Leadership Challenges: How to Get Extraordinary Things Done with Ordinary People* 2d ed. (San Francisco: Jossey-Bass, 1995).

5. K. C. Green and D. T. Seymour, *Who's Going to Run General Motors?* (Princeton, N.J.: Peterson's Guides, 1991), 134.

6. R. H. Kilmann, M. J. Saxon, and R. Serpa, "Issues in Understanding and Changing Culture," *California Management Review,* 28, 1986, 87–94; E. H. Schein, *Organizational Culture and Leadership* (San Francisco: Jossey-Bass, 1985), 223–43.

7. J. S. Ott, *The Organizational Culture Perspective* (Monterey, Calif.: Brooks Cole Publishing, 1989).

8. L. R. Beach, *Making the Right Decision: Organizational Culture, Vision, and Planning* (Englewood Cliffs, N.J.: Prentice-Hall: 1993); G. Morgan, *Imaginization: The Art of Creative Management* (Newbury Park, Calif.: Sage Publications, 1993).

9. T. Martin, "Ten Commandments for Managing Creative People," *Fortune,* January 16, 1995.

10. L. R. Beach, *Making the Right Decision.*

11. G. G. Gordon, "Industry Determinants of Organizational Culture," *Academy of Management Review,* 2, 1991, 396–415.

12. J. Martin, "Tomorrow's CEO."

13. H. M. Trice and J. M. Beyer, "Using Six Organizational Rites to Change Culture," in *Gaining Control of the Corporate Culture,* eds. R. H. Kilmann, M. J. Saxton, and R. Serpa, (San Francisco: Jossey-Bass, 1985).

14. Ibid.

15. Adapted from ibid., 372.

16. K. Rebello and E. Schwartz, "The Magic of Microsoft," *Business Week,* February 24, 1992, 60–64.

17. For a very detailed discussion of metaphors and metaphorical thinking, see G. Morgan, *Imaginization: The Art of Creative Management.*

18. R. Semler, *Maverick: The Success Story behind the World's Most Unusual Workplace* (New York: Warner Books, 1993); F. O'Donnell, "When Workers Are Bosses," *Washington Post,* September 14, 1993, B-2.

19. Adapted from T. J. Peters and R. H. Waterman Jr., *In Search of Excellence: Lessons From America's Best-Run Companies* (New York: Harper & Row, 1982), 224–34; J. Galbraith, "The Innovating Organization," *Organizational Dynamics,* Winter 1982; 5–25; B. Dumaine, "Ability to Innovate," *Fortune,* January 29, 1990, 43, 46; C. Knowlton, "What America Makes Best," *Fortune,* March 28, 1988, 40–54.

20. T. J. Peters and R. H. Waterman Jr., *In Search of Excellence.*

21. D. Woodruff, "May We Help You Kick the Tires?" *Business Week,* August 3, 1992, 49–50.

22. P. F. Drucker, "Don't Change Corporate Culture—Use It!" *The Wall Street Journal,* March 28, 1991, A14.

23. J. Martin, "Tomorrow's CEO".

24. F. Rice, "Denny's Changes Its Spots," *Fortune,* May 13, 1996, 133-42.

25. T. Paulson, "They Shoot Managers, Don't They?," *Ten Speed Press,* 1991, 137.

26. R. Stevenson, "Slot Machine Maker Hits Jackpot," *New York Times,* September 12, 1989, C1.

27. J. Martin, "Tomorrow's CEO".

28. J. Kennedy and A. Everest, "Put Diversity in Context," *Personnel Journal,* September 1991, 50-54.

29. C. Carson, K. Eckart, C. Flash, and G. Fysh, "It's Going the Way It Was Programmed," *News Tribune,* Tacoma, Wash., September 8, 1996, D1.

30. C. Borucki and C. Barnett, "Restructuring for Self-Renewal: Navistar International Corporation," *Academy of Management Executive,* 4, 1990, 37-49.

31. N. M. Tichy and S. Sherman, *Control Your Destiny or Someone Else Will* (New York: Doubleday, 1993).

32. R. M. Kanter, *The Change Masters* (New York: Simon & Schuster, 1983).

33. L. L. Cummings, "Compensation Culture, and Motivation: A System Perspective," *Organizational Dynamics,* Winter 1984, 33-44.

34. R. L. Mathis and J. H. Jackson, *Personnel/Human Resource Management,* 7th ed. (St. Paul, Minn.: West Publishing, 1994).

35. G. G. Gordon, "Industry Determinants of Organizational Culture."

36. Summarized from *Work USA Survey,* The Wyatt Company, Washington, D.C., 1996.

37. F. Rice, "Denny's Changes Its Spots."

38. J. P. Kotter and L. A. Schlesinger, "Choosing Strategies for Change," *Harvard Business Review,* March/April 1979, 109-12.

39. W. W. Burke, *Organizational Development* (Reading, Mass.: Addison-Wesley, 1987).

40. Adapted from W. L. French and C. H. Bell, *Organization Development: Behavioral Science Interventions for Organization Improvement,* 4th ed. (Upper Saddle River, N.J.: Prentice Hall, 1990), 169-72.

41. E. F. Huse and T. G. Cummings, *Organization Development and Change,* 4th ed. (St. Paul, Minn.: West Publishing, 1989).

42. W. G. Dyer, *Team Building: Issues and Alternatives,* 2d ed. (Reading, Mass.: Addison-Wesley, 1987).

43. D. G. Ancona, "Outward Bound: Strategies for Team Survival in an Organization," *Academy of Management Journal,* 33, 1990, 334-65.

44. C. Larson and F. LaFasto, *Teamwork: What Must Go Right, What Can Go Wrong* (Newbury Park, Calif.: Sage Publications, 1989).

45. Based on G. Boccialetti, "Organization Development Ethics and Effectiveness," in *The Emerging Practice of Organization Development,* eds. W. Sikes, A. B. Drexler, and J. Gants, (Alexandria, Va.: NTL Institute for Applied Behavioral Sciences, 1989), 83-92.

46. A set of ethical guidelines for OD practitioners was published in *Consultation,* Fall 1986, 21-218.

47. R. Denhardt, *The Pursuit of Significance* (Belmont, Calif.: Wadsworth Publishing, 1992).

IBAX: REORGANIZING TO ACHIEVE PERFORMANCE IMPROVEMENTS

Recall the IBAX situation, profiled in the integrative cases at the close of Parts I and II. IBAX, a vendor of health care information systems software, is a partnership between IBM and Baxter. The company had experienced significant strategic, operational, and financial problems since its inception in 1989. As we began the case, Jeff Goodman had just been hired as the CEO of IBAX. His challenge was to turn the company around.

In the integrative case that closed Part II, we learned about Goodman's strategic plan for IBAX. The plan was based on a retrenchment strategy. Goodman had closed several facilities and had reduced the work force from 750 to 580. Once the downsizing efforts were complete, Goodman started changing the internal functioning of IBAX. In this integrative case, we will examine the changes that Goodman made in the organizational design of the company, its human resource management practices, and its organizational culture.

CHANGING THE ORGANIZATIONAL DESIGN OF IBAX

Historically, IBAX had been organized in a traditional functional structure. A senior vice-president was in charge of each functional department such as human resources, finance, product development, sales and marketing, and so on. As with most functional structures, profit centers did not exist, and there was little direct accountability for the bottom-line performance measures that were most critical for the company (that is, net profit margins, product quality measures, customer satisfaction levels, and the like).

Goodman believed that a product-based structure would bring employees closer to the products and the customers that drove IBAX's performance. So he reorganized the company into six independent operating units based on the three core product lines of the company (Series 3000, 4000, and 5000), and three other categories of products offered by IBAX (Value-Added Products, Physician Series, and Point-of-Care Clinical Series). He called these units "businesses" and intended for them to operate as such. He identified teams of people to run each business, worked with them to establish performance objectives for their business with regard to such things as revenues, expenses, and customer satisfaction, and gave them the authority to do whatever necessary to make sure those objectives were achieved. Along with delegating the responsibility and authority associated with running the business, Goodman also made it very clear that these self-managed teams were accountable for the performance of their businesses. The locus of decision making in the organization shifted from being highly centralized to being very decentralized.

Once the teams understood their responsibilities, they began to reengineer their units, looking for redundancies in tasks and inefficient processes. Tasks were regrouped and jobs were redesigned. In many cases, both job scope and depth increased as employees took on additional tasks and responsibilites to improve the efficiency of their units. Where necessary, employees were provided with the training and development to do their job better or, in some cases, to do an entirely new job.

The product-based structure created relatively independent units, and therefore the need for integration between work groups was reduced to some degree. Nevertheless, there was still a need for some communication between work groups and with the functional managers that had remained part of the structure (such as the vice-presidents of human resources and finance). Team leaders served as liaisons with other groups where necessary, but it was generally understood that any employee could go directly to any other employee in the organization to get the information necessary to do her job. There was not a rigid hierarchy to be respected; doors were open, and everyone in the company was available to help as necessary.

A NEW APPROACH TO HUMAN RESOURCE MANAGEMENT

The human resource management (HRM) function changed dramatically as part of the retrenchment strategy. While the human resource management function had been fulfilled in very traditional ways in the past, Goodman and the vice-president of human resources, Meigann Putnam, designed more creative and innovative methods to better serve the HRM function.

Rather than providing the traditional services of recruitment, selection, compensation, training and development, and employee relations centrally, the HRM function was decentralized. An HRM advisor was assigned to each business unit at IBAX. This advisor worked within the business so he could better understand the products and markets of the business and, therefore, better assess its human resource needs. The advisor would involve the team members in the business in all elements of the HRM process. For example, the teams assumed responsibility for hiring their own people based on the assessed needs of their business. What had once been a top-down approach to human resource management was transformed into an integrated, team-based process.

INSTILLING A NEW ORGANIZATIONAL CULTURE

Changing the culture of IBAX was critical to the implementation of the organizational and human resource management changes. As you will recall from the integrative case at the close of Part I, there was no homogeneous culture at IBAX and no evolved, shared values among employees. Goodman knew from the outset that developing a strong and healthy corporate culture at IBAX would be a prerequisite to all the other changes that needed to take place.

Communication was the key to changing the culture at IBAX. From the beginning, Goodman was open with the employees about his concerns, goals, and plans. He involved them in both the assessment of the business and the development of the plan to turn it around. Employees started to believe that Goodman was committed to involving the employees in decision making. Further, he promised to reward organizational commitment, creativity, and hard work, and he followed through. Trust began to build within the ranks. As one person put it, "for the first time, the words and the music started to match." As trust continued to grow, the culture began to change. Morale began to improve, and employees started to feel empowered to make a difference at IBAX.

THE RESULTS

Much of the success of the retrenchment strategy can be attributed to the organizational changes described in this case. The move to a product-based structure put the focus of the company on the products it marketed and the customers it served. Responsibility and authority were delegated to those who could make a difference in product quality and customer service. Decision making was in the hands of self-managed teams who understood their performance objectives clearly and knew they wre accountable for achieving those objectives. The overall effect of these changes was improved product quality, greater productivity, better customer satisfaction, and stronger bottom-line profitability for all of IBAX's product lines.

For Discussion

1. Discuss the ways Goodman changed the organizational design of IBAX.
2. What were the benefits of decentralizing the HRM function?
3. How will the new organizational culture at IBAX help with the implementation of its retrenchment strategy?

PART 4

LEADERSHIP CHALLENGES IN THE 21ST CENTURY

Communicating Effectively within Diverse Organizations

■ CHAPTER OVERVIEW

Advances in technology and data management that have taken place over the past decade are making vast changes to the way individuals and organizations communicate. However, effective managers must be aware of the importance in building and sustaining human relationships through interpersonal communication.[1] Since managers spend the vast majority of their time in the disseminator role—informing, persuading, listening, and inspiring—communication skills will likely be the manager's most important asset or biggest liability. Recent studies show that managers spend from 66 to 80 percent of their time communicating with superiors, subordinates, peers, and outside constituents. If they do not understand the processes involved in good communication, their best-laid plans can fail. The challenge for effective communication is even greater for managers as organizations become more global and employees become more diverse.

This chapter is focused toward understanding communication in organizations and the task of achieving excellence in interpersonal communication. We start by defining communication and examining interpersonal communication, including oral, written, and nonverbal communication. Then we turn our attention to the basic elements in the communication process, such as the social context, sender and message encoding, receiver and message decoding, the medium, feedback, and noise. Next, we examine some of the barriers that prevent quality communication. These include cultural factors, trust and credibility issues, information overload, perception, and language characteristics. We move on to explore ways in which managers handle organizational communication, including both formal and informal communication channels. The role of technology in communication and information is changing the workplace and we would be remiss if we didn't examine this impact. Finally, we conclude by focusing on ways managers can achieve communication competency by improving their feedback and listening skills.

■ LEARNING OBJECTIVES

When you have finished studying this chapter, you should be able to:

- Describe the elements of the communication process and explain their relationship to one another.
- Give examples of the types of communication managers use.

C H A P T E R

12

- Explain the importance of feedback.
- Describe the barriers to effective communication.
- Discuss the differences between formal and informal communication channels.
- Discuss the changing role of technology in the communication process.
- Improve your feedback skills.
- Demonstrate your listening competency.

Managerial Incident

DESIGN CONTINUUM: BALANCING TECHNOLOGY WHILE MAINTAINING EFFECTIVE COMMUNICATION

"My company needs technology like I need air," says Gianfranco Zaccai, co-founder of Design Continuum. But this wasn't always the opinion of Zaccai, who created Design Continuum in 1983 and nurtured the company to annual revenues of approximately $10 million. With 100 employees in three countries; information technology has played an important role in the growth of the company. But before technology became a effective mechanism for Zaccai, he had to overcome some the challenges of balancing technology with maintaining effective interpersonal communication.

Design Continuum helps clients develop products and services for the international marketplace. Much of the research they did couldn't be conducted or shared by phone or through e-mail. The company's designs and drawings are very intricate, and clients needed to be intimately involved in all phases of a project. Sketches and diagrams couldn't be reproduced clearly or transmitted through electronic systems. Employees often traveled to customers and were away for lengthy periods of time. They met with clients, presented ideas, and answered questions. But once the team of designers had left, clients still needed more direct support to answer detailed questions and respond to changes. Zaccai doesn't mind referring to this as "hand holding."

It wasn't uncommon for miscommunication to occur because of distance or time differences. This often led to project overruns and time delays.

An important part of Design Continuum's business is market research. This was commonly bogged down in the information-gathering process because product-development questionnaires and surveys were slow to collect value data. This prolonged process and the delay in analyzing results were costly, and Design Continuum often took months to process and deliver results to its intended users.

Because Zaccai was a strong believer in communicating face to face and not just over a computer screen, he was reluctant to incorporate new technology into the workplace. Human contact, he believed, fostered creativity. In addition, Zaccai felt there was a lot to be gained by working in an interpersonal environment.

Zaccai knew that many of his competitors were beginning to incorporate new technology to reach international clients. He was faced with the challenge of using information technology to survive in the competitive global environment without sacrificing quality communication.[2]

INTRODUCTION

We see from reading about Design Continuum that the need for effective interpersonal communication is extremely important to remain competitive in the global environment.[3] The profound technological, economic, and business changes now underway in industrialized countries worldwide are radically altering the organizational environments in which we work. But they are not changing the need to maintain superior communication skills.

Communication is the process through which managers coordinate, lead, and influence their subordinates. The ability to communicate effectively is the characteristic managers consider most critical in determining managerial success. This ability involves a broad array of activities, including reading, listening, managing and interpreting information, serving clients, writing, speechmaking, and the use of symbolic gestures.[4] The Department of Labor considers these necessary for successful functioning in the workplace.[5]

Communication skills can make or break a career or an organization. Communication is essential to management because it encompasses all aspects of an organization and pervades organizational activity; it is the process by which things get done in organizations. Yet communication is a complicated and dynamic process with many factors influencing effectiveness.[6] First, communication is a process in which sender, messages, channels, and receivers do not remain constant or static. Second, communication is complex. A number of communication theorists suggest that even a simple two-person interaction involves many variables, such as the individuals, the setting, the experiences each person has had, and the nature of the task, that effect the efficiency and effectiveness of the process. Third, communication is symbolic. We use a variety of arbitrary words and signs to convey meaning to those with whom we are communicating. While there is some agreement about the meaning of most of our words and signs, these change over time.

The object of communicating is to create some degree of accurate understanding among the participants. Clearly then, communication skills are essential for managerial success. This chapter explores the ways managers communicate, both formally and informally. Like the other aspects of the business environment we have examined, communication is being affected by change. In particular, technology is changing the way managers communicate, and we will look at its effects in some detail. Throughout the chapter, emphasis will be placed on ways managers can develop communication competency.

WHAT IS QUALITY COMMUNICATION?

An accountant prepares a memo on the tax implications of a proposed business merger. A department chair praises the accomplishments of a faculty member. A crane operator signals directions. A professor writes a grade on a student's term paper. Employees in New York and Seattle attend a videoconference meeting. You will probably agree that all these incidents involve some form of communication. But what exactly is meant by communication?

Communication is a complex and dynamic process, and like other management terms, it has no universally accepted definition. For our purposes we will define **communication** as a process in which one person or group evokes a shared or common meaning to another person or group.[7] Indeed, the term *communication* stems from the Latin root word *communicare* which means "to make common." Often this is all that occurs and communication is considered a one-way process. One-way communication occurs when top executives in a large company send directions to subordinates. Often they do not expect any information in return, at least not immediately. But in most situations, the process of communication involves another aspect, when the receiver responds in some manner. For example, the person or group that receives the initial message returns a message to the person or group that initiated the communication. The receiver provides feedback to the sender. When this occurs, communication is a two-way, reciprocal event, involving the mutual exchange of information between two or more sides.

Communication network
A pattern of information flow among task group members.

Communication
A process in which one person or group transmits some type of information to another person or group.

Videoconferencing is one form of communication, the process in which one person or group evokes a shared or common meaning to another person or group. Communication may be a one-way process, but in most situations, the receiver responds, providing feedback to the sender.
© Steven Peters/Tony Stone Images

Defining communication is relatively simple, but achieving quality communication is both complicated and difficult. Successful and high-quality communication results when the message is received and conveys the exact meaning the sender intended. Before we look at the basic communication model, let's examine the basic types of interpersonal communication.

INTERPERSONAL COMMUNICATION

Managers use several different types of interpersonal communication in their work. Each type plays an important role in managerial effectiveness. We organize interpersonal communication into three broad types: (1) oral, (2) written, and (3) nonverbal.

ORAL COMMUNICATION

Oral communication
All forms of spoken information.

Oral communication consists of all forms of spoken information and is by far the most preferred type of communication used by managers. Research indicates that managers prefer face-to-face and telephone communication to written communication because it permits immediate feedback. For example, individuals can comment or ask questions, and points can be clarified. Managers spend most of their time sharing information by communicating orally.[8] The Experiential Exercise at the end of the chapter provides an opportunity for you to develop your communication skills and effectiveness within a group setting.[9] It takes practice and time to develop these valued managerial skills.

Every professional will eventually be called upon to use oral communication, such as in making a formal oral presentation to a large audience, small committee or team, client, customer, or national conference. As we discussed in Chapter 11, professionals are change agents. Changes have to be presented effectively and sold to achieve acceptance and implementation. As a manager, your oral communication skills are vital to your work and your career success.[10] Table 12.1 provides a checklist of key items to keep in mind when

TABLE 12.1   Checklist for planning more effective oral presentations

1. *Establish your goals.* Have a clear image of your goals or purpose. Ask yourself, What is it that I want to accomplish?

2. *Analyze the audience.* Know your audience so you can effectively select the appropriate content, vacabulary, and visual aids. When the members of your audience are from diverse backgrounds or occupations, it is especially important to find a common bond. Pinpoint some shared concerns members of the audience may have, whether they are economic, political, or cultural.

3. *Diagnose the environmental conditions.* Be aware of how much time you will have and use your time effectively. Determine in advance, if possible, the audience size, physical layout of the room and speaking area, and technical equipment.

4. *Organize your material.* Remember that your message can be followed easily if your material is organized. A logical flow of thoughts will help your listeners follow the message. Start with a brief introduction that provides a preview, follow with a body that develops, and finish with a conclusion that reviews.

5. *Design and use visual aids.* Keep in mind that visual aids not only help to clarify material and heighten its impact but also keep an audience alert. Keep the visual aids simple and use them to emphasize, clarify, or pull together important information.

SOURCE: Adapted from *Management Skills: Practice and Experience* by P. Fandt. Copyright ©1993. By permission of South-Western College Publishing, a division of International Thomson Publishing Inc., Cincinnati, Ohio 45227.

SHARPEN YOUR COMMUNICATION BEHAVIOR

How would you describe your communication behavior in a small-group environment? What are your strengths in communication, and in what areas do you still wish to build skills? After completing this chapter, take 20 minutes or so to write a description of how you see your communication behavior in a small group. Include a description of the way you encode and send messages, the receiving skills you use, the way in which you listen, and how you handle the barriers to communication. What type of feedback do you give to others? What is your reaction when someone gives you feedback?

After you have written your description, meet with two other small-group members or friends who know you well and discuss it with them. Is your description accurate? Can they add anything? Do they have other ideas that might help clarify and sharpen your communication behavior?

Create a goal for each specific behavior you want to work on to improve. Set a realistic time frame for improvement.

After each group member has provided feedback, make any changes in your communication competencies that you think are appropriate.

you are asked to make an oral presentation, whether to a small group or a large audience.[11]

WRITTEN COMMUNICATION

Written communication includes letters, memos, policy manuals, reports, forms, and other documents used to share information in an organization. Managers use written communication less often than oral communication, but there are many occasions when written documentation is important. Writing down a message and sending it as a letter or memo enables a precise statement to be made, provides a reference for later use, aids in systematic thinking, and provides an official document for the organization. Written messages can also be disseminated to many members of the organization at the same time in the form of newsletters or memos. Meeting the Challenge enables you to examine your communication behaviors and also offers you an opportunity to set goals for improvement and obtain feedback through peer evaluation.

Written communication
Letters, memos, policy manuals, reports, forms, and other documentation used to share information in the organization.

NONVERBAL COMMUNICATION

Nonverbal communication involves all messages that are nonlanguage responses. It can be anything that sends a message. Although managers recognize that communication has a nonverbal side, they often underestimate its importance. Nonverbal communication may contain hidden messages and can influence the process and outcomes of face-to-face communication.[12] Even a person who is silent or inactive in the presence of others may be sending a message that may or may not be what is intended.

Consider how nonverbal communication affects the impressions we make on others. For example, interviewers respond more favorably to job candidates whose nonverbal cues are positive (such as eye contact and erect posture) than to those displaying negative nonverbal cues (such as looking down and slouching).[13]

Nonverbal communication can also take place through the physical arrangement of space, such as that found in various office layouts. For example, visi-

Nonverbal communication
All messages that are nonlanguage responses.

tors tend to be uncomfortable in offices where a desk is placed between them and the person to whom they are speaking. Other things that communicate nonverbal messages about an individual are the artwork and decorations found in an office, as well as its orderliness and neatness.[14]

The following are six basic types of nonverbal communication:

1. *Kinesic behavior,* or body motion such as gestures, facial expressions, eye behavior, touching, and any other movement of the body.

2. *Physical characteristics,* such as body shape, physique, posture, height, weight, hair, and skin color.

3. *Paralanguage,* such as voice quality, volume, speech rate, pitch, and laughing.

4. *Proxemics,* such as the way people use and perceive space, seating arrangements, and conversational distance.

5. *Environment,* such as building and room design, furniture and interior decorating, light, noise, and cleanliness.

6. *Time,* such as being late or early, keeping others waiting, and other relationships between time and status.

UNDERSTANDING MANAGERIAL COMMUNICATION

Managers communicate for many reasons—to motivate, inform, control, and satisfy social needs. Motivational communication serves the function of influencing the behavior of organization members. Communication that is intended to motivate must be designed to influence employees to work toward the accomplishment of organizational goals. Communication has an informational purpose when it provides facts and data to be used for decision making. In addition, managers give employees information they need to perform tasks, and employees inform managers of their progress toward meeting their objectives.

Communication also serves a control function. While control is discussed more thoroughly later in the text, it is through communication that work is coordinated and integrated, tasks and responsibilities are clarified, and records are kept to create order. Communication that controls serves the purpose of creating order in an organization, so that multiple goals and tasks can be pursued.

Finally, managers communicate to satisfy social needs. Communication fulfills social needs relating to the emotional and non-task-oriented interactions that occur in every organization. For example, employees need to talk about football games, the weather, politics, the boss's personality, and so forth. While this communication may not directly affect the performance of organizational tasks, it serves important needs and can influence how employees feel about their work conditions and how connected they are with others at work.

Assess your personal level of communication in Meeting the Challenge. Does your communication behavior and style enhance teamwork? Do you develop trust and teamwork through your communication?

THE COMMUNICATION PROCESS

To improve the quality of communication, managers must understand how the process of communication works. The communication process begins when an individual or group has an idea or concept and wishes to make that information known to someone else. Let's explore the elements of the basic communication model in more detail.

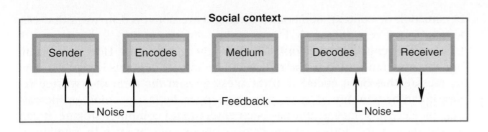

FIGURE 12.1
Basic elements in the communication process

The six primary elements of the communication process are shown in Figure 12.1.[15] These elements include the social context, the sender who encodes the message, the medium, the receiver who decodes the message, feedback, and noise.

Social Context: Considerations of Global Impact and Diversity

The **social context** is the setting in which the communication takes place. The setting has an impact on the other components of the communication process. For example, communication between a manager and a subordinate in the manager's office will likely be more formal and reserved than if it occurred at a football game. Fewer distractions may occur under these circumstances. However, the subordinate may be less inclined to give the manager candid feedback. The social context is an important consideration in light of the global nature of business and the diversity of employees' or customers' cultural backgrounds. Conducting business in this arena presents many challenges to managers.

Consider how technology has affected the social context of communication. On the positive side, electronic communication encourages more participation by lower-status employees and increases production of ideas. It reduces inhibitions stemming from status hierarchies. However, everything on the computer screen looks the same, and important business messages can get lost in the noise of routine messages.[16] Even legitimate business can clog the system. SmithKline Beecham, a pharmaceutical company, has taken several steps over the years to handle such overload, such as issuing a guide on do's and don'ts of e-mail and charging departments a fee, as for a telephone call.

Sender and Message Encoding

The sender initiates the communication process by encoding her meaning and sending the message through a channel. The **encoding** process translates the sender's ideas into a systematic set of symbols or a language expressing the communicator's purpose. The function of encoding, then, is to provide a form in which ideas and purposes can be expressed as a message.

Vocabulary, language, and knowledge play an important role in the sender's ability to encode. But our ability to encode ideas, thoughts, and feelings is far from perfect. Some professionals have difficulty communicating with the general public because they tend to encode meanings in a form that can be understood only by other professionals in the same field. For example, legal contracts that directly affect consumers often have been written with the assumption that only lawyers will decode them. Consumer groups have pressed to have such contracts written in language that everyone can understand.

Message and Medium

The result of encoding is the message. **Messages** are the tangible forms of coded symbols that are intended to give a particular meaning to the data. They are the thoughts and feelings that the communicator is attempting to elicit in the receiver. Words and symbols have no meaning in and of themselves. Their meaning is created by the sender and the receiver and, to a certain extent, by

Social context
The setting in which a communication takes place.

Encoding
Translating the sender's ideas into a systematic set of symbols or a language expressing the communicator's purpose.

Messages
The tangible forms of coded symbols that are intended to give a particular meaning to the data.

the situation or context. Sometimes messages are conveyed in ways that can be interpreted very differently.[17]

Once the encoding is accomplished, another issue arises. How can this information be transmitted to the receiver? The answer depends in part on how the message has been encoded. If the message is in the form of a written report, it can be transmitted by mail, by messenger, by fax machine, or increasingly by electronic means. If it has been entered into computer storage, it can be sent directly to another computer over phone lines or even by satellite. If it is expressed vocally, it can be presented directly in a face-to-face meeting or over the phone. The overriding consideration in choosing a method of transmission is to ensure that the receiver can comprehend the message.

Medium
The carrier of the message or the means by which the message is sent.

The **medium** is the carrier of the message or the means by which the message is sent. Organizations provide information to members through a variety of mediums, including face-to-face communication, telephone conversations, group meetings, fax messages, memos, policy statements, reward systems, production schedules, and technology. One critical impact is the improvement in technology that has made it possible to send and receive written messages thousands of times faster than was possible a few years ago.

Sometimes managers fail to understand or consider how the choice of a medium affects a communication's effectiveness. The results of a three-year study of managerial communication indicate that selection of the appropriate medium can have a major impact on communication effectiveness and even managerial performance.[18]

Receiver and Message Decoding: Challenges of Diversity

Decoding
The translation of received messages into interpreted meanings.

The receiving person or group must make sense of the information received. **Decoding** involves the translation of received messages into interpreted meanings. Once again, our abilities to accomplish this task are limited. As the work force becomes more diverse, managers are challenged to decode messages accurately. Since receivers interpret the message based upon previous experience, frames of reference, vocabulary, and culture, this process is not always successful.

Feedback

Feedback
Information about the status and performance of a given effort or system.

In our communication model, **feedback** refers to the process of verifying messages and the receiver's attempts to ensure that the message he decoded is what the sender really meant to convey. Feedback is a way to avoid communication failure because it provides preliminary information to the sender. Through feedback, communication becomes a dynamic, two-way process rather than just an event.

Many companies are beginning to realize the value of feedback from their customers. For example, look at the increasing number of companies that give toll-free phone numbers as well as Web page addresses to solicit customer input.[19] These types of activities provide organizations with valuable feedback that they can use to improve products as well as strengthen the quality of customer service.

Noise

Noise
Any internal or external interference or distraction with the intended message that can cause distortion in the sending and receiving of messages.

Noise is any internal or external interference with or distraction from the intended message, which can cause distortion in the sending and receiving of messages. In addition to physical conditions that make communication more difficult, emotional states can also create noise. For example, a radio playing loud music while someone is trying to talk, static on a line during a telephone conversation, or stressful working conditions are examples of noise. Noise can occur during any stage of the communication process, and it reduces the probability of achieving common meaning between sender and receiver. Messages that are poorly encoded (for example, are written in an unclear way), improperly decoded (for example, are not comprehended), or transmitted through inappropriate mediums may result in reduced communication effectiveness.

BARRIERS TO EFFECTIVE COMMUNICATION

Despite its apparent simplicity, the communication process rarely operates flawlessly. As we point out in the next section, communication barriers interfere with organizational excellence. Consequently, the information transmitted from one party to another may be distorted, and communication problems may result. We turn now to some common communication barriers that are summarized in Table 12.2.

CROSS-CULTURAL DIVERSITY

Communication, as an exchange of meaning, is bounded by culture. As we have seen, during encoding, an idea is translated into a message represented in symbols and language; then, during decoding, the message is translated into interpreted meanings. This means that the message must be encoded in a form

TABLE 12.2   Sources of communication breakdowns

• *Cross-cultural diversity*	When senders and receivers come from different cultural backgrounds, breakdowns in the communication process are more likely. Cultural differences may arise between people from different geographical or ethnic groups within one country as well as between people from different national cultures.
• *Trust and credibility*	Trust and credibility between the sender and receiver must be established. Without trust, the communicating parties concentrate their energies on defensive tactics, rather than on conveying and understanding meaning.
• *Information overload*	Individuals can experience information overload when they are asked to handle too much information at one time.
• *Perception*	A variety of factors such as experiences, needs, personality, and education can affect individuals' perceptions. As a result, two people may perceive the same thing in different ways.
• *Language characteristics*	The nature of our language means that many words or phrases are imprecise. Individuals often use different meanings or interpretations of the same word and do not realize it.
• *Gender differences*	Gender differences can result in breakdowns and lead to distorted communication and misunderstandings between men and women. Since males and females are often treated differently from childhood, they tend to develop different perspectives, attitudes about life, and communication styles.
• *Other factors*	Time pressures may cause us to focus on information that helps us make a choice quickly. Feedback may be impaired or absent.

One trend that will revolutionize American business in the 21st century is an increase in minorities and immigrants in the work force. Managers need to learn to embrace and value diversity.

© Michael Newman/PhotoEdit

that the receiver will recognize, but the symbols and language used for encoding depend on cultural background, which varies from person to person.

The Workforce 2000 study, commissioned by the U.S. Department of Labor in 1987, identifies demographic trends that will revolutionize American business in the 21st century. Four trends—increased minorities and immigrants in the work force, an increase in service jobs, an increase in information jobs, and a need for higher skill levels—indicate an urgent need for managers to embrace and value diversity.[20]

Managers need to understand that senders and receivers from different cultures may encode and decode their messages differently; they have different behaviors, styles, and ways of looking at things. All of these can lead to breakdowns in the communication process. These difficulties may arise between people from different geographical or ethnic groups in the same country, as well as between people from different national cultures.[21] Read the Global Perspective to be enlightened about the impact of cultural diversity in managing and organizing.[22]

A common problem in cross-cultural communication is *ethnocentrism,* or the tendency to consider one's own culture and its values as being superior to others. Very often such tendencies are accompanied by an unwillingness to try to understand alternative points of view and take seriously the values they represent. This attitude can be highly disadvantageous when trying to conduct business and maintain effective working relationships with people from different cultures.[23]

Studies show that the greater the differences between the sender's and receiver's cultures, the greater the chance for miscommunication.[24] A common criticism of some U.S. business managers is that although they have the technology and know the business, they are not prepared to deal with cultural differences. Among the cultural elements that affect cross-cultural communication are language and symbols, time orientation, personal achievement, personal space, social behavior, and intercultural socialization.[25]

TRUST AND CREDIBILITY

One potential barrier to effective communication is a lack of trust between the sender and the receiver. This lack of trust can cause the receiver to look for hidden meanings in the sender's message. A trusting relationship is almost a prerequisite for communication excellence. In the absence of trust and honesty, the communicating parties divert their energies to defensive tactics, rather than trying to convey and understand meaning.[26]

A work environment characterized by trust does not just happen. It takes time and effort to develop. It must be nurtured and reinforced by honesty and accuracy in communication and mutual respect between communication parties. Levi Strauss's approach to corporate aspirations, written by top management and guiding all major decisions, revolves around valuing trust. For example, one of the seven stated values is communication: "Management must be clear about company, unit, and individual goals and performance. Our people must know what is expected of them and receive timely, honest feedback and work in a trusting environment."[27] Other organizations such as Ford and Federal Express have created or adopted programs that break down the ad-

LEARNING THE LANGUAGE OF CROSS-CULTURAL COMMUNICATION

In organizations all over the world, people use time to communicate with each other. But the language of time varies from culture to culture. There are different languages of time just as there are different spoken languages. Deadlines may indicate a degree of urgency or relative importance in the United States, but in the Middle East, the time required to get something accomplished depends on the relationship between individuals.

The language of space refers to perceptions about interactions and status. The American businessperson, familiar with the pattern of American corporate life, has no difficulty appraising an individual's relative importance simply by noting the size of his or her office in relation to other offices nearby. In the American pattern, the president or board chair has the biggest office, and the more important offices are usually located at the corners of the building and on the top floor. The French, on the other hand, are much more likely to lay out space as a network of connecting points of influence, activity, or interest. The French manager will ordinarily be found in the middle of her subordinates to make it easier to supervise them.

The language of things refers to the status associated with material possessions. Lacking a fixed class system and having an extremely mobile population, Americans have become highly sensitive to how others make use of material goods. The French, English, and Germans, however, have different ways of using material possessions. Things that represent the height of dependability and respectability to the English would be considered old-fashioned and backward by most Americans. Middle Eastern people attach status to family, connections, and friendship rather than to material things. The Japanese take pride in tasteful though often inexpensive possessions that are used to create the proper emotional setting.

The language of friendship refers to the depth, length, and type of relationship that develops between individuals. Americans perceive friendships in terms of a series of favors that must be repaid, at least by gratitude. In India, however, friendship involves sensing a person's needs and filling them without any expectation of gratitude.

Finally, the language of agreements refers to the importance of knowing the rules for negotiating in different organizations and various countries. It's not essential to know the details of the legal practice, but one should be aware that differences exist. Sensitivity to these differences is critical.

Global Perspective

versarial relationships between management and the work force through communication training models. Based on a highly developed set of corporate ethical principles devised through employee participation, the programs look for ways the company can earn the trust and commitment of its employees.[28]

Managers must develop trust in their working relationships with subordinates and take advantage of all opportunities for face-to-face communication. *Management by wandering around* (MBWA), a phrase now popularly acclaimed as one way to do this, simply means that managers get out of their offices and communicate regularly with employees as they do their jobs.[29] Managers who spend time walking around can greatly reduce the perceived distance

TABLE 12.3   What makes some companies attractive?

Authors Robert Levering and Milton Moskowitz noted in their book, *The 100 Best Companies to Work for in America,* positive changes in five key areas. Notice how communication plays a role in defining successful companies that attract workers.

- *More employee participation.* A rarity in the early 1980s, genuine employee involvement in decision making about their jobs is a reality among the best companies. The quality movement—the management philosophy of the 1990s—provided specific techniques for increasing employee participation. Effective participation calls for open and honest communication.

- *More sensitivity to work/family issues.* Many of the best companies have made tremendous strides toward dealing with the problems of working parents, offering a variety of child-care options and flexible work schedules.

- *More two-way communication.* Accessibility of the top executives is much more common today than in the early 1980s. Even many large firms offer employees opportunities to ask questions—and get answers—directly from their CEOs. In the past, accessibility was too often more symbolic than real. Every manager proclaimed an "open-door policy," but many put up intangible barriers that made true openness unlikely.

- *More fun.* In many more companies, having fun seems to be part of the corporate mission. Fun is not inconsistent with operating a serious, profit-making business. Watch out for companies where there is no sense of humor. Hoopla, celebration, and good-natured fun are a hallmark of top companies.

- *More trust.* In the best workplaces, employees trust their managers, and the managers trust their employees. The trust is reflected in numerous ways: no time clocks, meetings where employees have a chance to register their concerns, job postings (so that employees can learn new skills), and employee committees empowered to make changes in policies, recommend new pay rates, or allocate the corporate charity dollars. Trust in the workplace simply means that employees are treated as partners and are recognized as having something to contribute beyond brawn or manual dexterity or strong legs and arms.

between themselves and their subordinates. They can also create an atmosphere of open and free-flowing communication, which makes more and better information available for decision making and makes decisions more relevant to the needs of lower-level personnel.

In their best-selling book, *The 100 Best Companies to Work for in America,* authors Robert Levering and Milton Moskowitz underscore the role trust has in creating a positive work environment.[30] Shown in Table 12.3 are five of the key features they discuss in their book. Notice how communication plays a role in defining successful companies that are highly rated by employees.

INFORMATION OVERLOAD

Information overload

Occurs whenever the capacity of a communication medium to process information is exceeded.

Although information is the lifeblood of the organization, it is possible for managers and organizations to have too much information. The increasing use of technology in organizations often leads to **information overload,** which occurs when the amount of information we can process is exceeded. The manager's responsibility in the disseminator role is to filter large volumes of information and distribute it appropriately.

With the widespread use of communication technology, the information age is upon us. With so much information available, managers are often dazzled and do not know what to do with it all. For example, businesses were quick to adapt to what was thought to be a timesaving technology, the use of e-mail. In 1994, we sent 764 billion e-mails from work. By 2000, the number is projected to balloon to 4 trillion.[31] E-mail, whether we like it or not, has changed communication and the way we work, by speeding up the business cycle from days to hours, even minutes, and by flattening organizations.[32]

In summary, information overload can lead to:

- Failing to process or ignoring some of the information.
- Processing the information incorrectly.
- Delaying the processing of information until the information overload abates.
- Searching for people to help process some of the information.
- Lowering the quality of information processing.
- Withdrawing from the information flow.

PERCEPTION

As we discuss in Chapter 14, perception is the process of selecting, organizing, and interpreting environmental stimuli to provide meaningful experiences. It encompasses both the sensory and mental processes used by an individual in interpreting information. A variety of factors such as experiences, needs, personality, and education can affect individuals' perceptions. As a result, two people may perceive the same thing in different ways and miscommunicate.

LANGUAGE CHARACTERISTICS

The very nature of our language constitutes a source of communication breakdown. Many words are imprecise. For example, suppose a manager tells a subordinate to do this task "right away." Does the manager mean for the subordinate to drop what she is doing and work on the new task immediately or to finish what she is currently working on and then do the new task?

When two individuals are using different meanings or interpretations of the same word and do not realize it, a communication barrier exists. For example, some words sound the same but have multiple meanings. *Write* (communicate), *rite* (ceremony), *right* (not left), and *right* (privilege) all sound alike, right (correct)? Don't assume that the meaning you give a word will be the one the receiver uses in decoding the message. Language characteristics can lead to encoding and decoding errors and mixed messages that create semantic barriers to communication. For example, a word may be interpreted differently depending on the facial expressions, hand gestures, and voice inflection that accompany it.

The imprecision and multiple meanings of words are one reason why jargon develops. **Jargon** is pretentious terminology or language specific to a particular profession or group. For example, at Disney, customers are called "guests" and employees are called "cast members." If cast members do a job correctly, it is called a "good Mickey"; if they do a bad job, it is a "bad Mickey."[33] At Microsoft Corporation, learning the company jargon is an important part of acceptance as an organizational member. Although jargon is designed to avoid communication breakdowns, in some cases it may lead to inefficiency because not everyone will understand what is being communicated, especially new members of the organization or group.

Language characteristics, including imprecision and multiple meanings, are posing an even greater threat to communication as society becomes more interconnected and mobile. The possibility of contact with someone from a different background or culture who uses words differently is increasing.

Jargon
Pretentious terminology or language specific to a particular profession or group.

PART 4 Leadership Challenges in the 21st Century

GENDER DIFFERENCES

Gender differences can result in breakdowns and lead to distorted communication and misunderstandings between men and women. Because males and females are often treated differently from childhood, they tend to develop different perspectives, attitudes about life, and communication styles. Historically, stereotypical assumptions about the differing communication styles of males and females have stimulated discrimination against female managers. In recent years, however, more realistic images of how professional men and women behave and communicate have replaced the old stereotypes.[34]

Communication barriers can be explained in part by differences in conversation styles. Research shows that women and men listen differently. Women tend to speak and hear a language of connection and intimacy while men tend to speak and hear a language of status and independence. Women are more likely to hear emotions and to communicate empathy.[35]

Women's oral communication differs from men's in significant ways. Women are more like to use *qualifiers,* phrases such as "I think" or "It seems to me." Generally, women tend to end statements with an upward inflection that makes the statements sound like questions. Female voices are generally higher and softer than male voices. This makes it easy for men to overpower women's voices, and men commonly interrupt women or overlap their speech.

Although a wide range of gender differences can exist in verbal communication, nonverbal differences are even more striking. Men lean back and sit in an open-leg position that takes up considerable space, thereby communicating higher status and a greater sense of control over their environment.[36] Women use much more eye contact than men, yet avert their gaze more often, especially when communicating with a man or someone of higher status. Women smile more frequently and are generally better at conveying and interpreting emotions.

Both men and women can work to change the perception that women are less capable of being competent managers. Women need to monitor their verbal and nonverbal communication and choose behavior that projects professionalism and competence. Men should become more aware of their communication behavior and its impact on female colleagues and choose responses that will facilitate an open exchange of ideas.[37]

OTHER FACTORS

Several other factors are considered barriers to effective communication. Time pressures may cause us to focus on information that helps us make decisions quickly, although the information may not be of high quality. Feedback may be impaired or absent. In one-way communication, such as a written memo, the sender does not receive any direct and immediate feedback from the receiver. Studies show that two-way communication is more accurate and effective than one-way communication, but it is also more costly and time-consuming.

Information technology
A broad category of communication techniques that includes videodisc recorders, telephone answering devices and services, closed circuit television systems, and fax machines.

INFORMATION TECHNOLOGY IN COMMUNICATION EFFECTIVENESS

Information technology is a broad category of communication techniques that are rapidly influencing how managers communicate. For example, video-tape recorders, telephone answering devices and services, closed-circuit tele-

Changes in information technology are influencing how managers communicate. Videotape recorders, telephone answering devices and services, closed-circuit television systems, fax machines, computers, and e-mail all provide new flexibility and opportunities.
© Michael Newman/PhotoEdit

vision systems, facsimile machines, computers, and electronic mail all provide new communication flexibility and opportunities. Computers networked together create an easy means to store and communicate vast amounts of information. Networking ties computers together, permitting individuals to share information, communicate, and access tremendous amounts of information. As we see in Managing for Excellence, this new information technology has led two organizations, Nintendo of America and DigiPen, to collaborate and create DigiPen Institute of Technology. This focus on information technology results in highly trained, specialized employees. This is not uncommon for organizations that seek to stay in touch and stay competitive. As we saw in the Managerial Incident at the beginning of the chapter, Gianfranco Zaccai, cofounder of Design Continuum, uses technology to run his design firm around the clock.[39]

Telecommuting refers to the practice of working at home or at a remote site by using a computer linked to a central office or other employment location. It may also include those who work out of a customer's office or communicate with the office or plant via a laptop computer or mobile phone. More than two million corporate employees are now telecommuting full-time, and three times that number are involved in this form of communication one or two days a week. When the small yet profitable Lepsch and Stratton Travel Agency faced the challenges of a shortage of office space and an unacceptably high turnover of support staff, it successfully implemented a program of telecommuting and had several employees conduct their work from home and communicate with the office by computer, telephone, and mail.[40] Many creative freelance workers, contract and temporary workers, and small companies are using this form of information technology, as are many better-known organizations, including IBM, Xerox, American Express, Du Pont, Apple Computer, and the Environmental Protection Agency.[41]

The emerging technology of **electronic mail (e-mail)**, a computer-based system that allows individuals to exchange and store messages through computerized text-processing and communication networks, provides a very fast, inexpensive, and efficient means of communication. Text-based messages can be sent and received by anyone who has access to a computer terminal and has a computer mailbox on the network. Messages can be transmitted in seconds to and from employees in the same building or overseas. The use of e-mail

Telecommuting
The practice of working at a remote site by using a computer linked to a central office or other employment location.

Electronic mail (e-mail)
A computer-based system that allows individuals to exchange and store messages through computerized text-processing and communication networks.

Managing for Excellence

NINTENDO TEAMS WITH DIGIPEN: INSTITUTE OF TECHNOLOGY CREATED

As the increased demand for qualified candidates schooled in 3-D animation, information technology, and computer simulations for organizational use outstripped the supply, DigiPen teamed with Nintendo of America to create the first four-year video college. DigiPen Institute of Technology plans to open its campus in Seattle, Washington, to 100 students, the first crop of candidates for a bachelor of science degree in Real Time Interactive Simulation, in September 1997.

According to the U.S. Bureau of Labor statistics, demand for computer system analysts, engineers, and scientists will grow faster than almost any other job category in the next ten years. In 1992, after approaching Nintendo about creating a program specifically for video gaming, Comair launched the DigiPen school. The college, which has been authorized by the Washington State Higher Education Coordinating Board, is receiving support from Redmond, Washington–based Nintendo in the form of software development tools and hardware. The school's founder and president, Claude Comair, says that this is a serious collaborative effort between Nintendo and DigiPen. The new video college is not fun and games. The curriculum is intense, including computer programming, advanced mathematics, physics, and communication skills.[38]

Videoconferencing
The technologies that use live video to unite widely dispersed company operations.

enhances vertical and horizontal communication because it can lead to greater information exchanges as well as the need to learn to manage the information.

Videoconferencing is an umbrella term referring to technologies that use live video to unite widely dispersed company operations. This technology offers tremendous savings of time, energy, and money. Business television networks enable companies to communicate to thousands of employees simultaneously. For example, televised instructions can provide training as well as technical assistance for employees. Videoconferencing enables organizations to hold interactive meetings in which groups communicate live with each other via camera and cable transmission of the picture and sound, even though they are hundreds or even thousands of miles apart.[42]

The norms of using information technologies have not been established in most organizations. Management needs to get smarter about what type of technology they are using. The traditional gatekeepers—administrative assistants and secretaries—are filtering out less and less, leading to information overload. Downsizing has shrunk the ranks of middle managers, forcing higher-ups to handle more extraneous information. Some managers who have suffered from information technology overload have resorted to so-called *bozo filters* that block certain messages and program commands or rules that automatically sort messages into folders of varying priorities.

Perhaps the greatest impact of the new technology on communication lies in the amount of information it makes available. While good communication is valuable and an essential part of the manager's job, he may drown in an overabundance of information. More information is not necessarily better information or even relevant information. It may encourage managers to make decisions too quickly. Rapid access to data can preclude thoughtful deliberation and make everyone a sender of messages worldwide at low cost. Managers often fail to build face-to-face relationships, so the personal touch in managing is lost. More, faster, and easier communication opens up the possibility for managers to waste a lot of time on junk communication.[43]

Used correctly, technology can exert a positive influence on nearly every aspect of productivity and quality. However, remember that although technology provides more choices, it does magnify the need to make careful, informed decisions about medium appropriateness. Technology can be the lifeline of the increasing number of global economic networks and an essential tool for people who want to stay in touch with the rest of the world.[44]

MANAGING COMMUNICATION WITHIN DIVERSE ORGANIZATIONS

Communication permeates every organization. Some messages are clear and effective; others cause confusion and errors. In addition, some messages sent throughout the organization contain misinformation or secret information that may impede organizational processes. As organizations become more diverse, managers must strive to provide clear guidelines for effective communication. In this section, we describe formal and informal communication channels.

FORMAL COMMUNICATION CHANNELS

Formal communication follows the chain of command and is recognized as official. One way to view formal communication in organizations, shown in Figure 12.2, is to examine how it flows—downward, upward, laterally, and externally. Specific types of communication are often associated with directional flow. Briefly examining each type of directional flow will help us appreciate the problems inherent in organizational communication and identify ways to overcome these problems.

Vertical Communication
Vertical communication is the flow of information both up and down the chain of command. It involves an exchange of messages between two or more levels in the organization.

Downward Communication   When top-level management makes decisions, creates strategic plans, conveys directions, and so forth, they are often communicating downward. **Downward communication** flows from individuals in higher levels of the organization to those in lower levels. The most common

Downward communication
Flows from individuals in higher levels of the organization to those in lower levels.

FIGURE 12.2
Formal communication flows

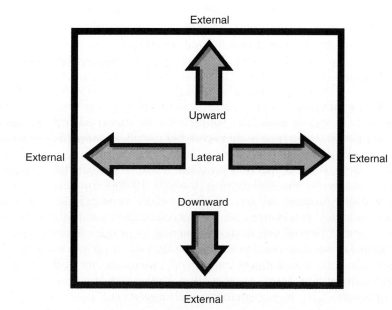

forms of downward communication are meetings, official memos, policy statements, procedures, manuals, and company publications. At the Walt Disney Company, a newsletter called *Eyes and Ears* informs employees of any new attractions and improvements and provides information on "Donald Deals," which offer discounts on meals and local amusements. This type of downward communication helps involve employees and makes them feel that they are an integral part of the organization.

Information sent downward may include new company goals, job instructions, procedures, and feedback on performance. Studies show that only 20 percent of the intended message sent by top management is intact by the time it reaches the entry-level employee. This information loss occurs for several reasons. First, managers tend to rely too heavily on written channels; an avalanche of written material may cause the overloaded subordinate to ignore some messages. This is especially true with the glut of information stemming from new technology that arrived in many offices without instruction on when to use it. Second, the oral face-to-face message, which commands more attention and provides immediate feedback, is often underutilized. Managers may e-mail the colleague or subordinate down the hall instead of walking over for a chat. They may e-mail a business client across town instead of picking up the phone. The experts agree that managers often forget that the best way to communicate, the "richest channel," is face to face, with its abundance of feedback.

Studies show that organizations that encourage effective downward communication have a stable work force. GE, Intel, Merrill Lynch, State Farm Insurance, and Hewlett-Packard are all organizations that excel at this. Employees become more productive and more valued when they receive quality information.[45]

Upward communication
Information flows to managers from their subordinates.

Upward Communication   **Upward communication** consists of messages sent up the line from subordinates to bosses. Openness to ideas and inputs from people in the lower organization is often the hallmark of healthy and enjoyable companies. Effective organizations need upward communication as much as downward communication. People at all levels can and will have ideas for organizational improvment. Companies that tap into those ideas can benefit tremendously.

Upward communication from subordinates to managers usually falls into one of the following types:

1. Personal reports of performance, problems, or concerns.
2. Reports about others and their performance, problems, or concerns.
3. Reactions to organizational policies and practices.
4. Suggestions about what tasks need to be done and how they can be accomplished.

This type of communication is frequently sent up only one level in the organization to the person's immediate supervisor. The supervisor may send some of the information to the next higher level, but usually in a modified form. Both written and oral channels may be used in those instances.

For example, Drexel University president Constantine Papadakis publicized his e-mail address to the Philadelphia school's 10,000 students and 55,000 alumni, with the promise that he would read every message, allowing senders to bypass traditional gatekeepers such as secretaries and administrations. "Contact me directly," he told one student gathering. "Consider it a privilege." Initially, Papadakis was inundated with 200 e-mails a day replete with suggestions and complaints. He would assess the urgency, then ask one of the vice-presidents to resolve the problem. At graduation, Drexel will announce the winner of a new award—best implementable e-mail suggestion.[46]

Upward communication is beneficial to both the manager and the subordinate. For the manager, it is often necessary for sound decision making. Upward communication helps managers know employees' accomplishments, problems, and attitudes, and allows employees to make suggestions and feel that they are part of the decision-making process. Additionally, it provides feedback, encourages ongoing two-way communication, and indicates the subordinates' receptiveness to messages. For the subordinate, upward communication may provide a release of tensions and a sense of personal worth that may lead to a feeling of commitment to the organization.

As we discussed previously, a trusting relationship is almost a prerequisite for effective communication. Trust cannot be mandated by policy or directives; it must be earned by the manager through credible behavior and communication. Suggestion boxes, employee surveys, and open-door policies are often used to encourage upward communication.

Achieving effective upward communication—getting open and honest messages from employees to management—is an especially difficult task. Upper-level managers often do not respond to messages from lower-level employees; if they do not take advantage of this information, they miss the chance to tap into a critical resource: their people.

Perhaps more important, we should note that upward communication often tends to suffer from serious inaccuracies.[47] The information loss in downward communication is shown in Figure 12.3. A recent study revealed that less than 15 percent of managers' total communication was directed toward their superiors.[48] When managers communicate upward, their conversations tend to be shorter than discussions with peers, and they often highlight their accomplishments and downplay their mistakes if the mistakes will be looked upon unfavorably.[49]

Lateral Communication
Lateral communication is the horizontal information flow that occurs both within and between departments. The purpose of lateral communication is co-

Lateral communication
The horizontal information flow that occurs both within and between departments. The purpose of lateral communication is coordination.

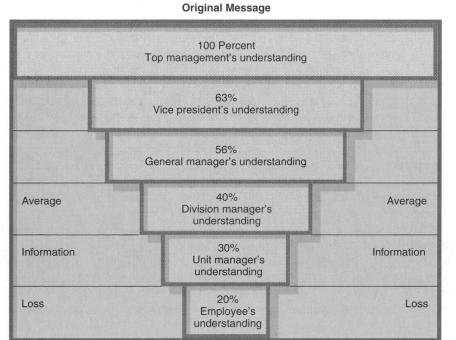

Original Message

FIGURE 12.3
Percentage of understanding lost in communication

ordination. As you will recall from the discussion of the coordination function in Chapter 4, communication provides a means for members on the same level of an organization to share information without directly involving their superiors. Examples include the communication that may occur between members of different departments of an organization and between co-workers in the same department. Self-managed teams create situations in which lateral communication can flourish. Both written and oral channels may be used for lateral communication. In addition, more formal liaison roles may be created to support horizontal information flows. These are important to coordinate activities that support the organizational objectives.

External Communication

External Communication

External communication
The sharing of messages with people outside the organization.

External communication is the sharing of messages with people outside the organization, especially customers, suppliers, and other stakeholders, or people who hold a stake in the success of the company. We often refer to this as *boundary-spanning communication* because it crosses the bounds between the organizations and its many publics. In recent years, companies have made extraordinary efforts to get input from outsiders, especially customers.

INFORMAL COMMUNICATION CHANNELS

The communication channels described so far are part of the formal sysems used to accomplish the work of the organization. In addition to these formal channels, organizations have informal channels of communication. Informal communication channels arise from the social relationships that evolve in the organization. These are neither required nor controlled by management.

Grapevine
The informal flow of messages throughout the organization.

The **grapevine** is the informal flow of messages throughout the organization. The grapevine is a useful and important source of information for managers and employees at all levels. It typically involves small clusters of people who exchange information in all directions through unsanctioned organizational channels and networks. The grapevine should be considered as much a communication vehicle as the company newsletter or employee meetings.

The grapevine can be quite beneficial. For example, research shows that the more involved people are in their organizations' communication channels, the more powerful and influential they become on the job.[50]

Information carried by the grapevine is often quite accurate. In fact, one well-known study found that approximately 80 percent of the information transmitted through the grapevine was correct.[51] The remaining 20 percent, though, can often lead to serious trouble. As you probably know from your own experience, a story can be mainly true but still be quite misleading because essential facts are omitted or distorted. The information in the informal network is usually unverified and often includes rumors that are exaggerated and frequently wrong. To help prevent incorrect rumors, the manager must keep the information that flows through the grapevine as accurate and rumor-free as possible. To do so, managers should share as much information as possible with employees, tell them of changes as far in advance as possible, and encourage employees to ask questions about rumors they hear.

To some extent, the grapevine is always present in any organization and is more than just a means of conveying corporate gossip. Its information may be less official but is no less important for understanding the organization. The grapevine is an influence to be considered in all management actions. Indeed, the grapevine's influence suggests that managers must listen to it, study it, and learn who its leaders are, how it operates, and what information it carries.

THE CHALLENGES OF COMMUNICATION COMPETENCY

Defining effective communication is much easier than accomplishing communication competence. Communication is both complicated and difficult. Managers agree that the ability to communicate effectively is crucial to enhancing career success.[52] More than ever before, your ability to communicate well affects your capability to thrive in today's organizations and professions. If you could strive for expertise in but one competence, communication would be the wise choice.

Even a fairly simple and straightforward exchange of factual information is subject to distortion and miscommunication. The three most important points to remember in meeting the challenge of communication competency are (1) to expect to be misunderstood by at least some listeners and readers, (2) to expect to misunderstand others, and (3) to strive to reduce the degree of such misunderstandings, but never expect total elimination of them or the ability to anticipate all possible outcomes. In this section, we will focus on ways to prevent misunderstandings and improve two critical aspects of communication—feedback and listening.

DEVELOPING FEEDBACK SKILLS

As we discussed earlier, *feedback* refers to the process of verifying messages from the sender. Through feedback, communication becomes a dynamic, two-way process, rather than just an event. Feedback can include very personal feelings or more abstract thoughts, such as reactions to others' ideas or proposals. The emotional impact of feedback varies according to how personally it is focused.

The first requirement of quality feedback is to recognize when it is truly intended to benefit the receiver and when it is purely an attempt to satisfy a personal need. A manager who berates an employee for a software error may actually be angry about personally failing to give clear instructions in the first place. If feedback is to be effective, managers need to observe the following principles:

- Feedback should be based on a foundation of trust between the sender and receiver.
- Feedback should be specific rather than general, with clear and preferably recent examples. Saying "You are a poor listener" is not as useful as saying "I watched you interact with that customer and you did not listen to what she was saying."
- Feedback should be given at a time when the receiver appears ready to accept it. Therefore, when a person is angry, upset, or defensive, it is probably not the time to bring up new issues.
- Feedback should be limited to things the receiver may be capable of doing something about.
- Feedback should provide descriptive information about what the person said or did and should avoid evaluative inferences about motives, intent, or feelings.
- Feedback should not include more than the receiver can handle at any particular time. For example, the receiver may become threatened and defensive if the feedback includes everything the receiver does that annoys the sender.

In addition to giving feedback, being able to receive feedback is also important for effective communication. Learning cannot occur without feedback. Unfortunately, many people and organizations do little to encourage or cultivate useful feedback. They protect themslevs from getting their feelings hurt. Many tune out anything that might undermine their self-confidence. In doing so, they also forfeit an enormous opportunity for growth. You do not have to agree with all feedback. An attitude of feedback receptiveness is vital to the development of your communication skills.[53]

IMPROVING LISTENING SKILLS

Of the four basic communication skills—reading, writing, speaking, and listening—only one is not formally taught in schools. Most of our learning is directed toward reading, speaking, and writing, with little attention given to training in listening.[54]

Since managers spend a large proportion of their time communicating, developing the skill of listening is a distinct asset. In his best-selling book *The 7 Habits of Highly Effective People,* Stephen Covey suggests that the key to effective listening is to seek first to understand, then to be understood.[55] Communication breakdowns are the result of misleading assumptions, particularly when the listener is in the process of evaluating, approving, or disapproving what another person is saying.[56]

How good a listener are you? Before we examine what contributes to effective listening and the ways you can improve, Experiential Exercise will help you assess your listening skills. Take the time now to measure your listening ability.

Before you can begin to improve your listening skills, you need to understand the demands placed on your listening capacities. Most important, listening is an active behavior; it involves careful attention and response to messages. Instead of evaluating the message or preparing a response, an effective listener tries to understand both direct and subtle meanings contained in messages. In other words, be attentive to the feelings of the sender and what he is *not* saying as well as to the verbal content of the message. Observe people while they are speaking. Watch facial expressions, gestures, body movements, and eye contact. This will help you to understand the real content of the message. Research indicates that listening skills are related to cultural norms. For example, Native Americans have a reputation for excellent listening skills; they do not feel compelled to fill up silence with idle chatter.[57]

The following guidelines will help you be an effective listener:[58]

- Listen for message content. Try to hear exactly what is being said in the message.
- Listen for feelings. Try to identify how the sender feels about the message content. Is it pleasing or displeasing to the sender?
- Respond to feelings. Let the sender know that you recognize her feelings, as well as the message content.
- Be sensitive to both the nonverbal and the verbal content of messages; identify mixed messages that need to be clarified.
- Reflect back to the sender, in your own words, what you think you are hearing. Paraphrase and restate the verbal and nonverbal messages as feedback to which the sender can respond with further information.

The only basic communication skill not taught formally in schools is listening. Listening is an active behavior that involves careful attention and response to messages.

© Bruce Ayres/Tony Stone Images

- Be attentive and listen to understand, not to reply. Most people are thinking about what they are going to say next or what is going on in the next office. Don't squirm or fidget while someone else is talking. Find a comfortable position and give 100 percent of your attention to the speaker.
- Be patient. Don't interrupt the speaker. Take time to digest what has been said before responding. Don't be afraid to ask questions to clarify and understand every word of what has been said. There is no shame in not knowing, only in not knowing and pretending to know.

Listening is an active process. Effective listening behaviors include maintaining eye contact, rephrasing what has been said, listening for the message beyond the obvious and overt meaning of the words that have been spoken, and observing nonverbal messages. The key to more effective listening competency is the willingness to listen and respond appropriately to the feelings being expressed, as well as to the content.

MANAGERIAL IMPLICATIONS

Organizational leaders are first and foremost in the communication business. According to Roger Smith, former chair of General Motors, effective communication has more impact on an organization's prospects than any other single factor.[59] Whether you are a financial planner, small-business owner, accountant, sales representative, minister, teacher, or any other type of professional, the following issues are key points to consider for managerial effectiveness:[60]

- You spend most of your time at work communicating.
- Your success is based on strong communication skills.
- Communication is becoming increasingly important in view of recent trends, such as increased globalization, diversity, and workplace specialization.
- Communication technology offers new opportunities to communicate more often and more efficiently than ever before. It is an essential tool for people who want to stay in touch with the rest of world.

Whatever you do in the future, communication will probably take up a large portion of your time, and the more effective you are at communicating, the more successful you are likely to be. Versatility in knowledge and skills is becoming more and more valued in today's global economy. Those individuals and organizations that can adapt from one job, product, service, customer, or partner to another are a step ahead of their competition.[61]

DESIGN CONTINUUM: BALANCING TECHNOLOGY WHILE MAINTAINING EFFECTIVE COMMUNICATION

The challenge faced by Design Continuum was how to use information technology effectively to survive in the competitive global environment without sacrificing quality communication. The primary change that Zaccai made was to invest in roughly $100,000 of videoconferencing equipment from Pictureted. By using this technology, Design Continuum employees could meet practically face to face to exchange important information.

Now Massachusetts employees can contact the Australia affiliate to demonstrate a new product or share ideas. Team members in Australia can then forge ahead with the project. Thanks to the time differences, work on any particular project continues virtually 24 hours a day.

Managerial
Incident
Resolution

Design Continuum helped Reebok develop the pump shoe and Spalding a new baseball glove through videoconference design meetings. The technology has brought clients and team members into a very cohesive working group and is increasingly used to communicate.

For example, one recent Sunday evening, Zaccai and a team of five employees teleconferenced with clients in Tokyo. It was Monday morning for them, but the team could see and interface in real time and could get their reactions. Though one of his managers was already in Japan, Zaccai said it was invaluable to have the rest of the team available in the United States. This meeting allowed the whole team to respond to questions that the representative in Tokyo couldn't answer. Better yet, the company avoided the expense of flying the team across the Pacific and the team avoided the lost work time and the accompanying jet lag.

To speed up the marketing research process, Zaccai began using e-mail and the Internet to keep the information-gathering process from getting bogged down. Product-development questionnaires and surveys are delivered via e-mail and are also posted on the firm's Web site to the intended users. A fast-paced project can be researched done in a matter of weeks instead of months.

Zaccai and Design Continuum are convinced that technology is too important to ignore. The key is to use technology more productively, train managers and employees to communicate effectively, and be sensitive to customers and peers, whether that communication is face to face or via a high-speed piece of technical wizardry. Without effective communication skills, you'll be falling behind your competitors.[62]

SUMMARY

- Communication is essential to management because it encompasses all aspects of an organization and pervades organizational activity. Managers communicate to motivate, inform, control, and satisfy social needs.

- Communication is a process in which one person or group transmits some type of information to another person or group. Managers use oral, written, and nonverbal communication, as well as information technologies, to communicate.

- The elements of the communication process include the social context, or the setting in which the communication takes place; the sender, who initiates and encodes the message; the medium, or the carrier of the message; the receiver, who decodes or translates the message; feedback, which refers to the process of verifying messages and the receiver's attempts to ensure that the message is what the sender really meant to convey; and noise, which is interference with or distraction from the intended message, which can cause distortion or miscommunication.

- There are six types of nonverbal communication: (1) kinesic behavior, or movement of the body; (2) physical characteristics; (3) paralanguage; (4) proxemics; (5) environment; and (6) time.

- Information technology is rapidly changing the way we communicate. Technologies such as computer networks, e-mail, videoconferencing, facsimile machines, and telecommuting all offer managers easier and more flexible means of communicating with subordinates, customers, suppliers, and stakeholders.

- Despite the apparent simplicity of the communication process, communication breakdowns may often interfere with communication excellence. Sources of breakdowns include cultural differences, trust and credibility, information overload, perception, characteristics of the language, time pressures, lack of feedback, and gender differences.

- Organizational communication functions under two systems, one formal and one informal. Formal communication flows downward, upward, and laterally and externally. Informal communication, referred to as the grapevine, flows in all directions.

KEY TERMS

Communication network	Medium	Electronic mail (e-mail)
Communication	Decoding	Videoconferencing
Oral communication	Feedback	Downward communication
Written communication	Noise	Upward communication
Nonverbal communication	Information overload	Lateral communication
Social context	Jargon	External communication
Encoding	Information technology	Grapevine
Messages	Telecommuting	

REVIEW QUESTIONS

1. Describe the elements of the communication process and their relationship to one another.

2. Give examples of the six types of nonverbal communication.

3. Discuss how advances in information technology are changing the communication process.

4. Explain the importance of feedback and listening.

5. Describe the sources of communication breakdowns.

6. Discuss the differences between formal and informal communication channels.

7. Evaluate the effects and implications of different types of information technologies.

8. What are the rules for giving effective feedback?

9. Why is it important that a manager ask for feedback from subordinates?

10. Explain how a manager can be an effective listener.

DISCUSSION QUESTIONS

Improving Critical Thinking

1. Discuss the difference between knowledge and information. Can there be an "explosion of information," but not an "explosion of knowledge"? Is information a prerequisite to knowledge?

2. What impact do electronic communications have on the feedback component of the communication process? On the encoding process?

Enhancing Communication Skills

3. How is nonverbal communication affected by gender differences? By cultural differences? Write a brief paper that demonstrates your understanding of these issues and prepare to present your findings to the class.

4. How can an organization respond to rumors or messages from the grapevine that are inaccurate and de-

structive? Prepare a brief written report on this subject.

Building Teamwork

5. Trust was identified as a prerequisite for good communication between a sender and a receiver, especially in upward communication channels. How can trust be established between two parties? Form a small group as directed by your instructor, and prepare a brief oral presentation on the subject.

6. How does managing by walking around affect the communication process in an organization? Form a small group, and develop some specific ideas on how this technique can help a manager be more effective. Be prepared to present your ideas to the class as directed by your instructor.

---

1. Use the Internet to search for and create a bibliography of recent articles about changes in business communication. List five such articles and write a brief summary of each. What common themes seem to be present in the articles you selected?

2. Select three organizations in the same industry and search for their Web sites on the Internet. Based on the message and the presentation of information provided, determine who their external stakeholders are. Do you see any common themes to the type of communication across organizations?

INFORMATION TECHNOLOGY: Insights and Solutions

3. Contact several human resource departments of large employers in your area to determine what information technology tools professionals in employee benefit positions use to obtain benefit-related information. How has this changed for the organization? Do they disseminate information to employees within the organization differently than they did five years ago?

ETHICS: Take a Stand

Pierce & Savon, Inc. was one of the most successful financial consulting firms to open in Olympia, Washington, in recent years. The partners prided themselves on a challenging and supportive work environment and they often attracted very assertive young graduates with MBAs or other graduate degrees. Zach was the latest addition to the associate team, with an undergraduate degree in computer science and an MBA. By his first month, it was clear that his sales and client accounts were far ahead of those of other new associates.

As the months passed, Zach proved to be a valuable member of the firm. He worked well with clients and seemed to know just the right approach to take with their portfolios. He often made risky buying and selling decisions with stocks and bonds, but continued to lead sales each month, win new clients, and draw positive feedback from regular accounts.

One evening while working late, Anni, another new associate, walked into Zach's office and saw confidential stock-trading information printing from Zach's computer. She realized that Zach was using his computer skills to tap into and use confidential corporate information such as code words, account references, and confidential e-mail files. By using sophisticated computer equipment, Zach knew in advance about trading that would take place, options that would be bought and sold by major stockholders, or critical decisions affecting stock prices..

When Anni mentioned what she had seen to Zach, he explained that the partners encouraged his creativeness and had purchased all of the computer technology that he requested knowing how it would be used. He offered her the opportunity to "learn the ropes" and share his knowledge and his financial gains.

Anni realized that competitive intelligence was important in devising effective strategies, but did not think this was an ethical way to obtain information. Zach seemed to be well respected and successful. The firm must encourage this behavior.

For Discussion

1. Is information technology being used wisely or inappropriately by the firm? By Zach?

2. Suggest how Anni can handle this situation ethically.

THINKING CRITICALLY: Debate the Issue

USE OR ABUSE OF THE INTERNET

Form teams of four or five students to assess whether or not managers should monitor employees' use of the Internet during working hours to be certain they are not abusing the freedom it allows. Half of the teams should take the stand that employees should be trusted not to abuse the system, and the other half of the teams should take the perspective that such monitoring is appropriate. Use current articles from magazines and even interviews with practicing managers to strengthen your team's arguments. Your instructor will select two teams to present their arguments to the class in a debate format.

BAREFOOT GRASS LAWN SERVICE

No Web Site Available

It is hard to imagine anything worse that could happen to a lawn care company. In the fall of 1987, Barefoot Grass Lawn Service of Madison, Wisconsin, routinely treated lawns of the majority of its 7,000 customers. What happened next was anything but routine. Some of the lawns mysteriously started turning brown. After investigating the damage on several lawns, and consulting with an expert from the University of Wisconsin, the company concluded that the fertilizer that it had been using was contaminated by the chemical atrazine.

Although the supplier of the fertilizer agreed to pay for the damages, Barefoot Grass Lawn Service knew that its reputation was on the line. How should it handle the crisis? Fortunately, the company kept good records and could identify the lawns that might be affected. Immediately, a letter was sent to the affected customers, explaining the mistake that had been made. The company then launched an aggressive compaign to solve the problem. Everyone that worked for Barefoot Grass Lawn Service, including the managers, pitched in. A local landscape company was contracted to help. One by one, the lawns were restored, either by neutralizing the atrazine with a charcoal solution or by replacing the lawn altogether. A total of 325 lawns were affected and successfully restored.

As a token of goodwill, after the lawns were repaired the company sent a box of steaks to each of its customers that had been affected. The company hoped that when the steaks were grilled, its customers would be reminded of how Barefoot Grass Lawn Service had taken care of them. In the end, Barefoot Grass Lawn Service kept the majority of its customers. The company now appears to have a bright future, and is growing at the rate of 20 percent per year. Some of its customers were astounded by how the company handled the crisis. One customer, the retired CEO of a company, wrote to the firm and remarked, "The way you handled this unfortunate situation should be taught in all business schools."

For Discussion

1. What role did communication play in the effective resolution of Barefoot Grass Lawn Service's problem?

2. Describe some negative consequences that could have resulted if Barefoot Grass Lawn Service had waited longer to contact its affected customers.

3. By handling the crisis in the manner in which it did, in what way was Barefoot Grass Lawn Service building trust and credibility for the future?

Video Case

CASE

THE PERFORMANCE REVIEW

Dave Jenkins was scheduled to receive his first performance review at 10:00 A.M. In his office, he prepared the packet of information required for the review session and left for the conference room with ten minutes to spare. He was nervous.

Dave enjoyed working in the branch office of the law firm Dieter, Smart, and Cohen. He expected his first review to be "above average" or possibly "excellent," since "outstanding" seemed beyond reach at the time. Although he was still learning his job, Dave felt positive about his work, the number of hours he put in weekly, client comments, and the fact that he was generating more revenue than most of his peers. If all went well, he thought he could make partner in a few years.

Five minutes before the meeting was to begin, Dave entered the conference room for his meeting with his immediate supervisor, Melissa Harris. He made himself comfortable, selected the chair at the head of the table, and began to prepare. Being nervous did not make this process any easier. At 10:15, Dave began to think he had the wrong time. He called the secretary to confirm his appointment with Melissa, or Ms. Harris, as she preferred to be called. Ms. Harris was running a little late—again—and Dave had no choice but to wait for her. By 10:45, he was becoming irritated. He had work to do and didn't like to be kept waiting.

Meanwhile Melissa Harris had had a very hectic morning. She was behind schedule and had an important client coming in at 11:15 A.M., so by 11:00 she had only fifteen minutes to spend on Dave's review. Walking down the hall to the conference room, she recalled that she had rated Dave's job performance as "average." Dave had the least seniority of any employee in the department, and she wanted to leave room for improvement. He was consistently bringing in more revenue than his peers, but telling Dave he was average would get him to work even harder.

As Melissa entered the conference room, she saw that Dave had taken her chair at the head of the table. She decided to stand, since this wouldn't take long. "Dave, in our firm, 'performance reviews' mean the systematic and regular evaluation of an individual's job performance and potential for development." Dave nodded in agreement. From a stack of papers that seemed a little disorganized, Melissa handed Dave his performance review form and asked him to sign it. Dave replied, "If you don't mind, I would rather sign after I have read the review and we have discussed it."

"I really don't have a lot of time for this right now," said Melissa. "You'll notice that your overall rating is 'average.' That is good for a new employee and that is how the numbers worked out." Dave was astonished. "'Average,'" he said in a quivering voice, "How can you rate me that low? My work has been very good. I have worked long hours to make sure I do a quality job, and you rate that 'average'?" Raising her voice, Melissa said defensively, "Are you questioning my evaluation of your work? You are not getting paid to be the judge here!"

Realizing that things were getting a little too heated, Dave tried to explain. "I'm saying I don't understand your low rating of my job performance." Melissa shuffled through more files and pulled out a piece of paper. "Well, for one thing, you don't know anything about our automated client billing procedure." Surprised and a bit defensive, Dave protested, "I did everything you asked me to do, Ms. Harris, and I did it well. I even asked you about the computerized billing system, and you told me that you wouldn't have time to show me until next year. Please give me a valid reason for my low performance rating."

Melissa decided to be more firm and said sternly, "I am your supervisor. You work for me and I evaluate your progress. I complete the performance reviews for all of the new lawyers. Nobody else has complained. What is your problem, Dave?" Dave was angry and dismayed. "This is just not fair. I know my work is better than half the others." Melissa looked at her watch and asserted emphatically, "It isn't your job to rate the performance of your peers. That's my job. We don't seem to be getting anywhere. If you'll sign and date this to indicate that we have had the required performance review interview, we'll be through here. I have an important appointment at 11:15."

Dave leaned forward and clenched his fist. "I'm not signing anything." Melissa gathered her papers and looked again at her watch. "Well, it's plain to me that you resent being rated as average. You don't respect my judgment and you won't follow my instructions. Time to get back to work." She left Dave sitting in the conference room astonished.

For Discussion

1. Describe the types of nonverbal communication that are present in this case.
2. Explain the nonverbal cues and their probable interpretation from both Dave's viewpoint and Melissa's perspective.
3. Offer feedback to Melissa and Dave about their behavior in this incident.

EXPERIENTIAL EXERCISE 12.1

Thinking on Your Feet: Improving Oral Communication Skills

Purpose: To improve your oral communication skills.

Procedure: Form small groups of four to six people. Each group member should write a lighthearted topic (for example, holiday excursions, your favorite hobby, postgraduation plans) on a slip of paper. Next, collect all the slips, and have the group members in turn draw a slip from the collection and give a one-minute impromptu talk on the topic. After each presentation, the group should provide feedback to the speaker on his oral and nonverbal communication.

Repeat this procedure until each member of the group has given a presentation and received feedback.

SOURCE: Adapted from P. Fandt, *Management Skills: Practice and Experience* (St. Paul, Minn.: West Publishing Co., 1994), 193.

ENDNOTES

1. T. Peters, *Crazy Times Call for Crazy Organizations* (New York: Random House, 1996).

2. T. Stein, "Global Connections: Staying in Touch to Stay on Top," *Success,* March 1996, 46–48.

3. T. Peters, *Liberation Management* (New York: Knopf, 1992).

4. T. Peters, *Liberation Management* ; J. A. Conger. "Inspiring Others: The Language of Leadership," *Academy of Management Executive,* 5, 1, 1991, 310–45.

5. D. L. Whetzel, "The Department of Labor Identifies Workplace Skills," *The Industrial/Organizations Psychologist,* July 1991, 89–90.

6. For more specific details and a thorough discussion, see M. Munter, *Guide to Managerial Communication,* 3d ed. (Upper Saddle River, N.J.: Prentice Hall, 1992).

7. K. H. Roberts, *Communication in Organizations* (Chicago: Science Research Associates, 1984).

8. M. Hammer and J. Champy, *Reengineering the Corporations: A Manifesto for Business Revolution.* (New York: Harper Business, 1993).

9. Adapted from P. Fandt, *Management Skills: Practice and Experience* (St. Paul, Minn.: West Publishing, 1994), 193.

10. For more specific details on making effective presentations, see P. Fandt, *Management Skills: Practice and Experience* (St. Paul Minn., West, 1994); M. Martel, *The Persuasive Edge: The Executive Guide to Speaking and Presenting* (New York: Fawcett Columbine, 1989); L. Harrisberger, *Succeeding: How to Become an Outstanding Professional* (New York: Macmillian, 1994); and A. Fischer and M. Northey, *Impact: A Guide to Business Communication* (Upper Saddle River, N.J.: Prentice Hall, 1993).

11. Adapted from P. Fandt, *Management Skills,* 193.

12. K. Blanchard, "Translating Body Talk," *Success,* April 1986, 10; J. Baird and G. Wieting, "Nonverbal Communication Can Be a Motivational Tool," *Personnel Journal,* September 1979, 609.

13. For an interesting discussion of how leaders communicate using nonverbal cues, see H. Sims Jr. and C. Manz, *Company of Heroes* (New York: Wiley, 1996); C. Manz and H. Sims Jr. *SuperLeadership: Leading Others to Lead Themselves* (Berkeley, CA: Prentice Hall, 1989).

14. P. C. Morrow and J. C. McElroy, "Interior Office Design and Visitor Response: A Constructive Replication," *Journal of Applied Psychology,* 66, 1981, 646–50.

15. K. H. Roberts, *Communication in Organizations.*

16. L. Kadaba, "Buried in E-Mail: Businesses Learn Timesaving Technology Can Waste Time When Unimportant Messages Pile Up," *Seattle Times,* September 18, 1996, SL-3.

17. J. Brownell, "Communicating with Credibility: The Gender Gap," *Cornell Hotel and Restaurant Administration Quarterly,* April 1993, 52–61.

18. R. Lengel and R. Daft, "The Selection of Communication Media as an Executive Skill," *Academy of Management Executive,* 2, 1988, 225–32.

19. "King Customer," *Business Week,* March 12, 1990, 88.

20. T. Peters, "Perpetual Job Insecurity," in *Lessons in Leadership*; S. Covey, "World-Class Leaders Take Global View," in *Lessons in Leadership* (Provo, Utah: Corey Leadership Center, 1996).

21. N. J. Adler, *International Dimensions of Organizational Behavior* (Boston: PWS-Kent, 1991).

22. F. Trompenaars, *Riding the Waves of Culture: Understanding Diversity in Global Businesses* (Chicago: Irwin Professional Publishing, 1994).

23. L. Holman, "Globalization in the Information Age," in *Lessons in Leadership;* S. Cady, P. Fandt, and D. Fernadez, "Investigating Cultural Differences in Personal Success: Implications for Designing Effective Reward Systems," *Journal of Value-Based Management,* 6, 1993, 65–80.

24. B. J. Reilly and J. A. DiAngelo, "Communication: A Cultural System of Meaning and Values," *Human Relations,* 43, 1990, 129–40.

25. G. Bonvillian and W. Nowlin, "Cultural Awareness: An Essential Element in Doing Business Abroad," *Business Horizons,* 37, 6, November 1994, 44–50.

26. A. Farnham, "Trust Gap," *Fortune,* December 4, 1989, 70.

27. R. Mitchell and M. O'Neal, "Managing by Values: Is Levi Strauss' Approach Visionary or Flaky?" *Business Week,* August 8, 1995, 61–62.

28. See, for example, P. Senge, *The Fifth Discipline: The Art and Practice of Learning Organizations* (New York: Doubleday, 1990).

29. T. J. Peters and R. H. Waterman Jr., *In Search of Excellence: Lessons from America's Best-Run Companies* (New York: Harper & Row, 1982).

30. R. Levering and M. Moskowitz, *The 100 Best Companies to Work for in America* (New York: NAL/Dutton, 1994).

31. Analysis for the Electronic Messaging Association, *1996 Report.*

32. A. Sprout, "Finally, Cyberchat Starts to Get Serious," *Fortune,* November 11, 1996; L. Kadaba, "Buried in E-Mail."

33. M. Cooper, D. Friedman, and J. Koenig, "Empire of the Sun," *U.S. News & World Report,* May 28, 1990, 44–51.

34. L. O'Connell, "For Success at Work, Bone up on Styles of Gender Chat, "*Orlando Sentinel,* November 13, 1994, B1.

35. John Gray, *Men are from Mars, Women are from Venus* (New York: HarperCollins, 1992); D. Borisoff, "Gender Issues and Listening," in *Listening in Everyday Life: A Personal and Professional Approach,* eds., D. Borisoff and M. Purdy, (Lanham, Md.: University Press of America, 1992); E. Aries, "Verbal and Nonverbal Behavior in Single-Sex and Mixed-Sex Groups," *Psychological Reports,* 51, 1982, 127–34; L. Hirschman, "Female-Male Differences in Conversational Interaction," in *Language and Sex: Difference and Dominance,* eds., B. Thorne and N. Henley, (Rowley, Mass.: Newbury House, 1975).

36. J. C. Pearson and E. Aries, *Gender and Communication* (Dubuque, Iowa: William C. Brown, 1991); L. Morrow,

"Men: Are They Really That Bad?" *Time,* February 14, 1994, 93.

37. J. Brownell, "Communicating with Credibility: The Gender Gap."

38. W. Bulkeley, "Computerizing Dull Meetings Is Touted as an Antidote to the Mouth That Bored," *The Wall Street Journal,* January 28, 1992, B1.

39. T. Stein, "The Global Connections: Staying in Touch to Stay on Top."

40. As discussed in A. DuBrin, *Contemporary Applied Management: Behavioral Science Techniques for Managers and Professionals,* 3d ed. (Homewood, Ill.: Irwin, 1989), 328-40.

41. R. O. Metzger and M. A. Von Glinow, "Off-Site Workers: At Home and Abroad," *California Management Review,* Spring 1988, 101-11; J. N. Goodrich, "Telecommuting in America," *Business Horizons,* July/August 1990, 31-37.

42. J. Zygmont, "Face to Face," *Sky Magazine,* February 1988, 10.

43. Pat O'Donnell, "The Biggest Loser at Solitare—The Company," *The Wall Street Journal,* December 19, 1994, A14.

44. D. Watley, "An Important Lesson from the Olympians," in *Lessons in Leadership.*

45. M. Loeb, "Wouldn't It Be Better to Work for the Good Guys?" *Fortune,* October 14, 1996, 223-24.

46. L. Kadaba, "Buried in E-Mail."

47. S. L. Kirmeyer and T. Lin, "Social Support: Its Relationship to Observed Communication with Peers and Superiors," *Academy of Management Journal,* 30, 1987, 138-51.

48. F. Luthans and J. K. Larsen, "How Managers Really Communicate," *Human Relations,* 39, 1986, 161-78.

49. M. J. Glauser, "Upward Information Flows in Organizations: Review and Conceptual Analysis," *Human Relations,* 37, 1984, 113-43.

50. D. J. Brass, "Men's and Women's Networks: A Study of Interaction Patterns and Influence in an Organization," *Academy of Management Journal,* 28, 1985, 327-43.

51. E. Walton, "How Efficient Is the Grapevine?" *Personnel,* 28, 1961, 45-48.

52. F. Luthans, R. Hodgetts, and S. Rosenkrantz, *Real Managers and Workplace Basics* (New York: Ballinger Publishing, 1988).

53. J. A. Sonnenfeld, "Director's Comments," *The Leadership Newsletter,* Fall 1996, 2.

54. S. Covey, *The 7 Habits of Highly Effective People* (New York: Simon & Schuster, 1989).

55. Ibid.

56. C. R. Rogers, "Barriers and Gateways to Communication," *Harvard Business Review,* 69, November/December 1991, 105-11.

57. E. T. Hall, "The Silent Language in Overseas Business," *Harvard Business Review,* May/June 1960, 58-64.

58. W. Kiechel, "Learn How to Listen," *Fortune,* August 17, 1987, 107-108.

59. See K. Green and D. Seymour, "Who's Going to Run General Motors?" Princeton, N.J.: Peterson's Guides, 1991, 45.

60. Adapted from M. Munter, *Guide to Managerial Communication,* xii.

61. F. Trompenaars, *Riding the Waves of Culture.*

62. T. Stein, " Global Connections: Staying in Touch to Stay on Top."

Understanding Leadership in a Dynamic Environment

C H A P T E R 13

CHAPTER OVERVIEW

The study of leadership and the demand for good leaders have fascinated people throughout the ages. In fact, thousands of articles and books have been published on the subject, looking at leadership from many different approaches—the study of traits, the study of leadership behaviors, the study of situations in which leaders act, the influence leaders have on others, and the role leadership has played in change. Obviously, leadership has been an important historical topic. Our society has been preoccupied with great military leaders, powerful political leaders, outstanding athletes, and visionary social reformers. How do we judge a good leader? Is being a leader an honor? Are the models we used to measure effectiveness a few years ago still appropriate in a changing world? Are leaders even necessary? These are some of the issues we examine in this chapter.

Our purpose in this chapter is to examine leadership as it relates to the manager's job and to provide a knowledge foundation for developing leadership effectiveness in a global and diverse organizational environment. Our emphasis is on "managerial leadership" in formal organizations such as business corporations, government agencies, hospitals, universities, and so forth. We examine the traditional approaches to leadership, explore several emerging leadership perspectives, and conclude with some guiding principles to get you started toward leadership effectiveness. Throughout the chapter, we offer many opportunities for you to apply leadership theories to practice and enhance your leadership skills.

LEARNING OBJECTIVES

When you have finished studying this chapter, you should be able to:

- Describe what is meant by the term *leadership*.
- Explain the sources of a leader's power.
- Explain the leadership and contingency variables in the situational leadership theory (SLT) and path-goal models.
- Identify leadership substitutes.
- Describe transformational leadership.
- Discuss transactional leadership
- Provide evidence of your understanding of developing followership.
- Explain how self-managed teams (SMTs) function.
- Suggest ways in which leaders influence quality-management programs.

THE BELL ATLANTIC WAY: SMITH'S WAKE-UP CALL

Since becoming CEO of Bell Atlantic, Raymond W. Smith has been challenged with providing the leadership needed to guide the company out of its old bureaucratic system. To do so, he has developed a program called the "Bell Atlantic Way"—a broad initiative to cut costs, spur sales, ensure a quality orientation, and promote independent thinking among employees at the $3 billion, Philadelphia-based regional Bell phone company. While all seven "Baby Bells" are striving to break out of their bureaucratic thinking, the Bell Atlantic Way program stands out for its sheer pervasiveness.

Smith, a Carnegie Mellon University engineering graduate, keeps a plaque on his desk reading "Be Here Now," a reminder to remain focused on the business at hand. He encourages employees to carry a blue poker chip, as he does, to keep them working on "blue-chip" priorities first, leaving less important tasks for later.

Smith began the Bell Atlantic Way process by becoming thoroughly immersed in a new leadership focus that stresses motivational techniques and employee partnerships. In the past four years, Smith has sent nearly 20,000 managers through a two-day training program to learn the Bell Atlantic Way. Similar training for nearly 60,000 other employees started in 1993. True believers wear "Coach Me" buttons, an invitation to co-workers and even subordinates to offer advice.

Smith's unrelenting message is expressed in company newsletters, training sessions, and ubiquitous Bell Atlantic Way posters. As he strives to lead Bell Atlantic in new directions, his biggest challenge will be to keep employees from slipping back into comfortable Bell habits. "We've largely overcome the old monopoly mindset, and I'd say we're in Act III, Scene IV of a five-act play," the CEO says. Can Smith provide the leadership necessary for Bell Atlantic to meet this challenge?[1]

INTRODUCTION

Raymond Smith obviously understands how important leadership can be to an organization. As we examine how he steered the changes at Bell Atlantic, two important behaviors emerge. First, he developed an agenda for himself and the company that included a new vision of what the organization could and should be. Second, he worked to gain cooperation from employees unleashing the power of self-leadership. Smith knew that he needed a company of leaders; this involved asking employees to work on changing corporate objectives instead of just fulfilling the narrow, bureaucratically defined objectives that marked the old Bell system. This is not an easy task for a leader.

Being an effective leader has never been more important or more challenging. As the global marketplace becomes more competitive and the workplace grows more diverse, leaders face many challenges. Meeting these challenges requires an unprecedented level of flexibility and responsiveness.

Accordingly, this chapter is devoted to exploring what leadership is and how managers can develop leadership skills. Our examination of leadership begins by discussing the nature of leadership and the sources of a leader's power. We will briefly discuss the historical perspective that includes traits and behavioral approaches. Then we take a look at several contingency models that are directed toward using resources effectively and developing relationships. The chapter will touch on how information technology is, and will be, influ-

WHAT IS EFFECTIVE LEADERSHIP?

How do you describe effective leadership? Take a few minutes and make a list on what effective leadership is to you. How do you visualize it? Is it a pattern of behavior? Characteristics that you identify with? Situations that you have found yourself in? How would you describe it to someone else?

In defining effective leadership, consider examples from as wide a range of experiences as possible; think globally and abstractly. See how creative you can be in recalling images of leaders you have known or known of, read about, worked with, or observed over the years from your family, social, school, and work life. You may also want to consider leaders you have encountered in fiction, history, and current events through books, television, and movies.

Form groups of six to eight members to share your impressions and thoughts. What common elements seem to emerge? Have a spokesperson make a list of these elements. Spokespersons should report the findings to the class as a whole.

encing leadership. Finally, the chapter concludes by examining several of the emerging developments and applications of leadership to better understand change-oriented leadership.

LEADERSHIP SIGNIFICANCE

We broadly define *leadership* as a social influence process. **Leadership** involves determining the group's or organization's objectives, motivating behavior in pursuit of these objectives, and influencing group maintenance and culture.[2] But leadership also produces change.[3] It is a group phenomenon; there are no leaders without followers.

Leadership
A social influence process that involves determining the group's objectives, motivating behavior in pursuit of these objectives, and influencing group maintenance and culture.

Typically, leadership involves creating a vision of the future, devising a strategy for achieving that vision, and communicating the vision so that everyone understands and believes in it. Leadership also entails providing an environment that will inspire and motivate people to overcome obstacles. In this way leadership brings about change.[4]

A debate in the popular management literature concerns whether leading and managing are different behaviors. One view is that managers carry out responsibilities, exercise authority, and worry about how to get things done, whereas leaders are concerned with understanding people's beliefs and gaining their commitment. In other words, managers and leaders differ in what they attend to and in how they think, work, and interact. A related argument contends that leadership is about coping with change, whereas management is about coping with complexity.[5]

Although the leader-manager debate has generated tremendous controversy in the literature, there is little research to support the notion that certain people can be classified as leaders rather than managers, or that managers cannot adopt visionary behaviors when they are required for success. We maintain that it is important for all managers to think of themselves as leaders, and consequently, we use the term *leadership* to encompass both leadership and management functions.[6]

Meeting the Challenge asks you to consider leadership and what it means to you.[7] Complete the exercise before continuing the rest of the chapter. It will enhance your understanding of what it means to become a leader.

We tend to associate leaders with power. In fact, power is central to successful leadership. Where does that power come from? In the next section, we examine the sources of a leader's power.

SOURCES OF A LEADER'S POWER

Power
The ability to marshal human, informational, or material resources to get something done.

Anyone in an organization, regardless of rank, can have power. **Power** is defined as the ability to marshal human, informational, or material resources to get something done. The concept of ability distinguishes power from authority. Authority is the right to get something done and is officially sanctioned; power is the ability to get results.

Power is important not only for influencing subordinates, but also for influencing peers, superiors, and people outside the organization, such as clients and suppliers. To understand this process better, we need to look at the various types of power. In addition, we must consider whether the power is prescribed by the person's position or is a result of personal attributes.

POSITION POWER

Power is derived, in part, from the opportunities inherent in a person's position in an organization. *Position power* includes legitimate power, coercive power, reward power, and information power.

Legitimate power
Power stemming from formal authority based on the particular positions in an organization or social system.

Legitimate Power
Power stemming from formal authority is sometimes called **legitimate power.**[8] This authority is based on perceptions about the obligations and responsibilities associated with particular positions in an organization or social system. Legitimate power exists when people go along with someone's wishes because they believe that person has the legitimate right to influence them and that they have a duty to accept that influence. For example, presidents, supervisors, and academic department chairs have a certain degree of legitimate power simply because of the formal position they hold. Other people accept this power, as long as it is not abused, because they attribute legitimacy to the formal position and to the person who holds that position.

Coercive power
The power to discipline, punish, and withhold rewards.

Coercive Power
Coercive power is the power to discipline, punish, and withhold rewards. As a source of leader power, coercive power is important largely as a potential, rather than an actual, type of influence. For example, the threat of being disciplined for not arriving at work on time is effective in influencing many employees to be punctual. Similarly, the possibility that we might get a speeding ticket is enough to cause many of us to drive within acceptable speed limits.

Reward power
Derived from control over tangible benefits, such as promotion, a better job, a better work schedule, a larger operating budget, an increased expense account, and formal recognition of accomplishments.

Reward Power
Another source of power that stems from the manager's position in the organization is influence over resources and rewards. **Reward power** is derived from control over tangible benefits, such as a promotion, a better job, a better work schedule, a larger operating budget, an increased expense account, and formal recognition of accomplishments. Reward power is also derived from status symbols such as a larger office or a reserved parking space. For reward power to be influential, the employee must value the rewards.

Information power
Control over information that involves the leader's power to access and distribute information that is either desired or vital to others.

Information Power
Information power is control over information. It involves the leader's power to access and distribute information that is either desired by or vital to others.

Managerial positions often provide opportunities to obtain information that is not directly available to subordinates or peers. However, some people acquire information power through their unique skill of being able to know all the latest news and gossip that others want to hear. With the vast changes in the use of information technology in most organizations, you can see how information power has become a centralized focal point.

PERSONAL POWER

Effective leaders cannot rely solely on power that is derived from their position in the organization. Other sources of power must be cultivated. *Personal power* is derived from the interpersonal relationship between a leader and her followers. It includes both expert and referent power.

Expert Power
A major source of personal power in organizations stems from expertise in solving problems and performing important tasks. **Expert power** is the power to influence another person because of expert knowledge and competence. Computer specialists often have substantial expert power in organizations because they have technical knowledge that others need. As we mentioned previously, not only is information technology driving many organizations, but the computer systems functions and the individuals with the knowledge to operate these areas provide expertise to everyone in the organization. The expertise of tax accountants and investment managers gives them considerable power over the financial affairs of business firms. A secretary who knows how to run the office may have expert power, but lack position power.

Expert power
The power to influence because of expert knowledge and competence.

Referent Power
Referent power is the ability to influence others based on personal liking, charisma, and reputation. It is manifested through imitation or emulation. There are numerous reasons why we might attribute referent power to others. We may like their personalities, admire their accomplishments, believe in their causes, or see them as role models. Much of the power wielded by strong political leaders and professional athletes, musicians, and artists is referent power. People who feel a deep friendship or loyalty toward someone are usually willing to do special favors for that person. Moreover, people tend to imitate the behavior of someone whom they greatly admire, and they tend to develop attitudes similar to those expressed by a person with whom they identify. Bill Gates (chair and CEO of Microsoft), Claudia Schiffer (supermodel), and Michael Jordan (Chicago Bulls basketball superstar) are just a few of the many individuals who influence potential buyers with their referent power.

Referent power
The ability to influence based on personal liking, charisma, and reputation.

Michael Jordan possesses tremendous referent power—the ability to influence others based on charisma, personal liking, and reputation. People tend to imitate his behavior and to develop attitudes similar to those he expresses.

© Robert Kusel/Tony Stone Images

Is power good or bad? Positive or negative? Keep in mind that power can be both positive and negative, good and bad. Although the concepts of power and influence are closely related, some research indicates that the two can be seen as different. A leader who has power may still have difficulty influencing subordinates' behavior, or influence may occur without a specific source of power. For example, in Managing for Excellence, former President Jimmy Carter's use of power is examined both as a U.S. president and as a president emeritus.

PRESIDENT EMERITUS AND EMPOWERING LEADER

History has not provided us with many models of past presidents who have made the transition out of office, failed a reelection campaign, failed at a personal business to the point of near-bankruptcy, and then become a highly respected, admired, and powerful person. We have one—former president Jimmy Carter. Carter has positioned himself as one of the most respected former presidents of all times. It is a remarkable study in the use of power and leadership, but not the kind you often hear about.

One of the fundamental aspects of this remarkable accomplishment is that Carter has used his reputation and prestige to influence others in positive, constructive ways. He has captured the essence of power in a positive way, by empowering those around himself.

First, Carter took a strong leadership role in support of Habitat for Humanity, a nonprofit organization that brings people together to construct private housing for the poor and homeless. Rather than being a vocal leader, he has been a behind-the-scenes leader. He's involved in the actual building projects that go on throughout the country. He doesn't want legitimate power, but instead has realized the value of referent power.

Next, Carter accepted the roles of conciliator and conflict resolver in North Korea, in the Sudan cease-fire, in the occupation in Haiti, in the cease-fire in Bosnia, and in the high-profile elections in Nicaragua and Panama. At Emory University, Carter created the Carter Center, where people come together to resolve conflict. Again, he has used his power, but as an expert or a referent to others who respect him.

Clearly there is a difference in Carter the president and Carter the president emeritus. One perspective is that as president, Carter led with the authority and legitimate power of the office. On the other hand, as a former president, Carter leads by reputation, prestige, expertise, and networking to influence and empower others by bringing out their best.

THE CHANGING FACE OF POWER: EMPOWERMENT

One of the major forces for cultural and structural changes in organizations has been the empowerment movement. *Empowerment* is designed to increase the power and autonomy of all employees in organizations. It has roots in perceptions of Japanese management, the quality-circle efforts of the 1970s and the quality-of-work-life (QWL) approach, and the psychological concept of self-efficacy.[9] The underlying theme of empowerment is the giving away and sharing of power with those who need it to perform their job functions. Such power sharing provides people with a belief in their ability and their sense of effectiveness. Research and observations of many leaders strongly suggest that equal power sharing contributes to an organization's effectiveness. Empowerment of employees can also be a powerful motivational tool, as we will discuss in Chapter 15, by providing them with both control and a sense of accomplishment.[10]

HISTORICAL LEADERSHIP APPROACHES

Now that we have considered some of the ways leaders gain power to influence others, we examine the different approaches used to determine what makes a leader effective. For purposes of our discussion, we have grouped lead-

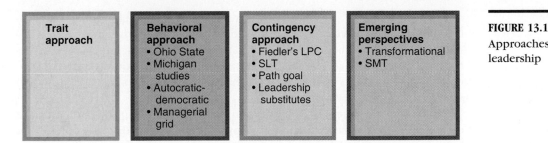

FIGURE 13.1
Approaches to understanding leadership

ership approaches into the four categories shown in Figure 13.1: the trait approach, behavioral approaches, contingency approaches, and emerging perspectives.

One of the earliest approaches to studying leadership was the trait approach. Underlying the **trait approach** is the assumption that some people are "natural leaders" and are endowed with certain traits not possessed by other individuals. This research compared successful and unsuccessful leaders to see how they differed in physical characteristics, personality, and ability. Evidence suggests that leaders and nonleaders do differ in a number of traits.[11] In general, leaders possess greater (1) drive (that is, achievement, ambition, energy, tenacity, initiative), (2) motivation, (3) honesty and integrity, (4) self-confidence, (5) cognitive ability, and (6) knowledge of the business.

Despite the evidence that leaders tend to differ from nonleaders with respect to the six traits listed, traits alone cannot predict leadership ability; leaders are not born but are much more than a combination of traits. To succeed, leaders do not have to be intellectual geniuses or all-wise prophets, but they do have to have certain capabilities. Therefore, the particular requirements for effective leadership in each situation may well outweigh drive, motivation, honesty and integrity, self-confidence, cognitive ability, and knowledge of the business, or make only certain ones important.[12] Possession of the listed qualities does not guarantee that you will become a leader, nor does the absence of any one of them rule out the possibility of becoming an excellent leader.

Trait research failed to predict leadership success consistently. As a result, some researchers began to examine what effective leaders *do* rather than what effective leaders *are.* We term this the **behavioral approach** to leadership. The researchers examined two independent patterns of behaviors or styles that are used by effective leaders. The behavioral approach assumed that what the leader does is the primary variable that determines effectiveness.

Behavioral models defined a leader's effectiveness based on **task orientation,** such as setting goals, giving directions, setting standards, supervising worker performance, and applauding new ideas. The other behavior found in effective leaders was **relationship orientation,** such as showing empathy for needs and feelings, being supportive of group needs, establishing trusting relationships, and allowing workers to participate in decision making.

Numerous studies have examined these behaviors, often with differing terms attached to the concepts of task orientation and relationship orientation.[13] The general consensus is that effective leaders use a combination of behaviors. However, it is still not obvious which behaviors are most effective, because numerous other factors can influence performance and success. Most important, the behavioral studies focused our attention on leadership training.

Take, for example, Jack Welch, hailed today as one of America's most successful CEOs. In his earlier years, he was nicknamed "Neutron Jack" and was labeled in 1984 as "the undisputed premier" among America's toughest bosses. He demonstrated all the task-oriented behaviors such as demanding high performance standards, establishing rigid rules and procedures, autocratic decision making, and high levels of control, but few if any of the relationship-

Trait approach
The assumption that some people are "natural leaders," and are endowed with certain traits not possessed by other individuals.

Behavioral approach
What the leader does is the primary variable that determines effectiveness.

Task orientation
Setting goals, giving directions, setting standards, supervising worker performance, and applauding new ideas.

Relationship orientation
Showing empathy for needs and feelings, being supportive of group needs, establishing trusting relationships, and allowing workers to participate in decision making.

oriented behaviors.[14] However, as we read about Jack Welch today and analyze his reign of success at General Electric, we realize what most of the behavioral leadership theorists learned: (1) effective leaders use a range of behaviors, (2) these behaviors can be learned, and (3) an important characteristic of effective leaders is their ability to change and adapt to the organizational settings in which they manage.

Thus we see a new era of leadership study ushered in, beginning in the early 1960s, called the **contingency approach.** We will discuss some of the key contingency models in the next section.

Contingency approaches
Examine the fit between leaders' behavior and the situations in which they manage.

CONTINGENCY APPROACHES: UNDERSTANDING LEADERSHIP QUALITY

The theme in earlier approaches to understanding leadership was the desire to identify traits or behaviors effective leaders had in common. A common set of characteristics proved to be elusive, however. Researchers were continually frustrated by the lack of consistent support for their findings and conclusions. As a result, research began to focus on leadership style and situational variables that are subject to changes. Overall, the contingency approach has four assumptions.

1. The appropriate leadership style depends on the requirements of the situation.
2. Leadership can be learned.
3. Successful leadership involves understanding situational contingencies.
4. The match between the leader's style, personality or behavior, and the situation leads to effectiveness.[15]

FIEDLER'S LPC CONTINGENCY MODEL

The first major contingency theory that clearly demonstrated the discipline of situational thinking was Fiedler's least preferred co-worker (LPC) model. The objective of the model is to predict work-group task performance or effectiveness.[16] The premise of **Fiedler's LPC model** is that group performance depends on a successful match between the leader's style and the demands of the situation. Let's look at what determines leader behavior and situational favorability and at how each can be used to determine an effective match.

Fiedler's LPC model
A contingency model that predicts work group effectiveness based on a match between the leader's style and the demands of the situation.

Leadership Behavior Assessment
The first step in applying the LPC model is to assess the leader's behaviors or characteristics. A characteristic that plays an important role in Fiedler's model is the behavioral tendency to be motivated primarily toward either task accomplishments or people relationships. Fiedler used an instrument called the **least preferred co-worker (LPC) scale** to measure a person's basic leadership style. The people completing the LPC scale are asked to describe the co-worker with whom they have been able to work least well (least preferred co-worker or LPC). A person who describes the co-worker in positive terms (such as *pleasant, helpful, supportive, open*) earns a high LPC score. A high LPC score suggests that the person has a behavioral tendency toward people relationships and thus has a relationship-oriented style. A person who describes a co-worker in negative terms (such as *unpleasant, frustrating, hostile, guarded*) gets a low LPC score. A low LPC score suggests that the person has a behavioral tendency toward task accomplishment and thus has a task-motivated style.

Least preferred coworker (LPC) scale
Designed to measure relationship-oriented versus task-oriented behaviors according to a leader's choice of descriptive terms.

According to Fiedler's LPC model, group performance depends on a successful match between the leader's style and the demands of the situation. The most favorable situation for the leader results when leader-member relations are good, when a leader has high position power, and when the task is structured,

© Loren Santow/Tony Stone Images

Situational Favorability

The next step in applying the LPC model is to understand the situation. The relationship between a leader's LPC score and group effectiveness depends on a complex situational variable called *situational favorability*. Fiedler defines *favorability* as the extent to which the situation gives a leader control over subordinates. Favorability is measured in terms of three aspects of the situation:

1. *Leader-member relations.* The extent to which the leader has the support and loyalty of subordinates.
2. *Task structure.* The extent to which there are standard operating procedures for accomplishing the task.
3. *Position power.* The extent to which the leader has authority to evaluate subordinate performance and administer rewards and punishments.

These three components—leader-member relations, task structure, and position power—combine in a number of ways to create specific organizational situations. Figure 13.2 shows the eight possible combinations and indicates the relative degree of control required in each situation. According to the LPC model, the situation is highly favorable for the leader (situation 1) when leader-member relations are good, the task is highly structured, and the leader has

	1	2	3	4	5	6	7	8
Favorability	Highly favorable						Highly unfavorable	
Leader-member relations	Good				Poor			
Task structure	High		Low		High		Low	
Leader position power	Strong	Weak	Strong	Weak	Strong	Weak	Strong	Weak

FIGURE 13.2

Fiedler's LPC leadership model

SOURCE: F. E. Fiedler, "The Effects of Leadership Training and Experience: A Contingency Model Interpretation," *Administrative Science Quarterly,* 17, 1972, 455. Reprinted by permission of *Administrative Science Quarterly.*

substantial position power. When leader-member relations are good, subordinates are more likely to comply with the leader's requests and direction, rather than ignoring or subverting them. When a leader has high position power, it is easy to influence subordinates. When the task is structured, it is easy for the leader to direct subordinates and monitor their performance. An example of this situation is the well-liked supervisor of a parts assembly-line crew.

The situation is highly unfavorable for the leader (situation 8) when relations with subordinates are poor, the task is unstructured, and position power is low. An example is the unpopular chair of a volunteer committee with a vague problem to solve.

Behavior-Situation Match

The final step in applying Fiedler's LPC model is to determine the appropriate leadership style for the situation. Based on the results of the LPC, a manager whose LPC score is low, or a task-oriented leader, will be more effective in a situation that is either highly unfavorable (situations 6, 7, and 8) or highly favorable (situations 1, 2, and 3) than a relationship-oriented leader. In contrast, relationship-oriented leaders, whose scores on the LPC are high, excel when conditions are moderately favorable. Moderately favorable situations lie somewhere between the extremes of high and low control.

What if the leader's style and the situational control requirement do not match? Fiedler contends that it is easier to alter a situation than to change a leader's LPC score, since LPC is a relatively stable and resistant measure. In fact, Fiedler developed a self-paced study program called Leader Match to train managers to apply his theory. The program shows trainees how to compute scores for LPC and situational factors and then suggests ways to alter the situation to match the trainee's LPC.

SITUATIONAL LEADERSHIP THEORY

A second contingency approach is the situational leadership theory. Hersey and Blanchard developed a contingency leadership model, which was originally called the *life-cycle theory of leadership,* but the name was later changed to *situational leadership theory (SLT).* According to the **SLT model,** quality leader behavior depends on the situational contingency of readiness and the appropriate behavior-readiness match.[17]

SLT model
States that effective leader behavior depends on the situational contingency of readiness and the appropriate behavior-readiness match.

Readiness is the extent to which a subordinate possesses the ability and willingness to complete a specific task. Subordinates have various degrees of readiness, as shown in Figure 13.3. In a specific situation, the leader provides some degree of task behavior and relationship behavior.

Task behavior is the extent to which a leader organizes and defines the role of followers by explaining what each person must do and when, where, and how tasks are to be accomplished. *Relationship behavior* is the extent to which a leader maintains personal relationships with followers by opening up channels of communication and providing support. Figure 13.3 shows the model linking task and relationship behaviors and subordinate readiness.[18] The appropriate style of leadership is shown by the curve running through the four leadership quadrants. As the subordinate's readiness increases from the minimum to a moderate level, the leader should use more relationship behavior and less task behavior. As the subordinate's readiness increases beyond a moderate level, the leader should decrease the amount of relationship behavior while continuing to decrease the amount of task behavior.

A leader using the *telling style* provides specific instructions and closely supervises performance. This style works best when follower readiness is low. The direction provided by this leadership style defines roles for people who

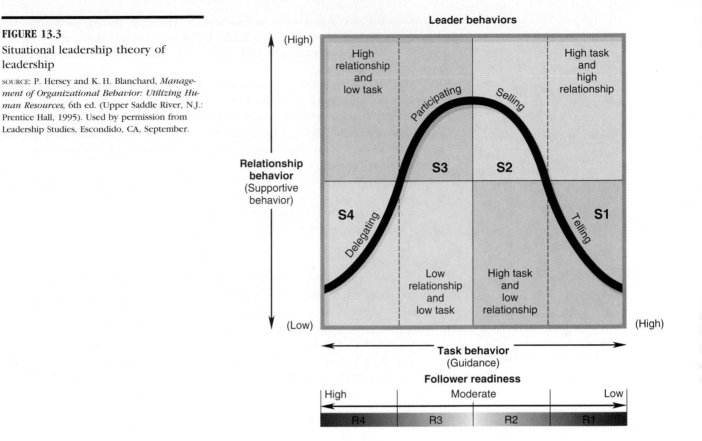

FIGURE 13.3
Situational leadership theory of
leadership

SOURCE: P. Hersey and K. H. Blanchard, *Management of Organizational Behavior: Utilizing Human Resources,* 6th ed. (Upper Saddle River, N.J.: Prentice Hall, 1995). Used by permission from Leadership Studies, Escondido, CA, September.

are unable or unwilling to take responsibility because it eliminates any insecurity about the task that must be done.

Using the *selling style,* the leader explains decisions and provides opportunities for clarification. This style offers both task direction and support for people who are unable but willing to take task responsibility. It combines a directive approach with explanation and reinforcement for maintaining enthusiasm.

The *participating style* involves sharing ideas and maintaining two-way communication to encourage and support the skills the subordinates have developed. It is most appropriately used for moderate-to-high follower readiness. Able but unwilling followers require supportive behavior to increase their motivation. This style helps to enhance a subordinate's desire to perform a task because it shares the decision making.

A *delegating style* occurs when the leader provides the subordinates with few task or relationship behaviors. When subordinates have reached a readiness level at which they decide how and when to do things and are able and willing to take responsibility for what needs to be done, it is appropriate for the leader to use a delegating style.

The SLT model shows that managers should be flexible in choosing a leadership style. It also implies that leaders must constantly check a subordinate's readiness level in determining the correct combination of task and relationship behaviors. Unlike Fiedler's LPC model, the SLT model has not been extensively researched, but it has been widely used in industry for manager training since it was originally published in 1969.

PATH-GOAL MODEL

Another well-known contingency approach is the **path-goal model** of leadership. This model is unique because its roots are in the expectancy theory of

Path-goal model
Used because of its emphasis on how a leader influences subordinates' perception of work goals and personal goals, and the links or paths found between these two sets of goals.

motivation that we will discuss in Chapter 15. The term *path-goal* is used be-cause the model emphasizes how a leader influences subordinates' perceptions of work goals and personal goals and stresses the links or paths found between these two sets of goals.[19]

Path-goal theory assumes that a leader's key function is to adjust his or her behavior to complement situational contingencies, such as those found in the work setting. When a leader is able to compensate for things lacking in the set-ting, subordinates are likely to be satisfied with the leader. Performance should benefit as the paths by which effort leads to performance and performance leads to valued rewards are clarified.

As shown in Figure 13.4, leader behaviors interact with several contin-gency factors to determine the employee's job performance and satisfaction. In the next section, we examine the situational contingencies and leader be-haviors that focus on leadership quality.

Leader Behaviors

Path-goal theory identifies four leader behaviors that affect subordinate per-ceptions of paths and goals: (1) supportive, (2) directive, (3) participative, and (4) achievement-oriented leadership.

Supportive leadership means giving consideration to the needs of sub-ordinates, displaying concern for their welfare, and creating a friendly climate in the work unit. This is similar to the concept of consideration. Supportive leadership is predicted to increase the satisfaction of subordinates who work on highly repetitive tasks or on tasks considered to be unpleasant, stressful, or frustrating. The leader's supportive behavior helps to compensate for these ad-verse conditions.

Directive leadership means letting subordinates know what they are ex-pected to do, giving specific guidance, asking subordinates to follow rules and procedures, and scheduling and coordinating work. This is similar to the con-cept of initiating structure. Directive leadership is predicted to have a positive impact on subordinates when the task is ambiguous and to have just the op-posite effect for clear tasks.

Participative leadership involves consulting with subordinates and tak-ing their opinions and suggestions into account. Participative leadership is predicted to promote satisfaction on nonrepetitive tasks that allow for ego involvement of subordinates. On repetitive tasks, open-minded or nonau-thoritarian subordinates will also be satisfied with a participative leader.

Achievement-oriented leadership refers to setting challenging goals, seeking performance improvements, emphasizing excellence in performance, and showing confidence. Achievement orientation is predicted to motivate sub-ordinates to strive for higher performance standards and to have more confi-

Supportive leadership
Giving consideration to the needs of subordinates, displaying concern for their welfare, and creating a friendly climate in the work unit.

Directive leadership
Letting subordinates know what they are expected to do, giving specific guidance, asking subordinates to fol-low rules and procedures, and sched-uling and coordinating work.

Participative leadership
Consulting with the subordinates and taking their opinions and suggestions into account.

Achievement-oriented leadership
Setting challenging goals, seeking per-formance improvements, emphasizing excellence in performance, and show-ing confidence.

FIGURE 13.4
Path-goal model of leadership

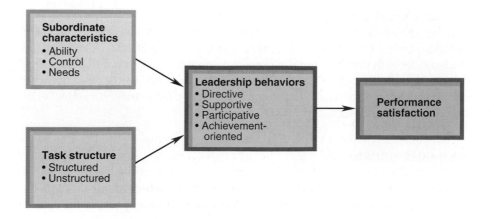

dence in their ability to meet challenging goals. For subordinates in ambiguous nonrepetitive jobs, achievement-oriented leadership should increase their expectations that effort will lead to desired performance.

Situational Contingencies

The situational contingencies defined by the path-goal model are subordinate characteristics and task structure. These characteristics influence how subordinates perceive the leader's behavior.

Subordinate Characteristics   The model uses three characteristics that help define the situation and relate to the most effective leadership behaviors: (1) ability, (2) locus of control, and (3) need structure. *Ability* relates to the subordinates' knowledge, skills, and expertise in completing a task. The greater employees' ability to perform the task, the less they will want directive leadership. High-ability employees will prefer achievement-oriented leadership.

Locus of control focuses on the employees' sense of internal and external control, or how much control over events or outcomes they believe can be gained. Research has shown that the more employees have an internal locus of control and desire control in a situation, the less they will be satisfied with directive leadership. Instead, such individuals will desire participative or achievement-oriented leadership.

Need structure refers to a hierarchy of needs. Do the employees have high- or low-level needs? The more high-level needs the employees have, the less they will want directive leadership. More specifically, people who desire safety and security will respond positively to directive leadership. Those who desire belonging will respond positively to supportive leadership. And those desiring self-esteem and self-actualization will respond positively to participative and achievement-oriented leadership.

Task Structure   If the task is structured, supportive and participative leadership behaviors will be more effective. When the task is stressful, boring, tedious, or dangerous, supportive leadership leads to increased subordinate effort and satisfaction by increasing self-confidence, lowering anxiety, and minimizing unpleasant aspects of the work.

Subordinates working on an unstructured task will want directive leadership. In these unstructured task situations, the manager's job is to initiate structure, clarify goals, and define expectations for the subordinates. In doing this, managers reduce uncertainty, which leads to increased motivation and performance. When the task is unstructured and complex, subordinates are inexperienced, and there are few formal rules and procedures to guide the work, directive leadership will result in higher subordinate satisfaction and effort. When the task is unstructured, participative and achievement-oriented leadership can increase subordinate effort and satisfaction.

The path-goal model is a complex leadership model. The principal contribution of this approach has been an expanded search for relevant contingency factors and clarification of ways that managers can influence employee behavior. The path-goal model of leadership can be used in guiding subordinates toward improved effort, performance, and satisfaction. This is a dramatic shift away from Fiedler's LPC model, where leadership style is considered to be relatively fixed and the solution may be to change leaders or aspects of the work situation rather than alter leadership behavior.

In sum, the contingency approach to leadership quality in diverse organizations generally concludes that effective leaders don't use a single style; they use many different styles and make adjustments based on the situation. An important but often overlooked contingency variable that may affect a leader's style is national culture. As we see in Global Perspective, national culture can

CULTURAL DIFFERENCES IN LEADERSHIP

According to some researchers, charismatic leadership emerges in some cultures more easily than in others. Particularly, cultures that have a strong tradition for prophetic salvation may be more amenable to charismatic leadership. For example, the Judeo-Christian beliefs of the coming of a savior create fertile ground for charismatic leaders. Prophets by definition are charismatic saviors. Israel, for example, has such a strong tradition. Another case in point is the recent rise of Islamic fundamentalism, which is typically tied to a prophetic spiritual leader, as is the case in both Sudan and Iran. The rise of Khomeini in Iran, for example, had all the elements of a typical charismatic relationship, including leader and follower characteristics, the intense and calculated image management on the part of the leader, and the sense of crisis due to the political climate of Iran in the 1970s.

On the other hand, some cultures do not have such prophetic traditions. For example, except for Mao Zedong, Chinese history has very few strong charismatic figures. Periods of crisis and change has certainly occurred. However, it appears that the relationship between leader and followers is based more on the social hierarchy and need for order, as is prescribed in the Confucian tradition, than on the intense emotional charismatic bonds that exist in Judeo-Christian religions. Furthermore, some have suggested that the development of a charismatic relationship in a culture such as Japan's needs to rely on the leader's development of an image of competence, moral courage, and the securing of respect from followers, while in India, charismatic leadership is associated with a religious, almost supernatural state.

SOURCES: Lutz, S., "A 'Lifetime' of Accomplishments by Age 38," *Modern Healthcare*, March 2, 1992, 41–44; reprinted with permission from *Modern Healthcare*, copyright Crain Communications, Inc., 740 N. Rush Street, Chicago, Ill. 60611. A. Nahavandi and A. R. Malekzadeh, *Organizational Culture in the Management of Mergers* (New York: Quorum Books, an imprint of Greenwood Publishing Group, Inc., Westport, Conn. 1996). R. Tsurumi, "American Origins of Japanese Productivity," *Pacific Basin Quarterly*, 7, 14–15.

affect leadership style, not because of the leader, but because of the subordinates. The cultural frame of reference and a subordinate's expectations can greatly influence what leadership style will be most effective.

LEADERSHIP SUBSTITUTES

Some argue that the importance of leadership is overrated and that in many situations leaders make little or no difference.[20] In contrast to traditional theories that assume hierarchical leadership is always important, the premise of the leadership substitutes model is that leader behaviors are irrelevant. The leadership substitutes model is fairly new, and only a few studies have been conducted to verify its propositions about specific substitutes and neutralizers.

Leadership substitutes
Situational variables that tend to outweigh the leader's ability to affect subordinate satisfaction and performance.

    Leadership substitutes are situational variables such as individual, task, and organizational characteristics that tend to outweigh the leader's ability to affect subordinate satisfaction and performance. They make leadership behavior unnecessary or redundant. A *neutralizer* is a condition that counteracts leader behavior and/or prevents the leader from having an effect on a specific situation.

Individual characteristics that can serve as leadership substitutes include a high level of experience, training, ability, professional orientation, or indifference toward organizational rewards. If, for example, employees have the skills and abilities to perform the job and a high need for independence, leadership is less important, and the employees may resent a leader who provides structure and direction. A professor in a graduate-level seminar may need to provide students with just a set of readings and materials to be studied rather than a structured course outline.

Various task attributes can serve as leadership substitutes. For example, if the task is simple and repetitive, subordinates can learn the appropriate skills without extensive training. Tasks that are characterized by structure or frequent feedback can also neutralize leader behavior, as can tasks that are intrinsically satisfying.

Characteristics of the organization can also substitute for leadership. When the organization possesses high levels of formality, inflexibility, cohesive work groups, staff support, managerially independent reward structures, and spatial distance between workers and managers, the need for formal leadership decreases.[21]

This employee, who possesses a high degree of experience, training, and independence, supports the argument that leadership is overrated; his leadership substitutes make leadership behavior unnecessary or redundant.

© Fernand Ivaldi/Tony Stone Images

EMERGING PERSPECTIVES TO UNDERSTANDING LEADERSHIP

The 1980s brought revolutionary change to many American businesses, and the pace of change is accelerating with political and economic developments in Europe, the Middle East, and other locations around the world. As we have been discussing throughout the book, the changing global environment is likely to continue to stimulate the transformation and revitalization of public and private institutions. Small as well as large U.S. companies such as IBM, AT&T, and General Motors recognize that they will have to change in order to survive. They have embarked on "transformation" programs of extensive change that must be accomplished in short periods of time. Such transformations require a new set of leadership guidelines.

What is fueling this change? Throughout this book we have been addressing many of the challenges that managers and organizations face as they prepare for the 21st century. These include internal and global competition; complex and fast-changing technologies; increasing demand for quality products and services; employee expectations of openness, participation, and autonomy; and demographic changes, just to name a few. In this section we look at several emerging perspectives in understanding leadership—transactional and transformational leadership, followership or self-leadership, the changing role of women in leadership positions, the influences of information technology on leadership, self-managed teams, and leadership influences on quality-management programs.

TRANSACTIONAL LEADERSHIP

Transactional leadership is centered on rational exchange; that is, the exchange of rewards for work performed. As you read about various leaders, you will be able to identify those who have a focus on goals and rewards as the driving motivator. This leader provides followers with resources and rewards in exchange for motivation, productivity, and effective task accomplishment. We teach leaders to provide rewards, to reinforce appropriate behavior, and to discourage inappropriate behavior. The leader's power stems from an ability to provide rewards in exchange for the followers' doing the work.

Transactional leadership
Provides followers with resources and rewards in exchange for motivation, productivity, and effective task accomplishment.

Organizations that have had to make dramatic changes in operating procedures or risk failure have had successful transactional leaders to motivate them. One such organization is the Denny's restaurant chain. Not long ago, Denny's was labeled one of America's most racist companies. Today it is a model of multicultural sensitivity. How? Ron Petty was brought in to begin repairing its image and taking charge of the metamorphosis by implementing a strategy of corporate restructuring, educating, eliminating, and rewarding. He began a system of specific goal setting, feedback, and reward contingencies. He used a model of motivating employees with money and other valued reinforcers to prove that diversity can make a difference and satisfy employees.[22]

TRANSFORMATIONAL LEADERSHIP

Transformational leadership

The process of influencing the attitudes and assumptions of organizational members and building commitment to the organization's mission and objectives.

Transformational leadership refers to the process of influencing the attitudes and assumptions of organizational members and building commitment to the organization's mission and objectives.[23] Transformational leaders do not accept the status quo. They recognize the need to revitalize their organizations and challenge standard operating procedures; they institutionalize change by replacing old technical and political networks with new ones. In other words, transformational leaders "transform" things from what could be to what is by generating excitement. Transformational leaders such as Steven Jobs, president and CEO of Next Corporation, Jack Welch, CEO of GE, and Bill Gates, CEO of Microsoft, create visions and mobilize employee commitment to that vision.

If we look more closely at Bill Gates's leadership style, we see that he involves employees by working with them as a team to share responsibility for managing. His leadership style, of course is all wrapped up with his personality, intelligence, and vision of Microsoft's complete market domination. By approaching his job with such intensity and doing his homework so diligently, Gates sets lofty standards. Despite his idiosyncracies and obsessions, associates and Microsoft employees rarely question his judgment. In fact, many who work around him have unconsciously adopted his singular lingo. Like him, they overuse terms such as *random* (inane), *drill down* (go into more detail), or *hard-core* (intensely dedicated); some even echo his precise, nasal, diphthong-laden speech.[24]

Though the literature on transformational leadership naturally focuses on CEOs and top managers, transformational leadership commonly involves the actions of leaders at all levels, not just those at the top. Transformational leadership increases follower motivation by activating the higher needs of followers, appealing to their moral ideas, and empowering them.

How do you see yourself—as a transactional or transformational leader? The Experiential Exercise at the end of the chapter provides an opportunity for you to consider this question and to compare your own style with those we have been discussing.

Most leadership research has concentrated on the leader's influence on followers. Followers are motivated to do more than was originally expected because of their feelings of trust, admiration, loyalty, and respect for the leader. This motivation occurs when the leader makes subordinates more aware of the importance and values of task outcomes, helps them think beyond their own self-interest to the needs of the work teams and the organization, and activates higher-order needs such as creative expression and self-actualization.[25]

FOLLOWERSHIP

While organizations spend millions annually to train potential leaders, they are also beginning to realize the value of followership or, more recently, the concept of self-leaders. This leadership paradigm is founded on a creating an organization of leaders who are ready to lead themselves.[26]

449

Teaching employees how to be effective followers may be a wise decision. In many respects, an effective follower resembles an effective leader, and subordinate leadership is a skill that every leader should master. After all, every leader, regardless of position, plays the role of follower at some point. Consider Raymond Smith at Bell Atlantic, profiled in the Managerial Incident. He plays the role of follower when he reports to Bell Atlantic's board of directors and stockholders.

Large organizations, discovering that an abundance of baby-boom managers in their 30s and 40s are concerned about career plateauing, have begun to adopt followership training programs to convince employees that they are contributing even when they are not moving up the corporate ladder. Lincoln Electric, a Cleveland-based manufacturer of welding machines and electrical motors, provides an example of the value of fostering organizational followership. The structure of the organization requires each employee to be accountable for his own behavior. Even in recessionary times, employees are loyal to the company and show their cooperation by performing duties not required by their contracts. Employees are asked to serve on an advisory board that meets weekly to assess how the company is doing in a variety of areas. The employees understand the organization and their contributions to it. They are adaptable and take responsibility for their own actions. In essence, the employees of Lincoln Electric are good followers.[27] Lincoln, along with many other companies, is aware of the importance of effective followership to organizational success.[28]

Studies show that effective followers have most of the following characteristics:

- Capacity to motivate themselves and stay focused on tasks.
- Integrity that demands both loyalty to the organization and the willingness to act according to beliefs.
- Understanding of the organization and their contributions to it.
- Versatility, skillfulness, and flexibility to adapt to a changing environment.
- Responsibility for their own careers, actions, and development.

Helen Gurley Brown was a pioneer executive who successfully faced obstacles that are not so apparent today, now that over 25 percent of the supervisory positions in U.S. industry are occupied by women.
© Frank Capri/Saga/Archive Photos

THE CHANGING ROLE OF WOMEN AS LEADERS

The number of women in leadership positions has increased steadily since 1970. In fact, over 25 percent of the supervisory positions in U.S. industry were occupied by women in 1990. The number of women enrolled in business schools is yet another sign of the increasing presence of women in management. In 1990, the number of men and women enrolled in U.S. business programs was nearly equal. Women's entrepreneurial spirit is also becoming apparent; more and more businesses, particularly in the service, retailing, and trade industries, are being started and managed by women.

Consider, for example, Gae Veit, chief executive of Shingobee Builders, a commercial and industrial contracting construction firm in Loretto, Minnesota. Veit liked the work she performed in a construction firm office and went into business for herself in the 1980s. According to Veit, a female general contractor had virtually no credibility with the corporate officers and potential commercial-building owners with whom she sought contracts. In spite of the obstacles, she met the challenge head-on. Veit's response to the gender problem was to "just be myself—to be confident and knowledgeable, but when I need help with an issue not be afraid or embarrassed."[29] She was recently named woman entrepreneur of the year by the Small Business Administration.

How well do men accept women as leaders? Research indicates that men's attitudes toward women in the workplace are gradually changing as more women enter the work force and assume leadership positions. Studies show, however, that both men and women executives believe that women have to be exceptional to succeed in the business world. Women leaders still face disadvantages in business and feel they must struggle harder than men to succeed.[30]

Do men and women differ in terms of leadership ability? In the past, successful leaders have been associated with stereotypical masculine attributes such as competitiveness, task orientation, and willingness to take risks. Recent studies, however, show that female middle- and top-level executives no longer equate successful leadership with these masculine attributes. Experienced female managers show no differences in leadership ability from their experienced male counterparts. Both groups possess a high need for achievement and power, and both demonstrate assertiveness, self-reliance, risk taking, and other traits and behaviors associated with leadership. Actually, once men and women have established themselves as leaders in their organizations, women do not behave differently than men.[31] The first female executives, because they were entering new territory, adhered to many of the "rules of conduct" that spelled success for men. Today, a second wave of women are making their way to the top and are not only adopting styles and habits that have proved successful for men, but are also drawing on the skills and attitudes they have developed from their experiences as women.[32]

INFORMATION TECHNOLOGY INFLUENCES ON LEADERSHIP

New technology will certainly create greater and more complex demands on leaders with the need for different approaches and incentives. Technology can be a tool that isolates. Research on top executives who have stumbled shows that they are impatient, impulsive, manipulative, dominating, self-important, and critical of others. Many are mechanical and fascinated by the power that technology awards them.[33]

CEOs in general have high needs for autonomy. The more entrepreneurial they are, the stronger their need to be in control. But many are poor communicators, so while they may be good at developing visions, their strategies aren't widely understood.

Successful leaders get to the top by producing financial results over the short run. A lot of companies reward independent leaders, especially in Silicon Valley, where the rate of change in high-tech companies is very fast and people often get promoted because of their technical skills.[34]

Great companies like Hewlett-Packard realize that they have a lot of technical people, so they need to create a culture that reinforces relationship building by managers. HP, for example, uses open cubicles so people can't isolate themselves in offices, and spends millions of dollars on training and development.

In the new era, leaders will be challenged more to manage relationships. This will include the ability to work effectively in interacting with a diversity of partners and other businesses and within the larger context of differing cultures.

SELF-MANAGED TEAMS: FOCUSING ON QUALITY AND DIVERSITY

You will recall from our discussion in Chapter 8 that the use of self-managed teams (SMTs) has become increasingly popular for diverse organizations such as Digital Equipment, Frito-Lay, General Electric, General Foods, Hewlett-Packard, Microsoft, and Pepsi-Cola, as well as numerous smaller firms.[35] SMTs appear in many forms, such as quality circles, task forces, communication teams, and new venture teams. They are used to solve complex problems, increase productivity, foster creativity, and reduce middle-management costs.

Most existing leadership theories assume a person-centered approach in which leadership is a quality that exists in one person—the leader. In contrast, the SMT is based on the premise of the distributed leadership model, which emphasizes the active cultivation and development of leadership abilities within all members of a team.[36] SMTs assume that leadership is a collection of roles and behaviors that can be shared and rotated. At any one time, multiple leaders can exist in a team, with each member assuming complementary leadership behaviors. At Microsoft, CEO Bill Gates believes that the only way to keep the company feeling small is by sticking to SMTs, a lesson he admits he borrowed from Hewlett-Packard. He contends that all employees at Microsoft must feel that they can make a difference and that they are accountable for their performance.[37]

How can an SMT be effectively managed? The leadership behaviors required for effective SMT functioning fall into four categories: (1) envisioning, (2) organizing, (3) spanning, and (4) social.[38]

Envisioning leadership behavior revolves around creating new and compelling visions. This requires facilitating idea generation and innovative thinking and helping others in the group to develop new ideas. *Organizing* leadership behavior focuses on quality issues such as details, deadlines, efficiency, and structure. Team members who fulfill this role help provide the group with direction and goal setting. Behaviors associated with *spanning* leadership include networking, developing and maintaining a strong team image with outsiders, bargaining, and being sensitive to power distributions. Spanning leadership links the SMT's effort to outside groups and individuals. *Social* leadership behavior focuses on developing and maintaining the team's diverse social environment. The effective social leader is concerned with members' needs, being sensitive to group processes, fostering an environment where individuals are respected, and mediating conflicts. These issues are most important as organizations become more diverse.

With the right leadership mix and enough time and support from outside, an SMT can achieve remarkable results. Although SMTs are becoming more common in the workplace, their usefulness depends on how well people in various leadership roles can communicate and unify the SMT to work toward a common goal. As we saw in the opening Managerial Incident, Raymond Smith brought a new perspective on teamwork to his position at Bell Atlantic. This new direction included a much greater stress on teamwork and multiple leadership roles. Smith pushed a strategy of using teams to manage and focused on developing his subordinates, motivating innovative behavior, and encouraging them to take a leadership role, even when that role was not formalized.

LEADERSHIP INFLUENCES ON QUALITY MANAGEMENT

Achieving quality and implementing quality management sound relatively simple: just put the customer first, empower employees to meet the needs of the customer, develop a measurement system to evaluate quality, and engage in continuous-improvement practices to ensure that quality improvements remain a high priority. Although it may be reduced to four easy steps, in practice implementing a quality-management program is more difficult than it sounds. Many argue that successful quality-management programs require a substantial change in the organizational culture and leadership of the firm. But, as you read in Chapter 11, culture doesn't change easily or quickly. How then can an organization improve its chances of implementing a quality-management program successfully?[39]

Perhaps the single most important prerequisite to effective quality management is a commitment on the part of the top management of the organization to play a leadership role in developing and implementing the program. In fact, the prestigious and coveted Malcolm Baldrige National Quality Award recognizes the importance of leadership from two important perspectives—symbolic acts and active involvement.

Symbolic acts are purposeful actions that convince employees that quality will be the priority of the organization—even above financial and efficiency goals. Unless the members of the organization truly believe that quality comes first, a quality-management program stands little chance of success. Consequently, it is essential that the organization's leaders do whatever is necessary to get the attention of their employees and convince them that quality is priority one.

Excellent examples of such symbolic acts of leadership come from the ranks of former Baldrige Award winners. Bob Galvin, former CEO of Motorola, changed the structure of his policy committee meetings so that quality appeared at the top of the agenda. To emphasize his point, Galvin would leave the meeting immediately after the quality issues had been discussed and before financial matters had been addressed. Despite strong protests on the part of the Xerox sales team, David Kearns, former CEO of Xerox, delayed the introduction of a major new product because of a "minor" quality problem. In each case, a highly visible action got the attention of the organization's employees and reinforced the quality message.[40]

Of equal importance is the *active involvement* of top managers in the daily management of the quality-improvement program. Slogans and "lip service" alone will never be enough to ensure the success of a quality-management program. Leadership at the top must be actively involved in ensuring that quality improvement is an organizational reality. Such involvement can take many forms. Top managers may actually teach quality-management training courses, meet with customer focus groups regularly, and visit employees on the shop floor to hear their ideas for improving the quality of the firm's output.

To determine top management's involvement in a quality-management program, the judges for the Baldrige Award review the calendars or logbooks of a firm's top managers for a given period prior to visiting the organization. The judges look to see how much time managers spend talking to employees and to customers.

While we have used examples of CEO involvement exclusively thus far, it is essential to note that leadership must come from all ranks of management. If quality management is on the agenda of top management only, the program is sure to fail. Bright and capable individuals in the line and staff functions throughout the organization must also be willing to play a leadership role in ensuring that quality becomes the priority for all employees.

MANAGERIAL IMPLICATIONS

We conclude this chapter on leadership with a list of guiding principles to start you toward leadership effectiveness. These ten items get to the core of what leadership is all about.[41] Following these principles will help you develop effective leadership skills.

- Know yourself. You cannot be an effective leader without knowing your own strengths and weaknesses. Knowing your capabilities will allow you to improve on your weaknesses and trade on your strengths.
- Be a role model. Expect no more than what you yourself are willing to give.
- Learn to communicate with your ears open and your mouth shut. Most problems that leaders are asked to solve are people problems created because of a failure in communication. Communication failures are the result of people hearing but not listening to one another.

- Know your team and be a team player. As a leader, make the effort to know what other members of the team are doing, not necessarily to monitor their progress but to seek ways and means of providing your own assistance.

- Be honest to yourself as well as to others. All good leaders make mistakes. Rarely do they make the same mistake more than once. Openly admit a mistake, learn from it, and forget it. Generally, others will forget it too.

- Do not avoid risks. If you are to become an effective leader, you will need to become an effective risk taker. See problems as challenges, challenges as catalysts for change, and changes as opportunities.

- Believe in yourself. All effective leaders share the characteristic of confidence in their own ability to get the job done. This personal confidence is often contagious and quick to permeate an entire organization, boosting confidence levels of all team members.

- Take the offense rather than the defense. The most effective leaders are quicker to act than react. Their best solution to any problem is to solve it before it becomes a problem. If they see something that needs fixing, they will do what they can to repair it before being told to do so by someone else.

- Know the ways of disagreement and the means of compromise. While people may disagree with one another, remember that who wins or loses is not important. The real winner is the leader who can facilitate the opposing side's goals while achieving his own.

- Be a good follower. Effective leaders lead as they would like to be led.

This chapter has explored many different facets of leadership effectiveness for the dynamic environment in which you are, or soon will be, working. As we noted earlier, a considerable amount of research has been done on leadership, and there are many books and articles on the topic. Although leadership means different things to different people, the focus of much leadership research has been on common qualities shared by all leaders. Many long lists of admirable qualities (aggressiveness, charisma, courage, wisdom) have been generated but have not been found to apply to all leaders in all situations. To be effective, a leader's qualities must be related in some way to the situation she is in and to the nature of her followers.

U.S. businesses desperately need better leadership. Companies that will be successful in the more competitive global economy will be more flexible, responsive, and leaner than those in the past. Small groups must tackle problems and seize opportunities as they arise. Individuals at all levels must be given the responsibility and authority to make decisions to be effective followers and leaders in the dynamic environment of the 21st century.

THE BELL ATLANTIC WAY: SMITH'S WAKE-UP CALL

Managerial
Incident
Resolution

The thrust of Raymond Smith's leadership style is to foster worker participation at all levels. His style could be interpreted as creating an organization of leaders. At a reinforcement session for Bell Atlantic supervisors, a blindfolded employee is told to hit a target with a Velcro-tipped dart. At first, no one lends any guidance. Then, people shout directions that help the employee hit the target. Such drills are more motivational than instructional. Indeed, employees whose esprit de corps appears to be slackening sometimes are advised to attend a "reinforcement" session.

The new leadership culture is already apparent in the executive suite. To set an example, Smith turned the executive dining room into an employee cafeteria. He also dispersed top brass from the executive floor and stationed them with the groups they oversee. "What kind of message do we send employees if we're all on the same floor and lunch in a private dining room?" Smith asks.

To some employees, Smith's leadership style seems a bit "hokey," but he says it is helping transform his executives into the kind of managers who can compete in all sorts of businesses. Smith is asking employees to work on changing corporate goals, instead of just fulfilling the narrow, bureaucratically defined objectives that marked the old Bell system. While Smith concedes that some people don't want to change under any circumstances, he vows that the new leadership focus, employee partnership, and independent thinking at the heart of the Bell Atlantic Way are here to stay.

SUMMARY

- Leadership is broadly defined as a social influence process that involves determining group or organization objectives, motivating behavior, and influencing group maintenance and culture. Leadership is a process whose function is to produce change.

- Power is the ability to marshal human, informational, or material resources to get something done. There are various types of power, including power that is prescribed by the person's position in the organization and power that is a result of personal attributes.

- The historical approach to leadership failed to find any specific traits or behaviors that guaranteed leadership success.

- Fiedler's LPC model was the first contingency approach to understanding leadership. The LPC model states that effectiveness depends on two factors, which were identified as the personal style of the leader and the degree of situational favorability.

- According to the SLT contingency model, effective leader behavior depends on the match between leader behavior and the situational contingency of subordinate readiness. The four leader behaviors are telling, selling, participating, and delegating.

- The path-goal model of leadership examines how four aspects of leader behavior influence subordinate

satisfaction and motivation. The four leader behaviors are supportive, directive, participative, and achievement-oriented leadership.

- Leadership substitutes are individual, task, and organizational characteristics that tend to outweigh the leader's ability to affect subordinate satisfaction and performance. They make leadership behavior unnecessary or redundant.

- Several emerging approaches to understanding leadership were discussed. Transformational leadership is the process of influencing the attitudes and assumptions of organizational members and building commitment for the organization's mission or objectives. Followership is being encouraged at many organizations as a way to influence individual accountability and independence. The emergence of women as leaders is influencing how leadership success is determined. SMTs are becoming more commonplace in high-performing diverse organizations. This concept is based on the distributed leadership model that emphasizes the active cultivation and development of leadership abilities within all members of a team. Finally, we discussed how leadership influences the successful implementation of quality-management programs.

KEY TERMS

Leadership	Trait approach	Path-goal model
Power	Behavioral approach	Supportive leadership
Legitimate power	Task orientation	Directive leadership
Coercive power	Relationship orientation	Participative leadership
Reward power	Contingency approaches	Achievement-oriented leadership
Information power	Fiedler's LPC model	Leadership substitutes
Expert power	Least preferred co-worker (LPC) scale	Transactional leadership
Referent power	SLT model	Transformational leadership

REVIEW QUESTIONS

1. Define the term *leadership.* Identify examples of effective leadership.

2. What are a leader's sources of power?

3. Distinguish between position power and personal power and provide examples of each.

4. Define the behavioral dimensions of initiating structure and consideration.

5. How does the behavioral approach to leadership differ from the contingency approach?

6. How does Fiedler's LPC model describe situational favorability?

7. Examine the differences between Fiedler's LPC model and path-goal leadership.

8. Describe the term *readiness* from the SLT contingency model.

9. How is a transformational leader different from other leaders?

10. Under what conditions would an SMT be effective?

DISCUSSION QUESTIONS

Improving Critical Thinking

1. Suppose that a leader's behavior does not seem to match the situation. Can the leader's behavior be changed to produce a better match? What would Fiedler's LPC model predict? The SLT model? The path-goal model?

2. Under what conditions would an organization want to promote followership? How would you feel about being trained to be a follower?

3. Watch a popular television show (or cable rerun) such as *Seinfeld, Friends, Melrose Place,* or *The X-Files* and examine how the main characters use power to influence. What types of power do they use most often? Least often?

Enhancing Communication Skills

4. Is a formal leader always necessary? If not, under what conditions does the leader not make a difference? After you have developed some understanding of this topic, share your ideas either in an oral presentation or in a short paper.

5. Give examples of situations in which you used your power to influence your peers, your family members, and your professor. Provide specific examples either as an oral presentation or in writing as directed by your instructor.

Building Teamwork

6. What are some of the major differences among the contingency leadership models? Form small teams to identify and discuss these differences.

7. Select any theory of leadership discussed in the chapter and analyze your own leadership behavior. When is your behavior effective? Ineffective? In a small group, exchange your ideas with others with whom you have worked.

8. Choose several internationally recognized individuals such as Queen Elizabeth II, Fidel Castro, Bill Gates, former president Jimmy Carter, Hillary Clinton, Elizabeth Taylor, Michael Jordan, and the like, and compare the types of power they possess. What commonalities do they share?

---

1. Select one of the more recent Web site magazines available and look for its listing of business-oriented Web sites such as AT&T Business Network {**http://www.bnet.att.com/**}, A Business Researcher's Interests {**http://www.brint.com/interest.html**}, or Four 11 {**http://www.four11.com**}. Describe, from a manager's perspective, the value they offer you. What type of information could be usual for you to use? How would you rate the sites? Compare eight to ten other sites that you locate on the Internet yourself.

2. Select several organizations in the same industry and search the Internet for information about them. How easy is it for you to obtain information on the companies' leaders? How well are the top executives known in the media? To what degree are the Web sites informational sources or public relations?

INFORMATION TECHNOLOGY: Insights and Solutions

ETHICS: Take a Stand

As the manager of a paper products division, Ken has shown remarkable leadership skills in achieving a 35 percent market share for his division's primary product. He has used his influence in many ways—to get the proper allocation of resources from top management and to motivate his staff to work hard to achieve the company's goals. Recently, Ken has had to deal with an employee problem, and he isn't sure how to proceed.

The problem is with Jeff, an employee who until recently had worked extremely hard and contributed significantly to the division's success. Unfortunately, the stress associated with meeting this objective seems to have taken its toll on Jeff. In the last few months, he has frequently come to work late or called in sick. Furthermore, he has made several critical errors and the quality of his work has begun to decline. Ken has approached Jeff several times about the problems, and Jeff has promised improvement. Ken has not seen any change, however. In fact, several clients have called to complain about Jeff's behavior on sales calls. Apparently, Jeff got into an unnecessary conflict with a member of a client's purchasing department. The client also said that Jeff seemed to have had several drinks at lunch. More than one client has mentioned that Jeff had alcohol on his breath before lunch.

Ken is not sure what action he should take. He feels obligated to reprimand Jeff because of these latest incidents. At the same time, Ken feels he should cover for Jeff until he has resolved his apparent alcohol dependency problem because of his valued contributions to the company in the past. The time has come for Ken to take some action.

For Discussion

1. What sources of power would be appropriate for Ken to use in his action toward Jeff?
2. Suggest the type of leader behavior that Ken can use to help Jeff.

THINKING CRITICALLY: Debate the Issue

LEADERSHIP—A NECESSARY EVIL?

Form teams as directed by your instructor. The teams will be responsible for debating the following question: Is leadership necessary? Half of the teams should take the position that every organization and group needs a leader to be effective. The other half of the teams should take the position that leadership is not always necessary for effective performance. Each team should research and prepare its position using organizational and group examples from current magazines, newspapers, and periodicals. Your instructor will select two teams to present their findings to the class in a debate format.

SUNSHINE CLEANING SYSTEMS

No Web Site Available

Video Case

Sunshine Cleaning Systems is a privately held company headquartered in Florida. The company offers janitorial services, pressure cleaning, and window cleaning to its customers. The CEO is Larry Calufetti, a former catcher for the New York Mets. Sunshine Cleaning Systems has some interesting clients, including the Miami Dolphins Training Center, the Orlando Arena (home of the Orlando Magic), the Orlando Convention Center, the Florida Turnpike, and the Smithsonian Institution in Washington, D.C.

What makes Sunshine Cleaning Systems unique is the company's Coaching Leadership Style. CEO Larry Calufetti has implemented a philosophy that encourages the managers at Sunshine to act as "coaches" rather than traditional managers in their relationships with their employees. This approach to leadership is based on the following set of principles, which are well understood by both the managers and rank-and-file employees:

- supportive management
- access to training
- providing employees with the tools they need to do quality work
- asking employees to accept responsibility
- encouraging innovation
- providing rewards
- promoting from within

In addition, employees are encouraged to feel good about their work and are reinforced by their managers on a continual basis. For instance, the company has an employee-of-the-month program for each branch, which is designed to reinforce outstanding work habits. This program, along with Sunshine's overall approach to leadership, is paying off. The company has very little turnover, which is unusual for a firm in the janitorial industry. Firm sales and profitability are also on solid ground.

By working together, the Sunshine team will continue to grow and provide quality service to its customers. The managers and employees at Sunshine believe that the company's Coaching Leadership Style is an important part of their collective success.

For Discussion

1. What model of leadership best fits the Larry Calufetti's philosophy of managing his company?
2. What type of power do the "coaches" at Sunshine Cleaning utilize when working with employees?
3. Think about your own strengths and weaknesses and how you relate to people. Would you fit in as a leader at Sunshine Cleaning Systems?

WEINTROP'S SEARCH FOR GOOD LEADERSHIP

While Tom Fiske was trying to earn enough money to finish graduate school, he worked full-time as a gas station attendant for Weintrop Oil, a large petroleum refiner with gas stations located primarily in the Southwestern United States. The station operated 24 hours a day and had a staff of 20 attendants and mechanics.

During his eighteen months of employment, there were two different managers. Alice Komasare, the first manager, had worked there for several months prior to Tom's arrival and stayed for twelve months until requesting a transfer to be closer to her family. The next manager, Tony Fitz, took over when Alice transferred and continued after Tom left.

Both Alice and Tony were in their late 20s, held bachelor's degrees in management, and had previous managerial experience. But that is where the similarities ended. Alice and Tony had very different styles of managing the station. Alice operated in ways that circumvented the regulations laid down in the Weintrop operations manual and sought to develop a sense of camaraderie and friendship with the crew. Her willingness to bend or disregard the rules was appreciated by everyone on the crew. As a result, the crew frequently helped each other out, even when they were not on the clock. Alice would often show up early in the morning with coffee and donuts for the morning crew or late in the evening with pizza for the evening crew. Her efforts on the crew's behalf were reciprocated whenever she needed an extra crew member or a task done that wasn't part of the official Weintrop job description. The crew felt a lot of loyalty to Alice and frequently would volunteer to work another eight-hour shift if the business needed them.

Alice also had good rapport with the customers. The crew often went against Weintrop's rules to help a stranded motorist, and Alice would always praise their efforts. Alice's station consistently set all-time sales records even though it didn't operate by the book. But, after a year, Alice accepted a transfer, and the crew, much distressed, greeted their new boss, Tony Fitz. Tony operated the station by the book in a no-nonsense attempt to establish discipline and order.

Where Alice fostered camaraderie, Tony deliberately attempted to foster individual accountability. Two crew members were fired for being two dollars short for four days' work because the operations manual set out strict rules about this situation. When the crew protested by saying that Alice had never done it that way, Tony responded by saying he was not Alice.

Tony altered the way the crew operated. Previously, the work crew had consisted of four attendants, one responsible for each island of gas pumps (three in all) and one floating assistant who was free to help wherever needed. In fact, any attendant who was free also helped out by wiping windows, checking oil, collecting money, or talking to the customers. Under Tony's system, the crew stopped helping each other and didn't leave their assigned areas. As a result of the new system, the crew's longstanding concern for customers diminished. They began to enforce the rules rigorously for fear of losing their jobs. Customers reacted at first by complaining to Tony and then by never returning.

The sales volume of the station declined sharply, despite Tony's rigorous application of Weintrop's rules. The district manager told Tony that service to customers was well below Weintrop's standards. Confronted with these problems and obvious crew hostility, Tony and the district manager found a solution: fire all of the crew members who had worked for Alice. So, one by one, the crew was fired.

For Discussion

1. How would you characterize the leader behaviors of Alice and Tony?
2. Compare and contrast the sources of power used by Alice and Tony.
3. Discuss the extent to which you think the leader behaviors of Alice and Tony are appropriate for the situation they faced. How would you go about deciding such appropriateness?
4. Who's to blame for the station's poor performance?

EXPERIENTIAL EXERCISE 13.1

Transformational or Transactional Leadership Questionnaire

For each of the following ten pairs of statements, divide 5 points between the two according to your beliefs, your perceptions of yourself, or which of the two statements characterizes you better. The 5 points may be divided between the A and B statements in any one of the following ways: 5 for A, 0 for B; 4 for A, 1 for B; 3 for A, 2 for B; 1 for A, 4 for B; or 0 for A, 5 for B, but not equally between the two, or $2\frac{1}{2}$ for each. Weigh your choices between the two according to the one that characterizes you or your beliefs better.

Please keep in mind that this is not a test and there are no right or wrong answers.

1. ____A   As leader I have a primary mission of maintaining stability.
   ____B   As leader I have a primary mission of change.

2. ____A   As leader I must cause events.
   ____B   As leader I must facilitate events.

3. ____A   I am concerned that my followers are rewarded equitably for their work.
   ____B   I am concerned about what my followers want in life.

4. ____A   My preference is to think long range: What might be?
   ____B   My preference is to think short range: What is realistic?

5. ____A   As a leader I spend considerable energy in managing separate but related goals.
   ____B   As a leader I spend considerable energy in arousing hopes, expectations, and aspirations among my followers.

6. ____A   While not in a formal classroom sense, I believe that a significant part of my leadership is that of teacher.

   ____B   I believe that a significant part of my leadership is that of facilitator.

7. ____A   As leader I must engage with followers at an equal level of morality.
   ____B   As leader I must represent a higher morality.

8. ____A   I enjoy stimulating followers to want to do more.
   ____B   I enjoy rewarding followers for a job well done.

9. ____A   Leadership should be practical.
   ____B   Leadership should be inspirational.

10. ____A   What power I have to influence others comes primarily from my ability to get people to identify with me and my ideas.
   ____B   What power I have to influence others comes primarily from my status and position.

Scoring:

Transformational Your point(s)	Transactional Your point(s)
1. B _____	1. A _____
2. A _____	2. B _____
3. B _____	3. A _____
4. A _____	4. B _____
5. B _____	5. A _____
6. A _____	6. B _____
7. B _____	7. A _____
8. A _____	8. B _____
9. B _____	9. A _____
10. A _____	10. B _____
Column totals: _____	_____

Interpretation: The higher column total indicates that you agree more with, and see yourself as more like, either a transformational leader or a transactional leader.

ENDNOTES

1. J. A. Lopez, "A Wake-Up Call for Bell Atlantic," *Business Week,* December 2, 1991, 133-35; R. M. Kanter, "Championing Change: An Interview with Bell Atlantic's CEO Raymond Smith," *Harvard Business Review,* January/February 1991, 119-30; P. Drucker, *The New Realities* (New York: Harper & Row, 1990); M. Hammer and J. Champy, *Reengineering the Corporation: A Manifesto for Business Revolution* (New York: HarperBusiness, 1993), 193-99.

2. G. A. Yukl, *Leadership in Organizations,* 3d ed. (Upper Saddle River, N.J.: Prentice Hall, 1993).

3. For a more thorough discussion of change and its impact on leadership, see H. Sims Jr. and C. Manz, *Company of Heroes* (New York: Wiley, 1996).

4. J. Kouzes and B. Posner, *The Leadership Challenges; How to Get Extraordinary Things Done with Ordinary People,* 2d ed. (San Francisco: Jossey-Bass, 1995); T. Peters, *Liberation Management* (New York: Knopf, 1992).

5. J. P. Kotter, *The Leadership Factor* (New York: Free Press, 1987).

6. C. Hickman, *Mind of a Manager, Soul of a Leader* (New York: Wiley, 1990).

7. Adapted from J. B. Lau and A. B. Shani, *Behavior in Organizations: An Experiential Approach,* 5th ed. (Boston: Irwin, 1992), 39.

8. J. French and B. Raven, "The Bases of Social Power," in *Studies of Social Power,* ed. D. Cartwright (Ann Arbor, Mich.: Institute for Social Research, 1959).

9. T. Kayser, *Building Team Power: How to Unleash the Collaborative Genius of Work Teams* (Burr Ridge, Ill.: Irwin, 1994).

10. Ibid.

11. Summarized in G. A. Yukl, *Leadership in Organizations.*

12. J. Kouzes and B. Posner, *Leadership Challenges.*

13. For example, task orientation may also be referred to initiating structure, concern for production, job-centered, authoritative; relationship orientation may also be referred to as democratic, people-centered, employee-centered, and consideration. Results can be reviewed from a number of earlier research findings, such as S. A. Kirkpatrick and E. A. Locke, "Leadership: Do Traits Matter?" *Academy of Management Executive,* 5, 1991, 48-59; R. M. Stogdill, *Handbook of Leadership* (New York: Free Press, 1974); R. M. Stogdill and A. E. Coons, *Leader Behavior: Its Description and Measurement* (Columbus, Ohio: Ohio State University Bureau of Business Research, 1957); R. Tannenbaum and W. Schmidt, "How to Choose a Leadership Pattern," *Harvard Business Review,* March/April 1958, 95-101; R. Blake and J. Mouton, "How to Choose a Leadership Style," *Training and Development Journal,* February 1986, 39-46.

14. See, for example, N. M. Tichy and S. Sherman, *Control Your Destiny or Someone Else Will* (New York: Doubleday, 1993); S. Flax, "The Toughest Bosses in America," *Fortune,* August 6, 1984, 90-107.

15. A. Nahavandi, *The Art and Science of Leadership* (Upper Saddle River, N.J.: Prentice Hall, 1997).

16. F. E. Fiedler, "The Contingency Model and the Dynamics of the Leadership Process," in *Advances in Experimental Social Psychology,* ed. L. Berkowitz (New York: Academic Press, 1967); and F. E. Fiedler, "The Effects of Leadership Training and Experience: A Contingency Model Interpretation," *Administrative Science Quarterly,* 17, 1972, 455.

17. P. Hersey and K. H. Blanchard, *Management of Organizational Behavior: Utilizing Human Resources,* 5th ed. (Upper Saddle River, N.J.: Prentice Hall, 1988).

18. Ibid.

19. R. J. House and T. R. Mitchell, "Path-Goal Theory of Leadership," *Journal of Contemporary Business,* Autumn 1974, 81-98.

20. S. Kerr and J. Jermier, "Substitutes for Leadership: Their Meaning and Measurement," *Organizational Behavior and Human Performance,* 22, 1978, 375-403.

21. See, for example, A. Zaleznik, "The Leadership Gap," *Academy of Management Executive,* 4, 1990, 7-22; C. C. Manz and H. P. Sims, "Leading Workers to Lead Themselves: The External Leadership of Self-Managing Work Teams," *Administrative Science Quarterly,* March 1987, 106-29; H. Sims Jr. and C. Manz, *Company of Heroes;* T. Peters, *Liberation Management.*

22. F. Rice, "Denny's Changes Its Spots," *Fortune,* May 13, 1996, 133-42.

23. J. Kouzes and B. Posner, *Leadership Challenges.*

24. B. Schlender, "What Bill Gates Really Wants," *Fortune,* January 16, 1995, 35-54; J. Maloney, "Larry Ellison is Captain Ahab and Bill Gates is Moby Dick," *Fortune,* October 28, 1996, 119-22.

25. J. Kouzes and B. Posner, *Leadership Challenges;* C. Lee, "Followership: The Essence of Leadership," *Training,* January 1991, 27-35; M. A. Abramson and J. W. Scanlon "The Five Dimensions of Leadership," *Government Executive,* July 1991, 20-25; and A. Zalenzik, "The Leadership Gap."

26. While this term is used by H. Sims Jr. and C. Manz, *Company of Heroes,* there are other contemporary perspectives that are developed around self-leadership. See, for example, T. Peters, *Liberation Management;* J. Kouzes and B. Posner, *Leadership Challenges.*

27. Adapted from C. Lee, "Followership"; M. A. Abramson and J. W. Scanlon, "The Five Dimensions of Leadership."

28. See the numerous examples from J. Martin, "Tomorrow's CEOs," *Fortune,* June 24, 1996, 76-90; T. Peters, *Liberation Management;* J. Kouzes and B. Posner, *Leadership Challenges.*

29. Adapted from "Shingobee Builders," in *Real-World Lessons for America's Small Businesses: Insights from the Blue Chip Enterprise Initiative* (*Nation's Business* on behalf of Connecticut Mutual Life Insurance Company and the U.S. Chamber of Commerce, 1992), 10-11.

30. J. B. Rosener, "Ways Women Lead," *Harvard Business Review,* November/December 1990, 119-25.

31. G. N. Powell, "One More Time: Do Female and Male Managers Differ?" *Academy of Management Executive,* 3, August 1990, 68-75; R. Sharpe, "The Waiting Game: Women Make Strides, But Men Stay Firmly in Top Company Jobs," *The Wall Street Journal,* March 29, 1994, B2.

32. J. A. Segal, "Sensitive Men: A Workplace Oxymoron?" *HR Magazine,* May 1993, 127-30; L. Grant "Rambos in Pinstripes: Why So Many CEOs Are Lousy Leaders," *Fortune,* June 24, 1996, 147.

33. L. Grant "Rambos in Pinstripes"; J. Martin, "Tomorrow's CEOs."

34. T. Peters, "Perpetual Job Insecurity," and J. Maloney, "Larry Ellison is Captain Ahab and Bill Gates is Moby Dick," in *Lessons in Leadership* (Provo, Utah: Covey Leadership Center, 1996).

35. B. Dumaine, "Who Needs a Boss?" *Fortune,* October 1990, 52-60.

36. H. Sims Jr. and C. Manz, *Company of Heroes.*

37. B. Schlender, "What Bill Gates Really Wants."

38. T. Kayser, *Building Team Power.*

39. For a more thorough discussion of this, see E. Holmes, "Leadership in the Quest for Quality," *Issues & Observations,* 16, 1996, 4-7.

40. D. A. Gavin, "How the Baldrige Award Really Works," *Harvard Business Review,* November/December 1991, 80-93.

41. Adapted from L. Ludewig, "The Ten Commandments of Leadership," *NASPA Journal,* Spring 1988, 297.

Effectively Managing Individual and Group Behavior

■ ## CHAPTER OVERVIEW

Management distinction in the 1990s will be achieved by those organizations with an organizational culture that allows them to move faster, communicate more clearly, react better to diverse customers and employees, produce higher-quality products and services, be globally oriented, and involve everyone in a focused effort to serve ever more demanding customers. To eliminate the barriers that separate functions within the organization, organizations must move toward a culture that helps people understand how to work together at both an individual and a group level.

In this chapter we lay the foundations of individual and group behavior. We first discuss some of the ways individuals differ—including attitudes, personalities, perceptions, and abilities. Merely placing people together does not guarantee success in organizations that are composed of individuals with diverse backgrounds and perceptions. The real challenge comes in encouraging individuals to pull together in a group and focus on common goals. Therefore, we turn our attention to understanding groups. We explore the dimensions that affect how groups operate in an organization and the ways managers can create more effective groups that make real contributions to the continuing success of the organization as a whole.

■ ## LEARNING OBJECTIVES

When you have finished studying this chapter, you should be able to:

- Explain why job satisfaction is important for managers to understand.
- Discuss the relationship between job satisfaction and performance.
- Explain personality and describe five personality traits that are considered important in the workplace.
- Identify and explain three perceptual biases.
- Discuss how to reduce perceptual errors.
- State the differences between formal and informal groups.
- Discuss the five-stage group developmental process.
- Identify five dimensions that influence group behavior and effectiveness.
- Describe the influences of information technology on group effectiveness.
- Explain what makes a group effective.

CHAPTER 14

Managerial Incident

TEAM LEADERS: MAGIC OR MANAGEMENT?

At age 33, J. D. Bryant, a supervisor overseeing a staff of fifteen circuit board assemblers at the Texas Instruments defense plant in Dallas, found out the company was moving to team-based management. He was told by his supervisor that it was a career-enhancing step. He would be a facilitator, teach the teams everything he knew so they could make their own decisions, and take a 5 percent pay cut. With no training or guidelines on how to do this, Bryant embraced teams in words only. He never gave operators the power to set schedules or do ordering; he still monitored performance and stepped in when a problem arose; he completed evaluations and budget data. Basically, he maintained his supervisory tasks and didn't share any power with the team.

Not long after the new team-based system had been in effect, Bryant became frustrated in his new role and applied to become a software writer at another plant. A few months after his move, that TI location also switched to a team-based system. He watched as some team leaders seemed to embrace the new style and be successful while he faced the same problems and concerns. He had a challenge—to figure out whether this team leadership was magic or a management style he could learn.

Eric Doremus had spent the past seven years in marketing at Honeywell before being asked to lead a team developing data storage systems for Northrop Grumman's B-2 bomber. How was a marketing specialist supposed to work with engineers when he would never have the technical skills nor understand what his teammates did? The first time Doremus met with the 40 members of the B-2 bomber team, he spent all of his time telling them what he couldn't do and what he didn't know. Is this why he was hired? His challenge was to determine what he could do to lead the team to success.

Reed Breland was a team facilitator at Hewlett-Packard's 180-person financial services center in Colorado Springs and handled all of the accounting for H-P's factories across the United States. Shortly after becoming a team facilitator, Breland saw that members of one of his teams were having a hard time working together. In his previous supervisory role, he would have just stepped in and settled the dispute. But now as a team facilitator, he decided that the team should handle it. To him it appeared to be a classic case of personality conflict, the two simply didn't like each other. With these two people on the eight-person team, the levels of disruptive behavior continued to increase. How much intervention was necessary for a team leader?

Bryant, Doremus, and Breland all faced challenges typical of team leaders with numerous questions and dilemmas. While they had all been successful middle managers, they were now placed in positions of uncertainty where they had to learn on the job. Not everyone is born a leader—but could these three managers learn to become one?[1]

INTRODUCTION

In the workplace, a new recognition and appreciation of individuals and groups is emerging. Effective organizations must pull together all their human resources to forge a strong, viable organizational culture that emphasizes teamwork. In recent years, U.S. industry has begun to see just how important teamwork is to quality and organization effectiveness. Indeed, the examples are all around us.

Procter & Gamble (P&G) is generally considered an important U.S. pioneer in applying teams to its operations. It began work with teams in the early 1960s, although these efforts were not publicized and virtually escaped media attention. P&G saw the team approach as a significant competitive advantage and up through the 1980s, it attempted to deflect attention away from its efforts. The company thought of its knowledge about the team organization as a trade secret and required consultants and employees to sign nondisclosure statements.[2]

Other prominent companies have been active with teams as well: Gaines, Cummins Engine, Digital Equipment, Ford, Motorola, Tektronix, Boeing, AT&T, Texas Instruments, and Xerox, to name just a few. In manufacturing, we now have extensive experience with self-managing teams, which started in the 1960s. Today teams in manufacturing are a proven system. It's no longer a question of why, but only of fine-tuning to specific sites.[3]

In the past few years, the use of teams in the service sector has been the most exciting area of application. Service teams are well past the experimentation phase, although we still have much to learn. Teams in government are the most readily changing areas of application. Until two or three years ago, there was very little interest in empowered teams in government agencies. Now, however, driven by downsizing, experimentation with teams seems to be active.

Perhaps the most promising area of team development now is in the professions and middle management. These include teams like concurrent engineering teams, cross-functional teams, product improvement teams, task force teams, ad hoc teams, and new venture teams.

As we will see in Chapter 17, teams are an important part of successful quality-management programs. These approaches foster top-quality products, individual employee concern for enhancing production, increased efficiency, and high employee morale.

This chapter provides the foundations of individual and group behavior. We begin by examining some of the ways individuals differ in attitudes, personalities, perceptions, and abilities. We will look at how job satisfaction and several personality factors affect performance. Since management effectiveness depends upon the ability of different individuals to pull together and focus on a common goal, we turn our attention to understanding group issues. We explore the different types of groups, how groups form and develop, the influences of information technology on groups, and several dimensions that influence group effectiveness. Finally, we take a look at how managers can work to make groups more effective.

UNDERSTANDING INDIVIDUAL BEHAVIOR: THE KEY TO MANAGING DIVERSITY

An individual's behavior will be determined to a great extent by several internal elements, such as attitudes, personalities, perceptions, and abilities. People respond differently to the same situation because of their unique combination of these elements. Managers are challenged to understand and recognize the importance of individual differences in their employees. We examine some of these elements that influence individual behavior in the next few sections.

ATTITUDES

Attitudes are relatively lasting beliefs, feelings, and behavioral tendencies held by a person about specific objects, events, groups, issues, or people. For example, when an organization first introduces its employees to quality-im-

Attitudes
Relatively lasting beliefs, feelings, and behavioral tendencies held by a person about specific objects, events, groups, issues, or people.

Job satisfaction includes five characteristics: the work itself—responsibility, interest, and growth; pay; relations with co-workers; technical help and social support; and promotional opportunities.

© Tim Thompson/Tony Stone Images

provement teams, they may express an attitude about the process and the organization.

Attitudes result from a person's background, personality, and life experiences. While these attitudes may not necessarily be factual or completely consistent with objective reality, managers still must be aware of those that have an impact on the organization, such as how satisfied individuals are with their jobs, how committed they are to the organization's values and goals, and how willing they are to expend considerable effort for the organization.[4]

The most commonly studied work attitude is job satisfaction. Job satisfaction is the degree to which individuals feel positively or negatively about their jobs. It is an emotional response to tasks as well as to the physical and social conditions of the workplace.[5] Job satisfaction can lead to a variety of positive and negative outcomes, from both an individual and an organizational perspective. It influences how employees feel about themselves, their work, and their organizations and can affect their contribution to achieving the organization's goals.[6]

The best-known scale that measures job satisfaction—the Job Descriptive Index (JDI)—evaluates five specific characteristics of a person's job:[7]

1. *The work itself*—responsibility, interest, and growth.
2. *Pay*—adequacy of pay and perceived equity.
3. *Relations with co-workers*—social harmony and respect.
4. *Quality of supervision*—technical help and social support.
5. *Promotional opportunities*—chances for further advancement.

Obviously, an employee can be satisfied with some aspects of a job, and at the same time be dissatisfied with others. A scale such as the JDI helps managers pinpoint sources of dissatisfaction so they can take appropriate action.

Of particular interest to managers is the possible relationship between job satisfaction and performance at work. Managers often struggle with the notion of trying to maintain high levels of performance along with employee satisfaction. Over the years, some research has shown that job satisfaction causes job performance, while other studies have indicated that job performance causes job satisfaction. The current view is that managers should not assume a simple cause-and-effect relationship between job satisfaction and job performance because the relationship between the two in any particular situation will depend on a complex set of personal and situational variables. An employee's job performance depends on a large number of factors such as his ability, the quality of equipment and materials used, the competence of supervision, the working environment, peer relationships, and so on.

PERSONALITY CHARACTERISTICS

Personality
The enduring, organized, and distinctive pattern of behavior that characterizes an individual's adaptation to a situation.

Personality is an enduring, organized, and distinctive pattern of behavior that describes an individual's adaptation to a situation.[8] It is used here to represent the overall profile or combination of traits that characterize the unique nature of a person. In short, personality characteristics allow us to tell people apart and to anticipate their behaviors.

Personality characteristics suggest tendencies to behave in certain ways and account for consistency in various situations. They can partly explain why learning certain new behaviors may be harder for some people than for others. A number of personality traits have been convincingly linked to work behavior and performance. Organizational researchers have tended to focus on specific personality characteristics or traits that are considered important in the workplace. We will examine five traits of special relevance to managers: self-esteem, locus of control, Machiavellianism, Type A orientation, and self-monitoring. Keep in mind, however, that these are not selection tools and should not be used for promotional or other job-related decisions.

SELF-ESTEEM

Self-esteem indicates the extent to which people believe they are capable, significant, successful, and worthwhile.[9] In short, a person's self-esteem is a judgment of worthiness that is expressed by the attitudes the individual holds toward herself. People have opinions about their own behavior, abilities, appearance, and worth. Research has shown that these assessments of worthiness are affected somewhat by situations, successes or failures, the opinions of others, and thus the roles that they assume.[10] Nevertheless, the assessments are stable enough to be widely regarded as a basic characteristic or dimension of personality that is credited with enhancing performance, increasing the likelihood of success, and fueling motivation.

Self-esteem affects behavior in organizations and other social settings in several important ways. For example, self-esteem is related to initial vocational choice. Individuals with high self-esteem take more risks in job selection, may be more attracted to high-status occupations, and are more likely to choose nontraditional jobs than individuals with low self-esteem.[11] Individuals with low self-esteem set lower goals for themselves than individuals with high self-esteem and tend to be more easily influenced by the opinions of others in organizational settings.[12]

Self-esteem
The extent to which people believe they are capable, significant, successful, and worthwhile.

LOCUS OF CONTROL

Locus of control is a personality characteristic that describes the extent to which individuals believe that they can control the environment and external events affecting them.[13] Do you have an internal or external locus of control? Before reading further, take a few minutes to complete Experiential Exercise 14.1 at the end of the chapter. This will give you some insight into this aspect of your personality and help you determine whether you have an internal or external locus of control. Please keep in mind that this is not a judgment but simply a way for you to learn more about your own possible managerial style.

Individuals who have an internal locus of control (a low score on the scale; see Experiential Exercise 14.1) believe that many of the events in their lives are primarily (but not necessarily totally) the result of their own behavior and actions. They feel a sense of control over their lives and tend to attribute both their successes and their failures to their own efforts. As a result of such an approach, individuals with an internal locus of control, or *internals,* tend to be more proactive and take more risks.[14] In contrast, individuals with an external locus of control, or *externals* (a high score on the scale), believe that much of what happens to them is controlled and determined by outside external forces such as other powerful people or luck. Such individuals do not generally perceive that they have control over their lives. As a result, they have been found to be more reactive to events and less able to rebound from stress-

Locus of control
The extent to which individuals believe that they can control events affecting them. Those with an internal locus of control believe that events are primarily the result of one's own behavior and actions. Those with an external locus of control believe that much of what happens is uncontrolled and determined by outside forces.

Entrepreneurial Approach

MASAYOSHI SON: ENCOURAGING THE ENTREPRENEURIAL SPIRIT

Before he was 20 years old, Masayoshi Son was a multimillionaire. While he was a student at the University of California at Berkeley, Son invented a pocket translator and sold the patent to Sharp Corporation for $1 million. Later the product became the Sharp Wizard. Not long after that, he built a software company and also quickly sold it for close to $2 million.

After graduating from Berkeley, Son returned to Japan to continue his entrepreneurial drive. His strong self-esteem and drive to be the best allowed him the confidence to take a year off and create 40 business prospects. Next, he tested each of the 40 ideas against 25 strict criteria. At the top of the list of criteria were such concepts as it would have to hold his interest for at least ten years and the company would have to generate at least $1 billion in sales before Son turned 40.

The Tokyo-based company Son started in 1981 was a software distribution business called Softbank Corporation. In a time when almost nobody owned a personal computer, Son took a risk that personal computers would make an impact and that the people who made software didn't necessarily know how to sell it. Son's original concept has grown to become Japan's largest distributor of computer software, hardware, and peripherals. Softbank Corp. recently acquired COMDEX, a computer trade-show organization, for $800 million and Ziff-Davis, publisher of *PC Week* and *PC Magazine,* for $2.1 billion. In 1995, Softbank's revenues were $1.6 billion. Son, who holds 57 percent of the public company, has an estimated personal net worth of $4.4 billion.

Unlike most Japanese businesses, Softbank is infused with the entrepreneurial spirit. Son's sense of purpose, strong drive to achieve, positive attitude, clearly focused goals, and high level of self-esteem keeps his 6,000 employees motivated. Son rewards them with stock in the company, a revolutionary idea in Japan. Even more extreme, Son plans to divide Softbank into 600 virtual companies with ten members each. This will create a dynamic environment where decisions can be made immediately and actions can be proactive rather than reactive to the market.

Obviously, Son is not afraid to challenge convention. He is socially active, has established high goals, is achievement oriented, is highly motivated, and believes he has control over his own destiny. Masayoshi Son is shaking up the corporate establishment in Japan and encouraging other entrepreneurs.

SOURCES: T. Stein, "Japan's Man with a Mega-Plan," *Success,* June 1996, 35–36.

---

ful situations. Externals tend to rely on others' judgments and conform to authority more readily than internals.

The many differences between internal and external locus of control can help explain some aspects of individual behavior in organizational settings. For example, since internals believe they control their own behavior, they are more active politically and socially and are more active in seeking information about their situations than are externals. Internals are more likely to try to influence or persuade others, are less likely to be influenced by others, and may be more achievement oriented than externals. For all these reasons, internals may be more highly motivated and set harder goals than externals. More differences between internals and externals are explained in the discussion section of Experiential Exercise 14.1.

An internal locus of control is an important personality characteristic of an entrepreneur, since these individuals are convinced that they play a role in determining their success or failure and tend to feel that they have control of

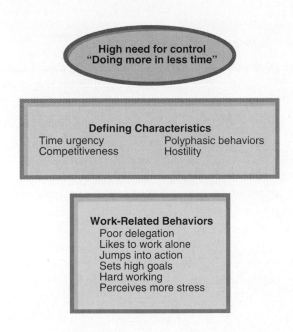

FIGURE 14.1
Type A characteristics and behaviors

their fate through their own efforts. As you read about software legend Masayoshi Son in the Entrepreneurial Approach, you'll be able to identify most of the traits of an internal locus of control that we have discussed: socially active, establishes high goals, achievement oriented, highly motivated, risk oriented, and likely to influence others. Masayoshi Son is an excellent example of an individual motivated to take the steps needed to set up and run a new business, even in the face of adversity.[15]

MACHIAVELLIANISM

Do you believe the ends justify the means? Are you a skilled negotiator? Do you manipulate others to get what you want? If you answered yes to these questions, chances are you have some degree of a Machiavellian personality. An individual with **Machiavellian personality** traits is someone who vies for and manipulates others for purely personal gain. Machiavellians feel that any behavior is acceptable if it achieves their goals. They are unemotional and detached, can be expected to take control, and try to exploit loosely structured situations. They perform well when there are substantial rewards for success and in jobs that require strong negotiation skills.[16]

As can be expected from a concept that relates to perception and use of power, there are differences among cultures in regard to Machiavellian behaviors. In cultures that respect high social power and broad authority, managers with high Machiavellian behaviors are more successful. The high-Machiavellian managers are tolerated and often successful, since they obtain results in a highly competitive and complex environment. While some organizations may seem to prosper under these conditions, the cost to employees and long-term success may be great.[17]

Machiavellian personality
Someone who vies for and manipulates others purely for personal gain and feels that any behavior is acceptable if it achieves one's goals.

TYPE A ORIENTATION

The concept of **Type A orientation** has received considerable attention not only as a risk factor for coronary disease but as a factor having significant implications for work and nonwork behaviors and reactions to stress.[18] Shown in Figure 14.1 are some of the common characteristics of the Type A personality.

Type A orientation
Characterized by impatience, a desire for achievement, aggressiveness, irritability, and perfectionism.

Meeting the Challenge

TYPE A AND TYPE B PERSONALITY ORIENTATION

Rate the extent to which each of the following statements describes your behavior most of the time. Place a 1 (not typical of me), 2 (somewhat typical of me), or 3 (very typical of me) before each statement.

_____ 1. My greatest satisfaction comes from doing things better than others.

_____ 2. I tend to bring the theme of a conversation around to things I am interested in.

_____ 3. I get impatient waiting in line or when someone pulls in front of me on the highway.

_____ 4. I move, walk, and eat rapidly.

_____ 5. I feel guilty when I relax or do nothing for several hours or days.

_____ 6. Having more than others is important to me.

_____ 7. I am extremely impatient, especially with people who are slow talkers; I often hurry their speech or finish sentences for them.

_____ 8. One aspect of my life (work, family, school) dominates all other aspects.

_____ 9. I am preoccupied with having rather than doing.

_____ 10. I frequently try to do two or more things simultaneously.

_____ 11. I simply don't have enough time to lead a well-balanced life.

_____ 12. I have nervous habits, such as finger tapping, clenching my fists, and/or rapidly blinking my eyes.

_____ 13. I always play to win, even with children.

_____ 14. I evaluate life strictly in terms of numbers—salary, grades, number of clients, number of pages read, and so on.

_____ 15. I get things done faster and faster and crowd more and more into my day.

_____ 16. I take out my frustration with my own imperfections on others.

_____ Total points

Scores from 16 to 25 indicate a Type B orientation. Scores from 35 to 48 indicate a Type A orientation. Scores that fall between 26 and 34 indicate neither Type A nor Type B. In general, the higher the score, the more Type A behaviors you exhibit.

Of particular interest to Type A orientation is the underlying need for control that is manifested in four general categories of behaviors. As summarized in Fig. 14.1, Type A individuals have a sense of being in a hurry, impatience with delays, and a concern of time urgency. They are competitive in work and social situations and measure their outcomes against others. Type A people often involve themselves in doing several things at once and understand several activities when pressured. Finally, Type A individuals often show hostility in the forms of diffused anger, intolerance for delays, irritability, and aggressiveness.

Type B orientation
Characterized as easygoing, relaxed, patient, able to listen carefully, and communicate more precisely than Type A individuals.

In contrast to Type A individuals, those with a **Type B orientation** are characteristically easygoing and less competitive in daily events. Type B individuals appear to be more relaxed and patient than Type A individuals, listen more carefully, and communicate more precisely.

Do you have a Type A or Type B personality? Before reading further, take a few minutes to respond to the sixteen descriptive statements found in Meeting the Challenge.[19] Then, calculate your score and determine whether you fit the Type A or Type B personality. This self-knowledge will help you learn about your own strengths and weaknesses and lead to being effective in a managerial role.

SELF-MONITORING

When observing individuals in the workplace, it is often easy to identify their style and personality characteristics. These individuals seem to behave consistently in many different situations. Herb Kelleher, CEO of Southwest Airlines, has a forceful but open style in all settings, whether he is dealing with the Southwest employees or stockholders, or presenting at a business conference.[20] Other individuals are very difficult to read, or their behavior seems to change from one situation to another. One explanation of why it is easy to read some people and establish their style and difficult to do so for others is the concept of self-monitoring.

Self-monitoring (SM) identifies the degree to which individuals are capable of reading and using the cues from their environment to determine their behavior. Individuals who score high on the SM scale (*high SMs*) seem to be able to read environmental and social cues about what is considered appropriate behavior and adjust their behaviors. For high SMs, behavior is likely to be the result of perception of the environment and is, therefore, likely to change depending on the situation. For *low SMs* (who score low on the SM scale), behaviors are more internally determined and they are likely to appear consistent across different situations.

Some interesting applications from research on SM in the workplace suggest that high SMs emerge as leaders more frequently and learn managerial skills more easily than low SMs. Also, high-SM managers are better able to cope with cross-cultural experiences. Therefore, since such situations are ambiguous and require ability to interpret environmental cues, high SMs have to be able to understand an increasing complex global environment.[21]

Self-monitoring
Identifies the degree to which individuals are capable of reading and using the cues from their environment to determine their behavior.

PERCEPTION

Perception can be defined as the way people experience, process, define, and interpret the world around them. It can be considered an information screen or filter that influences the way in which individuals communicate and become aware of sensations and stimuli that exist around them. Acting as a filter, perception helps individuals take in or see only certain elements in a particular situation.

Perceptions are influenced by a variety of factors, including an individual's experiences, needs, personality, and education. As a result, a person's perceptions are not necessarily accurate. But they are unique and help to explain why two individuals may look at the same situation or message and perceive it differently. For example, managers in the same organization but different departments, such as operations, marketing, and finance, will perceive the weekly sales data differently. In addition, an individual's cultural background may influence his perception and interpretation of certain company messages or symbols.

PERCEPTUAL PROCESS

The perceptual process is quite complex. It involves selection, organization, and interpretation of environmental stimuli. First, we select or pay attention to some information and ignore other information, often without consciously realizing that we are doing so. For example, a hungry person is likely to focus

Stereotyping may lead the perceiver to dwell on certain characteristics expected of all persons in the assigned category and to fail to recognize the characteristics that distinguish the person as an individual.

© Leslye Borden/PhotoEdit

Stereotyping
The tendency to assign attributes to someone, not on individual characteristics, but solely on the basis of a category or group to which that person belongs.

Halo-and-horn effect
The process in which we evaluate and form an overall impression of an individual based solely on a specific trait or dimension.

on the food pictured in an advertisement for china, whereas a person who is not hungry may focus on the color and design of the china.

After selecting, we organize the information into a pattern and interpret it. How we interpret what we perceive also varies considerably. Depending on the circumstances and our state of mind, we may interpret a wave of the hand as a friendly gesture or as a threat.

The perceptual process is filled with possibilities for errors in judgment or misunderstandings. While these perceptual errors or biases allow us to make quick judgments and provide data for making predictions, they can also result in significant mistakes that can be costly to individuals and organizations. We will explore several common errors, or distortions, in perception that have particular applications in managerial situations: (1) stereotyping, (2) the halo-and-horn effect, and (3) selective perception.

Stereotyping

Stereotyping is generalization, or the tendency to assign attributes to someone, not on individual characteristics, but solely on the basis of a category or group to which that person belongs. In many ways stereotypes lead to misunderstandings because they are inaccurate or biased. We readily expect someone identified as a professor, carpenter, police officer, poet, or surgeon to have certain attributes, even if we have not met the individual. Even identifying an employee by such broad categories as older, female, or Asian American can lead to errors and misperceptions. Stereotyping may lead the perceiver to dwell on certain characteristics expected of all persons in the assigned category and to fail to recognize the characteristics that distinguish the person as an individual.

When we face new situations, stereotypes provide guidelines to help classify people. Unfortunately, stereotyping based on false premises may lead to a distorted view of reality because it assumes that all people of any one gender, race, or age have similar characteristics, and this simply isn't true. Stereotypes based on such factors as gender, age, and race can, and unfortunately still do, bias perceptions of employees in some organizations.[22] A recent study even found gender bias in the college classroom and demonstrated that male professors were perceived to be more effective than females even though their performance ratings were identical.[23]

Some organizations, such as Texaco, Shoney's, and Denny's, have been forced by court orders and multimillion-dollar discrimination case settlements to institute classes to demonstrate how stereotyping can lead to inefficiency, turnover, and discrimination and to teach employees to manage a diverse work force.[24] However, for the majority of organizations, training and mentoring programs have been used to reduce stereotyping and help employees adjust to increasing workplace diversity.

One small organization that has been successful at integrating diversity is Cardiac Concepts, Inc., an outpatient laboratory specializing in cardiovascular testing. Emma Colquitt manages a staff of eleven women and minorities who are members of six different religions. While the small staff experienced very few problems. Colquitt brought in specialty training consultants to help employees handle the diversity of a workplace where religious, ethnic, and cultural differences had the potential to bring stereotyping issues to the surface and disrupt the effectiveness of the company.[25]

Halo-and-Horn Effect

The **halo-and-horn effect** refers to a process in which we evaluate and form an overall impression of an individual based solely on a specific trait or dimension, such as enthusiasm, gender, appearance, or intelligence. If we view the observed trait as positive, we tend to apply a halo (positive) effect to other traits. If we think of the observed trait as negative, we apply a horn (negative) effect. For example, a student who makes a good grade on the first test in a course may create a favorable impression with the instructor. The professor may then assume that the student is tops in all of her classes, a leader in many situations, efficient, honest, and loyal. Keep in mind that when evaluations are made on the basis of traits that really aren't linked, halo-and-horn effects result. Of course, many traits are, in fact, related. So, not all judgments based on the halo-and-horn effect are really perceptual errors.

Selective Perception

Selective perception is the tendency to screen out information with which we aren't comfortable or don't want to be bothered. We have all been accused of listening only to what we want to hear or "tuning out" what we don't wish to hear. Both are examples of selective perception.

A classic research study of how selective perception influences managers involved executives in a manufacturing company.[26] When asked to identify the key problem in a comprehensive business policy case, all executives in the study selected a problem consistent with their own functional area work assignments. For example, most marketing executives viewed the key problem area as sales; production people tended to see it as a production problem; human resources people perceived it as a personnel issue. These differing viewpoints demonstrate how errors can occur and affect the way the executives would approach the problem.

In organizations, employees often make this perceptual error. Marketing employees pay close attention to marketing problems and issues, research and development (R&D) engineers pay close attention to product technology or R&D funding, and accountants focus on issues specifically related to accounting. These employees selectively eliminate information that deals with other areas of the organization and focus only on information that is directly relevant to their own needs.

REDUCING PERCEPTUAL ERRORS

Since perception is such an important process and plays a major role in determining our behavior, managers must recognize the common perceptual errors. Managers who fall prey to perceptual errors such as stereotyping lose

Selective perception
The tendency to screen out information with which we aren't comfortable or that we do not consider relevant.

Employees often make perceptual errors, focusing their attention on areas with which they're familiar and screening out information with which they are uncomfortable or don't want to be bothered. Managers need to be aware of perceptual errors, such as halo-and-horn errors, stereotyping, and selective perception in order to avoid such mistakes.

© Alan Levenson/Tony Stone Images

sight of individual differences among people. The quality of their decisions can suffer, and the performance of capable people can also suffer. Simple knowledge of perceptual errors, such as stereotyping, halo-and-horn errors, and selective perception, is the first step in avoiding such mistakes.

Many of the topics we have just discussed are related to issues you have read about in Chapter 10. It is important to remember that whether we are conducting performance appraisals, interviewing, interacting with peers, or handling customers, the perceptual process can very easily be a factor in our behavior.

ABILITY

Ability is defined as an existing capacity to perform various tasks needed in a given situation. Abilities may be classified as mental, mechanical, and psychomotor. In the organizational setting, ability and effort are key determinants of employee behavior and performance. For example, mental or intellectual ability is important for problem solving because it involves the capacity to transform information, generate alternatives, memorize, and consider implications. Mechanical ability refers to the capacity to comprehend relationships between objects and to perceive how parts fit together. Psychomotor ability includes such things as manual dexterity, eye-hand coordination, and manipulative ability. The key point is that not only do employee' abilities vary substantially, but different tasks will require different abilities. Such recognition is crucial to understanding and predicting work behaviors.

Up to this point, we have focused on individual behavior. However, we can also examine the power of individuals who are encouraged to work together, as Managing for Excellence points out. U.S. West needed individuals to commit to a new technology in the workplace—one that would not only make the company more service oriented but would eventually make employees more efficient. Employees were provided the opportunity to experience the new technology. For those who wanted to be involved in the new system, the only requirement was that they had to work with and teach two other colleagues how to use it. It was a pyramid scheme that became known as "Global Village" and transformed the way U.S. West operates.[27]

We know that individuals act differently in groups than when they are alone. In the next part of the chapter, we explore groups since, in most organizations, group work has become a fact of life. In the corporate world, the supposed miracle cure for ailing organizations is team-based management. Unfortunately, many organizations try to adopt this concept without understanding that success is hard to achieve. Team-based management also takes effort, training, patience, group trust, and loyalty.[28]

Before we understand how managers can create and maintain successful, high-performance groups, we need to know more about the very basic aspects of group functioning. This includes how we define a group, different types of groups, group development, and some of the more influential variables on group effectiveness.

UNDERSTANDING GROUP BEHAVIOR: ESSENCE OF QUALITY

We define a **group** as two or more interdependent individuals who interact with and influence one another in order to accomplish a common purpose.[29] Our definition recognizes that a group can involve as few as two people, that

Group
Two or more interdependent individuals who interact with and influence one another to accomplish a common purpose.

A Pyramid Scheme at U.S. West: Bringing Employees Together through Technology

Margaret Turney, a top financial executive at U.S. West, was looking for a way to show employees how fast-changing technologies would affect the services the company offers. With 60,000 employees, she faced the usual employee concerns over lack of time to learn new technology, the possible isolation of individuals, and individuals who were not technically confident. With the support and innovative ideas of Sherman Woo, the company's director of information tools and technologies, Global Village was created, an internal web that now connects over 15,000 people at U.S. West and has transformed the way the company operates.

Woo believed the best way to interest individuals in new technology was for them to experience it themselves. He created a demonstration room, invited employees to visit, and gave a computerized demonstration tour of the products U.S. West might develop to take advantage of the new internal web technology. When an employee was interested in having the new browser software and being connected to the new web, Woo knew he had hooked her. In exchange, Woo demanded that each new user had to show at least two other colleagues how the web worked.

Woo's pyramid scheme has brought together employees working in fourteen states on the Global Village. Some meet in on-line chat rooms to exchange documents and discuss ongoing projects. Salespeople use the web to keep in touch with managers in locations all over the world. Customers may also benefit from U.S. West's internal web. The company plans to let service representatives use the intranet to fill orders for features such as call waiting immediately, while the customer is still on the phone.

The Global Village is so easy to use that nontechies help expand and maintain it. Workers in different departments create their own home pages and keep their own documents current. U.S. West has captured the energy of all those managers and employees who know how to type but don't know how to program. It has brought individuals together and encouraged positive working relationships. Rather than feeling more isolated, employees on the Global Village are very positively influenced by the technology and their new opportunities.

SOURCE: A. Sprout, "The Internet Inside Your Company: The Pyramid Scheme," *Fortune,* November 27, 1995, 161–68.

group success depends on the interdependent and collective efforts of various group members, and that group members are likely to have significant impacts on one another as they work together. This definition also helps us differentiate a group from a mere aggregate of individuals. In recent years, the word *team* has become a popular word in the business community, often replacing the word *group*. For our purposes in this chapter, we use the terms *group* and *team* interchangeably.

Simply placing individuals in groups and telling them to work together does not in and of itself promote productivity. Group effectiveness does not magically appear when a group is formed. Members must consciously work to build and maintain the effectiveness of their group in order to first achieve success and then to maintain it.

The critical requirements of an effective group are shown in Figure 14.2.[30] First, the group members must have an interdependent relationship with one another; they are dependent on one another to accomplish the group work. Second, this interdependence dictates that group members must interact through conversation or work activities. Third, a group is characterized by mu-

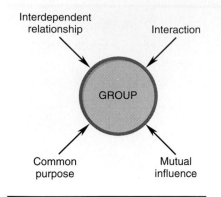

FIGURE 14.2
Requirements of a group

Formal groups
Groups that are deliberately created to accomplish goals and serve the needs of the organization.

Informal groups
Self-created groups that evolve out of the formal organization based on proximity, common interests, or needs of individuals.

tual influence between group members, rather than a situation in which all the power is held by a minority in the group. Fourth, groups must have a clearly understood goal or common purpose that evokes high levels of commitment from all members.

In the performance of organizational work, there are two basic types of groups—formal and informal. Both groups influence, either positively or negatively, the work performed. We examine the two types of groups and their influence on behavior in the next section.

FORMAL AND INFORMAL GROUPS

Groups come in many forms, shapes, and sizes. Most managers belong to several different groups at the same time: some at work, some in the community, some formally organized, and some informal and social in nature.

Formal groups are deliberately created by the organization's managers to accomplish goals and serve the needs of the organization. The major purpose of formal groups is to perform specific tasks and achieve specific objectives defined by the organization. The most common type of formal work group consists of individuals cooperating under the direction of a leader. Examples of formal groups are departments, divisions, task forces, project groups, quality circles, committees, and boards of directors. Boeing formed special quality-improvement teams when it was first testing the new 777 airplane. These are considered to be formal groups and will be maintained even after production of the plane.

Informal groups in organizations are not formed or planned by the organization's managers. Rather, they are self-created and evolve out of the formal organization for a variety of reasons, such as proximity, common interests, or needs of individuals. It would be difficult to design an organization that prohibits informal working relationships from developing.

Because human beings receive reassurance from interacting with others and being part of a group, informal groups can meet a range of individual needs. Perhaps the major reason informal groups evolve is to fulfill individuals' needs for affiliation and friendship, social interaction, communication, power, safety, and status. For example, individuals who regularly eat lunch, carpool, or go to a football game together are members of an informal group that fulfills some of these needs. While some informal groups may complement the organization's formal groups, at times they can also work against the organization's goals. A number of factors affect the way that groups operate and their ultimate effectiveness.

In the next sections we will first examine the group developmental sequence and then turn our attention to the five dimensions that influence group effectiveness.

GROUP DEVELOPMENT

The group development process is dynamic. While most groups are in a continuous state of change and rarely ever reach complete stability, the group development process does follow a general pattern. Groups appear to go through a five-stage developmental sequence: forming, storming, norming, performing, and adjourning.[31]

The types of behaviors observed in groups differ from stage to stage. The length of time spent in each stage can also vary greatly, with each stage lasting until its paramount issues are essentially resolved. The group then moves on. The stages are not clearly delineated, and there is some overlap between them. In other words, the process of group development is ongoing and complex. New groups may progress through these stages, but if the group's membership changes, the development of the group may regress to an earlier stage, at least temporarily.

Forming

In the *forming* stage, members focus their efforts on seeking basic information, defining goals, developing procedures for performing the task, and making a preliminary evaluation of how the group might interact to accomplish goals. There is often a great deal of uncertainty at this point, as group members begin to test the extent to which their input will be valued.

Groups in the forming stage often require some time for members to get acquainted with each other before attempting to proceed with the task responsibilities. It is a time for members to become acquainted, understand leadership and member roles, and learn what is expected of them.[32] The following behaviors are common for individuals in the forming stage of group development:

- Keeping feelings to themselves until they know the situation.
- Acting more secure than they actually feel.
- Experiencing confusion and uncertainty about what is expected.
- Being polite.
- Trying to size up the personal benefits and personal costs of being involved in the group.
- Accepting dependence on a powerful person.

Storming

In the *storming* stage, group members frequently experience conflict with one another as they locate and attempt to resolve differences of opinion about key issues, relative priorities of goals, who is to be responsible for what, and the task-related direction of the leader. Competition for the leadership role and conflict over goals are dominant themes at this stage. Some members may withdraw or try to isolate themselves from the emotional tension that is generated. Groups with members from diverse backgrounds or cultures may experience greater conflict than more homogenous groups.

It is important at this stage not to suppress or withdraw from the conflict. Suppressing conflict will likely create bitterness and resentment, which will last long after members attempt to express their differences and emotions. Withdrawal can cause the group to fail more quickly.

Norming

During the *norming* stage, a real sense of cohesion and teamwork begins to emerge. Group members feel good about each other and identify with the group. They share feelings, give and receive feedback, and begin to share a sense of success. The norming stage is a junction point.[33] If the issues have not been resolved, then the group will erupt into serious conflict and runs the risk of falling into groupthink. Groupthink, discussed in Chapter 6, occurs when the feeling of cohesion overrides the realistic appraisal of alternative courses of action.[34] But groupthink does not have to occur. The other option for the norming stage is to develop the potential for exchanging all kinds of information relevant to a task. An organized group is primed for the exchange of information that will help the members accomplish their task effectively.[35]

Performing

The *performing* stage, when the group is fully functional, is the most difficult to achieve. The interpersonal relations in this stage are marked by high levels of interdependence. The group is oriented to maintaining good relations and to getting its task accomplished. Group members can now work well with everyone in the group, communication is constant, decisions are made with full agreement, and members understand the roles they need to perform for the group to be highly effective.[36]

At the performing stage, the group has learned to solve complex problems and implement the solutions. Members are committed to the task and willing to experiment to solve problems. Cohesion has progressed to the point of collaboration. Confidence reaches a high level for the few groups who achieve this stage. Unfortunately, even if a group reaches this stage, it still faces the difficult job of staying there.

Adjourning

The *adjourning* stage involves the termination of task behaviors and disengagement from relationship-oriented behaviors. Some groups, such as a project team created to investigate and report on a specific program within a limited time frame, have a well-defined point of adjournment. Other groups, such as an executive committee, may go on indefinitely. Adjourning for this type of group is more subtle and takes place when one or more key members leave the organization.

Managers must understand the developmental sequence of groups because each stage can ultimately influence the group's effectiveness. In addition to the developmental process, research has identified several group dimensions that can affect group behavior and effectiveness. For example, a recent study investigated the relationship between an organization's executive team and organizational performance. The results indicated a strong relationship between performance, team structure, and the team's context.[37] The next section discusses several key dimensions that influence a group's behavior and its effectiveness.

DIMENSIONS THAT INFLUENCE GROUP BEHAVIOR AND EFFECTIVENESS

Numerous dimensions can affect how a group functions. Here we will examine five important factors that managers need to consider: size, membership composition, roles, norms, and cohesiveness. These are particularly important in the global environment where team members are often very diverse.

SIZE

Effective task groups can range from two members to a normal upper limit of sixteen. It is difficult to pinpoint an ideal group size because the appropriate size depends on the group's purpose.[38] Size affects how individuals interact with each other as well as the overall performance of the group. In groups of fewer than five members, there will be more personal discussion and more complete participation. As a group grows beyond several members, it becomes more difficult for all members to participate effectively. Communication and coordination among members become more difficult, and there is a tendency to split into subgroups. As a result, the interactions become more centralized, with a few individuals taking more active roles relative to the rest; disagreements may occur more easily; and group satisfaction may decline unless group members put a good deal of effort into relationship-oriented roles.

As group size increases, more potential human resources are available to perform the work and accomplish needed tasks. While this can boost performance, the expanded size tends to increase turnover and absenteeism, as well as provide opportunities for free riding. *Free riding* describes a tendency whereby one or more group members expend decreasing amounts of effort and just go through the motions because their contributions are less visible.[39] This phenomenon occurs because their contribution is less noticeable and they are willing to let others carry the workload.[40]

Free riding directly challenges the logic that the productivity of the group as a whole should at least equal the sum of the productivity of each individual in the group. In other words, group size and individual performance may be inversely related. Most students are acquainted with the concept of free riding, largely as a result of negative experiences they have encountered in working on group projects.[41]

MEMBERSHIP COMPOSITION

Two composition factors are particularly important influences on a group's effectiveness. The first factor is the members' characteristics, which include physical traits, abilities, job-related knowledge and skills, personality, age, race, and gender. The second factor encompasses the reasons why members are attracted to a particular group, such as their needs, motivations, and power.

Membership composition can be homogeneous or heterogeneous (diverse). A group is considered homogeneous when it is composed of individuals having similar, group-related characteristics, backgrounds, interests, values, attitudes, and the like. When the individuals are dissimilar with respect to these characteristics, the group is diverse. Rapidly growing global interdependence and the increasing emphasis on teamwork results in groups with quite diverse composition. This is no longer the exception; it is the everyday rule. Global Perspective addresses the challenge that cultural diversity creates for managers.

Does homogeneous or diverse composition lead to a more effective group? Managers face this difficult question every time they assemble a group. A manager needs to understand the purpose of the group and the nature of the task to determine whether the group is better served by a homogeneous or a diverse composition.

For tasks that are standard and routine, a homogeneous group functions more quickly. Membership homogeneity contributes to member satisfaction, creates less conflict and less turnover, and increases the chances for harmonious working relationships among group members. If a group is too homogeneous, however, it may exert excessive pressure on group members to conform to the group's rules and may lack the controversy and perspectives essential to high-quality decision making and creativity.[42]

For tasks that are nonroutine and require diverse skills, opinions, and behaviors, a heterogeneous group yields better results. We saw in our earlier example that Boeing's management created heterogeneous groups for their quality-performance teams. A diverse membership can bring a variety of skills and viewpoints to bear on problems and thus facilitate task accomplishment. The more diverse the membership, however, the more skilled the manager or group leader will have to be in facilitating a successful group experience.

ROLES

Roles are shared expectations of how group members will fulfill the requirements of their positions. People develop their roles and behaviors based on their own expectations, the group's expectations, and the organization's expectations. As employees internalize the expectations of these three sources, they develop their roles.

Roles
Shared expectations of how group members will fulfill the requirements of their positions.

CULTURAL DIVERSITY CHALLENGES MANAGERS TO CREATE EFFECTIVE TEAMS

What does it take to be an effective team member? As our organizations become more diverse, the chances are that the answer to this question often depends on the person's culture. Much the same way as what is considered effective leadership behavior depends on cultural factors, effective team membership is also culturally influenced.

An effective team member in Japan is above all courteous, cooperative, and avoids conflict and confrontation. In the United States, effective team members speak their mind, pull their weight by contributing equally, and participate actively. German employees are taught early in their careers to seek technical excellence. In Afghanistan, a team member is obligated to share his or her resources with others, making generosity an essential team behavior. In Israel, kibbutz team members are driven by values of hard work and contribution to the community. The Swedes are comfortable with open arguments and will publicly disagree with one another and with their leader.

Cross-cultural differences in team behaviors create considerable challenges for managers of culturally diverse teams. Success depends on accurate perceptions and careful reading of cues. Managers need to be flexible, patient, and willing not only to listen to others but to question their own assumptions. They also need to consider that many behavioral differences have individual rather than cultural sources. The only constant in the successful implementation of teams is the manager's sincere belief in the team's ability to contribute to the organization. Such belief is necessary regardless of the cultural setting.

SOURCES: R. M. Kanter and R. I. Corn, "Do Cultural Differences Make a Business Difference? Contextual Factors Affecting Cross Cultural Relationship Success," *Journal of Management Development,* 13, 2, 5–23; V. J. Marsick, E. Turner, and L. Cederholm, "International as a Team," *Management Review,* March 1989, 46–49.

People often have multiple roles within the same group.[43] For example, a professor may have the roles of teacher, researcher, writer, consultant, advisor, and committee member. Our roles also extend outside the workplace. The professor may also be a family member, belong to professional and civic organizations, and have social friends, all of whom may have very different expectations about the behaviors that are appropriate.

When operating in a work group, individuals typically fulfill several roles. Member roles fit into three categories and each has associated behaviors: (1) task-oriented roles, (2) relationship-oriented roles, and (3) self-oriented roles.[44] As Figure 14.3 shows, each of these categories includes a variety of different role behaviors.

Task-oriented roles focus on behaviors directly related to establishing and accomplishing the goals of the group or achieving the desired outcomes. They include seeking and providing information, initiating actions and procedures, building on ideas, information giving and seeking, consensus testing, opinion giving, summarizing progress, and energizing the quantity and quality of output.

Relationship-oriented roles include behaviors that cultivate the well-being, continuity, and development of the group. They focus on the operation

Task-oriented roles
Behaviors directly related to establishing and achieving the goals of the group or getting the task done.

Relationship-oriented roles
Behaviors that cultivate the well-being, continuity, and development of the group.

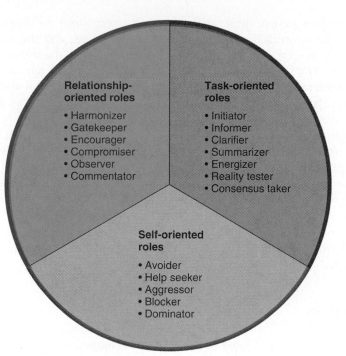

FIGURE 14.3
Group roles and associated behaviors

Self-oriented roles
Behaviors that meet some personal need or goal of an individual without regard to the group's problems.

Norms
Unwritten and often informal rules and shared beliefs about what behavior is appropriate and expected of group members.

Effective groups learn how to integrate relationship- and task-oriented roles. They can switch roles seamlessly, depending on the situation, and take on tasks, assume responsibilities, and take charge by plotting a strategy. Directions need not necessarily come from the highest-level member of the group.

© David Joel/Tony Stone Images

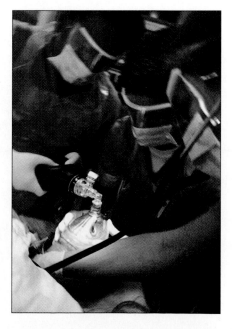

of the group and the maintenance of good relationships, and help the group survive, regulate, grow, and strengthen itself. They help foster group unity, positive interpersonal relations among group members, and the development of the members' ability to work effectively together. These behaviors include encouraging, harmonizing performance checking, standard setting, and tension relieving.

Self-oriented roles occur to meet some personal need or goal of an individual without regard for the group's problems. They often have a negative influence on a group's effectiveness.[45] Examples of such behaviors include dominating the group discussion, emphasizing personal issues, interrupting others, distracting the group from its work, and wasting the group's time.

Research indicates that the effective groups discover how to integrate relationship- and task-oriented roles. One group that has been consistently recognized for being exceptionally effective is the emergency-trauma team at Massachusetts General Hospital in Boston. They show how a flexible team switches roles (including leadership) seamlessly, depending on the crisis at hand. When patients are brought in for an emergency, individuals on the team take on tasks, assume responsibilities, and take charge by plotting a strategy. Directions may just as likely come from a doctor or attending physican as from an intern or nurse.[46]

NORMS

Norms are unwritten and often informal rules and shared beliefs about what behavior is appropriate and expected of group members. Norms differ from organizational rules in that they are unwritten, group members must accept them and behave in ways consistent with them before they can be said to exist.[47]

Norms cannot be imposed on a group, but rather develop out of the interaction among members. For example, a typical work group may have norms that define how people dress, the upper and lower limits on acceptable productivity, the information that can be told to the boss, and the matters that need to remain secret. If a group member does not follow the norms, the other members will try to enforce compliance through acceptance and friendship or through such means as ridicule, ostracism, sabotage, and verbal abuse.

As the Hawthorne studies demonstrated many years ago, work groups establish a variety of norms, which are not always aligned with the formal standards set by the organization. Group norms can be positive, helping the group meet its objective(s), or they can be negative, hindering the group's effectiveness. Although we know that disagreement among group members is beneficial for productive and critical thinking, it is often discouraged by group norms. Once a group reaches the performing stage of development, dissenters from group norm behavior are often pressured into conforming to new standards. Managers need to understand the norms of the groups they manage and then work toward maintaining and developing positive norms while eliminating negative norms.

COHESIVENESS

Cohesiveness
The strength of the members' desires to remain in the group.

Have you ever been a member of a group whose members seemed to get along and work well with one another, were highly motivated, and worked in a coordinated way? When a group behaves in this way, it is considered to be cohesive. **Cohesiveness** is defined as the strength of the members' desire to remain in the group, their commitment to it, and their ability to function together as a unit. It is influenced by the degree of compatibility between group goals and individual members' goals. A group whose members have a strong desire to remain in the group and personally accept its goals would be considered highly cohesive.

The degree of group cohesion is an important dimension influencing group effectiveness. Cohesiveness can influence communication and the job satisfaction of group members. For example, members of cohesive groups tend to communicate more frequently, are likely to feel more satisfied with their jobs, are more committed to working through issues, think more favorably of group members, and experience less conflict than members of groups that are not cohesive.[48]

Managers should strive to promote cohesiveness among work group members because group cohesiveness can be an extremely positive organizational force when it helps unite a group behind organizational goals. For example, when team members are committed, they know each other's strengths and weaknesses; they bring problems to the surface; and they work hard at being a team.[49] These abilities and people skills are basically the same regardless of whether you work for a large corporation like Nike or are employed by a small company with only a handful of employees.

Nevertheless, though we often assume that the more cohesive a group is, the better the group functions, it is important to recognize that cohesion may also have negative effects. High cohesiveness may actually be associated with low effectiveness if group goals are contrary to organizational goals or if members are more concerned with the group itself than with the goals of the organization.[50] Therefore, the relationship between cohesion and effectiveness cannot be anticipated or understood unless the group's goals and norms are also known. The realtionship between group cohesiveness, group effectiveness, and group norms is shown in Table 14.1.

In addtion, recall our discussion of groupthink, an agreement-at-any-cost mentality that results in ineffective group decision making. Highly cohesive groups may be prone to groupthink, which we discussed earlier in the text.[51]

TABLE 14.1   The relationship between group cohesiveness, group effectiveness, and group norms

NORMS	COHESIVENESS OF THE WORK GROUP	
	HIGH	LOW
Aligned with organization	Highest performance	Moderate performance
Not aligned with organization	Low performance	Moderate to low performance

As organizations become increasingly diverse in terms of gender, race, ethnicity, and nationality, this diversity brings potential benefits such as better decision making, greater creativity and innovation, and more successful marketing to different types of customers. But increased cultural differences within a work force can also make it harder to develop cohesive work groups and may result in higher turnover, interpersonal conflict, and communication breakdowns.[52]

Managers must be aware of these issues as they work to create high-performance groups. They need to be trained to capitalize on the benefits of diversity while minimizing the potential costs. Additionally, managers will need to work to integrate minority-culture members both formally and informally and strive to eliminate prejudice and discrimination to reduce alienation and build organizational identity among minority group members. The organization that achieves these conditions will create an environment in which all members can contribute to their maximum potential and in which the value of diversity can be fully realized.[53]

INFORMATION TECHNOLOGY INFLUENCES ON GROUP EFFECTIVENESS

Up to this point we have outlined numerous issues for managers to take into consideration to create and maintain high-performing groups. Now we examine the use of information technology as an additional variable that is widely being used by groups in organizations and has the potential to influence effectiveness.

Through the use of information technology, groups can be created that are composed of individuals who are widely separated geographically; they no longer have to work in proximity to each other. For example, in an electronically networked group, individuals can be anywhere in the world. Meetings require only that members are at their terminals. Communication between meetings can be extremely fast in comparison with telephone conversations and interoffice mail. Participation is more equalized and less affected by prestige, composition, and roles. Electronic communication, however, relies almost entirely on plain text for conveying messages, text that is often transient, appearing on and disappearing from a screen without any necessary tangible artifacts.[54] It becomes easy for a sender to be out of touch with her audience and easy for the sender to be less constrained by conventional norms and rules for behavior in composing messages.

Different kinds of technology can be effective for the different stages of group development. Research has shown us that during the forming and storming stages, groups function more effectively with face-to-face meetings to satisfy emotional needs. However, technological communications are very effective during the norming and performing stages.

Group members who meet electronically can feel a greater sense of anonymity, detect less individuality in others, feel less empathy, be less concerned over how they compare with others, and be less influenced by social conventions than members who meet face to face. Such influences can lead to more honesty and less tactfulness.

Groupware
A software package used to organize an electronic meeting in which participants' computers are interconnected from their various locations.

Work-group conferencing uses a software package call **groupware** to organize an electronic meeting in which participants' computers are interconnected from their various locations. Participants interact through microcomputers directly linked to a server and comments are broadcast to all others in the conference. The participants may be in the same room, linked by a local-area network, or geographically dispersed and interconnected over a wide-area network. The electronic conference centers on the entry of ideas, comments, and suggestions, and the retrieval and display of information.

Work-group systems are ideal for bringing far-flung individuals together via the network to tackle a problem. The group gets the benefits of shared thinking and distribution of information without the costs and time involved in travel. For example, in Boeing's Seattle Computer Services Group, team members and people from different functional areas use groupware frequently to exchange ideas and discuss challenges. Meetings are generally conducted by a moderator, who stands at the front and center of the conference room and manages the computer system.

While information technology has many positive influences on group effectiveness, face-to-face communication has a richness that electronic communication may never match.[55] According to Harold Beneen, the former head of ITT, groups that worked exclusively through electronic means took longer to develop and were less likely to become high performers because of the isolation and lack of warmth that evolves over time when relationships are developed.

CREATING SUCCESSFUL QUALITY GROUPS

Is there a secret to creating a successful group, one that achieves the performing stage of group development and has high levels of both task performance and human resource maintenance over time? Research indicates that effective and successful groups have specific, well-defined goals, develop interdependent and collaborative relationships, share leadership, provide feedback, recognize and reward performance, and celebrate victories. Successful groups also need team leaders and members who are willing to make a commitment.[56]

With respect to task performance, quality and effectiveness is measured in terms of achieving goals. With respect to human resource maintenance, an effective group is one whose members are sufficiently satisfied with their task, accomplishments, and interpersonal relationships to work well together on an ongoing basis. The following is a classic listing of the characteristics of a successful and quality-focused group:[57]

- Members are loyal to one another and the leader.
- Members and leaders have a high degree of confidence and trust in each other.
- The group is eager to help members develop to their full potential.
- The members communicate fully and frankly all information relevant to the group's activities.

- Members feel secure in making decisions that seem appropriate to them.
- Activities of the group occur in a supportive atmosphere.
- Group values and goals express relevant values and needs of members.

CHALLENGES FOR GROUP LEADERS

Most group leaders are not born with all the right skills or answers. Leading a group involves skills that few managers understand at first. The command- and control-type behaviors they were encouraged to demonstrate before leading a group are no longer appropriate. Some of the most critical skills needed immediately are communication, conflict resolution, and coaching. Other skills that can be learned but take much longer to develop include the patience to share information, trust to let others make decision, and the ability to let go of power,

To increase the likelihood that the group will be effective, a manager can diagnose the group dimensions discussed earlier—size, member composition, roles, norms, and cohesiveness. Next, consider how information technology will be involved in the group's work. For example, match the group size with the demands of the task that needs to be accomplished; determine if the task is routine or nonroutine before deciding if the group should be homogeneous or diverse; consider the roles that are required; and determine what the organizational norms are.

MANAGERIAL IMPLICATIONS

Developing effective work groups is an even greater challenge when a group or team consists of members from different cultures and with different ethnic backgrounds. Effective groups require that members shed some of their notions of individualism and accept a different set of philosophies in the workplace. We conclude this chapter by providing some guidelines for creating more effective groups. For a group to be successful, the following elements must be developed:[58]

- *Trust.* Group members must learn not be wary of each other. Lack of trust is an obstacle to flexibility and information flow.
- *Involvement.* Every group member's participation counts, and people are dependent on each other, regardless of where they fit into the hierarchy.
- *Emphasis on others' strengths, not weaknesses.* Group members must look for ways to complement, rather than compete with, each other.
- *Persuasive and nonpaternalistic leadership.* Managers must become good listeners and be willing to involve others in decision making. Everyone must take personal responsibility for completing the task.
- *Precise objectives.* Members need to have clearly defined, precise goals and specific deadlines.

This chapter has examined the foundations of individual and group behavior. We discussed some of the ways in which individuals differ, including attitudes, personality, perception, and ability. When organizations are made up of individuals with diverse characteristics such as job-related knowledge and skills, personality, age, race, and gender, merely placing employees in groups does not mean they will be effective. Clearly, the establishment of productive groups challenges managers. This is no easy task, although it can be important for organizational success.

TEAM LEADERS: MAGIC OR MANAGEMENT SKILLS

The three team leaders we profiled in the Managerial Incident at the chapter opening all faced new challenges. They were suddenly pushed into positions of team leadership without much training. The word from all three of their companies was that teams had the power to increase efficiency and productivity and reward workers with more control in their jobs. But overlooked in the midst of all this team talk was how confusing the experience could be.

Companies expect middle managers to metamorphose, effective yesterday, into star team leaders ready to coach, motivate, and empower. The problem is, few managers and even fewer companies understand the transformation process.

All three leaders profiled in the Managerial Incident accepted the challenge and developed a list of tips to pass on to other leaders in their organizations.

J. D. Bryant (Texas Instruments) had the opportunity to learn from other team leaders about planning, setting goals, and transferring responsibility. Currently he and three colleagues have taken training positions at TI's corporate services division to work with all new managers who need to be prepared and learn the necessary skills before they lead an effective team.

Bryant's tips: *Learn to truly share power. Worry about what you take on, not what you give up.*

Eric Doremus (Northrop Grumman) met with the 40 members of the B-2 bomber team a second time and told them what he could do for the team. He was hired primarily because they needed someone who could bring a much different perspective to the job, he was good at motivating people to do their best, and he could focus the team on the customer, which was not the way they were used to working. In addition, Doremus could help the team communicate better with its internal customer—Northrop Grumman—and see that the project was completed on time and within budget.

Doremus quickly learned that the most important task was not to be afraid to admit ignorance. Instead of trying to figure out everybody's job, he learned that he would succeed by helping this team feel as if they owned the project and by getting them whatever information they needed, financial or otherwise.

Doremus's tips: *Don't be afraid to admit ignorance. Get used to learning on the job.*

Reed Breland (Hewlett-Packard) at first let the team try to work out the problems, conflicts, and disruptive behaviors. He spoke to them about the problems, but was mainly interested in making sure the individuals understood that the work had to get done, regardless of how they got along. Nine months later the team was still squabbling. He knew he had to do something because it was beginning to affect the work of the whole unit.

Breland decided, rather than trying to determine who was right and wrong, to dissolve the team and had its members placed elsewhere. The team members are doing well in new assignments. He compares their dynamics with those of a sports team.

Breland's tip: *As a team leader it is important to know when to intervene in the group's process.*[59]

SUMMARY

- Attitudes are relatively lasting beliefs, feelings, and behavioral tendencies held by a person about specific objects, events, groups, issues, or people.

- Personality is the organized and distinctive pattern of behavior that characterizes an individual's adaptation to a situation; it endures over time and suggests tendencies to behave in certain ways. Several personality traits that have been linked to work behavior and performance include self-esteem, locus of control, Machiavellianism, Type A orientation, and self-monitoring.

- Perception is the way people experience, process, define, and interpret the world around them. Perceptual biases, such as stereotyping, halo-and-horn effects, and selective perception, cause managers to make errors that can be costly to the organization and to individuals.

- To reduce perceptual errors, managers must make a conscious effort to attend to relevant information, actively seek evidence of whether or not their perceptions are accurate, compare their perceptions with those of others, and look for objective measures in relation to their own perceptions.

- A group is defined as two or more interdependent individuals who interact with and influence one another in order to accomplish a common purpose. Groups can be classified as formal or informal.

- While most groups are in a continuous state of change, the group development process generally follows a five-stage developmental sequence: forming, storming, norming, performing, and adjourning.

- Achieving group effectiveness is no simple task, but awareness of the dimensions that influence groups should help in this endeavor. These dimensions include group size, composition, roles, norms, and cohesiveness.

- Information technology can influence groups in terms of the stage of development, the creation of groups, and the individual members' needs for communication richness.

KEY TERMS

Attitudes	Self-monitoring (SM)	Roles
Personality	Stereotyping	Task-oriented roles
Self-esteem	Halo-and-horn effect	Relationship-oriented roles
Locus of control	Selective perception	Self-oriented roles
Machiavellian personality	Group	Norms
Type A orientation	Formal groups	Cohesiveness
Type B orientation	Informal groups	Groupware

REVIEW QUESTIONS

1. Explain job satisfaction and why managers need to understand its importance in the workplace.

2. Describe self-monitoring and how it may affect the way team members of different cultures work together.

3. Identify and explain the difference between stereotyping and the halo effect.

4. Name a common stereotype. What attributes do you give that person?

5. Why would a manager need to understand an employee's locus of control?

6. Explain three types of ability.

7. Distinguish between a formal group and an informal group.

8. Define and discuss the five stages of group development.

9. Identify and discuss the five key dimensions that influence group effectiveness.

10. Describe the attributes of an effective group. Provide examples from your own experience or from an organization that you have read about in a recent publication.

11. How does information technology affect group development and performance?

DISCUSSION QUESTIONS

Improving Critical Thinking

1. Why would an organization be concerned with how satisfied employees are?

2. Have you ever violated a group norm? Discuss your behavior and the group's reaction.

3. Describe an effective and an ineffective group in which you have been a member. What role(s) did you play? What status did you have in the group? How cohesive was the group? What could you have done to make the group more effective?

4. Describe a stereotypical group to which you belong. What people or things belong to the group? Give an example of a member of the group who does not fit the stereotype.

5. Write a brief description of a junior in college majoring in business. How does your perception compare to others in your class? How would this description compare to students who attend a university different than yours?

Enhancing Communication Skills

6. Explain the ways managers can learn to reduce the perceptual errors that occur in the workplace. Prepare a presentation for a small group or the class that includes specific examples.

7. Identify and describe (either in writing or in a presentation) a formal group that you are a part of, and then describe any informal groups that exist within the formal group.

8. Interview a manager that participates in an electronically networked group. Explore this individual's attitude about the technique. How has this affected his job performance? Write up your interview results or present it to class as directed by your instructor.

Building Teamwork

9. Find an article in a current business magazine that describes how an organization is using groups to increase quality or organizational performance. Form a small group as directed by your instructor and share your findings with the group. Have the group select the best article and share it with the class.

10. Describe a group of which you have been a member and discuss its development over time. Did the group seem to proceed through all of the stages of group development? Why or why not? If you are not already part of a group for this class, form small groups as directed by your instructor and reach some consensus on your responses.

INFORMATION TECHNOLOGY: Insights and Solutions

1. Call several large consulting firms or organizations in your area to ask if they use any type of groupware for working with clients or customers. If organizations in your area do not use groupware products, check to see if this type of technology is available on your campus. If possible, ask to observe a group in session. What is your assessment of the differences in the way participants interact and solve problems?

2. Search the Internet for the most recent technology available for group meetings via videoconferencing and associated pricing. Next, using a spreadsheet such as Excel or QuattroPro, do a comparative analysis on the cost of buying and maintaining teleconferencing technology versus sending a group of individuals to a customer's site for a meeting. At what point does the equipment begin to become financially beneficial for an organization? What other benefits or negative considerations should be part of an organization's decision to use this type of technology?

3. As we discussed in the chapter, the public sector is only recently beginning to use groups as part of organizational decision-making and effectiveness measures. Search the Internet for articles that discuss where these have been tried and have been successful or not successful.

ETHICS: Take a Stand

Steve is a member of a group of four people assigned to write a report on ethics in the workplace for a management class. The irony of the situation is that he is faced with an ethical dilemma. It is the day the report is due, and he has discovered that Torri, another member of the group, has plagiarized her portion of the report.

Steve immediately told the other members of the group about the situation. The other members were good friends with Torri and were sympathetic to her personal situation. She was under a lot of pressure to perform well in this class. She had two children and was working her way through school on financial aid. Because of some personal demands last semester, she was put on academic probation. Anything less than a B in this course, and she would be forced to leave school. Besides, the group members did not want to be responsible for having her expelled. They felt justified in ignoring this new knowledge and taking their chances with the report as it was written. After all, "they hadn't plagiarized." Everyone in the group felt that the report would earn an A. "Why start trouble with the professor?" they asked. There was little time remaining. Steve felt his options were severely limited.

For Discussion

1. How would you suggest Steve handle the situation? What are his options?
2. Discuss the group's norms.
3. In which stage of development is the group? Will this affect the action taken?
4. Now, take the professor's position. How would you handle the situation if Steve told you what had happened?

THINKING CRITICALLY: Debate the Issue

ARE GROUP GOALS NECESSARY?

The class should be divided into groups of four. First, each group divides into pairs. One pair is assigned the position that group goals are of no use, and the other pair is assigned the position that groups cannot function without goals.

The pairs meet separately to prepare as forceful a three-minute presentation of their position as possible. The group of four meets. Each pair presents its position, being as forceful and persuasive as possible, while the other pair takes notes and asks for clarification of anything that is not fully understood. Each pair is allowed about three minutes to present its position.

The perspectives of each group are now reversed, each pair arguing the opposing pair's position. They should elaborate on the opposing position, seeing if they can think of any new arguments or facts that the opposing pair did not present.

The group of four should derive a position that all members can agree to and summarize the best arguments from each position.

Perspective of *Groups Cannot Function without Goals*

To support your position, use the rationale that goals guide actions and allow group members to plan and coordinate efforts. Groups cannot exist unless the activities of their members are directed toward achieving something.

Perspective of *Group Goals Are of No Use*

To support your position, use the rationale that goals are often stated in such vague terms that they could not possibly be effective guides for the actions of members. Appraisals of group progress usually reveal that groups have fallen short of their goals.

Video Case

GE MEDICAL SYSTEMS

Home Page: {http://www.ge.com/medical/}

In 1986, GE Medical Systems began forming work teams (called GEMS Teams) at its Florence, South Carolina, factory. Initially, some of the employees were skeptical. Teamwork meant a shift in responsibility from management to employee-directed work teams. The skepticism resulted from a disbelief on the part of many rank-and-file employees that management would give up any of their power. However, from the beginning, the teams were successful, and the employees could see that management had a genuine interest in seeing the teams succeed. By 1988, all of the employees at the plant were involved at some level in a work team. This was not accomplished at a small cost. To provide employees the skills that complement teamwork, a high level of training was required, particularly in the areas of communication and feedback skills. The move from traditional management to employee-directed work teams also demanded a change in the culture of the factory.

Today, there are 26 employee-directed work teams in the factory. The teams are involved in a wide variety of activities, ranging from routine production to problem solving and special projects. The case provides samples of interviews with managers and rank-and-file employees about the success of teamwork at the Florence factory. Most employees see teamwork as a positive development, which has increased their output and the pride that they have in their work. The employees also feel that the shift from traditional management to employee-directed work teams has had a positive effect on the culture of the factory. Because the managers of the plant often work closely with the teams, the traditional walls that separate management and rank-and-file employees are coming down. One employee remarked that she is no longer nervous when a manager walks through the factory. She said that she is now more nervous about disappointing a team member than a manager. Another employee remarked that for the first time she believes that everyone in the plant is working toward the same goals.

For the managers at the Florence plant, the movement toward employee-directed work teams has placed them in a coaching rather than a traditional management role. An example of how this works was illustrated in one of the interviews. A manager indicated that prior to the implementation of employee directed work teams, when he had a problem to solve, he would have simply found a solution to the problem and told the workers what to do. Now, he would take the problem to the team that would most likely be affected, and act as a coach in helping the team arrive at a solution. Once a solution was agreed upon, the team would then be implementing their solution, rather than his idea, in making the change.

Clearly, the implementation of employee-directed work teams at GE Medical in Florence has been a success. Hopefully, the experience of this organization will serve as a model for other firms interested in improving organizational effectiveness through employee-directed work teams.

For Discussion

1. In what ways has the implementation of employee-directed work teams at GE Medical in Florence increased employee job satisfaction, organizational commitment, and job involvement?

2. Has the implementation of teamwork in the plant had any other positive effects relative to managing individual behavior?

3. Would you enjoy being a part of an employee-directed work team? Why or why not?

ARE YOU SURE WE'RE IN THE SAME CLASS?

CASE

Teri was studying for her Management Principles exam when she spotted Clark, another student in her class. "Hey, Clark, would you like to study together for this exam? I could use some help reviewing these concepts from the chapter on individual behavior."

"Why bother studying?" Clark responded. "It doesn't matter how hard I try in that class, I just can't do well. Professor Danos's tests are impossible to study for—I do just as well guessing at the answers as I do studying. You know those multiple-choice questions are randomly selected, and it's just a matter of luck anyway. I guess I wasn't meant to be a management major."

"Clark, it sounds like you aren't doing well in the class. Maybe I can help. I really am enjoying the class and especially Professor Danos. I met Professor Danos at orientation my first summer on campus, and when I found out he was a scuba diver, I just knew he would be a great teacher! I like the way he explains things in language you can understand, and the examples he gives are always relevant to the topic. I think he makes the material in the text so interesting. I know I can do even better on this test if I spend enough time looking up all the sources of information that Professor Danos gave us to read."

Clark couldn't believe that Teri and he were in the same class! To Clark, the class was so disorganized. Professor Danos never followed the material in the book and was always going off on some unrelated topic that made the material even more confusing. "Professors are all alike, they just love to confuse students. If he would just tell you what you had to study and follow the textbook, the class might make sense. After all, isn't that what a textbook is for? Oh well, I guess there isn't anything I can do now anyway."

For Discussion

1. From the information given in the case, do you think Teri has an external or internal locus of control? What about Clark? Give some examples to justify your decision.

2. Why do Clark and Teri have different impressions of the same class?

3. Have Clark and Teri made any errors in perception? Has this ever happened to you?

EXPERIENTIAL EXERCISE 14.1

Locus of Control

For each of the following 10 questions, indicate the extent to which you agree or disagree using the following scale:

Strongly Disagree	Slightly Disagree	Disagree	Neither Agree nor Disagree	Slightly Agree	Agree	Strongly Agree
1	2	3	4	5	6	7

_____ 1. When I get what I want, it's usually because I worked hard for it.

_____ 2. When I make plans, I am almost certain to make them work.

_____ 3. On an exam or in competition, I like to know how well I do relative to everyone else.

_____ 4. I can learn almost anything if I set my mind to it.

_____ 5. My major accomplishments are entirely due to my hard work and ability.

_____ 6. I prefer games involving some luck over games requiring pure skill.

_____ 7. I usually don't set goals, because I have a hard time following through on them.

_____ 8. Competition discourages excellence.

_____ 9. Often people get ahead just by being lucky.

_____10. It's pointless to keep working on something that's too difficult for me.

Scoring: For questions 1 through 5, sum the values, and enter the results on the line: _____. For questions 6 through 10, reverse the scale so that 1 equals strongly agree, 2 equals agree, and so on. Now add the point values for questions 6 through 10, and enter the result on the line: _____. Sum both subtotals, and enter the total: _____.

Scores can range from a low of 7 to a high of 70. The higher you score on this questionnaire, the more you tend to believe that you are generally responsible for what happens to you. Higher scores are associated with an internal locus of control. In general, scores above 50 indicate an internal locus of control. In contrast, low scores (below 40) are associated with an external locus of control. Scoring low indicates that you tend to believe that forces beyond your control, such as other powerful people, fate, or chance, are responsible for what happens to you.

For Discussion

Internal versus External Locus of Control

1. *Use of information:* Externals make fewer attempts to acquire information and are more satisfied than internals with the amount of information they have. Internals are better at utilizing information than externals.

2. *Independence:* Externals are less independent than internals and more susceptible to the influence of others.

3. *Performance:* Internals perform better than externals on learning and problem-solving tasks when performance leads to valued rewards.

4. *Satisfaction:* Externals are less satisfied than internals and more alienated. Internals have a stronger job satisfaction/performance relationship than externals.

5. *Motivation:* Internals exhibit greater work motivation, expect that working hard leads to good performance, and feel more control over their performance and time commitment than externals.

6. *Risk:* Externals show less self-control and caution but engage in less risky behavior than internals.

SOURCE: D. Hellriegel, J. W. Slocum, R. W. Woodman, "Measuring Locus of Control," in *Organizational Behavior*, 6th ed. (St. Paul, Minn.: West Publishing Co., 1991), 97–98. Used with permission.

EXPERIENTIAL EXERCISE 14.2

Your Cohesion Behavior

How does your behavior affect group cohesion? When you want to increase group cohesion, what do you do? How would you describe your behavior in influencing group cohesion? The following statements should help you reflect upon how your behavior influences the cohesion of the groups to which you belong. Keep your responses to these statements in mind as you work in a group and experience the group's development.

Use a scale from 1 (almost never) to 9 (almost always) to respond honestly to each statement. Place the number (1 through 9) in the space to the left of the statement number.

Almost Never								Almost Always
1	2	3	4	5	6	7	8	9

_____ **1.** I try to make sure that everyone enjoys being a member of the group.

_____ **2.** I discuss my ideas, feelings, and reactions to what is currently taking place in the group.

_____ **3.** I express acceptance and support when other members disclose their ideas, feelings, and reactions to what is currently taking place in the group.

_____ **4.** I try to make all members feel valued and appreciated.

_____ **5.** I try to include other members in group activities.

_____ **6.** I'm influenced by other group members.

_____ **7.** I take risks in expressing new ideas and my current feelings.

_____ **8.** I express liking, affection, and concern for other members.

_____ **9.** I encourage group norms that support individuality and personal expression.

_____ Total

Scoring: Add all your answers together to get a total cohesiveness behavior score. Scores can range from a low of 9 to a high of 81.

Scores of 9-27 indicate low cohesion behavior. This often occurs early in the life of a group when the group first forms, it is trying to determine goals, and members are becoming acquainted.

Scores of 28-62 indicate a middle ground of cohesion behavior. There may be conflict occurring that you are not comfortable with or you may not be committed to the group. In this case, it is more important to examine which statements scored low and which scored high rather than examining the total score..

Scores from 63-72 indicate your behavior is very positive in establishing an effective group.

Scores above 72 are generally considered high. However, keep in mind that these are your perceptions of your own behavior. It is important to talk with other members of the group to see if they share your view.

All nine statements identify important factors for group cohesion. Discuss your answers with several other group members. These statements provide you a picture of your own group cohesion behavior and can be used to focus upon several ways of increasing group cohesion.

- Statement 1 describes a general attempt to keep cohesion high.

- Statements 2 and 3 pertain to the expression of ideas and feelings and the support for others expressing ideas and feelings; such personal participation is essential for cohesiveness and for the development of trust. Statements 4 and 8 also focus upon support for, and liking of, other group members.

- Statement 5 refers to the inclusion of other members, and Statement 6 concerns one's willingness to be influenced by other members.

- Statements 7 and 9 center on the acceptance of individuality within the group.

ENDNOTES

1. S. Caminiti, "What Team Leaders Need to Know," *Fortune*, February 20, 1995, 93-100.

2. H. Sims Jr. and C. Manz, *Company of Heroes: Unleashing the Power of Self-Leadership* (New York: Wiley, 1996); H. P. Sims and P Lorenzi, *The New Leadership Paradigm* (Newbury Park, Calif.: Sage Press, 1992).

3. H. Sims Jr. and C. Manz, *Company of Heroes.*

4. L. W. Porter, R. M. Steers, R. T. Mowday, and P. V. Boulian, "Organizational Commitment, Job Satisfaction, and Turnover among Psychiatric Technicians," *Journal of Applied Psychology,* 5, 1974, 603.

5. P. C. Smith, L. M. Kendall, and C. L. Hulin, *The Measurement of Satisfaction in Work and Retirement* (Chicago: Rand McNally, 1969).

6. L. Roberson, "Prediction of Job Satisfaction from Characteristics of Personal Work Goals," *Journal of Organizational Behavior,* 11, 1990, 29-41.

7. P. C. Smith, L. M. Kendall, and C. L. Hulin, *The Measurement of Satisfaction.*

8. E. Robinson, *Why Aren't You More Like Me?* (Dubuque, Iowa: Kendall/Hunt, 1991).

9. S. Coppersmith, *The Antecedents of Self-Esteem* (San Francisco: Freeman, 1967).

10. M. G. Mitchell and P. M. Fandt. "Examining the Relationship between Role-Defining Characteristics and Self-Esteem of College Students," *College Student Journal,* 33, 1995, 99-120.

11. A. Korman, "Self-Esteem Variable in Vocational Choice,"

Journal of Applied Psychology, 50, 1966, 479-86; A. Korman, "Relevance of Personal Need Satisfaction for Overall Satisfaction as a Function of Self-Esteem," *Journal of Applied Psychology,* 51, 1967, 533-38.

12. G. Mitchell and P. Fandt, "Confident Role Models for Tomorrow's Classrooms: The Self-Esteem of Education Majors," *Education,* 113, 1993, 556-62.

13. J. B. Rotter, "Generalized Expectancies for Internal versus External Control of Reinforcement," *Psychological Monographs,* 80, 1966, 1-28.

14. C. R. Anderson, D. Hellriegel, and J. Slocum, "Managerial Response to Environmentally Induced Stress," *Academy of Management Journal,* 20, 2, 1977, 260-72.

15. R. M. Kanter and R. I. Corn, "Do Cultural Differences Make a Business Difference? Contextual Factors Affecting Cross Cultural Relationship Success," *Journal of Management Development,* 13, 2, 1993, 5-23; V. J. Marsick, E. Turner, and L. Cederholm, "International as a Team," *Management Review,* March 1989, 46-49.

16. R. G. Vleeming, "Machiavellianism: A Preliminary Review," *Psychological Reports,* February 1979, 295-310.

17. D. A. Ralston, D. J. Gustafson, F. M. Cheung, and R. H. Terpstr, "Differences in Managerial Values: A Study of U.S., Hong Kong, and PRC Managers," *Journal of International Business Studies,* 2, 1993, 249-75.

18. Based on M. Jamal, "Type A Behavior and Job Performance: Some Suggestive Findings," *Journal of Human Stress,* Summer 1985, 60-68.

19. J. Bishop, "Prognosis for the 'Type A' Personality," *The Wall Street Journal,* January 14, 1992, 9H; M. Freidman and R. Roseman, *Type A Behavior and Your Heart* (New York: Knopf, 1974).

20. H. Sims Jr. and C. Manz, *Company of Heroes.*

21. G. H. Dobbins, W. S. Long, E. J. Dedrick, and T. C. Clemons, "The Role of Self-Monitoring and Gender on Leader Emergence: A Laboratory and Field Study," *Journal of Management,* 16, 3, 1990, 609-18.

22. "Throwing Stones at the Glass Ceiling," *Business Week,* August 19, 1991, 19.

23. P. Fandt and G. Stevens, "Evaluation Bias in the Business Classroom: Evidence Related to the Effects of Previous Experiences," *Journal of Psychology,* 125, 1991, 469-77.

24. The most recent case is Texaco, Inc., settled in November, 1996: J. Fitzgerald, "Texaco Settles Racial Bias Suit for Record $176 Million," The Associated Press. Denny's settled in 1993 but did not begin training until 1995: F. Rice, "Denny's Changes Its Spots," *Fortune,* May 13, 1996, 133-42.

25. M. Lee, "Diversity Training Brings Unity to Small Companies," *The Wall Street Journal,* September 2, 1995, 82.

26. D. Dearborn and H. Simon, "Selection Perception: A Note on the Departmental Identification of Executives," *Sociometry,* 21, 1958, 140-44.

27. A. Sprout, "The Internet Inside Your Company: The Pyramid Scheme," *Fortune,* November 27, 1995, 161-68. ©1995 Time Inc. All rights reserved.

28. K. Labich, "Elite Teams Get the Job Done," *Fortune,* February 19, 1996, 90-99; H. Sims Jr. and C. Manz, *Company of Heroes.*

29. This definition is adapted from M. E. Shaw, *Group Dynamics: The Psychology of Small Group Behavior* (New York: McGraw-Hill, 1981), 8.

30. For a thorough discussion, see D. W. Johnson and R. T. Johnson, *Cooperation and Competition: Theory and Research* (Edina, Minn.: Interaction Book Co., 1989); C. Larson and F. LaFasto, *Teamwork: What Must Go Right/What Can Go Wrong* (Newbury Park, Calif.: Sage Publications, 1989).

31. B. W. Tuckman, "Development Sequence in Small Groups," *Psychological Bulletin,* 63, 1965, 384-99; B. W. Tuckman and M. Jensen, "Stages of Small Group Development Revisited," *Group and Organization Studies,* 2, 1977, 419-27.

32. J. O'Brian, "Making New Hires Members of the Team," *Supervisory Management,* May 1992, 4; D. W. Johnson and F. P. Johnson, *Joining Together: Group Theory and Group Skills* (Boston: Allyn & Bacon, 1994), 18-21.

33. D. W. Johnson and F. P. Johnson, *Joining Together,* 20-22.

34. I. L. Janis, *Victims of Groupthink,* 2d ed. (Boston: Houghton Mifflin, 1982).

35. G. Whyte, "Groupthink Reconsidered," *Academy of Management Review,* 14, 1989, 40-55.

36. R. Poe, "The Secret of Teamwork," *Success,* June 1991, 72.

37. S. L. Keck, and M. Tushman, "Environmental and Organizational Context and Executive Team Structure," *Academy of Management Journal,* 36, 1993, 1314-44.

38. B. Berelson and G. Steiner, *Human Behaviors: An Inventory of Scientific Findings* (New York: Harcourt, Brace & World, 1964), 356-60.

39. N. Kerr and S. Bruun, "The Dispensability of Member Effort and Group Motivation Losses: Free-Rider Effects," *Journal of Personality and Social Psychology,* 44, 1983, 78-94.

40. For a more thorough discussion, see D. W. Johnson and P. F. Johnson, *Joining Together,* 248-52.

41. For more information see B. Latane, K. Williams, and S. Harkins, "Many Hands Make Light the Work: The Causes and Consequences of Social Loafing," *Journal of Personality and Social Psychology,* 37, 1978, 822-32; E. Weldon and G. Gargano, "Cognitive Effort in Additive Task Groups: The Effects of Shared Responsibility on the Quality of Multiattribute Judgments," *Organizational Behavior and Human Decision Processes,* 36, 1985, 340-61.

42. See reviews on group composition, diversity, and performance in M. E. Shaw, *Group Dynamics,* 232-33; D. W. Johnson and P. F. Johnson, *Joining Together,* 435-53.

43. D. W. Johnson and P. F. Johnson, *Joining Together,* 18-21.

44. T. L. Quick, *Successful Team Building* (New York: AMACOM, 1992).

45. Based on K. J. Benne and P. Sheats, "Functional Roles of Group Members," *Journal of Social Issues,* 4, 1948, 42-47.

46. K. Labich, "Elite Teams Get the Job Done."

47. K. L. Bettenhausen and J. K. Murnighan, "The Development of an Intragroup Norm and the Effects of Interpersonal and Structural Changes," *Administrative Science Quarterly,* 36, 1990, 20-35.

48. N. Evans and P. Jarvis, "Group Cohesion: A Review and Reevaluation," *Small Group Behavior,* 11, 1980, 359-70.

49. T. Kayser, *Building Team Power: How to Unleash the Collaborative Genius of Work Teams* (Burr Ridge, IL: Irwin, 1994); T. L. Quick, *Successful Team Building;* S. Cohen, "A Monkey on the Back, A Lump in the Throat," *Inside Sports,* 4, 1992, 20.

50. A more thorough discussion of this relationship appears in P. Fandt, S. Cady, and M. Sparks, "The Impact of Reward Interdependency on the Synergogy Model of Cooperative Performance: Designing an Effective Team Environment," *Small Group Research,* 24, 1993, 101-15.

51. I. L. Janis, *Victims of Groupthink.*

52. H. Park, P. Lewis, and P. Fandt, "Ethnocentrism and Group Cohesiveness in International Joint Ventures," in *Multinational Strategic Alliances,* ed. R. Culpan (Binghamton, N.Y.: International Business Press, 1993).

53. T. Cox Jr., "The Multicultural Organization," *Academy of Management Executive,* 5, 1991, 34-47.

54. R. McLeod Jr., *Management Information Systems,* 6th ed. (Upper Saddle River, N.J.: Prentice Hall, 1995).

55. T. Peters, *The Pursuit of Wow,* (New York: Vintage Books, 1994).

56. T. Kayser, *Building Team Power;* S. Caminiti, "What Team Leaders Need to Know."

57. Adapted from M. E. Shaw, *Group Dynamics;* W. Kiechell III, "The Art of the Corporate Task Force," *Fortune,* January 28, 1991, 104-106.

58. Combined from key points in T. Kayser, *Building Team Power;* S. Caminiti, "What Team Leaders Need to Know"; K. Green and D. Seymour, "Who's Going to Run General Motors?" (Princeton, N.J.: Petersen's Guides, 1991).

59. S. Caminiti, "What Team Leaders Need to Know."

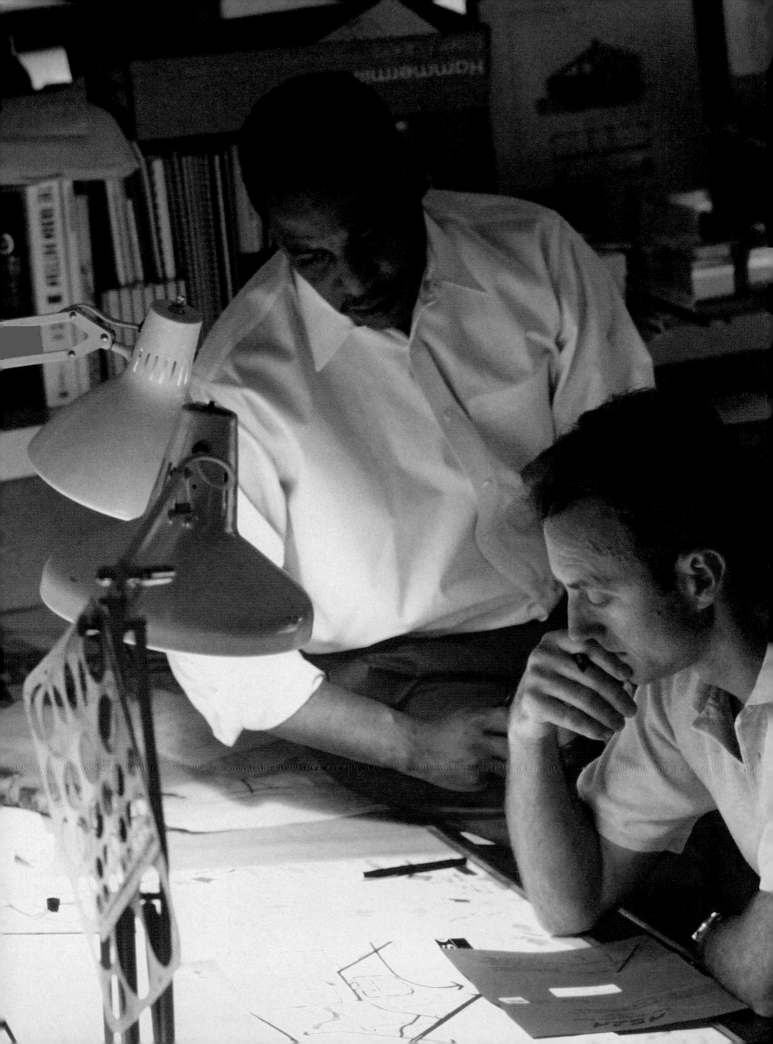

Motivating Organizational Members

■ CHAPTER OVERVIEW

An organization's energy comes from the motivation of its employees. Although their abilities play a crucial role in determining their work performance, so does their motivation. Managers must ensure that employees are motivated to perform their tasks to the best of their abilities. Through motivation, managers are better able to create a working environment that is conducive to good effort and where employees are inspired to work to accomplish the organization's goals.

In this chapter we discuss motivation as the force that energizes and gives direction to behavior. Many models of motivation and definitions have been developed and examined over the last 40 years. We examine need-based theories, process theories, theories that focus on how employees learn desired work behaviors, and several contemporary approaches to motivation. Finally, we will consider motivation from an international perspective and see how it differs from motivation in a purely domestic organization.

■ LEARNING OBJECTIVES

When you have finished studying this chapter, you should be able to:

- Explain the basic motivation process.
- Describe the different approaches to motivation.
- Define need-based theories of employee motivation.
- Explain the basic elements of Herzberg's theory of motivation.
- Describe how content and process theories differ.
- Explain how expectancy theory can be applied in the workplace.
- Describe the use of equity theory to motivate employees.
- Describe how reinforcement theory applies the principles of reinforcement to employee performance.
- Identify how goal setting is used to motivate performance.
- Discuss how information technology can affect employee motivation.
- Understand the importance of motivation from an international perspective.

USAA STRIVES FOR EXCEPTIONAL SERVICE

The United Services Automobile Association (USAA), located in San Antonio, Texas, is one of the nation's largest insurers of privately owned automobiles and homes. The company, which is owned by its policyholders, covers a phenomenal 95 percent of active-duty military officers. But USAA is faced with a myriad of difficult challenges, including changing demographics of its customers, changing demographics of its employees, and a market niche that is shrinking.

According to Robert Herres, chief executive of USAA, the underlying causes of the company's problems were the decline in the number of armed forces commissioned in the past few years, an employee pool that was becoming more and more diversified and harder to motivate, and employees' lack of motivation and the resulting lack of service to customers. Herres was challenged by the notion of expanding in a contracting market. How? His answer was to offer customers a progressively wider range of services. But transforming itself into a life and health insurance company, a discount brokerage firm, a mutual-fund manager, a travel agency, a buying club, and a bank requires that employees become knowledgeable and trained in every aspect of the company's mix of services.

To be effective, USAA employees would have to know how the whole organization fit together, rather than just about their own section of the company. Communication between departments that had often resulted in the serious problem of poor customer service needed attention, and an information system needed to be developed that was not only user-friendly but also applicable for all service units of USAA. Employees would need to be trained to use the information system and convinced that the system would make their jobs easier, not take jobs away.

Herres was determined to develop an aggressive motivational program to attack these problems. Could he successfully motivate employees and move USAA toward the goal of providing expanded and exceptional service in a shrinking market with dramatically changing customers and employees?[1]

INTRODUCTION

Robert Herres, CEO of USAA, is clearly facing motivational challenges. Like most effective managers, he is concerned about motivation because the work motives of employees affect their productivity and the quality of their work. Also like most managers, one of Herres's responsibilities is to channel employee motivation toward achieving organizational goals.[2]

As the concerns for productivity and quality are increasing at the global level, so is the search for the "right" theory or the "right" approach to work motivation. Many models have been developed and examined over the last four decades, and a variety of definitions have emerged in the process. In this chapter we explore several approaches to motivation, including a broad classification of need-based theories and process theories. We begin by looking at need-based theories that examine motivation based on specific human needs or the factors within a person. Next, we focus on expectancy and equity theories—two process theories of motivation. Reinforcement theory and its application in the workplace are discussed next. We then look at the impact of information technology on motivation before examining several contemporary approaches to motivation, including goal setting, participative management, and money as a motivator. Finally, we take an international perspective to better appreciate how diversity and the global environment can affect motivation of employees in the international arena.

BASIC MOTIVATION PROCESS

How does motivation occur? Since the early work of the scientific management and human relations theorists, management scholars have developed a number of different theories that help us understand what motivates people at work.[3] **Motivation** is generally defined as the forces acting on or within a person that cause that person to behave in a specific, goal-directed manner.[4] It is a psychological process that gives behavior purpose and direction. Although the process of motivation is quite complex, a general framework appears in Figure 15.1. As the model indicates, needs are drives or forces that initiate behavior. For example, people often need recognition, feelings of accomplishment, food, companionship, and growth. Needs are coupled with knowledge and thoughts about various efforts we might make and the potential rewards we might receive. When needs or cognitive activities become strong enough, we do something to satisfy them. If the activity leads to satisfaction, we usually feel rewarded. This reward also informs us that our behavior was appropriate and can be used again in the future.

The motivation theories that we present in this chapter are general approaches to the *what* and *how* of behavior. But we should remember that motivation is only one of many explanations of human behavior. Though some people view motivation as a personal trait—that is, some have it and others don't—this is not true. Certainly, individuals differ in their motivational drive, but motivation is the result of the interaction between the individual and the situation. Consequently, the level of motivation varies both between individuals and within individuals at different times.[5]

Motivation
The forces acting on or within a person that cause the person to behave in a specific, goal-directed manner.

APPROACHES TO MOTIVATION

Motivation can be studied through several broad approaches. Content or need-based theories emphasize specific human needs or the factors within a person that energize, direct, and stop behavior. Process theories take a more dynamic view of motivation. These theories focus on understanding the thought or cognitive processes that take place within the individual's mind and act to affect

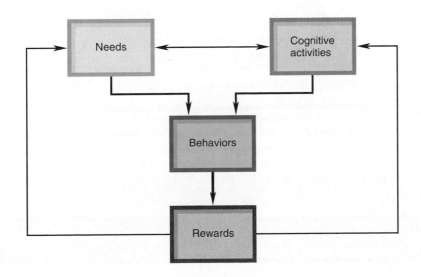

FIGURE 15.1
A general framework for the motivation process

behavior. More contemporary approaches to motivation include goal setting and participative management. We examine each of these approaches in the next sections.

NEED-BASED THEORIES OF EMPLOYEE MOTIVATION

Many factors are believed to influence a person's desire to perform work or behave in a certain way. Need-based theories explain motivation primarily as a phenomenon that occurs intrinsically, or within an individual. Here we look at three widely recognized need-based motivation theories: Maslow's hierarchy of needs, Herzberg's two-factor theory, and McClelland's acquired-needs theory.

Maslow's Hierarchy of Needs

Maslow's hierarchy of needs is the most widely recognized theory of motivation.[6] According to this theory, a person has five fundamental needs: physiological, security, affiliation, esteem, and self-actualization.[7] Figure 15.2 shows these five needs arranged in a hierarchy.

Maslow separated the five needs into higher and lower levels. He described physiological and security needs as lower-order needs, which are generally satisfied externally, and affiliation, esteem, and self-actualization as higher-order needs, which are satisfied internally.

Physiological needs
Food, water, air, and shelter are physiological needs.

Physiological Needs   At the bottom of the hierarchy are **physiological needs.** Food, water, air, and shelter are all physiological needs and are on the lowest level in Maslow's hierarchy. People concentrate on satisfying these needs before turning to higher-order needs. Managers must understand that to the extent employees are motivated by physiological needs, their concerns do not center on the work they are doing. They will accept any job that serves to meet their needs. Managers who focus on physiological needs in trying to mo-

FIGURE 15.2

Maslow's hierarchy of needs requiring fulfillment in the work environment

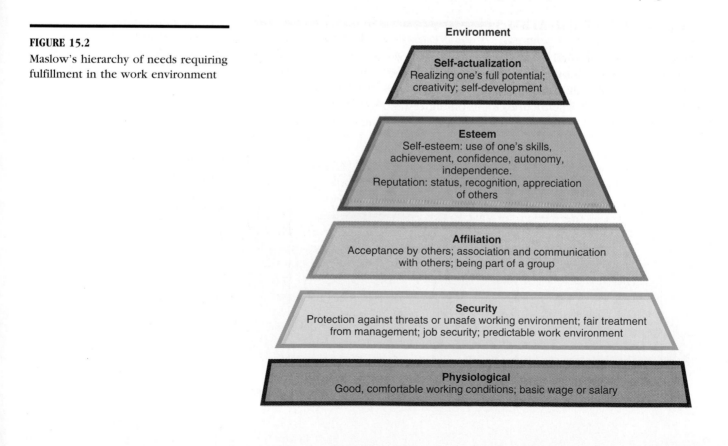

Environment

Self-actualization
Realizing one's full potential; creativity; self-development

Esteem
Self-esteem: use of one's skills, achievement, confidence, autonomy, independence.
Reputation: status, recognition, appreciation of others

Affiliation
Acceptance by others; association and communication with others; being part of a group

Security
Protection against threats or unsafe working environment; fair treatment from management; job security; predictable work environment

Physiological
Good, comfortable working conditions; basic wage or salary

tivate subordinates assume that people work mainly for money and are primarily concerned with comfort, avoidance of fatigue, and their rate of pay.

Security Needs   Next in the hierarchy are **security needs,** which reflect the desire to have a safe physical and emotional environment. Job security, grievance procedures, and health insurance and retirement plans are used to satisfy employees' security needs. Like physiological needs, unsatisfied security needs cause people to be preoccupied with satisfying them. People who are motivated primarily by security needs value their jobs mainly as a defense against the loss of basic need satisfaction. Managers who feel that security needs are most important will often emphasize rules, job security, and fringe benefits.

> **Security needs**
> The desire to have a safe physical and emotional environment.

Affiliation Needs   **Affiliation needs** include the desire for friendship, love, and a feeling of belonging. An individual with high affiliation needs focuses on obtaining love, affection, and a sense of belonging in her relationships with others. When physiological and security needs have been satisfied, affiliation needs become a more important source of motivation. When affiliation needs are primary sources of motivation, individuals value their work as an opportunity for finding and establishing friendly interpersonal relationships.

> **Affiliation needs**
> The desire for friendship, love, and a feeling of belonging.

Esteem Needs   Fourth in the hierarchy are **esteem needs.** These needs are met by personal feelings of achievement and self-worth and by recognition, respect, and prestige from others. People with esteem needs want others to accept them for what they are and to perceive them as competent and able. Managers who focus on esteem needs try to foster employees' pride in their work and use public rewards and recognition for services to motivate them.

> **Esteem needs**
> Personal feelings of achievement, self-worth, recognition, respect, and prestige from others.

As Managing for Excellence describes, Anson Dorrance, the UNC soccer coach, uses two of these need factors in motivating players. First, he focuses on affiliation needs by encouraging players to be connected and maintain a network of personal relationships. Second, he uses esteem needs by publicly recognizing excellent performance and personally recognizing and respecting them.[8]

Self-Actualization Needs   Finally, at the top of the hierarchy are **self-actualization needs.** Self-fulfillment and the opportunity to achieve one's potential are considered self-actualization needs. People who strive for self-actualization accept themselves and use their abilities to the fullest and most creative extent. Managers who emphasize self-actualization may involve employees in designing jobs or make special assignments that capitalize on employees' unique skills. Many entrepreneurs who break away from jobs in large corporations to start their own business may be looking for a way to satisfy their self-actualization needs.

> **Self-actualization needs**
> Needs for self-fulfillment and the opportunity to achieve one's potential.

Maslow's hierarchy provides a convenient framework for managers. It suggests that individuals have various needs and that they try to satisfy those needs using a priority system or hierarchy. Some research indicates that higher-order needs increase in importance over lower-order needs as individuals move up the organizational hierarchy. Other studies have reported that needs vary according to a person's career stage, organization size, and even geographical location. One of the major criticisms of Maslow's theory, however, is that there is no consistent evidence that the satisfaction of a need at one level will decrease its importance and increase the importance of the next-higher needs.

Herzberg's Two-Factor Theory

Herzberg's two-factor theory provides another way to examine employee needs. Herzberg examined the relationship between job satisfaction and productivity within a group of professional accountants and engineers.[9] He found that the factors leading to job satisfaction were separate and distinct from those that lead to job dissatisfaction—hence, the term *two-factor theory.*

Managing for Excellence

COACH DISCOVERS THE KEYS TO MOTIVATIONAL TECHNIQUES

In 1979, Anson Dorrance took over as head coach for the University of North Carolina women's soccer team. To prepare for this challenge, Dorrance went back to his own team experiences as a UNC soccer star and started reading some of the traditional motivational materials that were used in coaching, from sports stars and legendary sports. At first he tried using these traditional techniques until finally the team members' lack of any visible changes signaled that he was on the wrong track.

Dorrance must have learned from these early experiences, since he has put together the most dominant college athletic program in history. His women's teams have compiled an extraordinary 348-10-10 collegiate record since 1979, and in 1996 the team narrowly missed taking the UNC's tenth straight NCAA championship.

Dorrance traces much of that success to specific motivational techniques he has developed over the years. First, he has found that with women, the key is finding what will trigger their self-confidence. He works preseason charges ferociously to develop skills and confidence. However, once women begin to bond with teammates, they tend to lose their competitive edge. While men compete naturally, women prefer not to compete against people they like. To counteract this trait, Dorrance developed his next motivational technique. He rates every player's performance and very visibly posts updated rankings each week. Players use this information to compare themselves with others and maintain their motivational edge. Practices become more like a war.

The third motivational technique Dorrance uses is to establish a personal relationship with each player. According to Dorrance, men respond to leaders who demonstrate strength and competence, while women want to experience a leader's humanity. They do their best only if they believe they have a personal connection to the leader.

Finally, Dorrance encourages his players to be connected and maintain an intricate network of relationships. He has found that the women players are sensitive to the internal rhythms of the team; if two players are feuding, the whole group is thrown out of whack. The connectedness is also critical for players to allow them to handle the pressures of maintaining the UNC's extremely high record of success.

SOURCE: K. Labich, "Elite Teams Get the Job Done," *Fortune*, February 19, 1996, 90–99.

The two-factor model is shown in Figure 15.3. At the top are the sources of work satisfaction, otherwise termed *satisfiers* or *motivator factors*. The sources of dissatisfaction, or *hygiene factors*, are shown at the bottom.

Motivator factors
Related to job content or what people actually do in their work.

Motivator Factors **Motivator factors** are related to job content, or what people actually do in their work, and are associated with an individual's positive feelings about the job. Based on Herzberg's theory, motivator factors include the work itself, recognition, advancement, a sense of achievement, and responsibilities.

Hygiene factors
Associated with the job context or environment in which the job is performed.

Hygiene Factors **Hygiene factors** are associated with the job context or environment in which the job is performed. Company policy and administration, technical supervision, salary, working conditions, and interpersonal relations are examples of hygiene factors. These factors are associated with an individual's negative feelings about the job but do not contribute to motivation.

Studies on what managers value in their work support Herzberg's conclusion that factors such as achievement, recognition, and challenging work are

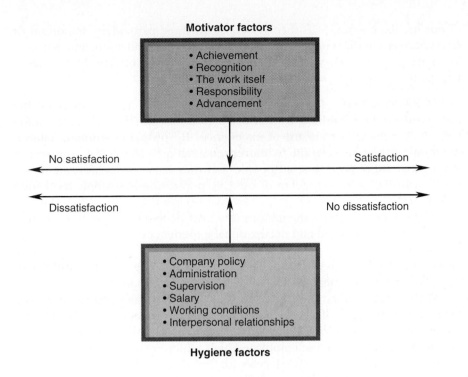

Motivator factors

- Achievement
- Recognition
- The work itself
- Responsibility
- Advancement

No satisfaction ←——————→ Satisfaction

Dissatisfaction ←——————→ No dissatisfaction

- Company policy
- Administration
- Supervision
- Salary
- Working conditions
- Interpersonal relationships

Hygiene factors

FIGURE 15.3
Herzberg's two-factor theory

valued more than things such as pay or security. For example, a recent survey of middle- and top-level managers by the American Productivity and Quality Center found that more than half of the sample respondents (all of whom were white males) believed that the most important characteristic of a job is that it involves work that is meaningful and provides a sense of accomplishment. They rated meaningful work most important three times more frequently than high income. Additionally, 90 percent or more of the respondents rated challenging work, participation in decision making, and recognition for their accomplishments as important or very important.[10]

But just because many people rate motivators above hygiene factors is no guarantee that the motivators will actually increase work motivation for all employees. These findings may not be applicable to the entire population, especially as the work force becomes more diverse. Moreover, these factors may only result in increasing employee motivation and satisfaction and have no effect on productivity.

Nevertheless, Herzberg's two-factor theory carries some very clear messages for managers. The first step in motivation is to eliminate dissatisfaction, so managers are advised to make sure that pay, working conditions, company policies, and so forth are appropriate and reasonable. Then they can address motivation itself. But additional pay and improvements in working conditions will not accomplish this. Instead, managers should strive to provide opportunities for growth, achievement, and responsibility—all things that the theory predicts will enhance employee motivation.

One example is the new program begun by AT&T in late 1996 that is aimed at motivating its work force to do something good for others by offering all 127,000 employees worldwide a paid day off to do volunteer work. It is by far the largest corporate-backed volunteer program ever. The move will cost the nation's number one long-distance carrier $20 million, but AT&T hopes it will raise employee motivation and morale, improve the company's public standing, and yield higher profits down the road.[11]

McClelland's Acquired-Needs Theory: Focus on Diversity

McClelland has proposed an *acquired-needs theory* of motivation that he believes is rooted in culture; that is, needs are acquired or learned on the basis

McClelland's acquired-needs theory of motivation states that, when a need is strong, it will motivate an individual to engage in behaviors to satisfy that need.

© Eric R. Berndt/Unicorn Stock Photos

Need for achievement
The drive to excel, accomplish challenging tasks, and achieve a standard of excellence.

Need for power
The desire to influence and control one's environment.

Need for affiliation
The desire for friendly and close interpersonal relationships.

of our life experiences. His theory focuses on three particularly important or relevant needs in the work environment: achievement, affiliation, and power.[12] McClelland argues that when a need is strong, it will motivate the person to engage in behaviors to satisfy that need.

Need for Achievement   Initially, McClelland's work centered on the **need for achievement,** represented by the drive to excel, accomplish challenging tasks, and achieve a standard of excellence. He primarily studied achievement motivation in relation to entrepreneurship.[13] McClelland's research shows that although almost all people feel they have an "achievement motive," probably only 10 percent of the U.S. population is strongly motivated to achieve.

The amount of achievement motivation that people have depends on their childhood, their personal and occupational experiences, and the type of organization for which they work.[14] Managers who want to motivate high achievers need to ensure that such individuals have challenging but obtainable goals that allow relatively immediate feedback about their progress.

High achievers often pursue a professional career in sales and are successful in entrepreneurial activities, as you will see in Entrepreneurial Approach. Here we provide the profile of Lisa Renshaw, President of Penn Parking, Inc., to illustrate an entrepreneur's self-motivated high achievement style. Renshaw likes to set her own goals and favors tasks that provide immediate feedback. She prefers to accept personal responsibility for success or failure rather than leave the outcome to chance or the actions of others.[15]

Research consistently demonstrates that high achievers are successful in entrepreneurial activities like running their own business, managing a self-contained unit within a large organization, or holding positions where success depends largely on individual achievement.[16] A high need to achieve does not necessarily lead to being a good manager, however, especially in large organizations. In contrast, the needs for affiliation and institutional power are closely related to management success.

Need for Power   McClelland's research also focused on the desire to influence and control one's environment as a particularly important motivator in organizations. This **need for power** may involve either personal power or institutional power. Individuals with a high need for personal power want to dominate others for the sake of demonstrating their ability to influence and control. In contrast, individuals with a high need for institutional power want to solve problems and further organizational goals.[17]

Need for Affiliation   Finally, the **need for affiliation** is the desire for friendly and close interpersonal relationships. Individuals high in the need for affiliation are likely to gravitate toward professions that involve high levels of interaction with others, such as teaching, counseling, and sales.

Though not all individuals have the appropriate needs profile to be a manager, McClelland argues that employees can be trained to stimulate their achievement needs. If an organizational position requires a high achiever, management can select a person with a high need for achievement or develop its own candidate through training.

In summary, need-based approaches to motivation provide managers with an understanding of the underlying needs that motivate people to behave in certain ways. However, these theories do not explain why people choose a particular behavior to accomplish task-related goals. As useful as they are, need theories still emphasize the *what* aspect of motivation by describing what motivates individuals, but do not provide information on thought processes or the *how* aspect of motivation. We examine a more complex view of motivation in the next section.

WHAT MOTIVATES ENTREPRENEURS?

At 21 years old, Lisa Renshaw already knew she wasn't like other aspiring business students. She didn't need the security of the corporate career or the structure that most young individuals are seeking. Instead, Lisa was seeking a challenge, immediate feedback, and an opportunity to take personal responsibility for success or failure. She was searching for ways to exert her energy and achieve the goals that she had established. In 1983, she met the owner of a troubled downtown Baltimore parking lot that was scheduled to be closed. She offered him a loan of $3,000 and free labor in exchange for equity in the property. Soon after, the owner left town, taking her $3,000. But Renshaw was willing to take a risk and stayed, renegotiated the lease, and persuaded the garage owner to lower the monthly payments so she would have a chance at breaking even.

By doing most of the work herself, Lisa built the business by greeting customers daily, handing out fliers, promoting heavily to Amtrak riders who used a nearby station, offering carpooling assistance, and giving free car washes to anyone who parked in her lot for five days. The lot's occupancy rate increased from less than 10 percent to more than 70 percent in three years. Within five years, Lisa had four lots, garnering a 20 percent margin on annual revenues of almost $1 million. In addition, Lisa Renshaw is now the president of Penn Parking, Inc.

SOURCE: J. Hyatt, "Entrepreneur of the Year," *Inc.*, January 1991, 35–51.

PROCESS THEORIES OF EMPLOYEE MOTIVATION

Managers need to have a more complete perspective on the complexities of employee motivation. They must understand why different people have different needs and goals, why individuals' needs change, and how employees change to try to satisfy needs in different ways. Not all employees want the same things from their jobs. Understanding these aspects of motivation has become especially relevant as organizations deal with the diverse managerial issues associated with an increasingly global environment. Two useful theories for understanding these complex processes are expectancy theory and equity theory.

Expectancy Theory

Expectancy theory is the most comprehensive motivational model. In general, expectancy theory seeks to predict or explain task-related effort. It provides a universal key to what motivates people to be productive on the job. Expectancy theory suggests that work motivation is determined by two individual beliefs: (1) the relationship between effort and performance, and (2) the desirability of various work outcomes that are associated with different performance levels.[18] Simply put, given choices, individuals choose the option that promises to give them the greatest reward. When you have three choices, you'll choose the one that provides you with the result you value the most. The theory applies to the career you select, the car you buy, the task you start the day with, where you go on vacation, and so on. However, when individuals make choices, they must be reasonably sure that the reward they are looking for is attainable without undue risk or effort.

To help you understand expectancy theory, the next paragraphs briefly define the key terms of the model and discuss how they operate. Figure 15.4 shows how these terms are related.

FIGURE 15.4
Expectancy theory

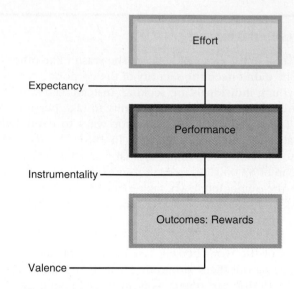

Expectancy
The belief that a particular level of effort will be followed by a particular level of performance.

Instrumentality
The probability assigned by the individual that a specific level of achieved task performance will lead to various work outcomes.

Valence
The value or importance that the individual attaches to various outcomes.

Expectancy   **Expectancy** is the belief that a particular level of effort will be followed by a particular level of performance. This is best understood in terms of the effort-performance linkage, or the individual's perception of the probability that a given level of effort will lead to a certain level of performance.

Instrumentality   **Instrumentality** is the individual's perception that a specific level of achieved task performance will lead to various work outcomes. This is the performance-reward, linkage or the degree to which the individual believes that performing at a particular level will lead to the attainment of a desired outcome.

Valence   **Valence** is the value or importance that the individual attaches to various work outcomes. For motivation to be high, employees must value the outcomes that are available from high effort and good performance. Conversely, if employees do not place a high value on the outcome, motivation will be low.

Motivation is the force that causes individuals to spend effort. However, effort alone is not enough. Individuals must believe that their efforts will lead to some desired performance level; otherwise they will not make much of an effort. Managers can influence expectancies by selecting individuals with proper abilities, training people to use these abilities, supporting people by providing the needed resources, and identifying desired task goals.[19] In addition, managers must try to determine the outcomes that each employee values.

One of the problems with expectancy theory is that it is quite complex. Still, the logic of the model is clear, and the steps are useful for clarifying how managers can motivate people. For example, managers should first find out which rewards under their control have the highest valences for their employees. Rewards are very important to people at work. It is not true that people are primarily motivated by money. For example, the best reward for a productive employee may be an office with large windows overlooking a scenic view of mountains or water. This type of motivator contributes to worker satisfaction, diminishes stress, and abets overall physical health.[20] In addition, many people value interesting work, challenge, advancement opportunities, and the chance to contribute more than they value money. Managers should then link these rewards to the performance they desire. If any expectancies are low, managers might provide coaching, leadership, and training to raise them.[21]

Equity Theory

Equity, or fairness in the workplace, has been found to be a major factor in determining employee motivation.[22] For example, before each sports season opens it is common to read about a baseball, basketball, or football star who is negotiating a higher contract. This in turn will trigger perceptions of inequity among teammates, many of whom called for renegotiation of their own contracts.

Although equity in the workplace is less visible than in the sports arena and on the playing field, feelings of unfairness were among the most frequently reported sources of job dissatisfaction found by Herzberg and his associates. Some researchers have made the desire for fairness, justice, or equity a central focus of their theories. For example, assume that you just received a 10 percent raise. Will this raise lead to higher performance, lower performance, or no change in your performance? Are you satisfied with this increase? What if you discovered that other colleagues in your work group received 15 percent raises?

Equity theory focuses on an individual's feelings about how fairly he is treated in comparison with others.[23] Figure 15.5 illustrates the basic components of equity theory. The theory makes two assumptions: First, individuals evaluate their interpersonal relationships just as they evaluate any exchange process, such as the buying or selling of a home, shares of stock, or a car. Second, individuals compare their situations with those of others to determine the equity of their own situation. Given the social nature of human beings, it should come as no surprise that we compare our contributions and rewards to those of others.

In the workplace, employees contribute things such as their education, experience, expertise, and time and effort, and in return they get pay, security,

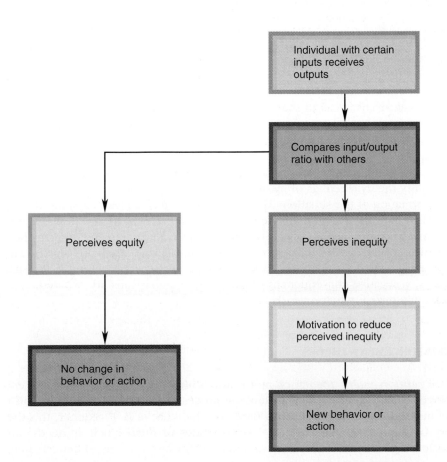

FIGURE 15.5
Equity theory

and recognition. According to equity theory, we prefer a situation of balance, or equity, that exists when we perceive that the ratio of our inputs and outcomes is equal to the ratio of inputs and outcomes of one or more comparison persons. If people experience inequity, they are generally motivated to change something.

This viewpoint also conveys several clear messages to managers. First, people should be rewarded according to their contributions. Second, managers should try to ensure that employees feel equity. Finally, managers should be aware that feelings of inequity are almost bound to arise, and when they do, managers must be patient and either correct the problem, if it is real, or help people recognize that things are not as inequitable as they seem.[24]

Equity theory suggests that maintaining one's self-esteem is an important priority. To reduce a perceived inequity, a person may take one of the following actions:

- Change work inputs either upward or downward to what might be an equitable level. For example, underpaid people can reduce the quality of their production, work shorter hours, or be absent more frequently.
- Change outcomes to restore equity. For example, many union organizers try to attract nonmembers by pledging to improve working conditions, hours, and pay without an increase in employee effort (input).
- Psychologically distort comparisons. For example, a person might rationalize or distort how hard she or he works or attempt to increase the importance of the job to the organization.
- Change the comparison person she is using to another person.
- Leave the situation. For example, quit the job, request a transfer to another department, or shift to a new reference group to reduce the source of the inequity. This type of action will probably be taken only in cases of high inequity when other alternatives are not feasible.

People often respond differently to the same situations, and therefore their reactions to inequity will vary. Some people are more willing to accept being under-rewarded than others. If the perceived inequity results in a change in motivation, the inequity may also alter effort and performance. You can probably think of instances in school where you worked harder than others on a paper, yet received a lower grade. Although working hard doesn't necessarily imply that you wrote a high-quality paper, your sense of equity was probably violated.

These points also reinforce the fact that perception is an important aspect of equity theory. Feelings of inequity are determined solely by the individual's interpretation of the situation. Thus, it would be inaccurate to assume that all employees in a work unit will view their annual pay raise as fair. Rewards that are received with feelings of equity can foster job satisfaction and performance; rewards received with feelings of inequity can damage key work results. The burden lies with the manager to take control of the situation and make sure that any negative consequences of the equity comparisons are avoided, or at least minimized, when rewards are allocated.[25]

REINFORCEMENT THEORY

The *reinforcement theory* of motivation shifts the emphasis from the employee's underlying needs and thinking processes to the rewards and punishments in the work environment. Based on the work of B. F. Skinner, this theory of motivation suggests that internal states of mind (such as needs) are misleading, scientifically unmeasurable, and in any case hypothetical. Reinforcement theory rests on two underlying assumptions: First, human behavior is determined by the environment. Second, human behavior is subject to observable laws and can be predicted and changed. The foundation of reinforcement theory is the **law of effect,** which states that behavior will be repeated or not, depending on whether the consequence is positive or negative.

Reinforcement Theory Application: Behavior Modification

Behavior modification is the application of reinforcement theory that managers can use to motivate employees. Managers and behavioral scientists need to pay attention to behavior—the observable outcomes of situations and choices, or what people actually do. Since people repeat behaviors that are positively rewarded and avoid behaviors that are punished, managers can influence employee performance by reinforcing behavior they see as supporting organizational goals.

The tools of behavior modification are four basic reinforcement strategies, in which either a pleasant or an unpleasant event is applied or withdrawn following a person's behavior. These four reinforcers are illustrated in Figure 15.6.

Positive Reinforcement   A **positive reinforcement** is the administration of positive and rewarding consequences following a desired behavior. This tends to increase the likelihood that the person will repeat the behavior in similar settings. For example, a manager praises the marketing representative's high monthly sales performance; a student gets a good grade; a professor receives high teaching evaluations.

Negative Reinforcement   **Negative reinforcement** or avoidance is the removal of negative consequences following a desired behavior. This also tends to increase the likelihood that the behavior will be repeated in similar settings. For example, a partner in an accounting firm scolds an employee about tardiness and then stops when the employee begins to be punctual.

Extinction   **Extinction** is the withdrawal of the positive reward or reinforcing consequences for an undesirable behavior. The behavior is no longer reinforced and therefore is less likely to occur in the future. For example, if an employee who is not meeting sales quotas fails to receive bonus checks, he will begin to realize that the behavior is not producing desired outcomes. The undesirable behavior will gradually disappear.

Punishment   **Punishment** is the administration of negative consequences following undesirable behavior. This tends to reduce the likelihood that the be-

Law of effect
Determines if a behavior will be repeated or not, depending on whether the consequence is positive or negative.

Behavior modification
An application of reinforcement theory that managers can use to motivate employees.

Positive reinforcement
The administration of positive and rewarding consequences following a desired behavior.

Negative reinforcement
The removal of negative consequences following a desired behavior.

Extinction
The withdrawal of the positive reward or reinforcing consequences for an undesirable behavior.

Punishment
The administration of negative consequences following undesirable behavior.

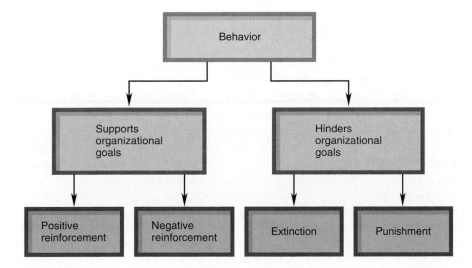

FIGURE 15.6
Four types of reinforcers

havior will be repeated in similar settings. For example, a manager docks an employee's pay for being rude to a customer. However, problems such as resentment and sabotage may accompany a manager's use of punishment.

Which type of reinforcer is most appropriate to use? As a result of considerable research and some popular management books such as *The One Minute Manager,* most managers prefer positive reinforcement to the use of punishment.[26] As Table 15.1 shows, there are several reasons for not using punishment. The manager who positively reinforces desirable behaviors among employees achieves performance improvements without generating the fear, suspicion, and revenge that are often the result of using punishment in the workplace.

When an employee's behavior is supportive of the organizational goals, a manager would use either positive or negative reinforcers to increase this desirable behavior. Managers must not allow excellent performance to be ignored or taken for granted. When employee behaviors do not support organizational objectives, a manager should use extinction or punishment (only as a last resort), since this behavior is considered to be undesirable.

Studies have shown that consistent rewards for organizationally desirable behavior result in positive performance in the long term. In contrast, punishment as a primary motivational tool contributes little to high motivation because employees learn to avoid the punisher rather than learning appropriate behaviors. Managers need to observe and manage the consequences of work-related behaviors carefully because individuals have different perceptions of what is a reward and what is punishment, depending on their values and needs. As the work force becomes increasingly diverse, this issue will present greater challenges to managers. For example, one employee may consider a day off a motivating reward, but another may prefer money to a day off. Consider how USAA rewards employees for contributing suggestions and ideas to improve the workplace. It offers employees a choice of gifts, such as power tools, bicycles, cameras, spa memberships, or certificates for meals at local restaurants.[27]

Schedules of Reinforcement

To use behavior modification effectively, managers need to apply reinforcers properly. **Schedules of reinforcement** specify the basis for and timing of reinforcement. The two basic types of schedules of reinforcement are continuous and partial.

Continuous Schedule of Reinforcement   With a **continuous schedule of reinforcement,** a desired behavior is rewarded each time it occurs. For example, a manager might praise an employee every time the worker performs a task correctly. This type of reinforcement is very effective during the initial learning process, but it becomes tedious and impractical on an ongoing basis. Further, the desired behavior tends to stop almost immediately unless the reinforcement is continued.

Schedules of reinforcement
Specify the basis for and timing of reinforcement.

Continuous schedule of reinforcement
Rewarding a desired behavior each time it occurs.

TABLE 15.1   The virtues of positive reinforcement or Why not use punishment?

WHY NOT USE PUNISHMENT?	WHY USE PUNISHMENT?
• May create distress for the punisher	• Temporarily stops or lessens behavior
• Attention is not focused on desired behavior	• Quick and easy to use
• May lead to negative side effects (fear, suspicion, and revenge)	
• May damage employee emotionally	

Partial Schedule of Reinforcement   As an alternative, a **partial schedule of reinforcement** can be used. In this case, the desired behavior is rewarded intermittently rather than each time it occurs. With a partial schedule, a desired behavior can be rewarded more often as encouragement during the initial learning process and less often when the behavior has been learned. The four major types of partial reinforcement schedules are compared in Table 15.2.

With a **fixed-interval schedule,** the manager rewards employees at specified time intervals, assuming that the desired behavior has continued at an appropriate level. An example is the Friday paycheck many employees receive.

With a **fixed-ratio schedule,** a reinforcer is provided after a fixed number of occurrences of the desired behavior. For example, a department store wants to increase charge card applications and offers to reward salesclerks each time they open four new accounts. Most piece-rate pay systems are considered fixed-ratio schedules.

With a **variable-interval schedule,** reinforcement is administered at random or varying times that cannot be predicted by the employee. For example, a division manager might visit a territory five times a month to comment on employee performance, varying the days and times each month.

A **variable-ratio schedule** provides a reinforcer after a varying, or random, number of occurrences of the desired behavior rather than after variable time periods. For example, slot machine payoff patterns, which provide rewards after a varying number of pulls on the lever, use a variable-ratio schedule. While people anticipate that the machine will pay a jackpot after a certain number of plays, the exact number of plays is variable.

Using Behavior Modification

To date, most behavior modification programs have been applied to employees at operating levels—clerical employees, production workers, or mechanics. Behavior modification is more easily applied to relatively simple jobs, where critical behaviors can be easily identified and specific performance goals readily set. For managerial jobs, these key factors may be more difficult to apply. Further, it is not clear that supervisor praise, recognition, and feedback are enough. Many times new reinforcers have to be introduced because the old ones become routine.

Partial schedule of reinforcement
Rewarding the desired behavior intermittently.

Fixed-interval schedule
Rewards at specific time intervals, assuming that the desired behavior has continued at an appropriate level.

Fixed-ratio schedule
Provides a reinforcement after a fixed number of occurrences of the desired behavior.

Variable-interval schedule
When reinforcement is administered at random or varying times that cannot be predicted by the employee.

Variable-ratio schedule
Reinforcement administered randomly.

TABLE 15.2   Comparing partial schedules of reinforcement

SCHEDULE	FORM OF REINFORCEMENT	INFLUENCES ON BEHAVIOR WHEN APPLIED	EFFECTS ON BEHAVIOR WHEN WITHDRAWN	EXAMPLE
Fixed Interval	Reward given on fixed time basis	Leads to average and irregular performance	Rapid extinction of behavior	Weekly or monthly paycheck
Fixed Ratio	Reward tied to specific number of responses	Quickly leads to high and stable performance	Moderately fast extinction of behavior	Piece-rate system
Variable Interval	Reward given at varying times	Leads to moderately high and stable performance	Slow extinction of behavior	Performance appraisals and rewards given at random times each month
Variable Ratio	Reward given at variable amounts of output	Leads to very high performance	Very slow extinction of behavior	Sales bonus tied to the number of new accounts opened, with random changes in the number needed

How successful has behavior modification been in the workplace? Its use has had some notable successes. For example, at Emery Air Freight, to use a classic case, managers wanted workers to use freight containers for shipments because of the cost savings. They established a program of positive reinforcement for employees that resulted in significant improvements in container use, cost savings of over $600,000 annually, and improved employee behavior. Dayton Hudson used behavior modification in the men's department of one of its stores. The goal was to increase the average sale from $19 to $25. Employees were taught how to make extra sales and were congratulated by a supervisor each time a sale went above $19. Within two months, department sales averaged $23. Other companies, such as General Electric, B. F. Goodrich, Michigan Bell, and Weyerhaeuser, are also using varied forms of behavior modification.

Criticisms of Behavior Modification

Critics of behavior modification charge that it is essentially bribery and that workers are already paid for performance. Because it disregards people's attitudes and beliefs, behavior modification has been called misleading and manipulative. One critic has noted that there is little difference between behavior modification and some key elements of scientific management presented more than 60 years ago by Taylor, particularly where money is involved. Is it a motivational technique for manipulating people? Does it decrease an employee's freedom? If so, is such action on the part of managers unethical? There are no easy answers to these questions.

Consider, for example, an organization that uses behavior modification as a solution to control health care costs and keep employees healthy. While this may sound like an impractical solution to rising health care costs, organizations with this strategy provide employees with financial incentives if they meet certain "wellness" criteria, such as not smoking, maintaining normal weight, and following a healthy lifestyle. The rewards or incentives used are typically either a lower premium contribution required from employees or higher benefits. For example, Baker Hughes, Inc., a Texas drilling and tool company, estimates it has saved $2 million annually by charging nonsmoking employees $100 less a year for health insurance than smokers. Adolph Coors Company claims it has saved $3 million a year by offering its employees incentives to meet weight, smoking, blood pressure, cholesterol, and other health criteria. Other companies adopting the strategy of rewarding healthy lifestyles include U-Haul, Control Data, and Southern California Edison. To avoid charges of unfairness and discrimination, some companies provide cost savings to employees actively involved in improving their health.[28]

Some organizations provide employees with financial incentives if they meet certain "wellness" criteria, such as not smoking, maintaining normal weight, and following a healthy lifestyle. In order to avoid charges of discrimination, some of these companies provide cost savings to employees actively involved in improving their health.

© 1996, Photo Disc, Inc.

INFORMATION TECHNOLOGY INFLUENCES ON MOTIVATION

Information technology has been and will continue to be a dynamic force in most organizations. Often the individual employee is forgotten or overlooked in the quest for faster, better, "new and improved" systems and more sophisticated methods that technology can deliver. If information technology is going to be implemented into organizations, it is important that individual considerations be central factors and, most important, that managers have a better understanding of how employee motivation can be affected.

How does a manager motivate her division to adopt a new technological system? Taken from management's perspective, the new system may represent a large investment that will have significant positive effects on overall quality and productivity of the division. However, taken from the employees' perspective, the system may be threatening, seen as the unknown, and possibly perceived as more work just to learn the system. Most important, managers need to understand what employees' values are and what types of goals have been established.

Consider some basic motivation theories we have discussed in the chapter. It is important to show users how the new system will benefit them and make their jobs easier, more challenging, or more rewarding (if that is what they value). The system may have more feedback built in, less direct supervision, greater work flexibility, or more opportunities for job enrichment than the old system. Training should always be included when new technology is added to the workplace, along with recognition for accomplishing new tasks and feedback.

CONTEMPORARY MOTIVATIONAL ISSUES ▬▬▬▬▬▬▬▬

Several contemporary issues involving motivation offer challenges to today's managers. We will look at three of these issues: goal-setting theory, participative management, and money as a means of motivating employees.

GOAL SETTING TO SUPPORT QUALITY INITIATIVES

Goal setting from a planning perspective was discussed in Chapter 4. But, as we pointed out earlier with regard to MBO, goal setting can also be applied on an individual level to increase employee motivation.[29] From a motivational perspective, it can be used to support quality initiatives. **Goal setting** is a process of increasing efficiency and effectiveness by specifying the desired outcomes toward which individuals, groups, departments, and organizations should work.[30] Goals are the future outcomes (results) to achieve. You may have a set goal, such as "I am planning to graduate with a 3.7 grade point average by the end of the summer semester."

As a motivational tool, goal setting can help employees because goals serve three purposes: (1) to guide and direct behavior toward supportive organizational goals, (2) to provide challenges and standards against which the individual can be assessed, and (3) to define what is important and provide a framework for planning.

For goal setting to be successful and lead to higher performance levels, goals must be specific and challenging but achievable, establish a time frame, be realistic, and be measurable. Though it is not always necessary to have employees participate in the goal-setting process, participation is probably preferable to managers assigning goals when they anticipate that the employee will resist accepting more difficult challenges. Managers must also provide feedback to employees about their performance. A current study found that performance-review feedback followed by goal setting favorably influenced employee work satisfaction and organizational commitment to a greater extent than performance review feedback alone.[31]

To use goal setting effectively to motivate employees, managers need to (1) meet regularly with subordinates, (2) work with subordinates to set goals jointly, (3) set goals that are specific and moderately challenging, and (4) provide feedback about performance. When subordinates accept the goal-setting process, they are more likely to be committed and work hard to accomplish goals. The evidence thus far suggests that goal setting will become an increasingly important part of the motivational process in the future. Though limited, some research has suggested that employees achieve high levels of job

Goal setting
A process intended to increase efficiency and effectiveness by specifying the desired outcomes toward which individuals, groups, departments, and organizations work.

Meeting the Challenge

EFFECTIVE GOAL-SETTING PRACTICES

Place yourself in a management role and use the following ten self-evaluation guidelines to channel your behavior toward effective goal-setting practices. You may also want to evaluate your own manager to see if she practices these guidelines.

1. I try to have goal-setting sessions at least once a year with all my employees as individuals, and with each team as necessary.
2. When possible, I invite employees to join with me in setting worthwhile goals for the department.
3. With employees whose performance is reliable, I often leave it to them to determine the methods they will use to reach their goals.
4. I invite employees to set personal goals for their growth and advancement.
5. I try to know what employees want out of their work, and what their needs and goals are.
6. Once I have agreed on a goal, I make sure it is addressed.
7. I let employees know at the time of setting goals how important they are to me.
8. I usually incorporate goals in appraisals.
9. I make sure to find out how realistic the goals are to employees who are charged with reaching them.
10. I periodically make sure that all employees understand not only my goals but the performance standards I expect of them.

---

satisfaction when they perceive that the probability of attaining goals at work is high. Also, they are more satisfied when they perceive more positive than negative goals in their environment.[32] Meeting the Challenge is an exercise that can help you develop your managerial competency at goal setting.

PARTICIPATIVE MANAGEMENT: IMPROVING QUALITY AND PRODUCTIVITY

Participative management
Encompasses varied activities of high involvement where subordinates share a significant degree of decision-making power with their immediate superiors.

The use of **participative management,** an umbrella term that encompasses various activities in which subordinates share a significant degree of decision-making power with their immediate superiors, involves any process where power, knowledge, information, and rewards are moved downward in the organization.[33] For example, at a mature General Motors automobile battery plant, when employees organized around teams and participative management, company officials reported productivity savings of 30 to 40 percent and a 25 percent decrease in worker complaints when compared with traditionally organized plants.

It is often difficult to determine exactly why participative management is successful, because many changes are occurring simultaneously in several areas, including human resources, work structure, technology, training, and reward systems. Involvement of individuals throughout the organization is now considered essential to organizational survival.

As a result of social and political developments over the past couple of decades, people today expect greater participation in choosing directions for their lives in general and their lives at work more specifically.[34] Participative management draws on and is linked to a number of motivation theories. For example, employee involvement can motivate workers by providing more opportunities for growth, responsibility, and commitment in the work itself. Similarly, the process of making and implementing a decision and then seeing the results can help satisfy an employee's need for responsibility, recognition, growth, self-esteem, and achievement.

Participative management programs represent a shift away from traditional management styles and ways of doing business.[35] For participative management to work, however, a company must change. As we discussed in Chapter 11, it is often extremely difficult for managers to give up authority and for employees to translate that surrender of power by higher-ups into lasting improvements in quality and productivity. When companies increase the amount of control and discretion workers have over their jobs, they are **empowering employees** and may improve the motivation of both employees and management.[36]

Empowering employees
Increasing the amount of control and discretion employees have over their job as a means of motivating behavior.

Do employee participation and involvement really work to motivate individuals? U.S. executives have indicated optimism toward employee involvement and participative management.[37] Participative management programs have been viewed as having positive influences on corporate quality, productivity, and customer service. For example, Corning Glass eliminated one management level at its corporate computer center, substituting a team advisor for three shift supervisors. They produced $150,000 in annual savings and increased the quality of service. Perceptions of autonomy and responsibility among workers increased because they felt they experienced more meaningful and productive work. Levi Strauss managers responded to employees on the factory floor when they proposed ways to curb boredom and boost productivity. Machine operators designed a system to team up to learn each other's jobs. The team idea was such a positive motivation for employees that the company is adopting it in other Levi Strauss plants around the globe.[38] At its DuPont, Washington, desktop computer–assembly operation, Intel successfully developed an employee participative system with operators working in two shifts of three teams. These teams are involved in everything including training, selection, scheduling production, scheduling overtime, and rejecting products not up to quality standards.[39]

Participative management is one way that an organization can establish a supportive environment. One of the many ways in which the work force is changing is that employees are less accepting of top-down control and expect growth, fulfillment, and dignity from their work.

MONEY AS A MOTIVATOR

The issue of whether money motivates is particularly relevant to many managers. However, the answer to a common management question, "Does money motivate my subordinates?" depends on which theory the manager accepts. As we discussed earlier, expectancy theory asserts that money motivates people if it is contingent on performance and satisfies their personal goals. Herzberg's two-factor theory would argue that money is a hygiene factor, so it does not act as a motivator.

As a medium of exchange, money should motivate to the degree that people perceive it as a means to acquire other things they want. For example, in the Entrepreneurial Approach, examine how Lisa Renshaw's motivation changed from money to achievement and recognition. Money also has symbolic meaning that managers must consider. In general, to motivate, money must be important to the employee and must be perceived as a direct reward for performance.

INTERNATIONAL PERSPECTIVES: VALUING DIVERSITY

Studying theories of motivation can lead us to assume that we are dealing with "human nature"—the way people really are. We must be aware, however, that most of the research for these theories has been by Americans with Americans, although some of Herzberg's work did include cross-cultural comparisons. Americans' motivation patterns and social character arise out of our unique history; they are not universal and to some degree differ from those of other cultures. These differences should be remembered when we hear that we should apply management practices from another culture to the American work scene; the past and present preoccupation with Japanese methods is a good example.[40] Further, American corporations with multinational divisions cannot assume that management practices that work well in the United States will apply to individuals in their overseas operations.

Don't be convinced that U.S. practices never work. Some concepts can be translated and applied and have been successful, especially those conceived by entrepreneurs who are motivated to conquer global opportunities. In Global Perspective, we present five guidelines that have been proven to ensure that an organization plays a major role in the international arena.

The United States is an achievement-oriented society that has historically encouraged and honored individual accomplishment and the attainment of material prosperity. Individualism, independence, self-confidence, and speaking out against injustice and threats are important elements of the American character. Japanese motivations and values are quite different, with obvious implications for management practices.[41] The Japanese place greater emphasis on socially oriented qualities. Their collective society is arranged in a rigid hierarchy, and all members are expected to maintain absolute loyalty and obedience to authority. Dependency and security are part of the Japanese upbringing, whereas autonomy and early independence are typically American. In their corporate life, the Japanese show great dependency and are highly conforming and obedient. Japanese managers recognize that these characteristics can inhibit creativity and innovation and are consequently encouraging programs in their schools that will develop the creativity and ingenuity they envy in Americans.[42]

The cross-cultural research on achievement has been relatively consistent across cultures, stimulated by the realization that managers in multinational corporations must be sensitive to the underlying values and needs of their diverse employees.[43] For example, managers in New Zealand appear to follow an achievement pattern developed in the United States. In general, managers in Anglo countries such as the United States, Canada, and Great Britain tend to have a high need for achievement as well as a high need to produce and a strong willingness to accept risk. In contrast, managers in countries such as Chile and Portugal tend to have a lower need for achievement. Keep in mind, however, that the word *achievement* itself is difficult to translate into other languages and this influences any cross-cultural research findings.

The implications for managerial style, practices, and motivational planning for an American firm operating branches in foreign countries are apparent. Managers must take the social character, values, and cultural practices of each coun-

All members of Japanese society are expected to maintain absolute loyalty and obedience to authority, in contrast to the American ideals of autonomy and early independence. Japanese managers have begun encouraging programs in their schools that will develop the creativity and ingenuity they admire in Americans.

© Reuters/Corbis-Bettmann

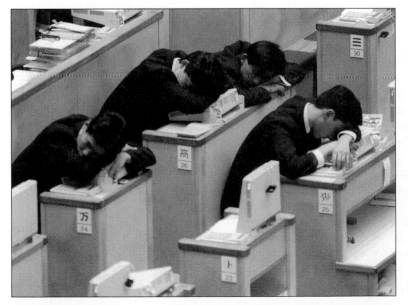

HOW TO ADAPT AND CONQUER FOREIGN MARKETS

Are you motivated to conquer global opportunities? Here are a few guidelines to ensure that your organization plays a major role on the international stage:

Learn to scan for opportunities: The entrepreneurial drive develops a knack for finding meaningful patterns in an assortment of data. New business can result from a change in diplomatic relations with China; a demographic shift can create a new market for herbal tea.

Adapt to your target market: Campbell Soup failed to sell its vegetable and beef soups in Brazil because natives prefer to add their own fresh vegetables to the dehydrated products of competitors. Often you can adjust a product to meet local consumer needs.

Steal ideas from the best: Develop a methodology for gathering competitive intelligence. Successful international companies are a great resource. While building his retail chain, Jimmy Lai of Hong Kong studied McDonald's, Marks and Spencer, and Benetton. He applied their best business practices to create his own $350 million clothing company.

Know that experts are often wrong: People can become so close to their particular field that they may be the last to see the light. For example, Starbucks founder Harvard Schultz was turned down by more than 200 investors before he found someone who believed in his coffee concept.

Let failures motivate you: Entrepreneurs pursue a number of ideas before they find a winner. The founders of Hewlett-Packard Company had no success with a bowling-alley foul-line indicator or an automatic urinal flusher. But they persevered. Learn from things that don't always work.

SOURCE: T. Stein, K. Callan, D. Menaker, and C. Brown-Humes, "The World's Greatest Entrepreneurs," *Success,* June 1996, 35–46.

try into consideration.[44] Our large corporations operating abroad have long known this but have often failed to put it into practice. American managers seem to forget that people of other cultures perceive work differently. Individual values and attitudes, including attitudes toward work, have strong cultural ties. Managers, therefore, must be careful in designing reward systems to ensure that the rewards are truly motivational in the local cultural framework.

A well-managed, diverse work force is instrumental for a firm's competitive advantage. In order to develop or maintain such an advantage, policymakers must consider a broad definition of motivation when determining compensation packages, responsibilities, rules and procedures, organizational structure, control systems, job design, and management techniques.[45]

MANAGERIAL IMPLICATIONS

As a manager you probably can't motivate your workers. You can, however, create an environment that lends itself to greater motivation. We conclude this chapter with a prescription for greater motivation that involves building value into people's work and increasing their expectation that they can be successful in attaining the rewards they want, by following these five steps:

- *Tell people what you expect them to do.* On a regular, periodic basis, tell employees what your goals are as well as your standards of performance. People need goals. There is no human activity without them. Don't assume that they know what you want. Tell them as specifically as possible.

- *Make the work valuable.* When you can, assign people to the kinds of work they like and can do well—work that they regard as valuable to them. Give them work that enables them to achieve their personal goals, such as growth, advancement, self-esteem, professional recognition, status, and the like.

- *Make the work doable.* Increase employees' confidence that they can do what you expect by training, coaching, mentoring, listening, scheduling, providing resources, and so on.

- *Give feedback.* When employees try to do what you expect, give them feedback on how well they are doing. Positive feedback tells them what they need to continue doing; criticism helps them correct mistakes.

- *Reward successful performance.* When employees have done what you asked them to do, reward them with both monetary and nonmonetary recognition.

In this chapter we have examined motivation as a key management tool that organizations can use to energize employees. An organization can help create a motivating atmosphere by making the work environment pleasant and conducive to productive output. The organization that achieves these conditions will create an environment in which all members can contribute to their maximum potential and in which the value of diversity can be fully realized.[46] Many companies are attempting to improve working conditions for employees based on the premise that a motivated work force can reduce absenteeism, increase productivity, encourage labor-management harmony, and lead to a better product or service. As we see from the Managerial Incident Resolution, USAA is finding that its motivational plan is continuing to pay off.

Managerial Incident Resolution

USAA GROWING AND STRIVING FOR EXCEPTIONAL SERVICE

Robert Herres, who has served as vice chair of the Joint Chiefs of Staff under Presidents Reagan and Bush, considered the challenges ahead of USAA. How could they conquer new markets and continue to grow even though the market was declining? Robert Herres focused on providing expanded quality service to customers. The plans for USAA were to begin offering customers progressively more services—life and health insurance, brokerage service, mutual-fund management, a travel agency, a buying club, and a bank. To accomplish all of this, the biggest challenge for Herres was the employees of USAA.

First, he says he had to win the hearts and minds of his own troops. "It's hard to convince the work force that this growth opportunity is for real, that there are job opportunities here, that there won't be pink slips. They've read so much about downsizing, and they think it will happen here. I tell them the only real limitation to growth is how well we do our jobs."

Once he had employees motivated to be part of the team, they had to become knowledgeable and trained. The company's employees were going to need even more education in the years ahead. As a company objective, Herres places customer service before everything else and believes that the emphasis on service motivates employees. For example, what makes USAA's growth recipe work isn't just the ingredients. It's the execution. The company answers 80 percent of all phone calls in 20 seconds, and it provides its 16,500 employees with the information technology and the training to do more than one task. An associate selling a customer car insurance, for example, can also help the customer open a bank account.

USAA has tried to make it easy for its employees to work hard. Its campus-like setting boasts restaurants, convenience stores, fitness centers, playing fields, a child-care center, a dry cleaner, and a post office. Most employees work a four-day, 38-hour week, and they often commute in company-sponsored van pools. But what really distinguishes USAA is its career development programs. The company shells out some $2.7 million per year in tuition reimbursement for college courses—some of which are taught right inside corporate headquarters.

It appears that USAA, headed by Robert Herres, has taken an approach that is focused on the employees and what they value. He has instilled a culture that creates a working environment conductive to good effort and where employees are inspired to work to accomplish the organization's goals.[47]

SUMMARY

- Motivation is defined as the forces acting on or within a person that cause that person to behave in a specific, goal-directed manner. It is a psychological process that gives behavior purpose and direction.

- Managers can draw upon several different approaches to motivation. Content or need-based theories emphasize specific human needs or the factors within a person that energize, direct, and stop behavior. They explain motivation as a phenomenon primarily occurring intrinsically, or within an individual.

- Herzberg's two-factor theory examines the relationship between job satisfaction and productivity. The sources of work satisfaction are termed *satisfiers* or *motivator factors*. The sources of dissatisfaction are called *dissatisfiers* or *hygiene factors*.

- Need theories of motivation provide managers with an understanding of the underlying needs that motivate people to behave in certain ways, but they do not promote an understanding of why people choose a particular behavior to accomplish task-related goals.

- Process theories take a more dynamic view of motivation than do need theories. Equity theory and expectancy theory focus on understanding the thought or cognitive processes in the individual's mind that influence behavior.

- Managers use expectancy theory in the workplace by first finding out which rewards under their control have the highest valences for their employees.

Then they link these rewards to the performance they desire.

- Reinforcement theory focuses on how employees learn desired work behaviors and rests on two underlying assumptions: First, human behavior is determined by the environment. Second, human behavior is subject to observable laws and can be predicted and changed. The foundation of reinforcement theory is the law of effect, which states that behavior will be repeated or not, depending on whether the consequence is positive or negative.

- Information technology can have an impact on employee motivation. Managers need to show users how the new system will benefit them and make their job easier, more challenging, or more rewarding (if that is what they value). Information technology systems should always include education and training systems when added to the workplace, along with employee recognition and performance feedback.

- Goal setting is a process for increasing efficiency and effectiveness by specifying the desired outcomes toward which individuals, groups, departments, and organizations should work. To be successful and lead to higher performance levels, goals must be specific and challenging rather than vague and easy. Employees should participate in goal setting, especially when the manager anticipates that the employee will resist accepting more difficult challenges.

KEY TERMS

Motivation
Physiological needs
Security needs
Affiliation needs
Esteem needs
Self-actualization needs
Motivator factors
Hygiene factors
Need for achievement
Need for power
Need for affiliation

Expectancy
Instrumentality
Valence
Law of effect
Behavior modification
Positive reinforcement
Negative reinforcement
Extinction
Punishment
Schedules of reinforcement

Continuous schedule of
   reinforcement
Partial schedule of reinforcement
Fixed-interval schedule
Fixed-ratio schedule
Variable-interval schedule
Variable-ratio schedule
Goal setting
Participative management
Empowering employees

REVIEW QUESTIONS

1. Explain what is meant by motivation.

2. What are the basic approaches to motivation?

3. Describe the main components of Maslow's hierarchy of needs.

4. Distinguish between motivator and hygiene factors.

5. What are the characteristics of an individual who has a high need for achievement?

6. What is the basic premise of expectancy theory?

7. What possible actions would an individual take to reduce inequity?

8. Describe the four types of reinforcers. Develop specific examples of the four types of reinforcers.

9. When should a manager use punishment? Under what conditions should a manager not use punishment?

10. How can a manager apply goal-setting theory to motivate employees?

11. What makes participative management or employee involvement programs motivational?

12. Explain why managers need to be aware of cultural differences in motivation.

DISCUSSION QUESTIONS

Improving Critical Thinking

1. What is the value of Herzberg's two-factor theory?

2. Think about the best job you have ever had. What motivation approach was used in that organization?

3. How can managers apply behavior modification to improve an employee's performance?

4. What ethical considerations should be considered before using a behavior modification program at work?

5. What occupations or professions are people with a high need for affiliation likely to choose? What about people with a high need for autonomy?

Enhancing Communication Skills

6. Think about the worst job you have ever had. What motivation approach was used in that organization? Prepare a short presentation that describes this job, citing specific examples of motivation approaches that you feel are or were used incorrectly. Make suggestions for possible changes.

7. How could a manager apply Maslow's hierarchy of needs theory to motivate employees on the job? To practice your written communication skills, write a brief paper and provide specific examples.

Building Teamwork

8. What motivational lessons can be learned from better understanding how individuals may react to information technology introduced in the workplace? Develop a training program that could be used to train individuals who value (1) primarily monetary rewards, (2) primarily recognition, (3) primarily achievement. Form a small group as directed by your instructor and discuss. Be prepared to present your group's training programs to the class.

9. In a small group, visit a local health club or diet center and ask for an interview with the manager. What kinds of rewards does the organization give members who achieve targeted goals? Does it use punishment? Be prepared to present your findings.

1. Use the Internet to search for current information on motivation that is available. Start your search with the search engine Yahoo and use the search keywords "motivation" and "motivation and employees." How many different hits do you get? Of what value are they?

2. After completing Item 1 above, complete several of the questionnaires that you found on-line. How valuable do you think this information would be for smaller organizations or for individuals? How much of the information you found would you consider to be just another form of commercialization?

3. Compare the information and questionnaires found in Items 1 and 2 with the concepts and theories presented in the text. How much of this information would you as a manager want to use for employees?

4. Use an alternative search engine than Yahoo (such as Alta Vista) to search for information on the Internet. Compare the results of the two strategies. Did you find differences in the type of information you retrieved? In the ease with which you retrieved information on motivation?

ETHICS: Take a Stand

Don Richards has recently been promoted as the manager of the Product Support Services (PS) department at McPhillards in Boston, Massachusetts. Because Don has been a part of this department since it started in 1985, he knows most of the individuals and has worked with them as a peer for many years. Everyone in the department seemed pleased when Don was offered the promotion to management and responded with supportive behavior.

Now that Don oversees these individuals, he has seen some changes in performance. For example, employee attendance has dropped and performance is slightly below expectations. Deadlines have begun to slip and are not being met. Hearing the same excuses every week, Don is becoming frustrated. He feels as though it will only get worse if he does not crack down now.

Don is considering establishing a set of policies; if an employee chooses not to abide by them, he or she will be given a warning and then suspended or fired. However, his primary concern is that although the new policy may get employees back on track, it may affect morale. Also, how will it affect his friendship with many of these individuals? He is also concerned that the employees might treat the policy as though it is them against him (employees versus management). This could possibly have the long-term effect of damaging team behaviors.

For Discussion

1. What type of employee system or policy do you recommend for Don to establish? How should he implement it?

2. What are the ethical issues involved when a manager is friends (outside of work) with one of his employees?

3. Should Don leave the situation alone and use negative performance evaluations to get employees back in line with performance objectives?

4. How effective would a system of behavior modification be? How ethical?

THINKING CRITICALLY: Debate the Issue

BEHAVIOR MODIFICATION: USEFUL OR MANIPULATIVE?

Form teams as directed by your instructor to debate the issue of how managers can apply behavior modification in the workplace. Half of the teams should research and prepare to argue that behavior modification can be a useful management technique for increasing performance and productivity in the organization. The other teams should research and prepare to argue that behavior modification is essentially a technique for manipulating employee behavior.

Video Case

SCIENTECH

Home Page: {http://www.scientech-inc.com:80/}

Scientech is an engineering firm that finds solutions for problems associated with the world's most sophisticated technologies, including nuclear power plants, commercial airliners, jet fighters, and computers. Early in the history of the company, Dr. Larry Ybarrondo, founder of Scientech, read an article in the *Harvard Business Review* that helped grow his business. The article identified three kinds of employees necessary in a service business: finders, who get new business for the company; minders, who manage the business; and grinders, who perform the actual work. Dr. Ybarrando used this article to set the tone for the type of people and the type of employee incentives that he put into place at Scientech.

What Dr. Ybarrando did was proceed under the philosophy that a company has to "give to get." Initially, this prompted Dr. Ybarrando to expand his management team and share responsibility with the new leadership. Frequently, this is a difficult step for an entrepreneur. A stock ownership plan was then created so that each employee could share in the growing value of the company. Additional employees were hired, based on the heuristic that an employee had to have skills in two areas. In addition, everyone in the firm, including Dr. Ybarrando, was responsible for maintaining customer accounts. To promote a positive atmosphere, employees were provided a significant voice in company affairs, and extra effort was rewarded. Employee empowerment was implemented at every level of the firm, with an emphasis on quality and integrity. All of these steps contributed to the progressive growth of the company.

This formula has worked for Scientech; the Idaho Falls–based company is experiencing increased sales and market share. Dr. Ybarrando has also become an advocate of the philosophy that corporations have to "give to get" if they expect a high level of performance from their employees.

For Discussion

1. Describe some of Scientech's approaches to employee motivation.
2. How does equity theory relate to the concept of employee stock ownership plans? Would an employee stock ownership plan be an attractive benefit to you? Why or why not?

CAN THEY DO IT AGAIN?

The spectators are on their feet. The clock is ticking down from 30 seconds. The score is tied and the Eagles have the ball. As the guard brings the ball down the court, the crowd chants, "Defense, defense, defense." The wave goes around the arena. A crisp pass crosses the floor to the forward. He shoots. It's off the rim. No basket is made. The Eagles get the rebound. Now there are ten seconds, five, four, three, two, one. The shot is off just as the buzzer sounds. It's good! The crowd goes wild. The Eagles win their first CBA championship.

Later, at the press conference, Coach Long was asked about next year. Could the Eagles repeat their victory? He answered with a resounding "yes." Privately, Coach Long wondered if he could continue to motivate the players and control some of the behaviors that caused problems this past year. He also wondered about the off-season. Would the players be motivated to stay in physical shape and develop their skills without the staff's constant supervision? The players certainly made a lot of money playing ball, but they didn't seem to take any responsibility for their behavior off the court.

Coach Long pondered several problems that he and his staff had confronted this past year. First, certain players were consistently in some kind of trouble. Recently, one player was arrested for possession of cocaine, another got into a fight at a local bar, and a third was arrested for DUI. Although the player involved in the fight claimed self-defense, and the other team members said the drug charges were false, the team had received negative publicity. The players were role models to hundreds of youngsters, and the Eagle organization just couldn't tolerate such behavior.

Other problems involved punctuality, absenteeism, and general courtesy. Three or four of the players were consistently late for practice. A few players invariably missed flights for away games. Some of the players were rude to the fans or refused to give autographs to fans who waited after the games. Several players took shortcuts across the running field to cut down on the required running distances. Heavy fines were imposed for these behaviors, but that didn't seem to work. The staff had to call players to remind them of practice times, pick them up for practice, watch them at practice, make special travel arrangements, and apologize to the fans for the players' surly attitudes.

Considering all this, Coach Long wondered how the team won the championship in the first place. He reminded himself that despite all the problems, the players did get along well together. After a two-week vacation, the staff had their first meeting. Coach Long mentioned the concerns he had about the previous year and his doubts that the team could win another championship under the same circumstances. The staff members agreed and voiced their concerns as well. They concluded with the commitment to making the changes necessary to produce another successful year.

For Discussion

1. What seems to be the central motivational problem that plagues the Eagles?
2. Using the reinforcement theory of motivation, describe the types of reinforcers the staff is using. What works? What is not working? Why?
3. What changes should the staff make? How should the changes be implemented?

EXPERIENTIAL EXERCISE 15.1

Working either in a small team or individually, design a contest that will motivate employees or peers where you are employed. If you do not have work experience, then develop a contest for students in the classroom. What concepts from the chapter are you going to use? Be sure your contest is well explained.

Before running the contest, check the following items to be sure you have answered them.

1. To what degree do contests work?
2. What behaviors are you trying to encourage?
3. Is the prize valued? How do you know?
4. Is the contest outcome tied to performance or chance? What are specific measurable standards?
5. Do employees believe they have a chance for winning?

EXPERIENTIAL EXERCISE 15.2

Your Goal-Related Behavior

The purpose of this exercise is to allow you to examine your goal-related behavior in problem-solving groups. Working by yourself, answer the following three questions. Be honest. Check as many responses to each question as are characteristic of your usual and regular behavior. Then form a group with two of your classmates and discuss your answers to the questions and why you answered them as you did. Develop as much awareness of your behavior in goal-related situations as possible.

1. When I am a member of a group that does not seem to have clear awareness of what its goals are or how they are to be achieved, I usually

_____ ask the group to stop and discuss its goals until all group members clearly understand what they are and what actions the group needs to take to accomplish them.
_____ feel disgusted and refuse to attend meetings.
_____ state as specifically as possible what I consider the goals to be and comment on how the present actions of the group relate to goal accomplishment.
_____ ask the designated leader to stop messing around and tell the group what it is supposed to be doing.

2. When I am a member of a group that has clear understanding of its goals but seems to have little commitment to accomplishing them, I usually
_____ try to shame other group members into being more motivated.
_____ blame the designated leader for being incompetent.

_____ ask the group members to look at how meaningful, relevant, and acceptable the goals are to them.
_____ try to change the group's goals in order to make them more relevant to members' needs and motives.
_____ point out the sacrifices some members have made in the past toward goal accomplishment and hope that all members become more committed.

3. When I am a member of a group that has conflicting opinions on what its goals should be, or that has members with conflicting needs and motives, I usually

_____ figure out how much cooperative and competitive behavior exists in the group and give the group feedback based on my observations, in an attempt to increase cooperativeness among its members.
_____ start a group discussion on the personal goals, needs, and motives of each group member in order to determine the extent to which there are competing goals among them.
_____ declare one member of the group to be the winner and ask all other group members to work toward accomplishing that person's goals.
_____ ask the group to determine how the members' actions can become more coordinated.
_____ form a secret coalition with several other group members so that our goals will become dominant in the group.

ENDNOTES

1. Adapted from A. Kover and R. Henkoff, "Growing Your Company: Five Ways to Do It Right!" *Fortune,* November 25, 1996, 78–98; T. Teal, "Service Comes First: An Interview with USAA's Robert F. McDermott," *Harvard Business Review,* September/October 1992, 117–27.

2. *Creating and Motivating a Superior, Loyal Staff* (New York: National Institute of Business Management, 1992).

3. For an integrated motivational model, see H. J. Klein, "An Integrated Control Theory Model of Work Motivation," *Academy of Management Review,* 14, 1989, 150-72.

4. R. M. Steers and P. W. Porter, eds., *Motivation and Work Behavior,* 3d ed. (New York: McGraw-Hill, 1983).

5. This discussion is based on *Creating and Motivating a Superior, Loyal Staff.*

6. For a research perspective, see M. A. Wahba and L. G. Bridwell, "Maslow Reconsidered: A Review of Research on the Need Hierarchy," *Organizational Behavior and Human Performance,* 16, 1976, 212-40.

7. A. H. Maslow, "A Theory of Human Motivation," *Psychological Review,* 50, 1943, 370-96.

8. K. Labich, "Elite Teams Get the Job Done," *Fortune,* February 19, 1996, 90-99. ©1996 Time Inc. All rights reserved.

9. F. Herzberg, "One More Time: How Do You Motivate Employees?" *Harvard Business Review,* January/February 1968, 53-62.

10. "What Motivates Managers," *Inc.,* June 1989, 115.

11. C. Wild, "AT&T Starts Volunteer Program," *1996 Conference Board Report.*

12. D. C. McClelland, *The Achieving Society* (New York: Van Nostrand Reinhold, 1961).

13. D. Miron and D. McClelland, "The Impact of Achievement Motivation Training on Small Businesses," *California Management Review,* Summer 1979, 13-28.

14. D. C. McClelland, *Human Motivation* (Glenview, Ill.: Scott, Foresman, 1985).

15. J. Hyatt, "The Entrepreneur of the Year," *Inc.,* January 1991, 35-51.

16. D. Miron and D. McClelland, "The Impact of Achievement Motivation Training on Small Businesses."

17. For a classic discussion of power, see D. McClelland and H. Burnham, "Power Is the Great Motivator," *Harvard Business Review,* 54, March/April 1976, 100-10.

18. V. H. Vroom, *Work and Motivation* (New York: Wiley, 1964).

19. *Creating and Motivating a Superior, Loyal Staff.*

20. "It's the Nature of the Job," *Psychology Today,* November/December 1993, 28.

21. R. W. Griffin, "Effects of Work Redesign on Employee Perceptions, Attitudes, and Behaviors: A Long-Term Investigation," *Academy of Management Journal,* 34, 1991, 425-35.

22. S. J. Adams, "Toward an Understanding of Inequity," *Journal of Abnormal and Social Psychology,* 67, 1963, 422-36.

23. See Ibid; S. J. Adams, "Inequity in Social Exchange," in *Advances in Experimental Social Psychology,* Vol. 2, ed. L. Berkowitz (New York: Academic Press, 1965), 267-300.

24. J. D. Hatfield and E. W. Miles, "A New Perspective on Equity Theory: The Equity Sensitivity Construct," *Academy of Management Review,* 12, 1987, 222-34.

25. E. W. Miles, J. D. Hatfield, and R. C. Huseman, "The Equity Sensitivity Construct: Potential Implications for Work Performance," *Journal of Management,* 15, 1989, 581-88.

26. K. Blanchard and J. Johnson, *The One Minute Manager* (New York: Morrow, 1982).

27. Adapted from A. Kover and R. Henkoff, "Growing Your Company: Five Ways to Do it Right!"; T. Teal, "Service Comes First."

28. G. Koretz, "Economic Trends," *Business Week,* April 29, 1991, 22.

29. For a detailed review, see E. Locke, K. Shaw, L. Saari, and G. P. Latham, "Goal Setting and Task Performance, 1969-1980," *Psychological Bulletin,* 90, 1981, 125-52.

30. The work on goal-setting theory is well summarized in E. Locke and G. P. Latham, *Goal Setting: A Motivational Technique That Works!* (Upper Saddle River, N.J.: Prentice Hall, 1984).

31. A. Tziner and G. P. Latham, "The Effects of Appraisal Instrument, Feedback and Goal-Setting on Worker Satisfaction and Commitment," *Journal of Organizational Behavior,* 10, 1989, 145-53.

32. L. Robertson, "Prediction of Job Satisfaction from Characteristics of Personal Work Goals," *Journal of Organizational Behavior,* 11, 1990, 29-41.

33. G. Pinchot, "Creating Organizations with Many Leaders," in *The Leader of the Future,* F. Hesselbein, M. Goldsmith, and R. Beckhard (eds.) (San Francisco: Jossey-Bass Publishers, 1996).

34. J. B. Miller, *The Corporate Coach* (New York: St. Martin's Press, 1994).

35. T. Kayser, *Building Team Power: How to Unleash the Collaborative Genius of Work Teams* (Burr Ridge, Ill.: Irwin, 1994); H Sims Jr. and C Manz, *Company of Heroes: Unleashing the Power of Self-Leadership* (New York: Wiley, 1996).

36. J. Hirsch, "Now Hotel Clerks Provide More Than Keys," *The Wall Street Journal,* March 5, 1993, B1.

37. C. Manz and H. Sims, *Business without Bosses: How Self-Managing Teams Are Building High Performing Companies* (New York: Wiley, 1995); M. Hammer and J. Champy, *Reengineering the Corporation: A Manifesto for Business Revolution* (New York: HarperBusiness, 1994).

38. R. Mitchell and M. Oneal, "Managing by Values," *Business Week,* August 1, 1996, 46-52.

39. C. Carson, K. Eckart, C. Flash, G. Fysh, M. Maharry, and J. Szymariski. "It's Going the Way It Was Programmed," *Tacoma News Tribune,* September 8, 1996, D1.

40. N. Adler, "A Typology of Management Studies Involving Culture," *Journal of International Business Studies,* Fall 1983, 29-47.

41. A. Howard, K. Shudo, and M. Umeshima, "Motivation and Values among Japanese and American Managers," *Personnel Psychology,* 36, 1983, 883-98.

42. J. T. Spence, "Achievement American Style: The Rewards and Costs of Individualism," *American Psychologist,* 40, 1985, 1285-94.

43. S. Cady, P. Fandt, and D. Fernandez, "Investigating Cultural Differences in Personal Success: Implications for Designing Effective Reward Systems," *Journal of Value*

Based Management, 6, 1993, 65–80; N. J. Adler, *International Dimensions of Organizational Behavior* (Boston: Kent, 1986); M. Dolecheck, "Cross-Cultural Analysis of Business Ethics: Hong Kong and American Business Personnel," *Journal of Managerial Issues,* 4, 1992, 288–303.

44. This discussion is from G. Hofstede, "The Interaction between National and Organizational Value Systems," *Journal of Management Studies,* 22, 1985, 347–57; G. Hofstede, *Culture's Consequences: International Differ-*

ences in Work-Related Values (Beverly Hills, Calif.: Sage, 1980).

45. This discussion is based on the research results found in S. Cady, P. Fandt, and D. Fernandez, "Investigating Cultural Differences in Personal Success."

46. T. Cox Jr., "The Multicultural Organization," *Academy of Management Executive,* 5, 1991, 34–47.

47. Adapted from A. Kover and R. Henkoff, "Growing Your Company: Five Ways to Do it Right!"; T. Teal, "Service Comes First."

IBAX: Facilitating Change through Leadership, Communication, and Motivation

By now you should be very familiar with IBAX, the company profiled in the integrative cases at the close of the major sections of the book. IBAX, a partnership between IBM and Baxter, had experienced significant strategic, operational, and financial problems since its inception in 1989. As of the beginning of 1991, Jeff Goodman, the newly hired CEO of IBAX, was in the process of implementing a retrenchment strategy designed to restore the company's product quality, customer satisfaction levels, productivity, and financial performance.

As we saw in the last integrative case, Goodman implemented major changes in the organizational structure of IBAX, its human resource management practices, and its organizational culture. In this case, we will examine how leadership, communication, and motivation changed at IBAX.

LEADERSHIP

Goodman knew that the successful implementation of a retrenchment strategy would require strong leadership throughout the organization. He felt strongly that "leading by example" would be critical in getting employees to deal more effectively with each other, the customers, the partners, and other stakeholders of the organization.

Upon his arrival, Goodman assessed the individuals who occupied managerial positions in the company, as well as those who appeared capable of assuming such roles. Based on that assessment, he was able to identify a core group of individuals who could fulfill senior management leadership roles within IBAX, as well as other leadership roles throughout the organization. The next challenge was to turn this group of individuals into a team that would be committed to the company, as well as to each other.

He began by taking the senior management group through an intensive off-site team-building program that involved everything from classroom lectures to scaling walls and swinging on ropes. The intent of the program was to build the trust and commitment of the team. Once Goodman was convinced that his senior management group had become a team, he turned his efforts to infusing the team philosophy throughout the organization. The other managers who had been identified as leaders within the company went through the same training with their work groups. Eventually, everyone in the organization had participated in the team-building program.

Goodman's challenge was to ensure that the team-building training was transferred back into the workplace. He continued to stress the importance of the concepts within the work environment, and eventually, the team philosophy became part of the organizational culture at IBAX. The ongoing behavior of the employees began to reflect their dedication to the company and their teams. This was evidenced by a growing commitment to deliver better quality products and services to the customers.

COMMUNICATION

As was mentioned previously, communication at IBAX prior to Goodman's arrival had been limited and primarily one-way—from the bottom up. Top management rarely communicated with the employees at the lower levels of the organization. As a result, the employees were literally unaware of the severity of the problems facing the company in early 1991. Therefore, one of Goodman's primary challenges was to inform the employees of the reality of the situation at IBAX and then develop the communication infrastructure to ensure that they had the information they needed to do their jobs effectively.

Goodman began by holding companywide meetings in which "he threw open the financial statements of the company and let the numbers tell the story." Where necessary, he explained what the financial statements said and what they meant. He also provided measures of customer satisfaction and perceived product quality to the employees. These were objective measurements that were visible to everyone and led to obvious conclusions regarding the performance of the company in the short term, as well as its long-term viability. These sessions provided employees with new insights about the situation at IBAX. They began to understand that survival depended on their ability to make radical and dramatic changes in the way the company operated.

Once Goodman knew that he had successfully communicated the need for change, he began to build a communication infrastructure that kept everyone apprised of the condition of the company and provided open access to the information they needed to do their jobs well. Everyone in each business unit had open access to revenues, expenses, statistics, and other decisional information that was relevant for their business. This information was posted on bulletin boards and distributed in reports; it was updated monthly and discussed among peers regularly. For the first time, employees had access to the information they needed to do their jobs effectively and efficiently and with a focus on achieving high-level performance as measured by critical financial and performance variables.

MOTIVATION

Goodman had a broad-based leadership team in place, had communicated the need for change to the employees, and had set up a well-defined communication infrastructure within the company. Yet he also needed to establish methods for motivating employees to do what was necessary to improve product quality, customer service, and customer satisfaction. This required an understanding of what motivates people and the development of a reward system that was based on realistic but aggressive performance goals.

Goodman's philosophy of motivation was simple. He believed that people are motivated by the ability to be involved, make decisions, and make a difference. They want to "buy in" to their company and its products, and they want to reap the rewards associated with doing a good job. With this philosophy in mind, Goodman knew that he had to encourage the employees of IBAX to take ownership in the turnaround—to feel responsible for the company's success.

From Goodman's perspective, this translated into empowerment. He felt strongly that the employees had to be empowered to make a difference in the performance of the company. But he also knew that you can't just empower people and expect positive results. Many employees need support and development to be effectively empowered—in other words, they need to be "enabled." Some employees simply weren't capable of assuming responsibility for important tasks within the organization. Others were capable, but did not have access to the information or resources they needed to do their jobs well. Others lacked the organizational authority to get their jobs done. In all of these cases, Goodman and his leadership team stepped in and provided what was needed. For some employees, that meant additional education and training; in other cases it simply required providing information, resources, or authority. But in virtually all cases, the employees at IBAX were enabled and empowered to do their jobs well.

Even empowered employees need performance standards to work toward. And the employees at IBAX had them. Employees engaged in what Goodman calls "covenant defining." As he explains it, "when one has a job to do, they should build a covenant with the person to whom they report. This covenant should define their responsibilities and how they will be measured and evaluated in light of those responsibilities. This covenant becomes a binding agreement between the parties involved as to their commitment to one another." The performance standards that resulted from this process of covenant defining provided the measures by which employees were evaluated and rewarded.

The formal reward system was based on these performance standards, as well as on attributes and behaviors related to team leadership and team behavior. Employees were measured over time, and those who met their standards and contributed to the team were rewarded. Beyond the formal reward system, IBAX implemented an awards program that was based on both individual and team performance. For example, one award, the Best Demonstrated Practices Award, recognized work teams that showed substantial creativity or significant performance improvements.

THE RESULTS

Through effective leadership, enhanced communication, and a well-defined system of motivating and rewarding employees, IBAX began to realize gains in quality, productivity, and financial performance. When the employees who are closest to the products and customers are enabled and empowered to make decisions and are rewarded for their efforts, dramatic improvements in organizational performance can be achieved.

For Discussion

1. How did Goodman develop his leadership team and what role did the team play in facilitating organizational change?

2. Why was improved communication so important to the retrenchment efforts at IBAX?

3. Describe how Goodman used motivation and reward systems to effect change within the company.

5

P A R T

CONTROL CHALLENGES IN THE 21ST CENTURY

Organizational Control in a Complex Business Environment

C H A P T E R

■ CHAPTER OVERVIEW

Control is the last of the four major management functions to be covered in this text. It is a critically important managerial function because it helps to ensure that all of our planning, organizing, and leading have gone as we had hoped they would. In today's rapidly changing and highly competitive global business environment, organizations can experience a very rapid reversal of their fortunes if they fail to control all aspects of their operations adequately. Individual and group behaviors and all organizational performance must be in line with the strategic focus of the organization. When economic, technological, political, social, global, or competitive forces change, control systems must be capable of adjusting behaviors and performance to make them compatible with these strategic shifts. The essence of the control process requires that managers determine performance standards, measure actual performance, compare actual performance with standards, and take corrective action when necessary.

In this chapter we begin by examining the steps in the control process. After this, we discuss several control system design considerations, criteria for effective control, and keys to selecting the proper amount of control. Since the control process can be implemented at almost any stage in an organization's operations, we examine the three basic organizational control focal points. In addition, we explore two opposing philosophies toward control and raise some thought-provoking ethical issues in the control of employee behavior.

■ LEARNING OBJECTIVES

When you have finished studying this chapter, you should be able to:

- Define and discuss the importance of organizational control.
- Identify the sequence of steps to be undertaken in a thorough control system.
- Identify the factors that are important considerations in the design of a control system.
- Describe the various characteristics of effective control.
- Identify the factors that help determine the proper amount of control.
- Define feedforward control, concurrent control, and feedback control.

- Describe the difference between the philosophies of bureaucratic control and organic control.
- Describe some of the more important techniques and methods for establishing financial control.
- Discuss some of the ethical issues related to the control of employee behavior.

Managerial Incident

MOTOROLA, INC.—SURVIVAL THROUGH CONTROLS

Motorola, Inc., headquartered in Schaumburg, Illinois, is an engineering-oriented company whose principal product lines are communications systems and semiconductors. With over 50 facilities worldwide and more than 100,000 employees, Motorola is recognized as one of the leading manufacturers of electronic equipment, systems, and components in the global marketplace. Its products are highly regarded for their quality and reliability. However, this was not always the reputation of Motorola.

Since its founding in 1928, the company has had its share of incidents that caused some corporate red faces. Some of these incidents were almost comical, and all could have been avoided with better control mechanisms. For example, in the early 1930s, while tinkering with a design problem on their Model 55 car radio, Motorola engineers managed to set on fire the car of Motorola's founder, Paul Galvin. Much to his dismay, this dubious feat was accomplished twice in one month! Such fires were not limited to the test track. There were reported incidents of cars, garages, and attached homes going up in flames. And, in one rather bizarre incident, a hearse equipped with a Model 55 radio and carrying a body destined for a traditional burial suffered one of these fires. The radio, hearse, and body were all cremated in ignominious fashion.

More recently, Motorola's Quasar TV plant in Chicago had a history of severe defects (between 150 and 180 per 100 TV sets) and high warranty costs ($16 million yearly). Results such as these were consistent with Motorola's historical unstated philosophy to "make the product right eventually." This approach required that, in general, 20 percent of Motorola's employees were doing testing, and countless hours were being spent servicing failures in the field. Within two years of the Japanese company Matsushita's purchase of Motorola's TV division, production doubled, quality improved astronomically (3 or 4 defects per 100 TV sets), warranty costs dropped to only $2 million (for twice as many TV sets), and the in-plant repair staff dropped from 120 to 15. These dramatic improvements were accomplished with the same hourly work force!

Although Motorola commanded almost 50 percent of the market, its share was dwindling as customers increasingly complained about delivery time, product quality and reliability, and many other areas of dissatisfaction. These problems led then-chairman Robert Galvin to throw down the gauntlet. In this increasingly competitive, global industry, relatively high quality was not good enough. Motorola needed control mechanisms that would ensure that worker performance and production output were close to perfect. This was the challenge facing Motorola—it needed to design and implement effective systems for control so that it could compete on an even basis with its Japanese competitors.[1]

INTRODUCTION

As we saw in the Managerial Incident, Motorola was facing a difficult situation. Poor control of product quality had driven Motorola out of many of its long-time businesses and was now threatening its very existence. To survive in the highly competitive electronics market, Motorola would have to develop control mechanisms that would ensure that its products could compete in quality with those of its Japanese competitors. This would require the institution of control mechanisms that could ensure that worker behavior and performance were consistent with newly defined, high standards.

Control is the last of the four major management functions that we have been discussing. By its very nature, control is concerned with making sure that all of our planning, organizing, and leading have gone as we anticipated. Control is a critical managerial function because the consequences of not meeting the standards of performance can be very negative for the organization. For example, poor inventory control can result in lost business because of a product shortage. Poor quality control may result in angry customers, lost business, and the necessity to provide customers with replacement products. Poor cost control can lead to negative profitability and perhaps even bankruptcy. The list of potential control problems is almost limitless. These problems all point to the fact that improving operational effectiveness and quality is virtually impossible without stringent control mechanisms.

Furthermore, in a world where quality often means the difference between success and failure, organizations simply cannot tolerate substandard product or service outputs. Organizations must develop and maintain control mechanisms capable of identifying and responding to deviations in organizational performance. And while the need for control is evident in all organizations, multinational organizations have particularly challenging and unique control needs. Maintaining internal control of units located in markets and regions around the globe can be far more problematic than maintaining control over a set of domestic operating units. Thus, control mechanisms must often be specifically designed to meet the challenges of global management.

In this chapter we examine several aspects of the control process. We begin by describing the basic steps in the control process and then build upon these basics.

A PROCESS OF CONTROL FOR DIVERSE AND MULTINATIONAL ORGANIZATIONS

Organizational control is defined as the systematic process through which managers regulate organizational activities to make them consistent with the expectations established in plans and to help them achieve all predetermined standards of performance.[2] This definition implies that managers must determine performance standards and develop mechanisms for gathering performance information in order to assess the degree to which standards are being met. Control, then, is a systematic set of steps that must be undertaken. Figure 16.1 illustrates this sequence of steps. As you can see, the process of control involves four steps: (1) setting standards of performance, (2) measuring actual performance, (3) comparing actual performance with standards, and (4) responding to deviations.[3] Let's now examine each of these steps in greater detail.

> **Organizational control**
> A process through which managers regulate organizational activities to make them consistent with expectations and help them achieve predetermined standards of performance.

SETTING STANDARDS OF PERFORMANCE

The control process should begin with the establishment of standards of performance against which organizational activities can be compared. Standards of performance begin to evolve only after the organization has developed its overall strategic plan and managers have defined goals for organizational departments. In some instances the performance standards are generated from within the organization. Sometimes, however, the impetus for specific perfor-

FIGURE 16.1
Steps in the control process

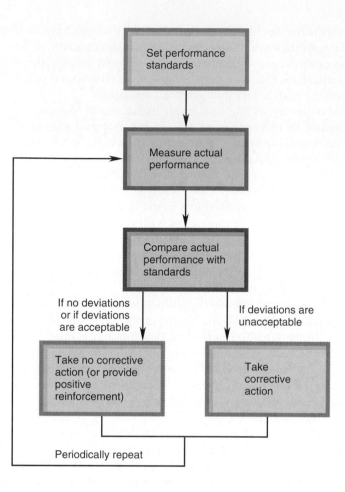

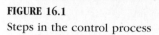

mance standards may originate with some outside source. For example, government laws on safety standards for electrical appliances will have a huge impact on what a manufacturer sets as the allowable current leakage from its hand-held hair dryers. Entrepreneurial Approach describes the situation local municipalities face as they try to dispose of garbage and at the same time adhere to increasingly rigid state and federal government standards. Here we see the rather novel landfill remodeling approach used by a small Massachusetts company.

In other cases the desires and needs of the customer may dictate the standards set by both manufacturers and the providers of services. In fact, in today's environment, the emphasis on quality and customer satisfaction is increasing the influence that customers have on organizational standards of performance. Global Perspective describes how this focus on the needs and desires of the customer has been put to good use by Nokia, the world's second leading manufacturer of cellular telephones.

The organizational activities to be controlled may involve individual behavior, group behavior, production output, service delivery, and so forth. Whenever possible, the standards should be set in a manner that allows them to be compared with actual performance. For example, it would not be very useful for Motorola to state that "output quality in the integrated circuit manufacturing operation should be high." Such a standard lacks the detail needed to make comparisons with performance. A more appropriate statement of performance standard might be "the integrated circuit manufacturing operation should have no more than five defects per 1,000,000 manufactured units." Such a standard contains the degree of clarity needed for comparative purposes.

Or consider the professor who wishes to communicate to students the standards of classroom performance for his management class. Simply stating

BioSafe: One Person's Trash Is This Company's Treasure

The town of Fairhaven, Massachusetts was facing a problem common to many local municipalities. What do you do when the government wants to shut down the town dump? Outright closure of landfills costs about $200,000 per acre, a figure that would be a tremendous burden for Fairhaven with its 23-acre landfill. Fairhaven's solution was to turn to BioSafe International, Inc., a small Cambridge, Massachusetts, company that has developed the concept of landfill remodeling, which is an improvement over traditional landfill mining. For BioSafe, the Fairhaven site is the company's first commercial remodeling project.

Traditional landfill mining tactics have attempted to excavate landfills and process the garbage by separating recyclable materials that were disposed of before the stricter government recycling standards were established. The landfill that has been excavated is then relined to meet federal standards, and the nonrecyclable waste is compacted and reburied. BioSafe's process improves on this practice by remodeling these landfills and opening as much additional landfill capacity as possible. This process is best suited for markets where space is at a premium, such as the northeastern United States.

Although BioSafe had sales of just $1.5 million in 1995, it estimates that it could reap more than $55 million in revenue between 1997 and 2006 from the Fairhaven facility alone. The Fairhaven remodeling project will create 70 percent more space and add 10 years to the life of that facility. And with more than 400 landfills in the northeastern United States that will have to be closed because they fail to meet federal standards, the potential for BioSafe is indeed huge.[4]

that "students should be prepared for class" is vague and provides little guidance to the students. But, if the syllabus says that "students should have read the assigned material prior to each class and should be prepared to discuss the issues when called upon in class," much more clarity is provided.

These two examples hardly illustrate the wide diversity of performance standards that might be established. Standards of performance can be set for virtually any activity or behavior within an organization. For example, it is not unusual to find organizations that set standards for employee dress or grooming. For many years IBM required the men in its male-dominated supervisory positions to wear white dress shirts. The Walt Disney Company maintains strict standards for employee dress, grooming, jewelry, cosmetics, and even artificial hair coloring. As today's work force becomes more diverse, setting and enforcing standards of individual behavior and performance can sometimes be more difficult. We have seen repeatedly throughout this book that the workplace is no longer composed of homogeneous individuals. Ethnic, racial, and gender differences often lead to different sets of individual values and expectations.

Furthermore, multinational corporations with operations in several countries often find it difficult, if not impossible, to maintain the same standards in all countries. It is difficult to establish corporationwide standards for subsidiaries that function within diverse sociocultural, technological, political-legal, and economic environments. For example, a multinational organization's facilities may have very different productivity targets in light of the different work attitudes in the various countries. Similarly, plants in different nations may employ technologies with various levels of sophistication suitable to the education/skill levels of the local work force; consequently, the plants may experience significant variation in productivity rates. Clearly, such circumstances can impede the development of corporationwide performance standards.

NOKIA: NUMBER TWO BUT TRYING JUST AS HARD

Through the Managerial Incident in this chapter, we are all familiar with Motorola, the world leader in mobile cellular telephones. However, many would be surprised to learn that the number two global company in this industry is Finland-based Nokia. With similarly manufactured products, Nokia has faced many of the same control issues that were facing Motorola. One of the keys to Nokia's global success has been its receptiveness to its customers when establishing standards. Nokia is committed to providing what the customer wants. For example, Nokia was able to introduce its digital cellular telephone, which allows users to send and receive e-mail and faxes, eight months before Motorola. Nokia was also the first company to accommodate the new European digital standards for cellular networks. And Nokia seemed to be the only company willing to provide the special features that one mobile network in England was looking for.

Nokia strives to maintain its enviable global position in the mobile cellular telephone marketplace. To accomplish this, the company has focused on standardizing products. Despite the fact that technology standards are different between the United States, Japan, and Europe, Nokia designs phones that are as similar as possible for those markets. This facilitates their manufacture on the same production line, which aids in cost reduction, further strengthening the company's hold on its global market share.[5]

MEASURING ACTUAL PERFORMANCE

In some cases measuring actual performance can be relatively simple, but in others it can be quite complex. We have to decide such things as (1) what to measure (that is, a single item or multiple items such as sales, costs, profits, rejects, or orders), (2) when to measure, and (3) how frequently to measure. As we noted earlier, standards should be stated as clearly as possible so they can be compared with performance. Doing this is quite simple when the performance criteria are quantitative in nature and can be objectively measured. The standard in our earlier Motorola example—"the integrated circuit manufacturing operation should have no more than five defects per 1,000,000 manufactured units"—is a quantitative performance criterion. Sometimes, however, performance criteria are more qualitative in nature and do not easily lend themselves to absolute units of measure. Instead, they require a subjective assessment to determine whether the standard is being met. For example, even though a management student has read the assigned material and discussed the issues when called upon in class, the professor's assessment of the student's performance can be quite subjective when the issues do not have a single correct interpretation.

Suppose that the Chicago Cutlery Company states that its knives "must be honed to a high degree of sharpness, and the wooden handles must be polished to a bright luster." This is also a qualitative performance measure, for determining whether a particular knife was sharp enough or bright enough would not be easy. But regardless of whether the stated performance measure is quantitative or qualitative in nature, actual performance must be recorded for subsequent comparison with the performance standard.

Measurement of performance in an assembly plant is relatively simple because standards are quantitative. But more qualitative performance criteria are more difficult to measure because they require a subjective assessment to determine whether the standard is being met.

© Mark Segal/Tony Stone Images

COMPARING ACTUAL PERFORMANCE WITH STANDARDS

The first two steps of the control process provide managers with the information that allows them to make comparisons between actual performance and standards. If the actual performance is identical to the standard, then no deviation has occurred. Rarely, however, is there absolutely no deviation between actual and planned performance. Fortunately, in most real-world situations, actual performance does not always have to be identical to the standard. Typically, the performance standard has a stated acceptable deviation. For example, suppose Motorola management set an average productivity standard of 50 cellular telephones per worker per hour, with an acceptable deviation of plus or minus 5 telephones per worker per hour. The acceptable deviations would define the control limits for this process. If productivity is between 45 and 55 cellular telephones per worker per hour, then the process is said to be "in control," meaning that no corrective action is necessary. Measurements outside this range indicate an "out of control" situation that requires corrective action.

Continuing with the Motorola example, if actual productivity is 47 telephones per worker per hour, then the deviation from the standard is acceptable, and no corrective action is required. Suppose, on the other hand, that productivity is 58 telephones per worker per hour. Now the deviation from the standard is unacceptable, and the subsequent steps in the control process should attempt to correct it. One might initially think that this deviation (with its extra output) would be considered desirable and that no attempts would be made to correct it. But this deviation could lead to problems if the company has no market for the excess output or no room to store it; possibly, too, the extra production is using resources that were to be used elsewhere.

For a more personal example, suppose that you have established a performance standard of at least 85 for your scores on the mid-term and final exams to help you achieve your goal of receiving a grade of B in your management course. If your mid-term exam score is only 75, you would have an undesirable deviation. But if your score is greater than 85, you would have an acceptable deviation from your established standard.

RESPONDING TO DEVIATIONS

After comparing actual performance with standards, we can choose to either (1) take no corrective action or (2) take corrective action. If the deviation was acceptable or if there was no deviation, then the response should be to take no corrective action, since the performance or behavior is acceptable in light of the standards. If, however, the deviation was unacceptable, then the response should be to take corrective action. Corrective action usually requires making a change in some behavior, activity, or aspect of the organization to bring performance into line with the standards. Even when no corrective action is necessary, it is often useful to provide positive feedback (and in some cases even rewards) to the responsible individuals so that they are motivated to continue performing to the standards.

Return to the earlier example in which you set a standard of 85 for your mid-term and final exam scores. If your mid-term exam score is only 75, the undesirable deviation would require a response on your part. You might attempt to compensate by preparing more thoroughly for the final exam. (Or you might decide to drop the course and try again in another semester!) If your score on the mid-term exam is 90, you would not need to take corrective action in preparing for the final exam (unless, of course, you decide to raise your goal to a course grade of A and reestablish your performance standard for the final exam to achieve this goal).

When exercising control in business organizations, a variety of types of changes are possible, depending upon the particular situation. Changes in materials, equipment, process, or staffing might be made. In some cases the corrective action might even involve changing the original performance standards. For example, the company might determine that the standards were set unrealistically high, making them too difficult to achieve consistently. Regardless of whether or not corrective action is taken, the control process does not end here. Even if performance standards are currently being achieved, there is no guarantee that this will be true in the future. Consequently, the measurement and comparison steps must be periodically repeated.

Developing and implementing creative and constructive responses to undesirable deviations can be exceptionally difficult for multinational organizations. Because the company's understanding of each individual unit is less when units are scattered around the globe, developing solutions requires a substantial amount of information gathering. Further, the development of solutions that are acceptable to both subsidiary and headquarters management may require active participation by key personnel at each level. Consequently, it may take longer to determine and implement the necessary corrective action, and that action may come at the expense of significant managerial time and energy.

Up to this point, we have seen that the basic process of control involves a few very fundamental steps: (1) establishing standards of performance, (2) measuring actual performance, (3) comparing actual performance with standards, and (4) responding to deviations when necessary. But knowing the four steps in the control process is not enough to ensure that an effective control system will be developed. As we will see in the next sections, several other issues must be considered.

DESIGNING QUALITY AND EFFECTIVENESS INTO THE CONTROL SYSTEM

Designing an effective control system can be far more complex than simply performing the four steps in the control process. Several other important factors must be considered as well. Once the control system has been designed

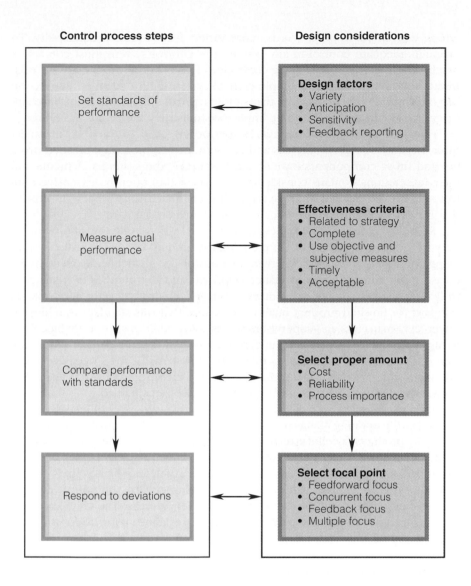

Control process steps   Design considerations

FIGURE 16.2
Control system design issues

and implemented, several criteria are available to help determine how effective it will be. Finally, it is necessary to select the amount of control to be used and the point in the organization where the control effort will be focused. These issues must be considered as each step in the control process unfolds, as Figure 16.2 illustrates. We begin our treatment of control system design issues by examining several important design factors.

DESIGN FACTORS AFFECTING CONTROL SYSTEM QUALITY

When designing a control system, four important factors must be considered: (1) the amount of variety in the control system, (2) the ability to anticipate problems, (3) the sensitivity of the measuring device, and (4) the composition of the feedback reports. Let's examine each of these factors more thoroughly.

Amount of Variety in the Control System

One important design consideration is the amount of variety in the control system. *Variety* refers to the number of activities, processes, or items that are measured and controlled. Systems become more complex as the number of system elements and number of possible interactions among them increase. There is more uncertainty in complex systems because more things can go

Law of requisite variety
Control systems must have enough variety to cope with the variety in the systems they are trying to control.

wrong with them. In other words, more variety leads to less predictability. To maintain adequate control in any system, the control system must contain as much variety as the system being controlled. This is known as the **law of requisite variety.**[6] Although a simple control system might seem attractive, the law of requisite variety suggests that simple control systems may not have sufficient variety to cope with the complex systems they are trying to control.[7]

Consider the plight of General Motors or any other automobile manufacturer. Because so many materials and parts go into the complex finished product and those components have so many sources, the system's elements and their interactions contain considerable variety. Consequently, extensive control systems are needed at all stages in the manufacturing process to ensure that the finished automobiles meet the performance standards.

Requisite variety can be achieved by either (1) increasing the amount of variety in the control system or (2) reducing the amount of variety in the system being controlled. Increased variety in the control system can be achieved by increasing the number of performance standards and the number of items controlled. In the case of General Motors, top management will set a performance standard for finished product quality. To ensure that this standard is achieved, lower-level managers and supervisors will employ additional performance standards to provide raw-material input control, production scrap control, labor control, quality control, and similar other control systems. If the lower-level managers and supervisors are successful in achieving these standards, it is likely that the top-level standard for product quality will also be achieved.

Let's now look at an example of how Motorola, whose problems were described in the opening Managerial Incident, might achieve requisite variety with one of its products, a cellular telephone composed of nearly 400 parts. To avoid repairs after final assembly, all 400 parts must be free of defects. But consider this sobering law of basic statistics. Because this product contains so many parts, unless each of the component parts is of very high quality, the probability that the finished product will be defect-free is low. To increase the chances of defect-free telephones, the company would have to establish controls for the manufacturing of all 400 parts. As an alternative, Motorola might consider reducing the amount of variety in the telephone by designing a phone with fewer parts. This would reduce the variety in the elements and their interactions. Since there would be fewer places where failures could occur, a simpler set of control systems could be put into place. Such actions were central to Motorola's survival, as we will see in the Managerial Incident Resolution.

Ability to Anticipate Problems

A second consideration in designing a control system is its ability to anticipate problems. When the control process is instituted, several distinct events occur when performance fails to meet the established standards. First, the undesirable deviation from standards is observed. Then, the situation is reported to the person or persons responsible for taking corrective action. Next, corrective action is instituted, and eventually, performance should return to an acceptable value. Inevitably, time lags occur between observation, reporting, instituting, and return. During these time lags, the performance continues to be unacceptable. Figure 16.3 illustrates this sequence of events.

The damage caused by these time lags can be reduced by building the ability to anticipate problems into the control system. If a deviation can be anticipated before it occurs, corrective action can be instituted more quickly and the negative consequences of the deviation reduced. To illustrate, consider how Weyerhauser Company manages its timber reserves. It is a fact of nature that forest fires sometimes occur. If standard performance is defined as a fire-free forest, then a forest fire represents an undesirable deviation that needs corrective action. Weyerhauser can anticipate that fires are more likely to oc-

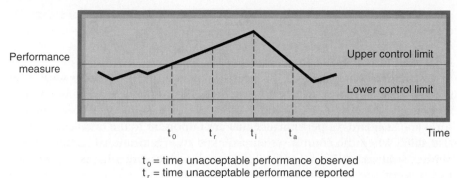

FIGURE 16.3
Time lags in control

t_0 = time unacceptable performance observed
t_r = time unacceptable performance reported
t_i = time corrective action instituted
t_a = time acceptable performance returns

cur during prolonged dry periods. By staffing watch towers, using spotter air-craft and reconnaissance satellites, and keeping fire-fighting equipment in a state of readiness during these periods, the company increases its anticipatory capability, enabling it to respond more quickly to the undesirable situation.

Sensitivity of the Measuring Device

A third consideration in control system design is the sensitivity of the measuring device. *Sensitivity* refers to the precision with which the measurement can be made. Care must be taken to use the appropriate device for the system under consideration. For example, the Teac Company, which manufactures computer components and other electronic equipment, might need a high-precision micrometer to measure the diameter of the spindles used in its computer disk drive. But, for Georgia-Pacific, a lumber company, to use such a measuring device to check the thickness of two-by-four wall studs would be highly unnecessary. A simple tape measure will suffice in this situation, for tolerances need to be expressed only in fractions of inches, not microns. The old maxim applies here: you don't need a sledgehammer to insert a thumbtack!

Composition of Feedback Reports

A final consideration in control system design involves the composition of feed-back reports. As the control process measures performance and compares it with standards, much information and data are generated. Reports to management will be based upon these data. But what data should be included in the reports? A simple answer, and one that users of such reports will view favor-ably, is "Don't tell me what is right with the system; tell me what is wrong." **Variance reporting** fulfills this desire by highlighting only those things that fail to meet the established standards. Focusing on the elements that are not meeting the standards provides the capability for **management by exception.** In this approach, management targets the trouble areas. If the system is operating acceptably, no information needs to come to the manager's attention.

Now that we have examined the factors that are important in the design of a control system, let's look at several criteria that measure the system's effectiveness.

Variance reporting
Highlighting only those things that fail to meet the established standards.

Management by exception
Focusing on the elements that are not meeting the standards.

CRITERIA FOR EFFECTIVE CONTROL

To be effective in detecting and correcting unacceptable performance, a control system must satisfy several criteria. The system must (1) be related to organizational strategy, (2) utilize all steps in the control process, (3) be composed of objective and subjective measures, (4) be timely in feedback reporting, and (5) be acceptable to a diverse work force.[8] The next sections examine these criteria more closely.

Is Related to Organizational Strategy

In designing a control system, one must make sure that it measures what is important now and what will be important in the future, not what was important in the past. As an organization's strategic focus shifts over time, the measures and standards of performance that are important to the organization must also shift. When the control system is linked to organizational strategy, it recognizes strategic shifts and is flexible enough to measure what is important as indicated by the firm's strategy.

This issue also has implications for the standards of behavior and performance that are set for individuals and groups within the organization. As the work force becomes more racially, ethnically, and gender diverse, organizations will often have to adjust their expectations of workers and performance standards in response to the differing attitudes, abilities, and cultural biases of their employees.

Multinational corporations often find it useful to maintain a centralized, integrated system of controls consistent with the strategic orientation of the organization. If the network of organizational units is to benefit from the company's global orientation, there must be sufficient coordination and control of the units to ensure that such benefits are achieved. For example, General Motors maintains a number of units that are interdependent through each of the sequential steps in the manufacturing process (for example, GM's Brazilian subsidiary supplies its U.S. subsidiary with engines); therefore, GM must have control systems that ensure that production processes are not disrupted.[9]

Utilizes All Steps in the Control Process

To be effective, a control system must employ all of the steps in the control process. Standards of performance must be set, measurements of actual performance taken, comparisons of standards with actual performance made, and, when necessary, corrective action taken. Omitting any of these steps will detract from the system's effectiveness. For example, we will see in the Managerial Resolution that Motorola set some very lofty quality-performance standards. What if Motorola managers measured actual performance and made comparisons with standards, but then failed to take corrective action when they observed undesirable deviations (the final step in the control process)? By omitting this step, performance would never be brought into line with the standards, and the survival of the company would be doubtful.

To return to our more personal example of your quest for a grade of B in your management course, suppose you never bothered to check your posted grade on the mid-term exam. In that case, your control system would be incomplete. Without knowing your mid-term exam score, you could not compare your actual performance with your standard. Consequently, you would not know whether there was an undesirable deviation and whether you should study harder for the final exam.

Is Composed of Objective and Subjective Measures

It is very unlikely that a control system will lend itself to the use of a single performance measure. More often than not, a number of performance measures are needed. As we discussed earlier, some of these performance measures may be objective and very easily quantified, while others may be qualitative and more subjective. For example, management may have set specific targets for productivity. This performance objective has a precise formula for measurement, as we will see in the next chapter. Suppose that in that same situation, management has also expressed a desire to achieve high levels of worker satisfaction. Such a qualitative criterion is more difficult, if not impossible, to measure accurately. Situations like this often require managers to blend quantitative (objective) and qualitative (subjective) performance measures in their control systems.

Incorporates Timeliness in Feedback Reporting

Timeliness is the degree to which the control system provides information when it is needed. The key issue here is not how fast the feedback information is provided, but whether it is provided quickly enough to permit a response to an unacceptable deviation. For example, consider the air traffic controller at Chicago's O'Hare Airport who observes on the radar screen that the positions of two aircraft are becoming alarmingly close. Feedback information on the changing positions of the two aircraft is needed very quickly if a tragedy is to be avoided. Here timeliness would be measured in seconds. Now consider the manager of a Christmas tree farm who monitors the annual growth rate of the trees. If the amount of growth falls below standards in a particular year, an application of fertilizer might be called for as a corrective action. In this case, timeliness might be measured in weeks or even months.

In an air traffic control situation, timeliness—the degree to which a control system provides information when it is needed—would be measured in seconds. But the monitoring of the annual growth rate of trees at a Christmas tree farm would be measured—just as effectively—in weeks or even months.

© /AP/Wide World Photos

Return again to the personal example of your grade. Suppose that the mid-term exam was administered in the eighth week of the semester and the results were not posted until the tenth week. This feedback would not be timely if the deadline for dropping the course was in the ninth week of the semester.

Is Acceptable to a Diverse Work Force

To be effective, organizational controls must be accepted by employees. The control system should motivate workers to recognize standards and act to achieve them. If the control system discourages employees, they are likely to ignore the standards, and undesirable deviations are likely to follow. The more committed employees are to the control system, the more successful the system will be.[10] In the increasingly diverse workplaces of today's organizations, one of the challenges to management is to develop control systems and establish standards that are acceptable and understandable to all workers.

To illustrate acceptability, consider your situation as a student in a management course. Suppose that your professor has no problem assigning course grades of B or lower, but says that a grade of A can be achieved only by students who read a new chapter and five related journal articles every day and submit a 20-page, typewritten synopsis of these readings each day. Would you be discouraged from attempting to earn a grade of A? Most, if not all, students probably would be discouraged and would resign themselves to a grade of no higher than a B for the course.

Up to this point, we have seen several factors that are essential to the design of an effective control system. To assist managers in developing effective control systems, Meeting the Challenge presents a checklist that can be used to make sure that all important factors and characteristics have been included in any control system that has been designed.

Now that the control system has been established, it is necessary to determine how much control should be used. The amount of control needed depends upon several factors, as we will see in the next section.

CHECKLIST FOR DESIGNING EFFECTIVE CONTROL SYSTEMS

Frequently, systems for management control of some process in an organization are inadequately designed or ill-thought-out. After designing your system for control, answer the following questions to ensure that all important aspects of the control system have been included.

_____ Have performance standards been explicitly stated with a degree of clarity that allows them to be compared with actual performance?

_____ Have standards been defined in a manner that permits measurement of actual performance?

_____ Are guidelines in place for responding with corrective actions to undesirable deviations?

_____ Is there sufficient variety in the control system to deal with the variety in the processing being controlled?

_____ Does the control system have the capability to anticipate problems before they get out of hand?

_____ Is the precision of the measuring devices appropriate for the performance being measured?

_____ Is the feedback system designed to report what is wrong with the process rather than what is right with the process?

_____ Is the control system measuring what is important as indicated by the firm's strategy?

_____ Is feedback information provided in a timely fashion?

_____ Is the control system acceptable to your employees?

SELECTING THE PROPER AMOUNT OF CONTROL

In almost any task, there are reasonable limits on the amount of energy that should be expended. This is also true in the area of control. In theory, the amount of control that a manager exercises over some aspect of the organization can vary from a minimum of zero control to a maximum of infinite control. It is possible for management to go too far and overcontrol some aspect of the organization, or not go far enough and thereby undercontrol. The result in either case is a suboptimal control system and suboptimal performance, which will decrease the overall effectiveness and efficiency of the organization.

Choosing the proper amount of control is critical to organizations that strive for quality in everything they do. Deciding how much control is enough is not a simple matter, however. Several factors can be used to help determine the proper amount of control. These factors, which vary in their degree of objectivity, include the costs and benefits of a control system, the reliability of the thing or process being controlled, and the importance of the thing or process being controlled.[11]

Costs in Control Systems

Two basic categories of costs need to be considered in control systems: (1) the costs associated with the information needed to perform the control process, and (2) the costs associated with undesirable deviations from standards. These costs behave differently as the amount of control effort varies.[12]

Control systems rely on information. As the amount of control effort increases, information feedback is needed in greater amounts and with greater frequency. This information does not come without a cost. Time, effort, resources, and money must be expended to gather and assimilate information. Consequently, as the level of control effort increases, the information costs of the control system also increase.

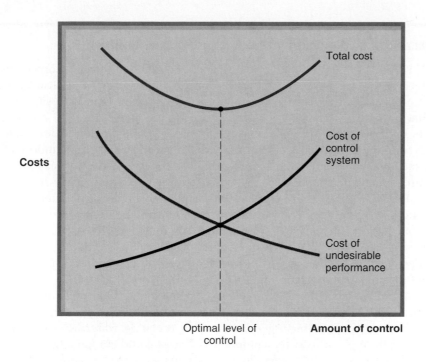

FIGURE 16.4
Cost trade-offs in a control system

As the level of control effort increases, undesirable deviations from performance standards will decrease. As a consequence, the costs associated with undesirable performance will also decrease. Reductions in the costs due to undesirable performance represent the benefits of control systems. Examples of these costs include costs to correct the problem that is causing the undesirable deviations; material scrap costs and rework costs when defective parts are detected in the manufacturing process; product warranty, repair, and replacement costs when defective output reaches the consumer; and worker compensation costs when workers are injured due to behaviors or actions that do not conform to standards. When these relationships are displayed in a graphical format as in Figure 16.4, they reveal that, from an economic standpoint, there is an ideal amount of control to be exercised. This optimal amount of control corresponds to the minimum total cost.

To help clarify the relationships in Figure 16.4, let's again consider the situation that Motorola faced in manufacturing the 400-part cellular telephone described earlier. Management can increase the level of control by increasing the number of parts, components, and finished products that are inspected and tested. Additionally, more sophisticated testing and measuring devices might be obtained. These actions will increase the costs of obtaining the information needed in the control process, but will also reduce the likelihood that defective units will be produced. When fewer defective units are produced, scrap, rework, product repair, product warranty, and product replacement costs all decline. When the opposing costs are combined, the total cost is U-shaped, and its lowest point indicates the optimal level of control.

From a practical standpoint, this optimal value is not always easy to identify. When performance improvements are many and varied, it may be difficult to quantify the precise cost benefit of the control system. In such cases, the value of the control system might be assessed by simply examining the number of areas of improvement and the level of improvement in each area.

Reliability of the System

Reliability refers to the probability that the object or process being controlled will consistently behave in an acceptable manner. The basic premise is that the more reliable the process, the less control is needed. The GPU Nuclear

Managing for
Excellence

THREE MILE ISLAND: FROM MELTDOWN TO INDUSTRY LEADER

The Three Mile Island nuclear facility, operated by GPU Nuclear Corporation, is located on the Susquehanna River outside Harrisburg, Pennsylvania. The Three Mile Island facility has the dubious distinction of being the site of the worst nuclear power plant accident in the United States. In 1979 one of its units underwent a core meltdown when safety systems failed to lift nuclear rods from the core. This accident resulted in a six-and-a-half-year shutdown for the facility. Shortly after GPU reopened the facility in late 1985, it realized that control would be simplified if the processes involved were made more reliable. In 1987 GPU began to consider the benefits of a reliability-centered maintenance (RCM) approach to preventive maintenance. The RCM process is based on four basic principles: (1) system functions must be preserved, (2) equipment failures that can defeat those functions must be identified, (3) failure modes must be prioritized, and (4) preventive maintenance tasks must be defined for high-priority failure modes.

GPU embarked on an RCM project that spanned a period from mid-1988 until mid-1994. They identified such key systems as the main turbine, the cooling water system, the main generator, and circulating water as viable candidates for RCM. Eventually they pinpointed almost 4,000 components in the 28 systems selected for RCM. Preventive maintenance policies were established for more than 5,400 tasks in these components. Although the costs were substantial (about $30,000 per system), they were more than offset by the benefits. During the period from 1990 to 1994, many improvements were observed; most noticeable among them were a significant decline in plant equipment failures and an increase in plant availability. In fact, this program was so successful that the Three Mile Island nuclear power generating facility was recently ranked top in the world on the basis of its proportion of uptime.[13]

Corporation put this principle to good use in the aftermath of the Three Mile Island nuclear disaster. In Managing for Excellence we can see how GPU's focus on reliability helped the Three Mile Island facility rise to a very enviable position in nuclear power generation circles. Process reliability is difficult to assess because it will be affected by the operating characteristics of the physical equipment and by the experience and attitudes of the workers. Equipment reliability can often be objectively measured. Human operators present a bit more uncertainty. Although reliability can be expected to increase with worker experience, there is no way to accurately predict when a worker will have a "bad day." Management must often make subjective judgments on the human aspect of reliability to aid in determining the proper amount of control.

Importance of the Process Being Controlled

Common sense would suggest that the more important the object or process being controlled, the greater the amount of control that should be exercised. The difficulty here lies in selecting a measure for importance. Frequently, cost or value is used as a substitute for importance. The more valuable the item, the more important it is; therefore, the more control it deserves. In the area of inventory control, a relatively small percentage of a company's inventory items (perhaps 20 percent) often account for a large percentage of the total inventory value (perhaps 80 percent). Although the percentages may vary, this "20/80 rule," as it has become known, would suggest that an "important few" items deserve close inventory control. The others (the "trivial many") require considerably less control.[14]

You should not automatically assume that importance can always be measured by cost or value. At first glance it might seem that extensive control systems are not needed to monitor quality in the manufacture of an inexpensive bolt. However, if that bolt is used to secure a window washer to the outside of a high-rise building, it has assumed a high level of importance despite its low cost. In a similar vein, recall the disaster that struck the space shuttle *Challenger.* Although the O-rings in the shuttle booster rockets were relatively inexpensive items, we are all painfully aware of the importance they played in this highly complex spacecraft.

Now that the question of how much control is needed has been addressed, let's examine where in the transformation process control should be used. The place where control is applied is called the focal point for control.

SELECTING THE FOCAL POINT FOR CONTROL

Before managers design and implement a control system, they must decide where the control effort will be focused. Virtually all organizations maintain a structure in which inputs are subjected to a transformation process that converts them into usable and marketable outputs. Despite this similarity, inputs, transformations, and outputs can vary considerably among organizations.

Although Chapter 17 provides a much more extensive examination of the operations aspects of the input transformation process, we do need to note here that inputs can include such items as raw materials, supplies, people, capital, land, buildings, equipment, utilities, and information. Outputs of the transformation process will be either physical products or services. The list of transformation processes is lengthy and quite varied. Table 16.1 provides descriptions and examples of these processes.

TABLE 16.1   Descriptions and examples of operations transformation processes

TRANSFORMATION	DESCRIPTION	EXAMPLES
Physical or chemical	Cutting, bending, joining, or chemically alternating raw materials to make a product	Manufacturing company, chemical processor, oil refinery
Locational	Provide transportation function	Airlines, trucking companies, package delivery services, U.S. Postal System
Storage	Hold and then release a commodity or item	Warehouses
Exchange	Transfer possession and ownership of a commodity or item	Wholesale and retail organizations
Physiological	Improve the physical or mental well-being of sick and injured people	Hospitals, health-care clinics
Informational	Transmit information to customers	Radio and television news departments, computer information services
Entertainment	Impart an attitudinal change to their customers	Motion picture industry, programming departments of television networks
Educational	Impart knowledge to customers	Schools, universities

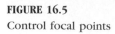

Control can focus on the inputs, the transformation process, or the outputs of the operating system. The three different focal points yield three different types of control: (1) feedforward control, (2) concurrent control, and (3) feedback control.[15] These control focal points are illustrated in Figure 16.5. The next sections examine them in greater detail.

Feedforward Control

Feedforward (preventive) control
Focuses on detecting undesirable material, financial, or human resources that serve as inputs to the transformation process.

When control focuses on the material, financial, or human resources that serve as inputs to the transformation process, it is referred to as **feedforward control.** This type of control is sometimes called **preventive control** because it is designed to ensure that the quality of inputs is high enough to prevent problems in the transformation process. For example, think about the preventive controls that might take place prior to the manufacture of blue jeans. A primary input for manufacturers such as Levi Strauss is denim fabric. Long bolts of this material will have patterns overlaid and cut prior to the sewing operations. Before the patterns are laid out on the fabric, a system of feedforward control could be used to inspect the denim fabric for knots, runs, tears, color variations, and other similar imperfections. If the fabric contains many imperfections, there could well be excessive levels of imperfections in the finished blue jeans. In such a case, the corrective action suggested by the feedforward control system might be to reject the entire bolt of fabric rather than trying to cut around the imperfections.

Concurrent Control

Concurrent control
Focuses on the transformation process to ensure that it is functioning properly.

When control focuses on the transformation phase, it is referred to as **concurrent control.** This form of control is designed to monitor ongoing activities to ensure that the transformation process is functioning properly and achieving the desired results. To illustrate, consider again the manufacture of blue jeans by Levi Strauss. Sewing-machine operators must continuously monitor their process to ensure that seams are being sewn straight and threads are interlocking appropriately. If these standards are not being met, it may be necessary to take such corrective actions as changing needles, adjusting thread tension, lubricating machines, and so forth.

Feedback Control

Feedback (corrective) control
Focuses on discovering undesirable output and implementing corrective action.

When control focuses on the output phase of Figure 16.5, it is referred to as **feedback control.** This type of control is sometimes referred to as **corrective control** because it is intended to discover undesirable output and implement corrective action. We can illustrate this focal point by again considering the manufacture of blue jeans. After the jeans have been assembled, a final inspection is normally performed. Individuals responsible for assessing the quality of the jeans compare the finished product with established standards of performance. If there is an undesirable amount of deviation from the standards, then corrective action must be prescribed. For example, if the design

stitching on the back pockets is misaligned, corrective action would be needed at the pocket-
stitching operation to correct this problem.

Multiple Focal Points

Very few organizations rely on a single point of
focus for their control process. Instead, most organizations use several control systems focused
on various phases of the transformation process.[16]
This way managers are better able to control resource inputs, ongoing transformation activities,
and final outputs simultaneously. This approach
gives the manager the capability to determine (1)
whether current output is in accordance with
standards, and (2) whether there are any impending problems looming on the horizon.

The McDonald's restaurant chain provides a
familiar example of a company that uses control mechanisms that are focused
on inputs, transformation processes, and outputs. In its attempts to maintain
consistency in its french fried potatoes, McDonald's utilizes feedforward control with a stringent set of standards for purchased raw potatoes. It utilizes concurrent control by monitoring the oil temperature and frying time used in the
cooking process and the amount of salt used in seasoning the french fries. Finally, it utilizes feedback control when the output (cooked french fries) is examined. If examination reveals improper color, it may be necessary to change
the cooking oil, the temperature of the cooking oil, the cooking time, or perhaps some combination of all three to attain the desired results. Multiple focal
points are important here, for if only the finished product were monitored, potential problems caused by a bad batch of raw potatoes or a defective fryer
thermostat would not be revealed until defective french fries were produced.

McDonalds uses multiple focal points
in its production of french fries: feedforward control for standards for purchased raw potatoes; concurrent
control in the monitoring of oil temperature, frying time, and amount of
salt; and feedback control when the
fries are examined. Problems in any
focal area affect the other areas.
© Dennis MacDonald/PhotoEdit

Not only are control systems focused on inputs, transformations, or outputs, they are also implemented in all functional specialty areas of the organization. Today's business organizations incorporate many highly interrelated and
overlapping functional specialties. Management, marketing, finance, and accounting activities all play a critical role in the success of the organization, and
as such, each will have many aspects that require control mechanisms. Noted
management theorist Peter Drucker has identified eight areas in which performance objectives should be set and results measured. These areas—marketing, financial resources, productivity, physical resources, human organization, profit requirements, social responsibility, and innovation—extend through
all of the interrelated functional specialties of the business.[17]

MANAGERIAL CONTROL PHILOSOPHIES

Instituting a control system requires that managers do more than simply select
the appropriate focal points. It is also necessary to make a choice between two
philosophical control styles: (1) bureaucratic control and (2) organic control
(often referred to as clan control).

BUREAUCRATIC CONTROL

Bureaucratic control involves the use of rules, procedures, policies, hierarchy of authority, written documents, reward systems, and other formal mechanisms to influence behavior, assess performance, and correct unacceptable
deviations from standards.[18] This type of control is typical of the bureaucratic

Bureaucratic control
Use of formal mechanisms to influence behavior, assess performance,
and correct unacceptable deviations
from standards.

style of management introduced in Chapter 2 and described elsewhere in this book. In this method of control, standard operating procedures and policies prescribe acceptable employee behavior and standards for employee performance. There is a rigid hierarchy of authority that extends from the top down through the organization. Formal authority for the control process lies at the supervisor level, and lower-level employees are not expected to participate in the control process. Bureaucratic control relies on highly formalized mechanisms for selecting and training workers, and it emphasizes the use of monetary rewards for controlling employee performance. Formal quantitative tools such as budgets or financial reports and ratios are frequently used to monitor and evaluate performance in bureaucratic control systems.

As we discussed in Chapter 2, the bureaucratic style often has a negative connotation due to its very formal structure and perceived lack of flexibility. However, this method of control should not be viewed as a mechanism to restrain, force, coerce, or manipulate workers. Instead, it should be viewed as an effective, although rigid, mechanism to ensure that performance standards are met.

ORGANIC CONTROL

Organic (clan) control
Reliance upon social values, traditions, shared beliefs, flexible authority, and trust to assess performance and correct unacceptable deviations.

Organic control, often called **clan control,** is quite different from bureaucratic control. It relies upon social values, traditions, shared beliefs, flexible authority, looser job descriptions, and trust to assess performance and correct unacceptable deviations. The philosophy behind organic control is that employees are to be trusted and that they are willing to perform correctly without extensive rules and supervision. This type of control is particularly appropriate when there is a strong corporate culture and the values are shared by all employees. When cohesive peer groups exist, less top-down bureaucratic control is necessary because employees are likely to pressure co-workers into adhering to group norms. When employees exercise self-discipline and self-control and believe in doing a fair day's work for their pay, managers can take advantage of this self-discipline and use fewer bureaucratic control methods.

Such cohesiveness and self-discipline are characteristic of self-managed teams (SMTs), as you will recall from earlier chapters.[19] Organic control is a very appropriate style to use in conjunction with SMTs. Although organic control is less rigid than bureaucratic control, it would be a mistake to assume that it is a better method. Both the bureaucratic and organic approaches can be useful for organizational control, and most organizations use some aspects of both in their control mechanisms. Table 16.2 provides a brief comparison of the bureaucratic and organic methods of control.

Before selecting one of these two control styles, managers must first evaluate several factors of their organization. The next sections describe the factors that help determine an appropriate choice of control style.

SELECTING A CONTROL STYLE IN TODAY'S DIVERSE AND MULTINATIONAL ORGANIZATIONS

The bureaucratic and organic approaches present two distinctly opposite control philosophies. Top management is often faced with a dilemma in choosing a style for their organization. This decision can be made more easily if managers first evaluate these four factors: (1) individual management style, (2) corporate culture, (3) employee professionalism, and (4) performance measures.[20]

Individual management style refers to whether the manager has a task-oriented or a people-oriented leadership style. These concepts were described in Chapter 12, where we discussed behavioral approaches to understanding

TABLE 16.2   Bureaucratic and organic methods of control

	BUREAUCRATIC	ORGANIC
Purpose	Employee compliance	Employee commitment
Technique	Rigid rules and policies, strict hierarchy, formalized selection and training	Corporate culture, individual self-discipline, cohesive peer groups, selection and socialization
Performance expectation	Clearly defined standards of individual performance	Emphasizes group or system performance
Organizational structure	Tall structure, top-down controls	Flat structure, mutual influence
	Rules and procedures for coordination and control	Shared values, goals, and traditions for coordination and control
	Authority resides in position	Authority resides with knowledge and expertise
Rewards	Based upon individual employee achievements	Based upon group achievements and equity across employees
Participation	Formalized and narrow	Informal and broad

SOURCE: Adapted and reprinted by permission of *Harvard Business Review*. An exhibit from "From Control to Commitment in the Workplace" by R. E. Walton, March/April 1985, 76–85. Copyright ©1985 by the President and Fellows of Harvard College; all rights reserved.

leadership. If a manager uses more relationship-oriented behaviors when interacting with subordinates, then an organic control style would tend to be more compatible with his leadership style. Examples of relationship-oriented behaviors include extending a high degree of trust, friendship, and respect to subordinates. In contrast, if a manager displays more task-oriented behaviors when interacting with subordinates, then a bureaucratic control style would tend to be more compatible with her leadership style. Task-oriented behavior occurs when the leader assumes the responsibility for planning, directing, providing job information, and maintaining standards of performance for subordinates. The key is that the control style needs to be consistent with the manager's leadership style.

The second factor that determines a control style is corporate culture. If the corporate culture encourages employees to participate in decision making and rewards them for this participation and loyalty, then an organic control style is more appropriate. If the culture of the organization favors decision making at the top and avoids employee participation, then a bureaucratic control style will be the better choice. As we will see in the resolution to the opening Managerial Incident, Motorola created a common culture and a common language before adopting its targets for quality improvement.

Employee professionalism can also influence the control style an organization uses. Employees who are highly educated, highly trained, and professional are more likely to want to participate in decision making and are more likely to accept the high standards of behavior displayed in the group's norms. These employees will be good candidates for an organic control style. Employees who lack experience, training, or the desire to participate would be better candidates for a bureaucratic control style.

Finally, performance measures influence the choice of control style. If performance can be quantified and explicitly measured, then a bureaucratic control style would work well. If task performance is difficult to measure or quantify, however, then an organic control style would be more appropriate.

You should recognize from the preceding discussion that achieving quality in the control process requires a good fit between the situation and the control system. Care must be taken to accurately assess management style, corporate culture, employee professionalism, and types of performance measures before selecting a philosophical approach to control. The choice of a control style is contingent upon all of these situational factors.

The selection of a control style for a multinational organization presents some unique challenges. Although most multinational organizations develop control systems that are a blend of bureaucratic and organic control, the high level of standardization in many multinational organizations permits a heavier use of bureaucratic control, as company manuals and specific rules, procedures, and policies may be applicable across certain subgroups of operating units. For example, since General Motors maintains a number of subsidiaries around the globe that manufacture the same types of engines, it has the potential to use bureaucratic controls in these units. Nevertheless, organic control mechanisms may also play an important part in the control process for multinational firms, for it is critical that each organizational subunit understand the role it plays in the network of subsidiaries. Strong shared values and philosophies help to ensure that behaviors and output at the subsidiary level are compatible with corporationwide initiatives.[21]

IMPACT OF INFORMATION TECHNOLOGY ON ORGANIZATIONAL CONTROL

Advances and developments in information technology have had a profound and positive effect on organizational control. The very essence of control is deeply rooted in information. Just look at how the topics have progressed in this chapter. One of the basic steps in the control process involves gathering information on actual performance and then comparing it with pre-established standards of performance. Furthermore, the final step in the control process requires that feedback be provided, which is nothing more than the dissemination of information. As the chapter unfolded we saw that it was critical to gather information and also to disseminate feedback information in a timely fashion. We live in an age when advances in information processing hardware and software occur with almost dizzying speed. All of these technological advances and improvements serve to get critical control information to management in a more timely fashion, allow management to make the proper control responses more quickly, and finally disseminate the information on those decisions more quickly so that the negative consequences associated with out-of-control situations can be minimized.

Balance sheet
Summary of an organization's financial position at a given point in time, showing assets, liabilities, and owner's equity.

A company's assets are the things of value that it owns. Current assets are those items, such as inventory, that can be converted into cash in a short time period; fixed assets include such items as buildings, land, and equipment.

© George Kavanagh/Tony Stone Images

MECHANISMS FOR FINANCIAL CONTROL

One of the most important areas where control must be exercised is in the finances of an organization. At times financial performance may not be meeting standards, or it may fall short of expectations. If such situations go undetected and corrective actions are not taken, the company's survival might be at stake. We will only briefly examine some of the more important techniques and methods for establishing financial control. More thorough coverage of these topics is left to your accounting and finance classes.

FINANCIAL STATEMENTS

Two financial statements provide much of the information needed to calculate ratios that are used to assess an organization's financial health. These statements are the balance sheet and the income statement.

Balance Sheet
The **balance sheet** provides a picture of an organization's financial position at a given point in time. It usually shows the financial status at the end of a fis-

cal year or a calendar year, although the time interval can certainly be shorter (for example, at the end of each quarter). The balance sheet summarizes three types of information: assets, liabilities, and owner's equity.

Assets are the things of value that the company owns; they are usually divided into current assets and fixed assets. **Current assets** are those items that can be converted into cash in a short time period; they include such items as accounts receivable, inventory, and, of course, cash. **Fixed assets** are longer term in nature and include such items as buildings, land, and equipment.

Liabilities include the firm's debts and obligations. They can be divided into current liabilities and long-term liabilities. **Current liabilities** are the debts that must be paid in the near future; they include such obligations as accounts payable and not-yet-paid salaries earned by workers. **Long-term liabilities** are the debts payable over a long time span and include such obligations as payments on bonds and bank loans and mortgages for buildings and land.

Owner's equity is the difference between the assets and liabilities. It represents the company's net worth and consists of common stock and retained earnings. Table 16.3 shows an example of a balance sheet. Note that the totals on both sides of the balance sheet are equal; this must always be the case.

Income Statement

The **income statement** summarizes the organization's financial performance over a given time interval, typically one year. It shows the revenues that have come into the organization, the expenses that have been incurred, and the bottom-line profit or loss realized by the firm for the given time interval. For this reason, the income statement is often called a *profit-and-loss statement.* Table 16.4 shows the general structure of an income statement.

FINANCIAL RATIOS

Several financial ratios can be used to interpret company performance. Each ratio is simply a comparison of a few pieces of financial data. These ratios can be used to compare a company's current performance with its past perfor-

Assets
The things of value that an individual or organization owns.

Current assets
Items that can be converted into cash in a short time period.

Fixed assets
Assets that are long-term in nature and cannot be converted quickly into cash.

Liabilities
The firm's debts and obligations.

Current liabilities
Debts that must be paid in the near future.

Long-term liabilities
Debts payable over a long time span.

Owner's equity
The portion of a business that is owned by the shareholders. The difference between the assets of an organization and its liabilities.

Income statement
A summary of an organization's financial performance over a given time interval, showing revenues, expenses, and bottom-line profit or loss.

TABLE 16.3 Balance sheet

	CESTARO MANUFACTURING COMPANY BALANCE SHEET DECEMBER 31, 1997			
ASSETS			**LIABILITIES AND OWNER'S EQUITY**	
Current assets:			Current liabilities:	
Cash	$ 30,000		Accounts payable	$ 20,000	
Accounts receivable	50,000		Accrued expenses	10,000	
Inventory	200,000		Income tax payable	40,000	
Total current assets		$280,000	Total current liabilities		$ 70,000
Fixed assets:			Long-term liabilities	
Land	150,000		Mortgages	300,000	
Buildings & equipment	400,000		Bonds	100,000	
Total fixed assets		550,000	Total long-term liabilities		400,000
Total assets		830,000	Owner's equity	
			Common stock	300,000	
			Retained earnings	60,000	
			Total owner's equity		360,000
			Total liabilities & equity		$830,000

TABLE 16.4   Income statement

CESTARO MANUFACTURING COMPANY INCOME STATEMENT FOR THE YEAR ENDING DECEMBER 31, 1997		
Gross sales	$2,400,000	
Less sales returns	100,000	
Net sales		$2,300,000
Less expenses and cost of goods sold:		
Cost of goods sold	1,600,000	
Depreciation	50,000	
Sales expense	150,000	
Administrative expense	80,000	1,880,000
Operating profit		420,000
Other income		10,000
Gross income		430,000
Less interest expense	40,000	
Taxable income		390,000
Less taxes	160,000	
Net income		230,000

mance, or they can be used to compare the company's performance with the performance of other companies in the same industry.

Liquidity Ratios

Liquidity ratios indicate the firm's ability to meet its short-term debts and obligations. The most commonly used liquidity ratio is the current ratio, which is determined by dividing current assets by current liabilities. The current ratio for the Cestaro Manufacturing Company, as illustrated in Tables 16.3 and 16.4, is 280,000/70,000, or 4. This ratio indicates that Cestaro has four dollars of liquid assets for each dollar of short-term debt. Another liquidity ratio is the *quick ratio,* which is calculated by dividing current assets less inventory by the current liabilities. This ratio assesses how well a firm can expect to meet short-term obligations without having to dispose of inventories. For the Cestaro Company, the quick ratio is (280,000 − 200,000)/70,000, or 1.14.

Profitability Ratios

Profitability ratios indicate the relative effectiveness of the organization. One important profitability ratio is the *profit margin on sales,* which is calculated as net income divided by sales. For the Cestaro Company, this ratio is 230,000/2,300,000, or .1 (10 percent). Another profitability measure is *return on total assets (ROA),* which is calculated by dividing the net income by total assets. For Cestaro, this ratio is 230,000/830,000, or .28 (28 percent). ROA is a valuable yardstick for potential investors, for its tells them how effective management is in using its assets to earn additional profits.

Debt Ratios

Debt ratios indicate the firm's ability to handle long-term debt. The most common debt ratio is calculated by dividing total liabilities by total assets. The debt ratio for Cestaro is 470,000/830,000, or .57 (57 percent). This indicates that the firm has 57 cents in debt for each dollar of assets. The lower the debt ratio, the better the financial health of the organization.

Activity Ratios

Activity ratios measure performance with respect to key activities defined by management. For example, the total cost of goods sold divided by the average

Liquidity ratios
Indicators of the firm's ability to meet its short-term debts and obligations.

Profitability ratios
Indicators of the relative effectiveness, or profitability, of the organization.

Debt ratios
Indicators of the firm's ability to handle long-term debt.

Activity ratios
Indicators of performance with respect to key activities defined by management.

daily inventory indicates how efficiently the firm is forecasting sales and ordering merchandise. When total sales are divided by average inventory, an inventory turnover ratio is calculated. This ratio indicates the number of times inventory is turned over to meet the total sales. A low figure means that inventory sits too long, and money is wasted.[22]

These and other similar ratios should be used to gain insights into a company's financial relationships and to identify areas that are out of control so that corrective action can be taken. When a ratio is out of line with either past company performance or the performance of comparable companies within the industry, managers must carefully probe through the numbers to determine the cause of the problem and devise a solution. Many of the numbers on the balance sheet and income statement are interrelated, and making a change to improve one ratio may have an undesirable impact on another. Therefore, managers must be very familiar with company operations in order to arrive at a proper remedy when using financial controls.

ETHICAL ISSUES IN THE CONTROL OF A DIVERSE WORK FORCE

Organizations are increasingly employing controversial mechanisms to control the behavior of individuals and groups within the organization. Sometimes these control mechanisms are known to the individuals, and sometimes the individuals are totally oblivious to their existence. There is considerable controversy over the ethics of using such control methods as drug testing, undercover surveillance, and computer monitoring. The next sections briefly review the debates over these practices.

DRUG TESTING

It has been estimated that the use of illegal drugs is costing U.S. organizations close to $100 billion per year.[23] Drug abuse results in increases in defective output, absenteeism, workplace accidents, increased health care costs, and more insurance claims. To combat the costs associated with these drug-related problems, organizations have increasingly turned to drug testing. One type of drug testing is pre-employment testing.[24] As the name suggests, organizations that use this approach require job applicants to submit to a drug detection test. In Ethics: Take a Stand at the end of this chapter, you will see how the Home Depot Corporation uses drug testing on job applicants.

Another type of drug testing focuses on testing current employees. Organizations that test existing employees can follow any of three policies. Random testing subjects employees to unannounced and unscheduled examination. Testing can also be based upon probable cause. If an employee exhibits suspicious or erratic behavior, or if drug paraphernalia are found in an employee's locker, there may be probable cause for testing. Finally, testing may be prescribed after an accident. Since it is conceivable that impaired motor skills may be the cause of the accident, this is a reasonable time for a drug test. The Motorola Corporation, described in the opening Managerial Incident, began screening all employees for illegal drugs in 1990. Motorola estimates that lost productivity and absenteeism costs could be reduced by $190 million annually if drug addicts are removed from the workplace.[25]

The ethical issue posed by drug testing hinges on whether it constitutes an invasion of privacy. Do individuals have the right to do as they please with regard to drugs while on their own time, or do organizations have the right to test for drugs in an effort to reduce medical costs, lost-productivity costs, absenteeism costs, and accidents in the workplace?[26] This ethical issue has even spilled out of the workplace and onto the home front. Because of the large number of drug- related crimes in and around its South Florida Congress Park housing project, Atlanta-based developer Trammel Crow Residential is now requiring prospective residents to pass drug tests to gain entry. Furthermore, current residents must do the same before their leases are renewed.[27] There is no easy answer to this question. The debate over drug testing continues and will undoubtedly continue for quite some time.

UNDERCOVER SURVEILLANCE

Businesses are constantly subjected to a variety of illegal activities that add to operating costs and decrease the bottom-line profit. Therefore, they are constantly looking for ways to control such activities. These activities include theft (pilferage, shoplifting, embezzlement, burglary), fraud (credit card, check, insurance), and malicious destruction of property (vandalism, arson).[28] Businesses often resort to a variety of surveillance techniques in order to control these illicit activities. Surveillance may be conducted by undercover internal security staffs, external security firms, or electronic devices. For example, General Electric uses tiny cameras hidden behind walls and ceilings to watch employees suspected of crimes, DuPont uses hidden cameras to monitor its loading docks, and Las Vegas casinos use ceiling-mounted cameras to observe activities on the gaming floors.[29]

Few would find fault when surveillance attempts to detect illegal activities being performed by individuals who are not part of the organization. However, undercover surveillance becomes a rather delicate issue when an organization's own employees are the subject of the scrutiny.[30] Again, the issue of invasion of privacy often surfaces in such instances, as does the concern that management has a low regard for and little trust in its own employees.

COMPUTER MONITORING

In many businesses, employees spend much of their time working at computer terminals and other similar electronic devices. Among these employees are data processors, word processors, airline reservations clerks, insurance claims workers, telemarketers, communications network personnel, and workers in many other occupations. Technology has evolved to the point where the work of these employees can be monitored electronically without their knowledge through the computers with which they interface.[31]

Although it is a form of undercover surveillance, computer monitoring is concerned with measuring employee performance rather than detecting illegal activities. This form of surveillance raises serious questions as to whether it violates a worker's right to privacy.[32] Many would question the appropriateness of the organization "electronically peeking over the workers' shoulders" to monitor their actions. They might argue that it is more appropriate to judge the net output of employees' efforts periodically (daily, weekly, monthly) rather than to constantly monitor their every action and/or decision.[33] There are no easy answers to the ethical questions raised by these control methods.

MANAGERIAL IMPLICATIONS

Throughout this book, we have been continually stressing that the successful organizations in the 1990s and beyond will be those that achieve quality in all aspects of their operations. Successful managers in these organizations will be those who can ensure that once plans have been set into place, all activities will be directed toward successfully carrying out those plans. The most effective device managers have for assessing the success of organizational activities is a basic control system. In a sense, control systems help managers to chart a course, or set a direction, when standards of behavior or performance are established. Control systems also help to tell them whether they are on course by providing a way to monitor performance. Managers monitor their behavior or performance by measuring what has been done and comparing it to what should have been done. Finally, when organizations stray off course, control systems help to guide them back onto the right path by forcing managers to consider corrective actions to remove undesirable deviations from standards.

Successful managers of the future will be those who:

- Develop a control system for each important product, service, process, or activity within the organization.
- Incorporate sufficient variety, sensitivity, anticipation capability, and feedback into the control system.
- Gauge the control system's effectiveness by considering its relationship to corporate strategy, its completeness, the degree to which it incorporates objective and subjective performance measures, its timeliness, and its acceptability to individuals within the organization.
- Determine the appropriate points within the organization where control systems should be focused.
- Understand the intricacies of the financial data contained in the organization's financial statements, and can use various financial control techniques to assess the firm's financial health.
- Adopt a philosophy of control that is consistent with the management style, corporate culture, employee professionalism, and performance measures present within the organization.

The checklist shown earlier in Meeting the Challenge can be helpful in determining whether a control system has been designed effectively.

In short, the concepts of control presented in this chapter provide us with a mechanism for determining whether our plans and actions have turned out as we had expected or hoped they would. If they haven't, we would be alerted to that fact, allowing us to take the appropriate corrective action to keep matters on their proper course. By remaining on course, we stand a better chance of being successful in our organizational activities.

Managerial Incident Resolution

Former Motorola chairman Robert Galvin knew that serious changes had to be made in the face of mounting customer discontent and shrinking market share. Contributing to the problems was the fact that each division had its own performance measures. These dissimilar systems made it virtually impossible for top management to assess and compare performance across the corporation, much less work toward common objectives. Galvin began by creating a common culture and a common language. A single measure for quality, total defects per unit of work, was chosen. The company launched a crusade to implement a wide range of control techniques to improve quality, reliability, and cycle time.

Management set a goal to gradually improve quality to the point where defects would be fewer than four per million (its renowned "six sigma" level) by the mid-1990s. Sampling inspection was to be used as a temporary means of control until permanent corrective actions could be implemented. Control processes were to be applied to cycle times, with the ultimate goal of a 90 percent reduction in the time to bring a product to market. Frontline employees were assigned the task of tracking defects, charting problems, and solving problems in cross-functional teams. To train its workers, the company established Motorola University, which provides one of the most comprehensive and effective corporate training programs in the world. Each Motorola employee receives a minimum of 40 hours training per year. To better control the quality of its inputs, a certification program was instituted for Motorola suppliers, each of whom must adhere to the Motorola standards.

To illustrate how successful these moves have been, consider the MicroTac cellular telephone. By effectively controlling the design and developmental time, Motorola was able to bring it to market two years ahead of the competition, and was able to sell over $1 billion worth of the 10.7-ounce pocket-sized telephone before there was a comparable competitor. In addition, the product even won two of the highest Japanese awards for quality. By the mid-1990s Motorola was rapidly approaching its "six sigma" goal of only 3.4 defects per million.[34]

SUMMARY

- Organizational control is the systematic process through which managers regulate organizational activities to make them consistent with the expectations established in plans, targets, and standards of performance. Control is an extremely important managerial function because it ensures that all of the planning, organizing, and leading has gone as we hoped it would. If things have not gone as planned, this situation can result in a variety of negative consequences to the organization.

- An organized system for control would require that (1) standards of performance be established, (2) actual performance be measured, (3) comparisons be made between standards and actual performance, and (4) corrective action be taken when there are unacceptable deviations of the actual performance from the standards.

- When designing a control system, one should consider the amount of variety to include in the system, its ability to anticipate problems before they occur, the amount of sensitivity needed in the measuring instruments, and the type of data and information to be included in the feedback report.

- To be effective, the control system should be related to the organizational strategy, incorporate all the steps in the control process, blend both objective and subjective performance measures, provide feedback in a timely fashion, and be accepted by members of the organization.

- To determine the proper amount of control to be exercised in a given situation, several factors must be examined. The costs and benefits of the control effort must be assessed. The amount of control can also be affected by the reliability of the system being controlled or the importance of the item being controlled.

- Feedforward (preventive) control systems focus on the inputs to the transformation process. Concurrent control systems focus on the ongoing activities of the transformation process. Feedback (corrective) control systems focus on the outputs of the transformation process.

- Bureaucratic control is a more rigid philosophy of control that relies on prescribed rules and policies, a hierarchy of authority, written documents, and other formal mechanisms to influence behavior, assess performance, and correct unacceptable deviations from standards. Organic control is a more flexible philosophy that relies on social values, traditions, flexible authority, and trust to assess performance and correct unacceptable deviations.

- Several financial control devices are available to assess an organization's financial health. The balance sheet and income statement are two important financial statements. In addition, there are several financial ratios that can be used to interpret company performance.

- It is becoming more common for organizations to test their employees for drug use, conduct undercover surveillance of their employees, and engage in computer monitoring. Such control procedures raise ethical questions of invasion of privacy and lack of confidence and trust in the employees.

KEY TERMS

Organizational control	Organic (clan) control	Owner's equity
Law of requisite variety	Balance sheet	Income statement
Variance reporting	Assets	Liquidity ratios
Management by exception	Current assets	Profitability ratios
Feedforward (preventive) control	Fixed assets	Debt ratios
Concurrent control	Liabilities	Activity ratios
Feedback (corrective) control	Current liabilities	
Bureaucratic control	Long-term liabilities	

REVIEW QUESTIONS

1. Why is control such a critical managerial function?
2. Discuss each of the steps in the control process.
3. Explain the difference between feedforward, concurrent, and feedback control.
4. Describe the difference between bureaucratic and organic control.
5. Discuss the factors that should be considered in selecting a control style.
6. Describe the factors that help determine the proper amount of control to be exercised.
7. Discuss the factors that should be considered in designing a control system.
8. Discuss the various criteria for effective control.
9. Discuss some of the organizational control practices that raise ethical dilemmas.
10. Describe the cost trade-offs in a control system.

DISCUSSION QUESTIONS

Improving Critical Thinking

1. Through your personal observations, identify a situation in which bureaucratic control is being used and one in which organic control is being used. Discuss the reasons you feel each situation exhibits the type of control you have said it displays.
2. Identify some situations that you have encountered where electronic or undercover surveillance was being performed. Discuss how you felt about those practices.

Enhancing Communication Skills

3. Select some aspect of your life (some activity you engage in) and then design a system by which you could control that activity. Be specific in describing the activity, how you would perform each of the steps in the control process, and the potential corrective actions you could take if your performance was not up to your standards. To enhance your written communication skills, write a short (1–2 page) essay in which you describe the aspect of your life being controlled and the design of the control system.
4. The chapter cited two brief examples (air traffic controller and tree farm manager) in which the response times for control feedback were quite different. Identify several situations with varying response-time requirements. Try to come up with examples having response times in seconds, minutes, hours, days, and months. To enhance your oral communication skills, prepare a short (10–15 minute) presentation for the class in which you describe your examples for each of these categories of response time.

Building Teamwork

5. Identify two situations that you have observed where you think the sensitivity of the measuring device is inappropriate. One of those situations should have a device that is too sensitive and the other a device that is not sensitive enough. Thoroughly describe what is being measured and the device that is being used to measure it. Indicate why you feel that the sensitivity of the devices is inappropriate. To refine your teamwork skills, meet with a small group of students who have been given this same assignment. Compare and discuss your selections, and then reach a consensus on the two best choices (one overly sensitive device and one insufficiently sensitive device). Select a spokesperson to present your choices to the rest of the class.
6. Try to identify two situations in which the costs would suggest very different levels of control. In one situation, the cost trade-offs should suggest that high levels of control are warranted, and in the other they should suggest that low levels of control

are appropriate. To refine your teamwork skills, meet with a small group of students who have been given this same assignment. Compare and discuss your selections, and then reach a consensus on the two best choices (one requiring low levels of con-

trol and one requiring high levels of control). Sketch the cost trade-off graphs for each situation. Then select a spokesperson to present your team's choices and graphs to the rest of the class.

INFORMATION TECHNOLOGY: Insights and Solutions

1. The General Electric Company has recently indicated that it would implement control measures to help it emulate Motorola's "six sigma" standard. Use the Internet to locate information on this new GE initiative. Then use a word-processing package to prepare a one-page synopsis of GE's plan.

2. Use whatever search vehicle is most convenient (Internet, e-mail, fax, newspaper/magazine advertisements, and the like) to gather information on the technical capabilities of Nokia's most advanced cellular telephone, and the services it can provide. Then use presentation software to display your findings to your classmates.

3. Use the Internet to gather information on nuclear power plant incidents in which problems occurred due to failed controls. Organize this information in a spreadsheet that can be sorted on such parameters as date of occurrence, country of occurrence, severity (length of shutdown), and any other parameters you find that might seem relevant. Compare the thoroughness of your spreadsheet data with that of your classmates.

ETHICS: Take a Stand

As this chapter mentioned, the use of illegal drugs is costing U.S. organizations close to $100 billion per year. Home Depot Corporation, a large chain of stores that specializes in the sale of home construction, home repair, home decorating, household, and gardening items, has a very strict policy on drugs. Anyone who approaches the front entrance of a Home Depot store is greeted by a sign in the window proclaiming: "We test all applicants for illegal drug use. If you use drugs, don't bother to apply!"

For Discussion

1. Discuss the ethical issues associated with this control mechanism for individual behavior.

2. Do you feel that pre-employment, or even post-employment, drug screening constitutes ethical behavior on the organization's part, or is it an invasion of personal privacy?

THINKING CRITICALLY: Debate the Issue

BUREAUCRATIC VERSUS ORGANIC CONTROL

Form teams of four to five students as directed by your instructor. Half of the teams should prepare to argue the benefits of bureaucratic control. The other half of the teams should prepare to argue the benefits of organic control. Where possible, identify companies that use these methods of control and assess their relative effectiveness. Two teams will be selected by the instructor to present their findings to the class in a debate format.

ELECTRONIC SURVEILLANCE OF EMPLOYEES

This case portrays a lighthearted look at a serious dilemma—the ethical propriety of electronic surveillance of employees as a means of organizational control.

The vignette takes place in the automobile showroom of Rally Motors, a fictitious auto dealership. The manager has placed a hidden microphone in the showroom and is listening in on the sales pitch of one of his salespeople, Tony. Tony is assuring a prospective customer that gas is cheaper than food, that interest rates are so low that car payments are virtually nonexistent, and that the oil in the car needs to be changed only once every 10,000 miles. The manager storms out of his office and interrupts Tony to ask him to come to his office. When the manager and Tony are alone, the manager says, "What are you saying? Are you nuts?" Tony assures the manager that he will eventually tell the truth, and goes back to his customer. In the meantime, another employee, Shelly, becomes suspicious and confronts the manager. She asks that manager how he can justify listening in on private conversations. The manager replies, "I have to know that my salespeople are honest. Do you know what kind of reputation car dealers have? I want to change that." Shelly asks the manager who is protecting *her* privacy. The manager replies, "Why do you want to know? Do you have something to hide?" At that point, Shelly quits her job in frustration and walks out.

The case depicts the tension that exists between using electronic surveillance as a means of organizational control versus invading the rights of employees and customers. What do you think?

For Discussion

1. What do you think? Was the manager of Rally Motors within his rights to listen in on Tony's conversation with his prospective customer? If you had been in Tony's shoes, what would your reaction have been?

2. Was Shelly's reaction realistic? What would your reaction have been had you been in Shelly's place?

3. Many managers watch their employees by means of live surveillance. Why is electronic surveillance any different?

4. The manager seemed sincere, yet his practice of listening in on private conversations seems obtrusive. What techniques would you suggest for accessing the honesty of car salespeople, short of listening in on their private conversations with customers?

Video Case

CASE

MINCO TECHNOLOGY LABS

At Minco Technology Labs, Inc., of Austin, Texas, internal errors were frequent, delivery performance was poor, the rate of returns was unacceptable, and overhead was soaring. "In a nutshell, we were in trouble," says Elizabeth Coker, owner and CEO of the company, which tests semiconductors and assembles hybrid microcircuits, primarily for the military electronics market. She had located the company in Austin because the area had a number of semiconductor companies, an educated work force, and modest housing and tax costs. It was equidistant from customers on both coasts and near a principal supplier ally, Texas Instruments.

When Coker realized that internal problems threatened Minco's existence, her first step was to simplify. She focused the company on its principal business—servicing the microcircuit processing market—and spun off services for customers in the custom packaging market. As changes proceeded, the overriding aim was "to ensure that any product going to our customers was correct and on time." The company established quality-control gates throughout its process to prevent any questionable product from being shipped. Each step from order taking to shipping was analyzed, through statistical process controls, to determine critical errors and their causes. Quality-status reports identified problems. Companywide training began.

Management was reduced to a single layer, with 12 managers and supervisors replacing 31. Responsibilities were shifted to teams of production-line workers. The number of meetings was cut. Quality, production, management visibility, team member suggestion, document review, and material review board meetings were combined into a single, one-hour daily meeting.

Team members met monthly. The CEO personally began teaching accounting principles and regularly provided every team member with full financial and budget details. Nonmanagement teams reviewed scrap and rework materials. A team would research a problem, resolve it, record it, and dissolve upon achievement of the goal.[35]

For Discussion

1. Describe how and where Minco used a structured control process to try to improve its performance.
2. Discuss the various focal points for control that Minco employed.
3. What types of performance improvements might you expect or predict Minco would experience after implementing these changes?

EXPERIENTIAL EXERCISE 16.1

Assessing Timeliness of Control Systems

Purpose: To gain a greater awareness of the importance of timely feedback in control systems.

Procedure: Make a list of all the offices, departments, and officials that you have interacted with and received feedback from at your university. Then construct a table using the following column headings:

Encounter	Actual Response Time	Ideal Response Time	Problems and Difficulties

In the first column (Encounter), list all of the areas of interaction. In the second column (Actual Response Time), indicate the amount of time that elapsed before you received the feedback that you desired. In the third column (Ideal Response Time), list what you feel would have been an appropriate amount of time in which receive the feedback. Finally, in the fourth column (Problems and Difficulties), note any problems or difficulties that you encountered because you did not receive the feedback in what you considered to be a timely fashion.

EXPERIENTIAL EXERCISE 16.2

Detecting Devices to Control Human Behavior

Purpose: To gain a greater awareness of the extent to which various devices are used to control individual behavior.

Procedure: Visit a shopping mall in your vicinity. Browse through several departments in a large department store and also visit several of the small specialty shops in the mall. See how many devices you can discover for controlling individual behavior. Compare and contrast the types of devices being used in the large department stores with those in small speciality stores. What factors seem to influence the use or nonuse of such devices?

ENDNOTES

1. Based on J. Moad, "Let Customers Have It Their Way," *Datamation,* April 1, 1995, 34–37; G. Bylinsky, "The Digital Factory," *Fortune,* November 14, 1994, 92–99; K. Parker, "Dynamism and Decision Support," *Manufacturing Systems,* April 1995, 12–24; R. Hall, *The Soul of the Enterprise* (New York: HarperBusiness, 1993), 67; L. J. Krajewski and L. P. Ritzman, *Operations Management: Strategy and Analysis* (Reading, Mass.: Addison-Wesley, 1996), 158; "Motorola: Training for the Millennium," *Business Week,* March 28, 1994, 158–62; J. Morkes, "How Motorola Keeps Beating the Competition," *R&D Magazine,* December 1993, 30–32; B. Smith, "Six Sigma Quality: A Must, Not a Myth," *Machine Design,* February 12, 1993, 63–66; P. L. Carter and S. A. Melnyk, "Time-Based Competition: Building the Foundations for Speed," *APICS 35th International Conference Proceedings,* October 18–23, 1992, 63–67; and "Pushing Design to Dizzying Speed," *Business Week,* October 21, 1991, 64.

2. K. A. Merchant, *Control in Business Organizations* (Marshfield, Mass.: Pitman, 1985).

3. T. Lowe and J. L. Machin, *New Perspectives on Management Control* (New York: Macmillan, 1987).

4. C. Williams, "'What a Dump' May Be a Compliment After BioSafe's Landfill Remodeling," *The Wall Street Journal,* September 9, 1996, B5A.

5. G. Edmonson, "Grabbing Markets from the Giants," *Business Week,* Special Issue: "21st Century Capitalism," 1994, 156.

6. W. R. Ashby, *Introduction to Cybernetics* (New York: Wiley, 1963).

7. S. Beer, *Cybernetics and Management* (New York: Wiley, 1959), 44.

8. M. Goold and J. Quinn, "The Paradox of Strategic Controls," *Strategic Management Journal,* January 1990, 43–57.

9. D. Cray, "Control and Coordination in Multinational Corporations," *Journal of International Business Studies,* Fall 1984, 85–98.

10. P. Lorange and D. Murphy, "Considerations in Implementing Strategic Control," *Journal of Business Strategy,* 4, Spring 1984, 27–35.

11. P. P. Schoderbek, R. A. Cosier, and J. C. Aplin, *Management* (San Diego: Harcourt Brace Jovanovich, 1991).

12. J. R. Evans and W. M. Lindsay, *The Management and Control of Quality* (St. Paul, Minn.: West Publishing, 1993).

13. B. H. Fox, M. G. Snyder, and A. M. Smith, "Reliability-Centered Maintenance Improves Operations at TMI Nuclear Plant," *Power Engineering,* November 1994, 75–78.

14. L. Krajewski and L. Ritzman, *Operations Management,* 163.

15. W. H. Newman, *Construction Control* (Upper Saddle River, N.J.: Prentice Hall, 1975).

16. P. Lorange, M. F. S. Morton, and G. Sumantra, *Strategic Control* (St. Paul, Minn.: West Publishing, 1986).

17. P. F. Drucker, *Management: Tasks, Responsibilities, Practices* (New York: Harper & Row, 1973), 100.

18. W. G. Ouchi, "Markets, Bureaucracies, and Clans," *Administrative Science Quarterly,* 25, 1980, 128–41.

19. H. P. Sims Jr. and C. C. Manz, *Super Leadership: Leading Others to Lead Themselves* (New York: Simon & Schuster, 1989).

20. C. Cortland and D. A. Nadler, "Fit Control Systems to Your Managerial Style," *Harvard Business Review,* January/February 1976, 65–72.

21. B. R. Baliga and A. M. Jaeger, "Multinational Corporations: Control Systems and Delegation Issues," *Journal of International Business Studies,* Fall 1984, 25–40.

22. E. Brigham, *Financial Management: Theory and Practice,* 4th ed. (Chicago: Dryden Press, 1985).

23. F. J. Tasco and A. J. Gajda, "Substance Abuse in the Workplace," *Compensation and Benefits Management,* Winter 1990, 140–44.

24. M. A. McDaniel, "Does Pre-Employment Drug Use Predict On-the-Job Suitability?" *Personnel Psychology,* Winter 1988, 717–30.

25. T. W. Ferguson, "Motorola Aims High, So Motorolans Won't Be Getting High," *The Wall Street Journal,* June 26, 1990, A19.

26. F. J. Tasco and A. J. Gajda, "Substance Abuse in the Workplace."

27. "Housing Complex Requires Drug Tests for Tenants," *Orlando Sentinel,* July 28, 1996, B3.

28. "Preventing Crime on the Job," *Nation's Business,* July 1990, 36–37.

29. J. Rothfeder, M. Galen, and L. Driscoll, "Is Your Boss Spying on You?" *Business Week,* January 15, 1990, 74–75.

30. N. H. Snyder and K. E. Blair, "Dealing with Employee Theft," *Business Horizons,* May/June 1989, 27–34.

31. B. Dumaine, "Corporate Spies Snoop to Conquer," *Fortune,* November 7, 1988, 68–76.

32. M. McDonald, "They've Got Your Number," *Dallas Morning News,* April 7, 1991, F1.

33. H. J. Chalykoff and T. A. Kochan, "Computer-Aided Monitoring: Its Influence on Employee Job Satisfaction and Turnover," *Personnel Psychology,* Winter 1989, 807–34.

34. Based on J. Moad, "Let Customers Have it Their Way"; G. Bylinsky, "The Digital Factory"; K. Parker, "Dynamism and Decision Support"; R. Hall, *The Soul of the Enterprise;* L. J. Krajewski and L. P. Ritzman, *Operations Management: Strategy and Analysis;* "Motorola: Training for the Millennium"; J. Morkes, "How Motorola Keeps Beating the Competition"; B. Smith, "Six Sigma Quality: A Must, Not a Myth"; P. L. Carter and S. A. Melnyk, "Time-Based Competition: Building the Foundations for Speed"; and "Pushing Design to Dizzying Speed."

35. Adapted from "Minco Technology Labs," in *Real-World Lessons for America's Small Businesses: Insights from the Blue Chip Enterprise Initiative* (*Nation's Business* on behalf of Connecticut Mutual Life Insurance Company and the U.S. Chamber of Commerce, 1993), 84–85.

Productivity and Quality in Operations

CHAPTER OVERVIEW

All business organizations engage in operations that transform inputs into outputs. Regardless of whether their organization manufactures a product or provides a service, operations managers have one fundamental concern—that is, to provide the customers what they want, when they want it. As simple as this concept sounds, operations managers must make many decisions prior to delivering the product or service. To achieve quality in operations, managers must (1) understand the nature of the various decisions they will face and (2) understand the various tools, techniques, and approaches that can help them to make these decisions. How managers should approach these decisions depends to a large extent upon whether their organization is predominantly product or service oriented and upon the structural characteristics of the operating system.

In this chapter we first examine the differences between manufacturing and service organizations and review the basic system configurations that these organizations may exhibit. We then briefly examine some of the more important managerial decision areas for the long-term design of these systems, as well as some of the important decisions for their short-term operation and control. Since productivity and quality have a major impact upon the efficiency and effectiveness of operations decisions, ways to measure and improve them are examined. We also present some contributions of the most prominent contemporary quality philosophers. We finish by discussing the roles that productivity and quality play in achieving excellence in operations.

LEARNING OBJECTIVES

When you have finished studying this chapter, you should be able to:

- Identify the major differences between manufacturing and service organizations.
- Describe the volume/variety continuum for identifying different operating system configurations and identify the different types of manufacturing and service organizations that might exist, as well as their locations on the volume/variety continuum.
- Identify the two broad categories of decision-making areas within operating systems and describe some of the important decisions in each category.
- Define the concept of productivity and identify the three approaches to improving productivity.
- Provide definitions of quality from both a consumer perspective and a producer perspective.

- Describe the four categories of quality-related costs.
- Identify the various areas of concentration and commitment for a program of total quality management.
- Describe the major contributions of the most prominent contemporary quality philosophers.

FENDER MUSICAL INSTRUMENTS CORPORATION

The year 1996 was a milestone for the Fender Musical Instruments Corporation. It marked the 50th anniversary of the day when Leo Fender, a radio repairman from Fullerton, California, introduced the first solid-body electric guitars. The Telecaster and Stratocaster were born, and the music industry was reshaped. Musicians were no longer at the mercy of hollow-body guitars with primitive pickups jammed under the strings. The sleek Strats and Teles, which haven't changed a bit since their birth, quickly became the darlings of the music industry. Such legendary performers and groups as Buddy Holly, Jimi Hendrix, Bob Dylan, Eric Clapton, Bruce Springsteen, the Beatles, and the Who are just part of the almost endless list of devotees to Fender guitars. Richie Sambora, Bon Jovi's lead guitarist, summed up this devotion best when he said of his Strat, "What could you possibly do to improve it? It's perfect right out of the box, and the only guitar I'll ever need."

The ride was not always a smooth one for the Strats and Teles, though. After guiding the company through its first two decades, Leo Fender sold the company to CBS, which began importing the instruments from Japan. Annual production topped the 40,000 level, and the company could sell virtually anything with the Fender name attached. But when interest rates soared with the recession of the late 1970s, CBS allowed quality to lapse. Dealers began sending guitars back to the plant, while many a Strat suffered the ultimate indignity of having its tuning head sawed off before being converted into a lamp. By the mid-1980s, Fender guitar sales had hit a 20-year low, production was down, the most recent annual loss was at the $5 million level, and the company was losing more than $1 million per month. At this point, William Schultz, current president of Fender, enters the picture. Schultz had worked for CBS during Fender's low point, and because of his musical background he was heartbroken to see the depths to which these once-revered instruments had sunk. Determined to correct this indignity, Schultz helped organize a buyout, acquired the Fender name and distribution for $12.5 million, and took the company private. The tall task that remained was to stop the flow of red ink and restore Fender guitars to their former prominence.[1]

INTRODUCTION

The Fender Musical Instruments Corporation was facing a very serious problem. Because Fender's productivity and quality had declined so dramatically, its market share was slipping and losses were mounting. Unless it could reverse this trend, Fender faced the possibility that this once-revered instrument would disappear from the music scene. Achieving excellence in its operations would require changes to correct its quality and productivity problems. As we will see as the chapter unfolds and in the closing resolution to this Managerial Incident, these changes would eventually pervade many aspects of Fender's operations.

In this chapter we will focus on issues of productivity and quality in operations. Recall that in Chapter 16 we presented a simple model for operations. It described a process in which inputs are subjected to a transformation process that converts them into the product or service outputs of the organization. We will see that operations management has a strong decision-making orientation and contains several design and operating decision areas. How managers should approach these decisions depends upon the structural characteristics of their own operating systems and whether their organizations are predominantly engaged in manufacturing products or providing services.

We begin by examining the differences between manufacturing and service organizations and the structural differences between various operating systems. Some of the more important system design and operating decisions are then described. We conclude the chapter by discussing the roles that productivity and quality play in achieving excellence in operations and examining ways organizations can improve productivity and quality.

WHAT IS OPERATIONS MANAGEMENT? ▬▬▬▬▬▬▬▬▬▬▬▬▬▬▬

Operations management is concerned with the design, planning, and control of the factors that enable us to provide the product or service outputs of the organization. Decision making is central to operations management. Operations managers must make decisions to ensure that the product or service output of the firm is provided (1) in the amount demanded, (2) at the appropriate time, (3) with the appropriate quality level, and (4) in a manner that is compatible with the goals of the organization.

The first three aspects of the operations manager's function are fairly straightforward: provide what the customers want, when they want it, and with a quality level that is acceptable to them. The last aspect can be a bit trickier. As we saw in Chapter 4, organizations often have multiple goals, and some may be in conflict with one another. When this happens, operations management decisions cannot simultaneously satisfy all organizational goals. Consider, for example, the dilemma you would face if you were in charge of operations in a steel mill. Suppose that two of your organization's many goals were to (1) maximize bottom-line profits and (2) reduce the amount of pollutants that the mill discharges into the atmosphere. Installing scrubbers in the mill's smokestacks would reduce pollution, but the expense of these scrubbers would detract from your organization's bottom-line profits.

The decisions faced by operations managers can be conveniently separated into two broad categories. The first set of decisions relates to the design of the operating system. After the system has been designed and built, operations managers must then make the operating and control decisions necessary to keep the system running in a smooth and efficient manner. Managers can draw on many tools, techniques, and models to help them make these decisions. For many operations decisions, the proper decision-making tools depend upon whether the system is a manufacturing or service system. We will see later in the chapter that the manufacturing-versus-service distinction also influences how quality and productivity are measured. Decision-making tool selection also depends upon the structural characteristics of the operating system. Consequently, before we explore the important operations management decision areas, we first examine the differences between manufacturing and service organizations and the structural differences among various manufacturing and service organizations.

MANUFACTURING VERSUS SERVICE OPERATING SYSTEMS

Although manufacturing and service organizations both display the same input-to-output transformation process, a fundamental output characteristic distinguishes manufacturing organizations from most service organizations. The out-

A hair salon, unlike a manufacturing company, cannot stockpile inventories of haircuts prior to the Saturday morning peak demand period. Its service capacity is often described as being time perishable; if it has excess capacity that goes unused, that capacity has been lost forever.

© Christopher Bissell/Tony Stone Images

put of manufacturing will always be a physical product—something that can be touched, measured, weighed, or otherwise examined. For example, IBM makes computers, General Motors makes automobiles, RCA makes audio and video equipment, and Nike makes athletic apparel.

Outputs of service organizations often lack physical properties. For example, H&R Block processes income tax returns, hospitals treat sick and injured people, and your college professors deliver lectures and convey knowledge to you. Sometimes, however, the outputs of service organizations do possess physical properties. When you eat in a fast-food restaurant, your lunch selection certainly has physical properties associated with it. Does this make the fast-food restaurant a manufacturing organization? Not really. The physical characteristic of outputs is not the only feature that distinguishes manufacturing from service organizations. As we take a closer look at other differences, continue to think about fast-food restaurants. You should have a definite opinion as to whether they are manufacturing or service organizations by the time we get to the end of the discussion.

Several of the differences between manufacturing and service stem from the physical nature of the output. Manufacturing can stockpile inventories of finished products in advance of customer demand.[2] Service organizations usually cannot. For example, a barbershop cannot stockpile a supply of haircuts prior to the Saturday morning peak demand period, and H&R Block cannot stockpile an inventory of completed income tax returns prior to April's peak demand. Service capacity is often described as being *time perishable.*[3] This means that if a service organization has excess capacity that goes unused, that service capability has been lost forever. On the other hand, a manufacturing organization with excess capacity can use the surplus capacity to produce additional product for later consumption.

Another difference is that production and consumption usually occur simultaneously in service organizations. In addition, the customer is normally a participant in the service process.[4] For example, you must show up at the barbershop or beauty salon to receive a haircut, and it will be performed while you sit in the barber's or hairdresser's chair. These two characteristics also demonstrate another difference between manufacturing and service—the system location considerations. Service systems, such as barbershops, restaurants, income tax preparation firms, and hospitals, need to be located close to their customers, while manufacturing systems would not consider this to be of prime importance.[5] Most adult Americans own an automobile, but few live within walking distance or an easy drive to an automobile manufacturing plant. However, most would like to have reasonable access to an automobile repair shop, for none of us would want to take our automobile back to Detroit (or Japan!) for repair service.

A final difference between manufacturing and service relates to the measurement of quality and productivity. The quality of a product is usually much easier to assess than the quality of a service.[6] Physical products are designed to meet various specifications that involve physical traits such as weight, dimensions, color, durability, and so forth. After manufacture, precise objective measurements of these characteristics can be made to determine the degree to which the product meets the quality standards. For example, once manufactured, an Apple Macintosh computer can be put through a variety of tests to ensure that

CHECKLIST FOR MANUFACTURING/SERVICE CLASSIFICATION

To determine whether a business firm is a manufacturing organization or a service organization, answer the following questions with a zero (0) for no and a one (1) for yes.

1. Does the firm provide a tangible, physical output?
2. Can the output be stored in inventory for future use or consumption?
3. Can the output be transported to distant locations?
4. Can excess capacity be put to productive use?
5. Can the output be produced well in advance of its consumption?
6. Can the system operate without having the consumer of the output as an active participant?
7. Is it reasonable to have the system located a great distance from the consumer of the output?
8. Is productivity relatively easy to measure?
9. Is quality relatively easy to assess?

Total the value of your responses. The closer the total is to 9, the more inclined we would be to classify the system as a manufacturing organization. The closer the total is to 0, the more inclined we would be to classify the system as a service organization.

it operates exactly as it was designed. Such precision is usually more difficult when assessing the quality of a service output. In many instances only subjective assessments can be made of the quality of the service output. Precise standards usually do not exist to determine how good the haircut is, how accurately the income tax return was prepared, or how tasty the hamburger was. Productivity, which gauges the relationship between inputs and outputs, is also easier to assess in manufacturing situations, where the physical nature of the inputs and outputs allows them to be precisely measured.[7] Meeting the Challenge presents a checklist for determining whether an organization is predominantly a manufacturing organization or a service organization. Apply the checklist to the Fender Musical Instruments Corporation as described in the opening Managerial Incident. Into which category (manufacturing or service) does Fender fall?

Now let's think again about fast-food chains and the checklist in Meeting the Challenge. The service capacity of the fast-food outlets is usually time perishable. Excess capacity early in the day will go unused; it cannot be used to satisfy the needs of the lunch-hour crowd. Using that early-morning excess capacity to stockpile inventory in advance of the lunch-hour rush is of limited practicality. Hamburgers and french fries cannot be cooked early in the day and then stored until the noon rush. In these situations, production and consumption must occur almost simultaneously, and the customer is an active participant in the process. The vast multitude of locations also points to a service orientation. One centralized McDonald's will not suffice. There must be plenty of outlets, scattered about so that they are near the customers in order to facilitate direct interaction between the customer and the service system. Thus, when all the tests are applied, a service classification proves to be more appropriate for fast-food restaurants.

Now carefully examine the situation described in Entrepreneurial Approach. Here we see that the Blue Rhino Corporation was started to relieve gas-grill owners of the need to find a propane filling station. Despite the fact

Entrepreneurial
Approach

BLUE RHINO CORPORATION: A GOOD IDEA "CATCHES FIRE"

As a backyard chef himself, Billy Prim certainly knew of the inconvenience that gas-grill owners faced when their tanks ran dry and a propane filling station had to be found. Prim decided to start a propane cylinder exchange business at the two convenience stores he owned. Customers could drop off their empty cylinders and exchange them for filled ones. The concept caught on, and his business quickly expanded. Prim realized that brand recognition would be important, so he adopted a powder-blue beast with a distinctive yellow flame for a horn as the corporate mascot for his company, which he named Blue Rhino Corporation. All Blue Rhino tanks feature factory valve seals, bilingual instructions, and a toll-free help line, adding to the company's image of safety and convenience. In its two years of existence Blue Rhino has grown to about 100 employees, with more than 3,000 exchange sites in 21 states. Prim has marketed his idea to retailers that sell gas grills but do not have propane gas available. These retailers include such giants as Wal-Mart, Home Depot, Kmart, and Sears. Prim's compelling logic, in his own words, was, "It didn't make sense to sell you a grill and send you off to the competition to get the tank filled."

With gas-grill sales booming, Blue Rhino is trying to establish itself as a national brand leader in cylinder exchange. During the 1980s, gas grills accounted for only 20 percent of all grills sold. By the end of 1995, that number had grown to 60 percent. More than 4.6 million gas grills were sold in 1995 alone, and over 33 million U.S. households own a gas grill. Figures like these will surely help Blue Rhino approach its goal to serve more than 9,000 exchange sites.[3]

that there is a physical commodity involved in its interactions with customers, Blue Rhino has many of the characteristics of a service operation. With thousands of sites geographically dispersed and the ultimate consumer involved in the transaction, Blue Rhino is well equipped to provide its customers with a quick and safe propane refill.

Let's now turn our attention to an examination of the structural differences that can exist among manufacturing and service organizations.

STRUCTURAL DIFFERENCES AMONG OPERATING SYSTEMS

Individual operating systems can be categorized along a volume/variety continuum, as illustrated in Figure 17.1. Companies can differ in the variety of outputs produced, as well as in the volume of each item that is provided. As you move toward the left extreme of low variety and high volume, you encounter systems that provide very few different types of output, but deliver a large quantity of each. Toward the right extreme of high variety and low volume, you encounter systems that provide a very wide variety of different types of output, but deliver a small number of each. The endpoints of this line represent two extremes in both manufacturing and service organizations. Let's take a closer look at these configurations, first in manufacturing organizations and then in service organizations.

Types of Manufacturing Systems
The left portion of the continuum represents systems that have a specific purpose.[9] The extreme left reflects companies that make only one product, but produce it in large quantities. In such a system, operations can be standardized. When the product being made takes the form of discrete, individual units, the system is called a **repetitive, assembly-line,** or **mass-production sys-**

Repetitive, assembly-line, or mass-production system
Produces a high volume of discrete items.

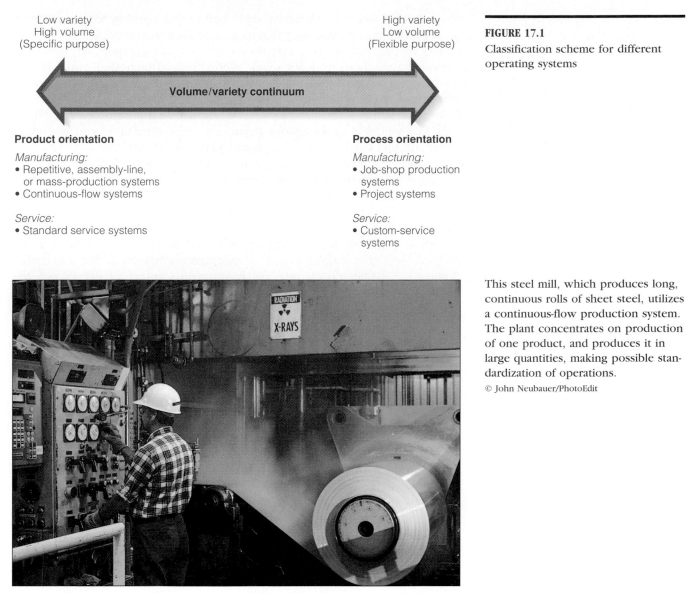

Low variety
High volume
(Specific purpose)

High variety
Low volume
(Flexible purpose)

Volume/variety continuum

Product orientation

Manufacturing:
• Repetitive, assembly-line, or mass-production systems
• Continuous-flow systems

Service:
• Standard service systems

Process orientation

Manufacturing:
• Job-shop production systems
• Project systems

Service:
• Custom-service systems

FIGURE 17.1
Classification scheme for different operating systems

This steel mill, which produces long, continuous rolls of sheet steel, utilizes a continuous-flow production system. The plant concentrates on production of one product, and produces it in large quantities, making possible standardization of operations.
© John Neubauer/PhotoEdit

tem. For example, a company that makes only yellow #2 pencils with an eraser would be at the left end of the continuum. When a product is made in a continuous stream, and not in discrete units, the system is called a **continuous-flow production system.** Examples here would include an Exxon oil refinery, a Coors brewery, or perhaps a USX steel mill that produces long, continuous rolls of sheet steel.

At the right end of the continuum are systems that have a flexible purpose. The extreme right reflects companies that make many different types of items, but produce only one of each. This would be a custom manufacturing situation. In such a system, operations cannot be standardized, but instead must be flexible enough to accommodate the wide variety of items that will be manufactured. When the items to be made require small to moderate amounts of resources and time (hours or days), the system is referred to as a **job shop production system.** The term *unit production* is often used to signify systems that manufacture only a single unit of a particular item. A sign shop that custom-fabricates neon advertising signs for small businesses would be an example of a company near the right extreme of this continuum. Another example of a facility near the right extreme of the continuum can be found in the Fender

Continuous-flow production system
Produces a high volume of output that flows in a continuous stream.

Job-shop production system
Produces small quantities of a wide variety of specialized items.

Musical Instruments Corporation, described in the opening Managerial Incident. Fender has a custom shop that handles requests for Stratocasters and Telecasters that are tailored to a customer's ego and budget. Here they will fashion you a guitar body from any exotic wood or metal requested. Furthermore, if you are so inclined, they will inlay your signature (or any design of your liking) across the frets in gems, jewels, abalone, or whatever material suits your fancy. The options are almost limitless to Fender's master craftspeople. However, you will have to wait about a year, and depending upon your specifications, you may have to pay as much as $50,000 for your guitar.

Project production system
Produces large-scale, unique items.

Sometimes flexible-purpose systems produce items that consume massive amounts of resources and require large amounts of time to complete (months or years). Such a system is referred to as a **project production system.** Examples here would include construction companies that develop shopping centers, build roads and bridges, and so forth.[10]

Although the endpoints have been neatly defined for the continuum of Figure 17.1, it is very unusual to find an organization that lies at either extreme. While Eberhard-Faber is a large pencil manufacturer, this company makes more than just yellow #2 pencils with erasers. It turns out pencils in a variety of colors with different types of lead. In addition to writing pencils, it also manufactures a variety of pens and marking pencils. All of these different writing instruments are produced in very large quantities. Consequently, Eberhard-Faber exhibits mass-production characteristics and would certainly be close to the left extreme of the volume/variety continuum. If the neon sign shop described earlier made a small number of several different signs, it would move slightly away from the right extreme. Even so, this system would still exhibit the basic characteristics of the job-shop system.

Types of Service Systems

The continuum of Figure 17.1 also applies to different types of service systems. The left extreme reflects organizations that provide standard services, while the right extreme reflects organizations that provide custom services. Consider, for example, a college dormitory cafeteria line. It has all of the characteristics of an assembly line, since each customer moving through the line is serviced in exactly the same manner at each serving station. The Blue Rhino Corporation, described earlier in Entrepreneurial Approach, provides another illustration of a standard service. All customer interactions with the company are for one purpose, that is, a propane cylinder exchange. In contrast, a walk-in emergency clinic might exhibit all the characteristics of a custom job shop, since most patients are likely to have different types of injuries and illnesses and consequently will require different services.

As in the case of manufacturing, service organizations can easily lie somewhere between the extremes. The cafeteria line might have *à la carte* selections, in which case some customers might receive slightly different service. Likewise, the emergency clinic might have a few patients with broken arms whose service requirements are virtually identical. The wound will be cleaned and dressed, X-rays taken, and a cast applied for each of them.[11]

Whether an organization is a manufacturing or a service entity and wherever it fits on the volume/variety continuum, its operations managers will have to make decisions. The next section examines the many decisions that must be made for both the design and the operation of manufacturing and service organizations.

OPERATIONS MANAGEMENT DECISION AREAS

When you operate any business organization, a number of decisions must be made. Based upon the time frame involved, these decisions can be conveniently categorized as long-term system design decisions or as short-term operating and control decisions.[12] It is not our intention to present a thorough description of each of the operations management decision areas. That level of detail is best left to separate operations management courses with their specialized textbooks. Instead, we provide you with a brief, introductory overview of some of the more important operations management decision areas.

Long-Term System Design Decisions

Long-term system design decisions require substantial investments of time, energy, money, and resources. As the name implies, they commit the decision maker to a particular system configuration (that is, an arrangement of buildings and equipment) that will exist for many years, if not the entire life of the organization. Once these decisions are made and implemented, changing them would be costly. Although a thorough treatment of these various decisions would require several chapters, the following brief overview will provide a basic understanding.

Choice of a Product or Service   Prior to the development and start-up of any business, a fundamental decision must be made about what product or service will be provided. This decision is directly linked to the corporate strategy, for it answers the question, "What business are we in?" The choice of product or service will ultimately dictate what inputs will be necessary and what type of transformation will be performed. To make a viable product/service selection decision, considerable interaction with the marketing function will be needed. This interaction will help the decision maker accurately assess the wants and needs of the marketplace as well as the strength of the competition, so that the product or service selected has a reasonable chance of success.

Product or Service Design   From a manufacturing standpoint, the development of a product involves a sequence of steps, as illustrated in Figure 17.2.[13] These steps might also be applied in certain service situations that involve physical output. The sequence of design steps requires (1) development of a concept, (2) development of a preliminary design or prototype, (3) development of "make versus buy" choices, and (4) selection of production methods, equipment, and suppliers.

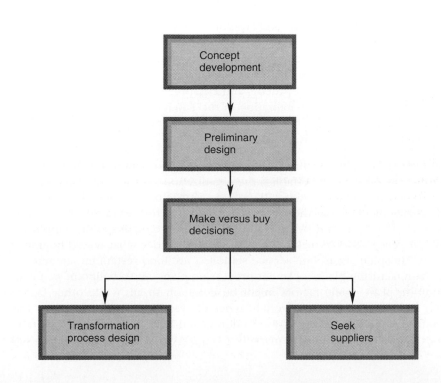

FIGURE 17.2
Steps in product design

Although each step in the design process is usually carried out by a different unit of the organization, design quality is facilitated when all participants from marketing, engineering, production, purchasing, and any other relevant areas work together as a design team. The instant feedback and enhanced interactions within the team help to achieve more rapid product development. The design process can also be facilitated by such recent high-tech developments as computer-aided design (CAD), computer-aided engineering (CAE), and computer-aided manufacturing (CAM). By using virtual prototypes on computers to design and test cars, the U.S. Big Three automakers have made marked progress in reducing the time required to develop new vehicles, which will save them billions of dollars in costs.[14]

System Capacity   Another decision to be made involves the capacity of the system.[15] This decision will determine the level of product or service output that the system will be able to provide. It is here that the firm will make its major investment decisions. The number of facilities to be built, the size of each facility, their individual capabilities, and the amount and type of equipment to be purchased must all be determined. In order to make high-quality decisions in this area, the decision maker must forecast the market demand for the product or service to be offered and assess the competition so that the organization's market share potential can be estimated. Next, the amount of labor and equipment needed to meet these market share projections must be calculated. Marketing will play a key role here, for accurate projections of market demand and competition will help to establish the size of the system being developed.

Process Selection   The selection of a framework for the transformation process will depend upon how the firm is likely to be categorized. Recall our classification scheme that categorized manufacturing and service organizations along a volume/variety continuum. An organization's self-assessment of the volume, variety, and type of product or service output likely to be generated will help to indicate the type of process to be selected. In a manufacturing setting, answers to these questions will indicate the types of material flows that can be expected through the system. This in turn will determine the process configuration to be selected; that is, will the organization be configured as a continuous-flow, repetitive, job-shop, or project system? In a service setting, the self-assessment of volume, variety, and type of service will determine whether the system process will provide custom or standard services. Once the process configuration has been selected, machinery and equipment compatible with that process can be obtained. We will see later in the resolution to the opening Managerial Incident that process and equipment selection was one of the key areas of focus in the revitalization of the Fender Musical Instruments Corporation. New state-of-the-art equipment was purchased to ensure consistency and quality in Fender's guitars.

Facility Location   The facility location decision involves the selection of a geographic site on which to establish the organization's operations. This decision is extremely important, for once the physical structure has been built, its high cost usually dictates that the location decision will remain in effect for a considerable amount of time. Manufacturing and service organizations emphasize very different factors in making this decision. Consider what would be important to a hospital, a gasoline service station, a fast-food restaurant, an automobile manufacturing plant, a cement processing plant, and a ballpoint pen manufacturing plant. Some factors might be common to all, while other factors might be important for only certain types of systems. Survey data show that manufacturing location decisions are dominated by five factors: (1) favorable labor climate, (2) proximity to markets, (3) quality of life, (4) proximity to sup-

TABLE 17.1   Major factors in manufacturing location decisions

1. *Favorable labor climate.* Management's assessment on the labor climate would be based on such parameters as union activity, wage rates, available labor skill levels, required labor training, worker attitudes, and worker productivity.

2. *Proximity to markets.* Consideration would be given to both the actual distance to the markets and the modes of transportation available to deliver the products.

3. *Quality of life.* Attention would be paid to the quality and availability of schools, housing, shopping, recreation facilities, and other lifestyle indicators that reflect the quality of life.

4. *Proximity to suppliers and resources.* When companies rely on bulky or heavy raw materials and supplies, this factor is of prime concern. Distance and transportation modes would influence this factor.

5. *Proximity to the parent company's facilities.* This factor is important for companies with multiplant configurations. When parts and materials must be transferred between operating facilities, frequent interactions, communication, and coordination will be necessary. Additionally, the time and cost of material transfers must be minimized. All of this can be facilitated by geographical proximity between the facilities.

pliers and resources, and (5) proximity to the parent company's facilities.[16] Table 17.1 describes these factors further.

In service organizations, proximity to customers is often the primary location factor to be considered. Since customers must usually interact directly with service organizations, convenient locations are crucial. Barbershops, dry cleaners, supermarkets, and gasoline service stations would do very little business if they were situated in remote, inaccessible areas. Traffic volume, residential population density, competition, and income levels all play an important part in the location decision for service organizations.

The location criteria mentioned here should not be interpreted as an exhaustive list. We will see in the resolution to the opening Managerial Incident that Fender decided to relocate its production facilities due to the high overhead associated with its rather expensive neighborhood in Orange County, California. And how about the rather bizarre factor considered by the Russell Stover Candy Company. Although it had committed to building a plant in Corsicana, Texas, that decision was put on hold when plans were announced for an animal parts processing plant in the same town. Russell Stover officials feared that odors from the animal rendering facility would contaminate its sweets. The candy company gave the go-ahead with its construction plans only after the animal rendering plant was paid by town officials to locate elsewhere.[17]

Facility Layout   The primary objective of the facility layout decision is to arrange the work areas and equipment so that inputs progress through the transformation process in as orderly a fashion as possible. This will result in a smooth flow of materials or customers through the system. The precise configuration for a given system will depend on where the system fits into the volume/variety continuum. Systems at the flexible-purpose extreme, which must be able to handle a wide variety of product or customer-service demands, will use a **process layout.** Conversely, systems at the specific-purpose extreme, in which all products or services are essentially the same, will use a **product layout.** Lying between these extremes are a variety of systems that need layouts combining aspects of each of the extreme cases. These systems would incorporate a **hybrid layout.** Finally, a system that produces extremely large or bulky items may use a **fixed-position layout,** in which the item remains stationary while

Process layout
A configuration flexible enough to accommodate a wide diversity of products or customers.

Product layout
A configuration set for a specific purpose, with all product or service demands essentially identical.

Hybrid layout
A configuration containing some degree of flexibility, lying between the extremes of process and product layouts.

Fixed-position layout
A configuration used for large or bulky items that remain stationary in the manufacturing process.

Global Perspective

TOYS R US: REVAMPING STORE LAYOUTS

Toys R Us, based in Paramus, New Jersey, is the world's largest children's retailer. Although superstores are now common for everything from pet supplies to office supplies, Toys R Us was the pioneer when it opened its first store in 1958. Initially Toys R Us stores commanded the lion's share of the toy market. Back then, few retailers carried toys on a year-round basis. And, because of its huge buying power, Toys R Us could offer prices that were 20 to 50 percent below the competition's. Although 1995 sales were up internationally, there was a 2 percent sales decline in the domestic market, and overall company profit was down 72 percent from the prior year. These declines were due in part to aggressive pricing policies of such discounters as Target, Wal-Mart, and Kmart, who have been matching Toys R Us on price.

Toys R Us has decided that a key to improving its market share and profitability is to cast off its time-worn warehouse look. Shoppers had been complaining that its stores were cluttered and confusing. They wanted less clutter, more service, and easier shopping. In response, Toys R Us has streamlined its product selection and redrawn store layouts. The maze of parallel aisles has been replaced with a hub-and-spoke pattern, with departments grouped around a central oval. Board games will be located in a department designed to resemble a Monopoly board. Popular characters such as Barbie, Mickey Mouse, and Bugs Bunny will get their own departments. In addition to the layout changes, the front wall of the stores will be removed and replaced with a glass grid designed to brighten the interior. These changes are called Concept 2000, and are part of a Toys R Us effort to recapture some of its youthful vigor.[18]

workers and equipment move to the item to provide processing. Just how important the layout decision can be is illustrated in Global Perspective. Here we see how Toys R Us, the world's largest children's retailer, embarked on a massive project to revamp the layout of its stores in an effort to rekindle customer interest and reverse recent declines brought on by aggressive competitors.

Some of these long-term system design decisions present unique managerial challenges to multinational organizations. For example, before selecting and designing a product or service, the sociocultural and economic environments of the global markets in which the organization will operate must be assessed. In addition, it would be unwise to select international locations for operating units of the organization without first considering the political-legal climate, economic conditions, state of technological development, and cultural values of the work force in the potential locations. Success will come more easily to multinational organizations that thoroughly research all of these parameters in their long-term system design decisions.

Short-Term Operating and Control Decisions

After the long-term system design decisions have been made and the system is operational, it is time to begin making the short-term operating and control decisions. These decisions are made frequently (daily, weekly, or perhaps monthly), are quite capable of being readily changed, and in many cases are directly involved with the scheduling of work activities. In today's organizations, managers face new challenges as they schedule, lead, and control labor in the increasingly diverse work force. Ethnic, racial, and gender differences often lead to different individual values and expectations. Hence, standards of individual behavior, performance, and productivity are sometimes more difficult to set and enforce.

Aggregate Planning   Before initiating any detailed day-to-day or week-to-week scheduling activities in a manufacturing firm, management must first make a series of decisions designed to set the overall level of operations for a planning horizon that generally spans the upcoming year. At this point, management makes rough production and labor scheduling decisions that will set the tone for the overall level of operations during the year. The goal is to ensure that customer demand can be satisfied, the firm's resources won't be overtaxed, and the relevant costs will be held to a minimum. These decisions constitute what is known as **aggregate planning.** This set of planning decisions represents the link between the more general business planning activities and the more specific master plans for short-range operation and control aspects of the firm.

Aggregate planning
Link between the more general business planning activities and the more specific master planning activities.

In aggregate planning, management formulates a plan that involves such factors as production scheduling, work force level adjusting, inventory scheduling, production subcontracting, and employment scheduling so that enough product or service will be available to satisfy customer demands.[19] By their very nature, aggregate plans are rather rough. They are usually stated in terms of product families rather than individual products. Further, their monthly or quarterly time periods are incapable of directing the day-to-day scheduling of operations. The main purpose of aggregate plans is to provide broad production scheduling, inventory scheduling, and human resource scheduling guidelines within which more detailed scheduling decisions will eventually be made.

Master Production Scheduling   Although the rough schedule provided by aggregate planning will be quite useful for projecting the overall levels of production and labor requirements over an intermediate planning horizon, it will not contain enough detail and information for scheduling the various production activities. Another schedule is needed that not only contains detailed information about individual product identities but also divides the planning horizon into finer increments of time. Such a schedule, which is known as the *master production schedule,* will be used to drive all of the ensuing production scheduling activities within the system.

The **master production schedule** is a detailed statement of projected production quantities for each item in each time period.[20] Time periods are typically weekly intervals. The master production schedule is often thought of as an anticipated build schedule for finished products. A major constraint in the development of the master production schedule is that the total number of units scheduled for production must be compatible with the aggregate plan. Since the master production schedule is simply a more detailed breakdown of the aggregate plan, the sum of the parts (the master production schedule units) must equal the whole (the aggregate plan).

Master production schedule
A detailed statement of projected production quantities for each item in each time period.

Inventory Management   One of the most studied of the short-term decisions deals with the control of inventories. Items in inventory may exist in any of four forms: (1) raw materials, (2) work in process, (3) finished goods, and (4) supplies. Raw materials are the basic inputs that have not yet been subjected to any processing transactions. Work in process represents semifinished items that are in various stages of completion. Finished goods are items that have had all processing transactions performed and are ready for delivery to the customer. Supplies represent purchased items that facilitate the completion of some production or service activity.[21] Two fundamental decisions must be made with respect to the replenishment of any item maintained in inventory:

TABLE 17.2   Economic order quantity model

- Relevant costs: Annual ordering cost and annual carrying cost
- Symbols used: D = annual demand or usage
                   S = cost per order (setup cost or purchase order cost)
                   H = carrying cost per unit per year
                   Q = order size (which is to be determined)

MODEL STRUCTURE

The total annual carrying cost is the average inventory level multiplied by the cost to carry a unit in inventory for a year. In symbolic form, the average inventory level is $Q/2$; therefore,

Total annual carrying cost = $(Q/2)(H)$

The total annual ordering cost is equal to the number of orders placed during the year times the cost per order. In symbolic form, the number of orders placed per year is D/Q; therefore,

Total annual ordering cost = $(D/Q)(S)$

Combining these two costs yields a total cost of

$$TC = (Q/2)(H) + (D/Q)(S)$$

DETERMINATION OF EOQ

Take the derivative of TC with respect to Q and set equal to zero, then solve for Q:

$$H/2 - DS/Q^2 = 0$$

An algebraic rearrangement of terms yields the following:

$$Q^2 = 2DS/H$$

and

$$Q = \sqrt{2DS/H} \qquad \text{(Also called the EOQ)}$$

This is called the EOQ since this is the most economic order quantity.

(1) how many should be ordered? and (2) when should they be ordered? These decisions are referred to as *lot-sizing* and *lot-timing decisions.* The objective of inventory management is to make those decisions in a manner that minimizes the total of inventory-related costs. Many models have been developed to aid in making lot-sizing and lot-timing decisions under varying conditions. The earliest and perhaps best-known of these models is the classic Economic Order Quantity (EOQ) model. Table 17.2 provides a brief overview of the specifics of this model.

Material Requirements Planning   Excellence in inventory control requires that lot-sizing and lot-timing decisions be made correctly for all items used to construct a product. EOQ models of the type described are quite capable of making the proper sizing and timing decisions for finished products. Unfortunately, they do a poor job of controlling the various raw materials, parts, and components that are assembled into those finished products. *Material requirements planning* (MRP) is a simple methodology devised for controlling these lower-level items.

The basic approach of MRP requires that lot-sizing and lot-timing decisions be made first for the finished product so that sufficient finished product will be available to support the master production schedule. These timing and sizing decisions for the finished product will determine the needs for the various components that combine directly into the finished product (that is, those components one level of production removed from the finished product). The timing and sizing decisions can then be made for these components so that suffi-cient amounts will be available to support the planned production of the fin-ished product. Once this has been done, attention is focused on the next lower level of manufacture. By continually linking the successive levels of manufacture, lot-sizing and lot-timing decisions for all raw materials, parts, and components used in making the finished product will be coordinated to ensure that the master production schedule will be met.[22] Since most multistage manufacturing systems have products that consist of hundreds or even thousands of individual raw materials, parts, components, subassemblies, and assemblies spanning dozens of levels of manufacture, a computerized system is necessary to perform the massive data handling and manipulation chores of the MRP process.

Just-in-Time Inventory Management   A recent phenomenon in the area of inventory control is a philosophy known as just-in-time (JIT) inventory management. This concept initially received considerable attention and refinement within the Japanese industrial community and is now quickly spreading worldwide. Despite its concern with inventory, JIT is more than just a technique for dealing with inventory. **Just-in-time inventory management** is an overall manufacturing philosophy that advocates eliminating waste, solving problems, and striving for continual improvement in operations.[23]

JIT attempts to reduce inventory because inventory can be costly and can hide problems. For example, problems such as machine breakdowns, high levels of defective output, and worker absenteeism may not cause noticeable disruptions to flow when high levels of inventory exist to "ride over" those problems. Inventory reductions can be achieved quite simply. Regardless of whether we are dealing with a manufacturing or service organization, whenever any item is to be replenished, the replenishment lot size can be made smaller. Raw materials and supplies can be ordered in smaller batches from suppliers. Parts and components can be manufactured in smaller batches, just as finished goods can be assembled in smaller batches. Because the ultimate goal is the almost total elimination of inventory, JIT systems are often referred to as *zero-inventory systems* or *stockless production systems.* To economically justify reductions in lot size, JIT users must attempt to reduce the setup cost or ordering cost as much as possible. Return for the moment to the EOQ formula in Table 17.2, where you can see that a reduction in the setup or ordering cost will lead to a smaller lot size. Setup cost can be reduced by studying and redesigning setup procedures to make them as short as possible, training workers in the proper setup procedure, redesigning tools and equipment, and perhaps even replacing equipment. All of these efforts are aimed at achieving quicker setups.[24]

Since there is little inventory in a JIT system, there can be little tolerance for problems because these will inevitably disrupt flow and perhaps stop system output. This is why JIT is regarded as a broader philosophy of problem solving, waste elimination, and continual improvement. In addition to the zero-inventory ideal, JIT also seeks to attain zero defects (perfect quality), zero breakdowns, and, in general, zero problems. In such systems, workers play an important role in attaining these goals. Not only are workers responsible for their own manufacturing efforts, they are also responsible for such things as quality control, equipment maintenance, housekeeping duties in the work area, and general problem solving in the workplace.[25]

Recall Managing for Excellence in Chapter 2, which told the story of Harley-Davidson. It was the successful use of the JIT philosophy by Japanese manufacturers that put Harley at such a severe competitive disadvantage. Harley's adoption of a JIT philosophy played a large role in the company's remarkable turnaround.

Just-in-time (JIT) inventory management
A philosophy that advocates eliminating waste, solving problems, and striving for continual improvement in operations.

Today most organizations face challenges and opportunities brought about by our continuously shrinking world and our global marketplace. Multinational organizations with operating units in different countries may have to set different productivity goals to accommodate differences in work attitudes across national boundaries. In addition, the level of technological development may differ among nations, resulting in significant differences in attainable productivity rates. Political factors may also affect the way the organization can operate in foreign countries.

Even organizations that view themselves as purely domestic are not untouched by aspects of our global marketplace. Raw material inputs, purchased parts, and supplies needed in their transformation processes often originate in foreign countries. In these instances, purchasing agreements must cut across national boundaries. Consequently, these "domestic" companies must be sensitive to the sociocultural, political-legal, technological, and economic environments of the supplying countries.

Thus far, we have seen that operations managers face a wide variety of decisions. To improve the quality of their operations, managers must make these decisions in a way that supports the goals of the organization. We have already noted that organizations can have a variety of goals. When this is the case, managers can move toward achieving excellence in operations by focusing on productivity and quality.

THE ROLE OF PRODUCTIVITY AND QUALITY IN OPERATIONS

Organizational goals can be many and varied. In firms operating on a for-profit basis, bottom-line profit will always have a high priority, while not-for-profit organizations will be more inclined to view service and customer satisfaction as the prime goals. But any of these firms might also strive to achieve other goals such as market share, improved satisfaction and welfare of its work force, heightened social and environmental responsibility, and so forth. Operations managers rarely find it easy to relate their decisions directly to these system goals. Fortunately, there are two measures of operations efficiency and effectiveness that indirectly relate to these system goals. In the next section, we will see that productivity is a measure of operations efficiency and quality is a measure of operations effectiveness. Every decision that an operations manager makes—whether a long-term design decision or a short-term operating and control decision—has an impact on productivity and quality. Let's turn our attention to the fundamentals of productivity and examine the ways in which productivity can be improved.

FUNDAMENTALS OF PRODUCTIVITY

Productivity
A measure of the efficiency with which a firm transforms inputs into outputs.

In Chapter 16 we saw a diagram that showed how all operating systems engage in the transformation of inputs into outputs. **Productivity** is a measure of the efficiency with which a firm performs that transformation process. In the broadest sense, productivity can be defined as the ratio of system outputs to system inputs, or

$$\text{Productivity} = \frac{\text{system outputs}}{\text{system inputs}}$$

Measuring productivity is often easier said than done, for outputs can be quite varied and inputs quite diverse. Table 17.3 shows some of the various inputs and outputs for a few manufacturing and nonmanufacturing examples.

TABLE 17.3   Examples of inputs and outputs for productivity measurement

OUTPUT	INPUT
Number of refrigerators manufactured	Direct labor hours, raw materials, machinery, supervisory hours, capital
Number of patients treated	Doctor hours, nurse hours, lab technician hours, hospital beds, medical equipment, medicine and drugs, surgical supplies
Number of income tax returns prepared	Staff accounting hours, desktop computers, printers, calculators, typewriters, supplies

Interest in productivity has increased during recent years in the United States, in large part because of the alarming decline in international competitiveness suffered by U.S. companies. Between 1960 and 1990, the United States had one of the lowest annual productivity increases of any of the industrialized nations. Its average annual increase of 3 percent was less than half of Japan's.[26] A lower level of productivity can result because less output is being produced from a given level of input or because more input is needed to achieve a given level of output. In either case, the cost incurred to produce a unit of the goods or services will be higher, as will the purchase cost for the customers. This leads to a decline in sales volume, which results in decreased revenues. With less operating revenue, business and industry are likely to lower employment levels, which leads to idle capacity. This is likely to reduce productivity even further, resulting in a snowball effect. Fortunately, most U.S. industries have recognized this phenomenon. Many firms are attempting to break this vicious cycle by instituting productivity improvement programs.

Over the past thirty-five years, the annual increase in production in the United States has been less than half of Japan's. But most U.S. industries recognize the problem and are attempting to break the vicious cycle by instituting productivity improvement programs.

© Kessler Photography

Improving Productivity

Any increase in the numerator or decrease in the denominator of the productivity equation will result in a productivity increase. Simply stated, to increase productivity, all that is needed is an increase in output, a decrease in input, or a combination of both. Such changes can be achieved in several ways. We can categorize the productivity-enhancing tactics as being related to technology, people, or design.[27] In Managing for Excellence, we can see how the Ford Motor Company used technology, people, and design to achieve very dramatic improvements in productivity.

Productivity Improvement through Technology   Productivity can be improved through the use of new technology. If, for example, old office equipment and computers are replaced with newer, faster versions, the number of tax returns prepared per labor hour might be expected to increase. Or, in the case of manufacturing, if faster equipment replaces slower equipment, more units might be produced per labor hour.

Another technological approach to improving productivity is to substitute capital for labor. For example, certain operations that are performed manually may be done by a machine or robot. If the machine has a lower hourly operating cost, higher output rate, and greater precision than a human operator, then the substitution should be considered as a possible means to improve productivity. Fender relied heavily on the use of technology to improve productivity, as will be seen in the resolution to the Managerial Incident.

Productivity Improvement through a Diverse Work Force   One of the most important inputs to the productivity equation is the human resource element. We have seen repeatedly throughout this book that the work force is becoming

FORD MOTOR COMPANY: REVERSING THE DECLINE

The Ford Motor Company, one of the Big Three U.S. automakers, experienced financial difficulties during much of the 1970s and 1980s, when foreign imports were capturing increasingly large shares of the U.S. automobile market. In fact, with losses of $1.5 billion in 1980, $1.1 billion in 1981, and $658 million in 1982, Ford had little cash in reserve and was in danger of becoming bankrupt. Even when there was a profit, it represented a much lower percentage of total sales than in the earlier "good times." For example, in the early 1960s Ford's return on sales had never fallen below 5 percent. In 1970 it dropped to 3.5 percent, perhaps foretelling the huge losses that were to come in the early 1980s. Contributing to this problem was Ford's low labor productivity—the foreign competitors' automobile output per worker exceeded Ford's capabilities. It was clear that Ford would have to improve its labor productivity and find ways to regain some of its lost market share if the firm was to prosper again.

In recent years, the Ford Motor Company has achieved stunning improvements in productivity and quality, and it is now regarded as the most effective U.S. automaker. Its cars are acknowledged to be as good as, or better than, those of its European and Japanese competitors. Ford emerged from the 1980s with the greatest productivity increase among the U.S. Big Three automakers. General Motors experienced a 5 percent gain, Chrysler showed a 17 percent increase, and Ford achieved a whopping 31 percent improvement. By 1992 Ford was able to produce as many vehicles as it did in the 1970s with half the number of workers.

Ford's dramatic productivity improvements were accomplished by focusing on the work force, technology, and product design. Ford promoted increased participation by its work force. Frontline workers were given more control over how they did their jobs. In addition, they were made directly responsible for monitoring the quality of their work and correcting defects. Finally, they were encouraged to contribute ideas and make suggestions for improving job methodologies. Ford also made a concerted effort to use state-of-the-art technologies. For example, many manual tasks are now performed by robots. Such technology provides the benefit of more consistent output, since robots do not suffer from fatigue, nor do they need periodic breaks. Furthermore, robots are advantageous for tasks that may be too dangerous or strenuous for humans. A new focus on product design also contributed to the productivity improvements. Ford adopted a team concept in developing and designing new models. Team members come from a variety of departments, including accounting, engineering, marketing, personnel, and production. One of the things Ford learned was that simpler is better. For example, an instrument console for the Escort was redesigned with 6 parts instead of the 22 parts in an earlier model. Improvements such as these enabled Ford to build its cars with one-third fewer labor hours than GM, giving Ford a cost advantage of almost $800 per vehicle.[28]

increasingly more racially, ethnically, and gender diverse. These groups of individuals all have their own unique sets of values, expectations, motivations, and skills. Their interaction often has a synergistic effect on the work team, enabling the team to achieve results that exceed previous norms.

Effective management of people can often result in significant increases in output without an appreciable increase in the labor cost. This feat can be accomplished through the use of employee compensation programs and employee teams. Many companies have found that compensation can encourage higher productivity. For example, the practice of paying employees bonuses based upon productivity and company profitability has become more popular in recent years.

The most common form of employee team in current practice is the quality circle, which is described more fully later in this chapter. Various companies have given their employee teams different names, but they all have the general objective of increasing employee satisfaction and productivity by providing them with more autonomy and a greater degree of involvement in the decision-making and problem-solving process. As will be seen in the resolution to the opening Managerial Incident, Fender has made use of this "people involvement" concept to improve both productivity and quality. Teams were established, and the company invested heavily in worker training programs.

Productivity Improvement through Design   Several system design issues were described earlier in this chapter. These design decisions can have a direct bearing on productivity. If a product is designed in a way that makes it easier to produce, less time will be spent producing the item, fewer defective units will be produced, and less scrap will result. These improvements will ultimately lead to an increase in productivity.

Process design can also have a significant impact on productivity. If the process has been designed poorly, material flow may be restricted by bottlenecks. Inappropriate placement of work areas and tools can lead to inefficient material flows through the system. These inefficiencies will ultimately lead to greater production time per unit and reduced productivity. Managing for Excellence provided a few rather dramatic examples of how simplified designs helped to improve Ford's productivity.

As we discussed in Chapter 8, job design is the third design area that can impact on productivity. If a worker's assigned job has been so narrowly defined that there is no job fulfillment, boredom and a lack of interest are likely to result. In such a situation, the quality of work can be expected to suffer. The resulting defects, scrap, and rework will diminish the level of productivity. To avoid these problems associated with excessive job specialization, many companies adopt philosophies of job enrichment, job enlargement, and job rotation.

As we continue through this chapter, we will encounter more and more evidence suggesting that productivity and quality are intertwined. Improvements in quality are likely to result in improved productivity. Later in this chapter, we will see more specifically how this occurs when we examine the five-step chain reaction of the late W. Edwards Deming, one of the world's foremost authorities on quality. But first, let's examine the fundamentals of quality.

FUNDAMENTALS OF QUALITY

People sometimes have an inaccurate perception about quality. Too often they assume that quality implies a high degree of luxury or expense. Grandeur, luxuriousness, shininess, and expense are not the prime determinants of quality, however. A more appropriate definition of quality can be approached from two different perspectives. From a consumer perspective, quality can be defined as the degree to which the product or service meets the expectations of the customer. From a producer perspective, quality can be defined as the degree to which the product or service conforms to design specifications. The more effective the organization is in meeting customer expectations and design specifications, the higher the implied quality level of its output.[29]

The Mercedes Benz and Honda Accord are two automobiles with very different prices and quite different features and accessories. However, this does not automatically mean that the more expensive and more elaborate Mercedes has a higher level of quality than the Honda. As the consumer perspective indicates, the test of quality is based upon user expectations. Each automobile has as its function the conveyance of passengers in a particular style, and those styles are different by design.

A similar observation could be made for service organizations. Ritz-Carlton Hotels and Holiday Inns both provide overnight lodging for guests. Ritz-Carlton Hotels feature larger, more elaborately decorated rooms with more amenities than Holiday Inns provide. But one fact remains—they both provide overnight sleeping and bathing accommodations for travelers. Ultimately, it is the individual guest who must determine the level of quality associated with these accommodations.

Once an organization selects the product or service that it will provide, design decisions are made that ultimately shape the product or service design characteristics. If the completed product or service output meets those design characteristics, the output would be viewed as high quality from the production perspective. If this output fails to meet customer expectations, however, then the initial design was probably inadequate, for the customer is not likely to purchase it regardless of the quality level that production perceives. Businesses are increasingly adopting this consumer perspective on quality. For example, if an Eckerd Photolab fails to have a customer's film developed by its promise date, there is no charge to the customer. Phar-Mor Drugs will pay customers $10 if its prescription price is not the lowest in town. Southtrust Bank of Orlando will pay customers $1 if they have to wait more than one minute for service, $5 if they are not treated courteously, and $10 if a mistake is made on a customer's bank statement. Time Warner will provide free cable TV installation if their installation technician does not arrive at the appointed time. This list could go on and on. Think about the service encounters that you have had. Do you know any companies that make similar provisions in their attempts to deliver quality service?

Although the terms *quality control, quality assurance,* and *total quality management* (or *total quality control*) are often used interchangeably, these concepts are not identical. **Quality control** (QC) has the narrowest focus; it refers to the actual measurement and assessment of output to determine whether the specifications are being met. The responsibility for taking corrective actions when standards are not being met is also in the domain of quality control. Statistical procedures are useful in quality control. **Quality assurance** (QA) concerns itself with any activity that influences the maintenance of quality at the desired level. It refers to the entire system of policies, procedures, and guidelines that the organization has established to achieve and maintain quality. Quality assurance extends from the design of products and processes through to the quality assessment of the system outputs. **Total quality management** (TQM) has an even broader focus than quality assurance, for its goal is to manage the entire organization in a manner that allows it to excel in the delivery of a product or service that meets customer needs. Before we look at TQM in more detail, it will be helpful to examine the factors for assessing quality.

Factors for Assessing Quality

A customer might evaluate many aspects of a product or service to determine whether it meets expectations. These aspects differ slightly for products and services.

Product Factors   When evaluating the quality of a product, a customer will probably first notice aesthetic characteristics, which are usually perceived by sensory reactions. Here the customer will observe how the product looks, sounds, feels, smells, or tastes. A product's features are also likely to be judged

Quality control
Focuses on the actual measurement of output to see if specifications have been met.

Quality assurance
Focuses on any activity that influences the maintenance of quality at the desired level.

Total quality management (TQM)
A systematic approach for enhancing products, services, processes, and operational quality control.

early. If you were about to purchase an automobile, for example, you might look for such features as a stereo system, air bags, and power seats. Performance is another aspect that helps determine whether the product meets the customer's needs and expectations. If you do a lot of highway driving, acceleration and passing power are probably important to you, so you would check these performance characteristics before making your purchase decision. Another important aspect of quality is reliability, which refers to the likelihood that the product will continue to perform satisfactorily through its guarantee period. You might ascertain this through product warranty information or by referring to a consumer magazine such as *Consumer Reports*.

The serviceability aspect refers to the difficulty, time, and expense of getting repairs. In the case of your automobile purchase, you might assess this by considering the location and business hours of the dealer's automobile service center. The durability aspect refers to the length of time the product is likely to last. Both the manufacturer and independent consumer agencies might be a source of data here. Conformance reflects the degree to which the product meets the specifications set by the designers. For example, you will undoubtedly check to be sure that the automobile possesses all the accessories that the advertising suggests it will have. A final aspect is perceived quality, which has been described as an overall feeling of confidence based upon observations of the potential purchase, the reputation of the company, and any past experiences with purchases of this type.[30]

Service Factors   The product quality factors can be relevant to a service encounter if some physical commodity is delivered to the customer. For example, when you dine at a restaurant, the meal can be judged according to most of those characteristics. Unfortunately, service quality is sometimes more difficult to assess with quantitative measures. Suppose you visit a dentist for emergency treatment of a broken tooth. In this case you would use other attributes to measure your satisfaction with service quality. Responsiveness reflects the willingness and speed with which the service personnel (that is, the dentist, nurse, and receptionist) attend to you. Reliability is a measure of the dependability and accuracy of the service performed. Assurance refers to the feeling of trust and confidence you have in the service personnel. Empathy reflects the degree of attention and caring that the service personnel provide to you. Finally, tangibles are an assessment of such factors as the appearance of the service personnel, cleanliness of the equipment and physical system, and comfort of the surroundings.[31]

Cost of Quality

Any costs that a company incurs because it has produced less than perfect quality output, or costs that it incurs to prevent less than perfect quality output, are referred to as the cost of quality. The cost of quality can be organized into the following four major categories:[32]

1. *Prevention costs.* Prior to the production of the product or the delivery of the service, several activities are performed in an attempt to prevent defective output from occurring. These activities include designing products, processes, and jobs for quality; reviewing designs; educating and training workers in quality concepts; and working with suppliers. The costs of these activities are the prevention costs.

2. *Appraisal costs.* Appraisal costs are incurred to assess the quality of the product that has been manufactured or the service that has been provided. They include the costs of testing equipment and instruments, the costs of maintaining that equipment, and the labor costs associated with performing the inspections.

FIGURE 17.3
Quality costs

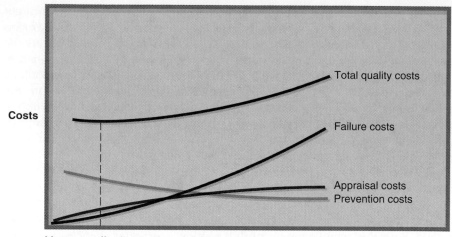

3. *Internal-failure costs.* Defective output that is detected before it leaves the system will either be scrapped (discarded) or reworked (repaired). If it is scrapped, the company incurs the cost of all materials and labor that went into the production of that output. If it is reworked, a cost is incurred for the material and labor that went into the defective portion that was replaced or repaired. In addition, more material and labor costs are incurred for the rework activities. These costs all contribute to the internal-failure costs.

4. *External-failure costs.* Defective output that is not detected before being delivered to the customer incurs external-failure costs. This category consists of the costs associated with customer complaints, returns, warranty claims, product recalls, or product liability suits.

The current popular view holds that prevention costs do not have to be increased substantially to reduce the number of defective units. Furthermore, this view suggests that as prevention costs increase, appraisal costs will decrease, since less testing and inspection will be necessary due to inherently lower numbers of defective units. Meanwhile, failure costs will also decrease with the reduced number of defective units.[33] Figure 17.3 displays these cost relationships and suggests that the most cost-effective way of doing business is close to, if not at, the zero-defect level.

Although these concepts of quality-related costs may seem to apply only to the physical products of manufacturing systems, service organizations can also benefit from paying attention to quality-related costs. Providing poor-quality service will lead to failure costs, just as with poor quality products. However, in the case of service organizations, external-failure costs tend to be much greater than internal-failure costs. This is a result of the customer's direct involvement in the service transaction. There is usually little opportunity to check the quality of the service before the service encounter with the customer. Defective service is generally not detected until the service act has transpired. At that point failure costs are by definition in the external category.

TOTAL QUALITY MANAGEMENT AS A TOOL FOR GLOBAL COMPETITIVENESS

Emphasis on quality is a key to achieving excellence in operations in today's global economy. This emphasis on quality is crucial for two reasons: (1) customers are becoming increasingly conscious of quality in their choice of products and services, and (2) increased quality leads to increased productivity and its associated benefits. It is no secret that in recent years U.S. manufacturers have struggled with the loss of market share to foreign competitors in the global marketplace. These losses have been attributed to the notion (in some cases real and in some cases perceived) that the foreign competitors have been able to supply products of higher quality and at a lower price. People who are trying to get the most from their disposable income have understandably been attracted to these products. These shifts to foreign manufacturers are evidence that consumers do consider the product factors discussed earlier prior to making purchase decisions. Any manufacturer who hopes to reverse this declining market share can begin to do so by focusing on the quality aspects of the product. A program of total quality management is one of the most effective ways to enhance an organization's competitive position. Fender's commitment to quality helped the company reverse the declining trends described in the opening Managerial Incident. They now have the number one product in the industry. A total quality management program involves several areas of concentration, commitment, and improvement.

Customer-Driven Standards

Since one definition of quality centers on meeting customer expectations, the **external customer** should play a central role in establishing product or service standards. Marketing will be instrumental in assessing the wants and needs of external customers. These wants and needs can then be conveyed to design engineers, who will make the product and service design decisions. Process design decisions will then follow. Ultimately, the products or services will be easier to sell if customers recognize that the products and services have been designed to satisfy their needs.

In some cases a customer may be an **internal customer** as opposed to an external end user. For example, the customer might be the next worker or next department in the production process. Internal customers also have quality requirements that must be considered in the product or service design stage. In essence, everybody in the organization is a supplier to some customer, and these supplier-customer links represent a major area of concern in total quality management.

External customer
The consumer who purchases the product or service output of the organization.

Internal customer
In the sequence of stages that extend from purchasing raw materials through to final delivery of the product or service, an internal customer is any individual or department that uses the output of a prior stage.

Management and Labor Commitment

Recall from Chapter 11 the concepts of organizational culture and organizational change. If total quality management is to pervade all levels of an organization successfully, management must develop an organizational culture in which all workers are committed to the philosophy. This requires a strong commitment from top management, where the values to be shared by the organization originate. If all parts of the organization are to coordinate toward a common goal, then this goal must be embraced at the top. Top management must not only communicate this goal, but must also demonstrate a commitment to the goal through its actions, policies, and decisions. Management must back up slogans and catchy phrases with a willingness to institute changes, a receptiveness to employee suggestions, and recognition and reward for improvements. As described in Managing for Excellence, Ford demonstrated total commitment in this area. Management asked assembly-line workers for advice before the design of the Taurus model was complete, and many of the suggestions were implemented. For example, all the bolt heads were made the same size so workers would not have to reach repeatedly for a new tool. Also, doors were designed with fewer pieces in order to improve assembly.

Organization and Coordination of Efforts

We have already seen that total quality management will result in a wide variety of diverse personnel interactions. Marketing serves as an intermediary between external customers and design engineers, who in turn interact with production personnel. The internal supplier-customer links lead to many interactions among production personnel. Purchasing must interact with external suppliers. If total quality management is to be successful, communication links must be established between all of these internal and external entities to achieve proper coordination. As we saw in Chapter 9, such coordination efforts lead to a teamwork philosophy among all participants in the organization.

Employee Participation

A central theme of the total quality management approach is that all employees should be brought into the decision-making and problem-solving process. After all, those who are doing the work are closest to the action and will probably have valuable opinions about methods for quality improvement. By providing the workers with an opportunity to express those opinions, worker morale and motivation are enhanced. Workers develop more of a sense of responsibility and connection to their jobs. Worker participation is further enhanced by the use of teams. The Motorola Corporation has been quite successful with teams at its microprocessor assembly plant in Austin, Texas. Management decided to build cross-functional teams (composed of representatives from management, first-line supervisors, line operators, internal vendors, and internal customers) in an effort to increase motivation, provide more creative problem solving, and stimulate ideas. Two of the more popular types of teams are quality circles and special-purpose teams.

Quality circle
A work team that meets regularly to identify, analyze, and solve problems related to its work area.

Quality Circles   A **quality circle** is a small group of supervisors and employees from the same work area.[34] Most quality circles have between six and twelve members, and membership is voluntary. Quality circles meet on a regular basis (usually weekly) to identify, analyze, and solve production and quality problems related to the work done in their part of the company. Many benefits accrue from quality circles. When workers are allowed to help shape their work, they usually take more pride and interest in it. Furthermore, quality circles have the potential to uncover and solve many problems or suggest ways to achieve improvements in operations. Even though some of these improvements may be very minor, collectively they can result in substantial cost savings, quality improvements, and productivity increases in the organization.

Special-purpose team
A temporary team formed to solve a special or nonrecurring problem.

Special-Purpose Teams   On occasion, a **special-purpose team** may have to be formed to solve a special or nonrecurring problem.[35] Unlike quality circles, special-purpose teams are likely to draw their members from many departments or work areas and bring together people from different functional specialties. For example, if some characteristic of a product no longer conforms to customer needs, marketing personnel will need to be on the team to explain the wants and needs of the customers. Design engineers would be needed to help translate those needs into new product design specifications. Production personnel would also be needed to determine if and how the redesigned product can be manufactured. Special-purpose teams also differ from quality circles in longevity. Quality circles are standing teams that continue in existence over time. Special-purpose teams are ad hoc groups that disband after the problem has been resolved.

PROMINENT QUALITY MANAGEMENT PHILOSOPHERS

Many of today's business organizations are placing more and more emphasis on quality because they are aware of how much it has helped their competition. It is safe to say that, in general, U.S. business organizations were a step behind many of their foreign competitors. Those competitors were able to get a head start in quality by taking the advice of some of the noted quality philosophers and consultants long before U.S. organizations did.

TABLE 17.4   Deming's 14 points

1. Create constancy of purpose for improvement of product and service, and communicate this aim to all employees.
2. Learn and adopt the new philosophy throughout all levels within the organization.
3. Understand that inspection only measures problems but does not correct them; quality comes from improving processes.
4. Reduce the number of suppliers, and do not award business on the basis of price tag alone.
5. Constantly improve processes, products, and services while reducing waste.
6. Institute modern aids to training on the job.
7. Improve supervision.
8. Drive out fear of expressing ideas and reporting problems.
9. Break down barriers between departments and get people working toward the goals of the organization as a team.
10. Eliminate slogans, exhortations, and targets for the work force.
11. Eliminate numerical quotas for production; concentrate on quality, not quantity.
12. Remove barriers that rob people of pride of workmanship.
13. Institute a program of education and self-improvement for everyone.
14. Put everyone in the organization to work to accomplish the transformation.

Perhaps the most prominent quality philosopher was W. Edwards Deming, an American who was considered the father of quality control in Japan. Deming emphasized the importance of improving quality through his five-step chain reaction, which proposes that when quality is improved: (1) costs decrease because of less rework, fewer mistakes, fewer delays, and better use of time and materials; (2) productivity improves; (3) market share increases with better quality and prices; (4) the company increases profitability and stays in business; and (5) the number of jobs increases.[36] Deming devised a fourteen-point plan to summarize his philosophy on quality improvement. Table 17.4 lists Deming's fourteen points.

Joseph Juran is another of the pioneers in quality management. Juran's experiences revealed that over 80 percent of quality defects are caused by factors controllable by management. This led Juran to develop a trilogy of quality planning, control, and improvement.[37] Quality planning involves linking product and service design with process design to achieve the quality characteristics desired. Quality control involves comparing products or services to standards and then correcting undesirable deviations. (This part of the trilogy relates directly to what we learned about control in Chapter 16). The final part of the trilogy involves getting into the habit of making significant improvements every year. An area with chronic quality problems is selected and analyzed, and an alternative is selected and implemented.

Other notable names in the area of quality are Armand Feigenbaum, Kaoru Ishikawa, and Phillip Crosby. Feigenbaum is credited with introducing the concept of total quality control and developing the quality cost categories described earlier in this chapter.[38] Ishikawa is credited with introducing quality-control circles, and he also developed the fishbone diagram (or cause-and-effect diagram), which helps to identify the causes of quality problems.[39] Crosby introduced the philosophy that "quality is free."[40] In his opinion, the most cost-effective level of defects is zero defects. Crosby contends that with no defects, rework costs are saved, scrap is eliminated, labor and machine time costs are reduced, and product failure costs are eliminated. Crosby believes that these

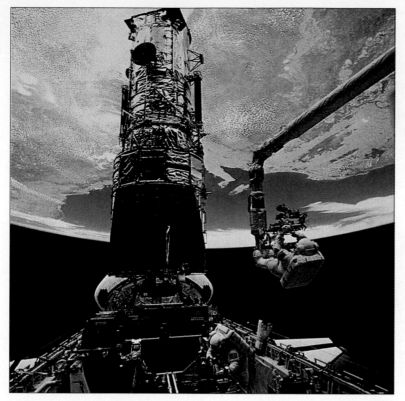

The repairs to the Hubble Space Telescope in 1993 at a cost of $750 million are an example of Crosby's philosophy that "quality is free." Crosby believes the costs incurred in creating an environment that promotes high quality result in cost reductions because they eliminate defects and product failure costs, save rework costs, and reduce labor and machine time.

© NASA/Consolidated News, Pictures/Archive Photos

cost reductions far outweigh the costs incurred in creating an environment that promotes the achievement of high quality. Crosby's philosophy is very much like the old adage, "An ounce of prevention is worth a pound of cure."

NASA's experience with the ill-fated Hubble Space Telescope dramatically illustrates this point. This $1.5 billion orbiting laboratory was launched for the purpose of viewing outer space. Not long after the launch, astronomers discovered that the telescope's view of the stars was somewhat blurred due to the incorrect grinding and polishing of its primary mirror. A relatively simple test costing a few hundred thousand dollars could have detected this flaw. As it turned out, repairs didn't come this easily or cheaply to NASA. To correct this defect and make a variety of other repairs, the space shuttle *Endeavour* embarked upon an eleven-day mission in early December 1993. The repairs required five separate space walks by astronauts spaced over five days. The mission cost $750 million—$250 million for replacement parts and $500 million for the shuttle flight.[41]

NASA continues to provide one of the most visible examples of increasing diversity in the work force. Astronaut crews on shuttle missions have become more diverse in race, nationality, and gender over the years. Kathy Thornton was one of the four astronauts who spent more than 35 space-walking hours repairing the ailing Hubble Telescope.[42] And in late 1996 astronaut Shannon Lucid completed more than six months aboard space station *Mir,* eclipsing the space endurance record for women, and in the process spending more time in space than any American astronaut before her.[43]

IMPACT OF INFORMATION TECHNOLOGY ON PRODUCTIVITY AND QUALITY

Advances and developments in information technology have had a profound and positive effect on productivity in operations. A quick reflection on the productivity formula (output divided by input) suggests that anything that enables one to achieve more output with the same amount of input, or the same amount of output with less input, will improve an organization's productivity. In the past few decades there have been many advances in information processing capabilities that have positively influenced productivity. Computer-aided design (CAD) and computer-aided manufacturing (CAM) allow firms to electronically link and manipulate information, allowing coordination of the design and manufacturing functions. Efficient designs and efficient manufacturing processes lead to less waste, smoother manufacturing, and a correspondingly higher level of productivity. On an even broader basis, information can be linked across all business functions within an organization by means of computer-integrated manufacturing (CIM). By linking the business functions with the engineering functions, companies are better able to respond to changes in the marketplace with new products or new designs of existing products.

Advances in information processing capabilities have also allowed companies to gravitate toward being lean production systems (LPS). These systems

RYDER SYSTEMS, INC.: BOOSTING PRODUCTIVITY THROUGH INFORMATION TECHNOLOGY

Although Ryder Systems, Inc., is a seemingly low-tech trucking company, don't let first impressions fool you. Ryder is actually on the cutting edge when it comes to using information technology to improve productivity. Its Fast Track Maintenance Service uses a computer chip to record information from electronic sensors on a truck's engine while the truck is being driven. When routine maintenance is due, or when a problem occurs, that information can be downloaded, resulting in greatly reduced downtime for maintenance or repair. Information technology is also used to track deliveries. When a driver picks up a load, an electronic device is plugged into an onboard computer, which indicates the load's destination, the optimal route to be taken, and the expected time duration of the trip. After the load is delivered, information is downloaded into Ryder's mainframe computer, generating performance reports for the customer.

Ryder's expertise and sophistication with these technologies has enabled it to be assigned responsibility for all shipping for the Saturn auto plant in Spring Hill, Tennessee. Ryder has been able to move parts between the Saturn plant and its 339 suppliers with trucks averaging 90 percent full. In spite of the fact that Saturn's just-in-time system maintains no inventory at the plant, it has had to shut down only once, for a total of eighteen minutes, due to a lack of parts.[44]

combine an understanding of quality with a desire to eliminate all kinds of waste. The just-in-time (JIT) and material requirements planning (MRP) systems described earlier in this chapter are compatible with this waste-elimination philosophy as they strive to have the right parts available in the right quantities and at the right time. The use of information technology to boost productivity is not restricted to manufacturing organizations. Turn your attention, for the moment, to Ryder Systems, Inc. described in Service Challenge. Here we can see that a seemingly low-tech trucking company is actually on the cutting edge when it comes to using information technology to improve productivity and become more competitive.

It should not go unnoticed in this discussion that these same technological advances that enhance productivity will also have a positive effect on quality. With more efficient and effective design tools, products and services that satisfy customer needs should result. And with more efficient and effective production and delivery systems, there is a greater likelihood that the delivered goods or services will meet their design specifications and at the same time satisfy the wants and needs of the customers. The simple translation: higher levels of quality will be delivered.

In this chapter we have seen that operations management has a strong decision-making orientation in both manufacturing and service organizations. We have also learned that the concepts of productivity and quality are extremely important for assessing the efficiency and effectiveness of operations decisions. Let's conclude the chapter by considering the implications of these concepts for tomorrow's managers.

MANAGERIAL IMPLICATIONS

Excellence in operations can be achieved only if management strives to achieve perfection in all of the decision-making areas related to operations. Particular attention should be paid to long-term system design decisions. Because of the difficulty in reversing decisions in this area, management may get only one chance at them. If a poor decision is made, operations may have to suffer the negative consequences for quite some time. Once the design decisions are behind them, managers must shift their attention to short-term operating and control decisions. These decisions will continue to recur throughout the life of the organization, so managers should strive for continual improvement in this decision-making focus. In short, tomorrow's manager must:

- Be prepared to make the tough decisions that commit to a long-term design for the operating system.
- Strive for perfection in making recurring short-term operating and control decisions.
- Focus on achieving continual improvement as these operating and control decisions are made repeatedly throughout the life of the organization.
- Be aware of the importance of productivity to organizational success, and understand the ways in which productivity can be improved.
- Recognize the links between productivity and quality.
- Focus on improving the quality of the product or service provided.

The quality-productivity link is best illustrated by the Deming five-step chain reaction, which states that improved quality leads to lower labor and material costs, which lead to an improvement in productivity, which results in higher-quality and lower-cost items (and an associated increase in market share), which lead to increased profitability and an increase in the number of jobs. Emphasis on quality will enable tomorrow's manager to reap the benefits of this quality-productivity chain reaction.

Managerial Incident Resolution

FENDER MUSICAL INSTRUMENTS CORPORATION

When William Schultz helped acquire Fender from CBS, many insiders questioned the wisdom of that venture. It hardly seemed prudent to pay $12.5 million for a company whose product quality was suspect, whose sales had just hit a 20-year low, and whose losses were $1 million per month. In Schultz's words, "We knew it wasn't going to be easy, but we also thought that, in the long run, it would be worth the effort." Schultz focused on five key areas to get Fender rocking and rolling again: people power, overhead overload, obsessive quality, return to roots, and special deliveries.

Schultz assembled a team of people who, much like him, possessed a musical background and a passion for Fender guitars. The guitar factory was then moved from its expensive Orange County, California, location to a smaller complex in Corona, which is in nearby Riverside County. The overhead savings gave the company some much-needed relief while it was regrouping. The Schultz team then invested in state-of-the-art woodworking equipment to ensure consistency and quality. To complement these new machines, nearly $2 million was spent to train workers in quality control and efficiency. Prior to shipping, each instrument now passes through a dozen inspection points. To win back musicians who had abandoned Fender, the company reissued the original electric-guitar designs and amps that had made it the industry leader in the 1950s and 1960s. Finally, Schultz established the Fender Custom Shop, where guitars are hand built to customer specifications. The market for these custom instruments is composed not only of professional musicians, but also a large number of successful professionals in a variety of fields (doctors, lawyers, business executives, and so on) who had musical roots in their youth and the means to indulge a middle-aged fantasy. Prices for these custom instruments range from $1,500 to $50,000.

Fender's turnaround has been astonishing. Although the company does not release income figures, it does claim sales of $160.1 million in 1996, which is a $30 million increase over the prior year. Fender has shown a profit each year since the takeover. The company manufactures 335,000 guitars annually, and each one is presold. Its current market share of 45 percent is likely to grow, for it has the number one product in the industry, a household name, and all the free advertising in the world thanks to MTV and a booming concert industry.[45]

SUMMARY

- Manufacturing organizations produce a physical product that can be stored in inventory and transported to different locations. Productivity and quality of this physical output are usually easy to measure. Service organizations differ in that their capacity is time perishable, customers are typically active participants in the service process, and their locations must be close to the customers.

- Operating systems can lie anywhere along a volume/variety continuum that extends from high volume and low variety on one extreme to low volume and high variety on the other extreme. Manufacturing organizations can be classified as repetitive manufacturing systems or continuous-flow systems at the high-volume/low-variety extreme and job-shop systems or project systems at the low-volume/high-variety extreme. Service organizations can be classified as standard service systems at the high-volume/low-variety extreme and custom service systems at the low-volume/high-variety extreme.

- Most operations management decisions can be classified as either long-term system design decisions or short-term operating and control decisions. Important long-term system design decisions include choice of a product or service, product or service design, system capacity, process selection, facility location, and facility layout. Important short-term operating and control decisions include aggregate planning, master production scheduling, inventory management, material requirements planning, and just-in-time inventory management.

- Productivity is a measure of the efficiency with which an organization converts inputs to outputs. It is measured as a ratio of system outputs to system inputs. Productivity can be improved through technology, people, or design.

- From a consumer perspective, quality can be defined as the degree to which the product or service meets the expectations of the customer. From a producer perspective, quality can be defined as the degree to which the product or service conforms to design specifications.

- There are four categories of quality-related costs. Prevention costs are incurred to prevent defective output from occurring. Appraisal costs are incurred to assess the quality of the output. Internal-failure costs are associated with defective units that are detected before they reach the customers. External-failure costs are associated with defective units that are not detected before they reach the customers.

- To achieve a successful total quality management program, concentration, commitment, and improvement should be focused on meeting customer expectations, attaining commitment to the philosophy and participation from every individual within the organization, and achieving coordination between all departments and functional specialties within the organization.

- W. Edwards Deming proposed a five-step chain reaction in which excellence in quality eventually leads to improved productivity, increased market share, increased profitability, and more jobs. Joseph Juran developed a trilogy of quality planning, control, and improvement. Armand Feigenbaum is credited with originating the concept of total quality control, Kaoru Ishikawa introduced the idea of quality circles, and Phillip Crosby developed the philosophy that quality is free.

KEY TERMS

Repetitive, assembly-line, or mass-production system	Process layout	Master production schedule
Continuous-flow production system	Product layout	Just-in-time (JIT) inventory management
Job-shop production system	Hybrid layout	Productivity
Project production system	Fixed position layout	Quality control
	Aggregate planning	

Quality assurance
Total quality management

External customer
Internal customer

Quality circle
Special-purpose team

REVIEW QUESTIONS

1. Discuss the differences between manufacturing and service organizations.

2. Discuss the volume/variety continuum for categorizing operating systems. Provide several examples of both manufacturing and service organizations for each of the major categories.

3. What are the two major categories for classifying the decisions faced by the operations function?

4. List and briefly discuss several of the long-term system design decisions faced by the operations function.

5. List and briefly discuss several of the short-term operating and control decisions faced by the operations function.

6. In addition to reduced inventory, what does the just-in-time philosophy advocate?

7. List and briefly describe the three categories of tactics that might be used to enhance productivity.

8. Provide a definition of quality from a consumer perspective and a definition from a producer perspective.

9. List and briefly describe the different aspects of a product that might be judged in an attempt to assess its quality.

10. List and briefly describe the different aspects of a service encounter that might be judged in an attempt to assess its quality.

11. Briefly describe the areas of concentration and commitment for a program of total quality management.

12. Describe the major contributions of several prominent quality philosophers.

DISCUSSION QUESTIONS

Improving Critical Thinking

1. JIT advocates a holistic view of workers that takes advantage of all their skills, knowledge, and experiences and gives them added duties and responsibilities. Discuss these added duties and responsibilities, and compare this view with the traditional manufacturing view of workers. How do you feel these enhanced responsibilities might affect worker motivation and dedication to the job?

2. It has often been said that poor quality and poor productivity will detract from a company's competitiveness. Discuss the chain of events that you think would lead from poor quality and poor productivity to the eventual loss of competitiveness.

Enhancing Communication Skills

3. Imagine the way material would flow through a custom machine shop that fabricates metal parts for customers. Then imagine the way patients would flow through a walk-in emergency clinic. Discuss the similarities between the flows in these two systems. To enhance your oral communication skills, prepare a short (10–15 minute) presentation for the class in which you describe the flow similarities in these two systems.

4. Consider the aggregate planning problem in which the demand for a product or service is seasonal. List as many strategies as you can that could be used to cope with the fluctuating demand pattern. Try to identify strategies that you might use from an operations standpoint, and also try to envision strategies that you might use from a marketing standpoint (in an attempt to induce changes in the demand pattern). Finally, indicate which of your strategies might not be viable in a service organization. To enhance your written communication skills, prepare a short (1–2 page) essay in which you describe the strategies in each category and explain which strategies probably aren't appropriate for service organizations.

Building Teamwork

5. The Crosby "quality is free" philosophy suggests that the only acceptable level of behavior is zero defects. Try to think of examples that might contradict this philosophy. That is, identify situations where the cost of totally eliminating defects might be higher than the failure cost incurred with a moderate level of defects. To refine your teamwork skills, meet with a small group of students who have been given the same assignment. Compare and discuss your selections, and then reach a consensus on the two best choices. Select a spokesperson to present your choices to the rest of the class.

6. Meet with a small group of students as directed by your instructor. To refine your teamwork skills, this

group will operate as a quality circle. Discuss with one another some of the problems you have encountered in conjunction with your college education. These problems can cover any aspect of your education, and may relate to interactions with administration, faculty, or support services (for example, the library, the computer center, and the like). Reach a consensus on the most important or urgent problem, then conduct a brainstorming session to develop potential solutions to this problem. Select a spokesperson to present your problem and potential solutions to the rest of the class.

INFORMATION TECHNOLOGY: Insights and Solutions

1. Using whatever search vehicle proves most fruitful (Internet, fax, telephone, and so on), gather information on model names, sales, and market share for the major guitar models offered by the Fender Musical Instruments Corporation and the Gibson Guitar Corporation. Then, using presentation software, prepare for your classmates a slide show presentation that compares the offerings of these two companies.

2. Use the Internet to research any major U.S. manufacturing company. Gather information on product variety offered and nature of the manufacturing process. Using the information gathered in conjunction with presentation software, develop a classification diagram similar to Figure 17.1 that places your selected company in its proper position on the diagram. Present your findings and interpretations to your classmates for their comments.

3. Use whatever search vehicle proves most fruitful (Internet, fax, telephone, and so on) to gather information on female U.S. astronauts, missions flown, duration of missions, nature of mission, vehicle flown, and so on. Organize this information into an electronic spreadsheet that allows the data to be sorted on any of the information items collected. Compare your list with the lists of your classmates to determine who performed the most thorough search.

ETHICS: Take a Stand

When the demand for a product or service is seasonal, aggregate planning suggests several strategies for coping with the seasonal variations. One strategy calls for adjusting the size of the work force by hiring and firing workers as demand fluctuates. This approach is often referred to as a chase strategy, since the organization is constantly varying its capacity to "chase" the contour of the fluctuating demand. The agricultural industry's need for people to harvest crops is highly seasonal. The industry typically follows a chase approach, hiring and firing migrant workers as the need arises.

For Discussion

1. Discuss the social and ethical implications of such a strategy. What alternative strategy or strategies might you suggest for such a situation?

2. Discuss the economic implications of your suggested strategies to agricultural firms and to you personally.

THINKING CRITICALLY: Debate the Issue

IS ZERO DEFECTS THE MOST COST-EFFECTIVE WAY?

Form teams of four or five students as directed by your instructor. Research the topic of quality costs and how they behave as one strives for higher levels of quality (that is, higher levels of conformance to standards or lower levels of defective output). You will find that one theory holds that total quality costs will continually decrease and be at their lowest at a zero-defects level. (This is the current popular theory described in this chapter). Another theory, however, holds that total quality costs will initially decrease, but then begin to increase as defective output is further reduced. (This is the classical theory on quality costs). Prepare to provide arguments in support of both of these theories. When it is time to debate this issue in front of the class, your instructor will tell you which position to take.

Video Case

WAINWRIGHT INDUSTRIES

Related Web Site: {http://www.fed.org/uscompanies/labor/n_z/Wainwright_Industries.html}

In the early 1980s, Wainwright Industries, a manufacturer of precision auto parts, faced nothing less than a crisis. Increased competition on a global level was forcing Wainwright to either increase quality or lose its competitive stature. In the face of this challenge, the employees of the firm decided to make radical changes. It was clear that business as usual with a few minor improvements would not save the company. What Wainwright needed was an entirely new philosophy based on quality and customer satisfaction.

Using the criteria for the Malcolm Baldrige National Quality Award as a road map, Wainwright set out to make a number of changes. First, the company decided to emphasize three principles: employee empowerment, customer satisfaction, and continuous improvement. As a creative way of demonstrating its resolve, the company adopted the duck as a symbol of employee empowerment, based on the fact that ducks fly in formation as a means of supporting one another while in flight. A number of specific employee-oriented initiatives were implemented, ranging from cross-training to profit sharing. The culture of the firm also changed, in visible ways. The employees of Wainwright now all wear the same uniform (including the CEO), signifying that everyone is working toward the same objectives and is on the same team. Office walls have literally been torn down and replaced with glass, based on the premise that if the managers can watch the frontline employees work, the frontline employees should be able to watch the managers work, too. Changes were also made pertaining to customer satisfaction and continuous improvement. The company implemented just-in-time manufacturing, statistical process control, benchmarking, and quality-minded manufacturing initiatives. The results of the company's activities are linked to five strategic indicators: safety, internal customer satisfaction, external customer satisfaction, six-sigma quality, and business performance. All of the results, including the firm's financial performance, are posted in "Mission Control," a room set aside for activities related to the company's quality initiatives. In addition, all of the firm's employees have access to the data after its accuracy has been verified.

As a result of these inititatives, Wainwright has met the challenge. Its market share, revenues, and profits are at record levels. Remarkably, the company was one of the recipients of the 1994 Malcolm Baldrige National Quality Award, the very award that the company benchmarked itself against in its early days of quality improvements.

For Discussion

1. Quality is important for any product or service, but may be especially important for the precision auto parts industry. Do you agree with this statement? Why or why not?

2. Why was it important for Wainwright to couple its initiatives in the areas of manufacturing quality improvements, through techniques such as just-in-time manufacturing and statistical process control, with employee initiatives like employee empowerment and profit sharing?

OREGON CUTTING SYSTEMS

CASE

Cutting technology is the science of designing and manufacturing cutting tools for various applications. This is the business of Oregon Cutting Systems (OCS). Each day OCS converts cold rolled steel into over 20 miles of cutting chain. Output varies from one-quarter-inch-pitch chain for consumer markets to three-quarter-inch-pitch chain used in mechanized forestry harvesters. OCS also manufactures related products, such as chainsaw bars. It is the industry leader with more than one-half the world's saw chain market. OCS is also an original equipment manufacturer, supplying the world's best-known brands of chainsaws through its own network of distributors and dealers.

In the early 1980s, it became apparent that business as usual was no longer going to be good enough for OCS. According to Noel Hingley, division vice-president for manufacturing, "the initial impetus for changing things came from a discomfort with quality problems that were too large, and problem solving that took too long and resulted in problems that weren't permanently solved." Self-inspection revealed an operation that was ripe with opportunities for improvement. Jim Osterman, president of OCS, noted that "when somebody came in with a problem or a complaint we were certain that it had to be their problem and not our product problem. As a consequence, we earned the reputation in the field of not covering our products." According to Charlie Nicholson, division vice-president for quality, "We felt we knew so much about the market and the needs of our customers (our end users) that we could pretty well design for them and we made a lot of assumptions regarding their needs and expectations. We did develop chains without direct data from them for a while and we did design chains for large market segments. We've learned since that there are a lot of different market segments out there that demand different types of products."

OCS began its improvement program by implementing a just-in-time (JIT) approach to inventory management. This was not without problems, though. OCS found that it could go only so far with JIT before it encountered obstacles in the form of machinery that wasn't reliable enough to maintain consistent production and interruptions in production because of quality defects. OCS found that it couldn't maintain as low a level of inventory as it wanted or make further gains. Then the company shifted its focus to quality and continuous improvement. A strong emphasis on statistical process control was adopted. Production workers were trained in its procedures and were given the authority to make decisions and solve problems. At that point, operations improved dramatically. Work in process was reduced to 30 percent of pre-change levels, and new goals were set for an additional 50 percent cut in inventory and a 20 percent reduction in costs. A major element in OCS's success is its effort to translate customer requirements into product characteristics. In a process it calls Strategic Product Development, OCS starts with customer inputs and designs products to meet those customer needs. As a result of these changes, OCS now delivers value that is far above what it previously delivered. Customer problems that were chronic in the past are now nonexistent. At the same time, OCS production workers have become happier and more fulfilled on the job and are proud of their accomplishments.

In retrospect, president Jim Osterman says, "I think what I would have done differently is understood the ramifications of total quality commitment a little better and started on the quality side before starting on the just-in-time side."[46]

For Discussion

1. Review the concepts of a consumer perspective on quality and a producer perspective on quality. Discuss how and when in the chronology of events each of these perspectives dominated the operating philosophy of Oregon Cutting Systems.

2. Discuss what you feel are the reasons that OCS met with limited success with JIT before it addressed the quality issue, and why such dramatic improvements were possible after the focus on quality and continuous improvement.

EXPERIENTIAL EXERCISE 17.1

Manufacturing versus Service Organizations

Purpose: To gain a better understanding of the characteristics of manufacturing and service organizations.

Procedure: Visit a local strip mall and a local industrial park in your town. Focus on five businesses in each location. Use the checklist in Meeting the Challenge to classify each of these ten businesses as either a manufacturing or a service organization.

EXPERIENTIAL EXERCISE 17.2

Assessing Quality

Purpose: To gain a better understanding of the aspects of a product and a service that might be used to assess its quality.

Procedure: Think of a product and a service that you recently purchased that did not totally meet your expectations. First, list the various factors for rating a product's quality, then give your product a rating from 1 to 10 (1 is the lowest rating, 10 the highest) for each of the factors. Jot down reasons for each of the ratings that you assigned to the product. Finally, calculate an overall average rating for the product to see where it falls on your 1–10 scale. Perform similar ratings and calculations for the service you chose.

ENDNOTES

1. B. Spitz, "And on the Lead Guitar," *Sky,* August 1996, 55–60.

2. L. J. Krajewski and L. P. Ritzman, *Operations Management: Strategy and Analysis,* 4th ed. (Reading, Mass.: Addison-Wesley, 1996).

3. J. R. Evans, *Applied Production and Operations Management,* 5th ed. (St. Paul, Minn.: West Publishing, 1997).

4. R. B. Chase and N. J. Acquilano, *Production and Operations Management: A Life Cycle Approach,* 6th ed. (Homewood, Ill.: Irwin, 1992).

5. L. J. Krajewski and L. P. Ritzman, *Operations Management: Strategy and Analysis.*

6. M. A. Vonderembse and G. P. White, *Operations Management: Concepts, Methods, and Strategies,* 3d ed. (St. Paul, Minn.: West Publishing, 1996).

7. L. J. Krajewski and L. P. Ritzman, *Operations Management: Strategy and Analysis.*

8. "Propane-Exchange Idea Catches Fire," *Orlando Sentinel,* August 24, 1996, C10.

9. M. A. Vonderembse and G. P. White, *Operations Management: Concepts, Methods, and Strategies.*

10. R. J. Schonberger and E. M. Knod Jr., *Operations Management: Improving Customer Service,* 5th ed. (Homewood, Ill.: Irwin, 1994).

11. R. B. Chase and N. J. Acquilano, *Production and Operations Management: A Life Cycle Approach.*

12. L. J. Krajewski and L. P. Ritzman, *Operations Management: Strategy and Analysis.*

13. M. A. Vonderembse and G. P. White, *Operations and Management: Concepts, Methods, and Strategies.*

14. R. Blumenstein, "Big Three Pare Design Time for New Autos," *The Wall Street Journal,* August 9, 1996, A3; M. Maynard, "GM Heads down Road to Quick Development Time," *USA Today,* August 9, 1996, B2.

15. M. A. Vonderembse and G. P. White, *Operations and Management: Concepts, Methods, and Strategies.*

16. R. W. Schmenner, *Making Business Decisions* (Upper Saddle River, N.J.: Prentice Hall, 1982).

17. "Plant's Plan Causes a Stink in Small Town," *Orlando Sentinel,* June 27, 1996, B5; "Candy Plant to Be Built in Corsicana," *Dallas Morning News,* August 14, 1996, D12.

18. B. Kuhn, "Toys R Us Plays Around with Image," *Orlando Sentinel,* July 13, 1996, C1*ff.*

19. L. J. Krajewski and L. P. Ritzman, *Operations Management: Strategy and Analysis.*

20. J. Heizer and B. Render, *Production and Operations Management,* 4th ed. (Upper Saddle River, N.J.: Prentice Hall, 1996).

21. J. R. Evans, *Applied Production and Operations Management,* 5th ed. (St. Paul, Minn.: West Publishing, 1997).

22. L. J. Krajewski and L. P. Ritzman, *Operations Management: Strategy and Analysis.*

23. N. Gaither, *Production and Operations Management,* 7th ed. (Belmont, Calif.: Wadsworth Publishing, 1996).

24. M. A. Vonderembse and G. P. White, *Operations Management: Concepts, Methods, and Strategies.*

25. Evans, *Applied Production and Operations Management.*

26. M. A. Vonderembse and G. P. White, *Operations Management: Concepts, Methods, and Strategies.*

27. Evans, *Applied Production and Operations Management.*

28. Adapted from N. Templin, "Team Spirit: A Decisive Response to Crisis Brought Ford Enhanced Productivity," *The Wall Street Journal,* December 15, 1992, A1; A. Taylor III, "Ford's $6 Billion Baby," *Fortune,* June 28, 1993, 76–81; A. Taylor III, "U.S. Cars Come Back," *Fortune,* November 16, 1992, 52–85; J. Main, "How to Steal the Best Ideas Around," *Fortune,* October 19, 1992, 102–106; E. L. Hennessy Jr., "Back to the Basics: To Regain Greatness, U.S. Manufacturer Must Retool Its Thinking," *Industry Week,* November 20, 1989, 23; "Smart Design," *Business Week,* April 11, 1988, 102–108; and "How Ford Hit the Bull's Eye with Taurus," *Business Week,* June 30, 1986, 69–70.

29. L. J. Krajewski and L. P. Ritzman, *Operations Management: Strategy and Analysis.*

30. J. R. Evans and W. M. Lindsay, *The Management and Control of Quality,* 3d ed. (St. Paul, Minn.: West Publishing, 1996).

31. Ibid.

32. Evans, *Applied Production and Operations Management.*

33. M. A. Vonderembse and G. P. White, *Operations Management: Concepts, Methods, and Strategies.*

34. Evans, *Applied Production and Operations Management.*

35. L. J. Krajewski and L. P. Ritzman, *Operations Management: Strategy and Analysis.*

36. W. E. Deming, "Improvement of Quality and Productivity through Action by Management," *National Productivity Review,* Winter 1981–1982, 12–22.

37. J. M. Juran and F. Gryna Jr., *Quality Planning and Analysis,* 2d ed. (New York: McGraw-Hill, 1980).

38. A. V. Feigenbaum, *Total Quality Control,* 3d ed. (New York: McGraw-Hill, 1983).

39. K. Ishikawa, *Guide to Quality Control* (Tokyo: Asian Productivity Organization, 1972).

40. P. B. Crosby, *Quality Is Free* (New York: McGraw-Hill, 1979).

41. S. Date, "No Gazing Off into Space on This Trip," *Orlando Sentinel,* December 4, 1993, A1*ff.*

42. S. Date, "Endeavour Opens Some Eyes as Hubble Mission Ends at KSC," *Orlando Sentinel,* December 13, 1993, A1*ff.*

43. "Shannon Lucid Leaves Mir, Boards Atlantis for Trip Back," *Orlando Sentinel,* September 20, 1996, A14.

44. R. Henkoff, "Delivering the Goods," *Fortune,* November 28, 1994, 64–78; I. Sager, "The Great Equalizer," *Business Week,* Special Issue on the Information Revolution, 1994, 100–107.

45. B. Spitz, "And on the Lead Guitar."

46. Adapted from "We're Getting Closer," Oregon Cutting Systems Segment, Association for Manufacturing Excellence Videotape #6, 1991.

Information Technology and Control

CHAPTER OVERVIEW

Consider all of the information that is available to assist organizational decision makers. Good information is necessary for good decision making. Information provides knowledge about past and current conditions in the organization and, if used carefully, can provide insights into possible future conditions. Ultimately, information provides a means of understanding the organization and its activities and making decisions on how to control the organizational system. The process of acquiring, processing, maintaining, and distributing this information increasingly involves information systems and information technology.

This chapter introduces the basic concepts of information and the information systems and technology that can be used to collect and distribute the information. First, we explore the differences between data and information and examine some characteristics of good information. We then introduce a basic model of an information system and the systems development process. Next, we look at the role of information technology in the organization and discuss several important categories of information technology. Finally, we look at the impact of technology on the organization and some of the limitations of computer-based information systems.

LEARNING OBJECTIVES

When you have finished studying this chapter, you should be able to:

- Explain the differences between data and information.
- Discuss the characteristics of useful information.
- Describe the various components in an information system.
- Illustrate the steps in the development of an information system.
- Explore the various roles of information technology in organizations.
- Describe a variety of types of technology that are changing the way we work.
- Discuss the impact of information technology on the organization.
- Explain the limitations of information technology.

NESTLÉ CORPORATION: GLOBAL INFORMATION SYSTEMS NEEDED FOR GLOBAL BUSINESS STRATEGY

The Nestlé Corporation is a multibillion-dollar food and pharmaceutical company with worldwide operations. From its corporate headquarters in Vevey, Switzerland, Nestlé oversees the operation of nearly 300 companies. So vast and diverse is the corporation that three official languages, English, Spanish, and French, are used. Although most of us are familiar with Nestlé's food division through its coffee, chocolate, and milk products, the company actually provides thousands of food products worldwide. Although Nestlé has developed many of those products itself, a large number has been added through acquisitions. In recent years Nestlé has acquired such familiar names as Carnation, Perrier, Stouffer's, Hills Brothers, and Buitoni. Nestlé's success has been such that in the mid-1990s, sales were at the $43 billion level and earnings had reached $2.2 billion.

Despite these glowing figures, market conditions had been changing in recent years. Nestlé's two largest markets, Europe and the United States, have become mature, and Nestlé has seen its profit margins decline there in the face of fierce competition. To counter these declines, Nestlé has begun to vigorously accelerate growth in less developed countries. Its strategy is to buy or develop products that fit well in local and regional markets and cultures. When developing new products in less developed countries, Nestlé attempts to develop them from ingredients native to these regions, thereby supporting local economies and keeping costs low. Nestlé also relies on local and regional staff to manage its interests. While this globalization focus has been paying off, Nestlé's information system has left something to be desired. The company's 200,000 employees are serviced by 80 information technology units. With so many different information technology units, its information technology infrastructure had been described as a "Tower of Babel." Several types of hardware and software were being used, with equipment supplied by several vendors. There was no way for units to communicate with one another, and with each additional acquisition, the condition only got worse.[1]

INTRODUCTION

Nestlé realized that major changes were needed in its information infrastructure if the diverse units of this global giant were ever going to be able to communicate with one another. Much of this change would be focused on gaining control of and better managing one of its biggest resources—information—through the development and use of information technology. How could its diverse units communicate with one another given the language, currency, and cultural differences that existed in this global corporation? How could corporate headquarters communicate on an individual basis with each of these diverse units? How would standards be established? And, would the benefits of this reengineering process outweigh its costs? These were but a few of the questions facing Nestlé.

Information technology in the world of business is barely 40 years old. It holds great promise for improving and even changing the way we manage and run our organizations. Yet, according to a recent special issue of *Fortune,* information technology has been described as "one of the most effective ways ever devised to squander corporate assets."[2] Investments in telecommunications, computer hardware and software, and technology-related equipment for the average large business can be as much as 8 percent of revenue every year.

In the mid-1990s, information technology accounted for over 14 percent of capital investment in the United States, up from 8 percent in 1980. Worldwide, investment in technology totals over $350 billion a year. Yet for the typical organization, productivity has barely improved. Still, a number of organizations are beginning to see results that can be directly linked to their investments in and better use of information technology.[3] In the opening Managerial Incident, Nestlé had reached the point where it became necessary to explore the opportunities technology presents and the capabilities it offers.

The fundamental purpose of information technology is to monitor, process, and disseminate information to assist in managing, decision making, and controlling the organization. In this chapter we explore the basic issues related to information technology and controlling information. We will examine the basic concepts of information systems and look at some of the roles that information technology can play in organizations. Finally, we will illustrate some of the limitations of information technology that must be managed.

INFORMATION AND MANAGEMENT

Before inspecting the specifics of information technology, we need to know what information is and how it differs from data. Also important is understanding the characteristics of information that are useful in making decisions.

INFORMATION VERSUS DATA

The words *data* and *information* are often used interchangeably. In the organizational context, however, there can be a significant difference in meaning. **Data** are the raw facts or details that represent some type of transaction or activity within an organization. For example, the sale of items at a grocery store or the sale of an automobile creates a great deal of data representing that event. Data, therefore, are the objective measurements of the characteristics of the objects or transactions that are occurring in an organization.

Information is the result of the process of transforming data into a meaningful and useful form for a specific purpose. In other words, data go through a process where meaning is added, yielding information. In data processing, the data are aggregated and organized, manipulated through analysis, and placed in a proper context for evaluation and use by the end user. In a grocery store, the price and inventory amount for a particular product are examples of raw data. As sales occur, the inventory changes. The changes in inventory for this product, as well as the broader inventory changes that occur for all items available in the store, are examples of information. Each individual transaction is not that important in isolation; once combined, however, the transaction and sales figures provide useful information.

Data
Raw facts or details that represent some type of transaction or activity within an organization.

Information
The result of the process of transforming data into meaningful facts useful for a specific purpose.

A grocery store checkout system provides an example of data versus information. The price and inventory amount for a particular product are examples of raw data. Each individual transaction is not important by itself, but combined with all other transactions in the store each day, the transaction and sales figures provide useful information.

© Bonnie Kamin/PhotoEdit

Other aspects of the data-information relationship also add complexity to organizational decision making and control. Information for one person may be data to another. For example, as customers make their purchases at the grocery store, the store's inventory is altered. If the store has automated cash registers, it can update the inventory immediately. If the store does not have automated registers, the inventory will have to be updated and reconciled manually at the end of the day. The transaction data, generated by and representing details of customer purchases, are important to the store manager. From these raw data, the manager derives information on the store's sales, the success or failure of specific specials, and inventories that need to be restocked, among other things. The regional manager for this chain of stores, however, is not as interested in the details of specific transactions. Instead, the regional manager is concerned with broader issues of how the stores as a whole are doing. Is one store in the region performing better than another? Do different specials or different store layouts generate better sales? Because the regional manager is interested in several stores as a unit, rather than in one store or individual customers, the information needs are different. In summary, information for the store managers is data for the regional manager.

EVALUATING INFORMATION

Currently, many organizations are not taking advantage of all their opportunities to collect data and use the information that can be produced. Collecting and manipulating data entails costs, however, which must be weighed against the benefits that can be obtained from using the information. This process is called *cost-benefit analysis.*

The opportunity presented by the collection, analysis, and use of data within an organization has both a positive side (benefits) and negative side (costs). The purpose of collecting data is to obtain useful information to improve decision making and control as managers strive to attain the organization's goals. Let's first examine the costs associated with data collection and information production.

Tangible costs
Costs that can be accurately quantified.

Intangible costs
Costs that are difficult or impossible to quantify.

These costs can be broken into tangible and intangible components. The **tangible costs** can be accurately quantified. For example, the costs of the hardware and software for a data collection system are tangible costs. They include the costs of maintaining and updating the system, as well as the cost of compensation and related expenses for personnel to run and monitor the system. **Intangible costs,** on the other hand, are hard to quantify, either due to the difficulty of precisely anticipating outcomes or the impossibility of predicting ultimate consequences. Examples of intangible costs include the loss of customer goodwill due to poor organizational performance, lower employee morale, and even work disruption due to changes in work procedures. In the opening Managerial Incident we saw that Nestlé had reached a point where changes had to be made to its information systems. When embarking upon such change, Nestlé would have to determine how to coordinate across many cultures, languages, and currencies, and at the same time communicate with existing systems of disparate hardware and software. Once the redesign had been finalized, specific costs for computer hardware and software could be explicitly defined. However, many of the intangible costs would remain unknown until the transition was finally completed.

Benefits also consist of tangible and intangible components. Tangible benefits include increases in sales, reduction in inventory costs, and identifiable improvements in worker productivity. Intangible benefits might include improvements in information availability, better employee morale, and improved customer service. Nestlé had suspected that a standardized and coordinated information system would reduce redundancies that existed in its 80 separate information technology units, thereby reducing costs in its information technology budget of $340 million per year. However, until the transition was finally completed, the full extent of the benefits to be derived could only be estimated.

The decision on whether to collect more data so as to produce more and better information is difficult. As in many situations, identifying the probable costs is easier than predicting the potential benefits because the additional information has not been used before. In fact, often the most important benefits of new information were not anticipated, but simply emerged as employees became more familiar with the new information. Many organizations have experienced this problem when they incorporated information technology. Not only were the anticipated benefits unrealistic, but the true benefits were often not foreseeable and, therefore, could not be quantified.

CHARACTERISTICS OF USEFUL INFORMATION

Information that is useful to decision makers in the organization has several characteristics. First, its quality must be very high. Second, it must be available to decision makers in a timely fashion. Finally, the information must be complete and relevant. Figure 18.1 shows the relationship among these three primary components of information.

Thus, in deciding whether to collect additional data and process it into information, the organization should consider the costs and the benefits. In a wholly rational decision-making environment, the costs and benefits will be known and can be carefully weighed against each other. As we discovered in Chapter 6, however, sometimes the decision-making environment is not entirely rational, and decision makers must weigh intangible benefits that are, at best, imperfectly known against known, tangible costs. As we saw, conclusions based on inaccurate or incomplete information often yield poor decisions. Nevertheless, decision makers must recognize that the decision of whether to incorporate information technology may have to be based on incomplete and imperfect information, especially about the potential benefits. Certain characteristics, however, make some information more useful than others, and we will examine those characteristics in the next section.

Quality
Quality is, perhaps, the single most important characteristic of information. Without high quality, the information is of little use. Quality consists of several

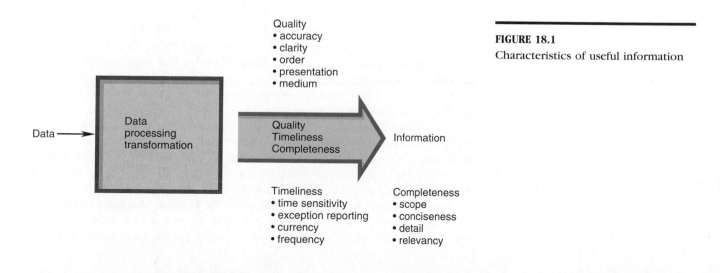

FIGURE 18.1
Characteristics of useful information

components. First, quality information must be accurate. If the details do not accurately reflect current conditions, then any decision made using the information may be adversely affected. Clarity is another characteristic of quality information. The meaning and intent of the information must be clear to the decision maker. Quality information has an orderly arrangement and is presented in a form that assists the decision maker. Finally, the medium through which the information is communicated is important. For example, providing the decision maker with a massive computer printout instead of several pages of summary information is an inappropriate means of communication.

Timeliness

Most organizational decision making requires timely information. Many day-to-day decisions are time sensitive. In other words, decisions on how to respond to situations in an organization must be made quickly. Timely information has several ingredients.

First, information should be provided when and as it is needed, so that the decision maker has the information when it is needed to support making a decision. For example, a decision maker might ask for exception reports, which are reports that are generated when things fall outside a normal range of activity within the organization. Thus, if production on an assembly line falls below a certain threshold due to a malfunction, an exception report is generated to inform those who need to know so they can make appropriate repairs and adjustments. Another key ingredient of timely information is currency. Information should be up to date when it is provided to the decision maker. A final characteristic of timely information is frequency. Information should be provided as often as needed. For example, reports should be generated and provided to the decision maker on a regular reporting schedule, such as daily, weekly, monthly, or quarterly. Managing for Excellence describes how timely feedback of information on package location is critical to United Parcel Service's successful monitoring of packages in the delivery process. Federal Express is another good example of an organization that uses technology very effectively to provide timely feedback of information on package location. In a manner similar to UPS's, each package is assigned a bar-coded identifier the moment it is picked up from the sender. The bar code is scanned at every change in its transport. Since this scanned information is communicated to a central computer, an up-to-date record of the status and location of each package is constantly maintained.[5]

Completeness

If information is to contribute to making good decisions, it must be complete. Information completeness consists of several primary components. The scope of the information must be sufficient to allow the decision maker to make an accurate assessment of the situation and to arrive at a suitable decision. Where appropriate, decision makers should have access not only to current information, but also to past history and to future plans for the organization. Conciseness and detail are two additional aspects of completeness. Information should be presented to the decision maker in as concise a form as possible, but there should be sufficient detail to provide the decision maker with enough depth and breadth for the current situation. Too much detail, however, can overwhelm the decision maker, causing information overload, distracting from the decision, or making it virtually impossible to focus on the important information. Finally, only information that is relevant to the decision at hand needs to be provided. Once again, too much information may do more harm than good.

Some examples of these concepts might be helpful. Imagine the job of air traffic controllers, who must manage a number of aircraft flying through a certain airspace. The relevant information consists of aircraft identification, speed,

UNITED PARCEL SERVICE: INFORMATION TECHNOLOGY BOOSTS COMPETITIVENESS

Managing for Excellence

United Parcel Service is the world's largest air and ground package distribution company, delivering close to 3 billion parcels and documents each year to any address in the United States, and to almost 200 foreign countries and territories. The company has long been recognized for its fast service and low rates in the area of traditional package delivery. More recently it has ventured into the overnight delivery business and has become very competitive with Federal Express, the world leader in that business. At the heart of UPS's high-quality service is a parcel tracking system that allows it to monitor packages throughout the delivery process. This system is loaded with advanced information technology. In fact, between 1992 and 1996 UPS expected to have invested $1.8 billion in information technology.

So, how does UPS keep track of every package? Through its TotalTrack, an automated package-tracing system, UPS monitors packages throughout the delivery process. An optical scanning device reads bar-coded information on the package label. UPS drivers are all equipped with a hand-held computer called a Delivery Information Acquisition Device (DIAD). The DIAD allows UPS drivers to collect customer signatures, pickup, delivery, and time-card information. All of this information is transmitted to the UPS central computer by way of the cellular telephone network. Once in the main computer, the information can be accessed worldwide to provide package location or proof of delivery. Not only can UPS officials access this information, but customers, using special package-tracking software provided by UPS, can access this information directly from their own microcomputers.

When UPS moved into overseas markets, it set up its own global communications network, UPSnet, as the information processing system for worldwide operations. In addition to the package-tracking capabilities of TotalTrack, UPSnet extends the system's capabilities into such functions as providing information for billing and delivery confirmation, expediting customs clearance, and package interception and rerouting. Investment in these sophisticated technologies has paid off, for UPS has been able to boost customer service, keep costs low, and streamline its global operations.[4]

direction, planned flight path, weather, other aircraft in the area, and so on. Clearly, high-quality, timely, and complete information are necessary if the controllers are to guide all the aircraft into and out of airports and airspace safely. Another example might be a stockbroker. Can you image the problems brokers would face if their information was more than an hour old? What if the most timely information the brokers had was yesterday's stock market results in the newspaper?

In October 1993 Bell Atlantic, a regional telephone company, announced that it would acquire Tele-Communications, Inc., often called TCI. Although this merger was not successfully completed, the stock market activity surrounding this announcement provides another example of what may happen when decisions are made with incomplete information. The day after the announcement, the stock with the ticker symbol TCI on the New York Stock Exchange quickly experienced 56 trades involving 55,000 shares; the price rose 15 percent.[6] Unfortunately, TCI is the NYSE symbol for Transcontinental Reality Investors, Inc., not Tele-Communications, Inc., which has the symbol TCOMA. Managers of the NYSE recognized the error after only a short time and halted trading in TCI before any major problems occurred. In this situation, intervention by the NYSE prevented investors from suffering serious financial damage as a result of their incomplete information.

In any business organization, the timeliness, quality, and completeness of information are important. Consider the manager of a manufacturing plant that practices just-in-time manufacturing. As we saw in Chapter 17, this means that raw material inventory must arrive in a timely fashion in order for production to continue, since the company maintains little excess, or spare, inventory. The manufacturing machinery must also be running according to schedule, so raw material inventory does not stack up. Scheduling of workers is also important, for the assembly line must have workers in order to run. Any deviation from plans—an exception—would be important to the facility's management, since they will have to adjust to current problems and conditions.

Finally, as the Managerial Incident described, Nestlé is attempting to redesign the way it manages, processes, and distributes information throughout the organization. All three of the characteristics of useful information—quality, timeliness, and completeness—are important to the ultimate success or failure of the redesigned information system.

INFORMATION SYSTEMS FOR MANAGEMENT

The fundamental idea behind information systems is that they provide a systematic approach to collecting, manipulating, maintaining, and distributing information throughout an organization. Despite the common misconception, an information system does not require a computer. Systems of managing information existed long before computers. And even with the rapid increase in computers in recent years, many organizations still maintain systems for managing information that are not computerized. Nevertheless, computer systems and other advances in information technology are providing organizations and their workers with virtually unlimited opportunities to collect, explore, and manage information, opportunities that were not available just a few years ago.

INFORMATION SYSTEM COMPONENTS

A general system consists of five basic components: inputs, the processing or transformation area, outputs, procedures for providing feedback to the system, and a means of controlling the system. As Figure 18.2 shows, this general system model closely resembles the traditional computer-based information system except that the latter also includes hardware, software, and a database. The next paragraphs discuss the components of a computer-based system.

Input

The input portion of a computer-based information system consists of any type of computer input device that can provide data to the system. For example, the scanner cash registers in stores, often called point-of-sale terminals, provide input to the information system. While we have all seen these devices in grocery stores and department stores, we were probably not aware of the fact that similar technology is also used by the United States Postal Service. While one person can manually sort only about 500 pieces of mail per hour, a scanning machine can sort 30,000 to 40,000 pieces in the same amount of time.[7] Sensors and monitoring equipment in a manufacturing or production facility can provide input. Input can also come via telephone lines, satellite transmission, and archival data stored on computer disks and tapes. Input data can also be directly entered into the system by a user at a terminal or microcomputer, through a bar-code reader, and now even through pen-based computer systems that recognize handwriting.

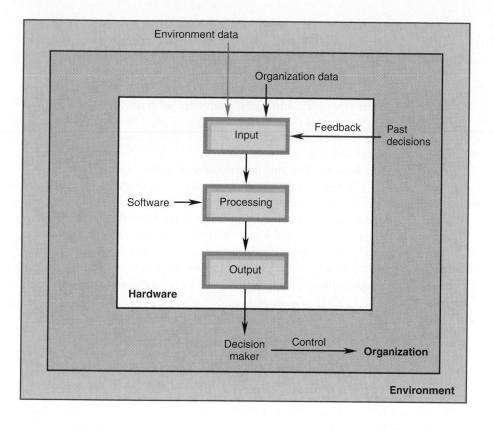

FIGURE 18.2
General information system

Processing

The processing component of an information system—what we typically think of as the "brains" of the computer—is often called the central processing unit (CPU). When we think of a computer, we usually mean the CPU. This is the portion of the system where the raw data are manipulated and transformed into meaningful and useful information that can then be distributed to the relevant decision makers.

Output

The output portion of the system is the actual distribution of the information that is the result of processing. Output can take a variety of forms, including paper printouts, electronic transmissions through telephone systems or via satellite, computer disks or tape, displays on computer monitors, and sounds or synthetic voices made available through speakers for audio use. It can even become available through the control and manipulation of computer-controlled machinery.

In the general systems model, the output process provides information to the decision makers, who can then manage and control the larger organizational system. Feedback occurs when the decision makers interpret the information to determine what should occur next. The decisions that result from the interpretation and use of the information are a means of controlling the system.

Hardware

The physical components of the information system—the computer, terminals, monitors, printers, and so on—are the hardware. The storage devices, such as hard disks, floppy disk drives, and tape drives, are also hardware components. An infinite variety of hardware components are available and can be combined as needed to meet organizational information processing needs.

Software

The software portion of an information system consists of the various types of programs that are used to tell the hardware how to function. Software controls how the data are processed. Examples of software include word-processing, spreadsheet, and accounting packages; other business applications; and even the games we commonly play. Ultimately, software governs how the information is stored and distributed.

Database

A database is the archived data and information that the organization uses. A database typically contains a vast amount of related information on company operations, financial records, employee data, customers, and so on. In the past, much of this information was maintained in separate files, which were often paper based. As a result, the data were often inconsistent and hard to locate and retrieve. Even early computerized systems often maintained data in separate files, leading to similar problems. A computerized database typically makes it easier for the organization to manage and use its data and information in decision making.

STEPS IN THE DEVELOPMENT OF HIGH-QUALITY MANAGEMENT INFORMATION SYSTEMS

End users
Those who will use and interact with the information system.

Most information systems are developed through a systematic process, in which system design specialists and programmers collaborate with the end users. **End users** are all the people who will use and interact with the information system, particularly the decision makers in the organization. This process, which is depicted in Figure 18.3, is often called *systems analysis and design.*

Investigation

The initial phase in the development of an information system is systems investigation. During this phase, the organization determines whether a problem or opportunity exists that can be addressed by an information system. In ad-

FIGURE 18.3
Systems development life cycle

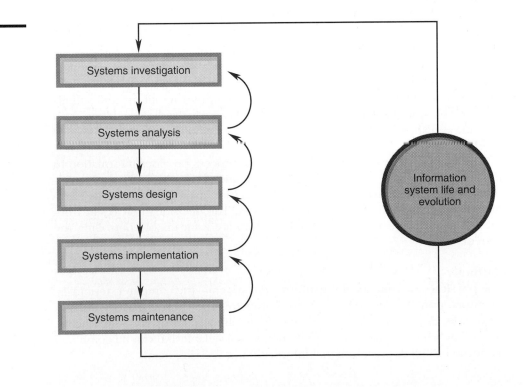

dition, a feasibility study is performed to determine whether a new information system is attainable. Once an organization ascertains that an information system is both appropriate and feasible, the organization develops a plan for managing the project and obtaining management approval. Nestlé, for example, conducted an initial investigation and found that information technology could provide a great deal of assistance in its attempts to coordinate and communicate between individual units, as well as between corporate headquarters and those diverse units.

Systems Analysis

Once the plan has been devised and management's approval has been obtained, the second phase, called systems analysis, begins. The purpose of this phase is to develop the functional requirements for the information system. In other words, this phase concentrates on what needs to be done to provide the desired information. This phase begins with an examination and analysis of the current systems in use, an assessment of the organizational environment, and a detailed assessment of the information needs of the end users. The organizational environment consists of both internal factors, such as the organization's structure, people, and activities, and external factors, such as industry considerations and the competition.

After studying these components, the system designers develop a set of functional requirements, or a detailed description of the necessary functional performance capabilities of the information system. These requirements focus on the type of information that decision makers require, the response times the users will need, and the format, frequency, and volume of information that should be produced and distributed. The specific hardware, software, and personnel that will ultimately be needed are not addressed in this stage. Nestlé, for example, realized that the variety and incompatibility of the information systems used throughout the organization created a significant problem that needed to be addressed.

Systems Design

Phase three is the system design phase. This is the first phase where the system's technological capabilities are addressed. The designers identify the hardware, software, people, and data resources that will be needed and describe the information products that will be produced to satisfy the functional requirements specified in the previous phase. More specifically, the user interface, or the point of interaction between the people and the information, is designed. The data, their attributes and structures, and the relationships among the various data elements are created. These data will ultimately become the input for the database. Finally, the software system—the various computer programs and procedures—is designed. For Nestlé, this part of the process was extremely important and complex, for it involved reconciling the company's many inconsistent and incompatible systems.

Computer-aided software engineering (CASE) tools are increasingly being used in this phase of the development process. CASE tools allow the system developers, or even the users themselves, to rapidly and easily develop prototype screens and report generators from a library of generic samples. In addition, once the prototypes have been designed, the CASE tools will generate the actual computer code that needs to be included in the larger system for those screens and reports. CASE tools are also more broadly used in business process planning, project management, database design, and software interface design.[8] Although much of the technical detail of Nestlé's eventual information system reengineering is not included in the resolution to the opening Managerial Incident, it should be noted here that CASE tools were a part of the final package.

Computer-aided software engineering (CASE)
Tools that allow system developers to create prototype screens and report generators rapidly and easily.

Systems Implementation

Once the analysis and design phases have been completed, systems implementation can begin. The outcome from this phase will be an operational system. The hardware and software that will be incorporated into the new information system are developed or acquired. As the system is put together, extensive testing is necessary to ensure that the system will meet all specified requirements. Any problems can be more easily corrected at this phase than at any later phase.

Documentation of the new system, or the relationship among the various pieces of hardware and software, should also be emphasized. The information system will not work perfectly, and the individuals who designed and developed it will not always be around to maintain it. Therefore, detailed and accurate descriptions of what was done, why it was done, and how it all works together are needed to assist in managing and maintaining the system.

Once the testing is completed, the system is ready for use, and the organization can switch from its old procedures to the new information system. This transition process may require operating both the new and the old system for a time in parallel. Operating the systems in parallel gives people time to learn and become comfortable with the new system and an opportunity to identify and correct most system bugs. Bringing the new system into operation on a trial basis, one location at a time, is called using a pilot system. Another alternative is the immediate cutover, where the old system is halted and the new system is started with no overlap in operations. All these transition methods have positive and negative aspects. The organization should carefully assess the benefits and potential costs before selecting an approach.[9]

Systems Maintenance

The final phase in the development of an information system is systems maintenance. Like an automobile, a house, or any piece of machinery, an information system will need to be maintained to keep it in top shape and to ensure that it will not encounter problems that could have been prevented. New hardware may be added to the system to address new needs or to replace older equipment. Software updates—new versions with added capabilities—are commonly available. In spite of extensive testing, most systems will contain errors, or bugs, some of them quite major. In addition, as the users work with the information system, they will discover additional things that need to be added, better ways of doing some things, and possibly areas that can be removed from the system.

Systems development life cycle (SDLC)

Recognition that investigating, analyzing, designing, implementing, and maintaining an information system is an ongoing process.

The **systems development life cycle (SDLC)** is the recognition that the process of investigating, analyzing, designing, implementing, and maintaining an information system is ongoing. All of the activities in the life cycle of an information system are highly interrelated and are very interdependent. For example, the design process is directly affected by the outcome of the analysis phase. Any issues that are missed or are not completely addressed during the analysis will not be a part of the functional analysis and, therefore, will not be effectively handled during the design phase. Obviously, if issues are not addressed during the design, there will be nothing to implement. So, as shown in Figure 18.3, as each new phase is entered, it may be necessary at times to go back to the previous phase, or even an earlier one, to address any deficiencies that are identified. But the SDLC goes beyond even this level of interrelationship. It recognizes that any system, no matter how well designed and maintained, will ultimately become obsolete and need to be replaced or will effectively be replaced as the organization and its information system evolve over time.[10]

One final aspect of any new information system is user training. The success of an information system depends on more than just thorough analysis, design, and implementation. Success is also, and perhaps ultimately, dependent upon the people who will use the system on a daily basis to assist in making decisions. To facilitate their use of the system, the users need to be trained in what the system can and cannot do and in how to accomplish the needed tasks. Training may be for simple tasks such as data entry or for very complex monitoring and operations of critical machinery within the organization. In larger organizations, the training role is commonly fulfilled by an information center.[11] As cultural diversity increases in the work place, the training process can become more difficult due to language barriers and communication problems. In addition, as with any type of change, the process can be slower and more tedious, when cultural backgrounds cause resistance to change.

PITFALLS IN SYSTEM DESIGN

Several types of pitfalls can affect the system design process. These pitfalls involve the project's feasibility, the system's ability to meet user needs, and user expectations of the system.

Feasibility

An assessment of the system's feasibility focuses on evaluating alternative systems that will best meet the needs of the organization and its workers. Feasibility has several dimensions.[12] **Organizational feasibility** examines how well the proposed system supports the strategic objectives of the organization as a whole. Systems that do not directly contribute to the short-range and long-range goals of the organization should be rejected. **Economic feasibility** focuses on whether the expected benefits will be able to cover the anticipated costs. A system whose benefits do not match or exceed the costs will not be approved unless mandated by other considerations, such as government regulations. The economic feasibility includes the cost-benefit analysis discussed earlier in the chapter.

Technical feasibility addresses the hardware and software capabilities of the proposed system. Is the system, as proposed, capable of reliably providing the needed information to the appropriate people? Can the decision makers get the right kinds and amounts of data to support the desired decision making? And will the information be available when needed? The last type is **operational feasibility,** which focuses on the willingness and ability of all concerned parties to operate, use, and support the information system as it is proposed and implemented. If any one of the relevant constituencies, such as management, employees, customers, and suppliers, does not support or use the system, it is doomed to ultimate failure. For example, if the system is too difficult for the employees to use successfully, they will reject it and use other approaches to do their work. Others who depend on the employees' use of the system for information will be unable to get what they need, leading to a further loss of opportunity.

Ability to Meet Needs of Diverse Users

A second concern in the system design process is whether the system will ultimately meet the users' needs. The investigation, analysis, and design process is time-consuming and can be very costly. Time and cost often put pressure on designers to take shortcuts that may lead to an inferior or flawed system that does not meet users' needs. Systems that do not meet the users' needs can also occur because users often have difficulty describing their information needs adequately. This problem is exacerbated when, as is often the case, the systems specialists have little or no previous experience with the types of problems currently under consideration. Therefore, if care is not taken, the resulting system may not

Organizational feasibility
Focuses on how well the proposed system supports the strategic objectives of the organization.

Economic feasibility
Focuses on whether the expected benefits of an information system will be able to cover the anticipated costs.

Technical feasibility
Focuses on the hardware and software capabilities of the proposed information system.

Operational feasibility
Focuses on the willingness and ability of all concerned parties to operate, use, and support the information system.

live up to the expectations of the users. In addition, as the users become more familiar with the system, their demands and expectations may increase.[13]

Another potential pitfall is that the users may resist the new system. This situation is especially common when workers are afraid that the new information technology may make some of the currently existing jobs unnecessary. Resistance is also more likely when the people who must work with the information systems are excluded from participating in its design and development. Not only does this lead to an incomplete analysis and design process, but it can also generate resentment toward the new system.[14] Meeting the needs of diverse users was a prime concern of Nestlé. As noted earlier, Nestlé was composed of units that spanned several languages, currencies, and cultures. In the past Nestlé had experienced resistance and heard a vocal outcry from local operating units when it tried to impose a strict standard for a specific microcomputer vendor. This experience taught Nestlé that it would have to provide local units some latitude and some input when it came to reengineering its information technology system.

User Expectations

Finally, in many instances the expectations of the users and the organization are too high. As we suggested earlier in the chapter, information technology has been touted as the savior of organizations, whereas in most cases the results have been minimal. In reality, however, the technology is not the key issue. Ultimately, the success or failure of the technology is dependent on how the organization and its employees align the capabilities of the technology with the needs of the organization.[15] The next section examines several aspects of this new realization.

Since management information systems frequently fail to do the job they were supposed to do, system designers can use the checksheet in Meeting the Challenge to improve their chances of achieving a successful information system design.

APPLICATIONS OF COMPUTER-BASED INFORMATION SYSTEMS

The traditional role of information systems has been to process data in order to assist the organization in maintaining control and in monitoring operations. That role still exists today, but it has become much broader as well. Organizations now depend much more heavily on information systems to manage their various functional areas, as well as to provide greater integration and sharing of information than were previously possible. And in the last ten years, information systems have even moved into the executive levels of organizations to provide support for strategic planning and decision making.

Managerial decision making is typically depicted as a pyramid, with operational control as the foundation, tactical or functional control as the middle, and strategic planning and control as the pinnacle. Note that the type of information, its focus, and the degree of detail will differ depending on the type of management decision making and control appropriate for that level of the organization. The use of information technology originated in the operational areas of the organization and is moving increasingly into the middle and upper levels of management.

ELECTRONIC DATA PROCESSING AND OPERATIONAL CONTROL

Computing in organizations usually originated at the operational levels of the organization, where it took care of basic data processing needs such as payroll operations, general accounting functions, and tracking transactions. These data

CHECKLIST FOR SUCCESSFUL INFORMATION SYSTEM DESIGN

Frequently, management information systems fail to do the job they were supposed to do because they were inadequately designed or poorly thought out. Before, during, and after the design of the information system, system designers should see if they can provide a positive response to the questions on the following checksheet:

_____ Is the information that is provided to the decision maker accurate and clear?

_____ Is the information that is provided to the decision maker current?

_____ Is the information provided to the decision maker in a timely fashion?

_____ Is the information provided to the decision maker frequently enough?

_____ Is the information that is provided to the decision maker complete?

_____ Have all of the steps in the information system development process been completely performed?

_____ Does the information system support the strategic objectives of the organization?

_____ Do the benefits of the information system outweigh the costs?

_____ Are the hardware and software capable of providing the needed information to the appropriate people?

_____ Does the information system meet the users' needs and expectations?

are still important, for they provide a detailed picture of the activities taking place within the organization. These detailed data are the foundation for the information that is generated and used for management decision making.

Operational control also includes what is commonly referred to as process control. In some industries, such as manufacturing and refining, information technology can be used to monitor and report on operations. Automated monitors of an oil refinery, for example, provide detailed status reports on the refining process and equipment. Additionally, an automated process control system can assist in automatically updating inventory, reordering materials when certain thresholds are reached, or adjusting material flow as production warrants.

Finally, office automation systems, which are discussed in more detail later in the chapter, provide for systematic approaches to handling and controlling business-related documents and communication.

MANAGEMENT INFORMATION SYSTEMS AND FUNCTIONAL CONTROL

A **management information system (MIS)** is typically focused on the routine, structured, regular reporting and information requirements of the organization. Regularly scheduled reports, delivered daily, weekly, monthly, or quarterly, are generated by MISs. These systems support the day-to-day decision-making needs that have been incorporated as part of normal operations. They also often contain information about conditions external to the organization, such as industry and economic trends and the performance of competitors.

In many MISs, information is available on demand to facilitate monitoring exception conditions and to monitor moment-by-moment activities if desired. These reporting capabilities typically support tactical or functional decision making in the organization. However, unanticipated reporting requirements and unusual operating conditions are not typically well supported by the systematic, structured nature of a traditional MIS.

Management information system (MIS)
Focuses on the routine, structured, regular reporting and information requirements of the organization.

DECISION SUPPORT SYSTEMS AND STRATEGIC PLANNING

Decision support system (DSS)
Focuses on assisting decision makers in analyzing and solving semistructured problems.

A **decision support system (DSS)** is an important type of computer-based information system that is becoming increasingly prominent in organizational decision making. A DSS helps decision makers formulate quality decisions for ad hoc, semistructured problems—situations in which procedures can be only partially specified in advance. Because the situations occur infrequently, the organization does not have routine procedures for dealing with them. This lack of routine means there are limited rules to guide decision behavior; therefore, outcomes are less predictable or obvious. These types of decision situations commonly arise at the middle and upper levels of the organization.

A DSS consists of several separate pieces, as shown in Figure 18.4. The user works with the DSS in an interactive, real-time basis. The DSS contains analytical models that can be used to examine and understand the situation, as well as specialized databases. The DSS allows users to combine their own insights and judgment with the analytical models and information from the database to examine alternative approaches and solutions to the situation. In particular, "what if" analysis can be performed using the DSS. In other words, the decision maker can assess a variety of decision choices by modeling the expected outcomes of those decisions with the information that is currently available.

Think of a DSS as a tool for simulating a situation. Just as an airline pilot in a flight simulator can experience a variety of scenarios that might be encountered, a manager using a DSS can use data from a database and analytical models to simulate what might happen if different decisions are made. American Airlines has developed a DSS called An Analytical Information Management System (AAIMS), which is used by a variety of airlines, airline financial analysts, and aircraft manufacturers. AAIMS can be used to analyze aircraft utilization and operations as well as traffic statistics. The analysis allows decision makers to assess forecasts of airline market share, revenue, and profitability. From these forecasts, users can decide on ticket pricing, aircraft assignments and maintenance, alternative route requests, and other complex scheduling issues.

The most common DSS-type of software tool is a spreadsheet program, which allows the user to quickly update data within the spreadsheet to see the effects on other variables. However, other specialized DSS tools also exist. For example, RCA has developed a DSS called Industrial Relations Information System (IRIS) to assist with personnel problems, labor negotiations, and other types of employee-related situations that cannot be anticipated. The National Audubon Society has developed a DSS called EPLAN (Energy Plan) to evaluate the impact of government energy policy on the environment. A DSS called Quality Decision Management has been developed by Hewlett-Packard to aid in raw material inspection, statistical analysis, and product inspection.[16] Bellcore has developed a DSS called SONET to help regional Bell operating companies plan and design telecommunications networks for local phone service.[17]

FIGURE 18.4
Decision support system (DSS)

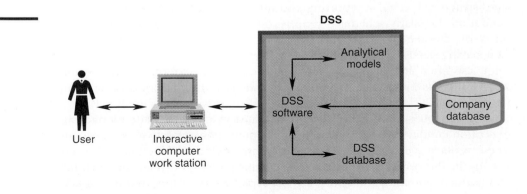

TABLE 18.1   Executive information and support systems

EXECUTIVE INFORMATION SYSTEM (EIS)
• Tailored to individual user
• Allows user to filter, expand, compress, and track critical information
• Provide an up-to-date status report
• Access to broad range of internal and external information and data
• User-friendly and easily learned

EXECUTIVE SUPPORT SYSTEM (ESS)
An ESS is an EIS with additional capabilities:
• Supports electronic communications
• Provides a variety of data analysis tools (such as spreadsheets, DSS, expert system support, database access)
• Often includes tools for personal productivity (such as electronic calendars, tickler files, Rolodex)

A more specialized type of DSS that has recently become popular is called an executive information system (EIS) or executive support system (ESS). Although there is some distinction between the two, for our purposes they can be viewed as essentially the same. An EIS is a general information system combined with a DSS for use primarily by upper-level management and executive decision makers to support strategic decision making in the organization. As we discussed at the beginning of the chapter, decision makers at different levels of the organization have different information needs. An EIS provides executives with the type of summary information they need and also gives them the opportunity to obtain additional details, that is, the data behind the information, if desired. Table 18.1 summarizes many of the characteristics of an EIS and an ESS.[18]

OTHER INFORMATION TECHNOLOGIES

In addition to the information systems we have just described, organizations may use several other types of information technology. Many of these are used at all levels of the organization to assist in communication, information transmission, and decision making. There is an interesting phenomenon that has accompanied the rapid advancements and new developments with information technology. An unprecedented number of entrepreneurial ventures by engineers, scientists, and technical experts is being spawned. Entrepreneurial Approach describes the conditions and climate that have fostered these ventures, and recounts a few interesting successes that have resulted.

TELECOMMUNICATIONS AND NETWORKING

Telecommunications is the transmission of information in any form from one location to another using electronic or optical means. This definition applies to all types of telecommunications, including the ordinary telephone call. Generally, however, the term implies that computer systems, and the people who use them, can communicate from almost any location.

The global integration of organizations is rapidly increasing the need for international phone calls and information transmission. For example, the num-

Entrepreneurial Approach

TECHNO-GEEKS CAN SURVIVE IN BUSINESS

As Microsoft Corp. chairman Bill Gates strengthened his hold on the title "World's Richest Person" in late 1996, many engineers, scientists, and technical experts have been concocting their own schemes to grab that elusive brass ring. Casting aside their pocket-protected, techno-weenie stereotypes, today's "geeks" aspire to the clout, cash, and charisma mold of Gates. In some localities, as many as one in every twelve business startups involves a technical area such as software engineering, computer services, or information technology. What is emerging is a new breed of engineer-entrepreneur who is in tune with not only bits, bytes, and nanoseconds, but also marketing, financing, networking, and management. Consider John Pelka, a former Harris Corp. engineer, who cofounded Quali-Tool, a successful computer hardware manufacturer. Or Don Schmaltz, former NASA engineer, and Peter Atwal, former Siemens engineer, who cofounded ISR Global Telecom, Inc. With a little help from a marketing consultant, they successfully launched their new telecommunications software package.

Technical-entrepreneur opportunities are not limited to professional scientists and engineers. Consider the success of the following four high school students. Chris Bray, Matt Baylis, James Ross, and Charles Ross became captivated when the World Wide Web became a phenomenon in the mid-1990s. While they were seventeen-year-old seniors at Orlando's Edgewater High School, they decided to start their own business when, in the words of one of the teens, "we looked around and saw what a lot of companies were doing, and we realized that we were just as good." PixelStorm, a company that specializes in the creation of World Wide Web sites for business clients, was born. It is a legally chartered corporation in the state of Florida, with corporate officers—the four partners—and shareholders—their parents. They have a business phone line, a separate fax number, and a corporate attorney, and have purchased business liability insurance. The best part is that they have paying clients, and they make real money. First-year revenue is estimated to be $24,000. By many standards, that's not a lot of money, but it sure beats what these students would earn by bagging groceries after school. In their eyes, the sky is the limit. After all, Bill Gates cofounded Microsoft with a friend when he was only nineteen years old. They couldn't have a more successful role model![19]

---

ber of international calls made annually to or from the United States has risen from 500 million in the early 1980s to almost 3 billion in the early 1990s.[20] These numbers do not include the data and information that are transmitted through private communication systems.

The more advanced ideas in telecommunications typically concern the connection of multiple computer systems and multiple users in what is usually called a network. A network that stretches over a wide geographic area, such as a city, a region, a country, and even the world, is typically called a **wide-area network (WAN).** For example, Wal-Mart and Sears, as well as many other companies, can easily communicate with their stores through a WAN. Network arrangements are becoming increasingly common in organizations that need to transmit and receive day-to-day information on business operations from their employees, customers, suppliers, and other organizations. And, each day more and more of us are adapting to that widest of WANs, the Internet's World Wide Web. Microsoft has developed software to facilitate the blending of desktop computing with the multimedia technology of the World Wide Web. This new technology will make it easier to find information, whether it is on the computer's hard drive or on the Internet. Furthermore, each piece of material

Wide-area network (WAN)
An information system that extends over a broad geographic area, such as cities, regions, countries, or the world.

created on a personal computer—whether an e-mail message, a memo to the boss, or any other type of document—could be easily embellished with images, audio, and video.[21]

A **local-area network (LAN)** connects information systems and users within a much smaller area, such as a building, an office, or a manufacturing plant. The computer network on a college campus is usually a LAN or may contain several LANs.[22]

Many activities are now possible due to the ease of access and relatively low cost of telecommunications. **Electronic data interchange (EDI)** is the electronic transmission of transaction data using telecommunications. These data can include sales invoices, purchase orders, shipping notices, and so on. EDI provides an almost immediate transmission of the data and allows for a significant savings in printing, mailing, and labor costs as well as in time. In addition, since the orders and information are electronically transferred, fewer people have to handle the data, thereby reducing the chances for data entry and mishandling errors. Some companies have reported decreases of 25 to 50 percent in the amount of time it takes to receive and fill customer orders since adopting EDI. RCA has estimated that the cost to fill an order will drop from $50 to around $4 due to labor-saving use of EDI. General Motors has required all of its suppliers to use EDI, leading to estimated savings of about $200 per automobile produced. And the U.S. Department of Defense is moving toward a similar requirement for its suppliers.[23] Ford Motor Company used telecommunications to transmit information to various units around the world when it designed the new version of the classic Mustang and prepared it for production.[24]

But EDI is not just for giant manufacturers and government. For example, InterDesign, of Solon, Ohio, makes plastic clocks, refrigerator magnets, soap dishes, and the like. Under pressure from a large retailer, the company adopted EDI. Now over half of the orders to InterDesign arrive via modems connected to its computer system instead of by mail or through a phone call. Virtually all order entry and shipping errors have been eliminated. Now employees who used to staff phones taking orders spend their time collecting valuable information the company couldn't afford to collect before. Sales are tracked by product, color, customer, region, and so on.[25] According to some predictions, by the turn of the century as many as one-half of all business documents will be transmitted by EDI.

The banking and retail industries are moving increasingly toward an environment of **electronic funds transfer (EFT),** where all financial transactions are done electronically. Many of us already depend on EFT for our banking and financial transactions. The automatic teller machine is an example of EFT. Being able to pay our bills over the phone is another example. And many of the point-of-sale terminals in retail stores, where our credit cards are checked, our checks are cleared, or our debit cards are used, depend upon EFT. Unlike a credit card, which it resembles, a debit card allows the money to be transferred from your account directly to the retailer's account upon completion of a transaction.

Many companies from around the world are discovering that they can benefit from telecommunications. Global Perspective describes a United Nations–sanctioned telecommunications network that has been designed to help businesses locate international trading partners and to negotiate contracts.[26]

Telecommuting, another facet of telecommunications, is a relatively new way to work. When workers telecommute, they operate from a remote location, such as a branch office or their home, and communicate with the office via telecommunications. Many jobs do not require an individual to be at the main office all of the time. In fact, some people find that working from a remote site, such as their home, provides some big benefits.

Local-area network (LAN)
An information system that connects users in a small area, such as a building, an office, or a manufacturing plant.

Electronic data interchange (EDI)
Electronic transmission of transaction data using telecommunications.

Electronic funds transfer (EFT)
Electronic manipulation of financial transactions.

Telecommuting
The practice of working at a remote site by using a computer linked to a central office or other employment location.

Scanning of credit cards and use of debit cards are only some of the operations that depend upon EFT, where all financial transactions are accomplished electronically.
© 1996, PhotoDisc, Inc.

Global Perspective

UNITED NATIONS TELECOMMUNICATIONS NETWORK

In its quest to help small and medium-sized businesses in developing countries become involved in world trade, the United Nations has established a global electronic trading network. It is the UN's hope that the network will stimulate growth in international trade by helping those target businesses locate information that would help them enter global markets. To this end, Global Trade Point Network, a pilot version of the network, was established in late 1994. GTPN has a service that companies can use to locate trade leads, negotiate business transactions, and make shipping and payment arrangements. Gateways into the network have been established at about 50 trade point sites around the world. These trade points also serve as information storage repositories. Businesses seeking information can access the trade points through their national telecommunications infrastructures, or by simply visiting any of the trade point sites. The network uses several existing telecommunications networks, including General Electric Information Systems (GEIS), AT&T's EasyLink, and the Internet.

The UN network is constantly incorporating additional services. Electronic data interchange (EDI) services for exchanging business transactions were added to several trade points shortly after the network's inception. The Bankers Association of Foreign Trade has established trade point databases that will help traders locate businesses that finance international trade. The United States Department of Commerce is making the National Trade Database accessible through the network. This database contains import/export guides, foreign trade indices, and assorted other foreign trade data. In addition, a number of U.S. manufacturers are making product catalogs available on-line. These catalogs allow users to access product information, product pictures, and animated product demonstrations. Plans exist to expand all of these services and to add many more. Ready access to the information on the Global Trade Point Network will greatly benefit businesses that aspire to be key players in the global marketplace.

American Express Travel Services has been experimenting with telecommuting for some of its employees. These jobs are oriented around providing customer service and information by telephone. Many employees located in the Houston area had a 60- to 90-minute commute to and from work each day. By telecommuting from their home, the workers found they had more time to spend with their families and were not stressed by the chore of driving in heavy traffic or bad weather. American Express has also seen some significant benefits. Thus far, workers have been able to handle 26 percent more calls with no reduction in the quality of service. In addition, the rent that would normally have been spent for office space for these employees could be saved. In New York, American Express estimates that it can save about $4,400 annually for every travel counselor who telecommutes. And, with advances in technology, managers can still monitor the employees' work performance in responding to customer phone calls.[27]

Recently, California instituted laws to encourage telecommuting to help reduce pollution caused by automobiles.[28] The January 1994 earthquake near Los Angeles did so much damage to the interstate highway system in the area that commuting times were significantly lengthened, sometimes by as much as two or three hours each way.[29] Telecommuting may be a way for companies to alleviate difficulties such as this.

Another advance that has grown out of telecommunications is electronic mail (e-mail) networks and bulletin board systems. E-mail systems, which are often a part of office automation systems, discussed later, are changing the way we work and communicate. You can think of e-mail as being like the postal system except that the messages and information are transmitted electronically through computer networks instead of being sent through the mail. Many companies, such as GTE, MCI, and TELENET, now offer e-mail services, and a number of personal computer networks, such as Prodigy, CompuServe, and Genie, are available for subscribers. Communication speeds are very fast. Whenever the people receiving messages are ready, they can read their mail.

In fact, e-mail received a lot of publicity immediately after the January 1994 earthquake near Los Angeles. The telephone companies purposely disabled long-distance telephone service into and out of the southern California area to allow for emergency communications. But this prevented many people from contacting and checking up on family and friends. For the most part, however, the local phone system remained in working order. Subscription e-mail is typically available to users through local phone service. So, in much the same way that ham radio operators often step to the fore after natural disasters, informal methods of sending and receiving messages and contacting family and friends via e-mail quickly and spontaneously developed. In the future, e-mail is expected to be able to handle audio and video messages as well.

ARTIFICIAL INTELLIGENCE

Artificial intelligence (AI) has the goal of developing computers and computer systems that can behave intelligently. Work in this area is derived from research in a variety of disciplines, including computer science, psychology, linguistics, mathematics, and engineering. Probably the most widely known application of artificial intelligence is in computer programs that play chess, some at or near the level of a grand master. But artificial intelligence applications go well beyond this. Two primary areas of research that have had some success in recent years are expert systems and robotics.

Expert Systems

An **expert system** is a knowledge-based information system. In other words, it is a computer-based system that contains and can use knowledge about a specific, relatively narrow, complex application. The knowledge the expert system contains and the way it is programmed to use this knowledge allow it to behave as an expert consultant to end users.

Expert system
A computer-based system that contains and can use knowledge about a specific, relatively narrow, complex application.

Fundamentally, an expert system is a type of software in which expert knowledge has been programmed to assist decision makers in a complex decision environment. The knowledge in an expert system has been painstakingly acquired from one or more experts in the knowledge domain of interest. Knowledge engineers, the expert system specialists, take this knowledge and carefully construct a knowledge base and the software that can use it. Users can then tap into this knowledge through the expert system and use it to provide expertise in difficult decision situations. Texas Instruments has developed an expert system called IEFCARES (Information Engineering Facility Customer Response Expert System) to assist in providing service and support for their CASE product called IEF. Like many other credit companies, both ITT Commercial Finance Corporation and American Express have expert systems to assist in managing and monitoring credit requests and approvals. Expert systems are also commonly used for tasks such as loan portfolio analysis, diagnostic troubleshooting, design and layout configuration, and process monitoring and control.[30]

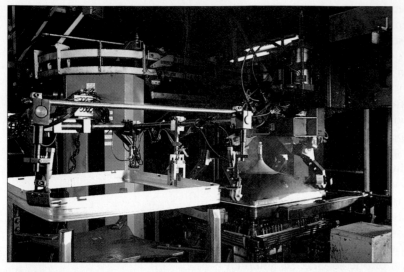

Robots are used extensively in manufacturing plants, offering significant benefits because they never tire or become ill, they're never absent, and they can work in areas and with tasks that are dangerous for humans.

© Kessler Photography

Robotics

Use of machines with humanlike characteristics, such as dexterity, movement, vision, and strength.

Robotics

The technology of building and using machines with humanlike characteristics, such as dexterity, movement, vision, and strength, is called **robotics.** A robot contains computer intelligence and uses research knowledge from AI, engineering, and physiology. Robots, often called "steel-collar" workers because they are used to perform manufacturing tasks that were previously performed by blue-collar workers, are programmed to do specific, repetitive tasks in exactly the same way each time. These automated machines offer significant benefits. They can be programmed to do very complex tasks that require a variety of movements and strength over and over again with precision. Robots don't have some of the faults of human workers, such as illness, fatigue, and absenteeism. In addition, robots can be very valuable in hazardous work areas and with tasks that are dangerous for humans.[31] Robots are being developed to dismantle nuclear power plants and to search for life on Mars. NASA has funded the Robotics Engineering Consortium, which is devoted to turning robotic ideas into practical machines. Some of its successful developments thus far include an excavator for Caterpillar, an off-road vehicle for Boeing, and a forklift system for Ford. An illustration of just how sophisticated these robots can be is provided by the computer-driven harvester being developed for New Holland North America. It uses the satellite-based Global Positioning System (GPS), wheel sensors, and a video camera to "see" a crop line so it can harvest a field without a driver or a remote operator.[32]

OFFICE AUTOMATION

One final area where information technology is having a major impact is in office automation. Systems for office automation are typically computer-based information systems that assist the organization in the processing, storage, collection, and transmission of electronic documents and messages among individuals, work groups, and organizations. Figure 18.5 shows the major categories of components in office automation systems. Many of these systems are important on their own merits, but when combined, they create an overall environment that supports all document and message processing.[33]

FIGURE 18.5

Components of office automation systems

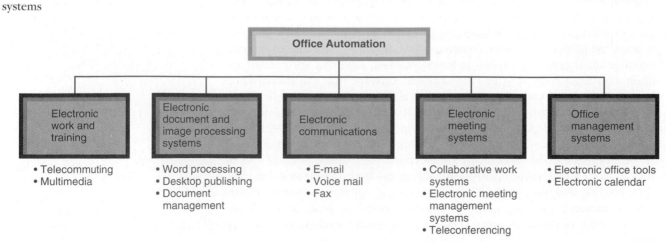

IMPACT OF INFORMATION TECHNOLOGY ON DYNAMIC ORGANIZATIONS

An organization is a sociotechnical system that consists of people and their tasks, as well as the organization's culture, structure, and environment. All of these things are affected by and will affect technology. Information technology will have a profound impact on management efficiency, social relationships, and organizational structure.

Information systems must produce useful and relevant information for management. Many of the areas that have been computerized have not yet resulted in the desired or expected gains. In part, this is because many organizations have used these new systems simply to replace traditional business practices instead of reassessing and redesigning the organization and the decision-making process to take advantage of the new technology's capabilities. Viewed another way, the primary, or first-order, effect of initial investments in information technology was simply to improve efficiency. Organizations still have a lot of room for improving the design and management of their information systems. Furthermore, we are discovering that the second-order effects, which are unintended and impossible to predict, are often more interesting and provide greater opportunities.[34] These unintended and unanticipated effects lead to a second area of impact.

If information systems were used only by isolated individuals, the systems would have minimal impact on the social relationships among people. Currently, however, the very essence of the use of information technology within organizations is to enhance communication between people. Therefore, whenever information systems are used in this manner, they have a social component and potential social effects.

For example, what are the new technologies doing to power relationships within the organization? Does the technology change the dimensions and directions of determining priorities? If the use of the technology has negative consequences, who is accountable for the results? And the expanding use and dependence on information technology have created an interesting paradox. Information technology, like globalization, can extend an organization, making it less personal and less social. Yet, the effect of the technology often rewards intimacy.[35] These social implications suggest other, broader effects of information technology.

In the early years of computer-based information systems, the technology was so limited that it was difficult to computerize even one division of the organization. As a result, data processing services tended to be decentralized. During the 1960s and 1970s, computer systems became much more powerful, and large systems were often able to handle many of the computing needs for the whole organization. This led to greater centralization of control over computer resources. The advent of the microcomputer in the late 1970s and the 1980s led to increased demands for computing access and power, creating a great deal of confusion and conflict within organizations as they struggled to manage the rapid proliferation of varieties of hardware and software.

Neither centralization nor decentralization alone is the appropriate response. Instead, organizations should examine their specific computing needs and try to align their information technology to those needs. Some aspects of information processing in an organization may require greater centralization of computing resources, while others may lend themselves to greater decentralization.

Many note that information technology can help managers control the interdependencies of their organizations. In particular, as the competitive environment has become more complex, so too have the information needs of the decision makers. Information technology can help managers respond to this

Because information systems enhance communication between people, they have a social component and an impact on the social relationships among people.

© Jeff Greenberg

competitive environment. For example, unlike the situation during the Industrial Revolution, when the goal was to simplify, routinize, and separate tasks, current trends in information technology and data communications are to flatten the organization, fuse departments, create cross-functional teams, and increase and improve communications among employees, suppliers, and customers.[36] The structure of the organization can then be adjusted to take advantage of the varying needs. But despite its great promise, information technology also has limitations. We turn to them in the next section.

LIMITATIONS OF COMPUTER-BASED INFORMATION SYSTEMS

As we have seen, although investments in computer-based information systems have been substantial, the improvements that can be directly traced to the investment in technology have been minimal. Several factors may explain this low return on investments in technology.

First, the technology has been changing so rapidly in the last ten years that organizations have had difficulty keeping up. In 1981 IBM produced its first microcomputer, marking for many the beginning of the rapid proliferation of computers in organizations and homes. Apple introduced its Macintosh system in 1984 as an easier-to-use alternative to the DOS (disk operating system) environment of IBM and IBM-compatible machines. In 1986 the Intel 386 microchip became the norm for microcomputer systems. Five years later the Intel 486 was released, and a few years later the Pentium microchip began to show up in microcomputers. And, in mid-1996, Microsoft Corporation unveiled its plans to introduce a microchip (code name Talisman) that will enable personal computers to display three-dimensional images at ultrahigh speed.[37] All of these versions of microchips and the microcomputers that use them have increased computing speed at a very low cost; they have also allowed larger and more sophisticated programs to be developed and have enabled almost all users to do types of computing that could be done only on mainframe computers just a few years ago. As computers have become more powerful, so have software programs. But this vast array of new hardware and software systems has made it difficult for organizations to maintain consistency throughout the organization. Furthermore, many people are reluctant to change their way of working to take full advantage of the capabilities of the technology.

MANAGERIAL IMPLICATIONS

Most organizations are only now coming to realize that the ways they incorporate technology into the workplace has a significant impact on their success or failure. A recent survey asked senior information system executives to name the ten issues that are most important for the management and organizational use of information technology as we move into the 21st century.[38] Their responses are listed in Table 18.2.

Successful managers of the future will be those who:

• Understand the importance of quality information that is obtained in a timely fashion.
• Employ information systems capable of providing quality information that is both timely and complete.
• Are able to use that information to their advantage in the organizational decision-making process.

TABLE 18.2   21st-century issues in the use of information technology

1. Information architecture—creating a high-level map of the information requirements of the organization.

2. Data resources—data are now viewed as the important factor of production.

3. Strategic planning—considered the most important issue of the 1980s, it involves the close alignment of technology with business plans.

4. Human resources—recognition of the limited number of information systems professionals available to develop and maintain increasingly technical and complex organizational computing environments.

5. Organizational learning—learning how to make appropriate use of information technology.

6. Technology infrastructure—a new issue for this survey, it involves building an infrastructure that will support current operations while remaining flexible enough to adapt to changing technology and evolving organizational needs.

7. Information system organization alignment—effectiveness of support for organizational activities and operations without constraining either the technology or the organization.

8. Competitive advantage—technology is no longer the sole arbiter of competitive advantage, but is becoming the necessary, but not sufficient condition. Competitive advantage comes from the proper role of information technology in streamlining internal business processes, forging electronic links with suppliers and customers, and shaping the organization's design.

9. Software development—developing new tools and techniques to facilitate the rapid and error-free development of needed software systems.

10. Telecommunications system planning—can be used to reduce structural, time, and spatial limits on organizational relationships.

- Are well versed in the latest technological innovations for information gathering, processing, and disseminating.
- Are aware of the impact of information technology on management efficiency, organizational social relationships, and organizational structure.
- Are aware of the limitations of computer-based information systems.

As we have seen throughout this chapter, the ultimate success or failure of information technology is not always immediately clear. Technology is not the solution for all organization problems, and technology will not, in and of itself, provide relief from poor organizational practices. The benefits that can be gained from technology are many. But the ultimate benefits from technology are the vast amounts of information that can be more easily processed and distributed. Management success—and, on a larger scale, organizational success—is still based primarily on the skills and insightful decisions of the managers. Still, it is up to the organization and its decision makers to take advantage of and properly use the information that becomes available.

NESTLÉ CORPORATION: GLOBAL INFORMATION SYSTEMS NEEDED FOR GLOBAL BUSINESS STRATEGY

Managerial Incident Resolution

Recognizing the problems presented by the inability of its nearly 300 companies to communicate with one another, Nestlé embarked upon a program to coordinate and standardize its information systems. Nestlé management had two main goals in mind with its focus on standardization. First, and foremost, standardization would promote communication between various units of the company. Furthermore, standardization would allow management at world headquarters in Vevey to communicate with each of its units and to monitor and control their activities, capabilities that were heretofore lacking. A second major goal of standardization was information system cost reduction. Manfred Kruger, assistant vice-president of management services in Vevey, felt that the development of information technology standards would prove to be cost-effective by building more efficient systems and eliminating redundancies. With an annual technology budget of about $340 million, there was plenty of room for information technology cost savings.

The Nestlé decision on information technology restructuring was to adopt an international client/server environment. Nestlé selected a package called R/3, an integrated software application developed by SAP A.G., Europe's largest vendor of IBM mainframe software and an emerging leader in software for client/server environments. The R/3 package includes integrated financial accounting, production planning, sales and distribution, cost-center accounting, order costing, materials management, human resources, quality assurance, fixed-assets management, plant maintenance, and project planning applications. In addition, R/3 provides word-processing, filing systems, e-mail, and other office support functions. The back-end server and front-end client portions of R/3 can run on a number of different operating systems and a wide range of computers. Since SAP has developed its programs in twelve languages, managers have the capability of generating reports in their local languages and currencies, and then having the same reports generated in the language and currency that are used as the corporate standards. These are just some of the aspects of the R/3 software that made it an attractive package to link Nestlé's global operations.

While several technical standards have already been adopted, standards are still being established in many other areas. Because of diversity in culture and customs throughout its worldwide empire, Nestlé has adopted a strategy of "a culture of working together," rather than stubbornly enforcing the same detailed standards to each of its units. To develop a core application, Nestlé gathers together a team representing different units. The team works to reach consensus on application requirements and development strategies. Once developed, the applications are sent to field organizations for adaptation to meet local needs. Nestlé has found that resistance at the local level is reduced when all key players have had a hand in the decision-making process.[39]

SUMMARY

- Data are the raw facts, details, or objective measures that represent some type of transaction or activity within an organization. Data processing is the process in which the data are aggregated and organized, manipulated through analysis, and placed in a proper context for evaluation and use by the end user. Information is the result of the process of transforming data into a meaningful form for a specific purpose.

- To facilitate good decision making, the people making decisions must have useful information. Useful information has three primary characteristics. The quality of the information produced and distributed to decision makers must be very high. The informa-

tion must be available in a timely fashion. Finally, the information must be complete in its scope.

- In general, the components of an information system consist of hardware, software, and data. The hardware consists of the input, processing, output, storage, and data transmission devices. The software consists of the various programs, which are the instructions that tell the hardware components what to do and how to do it. Data, which are often stored and maintained in a database, are the objective measures of an organization's activities.

- The development of an information system is a systematic process of examining and analyzing the current activities needed to maintain organizational operations. The systems design process involves several steps: (1) investigation, (2) systems analysis, (3) systems design, (4) systems implementation, and (5) systems maintenance. The systems development life cycle (SDLC) is a common model for how information systems evolve over time with an organization.

- Information technology has moved throughout the organization to assist at all levels of the organization. Information technology supports first-line managers in operational control activities; these include basic data processing activities such as payroll processing and general accounting. The mid-level functional aspects of managing an organization, such as routine, structured, and regularly required reports, are often processed using information technology. Even many strategic decisions and operations are now aided by technology, such as decision support systems (DSSs) and executive support systems (ESSs).

- Various types of information technology are changing the way we work. Telecommunications and networking are especially important. Electronic data interchange (EDI) and electronic funds transfer (EFT) are allowing organizations to establish and maintain business relationships without direct person-to-person contact. Telecommuting is allowing more workers to conduct business activities at home or on the road with the customer. Applications of artificial intelligence, such as expert systems and robotics, are enabling technology to do tasks that were previously done by workers. Office automation is creating a technology-supported office environment to assist in the management and processing of office work and information.

- Information technology will have an impact on management efficiency, social relationships, and the structure within an organization. Efficiency will improve only when the organization and the decision-making process are reassessed and redesigned to take advantage of the capabilities of the technology. When information systems are used to enhance communication between people in the organization, there is a social impact. Finally, as more aspects of an organization become integrated into the information system, more centralization of control over computer resources may occur.

- Among the limitations of information technology are (1) the difficulty in keeping up with technological advances, (2) the potentially high cost and time involved in changing technologies, and (3) the failure of many people to take advantage of the technology because of their reluctance to change the way they work.

KEY TERMS

Data
Information
Tangible costs
Intangible costs
End users
Computer-aided software
    engineering (CASE)
Systems development life cycle
    (SDLC)

Organizational feasibility
Economic feasibility
Technical feasibility
Operational feasibility
Management information system
    (MIS)
Decision support system (DSS)
Wide-area network (WAN)

Local-area network (LAN)
Electronic data interchange (EDI)
Electronic funds transfer (EFT)
Telecommuting
Expert system
Robotics

REVIEW QUESTIONS

1. How do data and information differ? Why is this distinction important?

2. Define and explain the characteristics of useful information.

3. What are the hardware and software components of an information system?

4. List and illustrate the steps in development of an information system. Is the process linear, or is it sometimes necessary to repeat previous steps? Explain.

5. List and briefly explain the various roles information technology can have in an organization.

6. What are four types of technology that are changing the way we work? What is the anticipated long-term effect of these technologies on the organization?

7. Identify and discuss the various effects information technology can have on an organization.

8. What are some of the limitations of information technology? Briefly discuss the causes and outcomes of each type of limitation.

DISCUSSION QUESTIONS

Improving Critical Thinking

1. Assume that the library at your school wishes to install an information system. Identify the major tasks necessary for each phase of a systems design process for the library. What difficulties in design and development might you expect to encounter in each phase?

2. Explain the concept of expert systems. If it is possible to capture the knowledge of an expert and place it in a expert system, one can argue that there is no longer a need for an expert. Furthermore, if the data are in a database, the knowledge of the expert becomes permanent. It can be transferred to different settings and even reproduced through copying processes. Can an expert system produce more consistent, reproducible results than the human expert on which it is based? Why or why not? Is it desirable to seek this result? Explain.

3. What can you do to ensure that you will have the technical knowledge and skills related to information technology that are necessary to compete effectively in the job market?

Enhancing Communication Skills

4. Examine the library at your school. What major types of activities must the library support as part of its mission? Which of these activities could be computerized? Can these various activities be integrated into one larger information system? Explain. Identify additional library functions that could be computerized. To enhance your oral communication skills,

prepare a short (10–15 minute) presentation of your answer for the class.

5. What news stories dealing with information technology have appeared in the news lately? What impact do you think these new technologies will have on organizations and management? To enhance your written communication skills, write a short (1–2 page) essay in which you discuss these impacts.

Building Teamwork

6. What do you think the office or organization of the future will be like? What technology do you think the office of the future will use? To refine your teamwork skills, meet with a small group of students who have been given this same assignment. Compare your visions of the office of the future, then reach a consensus about how this office will look. Select a spokesperson to present your team's vision to the rest of the class.

7. Identify several types of data that might be collected in an organization. Think about how the information that can be derived from the data would differ for each level of management. In other words, how might the various levels of management in the organization make different uses of the same basic data? To refine your teamwork skills, meet with a small group of students who have been given this same assignment. Compare your lists and then, by consensus, consolidate your lists into a single list of the best four types of data. Select a spokesperson to present your team's findings to the rest of the class.

INFORMATION TECHNOLOGY: Insights and Solutions

1. Use whatever search vehicle is most convenient (Internet, e-mail, fax, newspaper/magazine advertisements, and so on) to gather information on the technical specifications of the top three microcomputer models offered by the major name-brand computer companies. Prepare a spreadsheet that displays the information on the technical specifications for each model. Arrange that information in an orderly fashion so that potential computer shoppers could easily make model comparisons. Print a one-page spreadsheet comparison table and distribute it to your classmates for their review.

2. Use the Internet to research the Nestlé Corporation. Construct a list of as many of Nestlé's operating companies as you can locate. Compare your list with the lists of your classmates to determine who performed the most thorough search.

3. During a five-day school week, note each incident where you observe or encounter a device that might be construed to be a robot. These can be any machines or devices that are doing something, making something, or providing some service that a person might otherwise do. Organize your observations into meaningful categories and subcategories (for example, you might start with manufacturing, service, and government). Then use presentation software to display your findings to your classmates. Be prepared to defend your reasons for characterizing each device as a robot.

What kind of privacy rights do workers have? The rapid proliferation of information technology within many organizations is putting this question to the test.

Many organizations use electronic mail (e-mail) to communicate rapidly and easily among offices, suppliers, customers, and remote sites. Most of the computer systems that support e-mail automatically create archives of all messages that are sent. These archives are accessible to anyone with the administrative right to view the files or the technical skill to break into the system. Many organizations reserve the right to monitor the e-mail transmissions of their employees, telling new employees up front that the organization will be monitoring the employee's e-mail messages.

The privacy issues go well beyond monitoring e-mail messages. Employee activities can also be monitored and recorded by computer monitoring technology. For example, technology can allow a manager, even one who is miles away, to monitor employees' phone calls, read their e-mail messages, and even count the number of keystrokes an employee types in an hour or a day. The employee's activities provide a profile from which mangers, or the automated system, can draw inferences about employee performance and effectiveness.

Additional privacy issues revolve around electronically stored information concerning employees, customers, clients, and suppliers. One issue is what the company that owns that information can do with it. For example, in 1991 Lotus Development Corporation announced that it would publish and sell its Marketplace: Households compact disk. This database, which was to be updated quarterly, contained names, addresses, estimated incomes, and buying habits of 120 million Americans. After this announcement, more than 30,000 letters were sent to the firm in protest. Lotus stopped the product.

The Computer Professionals for Social Responsibility (CPSR) suggest that all companies should have a policy on privacy and should inform their employees and customers of the policy. The American Civil Liberties Union opposes companies reading an employee's electronic communications. Unfortunately, the laws dealing with these issues at both the federal and state levels are confusing, inconsistent, and badly out of date. Alan Westin, professor of public law and government at Columbia University, suggests: "The new office calls for us to redefine the reasonable expectations of privacy—what's fair and just to do."

For Discussion

1. Should organizations have the right to view an employee's e-mail messages without the employee's permission? Explain.

2. When might it be appropriate for an organization to examine an employee's e-mail messages without first receiving the employee's permission?

3. Justify the use of technology to monitor employee activities and productivity. What are the problems that can occur with this type of monitoring?

ROBOTICS—OPPORTUNITY OR THREAT TO BLUE-COLLAR WORKERS?

Form teams of four or five students as directed by your instructor. Research the topic of robotics in manufacturing, identifying aspects of their use that might be viewed as opportunities for blue-collar workers and aspects that might be viewed as threats. When it is time to debate this issue in front of the class, your instructor will tell your team which position (opportunity or threat) you will be assigned.

Video Case

CARR MATTSON ASSOCIATES

Home Page: **{http://www.mattsonassoc.com/}**

Carr Mattson Associates, established in 1986, provides staffing solutions to clients who use IBM mainframe and similar computers. The Edina, Minnesota, company's contract employees fill temporary vacancies, complete projects, help resident employees write computer programs, provide training in new computer technologies, and work in a variety of other computer-related capacities for client firms. The mission statement of the company provides a summary of its business philosophy:

> We want positive outcomes for our clients and our consultants. Carr Mattson and Associates is committed to making the best match possible for your organizational culture and your technical requirements for a position.

Although the company has remained true to its mission, in the early 1990s the firm went through a rough period. Two key people left the firm within a short time of one another, including one of the founders of Carr Mattson and the company's only salesperson. At roughly the same time, the economy turned sour, reducing the profitability of the firm, which resulted in employee pay cuts. These factors made Carr Mattson's bankers nervous and the company lost its financing. As a result, the remaining founder, Rhonda Mattson, had to finance the ongoing activities of the company by making a withdrawal from her personal IRA, borrowing on the cash value of her life insurance, and obtaining a loan from a relative. Fortunately, Rhonda Mattson had the resolve and business experience to take decisive steps. To compensate for the firm's financial stresses and win new clients, the company cut costs, made savvy personnel decisions, and formed an alliance with IBM and a foreign software firm. The alliance with IBM gave Carr Mattson the opportunity to provide technical consultants and employees to purchasers of IBM mainframe computers.

As a result of these initiatives, Carr Mattson is back on stride. To insure a proper match between the company and each of its clients, a comprehensive Needs Analysis/Organization Profile is completed for each potential customer. This profile, which includes information on each client's technical environment, corporate culture, organizational structure, products, work flow, and policies and procedures, is holistic in that it accesses the attitudes and expectations of each customer along with its technical needs.

Currently, Carr Mattson is growing at the rate of 30 percent per year. Its clients include not only many Fortune 500 companies but a variety of small and large companies located in the Minneapolis–St. Paul area. The company has won numerous awards from its customers. And Rhonda Mattson isn't borrowing against her life insurance any more. As a matter of fact, bankers are calling her.

For Discussion

1. Put yourself in the shoes of a potential customer of Carr Mattson. Discuss the pros and cons of hiring a company like Carr Mattson to pro-

vide skilled computer personnel, rather than building an internal staff that can handle all of your computer-related needs.

2. Is Carr Mattson's Needs Analysis/Organizational profile a good idea? What critical information does this profile provide Carr Mattson that may be instrumental in the staffing decisions that the company makes?

WCB ENTERPRISES

CASE

Lisa Fisher is in charge of marketing, sales, and purchasing for WCB Enterprises, a small company that manufactures a number of products that are sold primarily in retail stores. Lisa loves her job because of the variety and challenge involved. She is very good with people—customers, suppliers, and co-workers alike. As part of her job, Lisa has to travel to industry and sales conferences. These trips usually last no longer than two days, so she rarely falls more than a day or so behind company activities. This last trip, however, lasted a week because of a business-related side trip. On her return, Lisa found that she was facing more problems than usual.

Late this past Thursday, after Lisa left for her trip, one of the primary suppliers for WCB lost its main manufacturing facility due to a fire. Lisa did not find out about this until very late on Friday evening while she was still traveling. This past Monday, while making a sales call, Lisa heard on the radio that one of WCB's other suppliers had just shut down because of a strike. Other unions were honoring the strike, so deliveries from the supplier had essentially stopped.

Today, a Thursday, was Lisa's first day back in the office. Usually, after a trip of this length, Lisa would find a few phone messages and some correspondence to catch up on. This time, however, she found a stack of phone messages from concerned customers that had accumulated while she was gone. WCB, a relatively small operation, had never really faced a crisis before. WCB had only an informal answering service, with no specific mechanism for relaying phone messages to employees away from the office; thus, its procedures were not well organized for communicating with an employee who was out of town.

Lisa spent the whole morning trying to respond to the phone messages. In many cases, she had to contact others at WCB to find out about supplies, shipping, and so forth. Sometimes she was successful in reaching her co-workers; other times no one answered. To compound her problems, Lisa realized that WCB was heading into its busiest time of the year—the months leading up to Christmas, the busiest time of the year for retailers.

As Lisa picked up the phone once again, she realized that she really had very little information at her disposal. She was good at her job, but because of her absence from the office for a business trip, she was behind on her information. The problems of the suppliers made the situation even worse. Lisa realized that she would have to obtain a great deal of information from others before she would be able to respond to the ques-

tions of her callers and of those who would call in the coming days. She could solve this problem, but she wanted to make sure it never happened again. Before leaving late Thursday night, she made a note to herself to encourage WCB to reexamine its system of providing information within the company.

For Discussion

1. What problems did Lisa have in getting the information she needed to make decisions and answer questions from customers? What, if anything, do you think Lisa could have done to avoid these problems?

2. How could information technology be used to support Lisa in her job? How would your suggestions affect her relationships with her customers? Her suppliers? Her co-workers?

3. If you were Lisa, what kind of approach would you make to your superiors to help them understand your need for better technology support? What would you ask for?

EXPERIENTIAL EXERCISE 18.1

What Technology Do You Need?

The purpose of this exercise is to explore the variety of options available to support you as a traveling businessperson.

Step 1 Assume you are a mid-level manager for a moderate-sized organization. A significant portion of your job is to travel to meet with clients. You travel more than 100,000 miles a year, with trips ranging from a day to ten to fourteen days for important contracts. Since your office is on the road as much as it is at headquarters, you need to be able to accomplish your job while traveling.

Step 2 Your task is to identify your hardware and software needs. Then investigate your options as if you were really going to purchase the required equipment. Remember that system compatibility and reliability are important. In addition, remember that you will be carrying this equipment with you along with your luggage. Therefore, weight is also an important factor. You may also be using this equipment to assist you in presentations to potential clients and current customers. Therefore, a quality system display is also a factor to consider.

Step 3 Discuss your conclusion with others in your class.

For Discussion

1. What kind of trade-offs did you find yourself making in order to make your final selection of hardware and software? What hardware and software did you select?

2. What assumptions did you make about your job in the initial stages of working on this situation? What additional information would have been useful?

3. What maximum weight and cost limits, if any, did you use?

4. How did your decisions differ from those of others?

EXPERIENTIAL EXERCISE 18.2

Learning about E-Mail

If you have not done so before this time, see if you can acquire an account on your school's computer. Once this has been accomplished, learn about and try to use the e-mail system. With several of your classmates, explore the benefits, limitations, and difficulties of working via e-mail.

Step 1 Acquire a computer account and learn how to use the e-mail facility.

Step 2 Conduct a discussion/debate with several of your classmates using the e-mail facilities. As the discussion progresses, be aware of the problems of using e-mail to communicate about and coordinate activities. Keep a list of your comments and observations.

Step 3 Discuss how e-mail can enhance and limit organizational communication. Develop a list of suggestions for an organization that is attempting to use e-mail to improve organizational effectiveness.

For Discussion

1. How difficult was it to become comfortable with e-mail?

2. How effective was e-mail in supporting your discussion? What were the benefits? What were the limiting factors?

ENDNOTES

1. Based on J. Greenbaum, "Nestlé's Global Mix," *Information Week,* April 25, 1994, 18–21; J. Greenbaum, "Nestlé Makes the Very Best . . . Standard?" *Information Week,* August 23, 1993, 15–19; R. Cafasso, "SAP American Plans Improvements for R/3 Package," *Computer World,* June 6, 1994, 65–66; D. Bartholomew, "SAP Goes One Further," *Information Week,* October 31, 1994, 22–23; C. Rappaport, "Nestlé's Brand Building Machine," *Fortune,* September 19, 1994, 147–51.

2. "Information Technology Special Report," *Fortune,* Autumn 1993, 15.

3. "Welcome to the Revolution," *Fortune,* December 13, 1993, 66–78.

4. Based on J. Moad, "Can High Performance Be Cloned? Should It Be?" *Datamation,* March 1, 1995; L. Wilson, "Stand and Deliver," *Information Week,* November 23, 1992.

5. L. M. Grossman, "Federal Express, UPS Face Off on Computers," *The Wall Street Journal,* September 17, 1993, B1*ff*; "Blueprints for Service Quality: Federal Express Approach," *AMA Management Briefing,* American Management Association, New York, 1991.

6. "Can Bell Atlantic and TCI Pull It Off?" *Business Communications Review,* 23, November 1993, 8–10; "Bell-Ringer," *Business Week,* October 25, 1993, 32–36.

7. "Dynacorp Takes High-Tech to Mail-Carrying Business," *Central Penn Business Journal,* April 4, 1994.

8. J. L. Whitten, L. D. Bentley, and V. M. Barlow, *Systems Analysis and Design Methods,* 2d ed. (Homewood, Ill.: Irwin, 1989).

9. E. W. Martin, D. DeHayes, J. Hoffer, and W. Perkins, *Managing Information Technology: What Managers Need to Know* (New York: Macmillan, 1991), 299.

10. R. J. Benjamin, *Control of the Information Systems Development Cycle* (New York: Wiley-Interscience, 1971.)

11. D. Amoroso and P. Cheney, "Testing a Causal Model of End User Applications Effectiveness," *Journal of Management Information Systems,* Summer 1991; K. Christoff, *Managing the Information Center* (Glenview, Ill.: Scott Foresman/Little, Brown, 1990.)

12. J. A. O'Brien, *Management Information Systems: A Managerial End User Perspective,* 2d ed. (Homewood, Ill.: Irwin, 1993.)

13. R. R. Panko, *End User Computing: Management, Applications, and Technology* (New York: Wiley, 1988).

14. L. Fried, "A Blueprint for Change," *Computerworld,* December 2, 1991, 91–93.

15. H. R. Shrednick, R. J. Shutt, and M. Weiss, "Empowerment: Key to IS World-Class Quality," *MIS Quarterly,* 16, 1992, 491–505.

16. E. Turban, *Decision Support and Expert Systems: Management Support Systems,* 3d ed. (New York: Macmillan, 1993).

17. S. Cosares, "SONET Toolkit: A Decision Support System for Designing Robust and Cost- Effective Fiber-Optic Networks," *Interfaces,* 25, January-February 1995, 20.

18. J. Rockart and D. DeLong, *Executive Support Systems: The Emergence of Top Management Computer Use* (Homewood, Ill.: Dow Jones–Irwin, 1988).

19. Based on R. Burnett, "More 'Geeks' Braving Business World," *Orlando Sentinel,* September 1, 1996, H1*ff*; J. Kilsheimer, "Teenagers Spin Web into Cash, Business," *Orlando Sentinel,* September 18, 1996, B1*ff*; "Gates Gets 26% Raise," *Orlando Sentinel,* September 28, 1996, C1.

20. "Welcome to the Revolution."

21. "Microsoft to Blend Desktop Computing, Global Networking," *Orlando Sentinel,* July 22, 1996, B5.

22. W. Stallings and R. Van Slyke, *Business Data Communications,* 2d ed. (New York: Macmillan, 1994).

23. "The Strategic Value of EDI," *I/S Analyzer,* August 1989.

24. S. Sherman, "How to Bolster the Bottom Line," in "Information Technology Special Report," *Fortune,* Autumn 1993, 15–28.

25. "Welcome to the Revolution."

26. Based on S. N. Mehta, "On-Line Service Offers Fast Lane to Small Businesses," *The Wall Street Journal,* October 11, 1994, B2; T. L. O'Brien, "Entrepreneurs Raise Funds Through On-Line Computer Services," *The Wall Street Journal,* June 2, 1994, B1–2; L. Radosevich, "United Nations Launches Worldwide Network," *Computerworld,* October 24, 1994, 64.

27. "Information Technology Special Report."

28. "The Race to Rewire," *Fortune,* April 19, 1993, 42–61.

29. "Buildings, Roads Fall in Tremblers Onslaught," *Orlando Sentinel,* January 18, 1994, A1*ff*.

30. E. Turban, *Decision Support and Expert Systems.*

31. J. A. O'Brien, *Management Information Systems.*

32. "Center Devoted to Robotic Revolution," *Orlando Sentinel,* August 21, 1996, B1*ff*.

33. Ibid.

34. "Welcome to the Revolution."

35. D. Schuler, "Social Computing," *Communications of the ACM,* Special Issue, January 1994, 28-29.

36. "Welcome to the Revolution."

37. D. Clark, "Microsoft Will Describe Chip Project to Upgrade PCs," *The Wall Street Journal,* August 6, 1996, B4.

38. F. Niederman, J. C. Brancheau, and J. C. Wetherbe, "Information Systems Management Issues for the 1990s," *MIS Quarterly,* December, 1991, 475-500.

39. Based on J. Greenbaum, "Nestlé's Global Mix"; J. Greenbaum, "Nestlé Makes the Very Best . . . Standard?"; R. Cafasso, "SAP American Plans Improvements for R/3 Package"; D. Bartholomew, "SAP Goes One Further"; C. Rappaport, "Nestlé's Brand Building Machine."

IBAX: A NEW BEGINNING

When Jeff Goodman joined IBAX in 1991, the future of the organization looked very bleak. The company had lost millions of dollars, product quality was poor, customer satisfaction was devastatingly low, and employee commitment was nonexistent. But by the close of 1993, things had changed—dramatically. The company posted a profit of $2.1 million and financial projections for 1994 were favorable; product quality and customer service were greatly enhanced; productivity had been improved significantly; and the employees of IBAX were dedicated to making it a profitable and prosperous organization. What happened to cause such a turnaround? Many say it was strong leadership and a focus on using contemporary management practices to achieve success.

When Goodman and the IBAX partners (IBM and Baxter) realized that the company was no longer in danger of total collapse, they turned their attention to the long-term future. The company, though successful, was only the sixth largest player in an industry where economies of size and scope are critical. Consequently, IBAX appeared to have only two choices—become a larger company through the acquisition of competitors in the industry or be acquired by a bigger company that was large enough to compete effectively within the industry.

After much deliberation, it was determined that IBAX would be more successful as part of a larger organization. On June 1, 1994, IBAX was acquired by HBOC, an Atlanta-based company that is the market leader in the health care information systems industry. Although HBOC would not have been interested in acquiring IBAX in 1991, the company had become an attractive acquisition candidate by 1993. Goodman met his management challenge—he turned IBAX into a viable and prosperous organization.

APPENDIX

Career Development and Management

This appendix is designed to provide an overview of some important issues for you to consider as you begin thinking about entering a profession and developing plans for your lifetime of employment. Career development and management can help you take a proactive approach to planning and managing your career and can also help managers and organizations understand the experiences of their employees.

Since your job will be a major part of your life, you need to like what you are doing. According to Malcolm Forbes, former publisher of *Forbes* magazine, the foremost quality in selecting a career is to really love what you are doing. If you love it, you will do it well.[1]

But what exactly is meant by a career? We will suggest some answers and then examine the traditional career stages approach to career development and management. It is also possible to take alternative approaches to careers, and we will explore some of these before discussing a few current career management strategies. Finally, we conclude with some tactics and advice on achieving career success.

WHAT IS A CAREER?

A **career** is the individually perceived sequence of attitudes and behaviors associated with work-related experiences, activities, and positions over the span of a person's life.[2] As such, a career involves movement within an organization (such as moving up the organizational ladder) and between organizations, as well as the attitudes and behaviors that are associated with ongoing work-related activities and experiences. People build careers by moving among various jobs in different fields and organizations.

CAREER STAGES

The traditional and most common way to discuss career development and management is to view a career as a series of stages as shown in Figure 1. Regardless of the type of work or occupation, individuals typically move through four distinct career stages during their working lives: exploration and testing, establishment and advancement, maintenance, and withdrawal.[3]

EXPLORATION AND TESTING

The exploration and testing stage usually corresponds to the early years of an individual's career. During this period, the individual explores talents, interests, and values; tries to find a good fit or match between career and self-image;

FIGURE 1
Career Stages

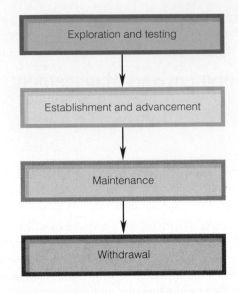

makes an initial choice of an occupation; and attempts to become established. Once the individual joins an organization, the orientation and socialization process by the organization and his or her peers is extremely important. **Socialization** is the process by which the newcomer is transformed from an outsider into an effective member of the organization.[4] For example, most organizations conduct an orientation program that introduces the new employee to the requirements of the job, the social environment in which he or she will work, and the organization's policies, rules, and procedures, as well as to key individuals, norms, and culture. Though orientation programs vary widely depending on the organization, the process itself is vital at this career stage.

During this career stage, the individual is often expected to follow directions and to play the role of a helper or a learner. A good supervisor provides a coaching relationship, feedback, guidance, and opportunities that will increase levels of understanding.

ESTABLISHMENT AND ADVANCEMENT

During the establishment and advancement stage, the individual first establishes career goals and strives to achieve them and then is heavily oriented toward building a record of significant accomplishments that relate to success.[5] The individual depends on her or his supervisor to provide challenging assignments and furnish feedback about performance. Many individuals begin to form a specific career strategy in this stage and ideally will find a mentor to assist them. They are likely to be involved in special assignments, transfers, and promotions and to become more visible to higher management. They often become specialized, develop an expertise in one area, acquire professional standing, and take on greater organizational responsibilities. Key relationships are now with peers and peer groups. The major personal issue at this time is the conflict that may develop between the career and the individual's personal life—spouse, family, and other nonwork interests.

MAINTENANCE

Movement into the maintenance stage is often associated with professional accomplishments, progress up the organizational hierarchy, high involvement in the job, and the responsibility for training and directing others. This is also a time when most managers review their careers and may become concerned because they have not achieved all the personal and work goals they had planned. They may reaffirm or modify earlier career goals and attempt to cope with unfulfilled dreams, a sense of lost youth, or prospects of mortality. For other managers, this stage is a time for finding ways to continue growing rather than stagnating or allowing their skills to become obsolete.

WITHDRAWAL

The main tasks during the withdrawal stage involve remaining a productive contributor with a strong sense of self-worth, developing and training possible successors, and completing major long-term projects and assignments. Supervisors should provide a lot of freedom and autonomy to complete these tasks. An individual in this career stage must develop a self-image that does not include work and is based on his or her life and activities outside work.

These four stages are simply general guidelines to the major career phases that individuals are likely to encounter. It is important to note that individuals pass through these stages at various ages. Rather than comprising a rigid progression, the stages simply provide some basic notions about the ways careers are likely to unfold and the means by which individuals address career issues at different stages in their lives.[6]

Individuals may make major changes in direction during the course of their careers and revert to earlier stages as they pursue alternative goals, accept new jobs, join other organizations, and progress through adult developmental stages that provide unique challenges. Because work and personal life are inseparable, a person's career experiences cannot be understood without also examining her or his personal experiences.[7]

CAREER SUCCESS

Career success is subjective because ultimately it is the individual who must decide whether he or she has been successful. Though success sometimes is framed in terms of advancement, career specialists increasingly emphasize that individuals should establish their own criteria for success and that those criteria can be as diverse as pay, adventure, challenges, or helping others.

In recent years, relatively slow growth in the economy has combined with the large number of baby boomers entering mid-career to limit severely the opportunities for promotion into upper-level management. As a result, success, which formerly was based solely on upward mobility in the organization, has been redefined. Four alternative career concepts that serve as models for the "ideal career" have been identified:[8]

1. *Linear career:* An individual decides on a field early in life, develops a plan for upward mobility, and executes it. The linear career is often linked to a need for achievement and power.

2. *Steady-state career:* An individual selects a specific field of work and may continue to improve professionally and financially within that field. The steady-state career-driven person does not necessarily strive to move up the corporate hierarchy, but may remain at the same level of the organization indefinitely. This career concept is motivated by a need for security and the desire to maintain a role in society.

3. *Spiral career:* An individual views a career as a series of infrequent but major shifts into different fields of work. Within each occupation the person works hard and excels in status and rank before moving on to new

opportunities and challenges. Individuals are motivated by a need for personal growth.

4. *Transitory career:* The individual explores alternatives while seeking to find a career identity. Transitory career individuals are often troubleshooters who are driven by the novelty and challenge of problem solving. These individuals are motivated by a need for independence and identity and often drift from one occupation to another with no particular pattern.

STRATEGIES FOR CAREER MANAGEMENT

Career management is a lifelong process of learning about yourself as well as about various jobs and organizations. Career management involves setting personal goals, developing strategies for achieving goals, and revising goals based on work and life experiences.[9] Most career experts suggest that individuals are primarily responsible for their own career management. One of the most important trends in American society is the new determination of many people to control their own career destinies and take full responsibility for their careers.[10]

Nevertheless, organizations also need to be involved in career management. Why would an organization be interested in careers or spend time on the career management of its employees? Effective career management results in a long-term fit between the individual and the organization. As we observed earlier, an individual's career is a process or sequence of work-related experiences. The organization has an important stake in the individual's career process, and its needs must be matched with the employee's needs and career goals. To the extent that the matching is done well, the organization is more effective and productive, and the individual is better satisfied, happier, and more successful.

Individuals can engage in career development and management on their own or in conjunction with career development programs sponsored by their organizations. Most organizations use informal career planning by human resource staff members. Career counseling may be a useful addition to an individual's efforts.

Significant reductions in the layers of middle management, restructuring, and rightsizing are common trends in many organizations. As a consequence, many individuals have been thrown off their career tracks. With more people competing for fewer promotions, individuals are likely to find themselves plateaued, at least periodically. A **career plateau** is a point in an individual's career where the likelihood of future promotion to a higher-level position is very low. Many professionals are attempting to overcome plateaus by: (1) using career counseling, (2) developing a strong network of other professionals, (3) becoming adaptable and less specialized, and (4) learning to be a team player.[11]

USING CAREER COUNSELING

Using personality and aptitude tests, career counselors help clients assess their skills and character traits. These are combined into a vocational profile that is matched with job options. Next, counselors help their clients target a field or job and determine how to transfer their skills, based on how much risk they can accept. The final step is a plan of action to get a new job. If the client does not want to change companies or professions, a counselor may recommend creating a special project to enhance the individual's value to the company or networking with other departments to make a lateral move.

Career counselors may charge $50 to $150 an hour and usually recommend 4 to 10 sessions. Some specialize in a field such as business or law, most counselors handle a broad range of professions. You can find career counselors through the yellow pages, personal contacts, university continuing education programs, or the National Association for Career Development.

DEVELOP A STRONG PROFESSIONAL NETWORK

Networking is a determined effort to meet other professionals with the goal of building a valuable resource of professional experience, knowledge, and friendship.[12] It involves developing collegial relationships with others because you need to know them and they need to know you. Networking can be described as congeniality at work. Successful professionals develop and nurture active friendships with a large and varied group of professionals. They make it a point to maintain periodic contact with each other and to share information.

Networking is most often conducted by telephone, fax, and computer networks. It is a two-way professional friendship that is focused on an exchange of ideas, new information, and new contacts. It is being genuinely interested in what others do and know.

Professional networks are vast interconnections that provide a huge intellectual resource. They are assets that provide access to talent, skills, experiences, innovations, and progressive action.

Most professionals devote a large portion of their workday to interacting with coworkers and a broad spectrum of other people. Every active professional has compiled a substantial list of phone numbers. Each of these phone numbers represents access to a potential networkee—a prospective adjunct to your network.

Building a network is a valuable and necessary strategy in career management. The following points may help you build your own network:[13]

- Join national organizations in your field and related areas. Become active in local and national organizations by attending meetings and conferences. Join committees, volunteer, and get involved.

- When you attend meetings, go up to people and introduce yourself. Show an interest in them and what they do.

- Exchange business cards with everyone you meet.

- Ask questions and learn to be an effective listener. Reinforce discussions and questions with your comments, opinions, and related experience.

- Develop strong relationships within your own company. Walk around and talk to people at their work stations. Show interest in their work. Be friendly, assertive, and congenial.

- Keep notes on the people you meet and talk to on the phone to remind you of the encounter.

As you build your professional network contacts, look down as well as up. Offering to help less powerful people is a highly effective career management and advancement strategy.

BECOME ADAPTABLE AND LESS SPECIALIZED

According to a recent article in *Fortune,* workers will be rewarded in the future for knowledge and adaptability. That notion translates to less emphasis on career specialization and more on generalization. A key career management strategy is to be flexible and willing to move from one function to another by integrating diverse disciplines and perspectives. Individuals who can operate comfortably in a variety of environments will fare better than those locked into the mind-set of a particular corporate or even national culture. People will need the ability not only to learn fundamental new skills but also to unlearn outdated ways.

LEARN TO BE A TEAM PLAYER

With teamwork predicted to become a dominant form of organizational design, a critical career management strategy is to learn to become an effective team player. Team designs require managers to share more power with people they once regarded as subordinates, and employees of lower rank are now experiencing increased responsibility. This means people skills have become extremely important, and even leaders will have to learn how to follow. As the paired forces of globalization and information technology increase the likelihood that teams will be working together across great distances, strong interpersonal and team player skills will be in demand.

TACTICS FOR CAREER SUCCESS

Regardless of how a career is defined, the following five tactics have been identified as important for career success:[14]

1. *Do excellent work.* High-quality performance and excellent work are the basics of a successful career. Though political savvy can sometimes give an average performer an advantage, politics can backfire. As a rule, the better the work, the greater are the chances of being promoted and given greater authority and responsibility.

2. *Increase your visibility.* To be rewarded for your performance, you have to be sure your superiors know about it. Some specific strategies for becoming visible are listed in Table 1. You can increase your visibility by taking or seeking a job with high visibility. A visible job has these characteristics:

   - Few rules and regulations.
   - Many rewards for unusual and/or innovative performance.
   - Many contacts with senior management; opportunities for participation in conferences and problem-solving task forces.
   - Relationships that cross departmental lines.

3. *Be mobile.* Mobility includes being flexible as well as being prepared to move. Experience in different functional departments (accounting, marketing, production, engineering, human resources) will help you develop a variety of skills needed to become a general manager. Take on new jobs

---

TABLE 1   Strategies for being visible

1. Send memos to your superiors when projects have been completed.
2. Submit periodic progress reports.
3. Actively solicit and use feedback.
4. Get assigned to special high-impact projects and task forces.
5. Pay honest compliments to people.
6. Volunteer for a variety of assignments.

or tasks and work with a variety of people. Experience at different geographical locations within the company can lead to an understanding of the organization as a whole and may attract the attention of top management. Keep in mind that mobility usually has some costs, especially personal ones.

4. *Find a mentor.* A higher-level manager can be a powerful mentor. Most successful managers have had several mentors and have learned valuable lessons from each. Having more than one mentor also minimizes the danger that you will be identified too closely with a single mentor. Keep in mind that having a single mentor is one reason why some executives fail to advance. Having a variety of mentors can help you learn how to motivate various types of people and develop a sensitivity to their needs. Notably, managers most often learn what *not* to do from their mentors.

5. *Avoid deadwood.* Incompetent supervisors can hinder a career because they may not appreciate your abilities. Furthermore, their recommendations will not be taken seriously, because they themselves have been bypassed. Asking for a transfer to escape deadwood can be ineffective in some companies because it is considered a sign of disloyalty. A better method is to make sure a superior in another department knows of your work and availability and let that manager arrange the transfer.

Developing a successful career doesn't happen by accident. It takes planning and hard work to become a successful professional. Those who are willing to put forth the effort needed to develop their careers will be the successful managers of the future.

NOTES

1. For more specific information about how to choose the career that is right for you, see R. N. Bolles, *What Color Is Your Parachute?* (Berkeley, Calif.: Ten Speed Press, 1993); and C. Carter, *Majoring in the Rest of Your Life* (New York: Noonday Press, 1992).

2. D. T. Hall, *Careers in Organizations* (Santa Monica, Calif.: Goodyear, 1976).

3. D. E. Super and D. T. Hall, "Career Development: Exploration and Planning," in M. R. Rosenzweig and L. W. Porter, eds., *Annual Review of Psychology, 29* (Palo Alto, Calif.: Annual Reviews, 1978); and D. T. Hall and Associates, *Career Development in Organizations* (San Francisco: Jossey-Bass, 1986).

4. D. C. Feldman, "The Multiple Socialization of Organizational Members," *Academy of Management Review* 6 (1981): 309–18.

5. J. Zahrly and H. Tosi, "The Differential Effect of Organizational Induction Process on Early Work Role Adjustment," *Journal of Organizational Behavior* 10 (1989): 59–74.

6. L. Baird and K. Kram, "Career Dynamics: Managing the Superior/Subordinate Relationship," *Organizational Dynamics* 11 (1983): 3–13.

7. For more specific information about the relationship between stages of adult development and career issues, see the variety of books and articles of D. J. Levinson and G. Sheehy.

8. M. J. Driver, "Career Concepts and Career Management in Organizations," in C. L. Cooper, ed., *Behavioral Problems in Organizations* (Englewood Cliffs, N.J.: Prentice-Hall, 1979).

9. J. H. Greenhaus, *Career Management* (Hinsdale, Ill.: CBS College Press, 1987).

10. S. Sherman, "A Brave New Darwinian Workplace," *Fortune,* January 25, 1993, 50–56.

11. "Getting Ahead: Jump-Starts for Stalled Careers," *Business Weekly,* July 1, 1992, 92; and Sherman, "A Brave New Darwinian Workplace."

12. W. E. Baker, *Networking Smart, How to Build Relationships for Personal and Organizational Success* (New York: McGraw-Hill, 1994).

13. A. Barber, and L. Waymon, *Great Connections: Small Talk and Networking for Business People* (New York: Impact Publications, 1992); L. Harrisberger, *Succeeding: How to Become an Outstanding Professional* (New York: Macmillan, 1994); O. Edwards, *Upward Nobility: How to Rise High in Business without Losing Your Soul* (New York: Crown Publishing, 1994); and Baker, *Networking Smart.*

14. K. C. Green and D. T. Seymour, *Who's Going to Run General Motors?* (Princeton, N.J.: Peterson's Guides, 1991).

GLOSSARY

Accountability   Employees must justify their decisions and actions with regard to the task they have been assigned.

Achievement-oriented leadership   Setting challenging goals, seeking performance improvements, emphasizing excellence in performance, and showing confidence.

Activity ratios   Indicators of performance with respect to key activities defined by management.

Adaptive organization (horizontal corporation)   An organization that eliminates bureaucracy that limits employee creativity and brings the decision makers of the organization closer to the customer.

Administrative management   Focuses on the managers and the functions they perform.

Affiliation needs   The desire for friendship, love, and a feeling of belonging.

Aggregate planning   Link between the more general business planning activities and the more specific master planning activities.

Alternative courses of action   Strategies that might be implemented in a decision-making situation.

Artifacts   Cultural routines that form the substance of public functions and events staged by the organization.

Assessment center   A controlled environment used to predict the probable success of job applicants based on their behaviors in simulated situations.

Assets   The things of value that an individual or organization owns.

Attitudes   Relatively lasting beliefs, feelings, and behavioral tendencies held by a person about specific objects, events, groups, issues, or people.

Authority   The formal right of an employee to marshal resources and make decisions necessary to fulfill work responsibilities.

Autonomy   The degree to which job holders have freedom, independence, and decision-making authority.

Balance sheet   Summary of an organization's financial position at a given point in time, showing assets, liabilities, and owner's equity.

BCG matrix   Business portfolio matrix that uses market growth rate and relative market share as the indicators of the firm's strategic position.

Behavior modification   An application of reinforcement theory that managers can use to motivate employees.

Behavioral approach   What the leader does is the primary variable that determines effectiveness.

Behavioral decision model   A descriptive framework for understanding that a person's cognitive ability to process information is limited.

Boundary-spanning roles   Lateral relationships that help to integrate and coordinate the activities of the organization (that is, liaisons, committees, task forces, integrating positions, and interfunctional work teams).

Bounded rationality   Recognizes that people are limited by such organizational constraints as time, information, resources, and their own mental capacities.

Brainstorming   A technique used to enhance creativity that encourages group members to generate as many novel ideas as possible on a given topic without evaluating them.

Breakeven analysis   A graphic display of the relationship between volume of output, revenue, and costs.

Budgets   Single-use plans that specify how financial resources should be allocated.

Bureaucratic control   Use of formal mechanisms to influence behavior, assess performance, and correct unacceptable deviations from standards.

Bureaucratic management   Focuses on the overall organizational system.

Business ethics   The application of general ethics to business behavior.

Business portfolio matrix   A two-dimensional grid that compares the strategic positions of each of the organization's businesses.

Business strategy   Defines how each business unit in the firm's corporate portfolio will operate in its market arena.

Cash cows   Businesses that fall into the low market growth/high market share cell of a BCG matrix.

Chain of command   The line of authority and responsibility that flows throughout the organization.

Changing   The second step in the change process, focusing on learning new required behaviors.

Charismatic authority   Subordinates voluntarily comply with a leader because of her special personal qualities or abilities.

Classical perspective   Comprising the oldest formal viewpoints of management, it includes the scientific management approach, the administrative management approach, and the bureaucratic management approach.

Closed systems   Systems that do not interact with the environment.

Code of ethics   The general value system, principles, and specific rules that a company follows.

Coercive power   The power to discipline, punish, and withhold rewards.

Cohesiveness   The strength of the members' desires to remain in the group.

Communication   A process in which one person or group transmits some type of information to another person or group.

Communication network   A pattern of information flow among task group members.

Compensation   Wages paid directly for time worked (base pay), incentives for better performance, and indirect benefits that employees receive as part of their employment relationship with the organization.

Competitive advantage   Any aspect of an organization that distinguishes it from its competitors in a positive way.

Computer-aided software engineering (CASE) Tools that allow system developers to create prototype screens and report generators rapidly and easily.

Conceptual skills The ability to analyze complex situations and respond effectively to the challenges faced by the organization.

Concurrent control Focuses on the transformation process to ensure that it is functioning properly.

Constraints Algebraic statements, in equation form, that reflect any restrictions on the decision maker's flexibility in making decision choices.

Contingency approaches The assumption that leadership can be learned and that leaders adapt to the varying situational factors in order to be effective.

Contingency perspective A view that proposes that there is no one best approach to management for all situations.

Contingency planning Development of two or more plans based on different strategic operating conditions.

Continuous-flow production system Produces a high volume of output that flows in a continuous stream.

Continuous schedule of reinforcement Rewarding a desired behavior each time it occurs.

Controlling Monitoring the performance of the organization, identifying deviations between planned and actual results, and taking corrective action when necessary.

Controls The mechanisms used to monitor the organization's performance relative to its goals and plans.

Corporate social responsibility The interaction between business and the social environment in which it exists.

Corporate strategy Decisions and actions that define the portfolio of business units that an organization maintains.

Cost leadership strategy A strategy for competing on the basis of price.

Current assets Items that can be converted into cash in a short time period.

Current liabilities Debts that must be paid in the near future.

Customer divisional structure A structure in which the tasks of the organization are grouped according to customer segments.

Data Raw facts or details that represent some type of transaction or activity within an organization.

Debt ratios Indicators of the firm's ability to handle long-term debt.

Decision making The process through which managers identify and resolve problems and capitalize on opportunities.

Decision support system (DSS) Focuses on assisting decision makers in analyzing and solving semistructured problems.

Decision tree A branching diagram that illustrates the alternatives and states of nature for a decision situation.

Decision variables The factors that the decision maker can manipulate.

Decisional roles The manager's responsibility for processing information and reaching conclusions.

Decoding The translation of received messages into interpreted meanings.

Delegation The process of transferring the responsibility for a specific activity or task to another member of the organization and empowering that individual to accomplish the task effectively.

Delphi technique Uses experts to make predictions and forecasts about future events without meeting face to face.

Devil's advocacy An individual or subgroup is appointed to critique a proposed course of action and identify problems to consider before the decision is final.

Dialectical inquiry Approaches a decision from two opposite points and structures a debate between conflicting views.

Differentiation strategy A strategy for competing by offering products or services that are differentiated from those of competitors.

Directive leadership Letting subordinates know what they are expected to do, giving specific guidance, asking subordinates to follow rules and procedures, and scheduling and coordinating work.

Diversity The heterogeneity of the work force in terms of gender, race, nationality, and ethnicity.

Divisional structure Members of the organization are grouped on the basis of common products, geographic markets, or customers served.

Dogs Businesses that fall into the low market growth/low market share cell of a BCG matrix.

Downward communication Flows from individuals in higher levels of the organization to those in lower levels.

Dynamic network A network structure that makes extensive use of outsourcing through alliances with outside organizations.

Economic feasibility Focuses on whether the expected benefits of an information system will be able to cover the anticipated costs.

Effectiveness Pursuing the appropriate goals—doing the right things.

Efficiency Using the fewest inputs to generate a given output—doing things right.

Electronic data interchange (EDI) Electronic transmission of transaction data using telecommunications.

Electronic funds transfer (EFT) Electronic manipulation of financial transactions.

Electronic mail (e-mail) A computer-based system that allows individuals to exchange and store messages through computerized text-processing and communication networks.

Employee assistance programs (EAPs) Designed to help employees cope with physical, personal, and emotional problems including substance abuse, alcoholism, stress, emotional illness, and family disturbances.

Employee-centered work redesign An approach whereby employees design their work roles to benefit the organization and satisfy their individual goals.

Employment test Any instrument, device, or information used to make an employment decision is considered a test by the EEOC's Uniform Guidelines of Employee Selection.

Empowering employees Increasing the amount of control and discretion employees have over their job as a means of motivating behavior.

Encoding Translating the sender's ideas into a systematic set of symbols or a language expressing the communicator's purpose.

End users Those who will use and interact with the information system.

Entropy The tendency for systems to decay over time.

Escalation of commitment The tendency to increase commitment to a previously selected course of action beyond the level that would be expected if the manager followed an effective decision-making process.

Esteem needs Personal feelings of achievement, self-worth, recognition, respect, and prestige from others.

Ethical behavior Behavior that is morally accepted as good or right as opposed to bad or wrong.

Ethical dilemma A situation in which a person must decide whether or not to do something that, although benefiting oneself or the organization, may be considered unethical and perhaps illegal.

Ethics The established customs, morals, and fundamental human relationships that exist throughout the world.

Expectancy The belief that a particular level of effort will be followed by a particular level of performance.

Expected monetary value (EMV) The sum of each expected value for an alternative.

Expected value The product of a payoff and its probability of occurrence.

Expert power The power to influence because of expert knowledge and competence.

Expert system A computer-based system that contains and can use knowledge about a specific, relatively narrow, complex application.

External communication The sharing of messages with people outside the organization.

External customer The consumer who purchases the product or service output of the organization.

External forces Environmental factors that are fundamentally beyond the control of management.

Extinction The withdrawal of the positive reward or reinforcing consequences for an undesirable behavior.

Feedback Information about the status and performance of a given effort or system.

Feedback controls Controls that compare the actual performance of the organization to its planned performance.

Feedback (corrective) control Focuses on discovering undesirable output and implementing corrective action.

Feedforward controls Controls designed to identify changes in the external environment or the internal operations of the organization that may affect its ability to fulfill its mission and achieve its strategic goals.

Feedforward (preventive) control Focuses on detecting undesirable material, financial, or human resources that serve as inputs to the transformation process.

Fiedler's LPC model A contingency model that predicts work group effectiveness based on a match between the leader's style and the demands of the situation.

Fixed assets Assets that are long-term in nature and cannot be converted quickly into cash.

Fixed-interval schedule Rewards at specific time intervals, assuming that the desired behavior has continued at an appropriate level.

Fixed-position layout A configuration used for large or bulky items that remain stationary in the manufacturing process.

Fixed-ratio schedule Provides a reinforcement after a fixed number of occurrences of the desired behavior.

Focus strategy A strategy for competing by targeting a specific and narrow segment of the market.

Force-field analysis A systematic process for examining the pressures that are likely to support or resist a proposed change.

Formal groups Groups that are deliberately created to accomplish goals and serve the needs of the organization.

Functional managers Managers who are responsible for managing a work unit that is grouped based on the function served.

Functional strategy Specifies the operations, research and development, financial, human resource management, and marketing activities necessary to implement the organization's corporate and business strategies.

Functional structure Members of the organization are grouped according to the function they perform within the organization.

GE matrix A business portfolio matrix that uses industry attractiveness and business strength as the indicators of the firm's strategic position.

General environment Those environmental forces that are beyond a firm's influence and over which it has no control.

General managers Managers who are responsible for managing several different departments that are responsible for different tasks.

Generic strategies The fundamental way in which an organization competes in the marketplace.

Geographic divisional structure A structure in which the activities of the organization are grouped according to the geographic markets served.

Global strategy A strategy for competing in multiple international markets with a standard line of products and services.

Goal setting A process intended to increase efficiency and effectiveness by specifying the desired outcomes toward which individuals, groups, departments, and organizations work.

Goals The results that an organization seeks to achieve.

Grand strategy A comprehensive, general approach for achieving the strategic goals of an organization.

Grapevine The informal flow of messages throughout the organization.

Group Two or more interdependent individuals who interact with and influence one another to accomplish a common purpose.

Groupthink An agreement-at-any-cost mentality that results in ineffective group decision making.

Groupware A software package used to organize an electronic meeting in which participants' computers are interconnected from their various locations.

Halo-and-horn effect The process in which we evaluate and form an overall impression of an individual based solely on a specific trait or dimension.

Hawthorne effect Phenomenon where individual or group performance is influenced by human behavior factors.

Human resource information systems (HRISs) Used to track and monitor economic, legislative, and competitive changes and to support and provide organized information to solve complex HR problems.

Human resource management (HRM) The management of the employees of the organization consisting of all the activities required to enhance the effectiveness of an organization's work force and to achieve organizational goals and objectives.

Human resource planning The process of determining future human resource needs relative to an organization's strategic plan and taking the actions necessary to meet those needs in a timely manner.

Human rights approach A situation in which decisions are made in light of the moral entitlements of human beings.

Human skills The ability to work effectively with others.

Hybrid layout A configuration containing some degree of flexibility, lying between the extremes of process and product layouts.

Hygiene factors Associated with the job context or environment in which the job is performed.

Hyperchange A condition of rapid, dramatic, complex, and unpredictable change that has a significant effect on the ways in which organizations are managed.

Income statement A summary of an organization's financial performance over a given time interval, showing revenues, expenses, and bottom-line profit or loss.

Informal groups Self-created groups that evolve out of the formal organization based on proximity, common interests, or needs of individuals.

Information The result of the process of transforming data into meaningful facts useful for a specific purpose.

Information overload Occurs whenever the capacity of a communication medium to process information is exceeded.

Information power Control over information that involves the leader's power to access and distribute information that is either desired or vital to others.

Information technology A broad category of communication techniques that includes videotape recorders, telephone answering devices and services, closed-circuit television systems, and facsimile machines.

Informational roles The manager's responsibility for gathering and disseminating information to the stakeholders of the organization.

Inputs Such diverse items as materials, workers, capital, land, equipment, customers, and information used in creating products and services.

Instrumental values Standards of conduct or methods for attaining an end.

Instrumentality The probability assigned by the individual that a specific level of achieved task performance will lead to various work outcomes.

Intangible costs Costs that are difficult or impossible to quantify.

Integrating mechanisms Methods for managing the flow of information, resources, and tasks within the organization.

Interdependence The degree to which work groups are interrelated.

Internal customer In the sequence of stages that extend from purchasing raw materials through to final delivery of the

product or service, an internal customer is any individual or department that uses the output of a prior stage.

Internal forces Inside factors that are generally within the control of management.

Internal network A network structure that relies on internally developed units to provide services to a core organizational unit.

Interpersonal roles The manager's responsibility for managing relationships with organizational members and other constituents.

Intuition An unconscious analysis based on past experience.

Jargon Pretentious terminology or language specific to a particular profession or group.

Job analysis Assimilating all of the information about a particular job, including job descriptions and job specifications.

Job depth The degree of control given to a job holder to perform his job.

Job description An outline of the responsibilities and tasks associated with a given job.

Job design The set of tasks and activities that are grouped together to define a particular job.

Job enlargement Programs designed to broaden job scope.

Job enrichment Programs designed to increase job depth.

Job rotation Assigning individuals to a variety of job positions.

Job satisfaction The degree to which individuals feel positively or negatively about their jobs.

Job scope The number of different activities required in a job and the frequency with which each activity is performed.

Job-shop production system Produces small quantities of a wide variety of specialized items.

Job specifications The identification of the knowledge, skills, abilities, and other employee characteristics needed to perform the job.

Justice approach A situation in which decisions are based on an equitable, fair, and impartial distribution of benefits and costs among individuals and groups.

Just-in-time (JIT) inventory management A philosophy that advocates eliminating waste, solving problems, and striving for continual improvement in operations.

Knowledge work Work that requires the acquisition, creation, or application of knowledge.

Labor-management relations The formal process through which employees and unions negotiate terms and conditions of employment including pay, hours of work, benefits, and other important aspects of the working environment.

Language systems and metaphors The way that organizational members typically express themselves and communicate with each other.

Lateral communication The horizontal information flow that occurs both within and between departments. The purpose of lateral communication is coordination.

Law of effect Determines if a behavior will be repeated or not, depending on whether the consequence is positive or negative.

Law of requisite variety Control systems must have enough variety to cope with the variety in the systems they are trying to control.

Leadership A social influence process that involves determining the group's objectives, motivating behavior in pursuit of these objectives, and influencing group maintenance and culture.

Leadership substitutes Situational variables that tend to outweigh the leader's ability to affect subordinate satisfaction and performance.

Leading Motivating and directing the members of the organization so that they contribute to the achievement of the goals of the organization.

Least preferred coworker (LPC) scale Designed to measure relationship-oriented versus task-oriented behaviors according to a leader's choice of descriptive terms.

Legitimate power Power stemming from formal authority based on the particular positions in an organization or social system.

Liabilities The firm's debts and obligations.

Line personnel Those organizational members that are directly involved in delivering the products and services of the organization.

Liquidity ratios Indicators of the firm's ability to meet its short-term debts and obligations.

Local-area network (LAN) An information system that connects users in a small area, such as a building, an office, or a manufacturing plant.

Locus of control The extent to which individuals believe that they can control events affecting them. Those with an internal locus of control believe that events are primarily the result of one's own behavior and actions. Those with an external locus of control believe that much of what happens is uncontrolled and determined by outside forces.

Locus of decision making The degree to which decision making is centralized versus decentralized.

Long-term liabilities Debts payable over a long time span.

Machiavellian personality Someone who vies for and manipulates others purely for personal gain and feels that any behavior is acceptable if it achieves one's goals.

Management The process of administering and coordinating resources effectively and efficiently and in an effort to achieve the goals of the organization.

Management by exception Focusing on the elements that are not meeting the standards.

Management by objectives (MBO) A method for developing individualized plans that guide the activities of individual members of an organization.

Management information system (MIS) Focuses on the routine, structured, regular reporting and information requirements of the organization.

Managers Organizational members who are responsible for planning, organizing, leading, and controlling the activities of the organization so that its goals can be achieved.

Market growth rate A measure of the annual growth percentage of the market in which the business operates.

Master production schedule A detailed statement of projected production quantities for each item in each time period.

Matrix structure A structure in which the tasks of the organization are grouped along to organizing dimensions simultaneously (such as product/geographic market, product/function).

Mechanistic systems Highly centralized organizations in which decision-making authority rests with top management.

Medium The carrier of the message or the means by which the message is sent.

Messages The tangible forms of coded symbols that are intended to give a particular meaning to the data.

Moral agent A business's obligation to act honorably and to reflect and enforce values that are consistent with those of society.

Motivation The forces acting on or within a person that cause the person to behave in a specific, goal-directed manner.

Motivator factors Related to job content or what people actually do in their work.

Multidomestic strategy A strategy for competing in multiple international markets by tailoring products and services to meet the specific needs of each host country market.

Myths Unproven beliefs that are accepted uncritically and used to justify current actions by communicating the practical benefits of certain techniques and behaviors.

Need for achievement The drive to excel, accomplish challenging tasks, and achieve a standard of excellence.

Need for affiliation The desire for friendly and close interpersonal relationships.

Need for power The desire to influence and control one's environment.

Negative reinforcement The removal of negative consequences following a desired behavior.

Network structure A contemporary organizational structure that is founded on a set of alliances with other organizations that serve a wide variety of functions.

Noise Any internal or external interference or distraction with the intended message that can cause distortion in the sending and receiving of messages.

Nominal group technique (NGT) A structured process designed to stimulate creative group decision making where agreement is lacking or where the members have incomplete knowledge concerning the nature of the problem.

Nonprogrammed decision Decisions made in response to situations that are unique, unstructured, or poorly defined.

Nonverbal communication All messages that are non-language responses.

Norms Unwritten and often informal rules and shared beliefs about what behavior is appropriate and expected of group members.

Objective function A symbolic, quantitative representation of the primary goal that the decision maker is seeking to optimize.

Objectives The desired results to be attained.

Open systems Systems that must interact with the external environment to survive.

Operational feasibility Focuses on the willingness and ability of all concerned parties to operate, use, and support the information system.

Operational planning   The process of determining the day-to-day activities that are necessary to achieve the long-term goals of the organization.

Operational plans   An outline of the tactical activities necessary to support and implement the strategic plans of the organization.

Opportunity   A situation which has the potential to provide additional beneficial outcomes.

Oral communication   All forms of spoken information.

Organic (clan) control   Reliance upon social values, traditions, shared beliefs, flexible authority, and trust to assess performance and correct unacceptable deviations.

Organic systems   Decentralized organizations that push decision making to the lowest levels of the organization in an effort to respond more effectively to environmental change.

Organization   A group of individuals who work together toward common goals.

Organizational change   Any alteration of activities in an organization, it can occur in the structure of the organization, the transfer of work tasks, the introduction of a new product, or attitudes among members.

Organizational control   A process through which managers regulate organizational activities to make them consistent with expectations and help them achieve predetermined standards of performance.

Organizational culture   The system of shared beliefs and values that develops with an organization. In simple terms, organizational culture is the personality of the organization.

Organizational design   The way in which the activities of an organization are arranged and coordinated so that its mission can be fulfilled and its goals achieved.

Organizational development (OD)   A process of planning change in organizations that use behavioral science knowledge, theory, and technology to help an organization improve its capacity for effective change.

Organizational feasibility   Focuses on how well the proposed system supports the strategic objectives of the organization.

Organizational mission   The reasons for which the organization exists; it provides strategic direction for the members of the organization.

Organizational structure   The primary reporting relationships that exist within an organization.

Organizing   The process of determining the tasks to be done, who will do them, and how those tasks will be managed and coordinated.

Orientation   The process of familiarizing new employees with the organization, their job, and their work unit, which enables them to become productive members of the organization.

Outputs   The physical commodity, or intangible service or information, that is desired by the customers or users of the system.

Owner's equity   The portion of a business that is owned by the shareholders. The difference between the assets of an organization and its liabilities.

Partial schedule of reinforcement   Rewarding the desired behavior intermittently.

Participative leadership   Consulting with the subordinates and taking their opinions and suggestions into account.

Participative management   Encompasses varied activities of high involvement where subordinates share a significant degree of decision-making power with their immediate superiors.

Path-goal model   Used because of its emphasis on how a leader influences subordinates' perception of work goals and personal goals, and the links or paths found between these two sets of goals.

Payoff table   A matrix that organizes the alternative courses of action, states of nature, and payoffs for a decision situation.

Payoffs   The outcomes of decision situations.

Performance appraisal   A systematic process of evaluating employee job-related achievements, strengths, and weaknesses, as well as determining ways to improve performance.

Personality   The enduring, organized, and distinctive pattern of behavior that characterizes an individual's adaptation to a situation.

PERT (Program Evaluation and Review Technique)   A network approach for scheduling project activities.

Physiological needs   Food, water, air, and shelter are physiological needs.

Plan   A blueprint for action that prescribes the activities necessary for the organization to realize its goals.

Planning   Setting goals and defining the actions necessary to achieve those goals.

Policies   General guidelines for decision making within the organization.

Pooled interdependence   Occurs when organizational units have a common resource but no interrelationship with one another.

Positive reinforcement   The administration of positive and rewarding consequences following a desired behavior.

Power   The ability to marshal human, informational, or material resources to get something done.

Problem   A situation where some aspect of organizational performance is less than desirable.

Procedures   Instructions on how to complete recurring tasks.

Process consultation   Involves structured activities directed toward key "processes" through which members of a group work with one another on specific issues and activities.

Process layout   A configuration flexible enough to accommodate a wide diversity of products or customers.

Product divisional structure   A structure in which the activities of the organization are grouped according to specific products or product lines.

Product layout   A configuration set for a specific purpose, with all product or service demands essentially identical.

Productivity   A measure of the efficiency with which a firm transforms inputs into outputs.

Profitability ratios   Indicators of the relative effectiveness, or profitability, of the organization.

Programmed decision   Decisions made in response to routine situations that have occurred in the past.

Programs   Single-use plans that govern a comprehensive set of activities designed to accomplish a particular set of goals.

Project production system   Produces large-scale, unique items.

Projects   Single-use plans that direct the efforts of individuals or work groups toward the achievement of a specific goal.

Protected class   Composed of individuals who fall within a group identified for protection under equal employment laws and regulations.

Punishment   The administration of negative consequences following undesirable behavior.

Quality assurance   Focuses on any activity that influences the maintenance of quality at the desired level.

Quality circle   A work team that meets regularly to identify, analyze, and solve problems related to its work area.

Quality control   Focuses on the actual measurement of output to see if specifications have been met.

Quality management   A formal approach to management where the overriding priority of the organization is to deliver a quality product or service and to work toward excellence and continuous improvement in all areas of the organization.

Question marks   Businesses that fall into the high market growth/low market share cell of a BCG matrix.

Rational-economic decision model   A prescriptive framework of how a decision should be made that assumes managers have completely accurate information.

Rational-legal authority   Subordinates comply with a leader because of a set of impersonal rules and regulations that apply to all employees.

Reciprocal interdependence   Occurs when information, resources, and tasks must be passed back and forth between work groups.

Recruitment   The process of finding and attracting job candidates who are qualified to fill job vacancies.

Reengineering   Radically changing the organizational processes for delivering products and services.

Referent power   The ability to influence based on personal liking, charisma, and reputation.

Refreezing   The third step in the change process, which centers on reinforcing new behaviors, usually by positive results, feelings of accomplishment, or rewards from others.

Relationship orientation   Showing empathy for needs and feelings, being supportive of group needs, establishing trusting relationships, and allowing workers to participate in decision making.

Relationship-oriented roles   Behaviors that cultivate the well-being, continuity, and development of the group.

Relative market share   The firm's market share divided by the market share of its largest competitor.

Repetitive, assembly-line, or mass-production system   Produces a high volume of discrete items.

Responsibility   An obligation on the part of an employee to complete assigned activities.

Restraining forces   Promote organizational stability or the status quo and resist change.

Reward power   Derived from control over tangible benefits, such as promotion, a better job, a better work schedule, a larger operating budget, an increased expense account, and formal recognition of accomplishments.

Rites   A relatively dramatic, planned set of recurring activities used at special times to influence the behavior and understanding of organizational members.

Robotics   Use of machines with humanlike characteristics, such as dexterity, movement, vision, and strength.

Roles   Shared expectations of how group members will fulfill the requirements of their positions.

Rules   Detailed and specific regulations for action.

Satisficing   The search and acceptance of something that is satisfactory rather than perfect or optimal.

Scalar principle   A clear line of authority must run throughout the organization.

Schedules of reinforcement   Specify the basis for and timing of reinforcement.

Scientific management   Focuses on the productivity of the individual worker.

Security needs   The desire to have a safe physical and emotional environment.

Selection   The process of evaluating and choosing the best qualified candidate from the pool of applicants recruited for the position.

Selective perception   The tendency to screen out information with which we aren't comfortable or that we do not consider relevant.

Self-actualization needs   Needs for self-fulfillment and the opportunity to achieve one's potential.

Self-esteem   The extent to which people believe they are capable, significant, successful, and worthwhile.

Self-managed teams   Groups of employees who design their jobs and work responsibilities to achieve the self-determined goals and objectives of the team.

Self-monitoring   Identifies the degree to which individuals are capable of reading and using the cues from their environment to determine their behavior.

Self-oriented roles   Behaviors that meet some personal need or goal of an individual without regard to the group's problems.

Sequential interdependence   Occurs when organizational units must coordinate the flow of information, resources, and tasks from one unit to another.

Sexual harassment   Actions that are sexually directed, are unwanted, and subject a worker to adverse employment conditions.

Single-use plans   Plans that address specific organizational situations that typically do not recur.

Skill variety   The degree to which a job challenges the job holder to use various skills and abilities.

SLT model   States that effective leader behavior depends on the situational contingency of readiness and the appropriate behavior-readiness match.

Social context   The setting in which a communication takes place.

Social contract   An implied set of rights and obligations that are inherent in social policy and assumed by business.

Span of control   The number of employees reporting to a particular manager.

Special-purpose team   A temporary team formed to solve a special or nonrecurring problem.

Stable environments   Environments that experience little change.

Stable network   A network structure that utilizes external alliances selectively as a mechanism for gaining strategic flexibility.

Staff personnel   Those organizational members that are not directly involved in delivering the products and services of the organization, but provide support for line personnel.

Staffing   Bringing or placing people into the organization and making sure they serve as productive members of the work force.

Stakeholders   People who are affected by or can affect the activities of the firm.

Standing plans   Plans that deal with organizational issues and problems that recur frequently.

Stars   Businesses that fall into the high market growth/high market share cell of a BCG matrix.

States of nature   Conditions over which the decision maker has little or no control.

Stereotyping   The tendency to assign attributes to someone, not on individual characteristics, but solely on the basis of a category or group to which that person belongs.

Stories   Accounts based on true events; they often contain both truth and fiction.

Strategic analysis   An assessment of the internal and external conditions of the firm.

Strategic control   The methods by which the performance of the organization is monitored.

Strategic decision-making matrix   A two-dimensional grid used to select the best strategic alternative in light of multiple organizational objectives.

Strategic goals   The results that an organization seeks to achieve in the long-term.

Strategic plan   A plan that identifies the markets in which an organization competes, as well as the ways in which it competes in those markets.

Strategic planning   The process by which an organization makes decisions and takes actions to enhance its long-run performance.

Strategy formulation   The establishment of strategic goals for the organization and the development of corporate- and business-level strategies.

Strategy implementation   The actions required to ensure that the corporate- and business-level strategy of the organization is put into place.

Supportive leadership   Giving consideration to the needs of subordinates, displaying concern for their welfare, and creating a friendly climate in the work unit.

Survey feedback   A method of improving relationships among members of groups or departments that gather information, perceptions, and attitudes through a customized survey questionnaire and present the information to participants to discuss.

Synergy   A phenomenon where an organization can accomplish more when its subsystems work together than it can accomplish when they work independently.

Systems analysis   An approach to problem solving that is closely aligned with the quantitative perspective on management.

Systems development life cycle (SDLC)   Recognition that investigating, analyzing, designing, implementing, and maintaining an information system is an ongoing process.

Tangible costs   Costs that can be accurately quantified.

Task environment   Those environmental forces that are within the firm's operating environment and over which the firm has some degree of control.

Task identity   The degree to which a job requires the completion of an identifiable piece of work.

Task orientation   Setting goals, giving directions, setting standards, supervising worker performance, and applauding new ideas.

Task-oriented roles   Behaviors directly related to establishing and achieving the goals of the group or getting the task done.

Task significance   The degree to which a job contributes to the overall efforts of the organization.

Team building   A process by which members of a work group diagnose how they work together and plan changes to improve their effectiveness.

Technical feasibility   Focuses on the hardware and software capabilities of the proposed information system.

Technical skills   The ability to utilize tools, techniques, and procedures that are specific to a particular field.

Telecommuting   The practice of working at a remote site by using a computer linked to a central office or other employment location.

Terminal values   Goals an individual will ultimately strive to achieve.

Theory X   Managers perceive that subordinates have an inherent dislike of work, and will avoid it if possible.

Theory Y   Managers perceive that subordinates enjoy work, and will gain satisfaction from their jobs.

Theory Z   Advocates that managers place trust in the employees and make them feel like an intimate part of the organization.

Total quality management (TQM)   A systematic approach for enhancing products, services, processes, and operational quality control.

Traditional authority   Subordinates comply with a leader because of custom or tradition.

Training   A planned effort to assist employees in learning job-related behaviors in order to improve performance.

Trait approach   The assumption that some people are "natural leaders," and are endowed with certain traits not possessed by other individuals.

Transactional leadership   Provides followers with resources and rewards in exchange for motivation, productivity, and effective task accomplishment.

Transformation process   The mechanism by which inputs are converted to outputs.

Transformational leadership   The process of influencing the attitudes and assumptions of organizational members and building commitment to the organization's mission and objectives.

Turbulent environments   Environments that are characterized by rapid and significant change.

Type A orientation   Characterized by impatience, a desire for achievement, aggressiveness, irritability, and perfectionism.

Type B orientation   Characterized as easygoing, relaxed, patient, able to listen carefully, and communicate more precisely than Type A individuals.

Unfreezing   Developing an initial awareness of the need for change and the forces supporting and resisting change.

Unity of command   A principle that each employee in the organization is accountable to one, and only one, supervisor.

Upward communication   Information flows to managers from their subordinates.

Utility approach   A situation in which decisions are based on an evaluation of the overall amount of good that will result.

Valence   The value or importance that the individual attaches to various outcomes.

Validity   A relationship between what a test proposes to measure and what is actually measured.

Values   Relatively permanent and deeply held preferences upon which individuals form attitudes and personal choices.

Variable-interval schedule   When reinforcement is administered at random or varying times that cannot be predicted by the employee.

Variable-ratio schedule   Reinforcement administered randomly.

Variance reporting   Highlighting only those things that fail to meet the established standards.

Videoconferencing   The technologies that use live video to unite widely dispersed company operations.

Vigilance   The concern for and attention to the process of making a decision that occurs when the decision maker considers seven critical procedures.

Whistleblower   Someone who exposes organizational misconduct or wrongdoing to the public.

Wide-area network (WAN)   An information system that extends over a broad geographic area, such as cities, regions, countries, or the world.

Written communication   Letters, memos, policy manuals, reports, forms, and other documentation used to share information in the organization.

NAME INDEX

Aaker, D. A., 149
Abell, Derek F., 231, 253
Abernathy, W., 328
Abrahams, J., 165
Abramson, M. A., 460
Acquilano, N. J., 603
Adams, S. J., 525
Adamson, Jim, 377, 378
Adler, A., 217
Adler, N. J., 217, 430, 525
Akers, Jim, 298
Akers, John, 22
Albert, Sam, 320
Albrecht, K., 149
Alexander, L., 111
Allen, M., 218
Altier, W. J., 328
Amelio, Gilbert, 316
Amoroso, D., 639
Ancona, D. G., 394
Anderson, C. R., 494
Anderson, D. R., 73, 603
Andrews, K., 111
Ansoff, H., 149
Aplin, J. C., 565
Aramony, William, 92
Aries, E., 430
Armellini, Joseph, 276
Armellini, Jules, 276
Ash, Mary Kay, 52
Ashby, W. R., 565
Atwal, Peter, 624
Austin, L., 74
Axline, L. L., 149

B

Baird, J., 430
Baird, L., 649
Baker, W. E., 649
Baldwin, S. R., 184
Baliga, B. R., 566
Barber, A., 649
Barnard, Chester, 56, 57, 67, 68, 74
Barnett, C., 394
Barnevik, Percy, 307
Barney, J., 185
Baron, R. A., 74
Barr, M., 149, 185
Barrier, M., 37, 149
Barry, D., 38
Bartholomew, D., 639, 640
Bartlett, Chris, 185, 307
Bassin, M., 295
Bayliss, Matt, 624
Bazerman, M. H., 217
Beach, L. R., 217, 218, 393
Beall, Donald, 24
Beals, Vaughn, 64
Beam H. H., 252
Beatles, 570
Beatty, R. W., 366
Becker, H., 112

Beckhard, R., 525
Beer, J. M., 393
Beer, S., 565
Beers, M. C., 328
Behling, O., 217
Bell, C. H., 394
Beneen, Harold, 484
Benjamin, R. J., 639
Benne, K. J., 494
Bennett, John G., Jr., 92
Bentley, L. D., 639
Berelson, B., 494
Berkley, J. D., 38, 327
Berkowitz, L., 460, 525
Berstein, A., 366
Bertrand, K., 37, 149
Bethune, Gordon, 123
Bettenhausen, K. L., 494
Bihler, D., 88, 111
Bildman, Lars, 78, 104
Birnbaum, Joel, 17
Bishop, J., 494
Blair, K. E., 566
Blake, R., 460
Blanchard, K. H., 217, 442, 443, 430, 460, 525
Blumenstein, R., 603
Boccialetti, G., 394
Bolles, R. N., 649
Bonvillian, G., 430
Borenstein, S., 252
Borisoff, D., 430
Borucki, C., 394
Boulding, K., 74
Boulian, P. V., 493
Bowen, H. R., 81, 82, 111
Bowyer, Jim, 303
Bracker, J., 157, 185
Bradley, S. P., 37, 328
Brady, F. N., 217
Branch, S., 37
Brancheau, J. C., 640
Brandon, K., 217
Brass, D. J., 431
Bray, Chris, 624
Breland Reed, 464, 486
Brett, J. M., 217, 366
Brickner, W. H., 148
Bridwell, L. G., 525
Brigham, E., 566
Brocka, B., 73
Brocka, M. S., 73
Brown, Helen Gurley, 449
Brown-Humes, C., 346, 355, 366, 517
Brownell, J., 430, 431
Bruun, S., 494
Bryant, J. D., 464, 486
Buchholz, B., 73
Bulkeley, W., 431
Burgelman, R. A., 149
Burke, W. W., 394
Burnett, R., 639
Burnham H., 525

Burns, J., 74
Burns, Stanley, 341, 365
Burns, Tom, 316, 326, 328
Burrow, Flois, 250
Burrow, Kevin, 250
Bush, George, 518
Bush, J. B., 328
Bushardt, S. C., 295
Bushnell, Nolan, 124
Butler, S., 111
Buzzell, R. D., 184
Bylinsky, G., 565, 566
Byrne, J. A., 38, 112, 184, 327, 328, 394

C

Cady, S., 430, 495, 525, 526
Cafasso, R., 639
Calfee, D. L., 185
Calingo, L. M. R., 184
Callan, K., 346, 355, 366, 517
Calufetti, Larry, 457
Caminiti, S., 493, 495
Campbell, Ronald, 443
Campion, M. A., 294, 295
Carnevale, A. P., 327
Carrard, Francois, 211
Carroll, A. B., 79, 86, 111
Carson, C., 394, 525
Carter, C., 649
Carter, J. H., 295
Carter, Jimmy, 437, 438, 455
Carter, P. L., 565, 566
Cartwright, D., 460
Cascio, W. F., 366
Case, T., 38
Castro, Fidel, 455
Caudron, S., 295
Cavanaugh, G. F., 111
Cederholm, L., 480, 494
Certo, S. C., 253
Chalykoff, H. J., 566
Champy, J., 430, 460, 525
Chance, P., 295
Chandler, Alfred D., 149, 174, 185
Change, Y., 149
Chaples, S. S., 185
Charan, R., 328
Charles, Ray, 223, 224
Chase, R. B., 603
Chavez, Cesar, 52
Chency, J. L., 328
Cheney, P., 639
Cheraskin, L., 294
Cheung, F. M., 494
Ching, C., 328
Cho, Fujio, 65
Christoff, K., 639
Ciampa, D., 217
Clapton, Eric, 570
Clark, D., 640
Clemons, E. K., 37
Clemons, T. C., 494

661

COMPANY INDEX

SUBJECT INDEX